I0007530

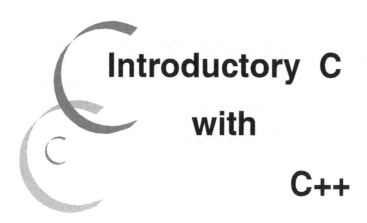

Introductory C
with
C++

Richard Petersen

Dedication

To my parents,

George and Cecelia

Introductory C with C++

Richard Petersen

Surfing Turtle Press
Alameda, CA
www.surfingturtlepress.com
Please send inquiries to: editor@surfingturtlepress.com

ISBN-13 978-1-949857-39-9

Copyright Richard Petersen, 2006

All rights reserved

Copyright 2006 by Richard Petersen. All rights reserved. Printed in the United States of America.

Except as permitted under the Copyright Act of 1976, no part of this publication may be reproduced or distributed in any form or by any means, or stored in a database or retrieval system, without the prior written permission of the publisher, with the exception that the program listings may be entered, stored, and executed in a computer system, but they may not be reproduced for publication.,

Information has been obtained by Surfing Turtle Press from sources believed to be reliable. However, because of the possibility of human or mechanical error by our sources, Surfing Turtle Press, the author Richard Petersen, or others, Surfing Turtle Press does not guarantee the accuracy, adequacy, or completeness of any information and is not responsible for any errors or omissions or the results obtained from use of such information.

Limit of Liability and Disclaimer of Warranty: The publisher and the author make no representation or warranties with respect to the accuracy or completeness of the contents of this work and specifically disclaim all warranties, including without limitation warranties of fitness for a particular purpose. The information and code in this book are provided on "as is" basis. No warranty may be created or extended by sales or promotional materials. The advice and strategies contained herein may not be suitable for every situation. This work is sold with the understanding that the publisher is not engaged in rendering legal, accounting, or other professional services. Surfing Turtle Press and anyone else who has been involved in the creation or production of the included code cannot and do not warrant the performance or results that may be obtained by using the code.

Trademark Acknowledgements
UNIX is a trademark of The Open Group
Microsoft and MS WINDOWS are registered trademarks of Microsoft Corporation
IBM and PC are registered trademarks of the International Business Machines Corporation
Macintosh is a registered trademark of MacIntosh Laboratory, Inc, licensed by Apple Computer, Inc.

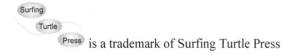 is a trademark of Surfing Turtle Press

 **Preface**

Preface

C differs from most programming languages in its use of expressions, pointers, and arrays. For those learning C, pointers are the greatest source of confusion. The primary aim of this text is to provide working models of how pointers are used in C as well as an introduction to their use in C++.

Most beginners falter on the use of pointers. Many try to avoid pointers completely, but quickly find that pointers are used extensively throughout C programs. Some attain a partial understanding of pointers which, at first, gets them by. However, when faced with complex programming tasks, they find that pointers become a necessity.

In most programming languages one learns about pointers only after most other topics have been discussed. Pointers are just one more added feature of the language. In C and C++, however, pointers are used with every feature. There are pointers to variables, pointers as parameters, pointers as arrays, pointers to structures, and even pointers to pointers. With each feature, pointers are used differently. The way pointers work with variables is different from the way pointers work with arrays. In this text, you learn pointers as you learn each feature of the language. With variables, you learn pointers to variables; with parameters, pointers to parameters; with functions: pointers to functions; with arrays, pointers in arrays; with structures, pointers to structures. Also, for C++ you will learn pointers to objects, to class members, and derived objects. Such an approach provides an understanding of the many ways pointers are used throughout the language.

The text is arranged in five sections. The first part focuses on the basic structure of the language. Variables, functions, and expressions are carefully examined. The second part deals with arrays. Arrays form an exception in C. Unlike structures they are not data objects. They are completely managed by pointers. The third part describes data structures and file management. The chapter on data structures introduces basic concepts such as linked lists and trees. A special examination is made of recursion and how it operates with lists, trees, and b-trees. The chapters on file management discuss the different types of files with special emphasis on record files b-tree indexes. The fourth part provides an introduction to C++, covering classes and objects, their use with pointers, as well as operator overloading and inheritance. The fifth part covers additional topics greater detail such as the pre-processor and bitwise operations.

Expressions play a primary role in C, whereas statements have more of an organizational function. Expressions define the tasks that are performed in a C program, including assignments and function calls. In a sense, there are no assignment statements in C. There are only assignment expressions. This reflects a design similar to function applicative languages such as Lisp. Assignments and function calls can be part of any complex expression. They can be found in the test expressions used in **while** or **if** statements. They may be nested within complex arithmetic expressions.

In C, arrays are deceptively familiar. Arrays can be declared and managed with a format called array notation that appears to operate like arrays in other programming languages. However, an array is not a valid C data object. Arrays are merely sections of designated memory manage by pointers. The array name itself is, in fact, used as a pointer. An attempt to understand the pointer operations that manage arrays can be overwhelming. The pointer operations on arrays involve pointer offset expressions, double indirection on a pointer, incrementation of pointers, arrays of pointer whose elements are themselves pointers, and the crucial difference between pointers to objects and pointers to arrays. Even coping with arrays of structures can become involved, especially when the member of a structure element is itself an array. For these reasons, arrays are handled with care in their separate part. Five separate chapters are devoted to examining arrays and their pointer operations.

There are a great many functions in C designed to manage files. Reflecting a design developed for UNIX, all C files have one logical structure, a byte stream. This stream can be accessed in different ways depending on the file function used. Certain file functions access a file as formatted text, while file functions access a file as a record file. In each case, one file is not considered to be physically different from the other. There is a distinction made between binary and text files that may or may not apply depending upon the operating system used. In UNIX there is no distinction, whereas in MS-WINDOWS there is.

The file functions can be organized according to the way they access a file. In this text, the file functions are categorized into character text, line text, formatted text, record sequential, and random access file functions. File management techniques involving data hiding and encapsulation are also discussed.

Building on an understanding of C, it is much easier to learn C++. The key component in C++ is the class which has similar features to that of structures in C. In this text, C++ structures are explained first, noting their similarities and differences from C structures. Then classes are discussed along with their impact on program organization and style. Using the same programs developed earlier in the text for C, C++ versions are examined. Comparison of C and C++ versions of the same programs helps to highlight the similarities and differences between C and C++. Though only an introduction to C++ can be presented in this text, all the key components are covered including pointers, overloading, constructors, and inheritance.

The programming styles used in C are another source of confusion to the beginner. Among programming languages, there are many kinds of programming styles, the most common being procedural, assembler, and function applicative styles. Usually, a programming language has only one programming style. Pascal has a procedural style. Lisp has a function applicative style. Assembly language has an assembler style. C, however, has all three. C can have a procedural style, assembler style, and a function applicative style. C programs will often integrate all three. This gives C great flexibility, but can easily lead to obscure code. Beginners can easily become lost. Beginners may start reading statements arranged in a procedural way and suddenly find themselves reading statements arranged in a function applicative way.

Therefore, it is best for beginners to work with C programs that use only one of these programming styles. Both assembler and function applicative styles tend to be obscure, while the procedural style is very clear. For this reason, this text uses a procedural style in its approach to the C language. There are some function applicative and assembler arrangements that are commonly used in most C programs. However, in this text, such arrangements are introduced within the context of a procedural style. Such an approach keeps a C program from becoming what C programs too often becomes - obscure. It is very easy to write unintelligible C programs.

For beginners in C, clarity is more important than cleverness. Because the language is so flexible, it is easy to lose one's way. For this reason, the text uses many short, clear, and simple programs. Each highlights a new feature of C. Slightly larger programs carefully integrate each new feature. Any program contained in a listing is a working program and can be compiled on any compiler.

 # Overview

Overview

Part 3: Data Structures and File Managment

Part 4: Introduction to C++

Part 5: C Topics

Part 6: Appendices

Contents

Contents

Part 3: Data Structures and File Managment

Part 4: Introduction to C++

Part 6: Appendices

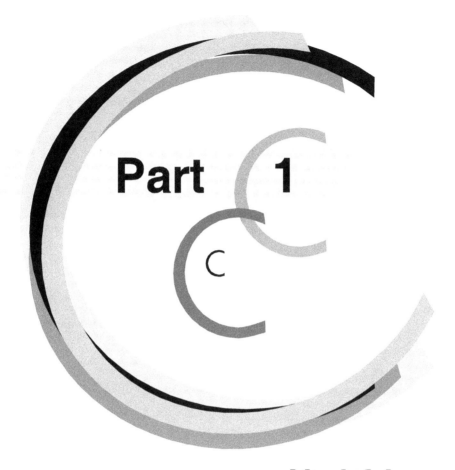

Part 1

Variables

Pointers

and

Functions

1

Introduction

The C Programming Language

Introduction

The C Programming Language

The C Programming language

Variables and Constants

Input/Output

Arrays and Strings

Expressions and Statements

Part 1: Variables, Pointers, and Functions

1. Introduction

C is a powerful, versatile, and sometimes obscure programming language. Some features of the C language will be familiar, while others will not. Declarations and loops operate much the same as they do in other computer languages, but input and output operations are very different. This chapter provides you with a basic overview of C that will allow you to write, compile, and run simple programs immediately. With C, using is believing.

C began as a research language and grew to become a widely used application language. Its development over the years has brought about changes in the language itself. There is now an ANSI standard version of C, commonly referred to as ANSI C. C++ is a further development that incorporates object-oriented programming capabilities. An earlier version of C known as K&R C can still be found in use and is discussed in Chapter 27. This text focuses on ANSI C with a special part on C++.

This chapter will provide a basic orientation to the C programming language. The origins and features of C are discussed first, followed by sections designed to show a beginning C programmer how to write simple C programs.

The complete set of source code files for both examples and exercise answers for this book are available at **www.surfingturtlepress.com**.

The C Programming Language

Dennis Ritchie developed the C programming language in 1972 at Bell Laboratories. At the time, he was working with Ken Thompson on the Unix operating system, and C became the primary language for Unix. It is a concise and powerful language originally designed for researchers. Its use slowly spread throughout the 1970s to universities and then to programmers in many different fields. C quickly became known as the small, concise, easy-to-use programming language that could tackle almost any task, no matter how complex.

C has its roots in languages such as ALGOL and BCPL. A precursor of C, called simply B, was used to program the UNIX operating system. C was later used for the same task. C contains many of the features required for complex systems programming. Complex tasks can be broken down into small, easy-to-write functions. The language itself contains many of the features found in structured programming languages. C has parameters, control structures, and scoped variables. At the same time, C has powerful lower-level capabilities. For example, C is capable of referencing almost any address in a computer's memory. A programmer can do almost anything in C.

C has a flexible and compact structure. Programs written in C tend to consist of many small functions. Though the functions themselves are simple, their interactions can be complex. C is a two-edged sword. Its flexibility allows for concise and versatile programming. However, the code can easily become obscure. A C program can be written in one section using a structured style and in another using an unstructured assembly-language-like style.

Because C is so simple and concise, features that are part of other languages must be simulated in C by other means. Call-by-reference operations, common in most programming languages, do not exist in C and must, therefore, be simulated using pointers. Array operations are actually pointer operations. Strings are simulated by manipulating character arrays. Such a design provides the programmer with a great deal of control, but at the same time, it can make learning C very confusing. Often, the most important part of learning C is to learn how to program the simple tasks, not how to program large projects.

Functions and Function Calls

The basic component of a C program is the function. In fact, a C program is composed of a collection of functions. These functions are defined independently from each other. Other languages, such as Pascal, will have an overall program structure within which procedures and functions are defined. In C, there is no overall program structure. A C program is only a collection of separately defined functions. C does not even have procedures. Instead, functions are used to perform the same roles as procedures.

A function is designed to hold a set of actions that you want your program to take. They are easy to write and help you organize your program into different tasks. Functions can be small or large, simple, or complex. You will find yourself writing programs consisting of many different functions.

A function definition consists of four components: a return type, a function name, a parameter list, and a block. All these terms will be examined in depth later. The function return type, name, and parameter list are often referred to as the header of the function. The return type is any data type. The function name is a name the user has chosen for the function. The parameter list is specified by opening and closing parentheses placed after the function name. The block is referred to as the body of the function. The block is specified with opening and closing braces. Variable declarations and statements are placed within this block. The different components of a function are described in Figure 1-1. This figure shows a simple function called `main` that has no parameter list (as indicated by the void keyword) and has a variable declaration and assignment statement in its block.

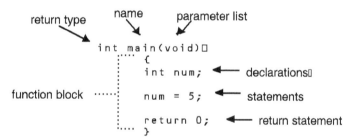

Figure 1-1: Function definition.

The return type and parameter list will be discussed in more detail in Chapter 6, on functions. Until then, programs are written without a parameter list. This lack of a parameter list is indicated by the keyword void. Below is an example of the function header for a function named `main`.

```
int main(void)
```

In the definition of the `main` function that follows, the keyword void indicates that there is no parameter list for this function. The subsequent open and close braces specify the function block. It currently has no statements in it. The `main` function returns a value of 0 with the return 0 statement, indicating a successful execution. A return statement takes an argument that becomes the return value of the function.

```
int main(void)
        {

        return 0;
        }
```

A function call consists of a function name followed by parentheses. Usually, arguments are placed within the parentheses. Often the function call will then be followed by a semicolon, forming a statement within a function block. A simple example of a function call is the call to the I/O function called `printf` that outputs characters to the screen. In the next example, `main` has been rewritten to include a function call to `printf`.

```
int main(void)
        {
        printf("Now in Calc\n");
        return 0;
        }
```

You need to write the functions that make up your program in a text file whose name has a **.c** extension. When you first create the file and name it, be sure to give the name a **.c** extension. The C compiler identifies files with a **.c** extension as C source code files. Most PC C compilers will include a text editor with which you can create your C source code files. Those using Unix-based C compilers will have to use a Unix text editor such as Vi or Emacs to create their source code files. A C source code file is only a standard text file that has a **.c** extension in its file name. As an exercise, you can create a source code file and write in the `main` function just described. You have then created your first C program.

This C program, however, is still not ready to run. To run a C program, you have to define all the functions that you use. However, in this program, the `printf` function has not been defined anywhere. The `printf` function is part of a set of functions used for standard input and output. These functions are already defined in a separate file known as the standard library that is automatically combined with your program by your compiler. However, in order to use these functions correctly, a source code file requires information about their parameters and return type. This information is provided in a file called **stdio.h**. All the information in the **stdio.h** file can be brought into a source code file by use of a preprocessor include operation. The syntax for this include operation is the pound sign, the keyword **include**, and the word **stdio.h** placed within less-than and greater-than signs.

```
#include <stdio.h>
```

The stdio.h file actually consists of a set of function declarations. Function declarations are also referred to as prototypes. These are explained in detail in Chapter 6. At this point, simply be careful to include the **stdio.h** file in your programs to ensure that they compile and run properly. The **myprog.c** program in LISTING 1-1 is a runnable version of a C program.

Simple programs may consist of only one function, the `main` function. However, a program will often consist of several functions. The program then progresses from one function to another through function calls. A function call begins execution of another function. As programs become more complex, a programmer will tend to define more and more functions. Often, a C program will consist of many small functions, rather than a few large functions.

LISTING 1-1:

myprog.c

```
#include <stdio.h>

        int main(void)
                {
                printf("Now in Main\n");
                return 0;
                }
```

Output for LISTING 1-1, **myprog.c**:

```
Now in Main
```

Though you can have a program made up of many functions, one of those functions must be named with the keyword `main`. All programs in C must have a function named with the keyword `main`. The `main` function is always the first function executed. Other functions in the program can then be called in `main`, just as the `printf` function is called in the **myprog.c** program.

In the next example, the programmer has defined another function called calc. Notice how **calc** has its own header and function block. There is also a function call to calc within the `main` function. This program will begin with the `main` function, executing the statements there. Then, through the function call to calc, the program will progress to the calc function.

```
        int main(void)
                {
                printf("Now in Main\n");
                calc();
                printf("Now in Main\n");
                return 0;
                }

        void calc(void)
                {
                printf("Now in Calc\n");
                }
```

The function call of `calc` in `main` consists of the function name and the open and close parentheses. A function call suspends execution in a function. Then the called function will begin execution. When all its statements have been executed, the called function returns control to the calling function. When `calc` is called, the execution of statements in `main` is suspended. The statements in calc are then executed, after which control returns to `main`, and the last `printf` in `main` is executed. The output of the **myfunc.c** program in LISTING 1-2 exemplifies this flow of control.

It often helps to write notes and explanations about your program within the program's source code file. These are known as comments. Comments are separated from the rest of the program by the special delimiter symbols `/*` and `*/`. The compiler ignores any characters within the comment delimiters, so you can write anything you want there. You can have as many comments as you want at any point in the program, each with its own set of delimiters, `/*` and `*/`. Be careful not to nest comments. If you do, the compiler will ignore all characters beginning from the first `/*` until the next `*/` is reached. Anything in between is ignored, whether it be a carriage return, a statement, or a function. In other words, before you can begin a new comment, be sure you closed the previous one with the $*/$ symbol.

LISTING 1-2:

myfunc.c

```
      /* Program to call a function */

#include <stdio.h>

      void calc(void);

      int main(void)
            {
            printf("Now in Main\n");
            calc();
            printf("Now in Main\n");
            return 0;
            }

      void calc(void)
            {
            printf("Now in Calc\n");
            }
```

Output for LISTING 1-2, **myfunc.c**:

```
Now in Main
Now in Calc
Now in Main
```

Compiling and Executing C Programs

Once you have written your program, you are ready to compile and then execute it. The actions you need to perform to compile your program will differ according to the particular C compiler you are using. Many PC compilers have user-friendly window- and menu- driven interfaces. Others, such as the standard Unix C compiler, will use simple line commands that you type in.

Despite the interface used, all C compilers perform the same basic steps. They all take a source code file identified by a **.c** extension and compile it into an executable program. The executable program will be a separate file consisting of binary machine instructions that can be directly executed by your computer. In MS WINDOWS such a file will have an extension .exe. In Unix, the file can be any name.

The next example describes the steps needed to compile and then execute a program in Unix, though the steps are the same on most other systems. First, the user compiles the source code file using the cc command to invoke the C compiler. In this example, a special option, the -o option, is used to specify the name for the executable program file. In this case, the executable file will be called simply myprog. In Unix, if no name is given, the executable file is, by default, named **a.out**. In MS WINDOWS, the executable file is, by default, given the same name as the source code file with the extension .exe. In this case, the default name in MS WINDOWS would be **myprog.exe**.

```
$ cc myprog.c -o myprog
```

Once the compiler has compiled the source code file and created the executable file, you can then execute that program by just entering the name of that executable file. In the next example, the user enters in **myprog** to execute the **myprog** program.

```
$ myprog
Now in Main
```

Your C compiler does more than just perform compilation. It actually includes three operations: preprocessing, compiling, and linking. All are needed to create an executable file. The preprocessor executes special preprocessing commands such as the #include operation described in the previous section. Preprocessing is described in detail in Chapters 2, 4, and 9. In effect it simply performs special text operations on a source code file, preparing it for actual compilation by the compiler.

The compiler then compiles the source code into what is referred to as object code. These are the binary machine instructions that can be executed by your computer. However, this is still not an executable program. The Linker then links the object code with any other needed code, including code for input and output such as printf, and then generates a final executable program. The process of compiling a source code file is described in Figure 1-2.

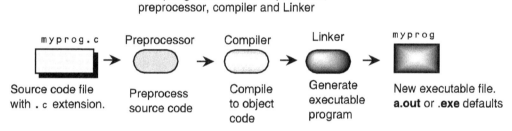

Figure 1-2: Compiling source code files to an executable file includes preprocessing, compiling, and linking, cc myprog.c -o myprog

As your programs become more complex, you will find it convenient to organize each program into several source code files. The process of managing a program composed of several source code files is described in Chapter 9.

Variables and Constants

Data in your program can take the form of values either contained by variables or represented by constants. A variable contains a value that can be changed. At one point in your program you could assign a variable a certain value, and then, at another point, assign it a different value. A constant, on the other hand, represents a specific value and cannot be changed. You can think of a constant as a kind of face-value representation.

In your program, you can create as many variables as you want. Variables are declared and defined with a data type and a name. They are placed after the open brace of the function block and before any statements in the function.

```
int main(void)
      {
      declarations;

      statements;
      }
```

There are several different data types in C, each with its own variations (see Table 1-1). The most common types correspond to those found in most programming languages: integer, floating-point, and character. Each data type has its own keyword. The integer type is specified with the keyword `int`. The floating-point type is specified with the keyword `float`. The character type is specified with the keyword `char`.

```
int           integer
float         floating-point
char          character
```

In a variable declaration, the data type is placed before the name of the variable. A semicolon is placed after the name. Below are declarations of two variables: the integer `num` and the floating-point `cost`.

```
int num;
      float cost;
```

Table 1-1: Data Types

```
      int
                  int num;

      long
                  long num;

      char
                  char  letter:

      float
                  float cost;

      double
                  double cost;
```

An example of a simple program consisting of the `main` function follows. The variable declarations have been placed after the opening brace of `main`'s function block.

```
#include <stdio.h>

int main(void)
        {
        int num;
        float cost;

        printf("Now in Main\n");
        return 0;
        }
```

There are four main types of constants in C: integer, floating-point, character, and string. An integer constant is represented by a sequence of numbers from 0 through 9. 127 is the integer constant for one hundred and twenty-seven. Floating-point values are specified with a decimal. `36.50` is the floating-point constant for thirty-six and a half. Character constants are represented by a single character enclosed in single quotes. `'A'` is the character constant for the letter A. `'?'` is the character constant for the question mark.

Variables and constants are often used together in assignment operations. In C, the assignment operator is the equal sign, `=`. The assignment operation assigns the value to the right of the assignment operator to the variable on the left.

```
num = 3;
cost = 4.50;
```

There is also a type of character known as a nonprinting character. The bell character and carriage return character are examples of nonprinting characters. These characters are used to perform certain actions. Nonprinting characters can be represented by an escape sequence. The escape sequence consists of a backslash followed by a character's octal value. Specially chosen characters are used in place of the octal value for the most widely used nonprinting characters. (See Table 1-2). The escape sequence \n represents the carriage return character. This character sends a message to the screen to perform a carriage return and line feed. The escape sequence \t represents the tab character. Both are often found within the string constants in `printf` function calls.

```
printf("\t Now in Main\n");
```

String constants consist of a sequence of characters enclosed within double quotes. An example of a string constant is the argument used in the `printf` function calls. `"\t Now in MAIN\n"`, in the previous `printf` example, is a string constant. For now, you will only see string constants used in `printf` and `scanf` function calls. Exactly how a string constant works requires an understanding of arrays. They will be discussed in the chapter on strings, Chapter 11. In the following examples, string constants are used simply as data to be output.

The **myvar.c** program in LISTING 1-3 incorporates all these aspects. Variables are declared, and constants are used to assign values to the variables. A string constant is used in a `printf` function call.

LISTING 1-3:

myvar.c

```
#include <stdio.h>

int main(void)
    {
    int num;
    float cost;

    num = 3;
    cost = 4.50;
    printf("Now in Main\n");
    return 0;
    }
```

Table 1-2: Escape Sequence Characters

Octal Characters
\0*oo*   \007   \7
Hexadecimal Characters
\X*oo*   \x7   \x6g
Line and Page Characters
\a   alert (beep) (ANSI)
\n   newline
\t   tab
\f   form feed
\r   carriage return
\v   vertical tab (ANSI)
\b   backspace
Quote and Backslash Characters
\\   backslash character
\'   single quote character
\"   double quote character (ANSI)

Input/Output: printf and scanf

You can perform simple input and output operations using the functions printf and scanf. These powerful and versatile functions are explained later in depth in Chapter 2 and Chapter 25. Here they are used to perform basic input and output operations on variables.

The printf function provides a method by which the values of variables can be output to the screen. To do this, the value of a variable, be it integer or floating-point, first, needs to be converted to characters. The corresponding characters are then printed out to the screen. For example, the integer 127 must be first converted into three characters, '1', '2', and '7' that can then be output to the screen.

The `printf` function has no information about the type of the value it is to print out. It must be told the type. That is accomplished by conversion specifiers you must provide in the `printf` function call. A conversion specifier consists of a percent symbol, `%`, followed by a code letter. The integer conversion specifier consists of the percent sign followed by a d for decimal, `%d`. The floating-point conversion specifier is the percent sign followed by an **f** for floating-point, `%f`, and the character conversion specifier is the percent sign followed by a **c** for character, `%c`.

`%d`	integer
`%f`	floating point
`%c`	character

A `printf` function call will always have a format string as its first argument. The format string is a string constant consisting of characters enclosed in double quotes. If you are outputting a value, this value will be placed after the format string. You then need to place the conversion specifier for that value within the format string. `printf` can then convert and display that value. Any other characters within the format string will also be displayed. The syntax for the `printf` function call follows, along with an example and its output.

```
printf("format string including conversion specifier", value1);

printf("The cost is %f \n", 3.50);
```

Output follows.

```
The cost is 3.50
```

If you want to output the value of a variable, you need to place the name of that variable after the format string. Be sure to include their appropriate conversion specifier in the format string. The `printf` function will only receive the values in this variable, not the variable itself. Technically, the `printf` function prints out a value, however, that value was obtained.

In the next example and in the program in LISTING 1-3, the variable num is printed out. The variable num is first assigned the value 32. num is an integer, and its conversion specifier is `%d`. When the program runs, the format string will be printed out. The value for num will be printed out as part of the format string and placed where the conversion specifier has been placed.
In the example,

```
num = 32;
printf("The number is %d \n", num);
```

Output:

```
The cost is 32
```

A `printf` function call can output several values at a time. It is not just limited to one value. Of course, for each value, you need to place a corresponding conversion specifier in the format string. In the **putvar.c** program in LISTING 1-4, the variables num and cost are output in the same `printf` function call. Conversion specifiers in the format string are matched sequentially with the list of values following the format string. The first conversion specifier is `%d`, and this is matched to the value of the first variable, num. The second conversion specifier is `%f`, and this is matched with the value of the second variable, cost. You can output as many values as you want to in a given `printf` function call, as long as you have a corresponding conversion modifier for each placed in the format string. The appropriate syntax for the `printf` function call follows, along with an example. The first conversion specifier, `%d`, matches the first value, the value of num, and the second conversion specifier, `%f`, matches the second value, the constant 4.50.

```
printf("format string", value1, value2, etc);

printf("The num = %d and cost = %f\n", num, 4.50);
```

LISTING 1-4:

putvar.c
```
#include <stdio.h>

int main(void)
        {
        int num;
        float cost = 7.25;

        num = 32;

        printf("The integer is %d \n", num);
        printf("The floating point is %f \n", 4.50);

        printf("Num = %d, cost = %f \n", num, cost);
        return 0;
        }
```

Output for LISTING 1-4, **putvar.c**:

```
The integer is 32
The floating point is 4.500000
Num = 32, cost = 7.250000
```

The `scanf` function performs the opposite operation from that of `printf`. `scanf` takes input from the keyboard and converts the data to appropriate integer and floating-point values. However, `scanf` takes a further step: these converted values are assigned to variables. The variables are listed after the format string. Whereas `printf` has a list of values, `scanf` has a list of variables. The format string in `scanf` consists only of the conversion specifiers needed for the variables it is converting values for.

There is a special twist to the `scanf` operation. For reasons to be explained later, an ampersand (`&`) must be placed in front of the variables in a `scanf` function call. The ampersand, in this context, represents the address operation. This address operation will allow the `scanf` function to assign the value it converts from the keyboard input to the variables in the `scanf` function call. (See Table 1-3). Without the ampersand, the program most likely will crash. The syntax for a `scanf` function call is listed next followed by an example. The format string in this example consists only of the conversion specifier for the num variable, `"%d"`, and the num variable has an ampersand placed before it, `&num`.

```
scanf("format string of conversion specifiers", &variable1, &variable2, etc);

scanf("%d", &num);
```

In the **invar.c** program in LISTING 1-5, scanf is used to read a value from the user first for the variable num, and then again for the variable cost. A printf is placed before each scanf to display a prompt for each input. The ampersand is placed before the variables num and cost.

LISTING 1-5:

invar.c

```c
#include <stdio.h>

int main(void)
    {
    int num;
    float cost;

    printf("Please enter number \n");
    scanf("%d", &num);
    printf("Please enter a cost \n");
    scanf("%f", &cost);
    printf("Num = %d, cost = %f \n", num, cost);
    return 0;
    }
```

Output for LISTING 1-5, **invar.c**:

```
Please enter number
96
Please enter a cost
28.30
Num = 96, cost = 28.300000
```

Table 1-3: Conversion Specifiers

Conversion Specifiers	
%c	character
%d	decimal
%f	float
%s	string (character array)

Arrays and Strings

Arrays are declared and used much like arrays in other languages. However, array elements are actually referenced with pointer operations. An explanation of how an array really works can easily lead to a great deal of confusion. For this reason, arrays are discussed in several chapters in Part 2 of the text. At this point, you will cover the basics of a simple character array.

An array is declared with a type, a name, and a number enclosed in brackets. Below, an array of 80 characters is declared with the name `lastname`.

```
char lastname[80];
```

Arrays of characters perform a special role in C. They are used to hold strings. There is no data type for a string in C. String operations, such as comparing two strings, are implemented by manipulating an array of characters.

Both `scanf` and `printf` can work with strings. The conversion specifier for a string is `%s`. In the **mystr.c** program in LISTING 1-6, the array `lastname` is treated as a string. The `scanf` function receives input for the string, and `printf` prints out the string.

In the `scanf` function call, an array name does not have an ampersand placed before it. An array name has special features that allow `scanf` to use it to copy characters into the array. This has to do with the fact that array operations are really pointer operations, as explained in Part 2 of the text.

LISTING 1-6:

mystr.c

```
#include <stdio.h>

int main(void)
    {
    int num;
    char lastname[80];

    printf("Please enter integer \n");
    scanf("%d", &num);
    printf("Please enter Lastname\n");
    scanf("%s", lastname);
    printf("Num is %d, Lastname is %s\n", num,lastname);
    return 0;
    }
```

Output for LISTING 1-6, **mystr.c**:

```
Please enter integer
37
Please enter Lastname
Petersen
Num is 37, Lastname is Petersen
```

Expressions

Your C programs will consist of expressions and statements. Expressions, in C, perform different tasks, whereas statements organize and control those tasks. A common example of an expression is the arithmetic addition expression that adds two values.

In C, expressions have a more aggressive role than in other programming languages. Expressions not only perform arithmetic or comparison operations, but also perform assignments and function calls. In fact, assignments are really expressions, not statements. Function calls are also expressions and can be placed anywhere you would place an expression. You will find function calls in test expressions and in assignment operations. Function calls are examined more fully in Chapter 6.

An expression consists of three components: an operator, operands, and a result. The operator performs an operation on the operands to obtain a result. You can then use this result in another operation such as another arithmetic operation or even a `printf` function call. Table 1-4 provides a listing of the more commonly used expression operators.

C has the same arithmetic operations found in most other programming languages. You can add, multiply, divide, or subtract. Next is an example of a simple addition expression. The two operands are the constants 4 and 7. The operator is the + sign denoting addition. The result will be 11.

```
(4 + 7)
```

Table 1-4: Operators

Arithmetic Operators

+	addition
−	subtraction
*	multiplication
/	division
%	modulo (remainder)

Comparison Operators

<	less than
>	greater than
<=	less than or equal
>=	greater than or equal
==	equal
!=	not equal
&&	and
||	or
!	not

Assignment Operator

=	Assign value to variable
	Variable = Value

Function Call Operator

()	Call Function
	function name(arguments)

Expressions can also perform comparisons, comparing one value to another. For example, you can check whether one value is greater than another. Such expressions are referred to as comparison expressions. Comparison expressions check for the truth or falsehood of a comparison. Their result is a true or false value. For example, if an expression checks to see if one operand is greater than the other, and this is, in fact, true, then the result of the expression is true. Comparison expressions are used primarily as test expressions for condition and loop statements described in the next section.

Like other programming languages, C has the standard relational operations, such as the greater-than and less-than operations. In the next example, the comparison expression compares the value of num to the constant 3 to see if that value is less than 3. If it is, the expression will be true; if not, it will be false.

```
(num < 3)
```

Unlike other programming languages, in C, the assignment operation is an expression, not a statement. The assignment operator is a single equal sign, =. An assignment operation consists of the assignment operator and two operands on either side. The left-side operand is a variable, and the right-side operand is a value. The value is assigned to the variable. The result of this expression is the value assigned. In the next example, the value 6 is assigned to the variable num.

```
num = 6
```

You can use as the value the result of yet another expression. In the next example, the result of an addition expression is assigned to the variable total.

```
total = (6 + 5 + 12)
```

An expression cannot be placed within your program by itself. You always need to place an expression within a statement. Statements are designed to hold expressions. Some statements perform complex operations such as loops. However, the simplest statement is designed only to hold an expression. It is called the expression statement and consists of an expression followed by a semicolon. The semicolon designates the end of a statement.

> *expression;*

Following are several examples of expression statements. Each consists of an expression terminated by a semicolon, ;. The assignment operation is an assignment expression, placed within an expression statement. It is not an assignment statement as it would be in other programming languages.

```
(4 + 7);
num = 6;                    total = (6 + 5 + 12);
```

LISTING 1-7:

myexpr.c

```c
#include <stdio.h>

int main(void)
    {
    int num, total;

    total = (6 + 5 + 12);

    num = (total / 3);

    printf("Total = %d, and Num = %d\n", total, num);

    printf("Square of Num = %d\n", (num * num) );
    return 0;
    }
```

Output for LISTING 1-7, **myexpr.c**:

```
Total = 23, and Num = 7
Square of Num = 49
```

In the **myexpr.c** program in LISTING 1-7, several arithmetic and assignment expressions are shown. The program consists of a series of expression statements. Since a function call is also an expression, the two `printf` function calls are also expression statements. Notice the use of an expression in the second `printf` function call. Instead of listing a variable, the expression (num * num) is used. The result of this expression is then output by `printf`.

Statements: Conditions and Loops

Statements organize and control the execution of your program. Condition statements allow you to choose one statement or another. Loops repeat different statements. Statements such as conditions and loops are often referred to as control structures. (See Table 1-5). Control structures provide a program with decision-making capability. They are examined in greater detail in Chapter 4.

Conditions: if

There are several kinds of condition statements, the most common of which is the `if` statement. An `if` statement consists of the keyword if followed by a test expression and then a statement. If the text expression is true, then the statement is executed. If the expression is false, the statement is not executed.

> `if` (*test-expression*)
> *statement*;

In the **myif.c** program in LISTING 1-8, the user is prompted to enter a number (notice the ampersand before the num variable in the `scanf` function call, `&num`). Then the `if` statement checks to see if the user entered 2. If so, the `printf` for the second greeting is output. If not, then the program just skips to the "Goodbye."

LISTING 1-8:

myif.c
```c
#include <stdio.h>

int main(void)
    {
    int num;

    printf("Please enter a number\n");
    scanf("%d", &num);

    if ( num == 2)
            {
            printf("2nd Greeting - Hello\n");
            }
    printf("Goodbye\n");
    return 0;
    }
```

Output for LISTING 1-8, **myif.c**:

```
Please enter a number
2
2nd Greeting - Hello
Goodbye
```

Loops: while

A loop will cause statements to be repeatedly executed until a test condition proves false. A commonly used loop in C is the `while` loop. It consists of the keyword while followed by a test expression and a statement or block of statements.

```
while(test-expression)
        {
        statements;
        }
```

In the **myloop.c** program in LISTING 1-9, a simple counting loop prints out the value of the variable `i` three times. The test condition is a less-than relational expression that will test to see if the value in `i` is less than 3. The variable `i` is used to control the loop. It is initialized before the loop, tested against the constant 3, and then incremented within the loop. The incrementation takes place by adding one to the value of `i` and then assigning the result back to `i`.

LISTING 1-9:

myloop.c

```c
#include <stdio.h>

int main(void)
        {
        int i;

        i = 1;
        while ( i <= 3)
                {
                printf("This is iteration %d \n", i);
                i = i + 1;
                }
        printf("Goodbye\n");
        return 0;
        }
```

Output for LISTING 1-9, **myloop.c**:

```
This is iteration 1
This is iteration 2
This is iteration 3
Goodbye
```

Table 1-5: Statements

`;`	*expression ;*

`{`
`}`
	`{`
	statement ;
	`}`

`while`	`while(`*test expression*`)`
	`{`
	statement ;
	statement ;
	`}`

`if`	`if(`*test expression*`)` *statement;*

`if-else`	`if(`*test expression*`)`
	statement ;
	`else`
	statement ;

Chapter Summary

A function is the basic component of a C program. The tasks that you want a function to perform are specified by statements that are placed within the function. A function is defined with a header and a body. The header consists of the function return type, the function name, and the list of function parameters. The body is a block that contains variable declarations followed by statements.

   Variable declarations are placed at the beginning of a function block. The declaration consists of the data type, followed by the variable's name. A semicolon ends the declaration. Statements follow the variable declarations and are usually terminated with a semicolon. You can place statements within loops to execute them repeatedly.

   To better organize your program, you can divide it up into several separate functions. C programs often consist of many different functions. Through function calls, your program can move from the execution of one function to that of another. After a function finishes executing all its statements, it returns control to the function that called it.

   A program's execution always begins with the function whose name is `main`. `main` is a keyword indicating that the program will begin with this function. If this `main` function is missing, then the functions do not constitute a program. It is possible for a program to consist of only one function, the `main` function. Many of the examples in the next few chapters will be simple programs consisting of only the `main` function.

   Basic input and output operations are executed with the `printf` and `scanf` functions. The arguments for a `printf` function are a format string and an optional list of values. If you want to output values, the format string needs to contain the appropriate conversion specifiers for those values. For example, if you want to output the value 3.50, you need to use the conversion specifier `%f` for floating-point values. The constant 3.50 would then follow the format string within the `printf` function call. If you want to output the value held by an integer variable called num, then you need the integer conversion specifier `%d` in the format string and the variable name num placed after the format string. The next example illustrates this operation.

```
printf("Value of num is %d \n", num);
```

The `scanf` function is used for input. Its format string consists only of a set of conversion specifiers. The format string is followed by a list of variables, each with an ampersand in front of it. An array name is the exception to the rule, as it has no ampersand placed before it. The next example allows you to input a value to the variable num.

```
scanf("%d", &num);
```

Arrays appear to operate much like arrays in other languages. However, the actual implementation of arrays in C is very different. Because arrays are so different, they are handled in Part 2 of this text.

Expressions perform a more aggressive role in C than in other languages. They include the standard arithmetic and comparison operations but also perform assignment operations and function calls. Expressions consist of three components; the operator, operands, and the result. The operator operates on the operands to obtain the result.

Statements organize and control expressions. All statements are terminated by a semicolon, *;* . The simplest statement is the expression statement consisting of an expression. Other, more complex statements control the execution of a program. These are known as control structures. There are two major types of control structures, conditions and loops. Conditions, such as the `if` statement, decide whether a statement is to be executed or not. Loops, such as the `while` statement, repeat a set of statements until a specified test fails.

With these basic components, programs can be written and run. It is helpful to write small programs to see how different features of the language operate. Suggested exercises are in the back of each chapter.

Table 1-6: Basic C Features

Data Types

```
        int
                    int num;
        long
                    long num;
        char
                    char  letter:
        float
                    float cost;
        double
                    double cost;
```

Escape Sequence Characters

Octal Characters
```
        \Ooo   \007   \7
```

Hexadecimal Characters
```
\Xoo    \x7    \x6g
```

Line and Page Characters

`\a`	alert (beep) (ANSI)
`\n`	newline
`\t`	tab
`\f`	form feed
`\r`	carriage return
`\v`	vertical tab (ANSI)
`\b`	backspace

Quote and Backslash Characters

`\\`	backslash character
`\'`	single quote character
`\"`	double quote character (ANSI)

Conversion Specifiers

`%c`	character
`%d`	decimal
`%f`	float
`%s`	string (character array)

Operators

Arithmetic Operators

`+`	addition
`–`	subtraction
`*`	multiplication
`/`	division
`%`	modulo (remainder)

Comparison Operators

`<`	less than
`>`	greater than
`<=`	less than or equal
`>=`	greater than or equal
`==`	equal
`!=`	not equal
`&&`	and
`||`	or
`!`	not

Assignment Operator

`=`	Assign value to variable
	Variable = Value

Function Call Operator

`()`	Call Function
	function name(arguments)

Statements

;	*expression ;*
{ }	{ *statement ;* }
while	while (*test expression*) { *statement ;* *statement ;* }
if	if (*test expression*) *statement ;*
if-else	if (*test expression*) *statement ;* else ¡ ;

Exercises

1. Write a short program to print out characters with the `printf` function. For example:

```
#include <stdio.h>

int main(void)
    {
    printf("Hello and how are you");
    printf("This didn't really work, did it?");
    printf("I forgot the newline \n");
    return 0;
    }
```

2. Write, compile, and run a short program that prompts you for your first name and your age and then displays those values on the screen.

3. Write, compile, and run a program that prompts you to enter a number and then displays the cube of that number.

4. Write a program using a counting loop to print out your name three times.

Data Types

Variables, Constants, and Conversions

2. Data Types

C has a wide range of data types, each with its own variations. In this chapter, each data type will be discussed in terms of how it is used with variables, constants, and input/output functions. At the end of the chapter, input and output functions such as `printf` and `scanf` will be explained in detail.

A data type specifies a way to interpret a sequence of binary bits. A set of bits is associated with a variable or constant. These bits can be interpreted as different kinds of data. The primary data types in C are integer and floating-point. An integer data type will interpret a set of bits as an integer value, and a floating-point data type will interpret the set of bits as a floating-point value.

The data types are specified in different ways for variables and constants. Variables use a set of keywords representing the different data types, whereas a constant relies on its format, sometimes using symbolic qualifiers. A variable declaration will specify the name of the variable and its data type. The name will be used to reference the set of bits associated with a variable. The data type will be used to interpret those bits as the specified type of data.

There are also data types that are only variations of the integer and floating-point types. `long` and `short` integer data types can hold values that are smaller or larger than that of a regular integer. The character data type, though an integer type, is used to represent characters. The `double` data type is a floating-point type that has greater precision than the regular floating-point type.

The simplicity of having only two primary data types in C can be misleading. C actually has several different kinds of data types. There are primary data types, aggregate data types, and derived data types. The aggregate types are structures, unions, and arrays. The structure type can be used to declare variables, but the array type cannot. Arrays are a special case, requiring an understanding of pointer operations. All these types can be combined further to form complex derived types. This chapter will only cover the primary types.

Declarations and Data Types

A variable declaration consists of a data type and an identifier, followed by a semicolon. Data types are used in declarations to specify an object's type. In the case of variable declarations, the identifier is the variable name, and the data type is specified by one of several keywords. The syntax for a declaration is described here followed by a sample declaration of an integer variable with the name **num**.

Data-Type	Variable-Name;
int	num;

The primary data types, integer and floating-point, are represented by the keywords `int` and `float`. Below are the keywords for the primary data types and examples of their use in declarations.

keyword	data type	declaration
int	integer	int num;
float	floating-point	float cost;

There are further variations on each of these data types. An integer can be a `long` or a `short`. A floating-point value can be either `float` or `double`. These types can be further specified as unsigned, signed, or constant. Following are the basic types and their keywords.

Basic Types: **Keywords:**
Integer   `int`
long integer   `long`
short integer   `short`
Character   `char`
Floating-point   `float`
                            `double`

For a variable name, you can only use letters, numbers, or underscores. There may be no spaces, commas, asterisks, slashes, hyphens, or any other kind of special character. Alphanumeric characters, characters '0' through '9', may be used as `long` as one is not the first character in the name. By convention, a variable never begins with an underscore. Such variable names are usually reserved for special variables used by your compiler or operating system. You also cannot use a keyword as a variable name. Keywords are the names used for data types and statements, such as `int` and while. Examples of valid variable names follow.

```
Aleina
Total78
Sub_total_89
count
```

In a declaration, the data type is placed before the variable name. This differs from the syntax of other computer languages such as Pascal. Here are some examples of variable declarations.

```
int count;
long id;
float cost;
char letter;
unsigned adder;
```

You can declare more than one variable of the same data type on the same line. In that case, you only write the data type once, and you then separate each variable name with a comma.

```
int count, num;
```

Declarations can also include initializations. An initialization uses the assignment operator, =. To the right of the assignment operator is the value with which to initialize the variable. In the next example, the variable **id** is initialized to 78. In the declarations of **count** and **num**, the initializations are incorporated into the comma-separated declarations.

```
long id = 78;
int count = 5, num = 1;
```

Integral and Floating-Point Data Types

Data is represented in memory by a sequence of bits. These bits are arranged into bytes, eight bits to a byte. The bits within a byte can be interpreted in several ways. In terms of numeric values, there are two qualitatively different ways in which bits are interpreted. Bits can be interpreted as an integral value or as a floating-point value. An integral interpretation interprets the bits as integers. A floating-point interpretation segments bits into an exponential number and a fractional number, which are then combined to construct a floating-point value.

Arithmetically, an integral value is best represented as an integer. An integer is a positive or negative number. 1, -1, 34, and -46 are all integer numbers. Floating-point values are best represented by real numbers, which are all the possible numeric values in between, and including, integer numbers. Real numbers have a fractional component. 3.5, 3.670, 57.10, 1.0, and -1.75 are all real numbers.

There are four different kinds of integral data types: character, integer, `short` integer, and `long` integer. These types vary only in terms of their size. A `long` integer uses more bytes and is thus able to represent larger integral values than a regular integer. A character has only one byte and has a limited range of integral values.

There are two kinds of floating-point values: single-precision and double-precision floats. These vary according to the number of bytes used. A double-precision `float` normally has twice as many bytes as a single-precision `float`. However, they do not differ in the range of their values. They only differ in terms of the accuracy of their floating-point values. Double precision has greater precision than single precision. Figure 2-4 displays the different range and size of each data type.

Integer Types: int, short, long, and unsigned

Integral types are used to represent integer numbers such as 4, 23, 10, or -7. They are signed and can have a positive or negative value. The integral types vary according to the range of integer values they can represent.

The keyword `int` is the name for the basic integer data type. An `int` usually takes the same number of bytes as a machine-level word. If on a given system, a word uses 2 bytes, an `int` will use 2 bytes. If 4 bytes are used for a word, then 4 bytes will be used for an `int`. The number of bytes used for an `int` will determine its range of possible values. A 2-byte `int` can represent signed integer values from +32767 to -32767. In C, an integer has a minimum range of +32767 to -32767. The range may be greater, but must at least meet these minimums. An `int` consisting of a 2-byte word has 16 bits, of which 15 are used for the integer value; its maximum value is 2^{15}-1 (32767). The remaining bit is the sign bit. In some systems, the sign bit is used to provide an added negative value, -32768. Figure 2-1 shows how an integer is implemented in a binary format.

The actual sequence of binary bits use to represent an integer value may further differ depending upon whether your system uses a big-endian or little-endian arrangement for its integer values. "Endian" refers to the end of the bytes at which the number begins. In a big-endian format, the number begins with the least significant bit, the 0 bit. In a little-endian format the number begins with the most significant bit; in a 2-byte integer, this would be bit 15. Windows systems use a little-endian format, while Unix and Mac systems use a big-endian format. The examples in this text use the little-endian format. For example, the number 0x11223344 represented here using a hexadecimal format would have a little-endian implementation of 0x44332211, whereas the big-endian implementation would be 0x11223344.

There are times when an integer value larger than that of an `int` is required, and there are times when only smaller integer values will be used. The other two integer data types, `long` and `short`, are used for these situations. A `long` usually has twice the number of bytes as a `short`. The size of a `long` is usually 4 bytes, and the size of a `short` is 2 bytes. The `long` is used to manage large integer values. In a 4-byte `long`, 31 bits are used for the integer values, providing a maximum value of 2^{31} - 1 (2147483647). Systems, where a `long` uses more bytes, will, of course, have a greater maximum value. The 32nd bit is reserved for the sign. In a 2-byte `short`, 15 bits are used for integer values, providing a maximum value of 2^{15} - 1 (32767). The remaining bit is a sign bit.

Integers

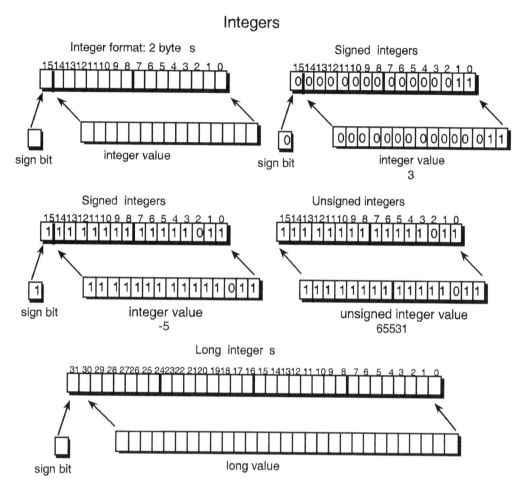

Figure 2-1: Integer binary 16-bit and 32-bit representation, signed and unsigned.

Depending upon the system, an `int` may be the size of a `short`, or it may be the size of a `long`. The deciding factor is usually the size of a word. An `int` is usually the same size as a word. In a system where a word is 32 bits (4 bytes), the `long` and the `int` may be the same size. A `short` remains 16 bits (2 bytes). In a system where the word is 16 bits (2 bytes), a `short` and the `int` may be the same size. A `long` remains 32 bits (4 bytes). In ANSI C, the actual sizes of integer types, as well as other types, are given in the **limits.h** file provided with your C compiler.

All three integer types can be qualified with the type qualifier unsigned, making them unsigned integers. An unsigned `int` is an `int` in which the sign bit is incorporated in the integer value. Instead of only 15 bits being used, all 16 bits are used for the integer value. The minimum required value for an unsigned `int` is $2^{16} - 1$ (65535) instead of $2^{15} - 1$ (32767). An unsigned integer has only positive values. In the case of a 2-byte unsigned integer, the values range from 0 to 65535. The same is true for unsigned `short` and unsigned `long`. The unsigned `long` values range from 0 to 4294967295 ($2^{32} - 1$). Table 2-1A and Table 2-1B summarizes signed and unsigned integer values.

Integer Constants: long, unsigned, Octal, and Hexadecimal

An integer constant is represented by a series of numbers. The numbers must not begin with zero or have a decimal point. Commas are not allowed. Numbers preceded by a minus sign represent negative integer values. Below are examples of integer constants:

```
3      756     25000    -72     -8
```

An integer constant qualified by an l or an L placed at the end is a `long` integer. An integer constant qualified by a U or u is an unsigned integer. You can combine the two to form unsigned `long` integer constants. Samples of each follow.

```
4L      -360000l      575U    42000u 9990000UL
```

An integer value can also be represented in octal or a hexadecimal form. The underlying representation of an integer is a binary value. This binary value can be interpreted using different bases. A standard integer interprets the binary value using a base of 10. An octal representation interprets the binary value using a base of 8. A hexadecimal representation interprets the binary value using a base of 16. Both octal and hexadecimal representations easily map into a binary value. Knowing a very few basic translation rules, you can easily tell the actual configuration of the binary value by simply seeing its octal or hexadecimal equivalent.

Octal integer constants are represented with a leading zero. Any set of numbers beginning with a 0 is considered an octal number. A hexadecimal integer constant is represented by the leading character x or X. Often a zero is placed before the x. Since a hexadecimal system has a base of 16, the values from 10 to 15 are represented by the letters a to f. Here are some examples of decimal, octal, and hexadecimal integer constants.

Integer	Octal	Hexadecimal
4	04	0x4
12	014	0xc
9	011	0x9
123	0173	0x7b

You can use the l and L qualifiers with the octal and hexadecimal numbers for large numbers:

```
075000L 0x77fff001
```

To have a C program display an integer value on your screen, you will need to use the appropriate conversion specifiers in a `printf` function call. To print out the value of an integer to the screen requires that an integer value first be converted to a sequence of characters. The number 127 must be converted into the characters '1', '2', and '7'. The functions `printf` and `scanf` use conversion specifiers to provide this kind of conversion. However, it is the programmer's responsibility to match the type of the conversion specifier with the data type of the value being output.

.The `printf` function provides conversion specifiers for all types of integers and their variations. The basic type of conversion specifier is the `%d`, for decimal. The `%u` conversion specifier is for unsigned integer values. The `%o` and `%x` conversion specifiers print out the octal and hexadecimal equivalents of the integer values. To convert a `long` value, you need to modify a conversion specifier with a lowercase `l`. The `l` modifier is placed between the percent sign and the conversion specifier. `%ld` converts a `long` integer, and `%lu` converts a `long` unsigned integer. The h modifier converts `short` integers. `%hd` converts a `short` integer. This is needed only on systems where `short` and `int` are different sizes. Here is a list of the different integer conversion specifiers.

`%d`	`%i`	int (decimal)
`%ld`		long
`%hd`		short
`%u`		unsigned int
`%lu`		unsigned long
`%o`		octal
`%x`		hexadecimal
`%lo`	`%lx`	long octal and long hex

In the **intypes.c** program in LISTING 2-1, the `printf` statements print out various kinds of integer values using different conversion specifiers. Each integer can be represented in decimal, octal, or hexadecimal form. This has no effect on the actual value of the integer. **num** is printed out in its integer, octal, and hexadecimal forms. The same kind of situation applies to the `printf` statement for small and little. In the last `printf`, the integer values of small and little are printed out in decimal form. The fact that they were assigned values using octal and hexadecimal constants makes no difference. The integer value is the same.

LISTING 2-1:

intypes.c
```
#include <stdio.h>
int main(void)
        {
        int num;
        short int small;
        short little;
        long int big;
        long large;
        unsigned int unum = 45000;
        unsigned long ubig= 3000000000Ul;
        num = 75;
        small = 0173;
        little = 0x7b;
        big = 85000;
        large =  -400001;

        printf("Num Dec = %d, Num Octal = %o, Num Hex = %x \n", num, num, num);
        printf("Small = %ho, Little = %hx \n", small, little);
        printf("Big = %ld, Large = %ld \n", big, large);
        printf("Unum = %u, Ubig = %lu \n", unum, ubig);

        printf("Small= %hd,Little= %hd\n", small, little);

        return 0;
        }
```

Output for LISTING 2-1:

```
Num Dec = 75, Num Octal = 113, Num Hex = 4b
Small = 173, Little = 7b
Big = 85000, Large = -40000
Unum = 45000, Ubig = 300000000
Small= 123,Little= 123
```

Table 2-1A: Signed Integers

int	int is the standard integer data type.
	Size: system-dependent, though usually size of a word.
	Range: For 2-byte word: -32767 to 32767
	Declaration:
	    `int num;`
	Constants:
	    `5  789`

long	long is used for large numbers.
	Size: usually 4 bytes.
	Range: -2147483647 to +2147483647
	Declaration:
	    `long num;`
	    `long int num;`
	Constants:
	    `7000000  5000001  5L  -3551`

short	short is used for small numbers.
	Size: usually 2 bytes.
	Range: -32767 to 32767 (2-byte size)
	Declaration:
	    `short count;`
	    `short int count;`

Character Types

Characters are represented in C by integer values. The correspondence between a given character and an integer value is determined by an agreed-upon character set. Depending on the compiler, C may use one of several character sets. One of the most popular is the ASCII character set.

The ASCII character set represents characters using integer values from a range of 0 to 127. For example, the character 'A' is represented by the integer value 65. This requires only one byte of memory. In an 8-bit byte, the range of ASCII values does not use the sign bit. The 7 bits used provide a maximum value of $2^7 - 1$ (127). Figure 2-2 displays the binary representation of different kinds of character values.

In some systems, the character set is extended by using the sign bit to represent an additional range of values. These extended configurations are system-dependent, though the most popular one is that for the IBM PC. An extended character set represents more characters, with an overall range of 0 to 255. Only one byte of memory is required. However, all eight bits, including the sign bit, are used. This provides a maximum value of $2^8 - 1$ (255).

Table 2-1B: Unsigned Integers

`unsigned int`	An unsigned integer has only positive values.
	Size: same as an `int`.
	Range: 0 to 65535 for 2-byte `int`
	Declaration:
	`unsigned id;`
	`unsigned int id;`
	Constants:
	`70000U  5u  355U`

`unsigned long`	A long integer without a sign bit.
	Size: usually 4-bytes.
	Range: 0 to 4294967295
	Declaration:
	`unsigned long id;`
	`unsigned long int id;`
	Constants:
	`9400000000u  751U`

`unsigned short`	Same size as a short `unsigned short int  id;`

In C, the `char` data type is used to declare a character variable with a size of 1 byte. This byte is treated as a 1-byte integer. You can use it in any kind of integral expression, whether it be arithmetic, relational, or an assignment. You can assign a variable of type `char` to an integer with no loss of information, or compare it to an integer in a relational operation, or even use it in an arithmetic operation with an integer. In most situations, a character and an integer are interchangeable, because a character is simply a smaller integer.

The `char` data type may, by default, be signed or unsigned. This often depends on upon whether or not a system uses an extended character set. An extended character set requires the use of the sign bit and would, therefore, default to an unsigned `char` data type. A system without an extended character set would not use the sign bit and would thus default to a signed `char` data type. The signed or unsigned type qualifier can force a character variable to be signed or unsigned in its declaration. In conversions from a signed character to an integer, an effect called sign extension can take place, making the integer value different from the character value. See Chapter 26 for a detailed discussion of sign extension. Following are examples of character declarations.

```
char letter;
signed char Sletter;
unsigned char Uletter;
```

Character constants are represented with a given character placed within single quotes. 'A' is the constant for the character A. Character constants have a character data type and, as such, have an integer value. The character constant, like variables of the `char` data type, can be used interchangeably with integers. However, keep in mind that there is a difference between a numeric character and an integer constant. The number 9 is the integer constant nine. The number nine placed within single quotes, '9', is a character constant representing the character symbol 9 in the character set. The integer constant 9 has an integer value of 9, whereas the character constant '9' has an integer value of 57.

In the **chartype.c** program in LISTING 2-2, integers and characters have been intermixed. The character variable letter is assigned a character constant, 'A'. The integer variable **num** is then assigned the value of the character variable letter. **num** and **letter** now have the same integer value.

In the first printf, **letter** and **num** are printed with their respective conversion specifiers, %c for character and %d for integer. In the second printf, the conversion specifiers are switched. **letter** is printed out as an integer, and **num** is printed out as a character. A character can be treated as an integer. An integer, if its value is less than 127, can be used as if it were a character. However, an integer whose value is greater than 127 has a value beyond the scope of the character set. In such a case, errors can result.

LISTING 2-2:

chartype.c

```
#include <stdio.h>

int main(void)
    {
    char letter;
    int num;

    letter = 'A';
    num = letter;

    printf("Letter = %c, Num = %d \n", letter, num);
    printf("Letter = %d, Num = %c \n", letter, num);
    return 0;
    }
```

Output for LISTING 2-2:

```
Letter = A, Num = 65
Letter = 65, Num = A
```

In the **intchar.c** program in LISTING 2-3, the character variable initial is assigned an integer value, 71, which happens to be equivalent to the character 'G' in the ASCII character set. The integer variable count is assigned the integer value of the character constant '9'. The integer value of '9' is 57. Both are printed out first as characters and then as integers.

The character set includes more than alphabetic characters. It was designed to represent the possible characters that could be typed on a keyboard. There are many keys on the keyboard that do not represent alphabetic or numeric symbols. These are keys that perform functions, such as the tab or the newline. There are also function keys and control keys. Most of these keys are represented in the character set. Some, like the function keys, require an extended character set.

All of these keys have integer values assigned by the character set. However, they do not have corresponding symbols that can be placed within single quotes and used as a character constant. The alphabetic symbol A can be placed within single quotes to represent the character A, 'A'. However, a tab or newline has no corresponding symbol. There are two solutions to this problem. First, you can simply use the integer value of the key needed. The integer value for a tab is 9, in the ASCII character set. The second approach is to use what is called in C an escape sequence. An escape sequence is used to represent an octal or hexadecimal equivalent of the character's integer value. All characters have an octal or hex equivalent, which can be specified in an escape sequence (see Table 2-2).

LISTING 2-3:

intchar.c

```
#include <stdio.h>

int main(void)
        {
        char initial;
        int count;

        initial = 71;
        count = '9';

        printf("Initial = %c,Count = %c \n",initial, count);
        printf("Initial = %d,Count = %d \n",initial, count);
        return 0;
        }
```

Output for LISTING 2-3:

```
        Initial = G, Count = 9
        Initial = 71, Count = 57
```

The escape symbol in C is the backslash, \. The integer equivalent of a character value can then be represented with an octal or hexadecimal constant. In the following example, the integer equivalent for a tab, represented by an octal and then by a hexadecimal value, is assigned to the character variable mytab. When an octal value is used in an escape sequence, its preceding 0 can be left out. '\07' can be represented as '\7'.

```
char mytab:

mytab = 7;
mytab = 07
mytab = '\7';
mytab = '\0x7';
mytab = '\07';           /* but not mytab = \7, or mytab = '07'*/
```

The escape sequence is enclosed in single quotes. The escape sequence literally represents a character symbol. It is a mistake to say mytab = \7 instead of mytab = '\7'. The backslash is required in order to specify the octal or hexadecimal equivalent of a character constant. The escape sequence instructs the compiler to read what follows not as a character, but as the octal equivalent of a character. '\7' is the octal equivalent of the ASCII tab character. However, '07' is an error, and '7' is the character constant for the character 7.

Often it is necessary to assign a zero value to a character variable. This zero value is usually referred to as a null value. A character variable could be assigned the integer constant zero, 0. But usually, for the sake of consistency and clarity, you should assign a character constant that is equivalent to zero. Such a constant is the escape sequence for an octal zero placed within single quotes, '\0'. It is often referred to as the null character. There is a crucial difference between the octal value '\0' and the character constant '0'. The octal value '\0' is the integer equivalent of zero, 0, whereas the character constant '0' is the ASCII integer equivalent of 48 and an octal equivalent of 060. In the next example, mynull is assigned a null character, whereas initial is assigned the numeric character '0'.

```
char initial
char mynull;

mynull = '\0';
initial = '0';
```

Many of the keyboard characters, such as tab and newline, are used so often that C provides a set of special symbols for them. These symbols operate only with an escape sequence. They replace the need to represent such characters with their octal or hexadecimal equivalent. The most commonly used escape symbols are those for the newline and tab. But there are others, used for such characters as the backspace and vertical tab. Some have been introduced with ANSI C only.

Table 2-2: Characters

char   A single character with integral value.
Size: one byte.
Range: ASCII character set, 0 to 127 characters
Range: Extended character set, 0 to 255 characters
Declaration:
```
        char  letter:
        signed char letter;
        unsigned char letter;
```
Constant:
Characters
```
                'h'
                '8'                letter 8, not integer 8
                '?'
```
Escape Sequence.
Octal
```
                '\n'
                '\007'
                '\7'
```
Hexadecimal
```
                \x7'
```

In the next example, 0101 and '\101' are two uses of an octal constant. The first is the normal use of an octal constant, and the second is the octal constant used in an escape sequence.

```
char letter;

letter = 'A'
letter = 65;
letter = 0101;
letter = '\101';
letter = '\x41';
```

Characters

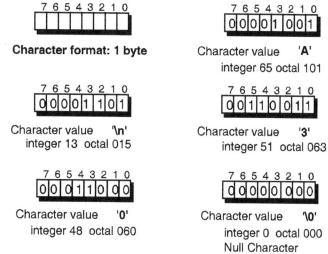

Character format: 1 byte

Character value   **'A'**
integer 65 octal 101

Character value   **'\n'**
integer 13 octal 015

Character value   **'3'**
integer 51 octal 063

Character value   **'0'**
integer 48 octal 060

Character value   **'\0'**
integer 0 octal 000
Null Character

Figure 2-2: Characters and corresponding integer and octal values. The values for the ASCII character set are used here.

LISTING 2-4:

escsym.c
```c
#include <stdio.h>
int main(void)
        {
        char mytab;
        char mynewline;

        mytab = '\t';
        mynewline = '\n';

        printf("The cost of oranges = \t 7.00. \n");
        printf("Below is a list of types of oranges.\n");
        printf ("\tValencia\n\tNavel\n\tJuice\n");

        putchar(mynewline);
        putchar(mytab);
        printf ("Goodbye");
        putchar('\n');
        putchar('\a');
        return 0;
        }
```

Output for LISTING 2-4:
```
        The cost of oranges =   7.00.
        Below is a list of types of oranges.
                Valencia
                Navel
                Juice

                Goodbye
```

The most common of these escape sequence symbols are the **n** for newline and the **t** for tab. A newline character constant can be specified with \n, and a tab character constant can be specified with a \t. The newline and tab are often used in the format string of a `printf` statement as shown in the **escsym.c** program in LISTING 2-4. However, you can just as easily assign them to character variables. Table 2-3 summarizes escape sequence characters in C.

Table 2-3: Escape Sequence Characters

Octal Characters
<code>\0oo</code>   <code>\007</code>
(0 may be omitted for octal: \7)

Hexadecimal Characters
<code>\Xoo</code>   <code>\x7</code>

Line and Page Characters

\a	alert (beep)
\n	newline
\t	tab
\f	form feed
\r	carriage return
\v	vertical tab
\b	backspace

Quote and Backslash Characters

\\	backslash character
\'	single quote character
\"	double quote character
\?	double question-mark character

The escape sequence is also used to allow those symbols used in both character and string constant specifications to be treated as characters themselves. A character constant requires the use of the single quote. However, the single quote itself is a character. Placing the single quote within its own single quotes simply confuses the compiler. ''' is invalid. This problem is overcome with the escape sequence. The escape sequence is used to specify a single quote character, '\''.

The same holds true for both the `double` quote and backslash characters. The `double` quote is used to specify string constants. To treat the `double` quote simply as a character constant requires placing it in an escape sequence. The backslash character is specified in the same way. The backslash character placed within an escape sequence is represented with two backslashes, \\.

'\''   The single quote character
'\\'   The backslash character
'\"'   The `double` quote character

```
printf(" This is a double quote \"  \n");
printf(" This is a single quote \'  \n");
printf(" This is a backslash \\  \n");
```

Table 2-4: Floating-Point Type

`float`	Floating-point value: single-precision.
	     Size: system-dependent (usually 4 bytes).
	     Range: 1.0e+37 to 1.0e-37
	     Declaration:
	          `float cost;`
	     Constant: `f` or `F`
	          `3.568f 3.568F`

`double`	Floating-point value: double-precision.
	     Size: twice the bytes of a float (usually 8 bytes)
	     Range: 1.0e+37 to 1.0e-37
	     Declaration:
	          `double cost;`
	     Constant:
	          floating-point notation.
	             `3.568`
	             `355.00`
	             `355.`
	             `0.98`
	             `.98`
	             `-355.98`
	          exponential (scientific) notation (E or e):
	            `4.78e+5` `4.78E+5`
	            `5.67e-8` `5.67E-8`
	            `.56e+7` `.56E+7`

`long double`	ANSI: Implementation is system-dependent,
	     but usually twice the number of bytes of a double.
	     Size: system-dependent (usually 16 bytes).
	     Range: 1.0e+37 to 1.0e-37
	     Declaration:
	          `long double cost;`
	     Constant: (L or l)
	          `3.568L 3.568l`

Floating-Point Data Type

The floating-point data type is used to represent real numbers. Real numbers include the fractional numbers between integers. The number 3 is an integer, whereas the number 3.56 is a real number.

The number 3.00 is the floating-point equivalent of the integer 3. Between two integer values, there can be an infinite number of real numbers. 3.2, 3.02, and 3.002 are all valid real numbers. Theoretically, the decimal places in a real number can be extended indefinitely. A floating-point data type places a limit on the extent of these decimal places, by limiting the range of possible real numbers that can be represented. In this sense, the floating-point data type only approximates real numbers.

A floating-point value is calculated from two components: an exponent and a fraction. In thinking of floating-point values, it helps to distinguish between the number of decimal places and the significant number. The fraction is the significant number in the floating-point value. The exponent will determine the number of decimal places the fraction value will be moved. In the value 37000.0, the significant number is 37, and the number of decimal places is 5. In the value 370.0, the significant number is again 37, but there are only 3 decimal places. Both are very different numbers: thirty-seven thousand and three hundred seventy.

Figure 2-3 shows how bytes, in a floating-point value, are organized into a sign, a fraction, and an exponent. In this example, the fraction of the `float` data type usually has 3 bytes, 24 bits. This allows a maximum significant number of 7 digits, meaning that a floating-point value can only contain 7 significant digits. The rest will be decimal placeholders, usually consisting of 0. The actual number of bytes used is implementation-dependent, differing from one system to another.

The data type `double` is a larger floating-point type in which the number of bytes allowed for the fraction is expanded. Usually, a `double` will consist of 8 bytes, 64 bits. The additional 4 bytes are usually assigned to the fraction, expanding the significant number to 14 digits, 56 bits. Since the `double` provides for a much larger fraction, it provides greater accuracy in any computation. It can be said to have greater precision.

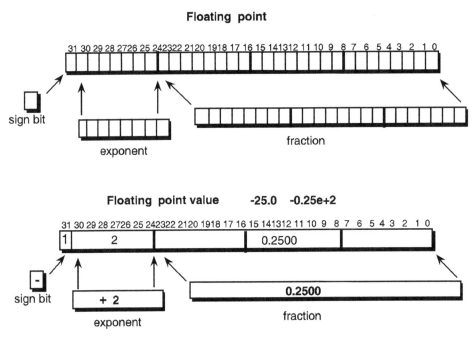

Figure 2-3: Floating-point values.

ANSI C provides for another floating-point data type that is called `long double`. The `long double` also increases the overall number of bytes for a floating-point value. However, it does not specify exactly how the components are to be expanded. The added bytes may all be used to increase the fraction, or some may be used to increase the exponent.

Figure 3-4 is a conceptual representation of a floating-point value. The actual implementation of floating-point values is more complex, requiring binary exponents and shift operations. The basic components are conceptually presented here: the sign, the exponent, and the fraction.

The exponent is implemented with 1 byte and has a range of 38. It can extend a number 38 decimal places to the right or left (this can vary with different systems). This allows the representation of large and small numbers.

The fraction and the exponent are used to calculate the floating-point value. The exponent is a positive or negative exponent with a base of 10. The number 370.0 has a fraction of 0.37 and an exponent of 3. The base of 10 is raised by the value of the exponent, 3, resulting in 1000. It is then multiplied by the fraction, 0.37 * 1000. The exponent can be negative, moving the decimal place to the left. The number 0.0037 has a fraction of 0.37 and an exponent of -2. The base of 10 is raised by an exponent of -2 to 0.01 and then multiplied by 0.37 to produce 0.0037.

The final floating-point value will have a sign, either plus or minus. This is different from the sign of the exponent. The sign of the exponent indicates whether the number is placed to the right or left of the decimal point. -370.00 has a negative sign and a positive exponent; 0.0037 has a positive sign and a negative exponent: -0.0037 has both a negative sign and a negative exponent.

Floating-Point Constants

A floating-point constant is a `double` by default. In ANSI C, it can be modified to a `float` with the qualifiers f or F to be a `float` data type. ANSI C also introduced a larger floating-point data type called a `long double`. The L or l qualifiers specify that a constant is a `long double`. Below, the same constant has been written as a `double`, a `float`, and a `long double`.

```
double  3.56
float   3.56F   3.56f
long double    3.56L   3.56l
```

Floating-point constants can be written using either decimal notation or exponential notation. Exponential notation divides a floating-point value into its fraction and exponent components. The fraction is written placing a decimal point after the first digit, followed by the letter e and the exponent. An example of exponential notation follows.

```
1.45e1
```

Exponential notation is another way of writing scientific notation. Scientific notation breaks a floating-point value into its components: the fraction and the exponent. The exponent is shown with its base of 10, which is then multiplied by the fraction. In C, exponential notation is used to represent scientific notation. The base of 10 is replaced by the symbol e or E.

Below are examples of floating-point constants in both decimal and exponential notations. Next to the exponential notation is the equivalent scientific notation. The exponent can have a negative value.

Decimal	Exponential	Scientific
14.5	1.45e1	1.45 * 101
0.0025 2.	5e-3	2.5 * 10-3
-0.0025	-2.5e-3	-2.5 * 10-3
-1500.00	-1.5e+3	-1.5 * 103
.003	3.0e-3	3.0 * 10-3

The exponential notation literally refers to the number of decimal places the significant number must be moved. Taking this into consideration, you can write the same floating-point value in several different ways. You only need to be sure that the exponent is correctly placing the decimal. For example, `1.45e1` can be written as `.145e2`. The e2 exponent moves the decimal two places to the right, giving you 14.5. You can even do away with decimals completely. `1.45e1` can be written as

145e-1. The e-1 exponent moves the decimal one place to the left, again giving you 14.5. In the next examples, each line holds equivalent floating-point values using different exponential notation.

```
1.45e1          145e-1          .145e2
3.57e1          357.0e-1        0.357e2
3e-3            30e-4           .3e-2
```

The ANSI C qualifiers for long double and float can also be used with exponential notation.

```
3e-3F           30e-4f          .3e-2L
1.45e1F         145e-1f         .145e2L
```

LISTING 2-5:

floatype.c

```c
#include <stdio.h>

int main(void)
    {
    float cost = 15.92;
    float total = 3.6e6;
    float strange ;
    double debt = 1.2e15;
    long double decrease = 5e-6;

    strange = 357e-1;       /* Value is 35.70 */

    printf("Cost = %f, Total = %f \n", cost, total);
    printf("Cost = %e, Total = %E \n", cost, total);
    printf("Cost = %g, Total = %G \n", cost, total);

    printf("Strange = %e\n", strange);

    printf("Debt=%f\nDecrease=%Lf\n", debt,decrease);
    printf("Debt=%e\nDecrease=%LE\n", debt,decrease);

    return 0;
    }
```

Output for LISTING 2-5:

```
Cost =15.920000, and Total = 3600000.000000
Cost =1.592e+1, and Total = 3.6E+6
Cost =15.92, and Total = 3.6E+6
Strange = 3.57e+1
Debt = 1200000000000000.000000
Decrease = 0.000005
Debt = 1.2e+15
Decrease = 5.0E-6
```

In most systems, the size of the exponent is the same for both float and double. This means that the maximum and minimum floating-point values for both float and double are 1.0e37 and 1.0e-37. Within this possible range of values are the two different levels of precision. In ANSI C, the smallest and largest possible values for floating-point data types are contained in the header file limits.h. Table 2-4 displays a summary of floating-point data types.

    `printf` has conversion specifiers that allow for printing floating-point values in either decimal notation or scientific notation. The `%f` is used for decimal notation, and %e is used for scientific notation. The `%g` will print out any floating-point value with an exponent less than 4 in decimal notation. Any value with an exponent greater than 4 will be printed out in scientific notation. For printing out a `long double` value, the conversion specifier must be modified with an uppercase L. `%Lf` converts a `long double`.

    The **floatype.c** program in LISTING 2-5 shows the different ways in which floating-point values can be printed out. The L modifier is used with the f conversion specifier when printing out `long double` values, `%Lf` and `%Le`. Some floating-point constants use a decimal point in their exponential notation, and others do not. The constant assigned to the variable **strange** uses no decimal in its exponential notation. strange is assigned the constant 357e-1, which is equivalent to the value 35.70. When **strange** is printed out, the exponential conversion specifier prints this in the format of 3.57e+1. The first digit is placed to the left of the decimal point, and the exponent indicates how many more decimal places the number must be moved to calculate the floating-point value 35.70.

Symbolic Constants: define, const, and enum

A literal constant is represented by a symbol that is literally equivalent to it. The integer constant 7 is represented by the numeric letter 7. The character G is represented by the letter G within single quotes, `'G'`. However, you can also represent a constant symbolically. You can use a name to represent a constant instead of its literal equivalent.

    There are three ways in which symbolic constants can be implemented. The first and most common is to use the preprocessor `define` directive to simulate a symbolic constant. The second is to declare a variable with the const qualifier. The third and most restrictive way is to define a new range of constant integer types using `enum`.

The define Directive and Symbolic Constants

The `define` directive is a preprocessor directive that you can use to simulate a symbolic constant. The `define` directive consists of the `define` keyword, a `define` symbol, and a replacement text. By convention, the `define` symbol is usually written in uppercase. The `define` directive can be thought of as a global substitution command. It replaces a symbol with a replacement text throughout the source code file. In the next example, the symbol RATE is defined as the text 0.50.

```
#define RATE    0.50
```

    There is a new line after the `define` directive and a cross-hatch (pound sign), #, before the word `define`. The pound sign and the newline form the boundaries, the beginning and end, of any preprocessor directive. The preprocessor looks for the pound sign, and when it finds it, it knows that it has been issued a directive. The pound sign should be placed in the first column of the source code file. In the **rate.c** program in LISTING 2-6, the `define` directive performs a global substitution. The collection of characters making up the symbol RATE, wherever it exists in the file, will be replaced with the text of characters 0.50.

LISTING 2-6:

rate.c

```
#include <stdio.h>

#define   RATE   0.50

int main(void)
        {
        float cost;

        cost = RATE * 5.0;
        printf("Cost = %f,  rate = %f\n",cost,  RATE);
        return 0;
        }
```

The preprocessor takes this source code and generates its own code with the text substituted in. This modified version is then passed to the compiler. Shown here is the version of this code that the compiler will actually see.

```
int main(void)
        {
        float cost;

        cost = 0.50 * 5.0;
        printf("cost = %f,  rate = %f\n",cost,  0.50);

        return 0;
        }
```

The preprocessor is not part of the compiler. It only performs simple word-processing-like operations on the text of the source code. It is the programmer's responsibility to make sure that the substituted text makes sense to the compiler. If the define directive in LISTING 2-6 were written as shown here, errors would result.

```
        #define RATE     0M5g
```

With such a define command, the preprocessor would make substitutions resulting in the version of the program listed next. This version would then be sent to the compiler, resulting in compiler errors.

```
int main(void)
        {
        float cost;

        cost = 0M5g * 5.0;
        printf("cost = %f,  rate = %f\n", cost,  0M5g);

        return 0;
        }
```

define symbols are particularly helpful if you are dealing with a value used throughout your program that you may need to change at a later date. If you had entered in the value as a constant in many different places, you would have to change each and every entry. But if you used a define symbol, you would only need to change the `define` symbol's replacement text in the `define` directive. This means you only need to make one editing change in one place, instead of searching through your program for each instance of a value. In the previous example, if the rate changes to 0.75, only the `define` directive needs to be changed. The preprocessor will then substitute 0.75 for the `RATE` symbol, wherever it is in the source code.

```
#define RATE    0.75
```

The const Qualifier and Declared Constants

The const qualifier is used to declare a variable whose value cannot be changed. An initialization is given in the declaration to provide the variable with an initial value. From that point on, the variable is effectively a constant. A constant variable has all the advantages of an ordinary variable. It is referenced with its declared name and can be scoped to a function. You can even use constant variables as function parameters, receiving their initial value from an argument in a function call.

To declare a constant variable, you precede a variable's data type with the keyword const. In effect, you are qualifying the type. After the type, you enter the variable name followed by an assignment operator and the constant value to be assigned. The next example declares a constant floating-point variable by the name of rate and assigns it the value 0.50.

```
const float rate = 05.50;
```

You can easily use the const qualifier in place of define symbols, as shown in the **ratecon.c** program in LISTING 2-7.

LISTING 2-7:

ratecon.c
```
#include <stdio.h>

int main(void)
    {
    float cost;
    const float rate = 0.50;

    cost = rate * 5;
    printf("Cost = %f, rate = %f\n",cost, rate);
    return 0;
    }
```

The enum Constant Types

The enumerator type, `enum`, allows you to define a set of integers represented by names as a new integral type. First, you need to define the `enum` type. Then you can declare integral variables of that type. The `enum` type definition consists of the keyword `enum`, followed by a user-chosen tag name, and then a set of names in braces. The `enum` type definition is usually placed outside of the functions at the beginning of the source file. The next example is an `enum` type definition for the weather `enum` type. This `enum` type has four possible integral value represented by the names clouds, rain, sun, and storm.

```
enum weather { clouds, rain, sun, storm };
```

The names in an `enum` type are named constants representing integers. The `enum` type is really a subset of the integer type. It specifies a range of integers for this type. The default range begins at 0 and continues through the count of the last name. In the **weather.c** program in LISTING 2-8, the name sun in the weather `enum` type represents the integer 2. If the names were to be printed out, their integer equivalents would be printed.

```
printf ("%d %d %d %d \n",clouds,rain,sun,storm);
```

Output:
```
0 1 2 3
```

Once you have defined an `enum` type, you can then declare an `enum` variable of that type. You declare an `enum` variable using the keyword `enum` followed by the type's tag name, and then the variable name. The next example declares the variable today whose type is the `enum` defined type weather.

```
enum weather today;
```

The today variable can only be assigned the integral values represented by the `enum` weather names: clouds, rain, sun, and storm. In effect, you can only assign one of these names to today. In the next example, the user assigns storm to the today variable.

```
today = storm;
```

In LISTING 2-8, an `enum` type definition is used to specify four possible values each representing a possible weather state. Notice the `enum` type definition for weather at the beginning of the file. The variable today is declared with the type `enum` weather. It is then assigned the weather value rain. An **if** test then checks to see if today holds the value of rain. It does, so the `printf` operation is executed, notifying us of rain.

LISTING 2-8:

weather.c

```c
#include <stdio.h>

enum weather { clouds, rain, sun, storm };

int main(void)
    {
    enum weather today;

    today = rain;
    if (today == rain)
            printf ("Sorry, but it is raining today");
    return 0;
    }
```

You can, if you wish, designate a specific integer value for each name in an `enum` type. In the `enum` type definition, after each name, just enter an assignment operator and the integer value you want. In the **weatinit.c** program in LISTING 2-9, an arbitrary set of integer values is used in the `enum` type definition for weather. This `enum` type definition will define a subset of the integer type, which will consist only of the integers 3, 6, 259, and 1.

LISTING 2-9:

weatinit.c

```c
#include <stdio.h>

enum weather {clouds=3, rain=6, sun=259, storm=1};

int main(void)
    {
    enum weather today;

    today = rain;
    if (today == rain)
        printf ("Sorry, but it is raining today");
    return 0;
    }
```

You can also use the `enum` type for practical applications, such as the definition of the `boolean` type in the **bool.c** program in LISTING 2-10.

LISTING 2-10:

bool.c

```c
#include <stdio.h>

enum boolean {BTRUE = 1, BFALSE = 0};

int main(void)
    {
    enum boolean quit = BFALSE;

    quit = BTRUE;
    if (quit == BTRUE)
        printf ("Goodbye\n");
    return 0;
    }
```

Input/Output Functions: Character and Formatted

In C, basic input and output operations treat data as a stream of characters. For values to be output or input, they must be converted to and from characters. Characters are retrieved and output one by one. This character I/O is the basic input and output operations upon which all other I/O functions in C rely. The two basic character I/O functions are `getchar` and `putchar`.

Formatted I/O allows input or output characters to be converted into different types of values. There are two functions for formatted I/O: `printf` and `scanf`. `printf` converts different types of values into output characters for printing to the screen. scanf converts input characters into different types of values and assigns them to variables and arrays.

Character I/O: getchar and putchar

The functions getchar and putchar access one character at a time. getchar receives a character from the keyboard, putchar prints a character to the screen. These functions are often used to manage the input of character strings. This topic is discussed in Chapter 11.

getchar must be able to return an EOF value. An EOF value indicates the end of input from the keyboard. The EOF value is an integer value, usually a -1. For this reason, getchar returns an integer value instead of a character value. When the result of getchar is assigned to a character, the integer return value will simply be converted to a character.

The following program receives a character from the keyboard and assigns it to the variable letter. The character value of **letter** is then printed out to the screen with putchar.

```
int main(void)
            {
            char letter;

            letter = getchar();
            putchar(letter);

            return 0;
            }
```

In the **outchar.c** program in LISTING 2-11, a while loop is used to read and print all characters keyed in until the newline is entered. Notice the use of the newline constant, '\n'. Chapter 4, on statements, describes how a while loop is implemented.

LISTING 2-11:

outchar.c

```
#include <stdio.h>

int main(void)
            {
            char letter;

            letter = getchar();
            while (letter != '\n')
                    {
                    putchar(letter);
                    letter = getchar();
                    }
            return 0;
            }
```

Formatted Output: printf

The printf function converts different types of values into output characters for printing to the screen. printf consists of a format string followed by a list of values. The list of values is optional. The format string is enclosed in double quotes and consists of constants and conversion specifiers. A conversion specifier is a special code that indicates the type of conversion that needs to take place on a listed value. In the format list, a conversion specifier is always preceded by a percent sign. For example, the conversion specifier for an integer value is a %d. See Table 2-5 for a list of C conversion specifiers. The syntax for a `printf` function call is shown here, along with an example of such a function call.

```
printf(" format string in quotes " , list of values );
printf("There are %d pages in this book", 75);
```

In certain cases, you will need to use modifiers in your conversion specifiers to correctly convert certain types of data. `Long` and `long double` values require the conversion modifiers `l` and `L`, as well as their respective conversion specifiers. A conversion modifier is placed between the percent sign and the conversion specifier. The correct conversion specifier for a `long` is %ld. For a `long double` it is %Lf. `printf` does not require an l modifier for a `double`. In `printf`, the %f conversion modifier works equally well with both floats and doubles. However, this is not the case for `scanf`. `scanf` distinguishes between floats and doubles. `scanf` requires that the lowercase l conversion specifier be included when converting a `double`. In `scanf`, %f converts floats only, whereas %lf converts doubles.

Another modifier, the precision modifier, is particularly useful for outputting floating-point values. Ordinarily, when floating-point values are output, the full number of decimal places are displayed. This can be up to eight characters. In most cases, users will only need to see two decimal places. You can limit the number of decimal places displayed by using the precision modifier. The precision modifier is simply a period followed by a number specifying the number of places to be printed out after the decimal. The precision modifier will round off the last place printed. The conversion specifier %.2f will only print out two places after the decimal in a floating-point value. The value 3.568 will be printed out as 3.57. You can see an application of the precision modifier in the **printvar.c** program in LISTING 2-12, when the floating-point value of cost is output. Here is the `printf` function call used in that program.

```
printf("The cost is %.2f \n", cost);
```

LISTING 2-12:

printvar.c

```c
#include <stdio.h>

int main(void)
    {
    int num = 35;
    float price = 7.50;
    long total = 750001;
    double cost = 100000.00;

    printf ("The number is %d.\n", num);
    printf ("The price is %f.\n", price);
    printf ("The total is %ld.\n", total);
    printf ("The cost is %.2f.\n", cost);
    printf("The num = %d, price is %.2f.\n", num,price);
    return 0;
    }
```

Output for LISTING 2-12:

```
The number is 35.
The price is 7.500000.
The total is 75000.
The cost is 100000.00.
The num = 35, price is 7.50.
```

In LISTING 2-12, integer and floating-point, as well as `long` and `double` values are printed out. Several `printf` operations use conversion modifiers their conversion specifiers. Notice how the precision modifier is applied to a floating-point value.

Table 2-5: Output Conversion Specifiers and Modifiers

`%c`	character
`%d`	integer (decimal)
`%ld`	long (decimal)
`%i`	integer (decimal)
`%l`	long integer
`%f`	double
`%.nf`	double with precision modifier to specify number of decimal places. `%.2f`
`%e`	double, exponential notation
`%E`	double, E notation
`%g`	double, use shorter of f or e notation
`%G`	double, use shorter of F or E notation
`%Lf`	long double
`%.nlf`	long double with precision modifier to specify the number of decimal places. `%.2lf`
`%Le %LE %Lg %LG`	long double, exponential notation
`%u`	unsigned integer
`%lu`	unsigned long
`%p`	pointer
`%o`	octal integer
`%lo`	octal long
`%x`	hexadecimal integer, 0-f
`%X`	hexadecimal with 0-F
`%lx %lX`	hexadecimal long
`%s`	string (character array)
`%%`	percent sign (percent sign character)

You can use a single `printf` operation to output several values, each with its own conversion specifier. In this case, there is a sequential correspondence between a conversion specifier and a value in the value list. The first conversion specifier will convert the first value. The second conversion specifier in the format string will convert the second value. In the next example and in LISTING 2-12, the values of `num` and `price` are printed out in the same `printf` operation.

```
printf("The num = %d, price is %.2f.\n", num,price);
```

The first conversion specifier, `%d`, matches up with the first value, the value held by the num variable, 35. It informs `printf` that the first value is an integer and needs to be converted from an integer to its character equivalent. The integer value 35 will be converted to the characters '3' and '5' for output. The second conversion specifier, `%.2f`, matches up with the second value, the value held by the price variable, 7.50. It notifies `printf` that the second value is a `float`. The floating-point value 7.50 will be converted to the characters '7', '.', '5', and '0'.

Formatted Input: scanf

`scanf` formats character input into values that can be assigned to corresponding variables. Whereas `printf` has a list of values to be formatted into characters, `scanf` has a list of variables into which converted character input will be assigned. A `scanf` format string usually consists of a series of conversion specifiers. There usually are no other characters in the format string. Many of the same conversion specifiers used for `printf` are also used for `scanf`. (See Table 2-6.)

    `scanf` conversion specifiers indicate the type of value the input characters are to be converted to. The `%d` specifier converts characters into an integer value. Numeric characters will be converted into an integer value and assigned to a corresponding variable. For example, the characters '4', '5', and '8' will be converted to the integer value 458 and then assigned to a variable.

    `scanf` operates on a list of variables, not on values as `printf` does. Variable names are listed after the format string. However, you need more than just a variable's name. You need to place an ampersand, `&`,before each variable's name. For example, if you use the num variable in a `scanf` operation, you need to enter &num. If you fail to do so, your program will crash when you try to run it. `scanf` actually requires the memory addresses of variables, and this is provided by the `&` placed before the variable name. This process is examined in detail in Chapters 5 and 6. The following shows the syntax for `scanf` and an example of its use.

```
scanf("conversion specifier", &variable);
scanf("%d", &num);
```

Using `scanf` in your program allows you to let the user enter in values to variables. Often, `scanf` is preceded by a `printf` that outputs a prompt, telling the user what value needs to be entered. In this particular case, `printf` has no values listed or conversion specifiers. It is only being used here to output the string of characters making up the format string.

```
printf("Please enter a number: ");
scanf("%d", &num);
```

It is important to match the right conversion specifier with the type of the corresponding variable. If they do not match, an invalid value will be assigned to the variable. Though `scanf` and `printf` share many of the same conversion specifiers, there is one crucial difference. Unlike `printf`, scanf requires the lowercase l conversion modifier when converting a `double`. The conversion specifier for a `double` is `%lf`. Without the l modifier, attempts to input data to a `double` variable will fail.

In the following example, input operations are performed on floating-point values, using scanf to read in values from the keyboard. Notice the use of the l and L modifiers to read in `double` and `long double` values. The value for salary is read in as a fixed field of five numbers.

```
int main(void)
     {
     double cost;
     long double total;

     scanf("%lf", &cost);
     scanf("%Lf", &total);

     return 0;
     }
```

In the **scanvar.c** program in LISTING 2-13, the user is prompted to enter the values for the different variables. Notice the conversion specifiers in the scanf function calls. The conversion specifier for cost is %lf using the l conversion modifier required for a `double`. However, when cost is printed out by printf, the conversion specifier has no l modifier, `%f`.

LISTING 2-13:

scanvar.c

```
#include <stdio.h>

int main(void)
     {
     int num;
     float price ;
     long total;
     double cost;

     printf ("Please enter a number: ");
     scanf ("%d", &num);

     printf ("Please enter a price: ");
     scanf ("%f", &price);

     printf ("Please enter a total: ");
     scanf ("%ld", &total);

     printf ("Please enter a cost: ");
     scanf ("%lf", &cost);

     printf ("\n");
     printf ("The number is %d \n", num);
     printf ("The price is %.2f \n", price);
     printf ("The total is %ld \n", total);
     printf ("The cost is %.2f \n", cost);
     return 0;
     }
```

Output for LISTING 2-13:

```
Please enter a number: 23
Please enter a price: 14.50
Please enter a total: 93000
Please enter a cost: 450000.00

The number is 23
The price is 14.50
The total is 93000
The cost is 450000.00
```

Table 2-6: Input Conversion Specifiers and Modifiers

(l modifier for long integer and double;
L modifier for long double)

%c		character	
%d		integer (decimal)	
%ld		long	
%i		integer (decimal, octal, or hexadecimal)	
%f		float	
%e		%g	float, exponential notation
%lf		double	
%Lf		long double	
%le %lg		double, exponential notation	
%Le %Lg		long double, exponential notation	
%u		unsigned integer	
%lu		long unsigned integer	
%p		pointer	
%o		octal integer	
%x		hexadecimal integer, 0-f	
%s		string (character array)	

Conversion Modifiers

Both scanf and printf may use conversion modifiers. Some modifiers are essential for correct conversion. The l and L modifiers are required for correct conversion of long integers, doubles, and long doubles. Other modifiers are used only to format output or to constrain input. Some modifiers are specific to either printf or scanf. For example, the + modifier is used with printf to print a plus sign before a numeric value. The conversion modifiers are examined in greater detail in Chapter 25, "Formatted I/O."

Table 2-7 lists and describes several of the most commonly used conversion modifiers. They are divided into three categories: `long` and `short` conversion modifiers, input modifiers used with `printf`, and output modifiers used with `scanf`. As described in the previous sections, the `long` and `short` conversion modifiers are required for the correct conversion of `long`, `double`, and `short` values. They are used in much the same way by both `printf` and `scanf`. Some modifiers are used by both `printf` and `scanf`, but in slightly different ways. For example, the field width modifier specifies the number of character read in or output. However, in `scanf`, this modifier strictly limits the number of characters read, whereas in `printf` it just pads output. Other modifiers are used exclusively for either output or input. The justification, sign, and form modifiers are used only with `printf` to format output. The field skipper modifier only applies to input. Certain modifiers apply only to a certain type of data. The precision modifier applies only to floating-point values, whether for input or output.

Table 2-7: Conversion Modifiers

Output Conversion Modifiers: printf

Long and Short Conversion Modifiers: l, `L`, h

`%ld`	Convert long integer.	
	`printf("long decimal %ld \n",25000000);`	
`%Lf`	Convert long double.	
	`printf("long double %Lf",989000000.34);`	
`%hd`	Convert a short integer. (`%hu` for short unsigned)	
	`printf("Decimal is a short %hd", 26);`	

Field Width Modifiers
Number for decimal and string specifiers: `%d`, `%i`, `%s`

`%5d`	Number less than three places padded.	___25
`%05d`	Specifies padding with leading zeros.	00025
`%10s`	String less than 10, pad with spaces.	_____RIC

Precision Modifiers: Floating-Point
Precision for floating-point specifiers: %f, %e, %g, %G, %E

`%7.2f`	Seven total spaces - two past decimal point.	___3.58

Justification:

Right justification with blanks is the default;
- indicates left justification with blanks.

`%-5d`	Number less than five places padded to right.	25___
`%-7.2f`	Seven total spaces - two past decimal point.	3.58___
`%-10s`	A string less than 10, pad with spaces.	RIC_____

Sign Symbols

+	Specifies that sign of value will be displayed, plus or minus	
	`printf("%+d", 25);`	+25
(space)	Print leading space instead of + sign for positive values.	
	`printf("% d,% d",-30,+25);`	-30, 25

Full Form

#	Specifies that full form is printed out.	
`%#o`	Octal. Prints leading 0 for an octal number.	
`%#x`	Hexadecimal. Prints leading `0x` for hex number.	
`%#7.2f`	Floating-point: `%f`, `%e`, `%g`, `%E`. Prints out decimal point even if there are only zeros after the decimal.	

`%#7.2g` Floating-point: `%g`, `%G`. Prevents trailing zeros from being removed.

Input Conversion Modifiers: scanf

Long and Short Conversion Modifiers: `l`, `L`, `h`

    `%ld`   Convert long integer.

    `%lf`   Convert a double. Required for scanf when reading a double.

                      `scanf("%lf", &price);`

    `%Lf`   Convert long double.

Field Width Modifiers

Restricted number of characters read: `%d`, `%i`, `%s`

    `%5d`   Read 5 characters for decimal conversion.

    `%05d`   The 5 characters read may be padded with leading zeros.

    `%5f`   Read 5 characters for float, including period used for decimal.

Precision Modifiers: Floating-Point

Read specified number of characters after the decimal: `%f`, `%e`, `%g`, `%G`, `%E`

    `%7.2f`   Read 7 characters for float, having two decimal places

Input Field Modifiers (see Chapter 16)

    `%*`   Field skipping modifier. Skips an input field.

Chapter Summary: Data Types

There are two basic data types: integer and floating-point. There are several types of integers: `int`, `long`, `short`, and `char`. `int` is the basic integer type. `long` has a greater range of integer values than an `int`. `short` may have a smaller range of integer values. `char` is used to represent characters.

There are two floating-point data types: `float` and `double`. A `double` has greater precision than a `float`. The implementation of a floating-point value is different from that of an integer.

Variables are declared using a data type's keyword and an identifier. The identifier is the variable name and may consist of any alphabetic character, as well as numbers and the underscore. However, a variable name may not begin with a number.

The data type of a constant is determined by its format. A number is an integer constant. A number with an `l` attached to it is a `long` integer. Octal constants are designated with a leading 0 in a number. A number with a decimal point is a floating-point constant. A floating-point constant can also be written in exponential notation. Character constants represent the character set. Some of these characters perform actions, such as newlines and tabs. They are represented using an escape sequence with either their octal value or, in some cases, a specially designated symbol. \n and \t represent the newline and tab characters.

Symbolic constants can be implemented using the preprocessor `define` command, the const qualifier, or the `enum` type definition. A `define` command really works like a word-processing global substitution operation. It enables the use of a name in place of a literal constant. The const qualifier is used to declare a constant variable. A constant variable may not have its value changed. It is essentially a variable that functions like a constant. The `enum` type definition defines a subset of integers as a new type. `enum` is an integral type, but its members are represented by names. Their values can be assigned to variables declared with the same `enum` type. `enum` names are equivalent to integer values.

Data type sizes in bytes

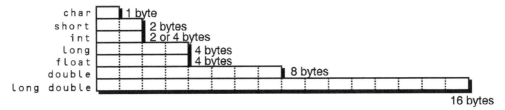

Data type value ranges

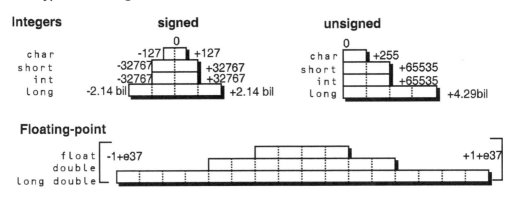

Minimum and maximum values

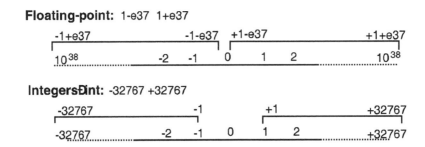

Figure 2-4: Data type sizes, value ranges for signed and unsigned integers, and minimum and maximum values for floating-point and integer types.

The output function `printf` is used to convert integer and floating-point values into their character representations for output. `scanf` converts characters to integer and floating-point values and assigns them to variables. `printf` and `scanf` use conversion specifiers to determine what type of values are being converted. Conversion specifiers sometimes require modifiers. The l and L modifiers must be used when converting longs and `long doubles`. The lowercase l modifier must be used in a scanf operation when converting doubles, %lf. Tables 2.8-2.14, and Figure 2-4 summarize the data types, conversion specifiers, escape sequence characters, and keywords covered in this chapter.

Table 2-8: Data Types (Review)

Integral Data Types

```
int
        int num;

long
        long num;
        long int num;

short
        short num;
        short int num;

char
        char  letter:
        signed char letter;
        unsigned char letter;

unsigned int
        unsigned id;
        unsigned int id;

unsigned long
        unsigned long id;
        unsigned long int id;

unsigned short
        unsigned short  id;
        unsigned short int id;
```

Floating-Point Data Types

```
float
        float cost;

double
        double cost;

long double
        long double cost;
```

Table 2-9: CONSTANTS (Review)

Integral Constants
Integers   5
                6045
                -355
Long integers (L or l)
                    700000
                    500001
                        5L
                    -355L
Unsigned integers
                    7000000U
                    5u
                    355U

Floating-Point - default is a double:
Double
                        3.568
                355.
                    0.98
            -355.98
Exponent (E or e)
                4.78e+5   4.78E+5
                7.86e-3   7.86E-3
                .56e+7   .56E+7
Long double (L or l)
                3.568l 3.568L
Float (f or F)
                3.568f 3.568F

Character (Placed within Single Quotes)
Characters
                'h'
                '8'   letter 8, not integer 8
                '&'
Escape Sequences
        Octal   Hexadecimal
                '\n'   '\x7'
                '\007'
                '\7'

Table 2-10: Escape Sequence Characters (Review)

Octal Characters
```
\Ooo    \007    \7
```

Hexadecimal Characters
```
\Xoo    \x7    \x6g
```

Line and Page Characters

\a	Alert (beep)
\n	Newline
\t	Tab
\f	Form feed
\r	Carriage return
\v	Vertical tab
\b	Backspace

Quote and Backslash Characters

\\	Backslash character
\'	Single quote character
\"	Double quote character
\?	Question mark character

Table 2-11: Output Conversion Specifiers (Review)

Integral Conversions

%c	Character
%d	Decimal
%i	Decimal
%u	Unsigned integer
%o	Octal integer
%x	Hexadecimal integer, 0-f
%X	Hexadecimal with 0-F

Floating-Point Conversions

%f	Double
%e	Double, e notation
%E	Double, E notation
%g	Use shorter of f or e notation
%G	Use shorter of f or E notation

Pointer Conversions (addresses)

%p	Pointer

String Conversions

%s	String (character array)

Table 2-12: Output Conversion Modifiers: printf

Long, Double, and Short Conversion Modifiers: `l`, `L`, `h`

`%ld`	Long integer
`%Lf`	Long double
`%hd`	Short integer (`%hu` for short unsigned)

Field Width Modifiers

`%nd`	Number of characters output for decimal value
`%nf`	Number of characters output for float value
`%ns`	Number of characters output for string

Precision Modifiers: Floating-Point

Precision for floating-point specifiers: `%f`, `%e`, `%g`, `%G`, `%E`

`%.nf`   Number of decimal places output

> `%.2f`   Output two places past decimal point

`%n.nf`   Combined width and precision modifier

> `%7.2f`   Seven total chars, two past decimal point

Justification:

Right justification with blanks is the default.
– indicates left justification with blanks.

`%-5d`	Number less than five places padded to right.
`%-7.2f`	Seven total spaces - two past decimal point.
`%-10s`	A string less than 10, pad with spaces.

Sign Symbols

`+`   Specifies that sign of value will be displayed, plus or minus:

> `printf("%+d", 25);`

`(space)` Print leading space instead of + sign for positive values

> `printf("% d,% d",-30,+25);`

Full Form

`#`	Specifies that full form is printed out.
`%#o`	Octal. Prints leading 0 for octal number.
`%#x`	Hexadecimal. Prints leading `0x` for hex number.
`%#7.2f`	Floating-point:
`%f`, `%e`, `%g`, `%E`	Prints out decimal point even if there are only zeros after the decimal.
`%#7.2g`	Floating-point: `%g`, `%G`. Prevents trailing zeros from being removed.

Table 2-13A: Input Conversion Specifiers (Review)

Integral Conversions
%c   character
%d   decimal
%i   decimal, octal, and hexadecimal
%u   unsigned integer
%o   octal integer
%x   hexadecimal integer,

Floating-Point Conversions
%f   float
%e %g   float, e notation

Pointer Conversions (Addresses)
%p   pointer

String Conversions
%s   string (character array)
%[a-b] valid string (character array)

Table 2-13B: Input Conversion Modifiers: scanf

Long, Double, and Short Conversion Modifiers: l, L, h

%ld   Long integer
```
                    scanf("%ld", &total);
```
%lf   Double. Required for scanf when reading a double
```
                    scanf("%lf", &price);
```
%Lf   Long double
```
                    scanf("%Lf", &cost);
```
%hd   Short integer (%hu for short unsigned)
```
                    scanf("%hd", &count);
```

Field Width Modifiers
        Restricted number of characters, read
%*n*d   Number of characters read for decimal value
%*n*f   Number of characters read for float value
%*n*s   Number of characters read for string

Precision Modifiers: Floating-Point
        Read specified number of characters after the decimal: %f, %e, %g, %G, %E
%.*n*f   Number of decimal places read.
         %.2f   Read only two places past the decimal point.
%*n*.if Combined width and precision modifier.
         %7.2f   Read seven characters for float, having two decimal places

Input Field Modifiers
%*   Field skipping modifier; skips an input field

Table 2-14: Keywords

auto	extern	int	struct
break	default	long	switch
case	double	register	typedef
char	else	return	union
const	float	short	unsigned
continue	for	signed	void
do	goto	sizeof	volatile
enum	if	static	while

Exercises

1. Write a short program using different kinds of variables. Assign values to them and print them out. The program should have at least five variables, one of each type. Make up your own names for variables. Below is a sample program.

```
#include <stdio.h>

int main(void)
    {
    int num;

    num =  10;
    printf("Num = %d \n", num);
    }
```

2. Write a program that prints out the octal, hexadecimal, and character equivalents of integers. Use the appropriate printf conversion specifiers. An example is written below.

```
#include <stdio.h>

int main(void)
    {
    int num;

    num = 65;
    printf("Num = %o \n", num);
    }
```

3. Write a program that prints out floating-point values using floating-point representation and scientific notation. Use the appropriate printf conversion specifiers. Below is a sample program.

```
#include <stdio.h>

int main(void)
     {
     float cost;

     cost = 75.90;
     printf("Cost = %.2f \n", cost);
     }
```

4. Write a program that asks the user to input a number associated with a tree and then prints out the name of the tree. Write the program first using the `define` command, assigning a number to a tree name. Rewrite the program using the `enum` type definition, again assigning a number to a tree name. You will have to use a simple if statement to print out the name. A simple example follows.

```
#include <stdio.h>

#define ORANGES 1
#define APPLES 2

int main(void)
     {
     int fruit;

     printf ("Please enter choice\n");
     scanf ("%d", &fruit);

     if (fruit == ORANGES)
            printf("You selected oranges\n");
     if (fruit == APPLES)
            printf("You selected apples\n");

     return 0;
     }
```

Expressions

Arithmetic, Comparison, and Assignment

3. Expressions

Expressions define the tasks to be performed in a program. They not only do calculations but also perform function calls and assignment operations. In this sense, expressions have a positive and aggressive role in C. Statements, on the other hand, simply order and select those tasks. If you were to compare a program to a company, then statements would be the managers organizing the work, and the expressions would be the workers, actually performing the tasks.

An expression is an operation performed on one or more operands. There are three elements to an expression: the operands, the operator, and the resulting value of the operation. The number of operands varies according to the type of operation. The unary and postfix expressions each have only one operand, whereas conditional expressions have three operands.

Most expressions consist of an operator and two operands. The expression 2 + 4 consists of the additive operator + with the operands 2 and 4. The resulting value of the expression is the result of the operation of the operator on the operands. In this sense, the expression can be said to have a value. In the expression 2 + 4, there are three values to be considered. There are the operand values 2 and 4, as well as the expression's result, 6. You can combine expressions to form complex expressions. In the expression 3 + (2 * 4), the result of the expression (2 * 4) becomes an operand in another addition expression.

There are eight kinds of expressions: primary, arithmetic, comparison, assignment, function call, comma, conditional, and cast. Comparison expressions include relational, equality, and logical expressions. There are several different kinds of assignment expressions. The comma and conditional expressions have specialized applications.

C expressions include operations that you may not usually think of as expressions. In C, the assignment operations and function calls are both expressions. An assignment operator, =, is an operation on two operands: a variable and a value. The value is assigned to the variable. The value assigned to the variable is also the resulting value of the assignment expression.

A function call is also an expression. The open and close parentheses in a function call constitute a postfix operator whose operand is a function name. The result of this function call expression is the return value of the function. The function call expression will be discussed in Chapter 6.

There is also one type of expression that consists of a single operand and no operator. This is known as a primary expression, and it usually consists of a variable or a constant. The resulting value of the primary expression is the value of the operand. You will see primary expressions used with control structures where the test will consist of just a single variable.

An expression is often placed in a program within an expression statement. An expression statement is a statement that consists solely of an expression. The syntax for an expression statement is an expression followed by a semicolon. Any expression may be used in an expression statement. Most of the program examples to this point have been made up entirely of expression statements. The following examples are all expression statements.

```
i = 3;
res = 4 + 5;
7 * 2;
num;
calc();
```

Primary Expressions

A primary expression consists of a single operand and no operator. The operand can be a variable, a constant, or a parenthesized expression. The result of a primary expression is the value of the operand. A single constant by itself can be a primary expression. The resulting value of the primary expression consisting of the constant **8** is the integer value **8**. A variable name by itself can also be a primary expression. The resulting value of the primary expression consisting of just the name of the integer variable `num` is the integer value held by `num`. Here are examples of valid primary expressions.

```
6
548
num
-54
```

A parenthesized expression is considered a primary expression in that it forces precedence. A parenthesized expression will be considered an operand whose value must be determined before evaluation can continue.

You can now see how operands can be subexpressions within a larger expression. The expression `4 + 5` is really the addition of the results of two primary expressions, 4 and 5. The expression `7 - num` is the subtraction of the results of two primary expressions, 7 and `num`. The expression `3 + (num *5 )` is the addition of the results of two primary expressions, 3 and `(num*5)`.

Arithmetic Expressions

Arithmetic expressions perform the standard arithmetic operations. Arithmetic operations are divided into three main categories: unary, additive, and multiplicative operations. Table 3-1 lists the arithmetic operators.

Table 3-1: Arithmetic Operators

Unary Arithmetic Operators		
+	Plus	
-	Minus	
Additive Operators		
+	Addition	
−	Subtraction	
Multiplicative Operators		
*	Multiplication	
/	Division	
%	Modulo (remainder)	

Unary Arithmetic Operations: Plus and Minus

The unary arithmetic operators affect the sign of an arithmetic value. Both are unary, meaning that they take only one operand. The minus operator, -, will result in a value that is the same as the operand's, except that the arithmetic sign will be changed. If the operand is a positive value, the unary minus will result in a value that is equivalent to the operand's negative value. If the operand is already negative, the unary minus operator will result in a value that is equivalent to the operand's positive value.

```
-6        negative 6
-(-6)     positive 6
-(3-7)    positive 4
```

A unary operation is an expression. The operator operates on an operand, which results in a value. The operand itself is not affected. A unary operation does not change the actual sign of an operand. It only results in a value that is the same as that of the operand, but with the sign changed.

The unary plus operator, +, simply takes the value of the operand as its result. The plus operator functions more as a programmer note, rather than as an effective operation.

Additive Operations: Addition and Subtraction

The additive operations are addition and subtraction. They perform standard addition and subtraction tasks. The plus sign, +, is the addition operator, and the minus sign, -, is the subtraction operator. Both operators must have two operands. An operand can be a primary expression, such as a variable or a constant, or it can be another arithmetic expression. Here are several examples of addition and subtraction used with an assignment operation.

```
total = 4 + 5;
total = num - 3;
res = total - (num + 4);
```

Multiplicative Operations: Multiplication, Division, and Modulo

The multiplicative operations are multiplication, division, and modulo. Multiplication and division perform standard multiplication and division tasks. The asterisk, *, is the multiplication operator, and the slash, /, is the division operator. As with the additive operators, they require two operands. Examples of multiplication and division follow.

```
total = 4 * 5;
total = 20 / 4;
```

The modulo operator is the percent sign, %. The modulo operation is the complement of the division operation. Whereas division results in the number of times one number is divided by another, the modulo returns the remainder of a division operation. A number rarely divides evenly into another number. There is usually a remainder. The modulo operation calculates this remainder. 23/4 returns a value of 5: 4 divides into 23 five times. However, 4 * 5 returns only 20. There is a remainder of 3. 23 % 4 will result in the remainder, 3. In the next example, the value assigned to resdiv is 3. The value assigned to remain is 4.

```
      int resdiv, remain;

          resdiv = 19 / 5;
          remain = 19 % 5;
```

The **multop.c** program in LISTING 3-1 illustrates the use of the different additive and multiplicative operators. First, three numbers are added together and the result, 23, is assigned to the total variable. Then the average of these three numbers is found by dividing that total by 3 and assigning the result, 7, to numavg. The remainder from dividing 3 into the dividend is then calculated using the remainder operator, %. Two different methods are used to calculate the nearest even number into which 3 divides into for the total, 23. The first subtracts the remainder from the total, and the second multiplies the average by 3.

LISTING 3-1:

multop.c

```c
#include <stdio.h>

int main(void)
        {
        int total, numavg, numrem, numeven1, numeven2;

        total = 6 + 5 + 12;

        numavg = total / 3;

        numrem = total % 3;

        numeven1 = total - numrem;
        numeven2 = numavg * 3;

        printf("Total = %d\n", total);
        printf("Average = %d\n", numavg);
        printf("Remainder = %d\n", numrem);
        printf("Even Total =%d and %d\n",numeven1,numeven2);

        return 0;
        }
```

Output for LISTING 3-1:

```
      Total = 23
      Average = 7
      Remainder = 2
      Even Total = 21 and 21
```

Arithmetic Precedence and Associativity

You can construct complex expressions consisting of several nested expressions. For example, as the operands of a multiplication expression, you could have an addition expression and a subtraction expression, as shown in the next example. However, in such complex expressions, one operator may take precedence over another. When a complex expression is evaluated, it is broken down into its subexpressions, one for each operator. The result of one subexpression may become the operand for another expression. The order in which these subexpressions are evaluated is determined by either parentheses or precedence. In the case of parentheses, the expressions with the innermost parentheses are evaluated first. Parentheses are the clearest and safest way to ensure proper evaluation of an expression. In the next example, the left and right subexpressions are evaluated first. 2 + 4 is 6, and 5 - 3 is 2. 6 * 2 is 12.

```
(2 + 4) * (5 - 3)
```

If there are no parentheses, the order of evaluation is determined by precedence. All operators are ranked according to their precedence. Those that have greater precedence will be evaluated first. The order of precedence for arithmetic operators ranks the multiplicative operators higher than the additive operators. *, /, and % take precedence over + and –. The unary operators have the highest precedence. In the next example, the multiplication operation, 4 * 5, is performed first. The two additive operations, 2 + 20 and 22 - 3, follow. The expression is interpreted as 2 + (4 * 5) –3, and the answer is 19.

```
2 + 4 * 5 - 3
```

Many operators share the same rank. If the operators do not share operands, their priority is undefined. It will not matter which is evaluated first. The decision is left up to the compiler in the interest of efficiency. In the next example, the division and modulo operations do not share the same operand. It does not matter when one or the other is evaluated.

```
4 / 2 + 11 % 5
```

Table 3-2: Precedence and Associativity of Operators (Non-binary)

Operators	Associativity
() [] -> .	Left to right
! ~ ++ -- + - * & (*type*) sizeof	Right to left
* / %	Left to right
+ -	Left to right
< > <= >=	Left to Right
== !=	Left to right
&&	Left to right
||	Left to right
? :	Right to left
= += -= /= *= %=	Right to left
,	Left to right

If the operators share the same operand, the priority of one operator over the other will be determined by its associativity. Associativity describes how an operator associates its operands. Is the left operand evaluated before the right operand or vice versa? Arithmetic operators associate left to right, whereas the assignment operators associate right to left (see Table 3-2 for a complete listing of associativity and precedence). Given two addition operators sharing the same operand, the first addition will be performed before the second. In the following example, the addition and subtraction operators share the same operand. Associativity is from left to right. Since the addition operation is placed before the subtraction operation, the addition is performed first.

```
2 + 10 - 5
```

An assignment operation has almost the lowest precedence. Only the comma operator is lower. This means that if an expression has an assignment operation, all other operators will be evaluated first. In the next example, all the arithmetic operations are performed before the assignment takes place.

```
num = 4 / 2 + 11 % 5;
```

Comparison Expressions: Relational, Equality, and Logical

Relational, equality, and logical expressions perform a comparison between their operands. The result of the comparison is the integer value of either one or zero. If an operation compares successfully, the result of the expression is an integer value of 1. If the comparison fails, the result of the expression is an integer value of 0. Since these are expressions, they can be combined with other kinds of expressions. In such a situation, their 1 or 0 resulting value can itself become an operand in a larger complex expression. Table 3-3 lists the various comparison operators.

Table 3-3: Comparison Operators

Relational Operators		
	<	Less than
	>	Greater than
	<=	Less than or equal
	>=	Greater than or equal
Equality Operators		
	==	Equal
	!=	Not equal
Logical Operators		
	&&	And
	||	Or
	!	Not

Relational Operations

A relational operator compares two operands and determines whether one is greater or less than the other. If the relational comparison is successful, the result of the expression is the integer value 1. If the comparison fails, the result is the integer value 0. There are four relational operators, two of which add in a further comparison for equality. The greater-than, >, and less-than, <, symbols are used to represent the relational operators.

Relational Expressions

<	less than
>	greater than
<=	less than or equal
>=	greater than or equal

Relational expressions are usually used as the test expression in a loop or condition. In the **hello.c** program in LISTING 3-2, a less-than relational expression is used as the test expression for a while loop. As long as i is less than 3, the relational expression i < 3 will result in a value of 1. This will be read as true for the while loop. As soon as the value of i is 3, the relational comparison will fail, resulting in a value of 0. The loop will cease.

LISTING 3-2:

hello.c
```
#include <stdio.h>

int main(void)
        {
        int i;

        i = 0;
        while ( i < 3)
                {
                printf ("hello\n");
                i = i + 1;
                }

        return 0;
        }
```

Output for LISTING 3-2:

```
hello
hello
hello
```

Relational expressions are only expressions and can be combined with other expressions. In the following examples, the relational expression num < 5, is combined with an assignment expression. If the value of num is 3, the value assigned to res is 1. In the next statement, the relational expression is first combined with an arithmetic expression and then assigned to res. If num is 6, the value in res is 4.

```
res = (num < 5);
res = 4 + (num < 5);
```

Equality Operations

The equality operations work much the same way as the relational operations. They test a relationship between two operands and result in 1 or 0. The equality operator consists of two equals signs, ==. The equality operator for inequality consists of an exclamation point and one equals sign, !=.

Equality Operators

| == | equal |
| != | not equal |

Take careful note that the equality operator is a double equal sign, not a single equals sign. A single equal sign is an assignment operation, whereas a double equal sign is an equality comparison. This can be confusing for those familiar with other programming languages; in Pascal, the = is a comparison operator, whereas in C it is the assignment operator. Writing only one equals sign for the equality operator is a common mistake.

```
more = 1;            assignment operation
more == 1            comparison operation for equality
```

Logical Operations

There are three logical operators: &&, ||, and !, which represent the three logical operations AND, OR, and NOT, respectively.

Logical Operators

&&	AND
||	OR
!	NOT (Unary)

Logical operators compare the truth or falsity of their operands. The truth or falsity of an operand is determined by whether or not it has a zero value. If an operand evaluates to zero, the operand is considered false. If an operand evaluates to a nonzero value, it is considered true. Depending on the logical operator used, different combinations of true and false operands will determine whether a logical operation is true or not. For example, a logical OR operation is true if either operand is true. The OR operation is only false if both operands are false. On the other hand, the logical AND operation requires both operands to be true for the logical operation to be true. Determining in your own mind the truth or falsity of different logical operations can be confusing. That is why it is helpful to use a truth table to determine whether a logical expression will succeed or fail. The truth tables for logical AND and OR operations are listed in the following discussions.

The logical expression itself has a result. Like other comparison expressions, if the logical expression is true, its result is an integer value of 1. If the logical expression is false, its result is 0.

The logical AND operator consists of two ampersands, &&. The AND operator is only true if both of its operands are true. In this respect, the AND operation is very restrictive. If one or the other is false, or both are false, the logical expression is false and results in the integer value 0. Here is the truth table for the AND operation.

(exp1)&&(exp2) exp1	exp2	((exp1)&&(exp2))
T nonzero	T nonzero	T 1
T nonzero	F 0	F 0
F 0	T nonzero	F 0
F 0	F 0	F 0

The logical OR operator consists of two bars, ||. The OR operation is less restrictive than the AND operation. The OR operation is only false if both operands are false. In all other cases, it is true. The truth table for the OR operation follows.

(exp1)||(exp2)	exp1	exp2	((exp1) || (exp2))
	T nonzero	T nonzero	T 1
	T nonzero	F 0	T 1
	F 0	T nonzero	T 1
	F 0	F 0	F 0

The NOT operator also tests for the truth or falsity of its operands. However, it inverses the result. If an operand is false, 0, then the NOT operation results in a true value, an integer 1. If an operand is true, nonzero, then the NOT operation results in a false value, an integer 0.

!(exp1)	exp1	!(exp1)
	T nonzero	F 0
	F 0	T 1

In many cases, you will find yourself using relational expressions as the operands in logical operations. Keep in mind that the truth of such an operand is determined by whether it results in a zero value or a non-zero value. When a relational expression succeeds, it results in an integer, 1, which is a nonzero value. The operand will be true. If the relational comparison fails, then the result will be zero. The operand will be false.

Logical operations are often used to validate input. The **numerics.c** program in LISTING 3-3 counts only the numeric characters '0'-'9' that a user enters. The logical AND expression uses two relational expressions as its operands.

LISTING 3-3:

numerics.c

```c
#include <stdio.h>

int main(void)
      {
      int ch, num = 0;

      while ((ch = getchar()) != '\n')
            {
            if((ch >= '0') && (ch <= '9'))
                        num = num + 1;
            }
      printf("Count of numbers = %d\n", num);

      return 0;
      }
```

Output for LISTING 3-3:

```
The zip is 34567 for this location.
Count of number = 5
```

Logical expressions in C use an early-out form of evaluation. For example, an && operation will stop evaluating operands at the first false one it reaches. The remaining ones are not evaluated. So if the first operand is false, the logical expression is known to be false and processing stops. The remaining operands are never evaluated. The same is true for the || operation. It will stop at the first true operand. This is of particular importance when you have an operand in a logical expression that is performing an action such as reading a file or assigning a value to a variable. If such operands are placed after the first operand, then they may never be executed.   Logical expressions, as well as relational expressions, can be combined easily with other expressions such as arithmetic or assignment expressions. In the **relexpr.c** program in LISTING 3-4, comparison expressions are combined with arithmetic and assignment expressions. The value of relres is 2, of equalres is 1, and of logicalres is 1.

LISTING 3-4:

relexpr.c

```
#include <stdio.h>

int main(void)
      {
      int relres, equalres, logicalres;

      relres = (3 < 5) + (6 >= 6);
      equalres = (5 == 4) + (3 != 2);

      logicalres = (((5>3) && (2<4)) || (5==5));

      printf(" Rel = %d, Eq = %d, Log =  %d",
                                          relres,equalres,logicalres);

      return 0;
      }
```

Output for LISTING 3-4:

```
Rel = 2, Eq = 1, Log = 1
```

Comparison Operators' Precedence

Comparison operators have precedence just like arithmetic operators. Relational operators are ranked above equality operators. Logical operators have the lowest ranking among comparison operators. All associate from left to right. This low ranking of the logical operators encourages code in which logical expressions are written without parentheses. As shown in the following example, you can safely write the logical expression in LISTING 3-3 without using any parentheses. The higher precedence of relational operators ensures that they will be evaluated before the logical operators.

```
if(ch >= '0' && ch <= '9')
```

All the comparison operators are ranked below arithmetic operators. This can sometimes lead to obscure code in which complex arithmetic expressions are combined with logical expressions using no parentheses.

Logical operators have a special associativity feature. Though for most expression operators, C does not specify which operand must be evaluated first, an exception is made for logical operators . The left operand of a logical operator will always be evaluated first. This associativity has a special effect on logical AND operations. Recall that if only one operand in a logical AND expression is false, the entire expression fails and results in zero. So if the first operand is false, there is no need to evaluate any of the others. This is, in fact, what C does. If the first operand in a logical AND operation is false, then the remaining operand is not evaluated. Processing of the AND operation stops immediately, and the result of that operation is false. In the previous example, if the value of ch is less than '0', then the relational operation will fail, and this first operand of the logical AND expression will be false, making the entire AND operation false. The second operand, `ch <= '9'`, will never be evaluated.

Assignment Operations

In C, the assignment operation is an expression. The resulting value of the assignment expression is the value assigned to the variable in the assignment operation. The result of the expression `(num = 5)` is the value 5. You can combine an assignment operation with other operators to form a complex expression. In the next example, the assignment operation is combined with an arithmetic addition operation. The addition expression is the right operand of an assignment operation. The result of the addition is assigned to the variable `num`.

```
(num = (4 + 2));
```

You can assign the result of this assignment expression, in turn, to yet another variable:

```
total = (num = (4 + 2));
```

Often such a combination of assignment expressions is used to assign the same value to several variables using a single constant. Parentheses can be left out because assignments evaluate from right to left. The next example combines four assignment expressions, the first of which assigns 0 to the variable tax. The result of this assignment expression is 0. This result is an operand in yet another assignment expression, assigning 0 to the price variable. This 0 result of the price assignment expression is an operand in yet another assignment operation, assigning this result to the `num` variable. You finally end with the total assignment expression.

```
total = (num = (price = (tax = 0)));

total = num = price = tax = 0;
```

You need to keep in mind that the assignment operation is an expression and, as such, can be used anywhere you could use any other expression. You will often find assignment operations embedded within complex expressions. In the **assignex.c** program in LISTING 3-5, there several examples of embedded assignment expressions. The **assignex.c** program takes the **multop.c** program from LISTING 3-1 and combines its assignment operations into complex expressions with embedded assignment expressions. First, all the values are initialized using the combined assignment operations previously described. Then the average of three numbers is calculated by first adding the numbers and assigning them to the variable total: the result of this assignment operation is used in a division operation and divided by 3. The result of the division operation is then assigned to the numavg variable.

```
numavg = (total = (6 + 5 + 12)) / 3;
```

The same kind of embedded assignment operation is used in the next statement to calculate the even number. First, the remainder is calculated and the result assigned to numrem. The result of this assignment operation is then subtracted from **total** to give us the even number that the average divides into. This result is assigned to numeven.

```
numeven = total - (numarem = total % 3);
```

You will find embedded assignment expressions used primarily in the test expressions of loop and condition statements as described in Chapter 4, as well as with function calls as described in Chapter 6.

LISTING 3-5:

assignex.c

```c
#include <stdio.h>

int main(void)
    {
    int total, num, numavg, numrem, numeven;;

    total = num = numavg = numrem = numeven = 0;

    numavg = (total = (6 + 5 + 12)) / 3;

    numeven = total - (numrem = total % 3);

    printf("Total = %d, Average = %d\n", total, numavg);
    printf("Remain = %d, Even = %d\n", numrem, numeven);

    return 0;
    }
```

Output for LISTING 3-5:

```
Total = 23, Average = 7
Remain = 2, Even = 21
```

Table 3-4: Assignment Operators

Assignment Operator
=   Assign value to variable

Increment Operators (Unary)
++   Increment variable
--   Decrement variable

Arithmetic Assignment Operators
+=   Add and then assign
-=   Subtract and then assign
*=   Multiply and then assign
/=   Divide and then assign
%=   Modulo, assign remainder

Though an assignment operation is an expression itself, the left-hand side of an assignment statement cannot be an expression. It must be a variable. The result of an expression is always, and only, a value. A value can only be assigned to a variable, not to another value. The following examples all have errors in which a value is used in the left-hand side of an assignment operation. In the first expression, the value of num is assigned to the constant, 6. In the second expression, the result of the expression (price = 0) is assigned to the result of another expression, (total = num). Values can be assigned only to variables, not to other expressions. In the third expression, the same thing happens. The value of num is assigned to the expression (total * 6).

```
total = 6 = num;
(total = num) = (price = 0);
(((total * 6) = num) + 2);
```

In many languages, an assignment operation is considered a statement. However, in C, an assignment operation is a statement only in that any expression can be part of an expression statement. An expression statement is simply an expression placed before a semicolon. The semicolon indicates the end of a statement. What looks like an assignment statement is really just a common expression statement whose expression happens to be an assignment expression. In this sense, there is no such thing as an assignment statement in C. There are only assignment expressions.

"Arithmetic" Assignment Operators

Often the assignment operation is used not simply to assign a value to a variable, but to assign a value that has been in part determined by the variable. The next example consists of an arithmetic expression and an assignment operation. i + 1 is an addition operation that adds 1 to i. The result is then assigned to i. The variable i has been changed using its own value.

```
i = i + 1
```

Some other value could be used instead of 1, as shown in the next example.

```
i = i + 5;
```

Instead of addition, you could use multiplication. In the next example, i will be increased by a multiple of 5.

```
i = i * 5;
```

Arithmetic assignment operators provide a shorthand for just this kind of operation. An arithmetic assignment operation consists of the equals sign and an arithmetic operator. There are additive as well as multiplicative arithmetic assignment operators A complete list of assignment operators appears in Table 3-4. The more common arithmetic assignment operators are listed here.

+=	Add and then assign
-=	Subtract and then assign
*=	Multiply and then assign
/=	Divide and then assign
%=	Modulo; assign remainder

The combination of a multiplication of i by 5 and assignment of the result back to i can be achieved using the multiplicative arithmetic assignment operator, *=.

```
i *= 5;
```

The combination of an addition of 1 to i and assignment of the result back to i can be achieved with the addition arithmetic assignment operator, +=.

```
i += 1;
```

The expression used in the arithmetic expression can be any expression. The following examples are both equivalent:

```
i *= (5 + (4 * 3));
i = i * (5 + (4 * 3));
```

The uses of the different arithmetic assignment operator are illustrated in the **assignop.c** program in LISTING 3-6. The num variable undergoes several changes in value in which it is first assigned a value, 6, and then has that value incremented using addition arithmetic assignment operations, adding first 5 and then 12. The value of num is then 23. At that point, this value of num is assigned to numrem. Then a division arithmetic assignment operation, num /= 3, changes the value of num to that of the average of these three numbers, 7. The following multiplication arithmetic assignment operation, num *= 3, changes the value of num to that of the even number that the average divides into. Then a remainder arithmetic assignment operation gives the variable numrem the remainder, 2, instead of the average. num is then changed back to the original total by using the addition arithmetic assignment operator to add the remainder to the current value of num.

LISTING 3-6:

assignop.c
```
#include <stdio.h>

int main(void)
        {
        int num, numrem;
        num = 6;
        printf("Num = %d\n", num);
        num += 5;
        printf("Num = %d\n", num);
        num += 12;
        printf("Num = %d\n", num);
        numrem = num;

        num /= 3;
        printf("Num as Average = %d\n", num);
        num *= 3;
        printf("Num as Even Number = %d\n", num);
        numrem %= 3;
        printf("Numrem as Remainder = %d\n", numrem);
        num += numrem;
        printf("Num as Total = %d\n", num);

        return 0;
        }
```

Output for LISTING 3-6:

```
Num = 6
Num = 11
Num = 23
Num as Average = 7
Num as Even Number = 21
Remainder = 2
Num as Total = 23
```

Increment and Decrement Assignment Operators

The increment operator increments a variable. The operand must be a variable, not a value. The increment operation can be thought of as an assignment operation in which 1 is added to a variable and the result assigned to that variable. The increment operation and the assignment operation below are equivalent.

```
i++;
i = i + 1;
```

The increment operator can operate in two ways: postfix and prefix. Prefix places the increment operator before its operand; postfix places the increment operator after its operand.

Prefix   **Postfix**
```
++i;            i++;
```

When the increment operator is the sole expression in a statement, as in the preceding examples, there is no difference between postfix and prefix formats. However, the increment operation is an expression and as such can be used as part of other expressions. When the increment operation is part of another expression, there is a great deal of difference between the postfix and prefix formats.

In postfix, the variable will first be used in the expression and then incremented. In prefix, the variable will be incremented first and then used in the expression. In the next examples, the postfix operation first uses i in an assignment to num and then increments it, whereas the prefix operation first increments i and then assigns the value of i to num. In the postfix example, if the value of i is 3, the value of num will be 3. However, in the prefix example, the value of num will be 4. Next to each example are equivalent expressions.

```
num = i++;                     num =  i ;
                               i = i + 1;

num = ++i;                     num = (i = i + 1);
```

The differences become more subtle when the increment operation is used in arithmetic or relational expressions. A common guideline is not to use the increment operation within an expression. However, if it is used, the prefix operation is preferable. In the next example, the prefix use of i, ++i, incorporates the increment of i into the expression, whereas the postfix operation will perform the increment after the expression.

```
num = (++i * 5);               num = ( (i=i+1) * 5);


num = (i++ * 5);               num = ( i * 5);
                               i = i + 1;
```

Just as you can increment a variable using the increment operator, you can also decrement a variable using the decrement operator. The decrement operator consists of two minus signs, --, and takes an integer variable as its operand. A decrement operation decrements an integer variable by 1. Like the increment operator, it also has a prefix and a postfix format. In the next examples, the postfix decrement of i first assigns i to num and then decrements i. In the prefix decrement, i is first decremented by 1 and then assigned to num.

```
i--;     and     --i;

num = i--;            num = (i = i - 1);

num = --i;            i = i - 1;
                      num =  i ;
```

The increment operator can also be applied to a pointer variable. However, the effect is slightly different. The increment operation on pointers is discussed in Chapter 11.

Increment Operator Errors

In certain circumstances, use of increment and decrement operators in expressions can have unintended results, possibly giving you runtime program errors. For instance, if the variable used in the increment operation is used again in the same expression, then the effect of the postfix increment operation may be undefined. In the next example, it is unclear whether `i` is incremented after the entire expression or before the next use of `i` within the expression. Different compilers may implement such an operation either way.

```
num = i++ * i;          num = i * i;            num = i * (i=i+1);
                        i = i + 1;
```

The postfix increment operation may, again, be undefined if more than one increment operation is used in an expression. In the next example, both instances of `i` could be incremented after the expression, or the first `i` could be incremented before the next.

```
num= i++ * i++;         num = i * i;            num = i * (i=i+1);
                        i = i + 1;              i = i + 1;
                        i = i + 1;
```

The postfix increment operation causes further problems when used as arguments in function calls. If the value of `i` is 3, the prefix example prints out 4, whereas the postfix example prints out 3.

```
printf("%d", ++i);      printf("%d", (i=i+1) );

printf("%d", i++);      printf ("%d", i);
                        i = i + 1;
```

Comma Operator Expressions

The comma operator expression is an expression that consists of a list of other expressions. These listed expressions are separated by a comma. The comma does not perform any operation on these expressions. The expressions are simply evaluated sequentially as if they were a series of separate statements. The comma operator expression is used primarily in the initialization and update expressions of the for loop statement, as described in Chapter 4. Though rarely used in any other situation, it is a valid expression in and of itself. Its basic structure and operation are described here. A simple example of a comma operator expression follows.

```
(3 * 5, 4.00 + 2.5, num = 5)
```

The comma operator expression allows you to include several separate expressions into one overall expression. The next example is one expression statement, as indicated by the ending semicolon. The expression statement's expression consists of a comma operator expression that includes three separate expressions.

```
(4 * 3, i = 1 , 7 / 2);
```

The comma operator can come in handy when you want to perform a series of assignment operations and place them all on one line for convenience' sake. In the next example, the user initializes several variables, all within one expression statement. The expression is a single comma operator expression, which is, in turn, made up of several assignment expressions.

```
(num = 3, i = 0, cost = 42.50, rate = 6);
```

You can, of course, do away with the parentheses, as shown in the next example. Such a listing of assignments is not the same as the combined assignment operations used in the previous section to initialize several variables to the same value, total = tax = i =0. The following example initializes different variables to different values.

```
num = 3, i = 0, cost = 42.50, rate = 6;
```

The comma operator expression does have a result. The result is the value of the last expression in its list. You can even use this result within another expression. The result of the comma operator expressions in the next examples is the integer value 5. In the first case, the expression is used in an assignment operation. In the second case, it is used in a relational operation.

```
res = (3 * 5, 4.00 + 2.5, num = 5);
if (i > (3 * 5, 4.00 + 2.5, num = 5))
```

Conditional Expressions

A conditional expression implements an if-else decision format. The conditional expression consists of three subexpressions: the test expression and the two alternative result expressions. If the test is true, the second expression will be evaluated, and its result will be the result of the conditional expression. If the test is false, the third expression will be evaluated, and its result will be the result for the conditional expression. Here is the syntax of the conditional expression.

```
(expression1) ? expression2 : expression3
```

The conditional expression is often used for simple operations such as testing for a maximum value. In the next example, if a is greater than b, the result of this expression is the value of a. Otherwise, the result is the value of b.

```
(a > b) ? a : b
```

You can use the conditional expression as you would any other expression. In the next example, the conditional expression is part of an assignment expression. Depending upon whether the test expression is true or false, the value of a or b will be assigned to maxval. The larger value will be assigned to maxval.

```
maxval = ((a > b) ? a : b);
```

When used in an assignment operation, the conditional expression is functionally equivalent to an if-else statement. However, an if-else statement does not result in a value, whereas the conditional expression does. The next example shows a conditional expression and its equivalent if-else statement.

```
maxval = ((a > b) ? a : b);

if ( a > b)
    maxval = a;
else
    maxval = b;
```

A conditional expression could just as easily be used in an arithmetic or relational expression. In the next examples, a conditional expression is first combined with an addition operation. If the value of a is 3 and that of b is 4, the result of this expression is 13. In the next expression, a conditional expression is combined with a relation expression. If the value of a is 3 and that of b is 4, the result of this combined expression is 1. Relational expressions result in a 1 or 0 value, depending on whether they are true or not.

```
(5 + (2 * ((a > b) ? a: b)) )

(6 > ((a > b) ? a: b))
```

The expressions used in a conditional expression can be of any type. The next example uses a logical operation for its text expression, an assignment and function call in its second expression, and an assignment operation for its last expression.

```
( ((a > b) && (a != c)) ? res = calc() : b = c )
```

Use of the comma operator expression can extend indefinitely the number of expressions executed in the conditional expressions. In the next example, the third expression is a comma operator expression that is, in turn, made up of three other separate expressions. Should the test expression be false, then these three expressions will be executed.

```
((a > b) ? maxval=a : (res=calc(), b=res*5, maxval=b))
```

A conditional expression can even include another conditional expression, allowing you to nest conditional expressions. In the next example, the third expression is itself another conditional expression. Such a format gives you the equivalent of a nested if-then-else statement as described in the chapter on statements.

```
( (a > b) ? maxval=a : (a < b) ? maxval=b : maxval=0 )
```

The previous conditional expression breaks down in the following nested if-then-else structure.

```
if(a > b)
     maxval=a
      else
           if (a < b)
                maxval=b
          else
                maxval=0
```

Cast Expressions

The cast operator consists of a type enclosed in parentheses. It is a unary operator that takes only one operand. This operand can be any valid expression. The syntax of the cast expression follows.

```
(type) expression
```

The cast operation takes the value of its operand and converts it to the type designated within the parentheses of the cast. The result of the operation is the converted value of the operand. The next example converts an integer value to a floating-point value. The integer value 7 is converted to a floating-point value, 7.00. This new floating-point value is the result of the cast expression.

```
(float) 7
```

The operand used in a cast operation can be any valid expression. An expression results in a value, and the cast operator can work on any value. In the following examples, the cast operator is applied to an arithmetic expression, an assignment expression, and a primary expression consisting of a single variable. In the case of the variable, it is important to note that the variable's type is not itself affected. The variable's value is first obtained and then converted. The cast operation is an expression that generates a resulting value, the result of a conversion on a value obtained from the operand.

```
(int) (5.5 * 2.6)
(double) (i = 10)
(float) num
```

Odd effects can result when using a cast. If a floating-point value is cast to an integer, the floating-point fraction is lost. In the next example, the cast of 3.75 to an integer value provides a result that cuts off the fraction. The resulting value is 3.

```
(int) 3.75
```

The cast operation itself does not cut off the fraction. In C, there is a set of conversion rules for converting a value of one type to that of another. These conversion rules take effect in any expression where operands of different types are used.

Conversions

Expressions can include operands of different types. An integer can be multiplied by a `float`. A `long` can be added to a `double`. A `double` can be assigned to an integer. C handles operands of different types by converting one of them into the same type as that of the other operand.

Conversion rules determine which operand to convert by a process of promotion and demotion. Though these built-in conversions are convenient, you may at times have to enforce correct conversions with an explicit cast operation. Should your compiler issue warnings about type mismatches, you should correct the problems using a cast, rather than rely on the default conversions. For example, when assigning a signed character value to an unsigned integer variable, the signed character should be explicitly cast as an integer to avoid sign extension. Floating-point: conversions;

Promotion

Types have different sizes in terms of the number of bytes each one uses. `int` uses 2 bytes, `float` uses 8 bytes, `long` uses 4 bytes. Because an `int` uses only 2 bytes, it can be said to be smaller than a `float`. In expressions with two different types of operands, the operand with the smaller type is always promoted to that of the larger type. In this sense, expressions always promote to the largest type. The result of an expression is promoted to the largest-size type in the expression.

Promotion and Arithmetic Expressions

Arithmetic operands are promoted according to the following rules. The operand of a smaller type is promoted to that of a larger. Character and `short` types used in expressions are always promoted to integers. Then, in expressions that mix integers, floats, or doubles, the smaller type is promoted to that of the larger type. In the next example, the integer `num` will be promoted to a `double`, and the result of the expression `(num * cost)` will be a `double`. `cost` is a `double` with a size of 8 bytes. But `num` is an integer with a size of 2 bytes. Since `num` is the smaller type, it will be promoted to a `double`. The result in this example will also be a `double` value 12.00.

```
int num = 4;
double cost = 3.00;

(cost * num)
```

In complex expressions, conversions will first affect the operands in the subexpressions. Expressions in the innermost parentheses are evaluated first. The intermediate results take on the size of the larger type. In the next example, even though the `double` variable rate is embedded deep within the complex expression, its type becomes the type of the expression's result. A `double` is the largest of all the variable or constant types in the expression.

```
int num = 9.50;
double rate = 30.00;
long disnum  = 5;
```

```
        ((num + 3)                      +       (rate /disnum))
        integer integer                         double long

        (num + 3)                               (rate / disnum)
        integer  12                             double  6.00

                    ( integer +  double )
                        double  18.00
```

Promotion and Assignment Expressions

Conversions in assignment expressions operate differently. The operands of an assignment operation consist of a variable and the assigned value. If the variable is of a different type than the assigned value, then the type of the assigned value is converted to that of the variable. If the assigned value's type is smaller than the variable's type, the assigned value is promoted. However, if the assigned value is smaller, then it will be demoted.

```
int num = 6;
float cost;

cost = (num * 5);
```

In the previous example, the assigned value is promoted the same type as that of the variable cost. The expression `num * 5` results in the integer 30. This value is then assigned to the variable cost, whose type is `float`. Since the type of cost is larger than the type of the assigned value (`float` is larger than `int`), the assigned integer value is promoted to a `float`, 30.00. This value is then assigned to the cost variable.

Demotion

Demotion occurs when an operand of a larger type must be converted to an operand of a smaller type. Demotion usually takes place in assignment operations. If the assigned value has a larger type than the variable to which it is assigned, then the larger type must be demoted to the smaller type. Demotion can have serious consequences. In the case of integer demotion, information can be lost.
Demotion operates differently for floating-point and integer values. Each will be examined separately. Then you shall see how demotion is applied to arithmetic and assignment expressions.

Demotion and Floating-Point

Demotion from a `double` to a `float` is achieved smoothly. The larger precision of a `double` value is rounded down to the lower precision of a `float` value. However, demotion from a floating-point type to an integer type results in the loss of the floating-point's fraction. In the case below, demotion from `float` to integer takes place. The fraction has been cut off, leaving just the integer, 31. 31 is then assigned to the variable `num`.

```
int num;
float cost = 31.56;

num = cost;
```

Demotion and Integers: Truncation

Demotion from a larger integer type to a smaller integer type is achieved by truncation. Truncation operates at the bit level. An integer consists of 16 bits. A character consists of 8 bits. When an integer is converted to a character, 8 of its bits are copied into the 8 bits of the character. The remaining 8 bits of the integer are simply discarded. This is truncation. Because information may be lost, it is possible for truncation to result in a radical change in value.
Truncation does not have an effect if the value of the larger type can be held within the smaller type. If an integer value has a value of 65, it will be converted easily to a character value

with no change in value. You could safely assign such an integer value to a character value. A character variable can easily handle the value 65 (0 to 129). Truncation takes place. But in a value of 65, the discarded bits are all zeros. ...

```
                Integer value            Character value
        65      00000000 00100001    65    'A'    00100001
```

Truncation has a very drastic effect if the value of the larger type cannot be held within the smaller type. In this case, the discarded bits are not zeros. They are part of the value. For example, a conversion of the integer value of 337 to a character will drastically change that value. The demotion will truncate all the higher-order bits, using only the lower-order bits. The value 359 will take on a value of 103. The character with the value of 103 is 'g'.

```
                Integer value            Character value
        359  00000001 01101000 103       'g'    01101000
```

The result of a truncation can be considered a modulo of the number of values of that type. The result of a truncation of an integer to a character is the modulo of 256, the number of values in one byte, including 0. To calculate the result of the truncation in the preceding example, 359 is divided by 256, which results in a remainder of 103, the value of the character 'g'.

Demotion and Assignment Expressions

Demotion is most easily detected in an assignment operation. If the assigned value is larger than the variable type, demotion takes place. The assigned value is cut down to the size of the type of the variable.

In the next example, the `long` value of the variable total is being converted to an integer value for the integer variable `num`. The `long` value of total will be demoted through truncation to an integer value. If the value of total is larger than 32767, then truncation will result in a change of value. In this case, the `long` value of 75000 will be truncated to 9464 and then assigned to **total**.

```
        int num;
        long total = 75000L;

        num = total;
```

Chapter Summary: Expressions

Expressions perform tasks. Expressions usually consist of an operator and operands. The operator designates the task to be performed on the operands. There are eight major kinds of expressions: primary, arithmetic, comparison, assignment, function call, comma operator, conditional, and cast.

Primary expressions consist of one operand and no operator. The operand is usually a variable or a constant. The result of the expression is the value of the variable or the constant.

Arithmetic expressions perform basic arithmetic operations. The modulo operator results in the remainder of a division. If no parentheses are used in a complex arithmetic expression, then precedence will determine which arithmetic expression is to be evaluated first. If two operators have the same precedence and share the same operand, then associativity will determine which expression is evaluated first.

Table 3-5: Operators

Primary Operands
Constants   `6`
Variables   `num`

Arithmetic Operators
Unary Arithmetic Operators
     +   plus
     –   minus
Additive Operators
     +   addition
     –   subtraction
Multiplicative Operators
     *   multiplication
     /   division
     %   modulo (remainder)

Comparison Operators
Relational Operators
     <   less than
     >   greater than
     <=   less than or equal
     >=   greater than or equal
Equality Operators
     ==   equal
     !=   not equal
Logical Operators
     &&   and
     || or
     !   not

Assignment Operators
Assignment Operator
     =   Assign value to variable
Increment Operators (Unary)
     ++   Increment variable
     ––   Decrement variable
Arithmetic Assignment Operators
     +=   Add and then assign
     –=   Subtract and then assign
     *=   Multiply and then assign
     /=   Divide and then assign
     %=   Modulo, assign remainder

Conditional Operators
     `((e1)?e2:e3)`   `((a>b)?a:b)`

Comma Operator
     `( , )`   `(num = 5, 3 * 5)`

Cast Operator
    (*type*)   (float) 7

Function Call Operator
    function name() calc()

There are three kinds of comparison operations: relational, equality, and logical. Relational operators compare whether one operand is greater or less than the other. Relational operations are expressions that result in a value. If a relational comparison succeeds, then the relational expression results in an integer value of 1. If it fails, it results in a 0. The same is true of equality expressions. A logical operation tests for the truth or falsity of its operands. An operand is true if it results in a nonzero value. It is false if it results in a zero value.

Assignment operations are expressions. The left operand of an assignment operation must be a variable. The result of an assignment expression is the value assigned to a variable. Assignment operations can be placed anywhere an expression can be placed.

Arithmetic assignment operators are a variation on assignment operators. They combine an arithmetic operation on a variable with an assignment operation on that same variable. An increment operation is a postfix or prefix operation that increases a variable's value by 1.

Conditional expressions implement the equivalent of an if-else condition to select between two alternative expressions. The result of the expression is the result of the expression chosen.

When operands of different types are used in the same expression, conversion may result. Types are ranked according to the amount of memory they use. Usually, an operand of a smaller type is promoted to that of a larger type. This is called promotion. However, sometimes a larger type is converted to a smaller type. This is called demotion. Demotion among integral types is carried out by truncation. Truncation may result in information being lost. Demotion usually occurs in assignment operations and should be avoided if possible.

Table 3-5 summarizes the operators discussed in this chapter. Table 3-6 reviews the precedence and associativity

Table 3-6: Precedence and Associativity of Operators

Operators	Associativity
() [] -> .	Left to right
! ~ ++ -- + - * & (type) sizeof	Right to left
* / %	Left to right
+ -	Left to right
<< >>	Left to right
< > <= >=	Left to right
== !=	Left to right
&	Left to right
^	Left to right
|	Left to right
&&	Left to right
||	Left to right
? :	Right to left
= += -= /= *= %= &= ^= |= <<= >>=	Right to left
,	Left to right

Exercises

1. Write a program that allows the user to enter the number of items purchased as well as the cost. Calculate a total price for all the items, including a tax of 15 percent. Print out the final price.

2. Ask the user to enter in the cost of an item and the number purchased. Items can be shipped 10 to a box or in individual boxes. Determine how many must be shipped in individual boxes. The modulo operator may be helpful. Add a shipping fee of $5.00 for each individual box. Calculate the final price, including the 15 percent tax.

3. There are three items designated by the integer values 1, 2, and 3. The user will select an item by entering in its integer. Declare and initialize three variables to work as counters for each item. Combine all three initializations into one expression consisting of three assignment operations and one 0 constant. When a 1 is entered, the counter for the 1 item is incremented. When a 2 is entered, the counter for the 2 item is incremented. When a 3 is entered, the counter for the 3 item is incremented. Place the prompt and `scanf` for the user within a loop. If the user enters a 0, the loop will stop. Print out the totals for each item and the combined total for all.

4. Write a program that receives two numbers from the user and prints out the lower number. Use a conditional expression combined with an assignment operation.

5. Write a short program with conversions. Print out the values converted. Convert different types (floating-point and integer), as well as different sizes (`long`, `int`, etc.). A sample program follows.

```
#include <stdio.h>

int main(void)
     {
     int num;

     num =  3.567 *  (2.1 + 4);
     printf("Num = %d \n", num);

     return 0;
     }
```

6. Experiment with demotion. Give examples for both expressions and assignments. Print out the values converted. A sample program follows.

```
#include <stdio.h>

int main(void)
     {
     int num;

     num =  (4 *  10000);
     printf("Num = %d \n", num);

     return 0;
     }
```

Statements

Expression, Iteration, and Condition

Expression Statements

Compound Statements

Iterations Statements

Conditions

Jump Statements

4. Statements

Statements control the execution of expressions. In C, expressions perform the program's tasks. However, a program does not consist of a set of expressions listed next to each other. Expressions must be organized into some kind of order. This is the role of statements. A program itself consists of a series of statements, which organize expressions. They select which expressions are to be executed and when. Statements are combined with other statements to form complex control patterns within a program. Because of this, statements are often referred to as control structures. They control the flow of the program's execution. This chapter will cover the role of statements and how they relate to expressions.

There is a kind of statement in C, called the expression statement that consists solely of an expression. Expression statements are commonly used to hold assignment and function call expressions. In C, what is commonly thought of as an assignment statement in other languages is really an expression statement whose expression is an assignment operation. The assignment operation is really an assignment expression.

The expression statement is the only simple statement in C. All other statements, such as iterations, conditions, or blocks, are control structures. Control structures are statements that control the execution of other statements. A compound statement groups together a set of statements. The two iteration statements, `while` and `for`, repeat the execution of statements. The two condition statements, `if` and `switch`, choose which statements to execute.

Expression Statements and Null Statements

An expression statement consists of any valid expression, followed by a semicolon. The expression used in the statement can be any expression. Often the expression is an assignment operation or a function call. But the expression could just as easily be an arithmetic expression or relational expression. An expression statement consisting only of an arithmetic expression does nothing, but is still a valid expression statement.

In the first example that follows, the assignment operation, count = 6, is an assignment expression that happens to be placed in a statement. It is not really an assignment statement as such. count = 6 is an expression. In the second example, the function call is a function call expression, calc(), placed within an expression statement. The function call is an expression itself. The parentheses form an operator that calls the function.

The third example, (4+2);, is also a valid expression statement. It consists of an arithmetic expression, (4+2), preceding a semicolon. The expression adds 4 to 2, with a result of 6, and then does nothing with the result. In the fourth example, the expression is a relational operation. If `i` is less than 3, the relational operation will have a result of 1. Nothing is then done with the 1.

Expressions
```
count = 6
calc()
4 + 2
(i < 3)
```

Expression statements
```
count = 6 ;
calc();
4 + 2 ;
(i < 3) ;
```

If there is no expression in the expression statement, nothing happens. This is still a valid statement and is referred to as the null statement. It is written as a semicolon with nothing preceding it.

Null statement

```
;
```

If you use a null statement, it is always advisable to place it on a line of its own. Otherwise, it can cause confusion. Null statements have a habit of showing up where they are least expected. The next example has a null statement following a declaration. The second semicolon is the null statement.

```
int count;
;
```

Compound Statements

A compound statement is a statement composed of one or more statements. The statements may be of any type. Often a compound statement is a list of expression statements. Compound statements can be placed anywhere within a function. They are usually attached to control structures, such as a `while` loop or an `if` condition.

A compound statement consists of a set of opening and closing braces. Statements are placed within the braces. Unlike other statements, the compound statement is not terminated with a semicolon.

```
{
cost = 5.30;
result = (4 + 5);
printf ("%f, %d", cost, result);
}
```

A compound statement can be more than just a statement. You can declare variables at the beginning of a compound statement. These variables are scoped to that compound statement. A compound statement with variable declarations is referred to as a block. The body of a function is a compound statement itself and is often referred to as the function block. In the **myblock.c** program in LISTING 4-1, the variable cost is declared locally within a compound statement. The variable result is known within the inner block; however, the variable cost is not known in the outer block. cost is scoped to the inner block. Block scoping is examined in greater detail in Chapter 8.

LISTING 4-1:

myblock.c
```
#include <stdio.h>

int main(void)
        {
        int result;
                {
                float cost;
                cost = 5.30;
                result = (4 + 5);
                printf ("%f, %d", cost, result);
                }
        /* cost is not known */

        return 0;
        }
```

Iteration Statements: while and for Loops

Loops are implemented with three iteration statements: while, do-while, and for. The while statement is very similar to the while statement in other programming languages. The do-while statement is a variation of the while statement. The for statement, however, is very different. In C, the for statement has as much flexibility as a while statement.

The for, while, and do-while statements consist of their respective keywords, a test expression, and another statement. The test expression can be any valid C expression.

Though the while, do-while, and for statements are considered to be statements themselves, each has a statement as part of its structure. This is the statement that is repeated by the while, do-while, or for loop. The statement can be anything the programmer chooses. Often it is a compound statement; sometimes it is another while statement. It can even be a null statement.

The while and do-while Statements

The valid syntax for a while loop consists of the keyword while, a test expression within parentheses, and a statement. The statement is repeated for as long as the test expression evaluates to a nonzero value. The statement can be a single statement or a compound statement. The syntax for the while statement is described here.

> while (*test expression*)
> *statement* ;

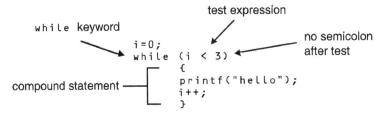

Figure 4-1: while statement.

Often, but not always, the test expression is a relational expression. In a simple counting loop, the test expression consists of a changeable variable compared to a predetermined constant. Figure 4-1 shows such a counting loop.

> while (i <= 3)
> *statement;*

Here the variable i is compared to the constant 3. If i is less than or equal to 3, the expression is true and evaluates to 1. 1 is a nonzero value, and so the loop continues execution. The statement is executed. If i is greater than 3, the relational expression is false and evaluates to zero. This zero value renders the test expression false and causes the loop to cease execution.

If the loop is to execute the statement three times, you need to explicitly manage the value of the variable i. i must first be set to a value less than 3 in order for the loop to be executed at all. This is done before the loop and is often referred to as the initialization.

```
i = 1;
while (i <= 3)
              statement;
```

Initialization allows entry into the loop, but it does not provide for an exit from the loop. In order to exit from this loop, the variable i must somehow be changed so that, eventually, it is larger than 3. Only when i is larger than 3 can the test expression be false and the loop ceases repetition. To do this, a statement is needed within the loop that changes the value of the variable i. This will require that more than one statement be placed within the loop. Yet the syntax for a while structure provides for only one statement. This restriction is overcome by the use of a compound statement. A compound statement is one statement that in turn consists of several statements.

To have the loop execute three times, the variable i can be incremented by 1 for each execution of the loop. On the third execution, i will be incremented to 4, rendering the test expression false on the fourth try. This incrementation of the test variable is referred to as either the increment or the update, as shown in Figure 4-2. The program **iter.c** in LISTING 4-2 is an example of a simple counting loop.

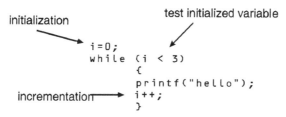

Figure 4-2: while initialization and incrementation.

The initialization and increment can be described as an entry condition and an exit condition, respectively, for a loop. All loops must have an entry condition and an exit condition in some form. Lacking an entry condition, a loop will not be executed. Lacking an exit condition, the loop will continue to execute without end, an infinite loop.

The entry and exit conditions can be supplied by the user through an input/output function. The variable used to control the loop will receive its value from the user. In this case, there are two input statements. One is placed before the loop to initialize the input variable. The other is placed at the end of the loop to update the input variable. In the **square.c** program in LISTING 4-3, the loop continues until the user enters a 0 value, which will stop the loop.

LISTING 4-2:

iter.c

```
#include <stdio.h>
#define MAX 3

int main(void)
      {
      int i;

      i = 1;  /* initialization */
      while (i <= MAX)
            {
            printf ("This is the %d iteration\n", i);
            i = i + 1;                  /* increment */
            }

      return 0;
      }
```

LISTING 4-3:

square.c

```
#include <stdio.h>

int main(void)
      {
      int quit, mynum, square;

      printf("Enter a number\n");
      scanf("%d", &mynum);

      while (mynum != 0)
            {

            square = mynum * mynum;
            printf("Square of %d = %d\n", mynum, square);

            printf("Enter a number (0 to quit)\n");
            scanf("%d", &mynum);
            }

      return 0;
      }
```

The do-while statement is a variation on the while statement. Instead of the test occurring at the beginning of the loop, it occurs at the end. The loop begins with the keyword do. A single statement or a compound statement may follow. The while keyword and the test expression are placed after the statement. Unlike the while statement, a semicolon will follow the do-while test. Figure 4-3 illustrates a sample do-while statement. In LISTING 4-4, the program in LISTING 4-2 is rewritten with a do-while statement.

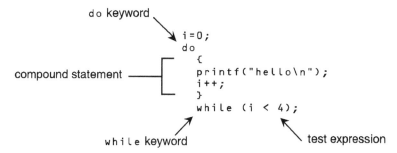

Figure 4-3: do-while statement.

LISTING 4-4:

iterdo.c

```
#include <stdio.h>
#define MAX 3

int main(void)
    {
    int i;

    i = 1;  /* initialization */

        do
        {
        printf ("This is the %d iteration\n", i);
        i = i + 1;              /* increment */
        }
        while (i <= MAX);       /* semicolon */

    return 0;
    }
```

The while Test Expression

The test expression for the `while` statement, as well as for the `for` and `if` statements, can be any valid expression. This means that a test expression can be an assignment operation. It can also be a simple primary expression consisting of just a variable or a constant. The truth or falsity of the test expression is determined by whether the expression evaluates to zero or nonzero. A zero result is considered false. Any nonzero result is true. This can lead to some odd combinations within the test expression.

Assignment and Equality Expressions

Since assignment operations are expressions, they can be used as test expressions. However, their use can lead to subtle runtime errors. In the next example, the test expression is an assignment operation. The value of k is assigned to `i`. The result of this expression will then be tested for truth or falsity. The result of the assignment expression is the value assigned, in this case, the value of k. If you use an assignment operation as your test expression, then the truth or falsity of the test depends on the value assigned. If you assign a 0 value, the test is false, and if you assign a nonzero value, plus or minus, the test is true. In the following example, if the value of k happens to be zero, the test will be false. However, if the value of k happens to be anything other than zero, the test will be true.

```
while(i = k)
```

If the assigned value is a constant, the loop becomes either an infinite loop or one that is never executed. In the next examples, the first test is always false because the value assigned in the assignment expression is always zero. Such a loop will never be executed. In the second example, the test expression assigns the constant 5 to i. The result of this expression is always 5. If the value assigned is a nonzero constant, then the test expression is always true. In such a case there is no exit condition. The loop will continue to repeat indefinitely. Such a while loop is referred to as an infinite loop.

```
while(i = 0)          /* Always False */

while(i = 5)          /* Always True */
```

Such test expressions are often mistakes. For example, the programmer, intending to write i == 5, forgets the second = sign for the equality operator and writes i = 5 instead. The single = sign is the assignment operator, not the equality operator. The result of an assignment is the value assigned, in this case, 5. If the value assigned is a nonzero value, the test is always true. If the value assigned is zero, the test is always false. In the next example, both test expressions are valid, but they are completely different. The expression i == 5 is an equality expression, a comparison. It is true only if the value of i happens to be 5. However, i = 5 is an assignment expression. The result of this assignment expression is always 5. This test expression is always true.

```
while (i = 5)          while (i == 5)
```

The same care must be taken when you compare a variable to the constant 0. If by mistake, you use an assignment operator instead of the equality operator, then the test expression is always false, and the loop is never executed. In the next example, the first while test is always false, and the loop is never executed. The second while test is false only if the value of i is 0. It is true if i is any other value.

```
while (i = 0)          while (i == 0)
```

Should you want to create an infinite loop on purpose, it is best to use either the while loop with the integer 1 as its expression or the for loop with no expressions.

```
while (1)
for (;;)
```

Flags are particularly prone to this mistake. A flag is a variable initialized to a certain value, such as 1, and used to control a loop. A change in its value will stop the loop. The **squareq.c** program in LISTING 4-5 shows how you would use a flag to control a loop. In this program, the square of numbers is printed out until the number 10 is reached. The variable quit is used as a flag to control the loop. It is initialized to 0. When quit is set to 1, the loop will stop.

LISTING 4-5:

squareq.c

```
#include <stdio.h>

int main(void)
        {
        int quit, mynum = 1, square;

        quit = 0;
        while (quit == 0)
                {
                square = mynum * mynum;
                printf("Square of %d =%d\n",mynum,square);

                if ( mynum == 10)
                                quit = 1;
                mynum++;
                }

        return 0;
        }
```

In the **squerr.c** program in LISTING 4-6, the programmer makes the common mistake of using an assignment operation in the while test instead of an equality comparison. In the test expression, the assignment operation quit = 0 has been used instead of the equality operation quit == 0. The quit flag is immediately assigned the value of 0. The while loop is never executed because the result of the assignment of zero to a variable is zero, which renders the test expression false. Even when this is corrected, the loop will only execute once, because there is still another error in the program. In the if statement's test expression, mynum = 10 has been written instead of mynum == 10. The result of the test expression is the value assigned, 10. This is not zero, so the test is true. The variable quit is changed to 1 the first time through.

LISTING 4-6:

squerr.c
```
#include <stdio.h>

int main(void)
        {
        int quit, mynum = 1, square;

        quit = 0;
        while (quit = 0)
                {
                square = mynum * mynum;
                printf("Square of %d = %d\n", mynum, square);
                if (mynum = 10)
                        quit = 1;
                mynum++;
                }

        return 0;
        }
```

Assignment and Function Call Expressions

Though assignments used with constants will lead to errors, assignments used with function calls can create powerful and complex test expressions. You will often find in C programs such combinations of assignments and function calls used in test expressions. Such a test expression will not just test for truth, but will call functions and assign values. You can begin to see how a test expression can be used to perform a great deal of work.

To see how a test expression can incorporate assignments and function calls, let us begin by examining a standard loop structure. Following is a loop that reads in and prints out characters until the user enters in a carriage return. The user provides a character from the keyboard through the function `getchar`. This initializes the variable `ch`. The `ch` variable is used to control the loop. If ch is not a newline, '\n', then the loop continues to execute. Within the loop, ch is updated with another character obtained through `getchar`. You do not know when the loop will stop, because it is up to the user to decide when to input a newline.

```
ch = getchar();
while (ch != '\n')
        {
        putchar(ch);
        ch = getchar();
        }
```

The combination of an assignment operation and function call allows the entry condition and exit condition to be combined into the test expression. In the loop in Figure 4-4, the function call to `getchar` and the assignment of its result to the variable `ch` are combined into the `while` test expression. Four actions take place in this test expression:

1.   Function call: A function call to `getchar`.
2.   Assignment: The character return value of `getchar` is assigned to `ch`.
3.   Relational comparison: The result of the assignment operation becomes an operand in a relational expression. It is compared to the newline constant, '\n'.
4.   The result of the relational expression is then used to determine whether the expression is true or false.

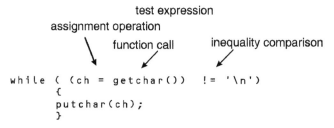

Figure 4-4: Complex test expression.

The parentheses are placed around the assignment operation within the test expression in Figure 4-4. The assignment operator, =, has a lower precedence than most other operators, including the relational operators. In order to force execution of the assignment before the relational operation, the assignment operation must be enclosed within parentheses. If the parentheses are missing, then the relational operation would execute first. The result of the relational operation, a 1 or 0, would then be assigned to the variable ch.

You can further combine such complex assignment expressions with logical expressions to form yet more powerful test expressions. However, placement of the assignment in a logical expression can be crucial. A logical expression evaluates from left to right. The next example works because the assignment to ch is in the leftmost operand of the logical expression. Because of this, ch has a value before it is used in any of the later relational expressions.

```
while( ((ch = getchar()) >= 'a') && ( ch <= 'z'))
        putchar(ch);
```

The **getalpha.c** program in LISTING 4-7 combines all these features in a program that allows the user to input lowercase characters only. Each valid character is printed out. The user terminates input by entering a newline character.

LISTING 4-7:

getalpha.c

```
#include <stdio.h>

int main(void)
        {
        int ch;

        while(((ch = getchar()) != '\n') && ((ch >= 'a') && (ch <= 'z')))
                {
                putchar (ch);
                }

        return 0;
        }
```

Primary Expressions: Variables and Constants

Though this may appear odd, a simple primary expression can be a valid test expression. A primary expression can be either a constant or a variable. The result of the expression is the value of the constant or the value in the variable. A primary expression consisting of a single constant is often used to write infinite loops. A primary expression consisting of a single variable can be used as a shorthand for comparing the value of the variable to zero.

In the next example, the test expression is the primary expression consisting of the variable i. The result of this primary expression is the value of the variable i. If the value of the variable i is zero, the test is false. If it is anything other than zero, the test is true.

```
while (i)
```

The use of a variable as the test expression is a shorthand for an inequality test of the variable against zero. The test for the value of i is equivalent to the equality comparison, $i!=0$. Both test expressions are equivalent, and both will be false when i is equal to zero.

```
while (i)                    while (i != 0)
```

You can also use a single constant as a test expression. In this case, the constant is a primary expression whose value is that represented by the constant. In the following example, the test expression is the constant 1. The value of the constant 1 is always 1. Because the constant is nonzero, the test is always true. The loop continues indefinitely. This is one way of writing an infinite loop.

```
while (1)
```

In the next example, the test expression is the constant 0. The value of the constant 0 is always zero and thereby always false. This loop will never execute.

```
while (0)
```

The while test and the Null Statement: Input Buffer Example

Taking into consideration the way function calls, assignments, and comparisons can be incorporated into a test expression, you can begin to see how you could write a while statement in which the test expression does all a loop's work. In this case, the statement following the test expression would simply be a null statement. A common example is a while statement designed to flush buffered input.

In the case of buffered input, characters typed in at the keyboard by the user are first placed in an input buffer. They remain there until retrieved by input functions, such as getchar. Characters are usually read into the input buffer one line at a time. The user terminates the input with a newline character, \n. As characters are retrieved from the input buffer by input functions, the buffer is emptied out. Many functions will leave extra characters in this input buffer that then need to be flushed out before new characters can be entered in by the user. Retrieving all characters up to and including the newline in effect flushes out the input buffer.

You can construct a simple while loop to flush the input buffer. Such a while loop, as shown in Figure 4-5, will perform all its tasks within the test expression. In this loop, three actions take place in the test expression. The first is a function call to the function getchar. The second is an inequality operation in which the return value of getchar is tested to see if it is not equal to the newline constants, \n. Finally, the result of the inequality expression is tested for truth or falsity.

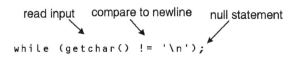

Figure 4-5: Null statement and buffer flush.

There are many different kinds of I/O functions, and all interact with the input buffer differently. Mixing different I/O functions requires flushing the input buffer at different times. In the **squflush.c** program in LISTING 4-8, both scanf and getchar are used in the same input buffer. The execution of the first scanf statement leaves a newline character in the input buffer. A subsequent call to getchar will simply take the newline character as the input. The newline character must first be flushed out. This is the purpose of the next `while` statement. The characters in the buffer are retrieved up to and including the newline character. The input buffer is now clear, and a subsequent call to `getchar` will allow the user to input a new character. The interactions of input functions with the input buffer are described in greater detail in Chapter 18.

LISTING 4-8:

squflush.c

```
#include <stdio.h>

int main(void)
      {
      int quit, mynum = 1, square;

      quit = 0;
      while (quit == 0)
            {
            printf("Please enter a number\n");
            scanf("%d", &mynum);

            square = mynum * mynum;
            printf("Square of %d =%d\n",mynum,square);

            while (getchar() != '\n');
            printf ("Do you wish another square ?");
            if(getchar() == 'n')
                        quit = 1;
            }

      return 0;
      }
```

When coding `while` statements, you need to take special care not to unintentionally enter a null statement after the test expression. To do so can result in an unintended infinite loop. Programmers that know other programming languages are particularly prone to making this mistake. In other programming languages such as Pascal, the test expression of a loop is terminated with a semicolon. However, in C, the semicolon ends the entire `while` statement. Should you forget the C syntax for a `while` statement and put a semicolon after the test expression, you will have unintentionally created an infinite loop. The syntax is valid. You can have a null statement follow a `while` test expression. However, if the test expression contains only a simple comparison operation, then the test will always be true and you will have an infinite loop.

In the next example, the programmer accidentally entered a semicolon after the `while` test expression. As far as the C compiler is concerned, this is a valid `while` loop that has as its statement a null statement. However, the test is always true, so it is an infinite loop. The `i` variable that is meant to control the loop is now being updated in what the compiler considers to be a separate compound statement that has nothing to do with the `while` loop.

```
i = 0;
while (i < 3) ;    /*semicolon for null statement */
        {
        printf ("Num = %d\n", i);
        i++;
        }
```

In the previous example, the compound statement following the `while` is simply a compound statement by itself. There are really three separate statements in this program, one of which is an infinite loop: the initial assignment, the `while` loop, and the compound statement. In the next example, the same program is written, but with better clarity so as to distinguish the different statements from one another.

```
i = 0;

while(i < 3)
        ;

{
printf ("Num = %d\n", i);
i++;
}
```

The for Statement

The `for` statement consists of three expressions followed by a statement. The three expressions are placed within parentheses and separated by commas. The statement to be executed within the `for` loop is placed after the expressions. Figure 4-6 displays a sample `for` statement. The syntax of the `for` statement follows.

```
for (expression1 ; expression2 ; expression3)
            statement;
```

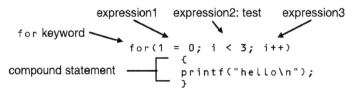

Figure 4-6: for statement.

The three expressions correspond to the three expressions used to manage a `while` loop: the initialization, test, and update expressions. The first expression is executed once before the loop begins. It is often used to initialize variables used in the test expression. The second expression is the test expression for the loop. When it evaluates to false, the loop stops. The last expression is an update expression. It is executed as the last statement within the loop and is usually used to update variables in the test expression.

for (*initialization ; test expression ; update expression*)
statement;

The for statement is often used to implement simple counting loops. The for statement in Figure 4-7 implements a counting loop to output hello three times using an i variable. In the initialization expression, i is assigned the value 0. This expression is executed once, before entry into the loop. Then the test expression checks to see if the value of i is less than three. When i is greater than or equal to three, then the test is false and the for loop ends. In each iteration of the loop, the statement following the for expressions is executed. In this case, the printf statement is executed. After this statement, the update expression is executed. The update expression here is an increment of the i variable. This increment is performed at the end of each iteration. You should think of the update expression as if it were the last statement in the loop. Whereas the initialization expression is executed only once before the loop, the update expression is executed with each iteration as the last statement within the loop. With each iteration, the update expression will increment the variable i by 1. On the third iteration, i will be set to 3, making the test expression false and ending the for loop.

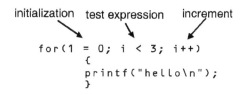

Figure 4-7: for loop initialization and incrementation.

The statement executed in a for loop can be any valid statement. If you need to perform several tasks within the loop, you can use a compound statement, listing statements within it. In the **squfor.c** program in LISTING 4-9 is an example of a for loop that uses a compound statement, which in turn consists of other statements.

LISTING 4-9:

squfor.c
```c
#include <stdio.h>
#define MAX 5

int main(void)
    {
    int mynum = 1, square;

    for(mynum = 1; mynum <= MAX; mynum++)
        {
        square = mynum * mynum;
        printf("Square of %d = %d\n", mynum, square);
        }

    return 0;
    }
```

Even if you are executing only one statement within a `for` loop, it is still advisable to use a compound statement. A compound statement will clearly designate the repeated task. Still, if you only need to execute one task, a simple statement will suffice. The **iterfor.c** program in LISTING 4-10 is an example of a simple `for` loop with one statement.

LISTING 4-10:

iterfor.c

```
#include <stdio.h>
#define MAX 3

int main(void)
    {
    int i;

    for(i = 1; i <= MAX; i++)
        printf ("This is the %d iteration\n", i);

    return 0;
    }
```

In other computer languages, the `for` loop operates under severe restrictions. It is usually just a counting loop using one variable. This is not the case in C. In C, the `for` loop has the same flexibility as a `while` loop. In fact, you can think of the `for` loop as just another way of writing a `while` loop. If a `for` loop is written as a `while` loop, the initialization expression would be an expression statement located just before the `while` statement. The update expression would be an expression statement located at the end of the `while` block. And the test expression would be the `while` loop's test expression. The translation of a `for` loop's expressions into corresponding `while` loop components is laid out in the following description.

```
for(initialization; test ; update)


initialization;
statement;
while(test)
        {
        statement;
        update;
        }
```

The next example shows how a `for` loop can be written as a `while` loop. The initialization expression, i = 0, becomes an expression statement just before the `while` loop begins. The update expression, i++, becomes the last statement within the body of the `while` loop. The test expression, i < 3, becomes the `while` test expression following the `while` keyword.

```
for(i = 0; i < 3 ; i++)                    i = 0;
        {                                  while(i < 3 )
        printf ("hi\n");                        {
        }                                       printf ("hi\n");
                                                i++;
                                                }
```

The for Statement and the Comma Operator Expression

The expressions in a `for` loop must be single expressions. For example, the first expression is one single expression. However, this one expression can be an expression that is made up of other expressions. An expression that in turn consists of several other expressions is the comma operator expression (see Chapter 3). The comma operator expression is a single expression whose components are themselves expressions. The comma operator expression allows the programmer to use several expressions where only one expression is permitted. Using a comma operator expression, you can now, in effect, list several expressions in the `for` loop's initialization expression. You could do the same for the update expression, listing several update operations to be performed.

The next example prints out the square of the first five odd numbers. The variable, num, is managed in the `for` loop using an initialization and an update operation, much in the same way it would be managed in a `while` loop. It is initialized in a statement before the `for` loop and updated in a statement at the end of the `for` loop. The for loop's initialization expression and update expression perform the same kind of management, initializing a variable before the loop and updating it within the loop.

```
num = 1;
for(i = 1; (i <= 5); i++)
        {
        square = num * num;
        printf("%d: Num = %d, Square = %d\n",i,num,square);
        num = num + 2;
        }
```

There is a way to incorporate the management of num into the `for` loop expressions. A comma operator expression can be used to expand a `for` loop expression into a series of expressions. The assignment expressions for both i and num can be combined into a comma operator expression and then used as the first expression in a `for` loop. The same can be done for their updates. In the next example, the `for` loop still has only one initialization and update expression, but each expression is a comma operator expression consisting of two other expressions. The initialization expression is a comma operator expression that has two assignment expressions, (i = 1, num = 1). The update expression is a comma operator expression consisting of an increment and an assignment, (i++, num=num+2).

```
for((i = 1, num = 1); (i <= 5); (i++, num=num+2))
        {
        square = num * num;
        printf("%d: Num= %d, Square= %d \n",i,num,square);
        }
```

Since the `for` loop assumes parentheses around its expressions, you can drop the enclosing parenthesis for the comma operator expressions. In the **comma.c** program in LISTING 4-11, the comma operator expressions do not include enclosing parentheses. They appear as a list of expressions separated by commas. However, you need to keep in mind that this is really just one expression.

LISTING 4-11:

comma.c

```
#include <stdio.h>
#define MAX 5

int main(void)
        {
        int i, num, square;

        for(i = 1, num = 1; i <= MAX; i++, num=num+2)
                {
                square = num * num;
                printf("%d:Num=%d,Square = %d\n",i,num,square);
                }

        return 0;
        }
```

As you incorporate more expressions into your `for` loop, the loop can become more difficult to understand. It often helps to conceptually map elements of a `for` loop to those of a `while` loop. The corresponding elements of the previously described `for` loop map into the `while` loop shown here.

```
(i = 1, num = 1);
while(i <= 5)
        {
        square = num * num;
        printf("%d: Num= %d, Square= %d \n",i,num,square);
        i++;
        num = num + 2;
        }
```

There is no limit to the number or kind of expressions that can be placed within the comma operator expressions used in a `for` loop. The use of the comma operator can be carried to great lengths. In the next example, the entire work of the loop is placed within the `for` loop expressions. The `printf` statement is now an expression in the comma operator update expression. The `for` loop's statement is reduced to a null statement. Though this example is exaggerated, there are many tasks for which a `for` statement does all the work within its expressions.

```
for(i=1,j=0;(i<3); printf("%d %d\n",i,j),i++,j++)
                ;
```

In such cases, the null statement is usually just placed at the end of the `for` loop on the same line.

```
for(i=1,j=0;(i<3);printf("%d %d\n",i,j),i++,j++);
```

The for Statement Expressions

The `for` statement does not in any way require that the first expression actually be an initialization. Nor does it require that the last expression be an update or increment operation. The expressions can be any valid expressions. The `for` statement only places these expressions in a loop structure. It is only a matter of location. The first expression is placed before the loop where an initialization is likely to occur. The last expression is placed at the end of the loop where an update is likely to occur. The next example shows the corresponding placement of `for` statement expressions in a loop structure.

```
for  (firstexpr; testexpr ; lastexpr)              firstexpr;
         {                                         while  (testexpr)
         statement;                                    {
         }                                             statement;
                                                       lastexpr;
                                                       }
```

In the next example, the first expression in the `for` loop is a `printf` function call, and the last expression is an arithmetic and assignment operation. To show how these expressions are organized, the loop is then rewritten as a `while` loop.

```
for (printf("hi"), res=0; (res < 30) ; res = num * rate)
            {
            printf("\nEnter rate and num ");
            scanf ("%d %d", &rate, &num);
            }

printf("hi");
res = 0;
while (res < 30)
            {
            printf("\nEnter rate and num ");
            scanf ("%d %d", &rate, &num);
            res = num * rate;
            }
```

The `for` loop does not require there actually be a first or last expression. In the next example, the last expression is left empty.

```
    for ( i = 0; i < 3;  )
            {
            printf ("hi\n");
            i++;
            }
```

Though the first and last expressions in a `for` loop may be any kind of expression, the middle expression is special in that it is a test expression. Its result will determine continual execution of the loop. You can, however, leave the test expression empty. An empty test expression evaluates to true. An empty test expression will give you an infinite loop, a loop that is always true. In fact, should you need an infinite loop in your program, an easy way to write one is to use a `for` statement with empty expressions. The next example shows two infinite loops, one using empty `for` loop expressions, and the other using a `while` loop with a constant expression.

```
for( ; ; )                              while (1)
    printf("Infinite");                     printf("Infinite");
```

Conversely, a zero constant in the test expression creates a loop that can never be executed.

```
for ( ; 0; )                    while (0)
    printf("Not Entered");          printf("Not Entered");
```

An infinite loop does not require that the other two expressions remain empty, only that the test expression be empty. In the next example, the first and last expressions are executed, and the test is always true, giving you an infinite loop.

```
for(i = 0; ; printf ("Infinite %d\n", i), i++);
```

The `for` loop can also be written to incorporate complex I/O tests. Following are three versions of the same loop. Characters are read in using `getchar`, assigned to ch,and printed out. This continues until the newline character is reached, '\n'. In the first version, the I/O operation is broken down into separate initialization, test, and update components. In the second version, the initialization and update are incorporated into a complex test expression. In the final version, the repeated statement, putchar, is made the update expression, leaving only the `for` expressions followed by a null statement. The **allfor.c** program in LISTING 4-12 is a rewritten version of the program in LISTING 4-7, incorporating all operations into the `for` loop expressions.

```
for (ch = getchar(); ch != '\n'; ch = getchar())
            {
            putchar (ch);
            }

for ( ; (ch = getchar()) != '\n' ;  )
            {
            putchar (ch);
            }

for ( ; (ch = getchar()) != '\n'; putchar (ch));
```

LISTING 4-12:

allfor.c

```
#include <stdio.h>

int main(void)
    {
    int ch;

    for( ;((ch = getchar()) != '\n') && ((ch >= 'a') && ( ch <= 'z')); putchar(ch));

    return 0;
    }
```

Nested Loops

There are many applications in which loops are nested within each other. For example, any task that operates on a table is a prime candidate for a nested loop. You shall later see that nested loops are used extensively for multidimensional arrays (see Chapter 13).

In the case of nested loops, the inner loop is executed with each iteration of the outer loop. The **matfor.c** program in LISTING 4-13 uses nested `for` loops to print out a matrix. For each iteration of the outer loop, the inner loop prints out a row of the matrix.

You can also nest `while` loops. The **matwhile.c** program in LISTING 4-14 uses nested while loops to print out a matrix. Notice how the different components of the `for` loop in LISTING 4-13 map onto those of the while loop in LISTING 4-14. The nested `while` loop in LISTING 4-14 has the same effect as the nested `for` loop in LISTING 4-13.

LISTING 4-13:

matfor.c
```c
#include <stdio.h>
int main(void)
    {
    int i, j, k;
    for (k = 0, i = 1 ; i <= 3 ; i++)
        {
        for (j = 1 ; j <= 3 ; j++)
            {
            k = k + 1;
            printf (" %3d", k);
            }
        printf ("\n");
        }
    return 0;
    }
```

Output for LISTING 4-13 and 4.14:
```
    1    2    3
    4    5    6
    7    8    9
```

LISTING 4-14:

matwhile.c
```c
#include <stdio.h>
int main(void)
    {
    int i, j, k;
    k = 0;
    i = 1;
    while( i <= 3)
        {
        j = 1;
        while (j <= 3) {
            k = k + 1;
            printf (" %3d",k);
            j++;
            }
        printf ("\n");
        i++;
        }
    return 0;
    }
```

Conditions: if and switch

The `if` and `switch` statements are flexible decision-making structures that determine which statements are to be executed and which are not. There are several different variations on the `if` statement, each of which allows varying degrees of complexity. In its simplest form, an if statement simply decides whether a statement will be executed or not. In combination with the else extension, an if statement becomes a decision between two possible statements: one or the other will be executed. Combining an else , in turn, with another if generates a decision making structure that chooses between a set of possible statements.

The switch statement also chooses among several possible statements. Though it can be approximated by an else-if, the switch statement provides a simple and clear way to organize a set of possible options. However, the switch statement is in some ways more restrictive in its decision-making capability than an if statement.

The if Statements

In its simplest form, an if is a condition placed on a statement's execution. If the condition is true, the statement is executed. If not, the statement is not executed. An if statement consists of the keyword if, a test expression, and a statement. The test expression is tested for truth or falsity. An expression with a zero result is false. Any nonzero result is true. There is no keyword then. Even though many programming languages have a **then** with their if statement, C does not. The syntax for the if statement follows. The test expression is enclosed within parentheses.

if(*test expression*)
            statement ;

The statement in an if condition may be any valid statement. It may be an expression statement, a compound statement, a while statement, or even another if statement. In most cases, you would find an if condition used with a compound statement (see Figure 4-8). Examples of several possible kinds of statements follow.

```
if(i < 3)
        printf("hello");        /*Expression Statement*/

if(i < 3)
        {                       /* Compound Statement */
        printf("hello");
        printf("goodbye");
        }

if(i < 3)
        if (j == 5)     /* If Statement */
            printf("hello");
```

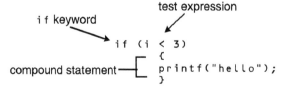

Figure 4-8: if statement.

LISTING 4-15:

ifgreet.c

```c
#include <stdio.h>

int main(void)
    {
    int i;

    for (i = 0; i < 3; i++)
            {
            if(i == 0)
                    printf ("hello\n");
            printf ("Number %d\n", i);
            if(i == 2)
                    printf ("goodbye");
            }

    return 0;
    }
```

Often, an `if` statement will be placed within a compound statement that, in turn, is part of another `if`, `while`, or `for` statement. In the **ifgreet.c** program in LISTING 4-15, `if` statements are placed inside a `for` statement.

The if-else Construct

An `if-else` construct consists of an `if` statement followed by the keyword `else` with its own statement. The `if-else` statement allows a decision between two possible statements. One or the other will be chosen. The syntax for an `if-else` statement follows.

```
if (test expression)
        statement;
else
        statement;
```

Figure 4-9 contains a simple test for equality. A test is made on the value of the variable formal in order to decide whether a formal or informal greeting should be printed out. If `formal` is equal to 1, then "greetings" will be printed out. Otherwise, "hello" will be printed.

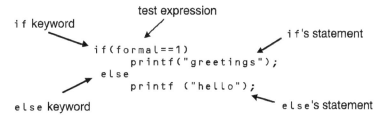

Figure 4-9: if-else statement.

An `if` statement is commonly used to do a simple calculation. In the next example, two values are compared to determine which is the maximum. The variable max will hold the maximum value.

```
if(i > j)
        max = i;
else
        max = j;
```

You can use any valid statement in your `if-else` constructs. The next example uses compound statements for both the `if` and the `else` segments of the overall `if-else` statement.

```
if(first > second)
        {
        max = first;
        printf ("The first is larger\n");
        }
  else
        {
        max = second;
        printf ("The second is larger\n");
        }
```

You can even use another `if` statement in an `if-else` construct, as shown in the next example.

```
if (i > j)
        max = i;
else
        if(j > 0)
                max = j;
```

If the `if` segment in an `if-else` construct has as its statement another `if`, the `else` will not match properly. An `else` matches with the most recent `if`. In the following case, the `else` is matching with `if(i>0)`. The indentation makes it appear as if the `else` matches the first `if`. In fact, it matches the second `if`.

```
if(i > j)                              if(i > j)
        if (i > 0)                             if (i > 0)
                max = i;                               max = i;
else                                       else
        max = j;                               max = j;
```

Such a problem can be easily fixed by placing the second `if` statement, `if(i>0)`, within a compound statement.

```
if (i > j)
        {
        if (i > 0)
                max = i;
        }
else
        max = j
```

Just as with the simple `if` statement, the `if-else` can be combined with other `while` and `if` statements. The program **ifnest.c** in LISTING 4-16 is a variation of LISTING 4-15. Here, the `if-else` statements are embedded within other *if* statements, which, in turn, are embedded within a `for` statement.

LISTING 4-16:

ifnest.c

```
#include <stdio.h>

int main(void)
        {
        int i, formal;

        formal = 1;
        for (i = 0; i < 3; i++)
                {
                if (i == 0)
                        {
                        if (formal == 1)
                                printf ("hello\n");
                        else
                                printf("greetings\n");
                        }
                printf ("Number %d\n", i);
                if (i == 2)
                        {
                        if (formal == 1)
                                printf("goodbye\n");
                        else
                                printf("farewell\n");
                        }
                }

        return 0;
        }
```

The `if-else` construct is an operation similar to that of the conditional expression. The question mark, `?`, in a conditional expression indicates the `if`, and the colon is an `else`. However, the conditional operation is an expression and as such has a resulting value, whereas the `if-else` construct is a statement and has no resulting value. Here are two versions of the same condition operations using first an `if-else` statement and then a conditional expression, (`?` :).

```
if (i > j)
        max = i;
else
        max = j;

max =  ((i > j) ? i : j );
```

The else-if construct

You can combine `if-else` statements in such a way as to allow a choice among several different options, instead of just two. To create such a construct you need to use another `if-else` as the statement for the `else` segment in an `if-else` condition. Such a construct is often referred to as an `else-if` construct, an `if` that follows an `else`. The syntax for an `else-if` construct follows.

> if (*test expression*)
> > *statement*;
>
> else
> > if (*test expression*)
> > > *statement*;
> >
> > else
> > > *statement*;

An `else-if` construct allows a flexible choice among multiple options. In an `else-if` construct, the `else` alternative becomes another decision rather than a simple statement. As long as the test expression of each `if` is false, there will be a cascade effect, moving from one `if` statement to the next. If a test is true, its statement is executed, and its else is skipped, halting the process. In the **elsegret.c** program in LISTING 4-17, the second option is printed out, `printf("hello")`.

LISTING 4-17:

elsegret.c
```c
#include <stdio.h>
int main(void)
        {
        int formal;
        formal = 2;
        if (formal == 1)
                printf("greetings");
        else
                if (formal == 2)
                        printf("hello");
                else
                        if (formal == 3)
                                printf("hi");
                        else
                                printf("Invalid Greeting");
        return 0;
        }
```

The if Test Expression

The test expression of an `if` statement can be any valid expression. Like a `while` test, an `if` test can include function calls, assignment operations, or simple primary expressions. In the **elsecom.c** program in LISTING 4-18, there is an `else-if` with complex test expressions.

LISTING 4-18:

elsecom.c

```c
#include <stdio.h>

int main(void)
        {
        int business = 1;
        int personal = 1;
        int formal = 3;

        if ((formal == 1)&&(business))
                printf("greetings");
        else
                if ((formal = getchar()) < '3')
                        printf("hello");
                else
                        if ((formal == 3)||(personal == 1))
                                printf("hi");
                        else
                                printf("Invalid Greeting");

        return 0;
        }
```

You can also use a primary expression consisting of a single variable as the test expression in an `if` statement. In this case, the test expression is equivalent to a test of inequality to 0.

```
        if(count)                       if(count != 0)
```

The same pitfalls apply to the `if` test as to the `while` test. Be careful to distinguish the assignment and the equality operators. An assignment operator consists of one equals sign, =, and the equality operator consists of two equals signs, ==. Assignment operations are valid expressions and can be used as test expressions. Keeping this in mind, an error occurs if you accidentally use an assignment operator where you intended to use an equality operator. In such a case you could end up with a condition that is either always true or always false. In the next example, the assignment of 0 to count will result in a condition that is always false. The assignment of a nonzero value such as 1 to count will result in a condition that is always true.

```
        if (count = 0)       Valid but always false.
        if (count = 1)       Valid but always true.
```

Though the equality and assignment operators appear similar, they perform different operations. In the next example, the assignment operation assigns 1 to count, whereas the equality operation compares the value of count to 1.

```
        if(count = 1)   if(count == 1)
        if(count = 0)   if(count == 0)
```

`if` statement test expressions will often consist of complex expressions. There is no limit to the complexity. In many cases, you will find a series of relational operations combined with logical operations to test for a special condition. In the next example, the test checks for any characters that are not what are known in C as whitespaces: spaces, carriage returns, and tabs. Any character other than a whitespace is counted by incrementing charcount.

```
if((ch == ' ') && (ch != '\t') && (ch != '\n'))
            charcount++;
```

In the **outalpha.c** program in LISTING 4-19, the if statement's test expression contains a logical expression used to check for lowercase characters. If a character is not an alphabetic lowercase character, the program prints out a dash.

LISTING 4-19:

outalpha.c

```
#include <stdio.h>

int main(void)
        {
        int ch;

        while((ch = getchar()) != '\n')
                {
                if ((ch < 'a')||( ch > 'z'))
                        putchar('-');
                else
                        putchar(ch);
                }

        return 0;
        }
```

As with loops, function calls and assignment operations are often incorporated into the test expression of an if condition. In the following example, getchar is made part of the test expression. Its result is assigned to ch. The result of the assignment is then compared to the newline character constant '\n'.

```
if((ch = getchar()) != '\n')
        putchar(ch);
```

Often the if statement will be used to check for errors returned from a function call. The actual function call will be nested in a test expression of the if statement. The return value of functions will be tested to check for errors. In the next example, scanf will return the number of successful conversions. In this case, scanf should return a 1. If the conversion fails, it will return 0. The return value is tested for 0 to see if an error message should be printed out. Functions and their use with if statements are examined in greater depth in Chapter 6.

```
if ((scanf("%d", id) == 0)
        printf ("scanf failed to read input \n");
```

The switch Statement

The switch statement provides a convenient way to choose among several alternatives. There are situations in which you will need to decide on one of several possible choices. The choices are usually predetermined and remain constant. Selection of a choice involves matching your decision with the possible choices presented. You could implement such a process using `else-if` constructs. However, the simplicity of such a task allows you to use the more convenient implementation of the `switch` statement.

The `switch` statement compares an integer value against a set of integer constants. The integer value can be any type of integral, including a char or long. They can also be signed or unsigned. Associated with each constant are statements. A match between the integer value and an integer constant executes the associated statements. The `switch` statement consists of a test expression, a set of integer constants, and statements associated with each constant. The integer constants are arranged sequentially and are preceded by the keyword case. Each constant is terminated with a colon. To the right of the colon are statements. The last statement among the statements associated with the constant may or may not be a `break` statement. The `break` statement will force an exit of the `switch` statement.

The `switch` statement compares the result of the test expression with the integer constants. When a match is found between the integer result and an integer constant, control shifts to the statements to the right of the colon. The statements are then executed until either a `break` statement is encountered or the end of the `switch` statement is reached. The syntax for the `switch` statement follows. A default option may be placed at the end of the list of constants. It is specified by the keyword default.

```
switch (integer expression)
       {
       case integer :
                       statements ;
                       break;
       case integer :
                       statements ;
                       break;
       default :
                       statements ;
                       break;
       }
```

In the **numsel.c** program in LISTING 4-20, the user is allowed to enter a number. That numeric value is placed in the variable, `mynumber`. The `switch`'s test expression is the primary expression consisting of the variable `mynumber`. The result of this expression is the value held by `mynumber`. This result is then compared with the constants 1, 2, and 3. When a match is made, the corresponding `printf` statement is printed out. Following the `printf` statement, a `break` statement then forces an exit of the `switch`. If no match is made, then the default statements will be executed. Figure 4-10 shows the syntactical structure of this `switch` statement. Figure 4-11 illustrates the control flow of the `switch` statement.

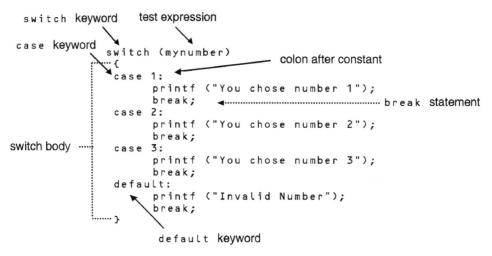

Figure 4-10: switch statement.

LISTING 4-20:

numsel.c

```c
#include <stdio.h>

int main(void)
    {
    int mynumber;

    printf("Please enter a Number:\n");
    scanf("%d", &mynumber);

    switch (mynumber)
        {
        case 1:
            printf ("You chose number 1");
            break;
        case 2:
            printf ("You chose number 2");
            break;
        case 3:
            printf ("You chose number 3");
            break;
        default:
            printf ("Invalid Number");
            break;
        }

    return 0;
    }
```

The switch statement is similar to an else-if construct. In the **greetsel.c** program in
LISTING 4-21, the greetings program is implemented with a switch instead of an else-if. The

default option is used for the last `else`. Notice the use of the symbolic constants set up with the define command. Symbolic constants are often used to clarify the choices in a `switch` statement.

LISTING 4-21:

greetsel.c

```c
#include <stdio.h>
#define FORMAL 1
#define COMMON 2
#define FRIENDLY 3
int main(void)
        {
        int greeting;
        printf("Enter Greeting Code\n");
        scanf ("%d", &greeting);
        switch (greeting)
                {
                case FORMAL:
                                printf("greetings");
                                break;
                case COMMON:
                                printf("hello");
                                    break;
                case FRIENDLY:
                                printf("hi");
                                break;
                default :
                                printf("Invalid Greeting");
                                break;
                }

        return 0;
        }
```

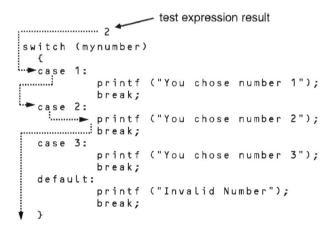

Figure 4-11: switch statement control flow.

It is tempting to think of the `switch` statement as a simple `else-if` construct. It is not quite that. An `else-if` will only execute the statements whose test expression is true. A `switch` statement might execute statements not associated with a true test. It helps to think of the colons in a `switch` statement as forming a kind of barrier between constants and statements. Execution of the `switch` begins by comparing the result of the test expression to each constant. Once a match is made, control transfers across the barrier of colons, and statements are executed. This execution of statements will continue through to the end of the `switch` unless a `break` is encountered. The natural state of affairs for the `switch` is to execute all statements from the point of the successful match. The `break` is a forcible interruption of this process.

In the **nums.c** program in LISTING 4-22, the `break` statements have been removed. If the user enters a 2, then the `printf` for number 2, number 3, and the default will print out. If 1 is entered, all will print out. If 3 is entered, only the `printf` for number 3 and the default will print. Figure 4-12 displays the control flow of the `switch` statement without breaks.

A `switch` statement is very restricted in terms of the type of objects it can compare. The `switch` statement can only compare integer values. The `switch`'s test expression must result in an integer value. This integer is then compared to a set of integer constants. Floating-point values cannot be compared. Nor can the case values be variables. They must be integer constants.

The integer constant used in the `switch` statement is an integer constant expression. An integer constant expression is any integer operation that can be performed by the compiler. For example, the expression $(2 + 4)$ is an integer constant expression. The compiler can determine the result and replace the expression with 6.

LISTING 4-22:

nums.c
```c
#include <stdio.h>

int main(void)
    {
    int mynumber;

    printf("Please enter a Number:\n");
    scanf ("%d", &mynumber);

    switch (mynumber)
        {
        case 1 :
            printf ("You chose number 1 \n");
        case 2 :
            printf ("You chose number 2 \n");
        case 3 :
            printf ("You chose number 3 \n");
        default:
            printf ("Invalid Number \n");
            break;
        }

    return 0;
    }
```

In any expression, characters are promoted to integers. For this reason, you can use any character constant as an integer constant for a `switch`. You can also use symbolic constants, specified by either define or `enum`, that define integer values. In the next example, `getchar` receives input from the user and places it in the character variable `inchar`. A `switch` on `inchar` then determines which character was input. If an 'a' was input, then `inchar` will match the 'a' option. Control will pass to the right side of the colon, and all statements from that point on will be executed until a `break` is reached. If the character 'b' was input, the `switch` statement would not match any of the available constants (a, f, q). It would then match on the default and execute the statement `printf("Invalid Entry");`.

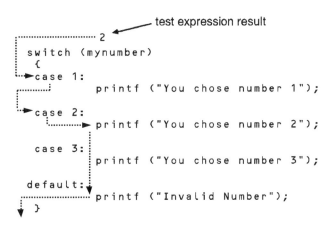

Figure 4-12: switch without break statements.

```
inchar = getchar();
switch (inchar)
        {
        case 'a' :
                printf(" Add a new record ");
                addrec();
                break;
        case 'f' :
                printf( " Find a record ");
                findrec();
                break;
        case 'q' :
                printf ( " Quit, Goodbye ");
                break;
        default:
                printf ( "Invalid Entry");
                break;
        }
```

With a `switch` statement, you can apply several tests to the same set of statements. For example, you could have both a test for an uppercase character and a test for its lowercase version executing the same statements. In the next example, the user can enter a lowercase 'a' or an upper case 'A' to add a record. You can implement such task by taking advantage of the fact that an integer constant need not have corresponding statements or a `break` statement. When a constant does not have a corresponding `break` statement, it operates like a logical OR with the next constant below it. In the next example, the constant 'A' has no corresponding `break` statement. 'A' and 'a' operate together like a logical OR. If a person enters either an uppercase 'A' or a lowercase 'a', the `addrec` function will be executed.

```
switch (inchar)
    {
    case 'A' :
    case 'a' :
            printf("Add a new record ");
            addrec();
            break;
    case 'Q' :
    case 'q' :
            printf("Quit, Goodbye ");
            quit = 0;
            break;
    }
```

Among tests that share the same statements, you can further organize your `switch` to allow certain of those tests to execute additional statements. In the next example, both the test for the 'F' and that for the 'D' constant share the same `disprec()` statement. If you enter a 'D', you will execute `disprec()`. However, if you enter an 'F', you will first execute `findrec()`, followed by an execution of `disprec()`. You use the 'F' constant not only to call `disprec` to display a record, as 'D' does, but also to call `findrec` to first search for a record. There is no `break` between the statements for the 'F' test and the statements for the 'D' test. A match on 'F' starts with its own statements and continues down through the 'D' test's statements, until finally reaching a `break`.

```
switch (inchar)
    {
    case 'F' :
            findrec();      /* Find a Record */
    case 'D' :
            disprec();      /* Display a Record */
            break;
    case 'Q' :
    case 'q' :
            printf("Quit, Goodbye ");
            quit = 0;
            break;
    }
```

Often a `switch` statement will be used to manage a menu, as shown in the **menu.c** program in LISTING 4-23. The constants in the `switch` will compare to menu selections. The `switch` itself will be placed in a loop. The test for the loop will be controlled by the quit option in the `switch` statement, 'q'. This program is incomplete for the sake of brevity, using empty functions for the different options.

LISTING 4-23:

menu.c
```c
#include <stdio.h>
void addrec(void);
void findrec(void);
void disprec(void);

int main(void)
        {
        int quit = 1;
        char inchar;

        while ( quit == 1)
                {
                inchar = getchar();    /* Get user response */
                switch (inchar)
                        {
                        case 'A' :
                        case 'a' :
                                addrec();       /* Add a record */
                                break;
                        case 'F' :
                        case 'f' :
                                findrec();      /* Find a record */
                        case 'D' :
                        case 'd' :
                                disprec();      /* Display a record */
                                break;
                        case 'Q' :
                        case 'q' :
                                printf("Quit, Goodbye\n");
                                quit = 0;
                                break;
                        default:
                                printf("Invalid Entry\n");
                                break;
                        }
                while (getchar() != '\n');     /* Flush buffer */
                }

        return 0;
        }


void addrec(void)
        {
        printf("Add a new record\n");
        }

void findrec(void)
        {
        printf("Find a record\n");
        }

void disprec(void)
        {
        printf("Display a record\n");
        }
```

The Jump Statements: break, continue, goto, and label

The jump statements are nonstructured control statements that allow a program to transfer control from one statement to another out of sequence, in effect jumping across statements. Instead of automatically transferring control to the next statement, with a jump statement you could force a transfer of control to some other statement in the program. The break and continue statements are specialized jump statements that are used only with while and for statements. The break is also used with the switch statement. The goto and label statements are more generalized, allowing jumps to anywhere in your program. You can even use the goto and label statements to implement assembly-language-like versions of loops and conditions.

break and continue Statements

The break statement breaks out of the while, for, and switch statements. You will often need to use break statements in a switch, as shown in the previous section. Only rarely will you ever use break statements in while or for loops. The break is nonstructured in that it provides an exit condition other than that of the statement's test expression. For example, in the next program, the break will force an exit from the loop when i is equal to 3.

```
i = 1;
while (i <= 10)
        {
        if (i == 3)
                break;
        printf ("This is %d iteration\n", i);
        i++;
        }
```

The continue statement is uniquely designed to work with loops. The continue statement skips over the rest of the statements in a loop and begins the next iteration. You can think of the continue as a statement that jumps over the rest of the statements in the loop and continues with the next execution of the loop. The following example prints out the iteration only when i is an odd number. On even iterations, continue skips over the printf statement.

```
i = 0;
while(i < 10)
        {
        i++;
        if (i % 2 == 0)
                continue;
        printf("This is an odd iteration %d\n", i);
        }
```

goto and label Statements

The goto statement is used in conjunction with labels. It allows jumps to be programmed into the code. With a goto statement and a label, the program can be made to jump from one statement to another. The goto encourages a style of programming found in assembly-language applications. It is rarely used in higher-level computer languages.

```
int main (void)
     {
     int i;

     i = 1;

     L1: if(i > 10)
               goto L2;
          printf ("This is %d iteration\n", i);
          i++;
          goto L1;
     L2: ;
     }
```

The preceding program implements a `while` loop using only `goto` and label statements. The syntax for a label statement is the label name, followed by a colon, followed by a statement. The statement can be a null statement. There are two `goto` statements in this program. `goto L1` drives the loop. Execution always returns to the L1 label placed before the `if` condition for the loop. The `goto` L2 statement breaks out of the loop when the 10th iteration has been reached. It does this by jumping over the `goto L1` statement to the L2 label. The L2 label has a null statement, L2: ;.

Chapter Summary: Statements

Statements are placed within the body of a function. Statements organize and control expressions. The most common type of statement is the expression statement. Expression statements are statements that consist of a single expression. Expression statements are generally used for assignment expressions and function calls. However, the expression can be any valid expression. If there is no expression, the statement is a null statement.

Compound, loop, and condition statements control the execution of other statements. They are referred to as control structures. Compound statements group several statements into one statement. Loops repeat statements. Conditions choose which statements are to be executed.

There are two types of loops: `while` and `for`. The `for` loop has the same flexibility as a `while` loop. Both have a test expression. The truth or falsity of a test expression is determined by whether the expression results in a zero or a non-zero value. A zero value is false. A non-zero value is true. The test expression can be any valid expression. However, care must be taken when using assignment expressions as test expressions.

There are two kinds of conditional statements: `if` and `switch`. The `if` statement can be combined with an `else` to form a choice between two statements. `if` statements can be nested within one another using blocks. An `if` statement may also be combined with other `if` statements in an `else-if` combination to form a choice among several statements.

The `switch` statement is more restrictive than the `if` statement. It tests only integer values. It presents a choice among several alternatives. However, depending on the placement of `break` statements within the `switch`, these alternatives may or may not be exclusive.

The jump statements are used to forcibly jump from one statement to another. The `break` and `continue` statements work with loops. The `goto` statement works with label statements to implement assembly-language-like jumps between statements. Table 4-1 reviews the statements discussed in this chapter.

Table 4-1: Statements (Review)

`;`	*expression;*

`{`
`}`
	`{`
	statement;
	`}`

`while`	`while`(*test expression*)
	           `{`
	           statement `;`
	           statement `;`
	           `}`

`do`	`do`
	           statement `;`
	           `while` (*test*)`;`

`for`	`for`(*expression1, expression2, expression3*)
	                statement;
	
	`for`(*initialization; test; increment*)
	                statement;

`if`	`if`(*test expression*) *statement;*

`if-else`	`if`(*test* expression)
	           statement;
	`else`
	           statement;

`switch`	`switch` (*integer expression*)
	           `{`
	           `case` *integer* `:`
	                     statements;
	                     `break;`
	           `case` *integer* `:`
	                     statements;
	                     `break;`
	           `default` `:`
	                     statements;
	                     `break;`
	           `}`

`break`	`break;`
`continue`	`continue`
`goto`	`goto` *label;*

Exercises

1. Calculate and print out a multiplication table from 1 to 10. The output should look something like that shown here. There is no need to use multiple functions. Use only the main function for now.
   (a) First, write the program using only `while` loops.
   (b) Rewrite the program using only `for` loops.
   This is what the output should look like. Be careful of spacing.

		1	2	3	4	5	6	7	8	9	10
1	|	1	2	3	4	5	6	7	8	9	10
2	|	2	4	6	8	10	12	14	16	18	20
3	|	3	6	9	12	15	18	21	24	27	30
4	|	4	8	12	16	20	24	28	32	36	40
5	|	5	10	15	20	25	30	35	40	45	50
6	|	6	12	18	24	30	36	42	48	54	60
7	|	7	14	21	28	35	42	49	56	63	70
8	|	8	16	24	32	40	48	56	64	72	80
9	|	9	18	27	36	45	54	63	72	81	90
10	|	10	20	30	40	50	60	70	80	90	100

2. Write a simple cash register program that adds up prices, calculates a tax, and prints out the total. In a loop, use `scanf` to input a price and then add the price to a total. The tax on everything is 10%.

3. Write a program that takes in a line of input from the user and counts all the vowels in the input (a,e,i,o,u). Use a `switch` statement that will check for both upper- and lowercase instances of a vowel. Use `getchar` to read in characters. Place the `switch` within a loop that stops at a newline, `'\n'`. Then, print out the total number of vowels in the input line.

4. Using a `switch` statement, write a program, similar to the one in Exercise 2, to ring a bell for each tab entered and to check to see if a character is numeric, 0-9. If a character is not numeric, print out the character and an error message.

5. Write a program to select several items to buy. Set up a menu and give a number to each item. Make up your own items. Classify each item as a luxury or a necessity. A luxury item is taxed 20%. A necessity is only taxed 5%. Assign your own prices. Allow the user to choose items. Use a `switch` statement for the items. Keep a subtotal for luxury items. When the user is finished, print out the total price, the total price of the luxury items chosen, and the total tax for these luxury items.

5

Pointers

Indirection and addresses

5. Pointers

Any object defined in a program can be referenced through its address. Your computer's memory is organized into bytes, each with its own address. When you declare a variable, a set of bytes is set aside for its use. This is where a variable's value will be stored. The beginning address of these bytes is often referred to as the address of that variable. Normally you will only need to use a variable's name to reference the value held in this memory. However, it is also possible to use the address of this memory, instead of the variable name, to reference that value. Using the address of a variable to reference its value is a pointer operation, and it is usually carried out by a pointer variable.

With a pointer variable, you can reference any object defined in a program. A pointer is a variable that has as its value the address of an object. The address held by a pointer can be used to reference a particular object. In this sense, a pointer can be said to point to an object.

A pointer is often used to reference a variable. In such a case, a pointer will have as its value the address of another variable. Since the pointer is a variable itself, a pointer can be described as a variable that holds the address of another variable. This chapter will cover pointers and addresses and how they are used to reference variables. The first part of the chapter will focus on how pointers are used. Then a detailed examination of how pointers operate using addresses will follow.

It is easier to describe what a pointer is used for than to explain how a pointer works. The use of a pointer can be conceived of in a very straightforward, task-oriented way. However, whenever you use pointers, errors can arise easily. Often, correction of pointer errors requires an understanding of how a pointer operates. This, in turn, requires a technical understanding of how objects are defined and referenced in memory. An understanding of how objects are arranged in memory helps us to understand how addresses can be used to reference those objects.

There are situations in which it makes sense to think of the address itself as a pointer. This is discussed at the end of the chapter. For the purposes of this chapter, the term pointer will refer to a pointer variable. An address will be referred to simply as an address.

Pointers and Object References

A pointer is used as a referencing mechanism. A pointer provides a way to reference an object using that object's address. There are usually three elements involved in this referencing process: a pointer variable, an address, and another variable (see Figure 5-1). The pointer variable holds the address of the other variable. A special operation, called an indirection operation, will use this address to reference the other variable.

Figure 5-1: Pointer reference and declaration.

A pointer variable is a variable itself. It is declared with a name and a type. Its type consists of two elements: the pointer type specifier-an asterisk-and a data type. The pointer specifier indicates that the variable is a pointer. The data type is the type of object the pointer variable points to, the type of variable it will be used to reference.

The value that a pointer variable holds is an address. An address is different from other kinds of values in that it is used to reference other objects you have declared in your program. Normally, a value is used to reference some real-world value. An integer value is an integer number that can be used in arithmetic calculations. A character value is a character symbol, such as an alphabetic character. An address, however, is the address of a program object. A pointer to an integer holds an address of an integer variable. Figure 5-1 illustrates a pointer declaration and its reference of a variable.

For a pointer to reference another variable, it must first be assigned that variable's address. The address of a variable is obtained with the address operation. The address operator is an ampersand, &. When applied to a variable, this operation will result in the address of that variable. This address can then be assigned to a pointer variable. Once the pointer variable has the address of another variable, it can be said to point to that variable.

An indirection operation on the pointer variable will actually reference the pointed-to variable. The indirection operation makes use of both the address held by the pointer and the pointer's data type. The address is used to locate the variable. The data type is used to determine the variable's type. For example, indirection on a pointer to an integer will reference an integer variable, whereas indirection on a pointer to a `float` will reference a floating-point variable. Figure 5-2 displays an address operation and indirection.

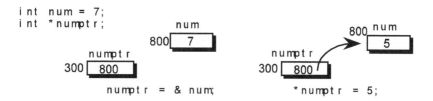

Figure 5-2: Address operation and indirection.

In the **numadd.c** program in LISTING 5-1, all these elements come into play. An address operation is used to obtain an address of a variable that is then assigned to a pointer. An indirection on the pointer then references that variable. The pointer variable `numptr` is declared as a pointer to an integer. `numptr` is then assigned the address of the variable `num`. At this point, `numptr` can be said to point to `num`. An indirection operation on `numptr` references the variable `num`, assigning 5 to `num`. In the `printf` statement, the value of `num` is printed out using both the variable `num` and its reference through an indirection operation on `numptr`. Then the address of `num` and the contents of `numptr` are printed out. They are the same. `numptr` holds the address of `num`.

LISTING 5-1:

numadd.c

```
#include <stdio.h>

int main(void)
        {
        int num;
        int *numptr;

        numptr = &num;
        *numptr = 5;

        printf("Num = %d, Indirection on Numptr = %d \n", num, *numptr);
        printf("Address of Num = %p, Address held in Numptr = %p \n", &num, numptr);
        return 0;
        }
```

Output of LISTING 5-1:

```
        Num = 5, Indirection on Numptr = 5
        Address of Num = 800, Address held in Numptr = 800
```

Pointers, Addresses, and Variables

To understand the relationship between pointers and variables, the implementation of each needs to be closely examined. Pointers are declared differently than other variables. A pointer's value and type are designed to provide information with which to reference other variables. An ordinary variable simply represents data values, such as integers or characters. A pointer can be said to represent the variables themselves.

Type, address, and memory are the three basic elements used to define a variable. A variable is defined and referenced in memory. When a variable is defined, a set of bytes is allocated for its use. The beginning address of those bytes is then associated with the variable's name. Each time the variable's name is used in a statement, the variable's address is used to locate those bytes. These bytes will hold a variable's value. The variable's declared data type is used to interpret that value. An integer variable will hold in its bytes an integer value. Figure 5-3 illustrates a variable's address and memory.

Each time a variable is used, the variable's address is used to locate its memory, and its type is used to interpret that memory. An integer variable will use its address to locate its memory and interpret that memory as an integer value. This location and interpretation process references a variable. Address and type are the two pieces of information that a variable needs to reference its memory.

In the next example, the integer variable `num` is assigned the integer value 7. The integer value held by the variable `num` is located at a specific address in memory. The integer value itself exists only as a series of binary bits. The `int` type in the `num` variable's declaration indicates that this series of bits is to be interpreted as an integer value.

```
        int num;
        num = 7;
```

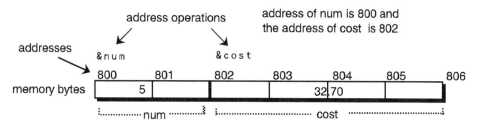

Figure 5-3: Addresses and variables.

A pointer has the same two pieces of information that a variable uses to reference its memory: an address and a type. A pointer variable is declared with a pointer type specifier and a data type. The pointer type is represented by an asterisk, *. The asterisk alone does not declare a pointer variable. The asterisk indicates that the value of this variable is an address. This address will be used to locate a variable. The data type placed before the asterisk in the pointer declaration is the type of the variable pointed to by the pointer. The data type is used to reference the memory at that address as a specific kind of variable. In the next example, the asterisk, *, indicates that numptr is a pointer variable. The data type, int, is the type of variable this pointer can reference, an integer.

```
int *numptr;
```

How, then, does a pointer obtain the address of a variable? First, the address operation has to be applied to the variable. The address operation is literally a unary expression consisting of an address operator and a single operand. The address operator is the ampersand, &, and the operand can be any variable. You simply place the ampersand next to the variable. The result of the address operation is the address of the variable. You can then use an assignment operation to assign this address to a pointer variable.

In the next example, the address of num is obtained by the address operation and then assigned to the pointer numptr. In the **costadd.c** program in LISTING 5-2, the address of the cost variable is assigned to the pointer costptr. The address held by the costptr pointer, as well as the address resulting from an address operation on the cost variable, is printed out. Both addresses are the same.

```
int num;
int *numptr;

numptr = &num;
```

A pointer variable has, as its value, an address, which is simply a number used to reference a location in memory. When an address is used as a pointer value, it is always treated as an address of an object. In C, an address is always used as an address of- an address of a type of object.

An address is similar to an unsigned integer. In C, a pointer can be easily converted to an integer, and vice versa. However, in C, an address is never used as an unsigned integer. It is instead always used as a pointer value: as the contents of a pointer variable, as the result of a pointer expression, or as a constant cast to a pointer value. In this respect, the type of an address is that of a pointer to an object. You can think of an address as not simply an address, but as an address of some type of object.

LISTING 5-2:

costadd.c

```
#include <stdio.h>

int main(void)
        {
        int num = 5;
        float cost = 32.70;
        int *numptr;
        float * costptr;

        numptr = &num;
        costptr = &cost;

        printf("Address of Num = %p \n", &num);
        printf("Address in Numptr = %p \n",  numptr);
        printf("Address of Cost = %p \n",&cost);
        printf("Address in Costptr = %p \n", costptr);
        return 0;
        }
```

Output of LISTING 5-2:

```
        Address of Num = 800,
        Address in Numptr = 800
        Address of Cost = 802,
        Address in Costptr = 802
```

The change of a pointer variable's value changes the address, but it does not change the data type. In the next example, the pointer variable `numptr` can be assigned many different addresses. However, those addresses will always be considered to be addresses of integers. In the same way, `costptr` may have many different addresses, but those addresses will always be addresses of `floats`. In this sense, one can speak of different types of pointer variables. A pointer variable is literally a variable of type pointer to a type of object. The data type restricts that pointer variable to addresses of that type of object. `costptr` can only be assigned addresses of `floats`; `numptr` can only be assigned addresses of integers.

```
        int * numptr;  int   address
        float * costptr;      float address
```

Two pointer variables can be compared only if their types match. However, as with most operations, you can use a cast expression to generate the same value with a different type. You can apply a cast operation to a pointer that will result in an address of a different type of object from that of the pointer. In the next example, the address held by `costptr` is changed in a cast operation from an address of a `float` to an address of an `int`. The address of an `int` held by `numptr` can now be compared to the address of an `int` generated by the `(int*)` cast operation on `costptr`. `costptr` is still a pointer to a `float`, but the cast operation has taken its value generated a different type of pointer.

```
int *numptr, *iptr;
float *costptr;

if (numptr == iptr)
        printf ("they are equal\n");

if (numptr ==  (int *) costptr)
        printf ("they are equal\n");
```

Printing out the contents of a pointer variable prints out the address of the variable being referenced by this pointer. The next examples show the different ways you can output addresses. For the sake of these examples, the address held by `numptr` is 534. If the contents of `numptr` are printed out, the output consists of the number 534. This is the address, 534. The output function `printf`, with its conversion capabilities, is usually used to print out addresses. In C, the letter 'p' is a special conversion specifier for pointer values, `%p`. L, l:%lu pointer conversion modifier;

```
printf("Value in numptr is address %p.",numptr);

        Value in numptr is address 534.
```

Indirection Operation

A pointer has the address and data type with which to locate and interpret memory. The actual location and interpretation remain dormant until the address and data type are operated on explicitly. By itself, a pointer is not capable of referencing that memory. You need to use a special operation that can take the information in a pointer and perform the same location and interpretation tasks as a variable. This special operation is called indirection, and it references memory as a variable would. The indirection operation uses the address and it's data type to locate and interpret memory.

The indirection operator is an asterisk. The indirection operation uses the address in a pointer to locate bytes in memory. However, the location part of indirection is only half the operation. The indirection operation then makes explicit use of the pointer's data type to interpret the located memory as a certain type of object. The location and interpretation, taken together, can be thought of as referencing an object. An indirection operation on a pointer to an integer can be thought of as referencing an integer variable. A direct reference using a variable name involves the same kind of location and interpretation of memory as that performed by the indirection operation.

In the next example, there is an indirection operation on the pointer variable `numptr`. `numptr` is first assigned the address of `num`. For the sake of this example, the address of `num` is 534. `numptr` holds the address 534 and has a data type of integer. The indirection operation locates that address and interprets the memory at that address as an integer. The indirection operation can be thought of as referencing the integer variable whose memory is located at address 534. Figure 5-4 illustrates the indirection operation on a pointer variable.

```
int num = 7;
int *numptr = &num;
        printf("%d", *numptr);
```

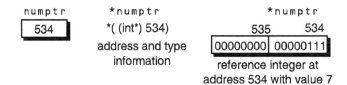

Figure 5-4: Indirection on a pointer to a variable.

Indirection on a pointer to a variable references a variable. This means that you can use indirection not only to interpret memory as some kind of value but also to assign a value to that memory. Just as you can change the contents of a variable, you can also change the contents of memory referenced by a pointer.

In the next example, the indirection operator works on the address in the pointer variable numptr. The indirection operation takes the address in numptr (534) and references that memory as an integer variable. The indirection is being used in an assignment expression, assigning the value 3 to the memory at address 534, as Figure 5-5 shows. The indirection operation can be seen as just another variable reference, subject to the same rules as any other variable reference. A variable reference used as the left-hand operand in an assignment operation will assign the right-hand value to that variable. In this case, the variable reference is carried out by an indirection on a pointer, not a variable name.

```
int num;
int *numptr = &num;

*numptr = 3;
```

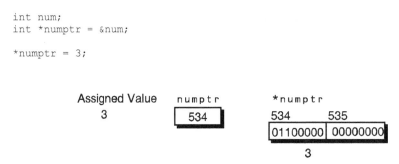

Figure 5-5: Assignment and indirection on a pointer.

In the next example, the indirection operation *numptr is operating just like the variable name num. The assignment expression *numptr=3 assigns the value 3 to the memory at 534, just as the assignment expression num=3 assigns the value 3 to the variable num. res=*numptr references the value of the memory at 534 and assigns that value to the variable res. res=num references the value of the variable num and assigns it to the variable res.

```
int num, res;
int *numptr = &num;

num = 3;
*numptr = 3;
res = num;
res = *numptr;
```

You can use the indirection operation in any kind of expression in which a variable can be used. Within an expression, both variable names and indirection operations can reference data. In the **numind.c** program in LISTING 5-3, indirection operations are used in several different kinds of expressions. An indirection on `numptr` is used in an arithmetic addition operation. Another indirection is used in a relational expression, `*numptr<5`. Still another indirection is used in a multiplication operation. All of these indirections use the same pointer variable, `numptr`. The address in `numptr` has remained the same throughout the program. This means that all indirections reference the same variable. As long as the address in the pointer variable remains the same, it is as if the same variable is being referenced.

LISTING 5-3:

numind.c

```
#include <stdio.h>

void  main(void)
      {
      int num, res;
      int *numptr;

      numptr = &num;
      *numptr = 3;

      res = *numptr  + num;
      if(*numptr < 5)
            res = num * *numptr;

      printf("num= %d,numptr=%p \n",num,numptr);
      printf("res = %d,\n", res);
      }
```

Output of LISTING 5-3:

```
      num = 3, numptr = 800
      res = 9,
```

In the multiplication operation, there are two uses of the asterisk., The asterisk, when laced next to the pointer variable, is an indirection operation. Placed between two integers, the asterisk is a multiplication operation. The space between the two asterisks is crucial. Without it, the compiler will interpret the two asterisks as two indirection operations.

There are, then, two kinds of variable references: the variable name and the indirection operation. In the case of pointer variables, the two must not be confused. When used with the indirection operator, the pointer variable is the operand in an indirection operation. Without the indirection operator, the pointer variable is like any other variable name. A pointer variable name by itself simply references a pointer variable, the contents of which are an address, whereas when the pointer variable name is used in an indirection operation, the data object at that address is referenced.

In the first `printf` in the next example, the value of the memory referenced by the indirection operation on `numptr` is printed out. The value of the memory at 534 is 3. In the second `printf`, only the pointer variable name, `numptr`, is used. The pointer variable `numptr` is referenced and its value printed out: the address 534.

```
printf("%d", *numptr);
printf("%u", numptr);
```

Output of printf statements:

```
3
534
```

A pointer variable is a variable, and as such you can assign to it different addresses. You can first assign one address to a pointer, and then use another assignment to replace it with another address. In this way, you can use the same pointer variable to reference different variables. Indirection operates on the address held by a pointer. If the pointer variable is assigned a new address, the next indirection will reference the variable at that new address. The referencing process relies on the address. When indirection operations work on different addresses, they are, in effect, referencing different variables.

In the **countadd.c** program in LISTING 5-4, numptr is first assigned the address of num. The first indirection references the same memory as that used by num. The value 5 is assigned. numptr is then assigned a new address, the address of count. The next indirection on numptr now references the same memory as that used by the variable count. The value 10 is assigned. An indirection on numptr will now reference the value 10.

LISTING 5-4:

countadd.c

```
#include <stdio.h>

void  main(void)
      {
      int num, count;
      int *numptr;

      numptr = &num;
      *numptr = 5;
      printf("num = %d,numptr = %p \n", num, numptr);
      numptr = &count;
      *numptr = 10;
      printf("count = %d,numptr = %p \n",count,numptr);
      printf("num = %d, count = %d, *numptr = %d \n",

                                          num, count, *numptr);

      }
```

Output of LISTING 5-4:

```
num = 5, numptr = 800
count = 10, numptr = 600
num = 5, count = 10, *numptr = 10
```

Addresses and Memory Maps

The contents of any variable are changed by assigning a new value to that variable. The contents of an integer variable are changed when an integer value is assigned to it. In the same way, the contents of a pointer variable are changed when an address is assigned to it. There are many places from which to obtain addresses. The most common source of an address is another variable. To understand how this works, you will need a rough outline of how memory is organized and used by a program.

Computer memory is a collection of bytes. Each byte has its own address. A pointer can reference any one of these addresses. When a program is loaded into memory from a file, the program is divided into segments. There are four major segments. The first segment is the set of program instructions. This is the program itself. It is usually protected by your operating system. The memory there cannot be referenced or changed. The second segment consists of memory reserved for global and static variables. These are variables that are defined once and remain in existence for the entire run of the program. The third segment is the free and unused portion of memory. Sometimes this is referred to as the heap or allocated memory. This is memory that can be allocated and used during the run of the program. The fourth and last segment is the stack. This is a dynamic part of memory where function variables are defined, and function call information is placed. This memory is constantly being used, freed up, and used again in different ways. Figure 5-6 illustrates these four segments.

Addresses can be obtained for all of these segments in many different ways. An address operation can obtain the address of a variable, whether it is global or function-based, referencing memory either in the stack or the data segments. An allocation function such as `malloc` can allocate part of the unused free memory in the third segment. The function will then return the address of that allocated memory. A function name represents the address of program instructions that make up the function, referencing memory in the program segment. You can assign this address of a function to a pointer to a function, as described in Chapter 6. Finally, a pointer cast operation can convert an integer to an address, referencing memory in any of the segments. In this way, an integer can be used to represent a global address, accessing any part of a computer's memory.

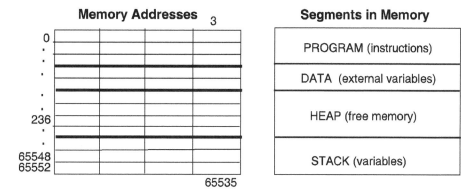

Figure 5-6: Memory map of program organization.

Addresses and Variables: The Address Operation &

When a variable is defined, it is given its own memory. The address of this memory can then be assigned to a pointer. When a pointer is assigned the address of a variable, it will be able to access memory that has been reserved for use by that variable. How, then, can a pointer obtain the address of memory used for a particular variable. By using the address operation.

The address operation is an expression whose result is the address of a variable. The address operator is a unary operator represented by the ampersand, &. The address operator can take a variable name as its operand. In this case, the address operation will result in the address of the memory used for that variable.

```
int num = 6;
```

Figure 5-7: Address operation.

In Figure 5-7, the address operation, &num, results in the address of the variable's memory. However, an address is always an address of a type of object. In this case, the type associated with the address is the same as the type of the variable. In Figure 5-8, the address operation, &num, returns an address, 534, which is the address of an integer. This address can then be assigned to a pointer variable. The pointer variable, in this example, must be a pointer to an integer. The type of the variable and the data type of the pointer must be the same. In Figure 5-8, numptr is a pointer to an integer and num is an integer.

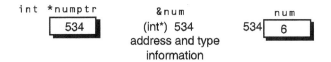

Figure 5-8: Address operation and pointer variable.

In the next example, the address operation on the variable num, &num, results in an address that is the address of the memory used by the variable num (534). This address, in turn, becomes the assigned value in an assignment operation. The address resulting from the address operation on num is assigned to the pointer variable numptr. As a result, numptr obtains the address of the variable num, 534. (Figure 5-10 later shows how this process is arranged in memory.) The pointer and the integer variables are both variables located at addresses in memory. The pointer variable is assigned the address of the integer variable. The indirection operation references the memory at that address.

```
int num;
int *numptr;

numptr = &num;
```

An indirection operation can reference the same memory used by a variable. In Figure 5-9, the pointer numptr holds the address of the variable num. An indirection operation on numptr will reference the same memory that num uses. There are now two ways to reference the memory at address 534: first, with the variable name num; and second, with an indirection on the address in numptr.

Figure 5-9: Indirection and assignments.

In the **numref.c** program in LISTING 5-5, numptr is assigned the address of num. Because of this, the variable name num and the indirection on numptr can be used interchangeably. Both reference the same memory. The printf statement prints out the same value for both num and *numptr because both access exactly the same memory. That memory was originally set to 2 by the second assignment expression using the variable name num. Then it was set to 5 by the third assignment expression using an indirection on the pointer, *numptr. The operands in the multiplication operation are actually the same. The first operand uses the variable name to reference the memory of num, and the second operand uses an indirection operation to reference the memory of num, *numptr. The multiplication operation is then 5 * 5, resulting in 25.

LISTING 5-5:

numref.c
```c
#include <stdio.h>

void  main(void)
       {
       int num, sqnum;
       int *numptr;

       numptr = &num;

       num = 2;
       *numptr = 5;
       sqnum = num * *numptr;

       printf("num = %d,*numptr = %d \n", num, *numptr);
       printf("Square of num = %d \n", sqnum);
       }
```

Output of LISTING 5-5:

```
num = 5, *numptr = 5
Square of num = 25
```

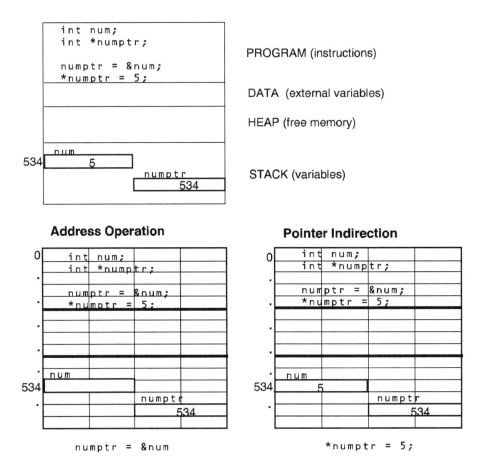

Figure 5-10: Address and indirection operations in memory.

It is just as easy to have more than one pointer variable set to the same variable's address. In the **varptrs.c** program in LISTING 5-6, both numptr and iptr are assigned the address of num. An indirection on either numptr or iptr will access the same memory as that used by num. First, both numptr and iptr are set to the address of num. An indirection on numptr changes the memory used by num to 5. The next indirection on iptr changes num's memory again, this time to 10. The multiplication operation works through two different pointers, numptr and iptr, but references the same memory, that of num. Then values of num, the indirection on numptr, and the indirection on iptr are printed out. Then the address of num and the addresses in the pointer variables numptr and iptr are printed out. These addresses are all the same. The value of sqnum will be the result of the multiplication operation 10 * 10 - 100.

LISTING 5-6:

varptrs.c

```
#include <stdio.h>

void  main(void)
      {
      int num, sqnum;
      int *numptr;
      int * iptr;

      numptr = &num;
      iptr = &num;

      *numptr = 5;
      *iptr = 10;
      sqnum = *iptr * *numptr;

      printf("num = %d,*numptr = %d,*iptr = %d \n",
                                          num, *numptr, *iptr);
      printf("&num = %p,numptr = %p,iptr = %p\n",
                                          &num, numptr, iptr);
      printf("Square of num = %d \n", sqnum);
      }
```

Output of LISTING 5-6:

```
num = 10, *numptr = 10, *iptr = 10
&num = 800, numptr = 800, iptr = 800
Square of num = 100
```

An error will occur if a programmer were to forget to type in the address operator, &, when the address of a variable is called for. This is a simple mistake that is easy to make. In the next example, the programmer has left out the & before the variable num in the assignment operation. The value of the variable num is assigned to numptr, not the address of num. numptr ends up with the address 6, instead of the address 534, the address of num. Some compilers may balk at this assignment. Others may simply convert the integer to a pointer and make the assignment, issuing only a warning. Figure 5-11 show the result of a pointer being assigned the value of a variable instead of its address.

```
int num;
float *numptr;

num = 3;
numptr = num; /* should be:  numptr = &num */
```

```
       int *numptr            num
          ┌──────┐        ┌──────┐
          │  6   │      534 │  6   │
          └──────┘        └──────┘
```

Figure 5-11: Pointer with value of variable instead of address.

Addresses and Allocated Memory: `malloc`

A program can call a function to cut out and set aside parts of the unused free memory in the heap segment for use by pointers. You can then use a pointer to access this memory. In this way, parts of this unused memory can be allocated and used as if they were variables.

For this free memory to be usable, it must first be allocated. The allocation function `malloc` allocates parts of this unused memory. `malloc` takes an argument that is the number of bytes it is to allocate. The number of bytes depends on the type of variable those bytes are to be used for. Types are of different sizes and vary from system to system. A common configuration is int = 2 bytes, float = 4 bytes, char = 1 byte. The programmer must make sure that there are enough bytes allocated for the type of object needed. In the next example, `malloc` has set aside 2 bytes (the usual size for an integer) for the program's use.

```
malloc(2);
```

However, on some systems, an integer may be 4 bytes. How can you make sure what the actual size of a variable is? The sizeof operator does this automatically for you. The sizeof operator can be applied either to the names of objects or to types. When it is applied to types, the type must be enclosed in parentheses. The operation `sizeof(int)` gives the correct size of an integer in bytes for your system.

In Figure 5-12, the result of the sizeof operation is used as the argument for `malloc`. The sizeof operation will be performed first, resulting in the number of bytes for an integer. Assuming that the size of an integer is 2 bytes, `malloc` has then set aside 2 bytes for the program's use.

```
malloc(sizeof(int));
```

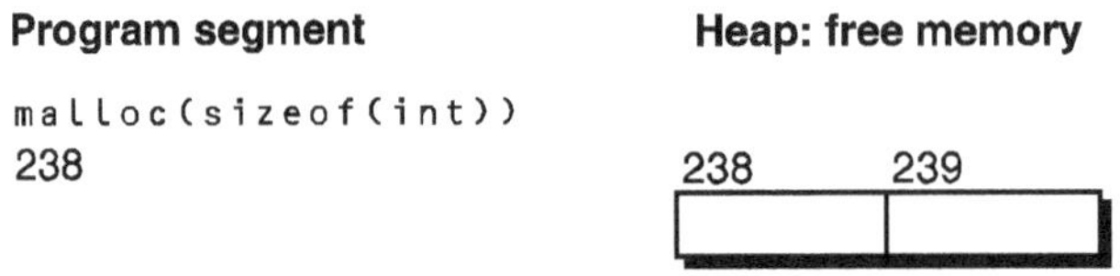

Program segment

```
malloc(sizeof(int))
238
```

Heap: free memory

238   239

Figure 5-12: malloc function.

`malloc` returns to the program an address of the first byte of all the bytes set aside. An address is always an address of a type of object. However, `malloc` does not know for what type of object the memory is allocated. It only receives an integer value that is the number of bytes to be allocated. The address it returns is a generic address whose type is specified by a generic pointer type. In C, a generic pointer is a pointer to void. The address returned from `malloc` is an address of an unknown type of object, a void object. An address whose type is a pointer to void can be assigned to any pointer variable of any type, with no conversions or casts required.

The address that `malloc` returns can then be assigned to a pointer variable. In Figure 5-13, the address returned by `malloc` is assigned to `numptr`. For the sake of this example, the address consists of the address location 238, and it is cast to the address of an integer. To hold this address, a pointer variable with a pointer type of int is needed.

```
int *numptr;

numptr = malloc(sizeof(int));
```

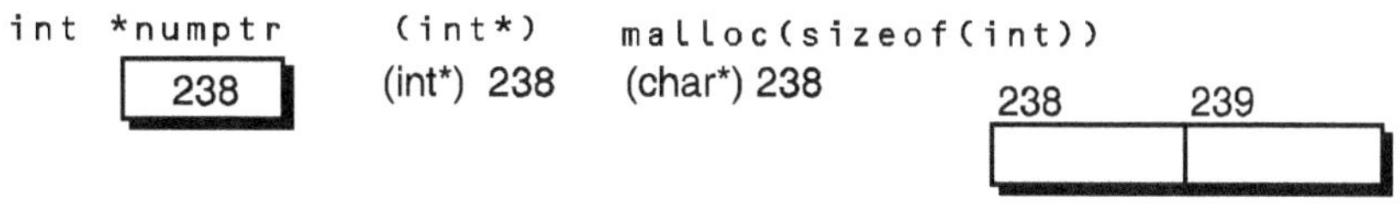

Figure 5-13: malloc and pointer variable.

`numptr` is a pointer variable. As a variable, it resides in the stack segment. However, its contents consist of the address 238. The address 238 is in the heap segment. A connection has been made between a pointer variable in the stack segment and memory in heap segment. The pointer holds the address of the allocated memory. It is through the pointer variable that your program can use that allocated memory. In the **allocptr.c** program in LISTING 5-7, `numptr` obtains its address from `malloc`. `costptr` obtains its address from an address operation on cost. Their addresses, being from different segments, will be different. Figure 5-14 illustrates how memory is allocated by `malloc` and its address assigned to `numptr`.

LISTING 5-7:

allocptr.c

```
#include <stdio.h>
#include <stdlib.h>

void  main(void)
      {
      float cost = 7.25;
      float *costptr;
      int *numptr;

      numptr = (int *) malloc(sizeof(int));
      *numptr = 5;
      costptr = &cost;

      printf("*numptr = %d, numptr=%p\n",*numptr,numptr);
      printf("cost = %f,costptr = %p \n", cost, costptr);
      free(numptr);
      }
```

Output of LISTING 5-7:

```
*numptr = 5, numptr = 65000
cost = 7.25, costptr = 700
```

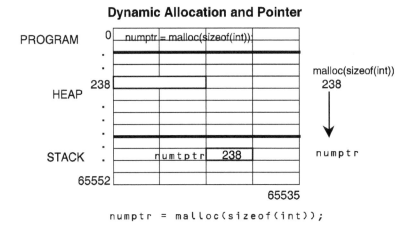

Figure 5-14: Dynamic allocation of memory and assignment of address to a declared variable.

An indirection operation on `numptr` can then reference the memory at 238 as an integer variable. In Figure 5-15, the memory at 238 was referenced as an integer variable and assigned the value 3.

```
*numptr = 3;
```

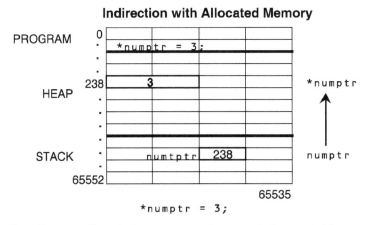

Figure 5-15: Indirection on allocated memory using a pointer variable.

The memory that has been obtained from the heap has not been designated for any other use, as was the memory used for variables. In a sense, what has happened here is a kind of simulation of a variable declaration. A variable declaration designates memory and then uses type and address information to reference that memory. The same thing happens in this situation, using only a pointer. `malloc` designates the memory, and the pointer holds the address and type information with which to reference that memory. An indirection on that pointer will reference that memory as an object. In the program in LISTING 5-7, an indirection on `numptr` references an integer object, even though no integer object has been declared. The memory at the address held by `numptr` is treated as the memory of an integer object.

The memory that `malloc` allocated is reserved and cannot be reallocated until it is freed. The function free will free allocated memory. In LISTING 5-7, the function free is called with the pointer `numptr` to free the memory at the address held by `numptr`. That memory could then be reallocated in a subsequent call to `malloc`.

The function declarations for `malloc` and free are held in a header file called **stdlib.h**. This file needs to be included in any program that uses `malloc` and free. To do this, you have to place a preprocessor include command for **stdlib.h** at the head of your program, just as you did for the **stdio.h** file: #include <stdlib.h>.

Addresses and Global Memory: Integer Conversions

Addresses are equivalent to unsigned integer values. For example, in a computer with 64,000 bytes of memory, each byte will be referenced by its own address. The 1000th byte will be referenced by the number 1000. However, an address in C is never represented as simply an address. An address can only be represented as an address of a type of object. In other words, an address can only be represented as a pointer. In this sense, an address cannot be written as an integer. It is possible, however, to take an integer and convert it to a pointer. In this case, the integer becomes an address of a type of object. This conversion is effected with a cast.

The type of such a cast operation is a pointer to an object. The cast for a pointer to an integer is `(int*)`. The type in this cast is literally the type used in the declaration of a pointer to an integer, the keyword `int` and the asterisk symbol: `int*`.

In the next example, the address resulting from the cast of the integer is assigned to a pointer variable. The pointer variable then uses the address to reference the memory at address 143. An attempt to assign the integer 143 directly to a pointer variable without using a cast may or may not succeed. Some compilers may assume an implied conversion and proceed with the assignment, giving only a warning. However, an attempt to use the integer 143 directly in an indirection operation, without first casting it as a pointer, is invalid.

```
void  main(void)
            {
            int *ptr;

            ptr = (int *) 143;
            *ptr = 5;
            }
```

In next example, a preprocessor define directive is used to define a symbolic constant for the pointer conversion. This makes for a clearer style. The preprocessor will replace the symbolic constant `IPTR` with the replacement string `(int*) 143` before the program is compiled. Symbolic constants provide a way to represent global addresses in your program.

```
#define IPTR  (int*) 143

int main(void)
          {
          int *ptr;

          ptr = IPTR;
          *ptr = 5;
          }
```

There is no restriction on the indirection operation in regard to memory. It may use the same memory a variable uses. It may use memory allocated by special allocation functions. It may even use memory that has not been allocated at all. In this respect, an indirection operation can use an address to access memory located anywhere. It can be used to access memory that has been reserved for other variables, the program itself, or even, in some cases, the operating system.

This pointer conversion of an integer constant is as close as C comes to an explicit pointer constant. Integer values have corresponding integer constants. Pointer values do not. Though technically, an address is equivalent to an integer, an address is always an address of a type of object, never just a bare address. To use an integer as an address, you first need to convert it to a pointer.

Addresses as Pointer Values: Pointer Expressions

You will find that the term "pointer" is used in several different ways. A pointer is defined as a variable that holds the address of another variable. At the same time, the term pointer is also used to refer to the address itself. A closer look at the pointer type may be helpful in clearing up this confusion. A pointer type consists of a data type and the pointer type specifier, the asterisk. The pointer type of an integer pointer is int*. The asterisk is the actual pointer specifier. The data type is the type of object the pointer points to. A pointer type always consists of both the pointer specifier (the asterisk) and the data type (the type of object it points to). A pointer is always a pointer to a type of object.

A pointer type is used to declare pointer variables. As such, pointer variables are referred to as pointers. However, there are expressions that result in addresses. The type of such an address is that of a pointer type. An address is not an integer, nor is there any special address type. Since this address's type is a pointer type, an address can also be referred to as a pointer value. It is an address of a type of object. This pointer value has not only address information but also type information. This means that the address resulting from a pointer expression has the information with which an object can be referenced. Such an address can be used to locate memory, and the address's pointer data type can be used to interpret that memory. An address with a pointer type, a pointer value, bears both address and type information. The indirection operation can be performed directly on it. The indirection operation is not restricted to pointer variables. It operates on any pointer value, whether that address is held in a pointer variable or is the result of a pointer expression.

The notion of a pointer expression is new. A pointer expression is an expression that results in an address. The address operation is a pointer expression whose result is a pointer value: an address of a variable. The malloc function call is a pointer expression that results in a pointer value: an address of allocated memory. A cast operation on an integer is a pointer expression whose result is a pointer value: an address designated by the integer value and cast to a pointer type. All of these addresses are pointer values that have pointer types through which they can reference specific types of objects.

The indirection operation can work directly on these addresses. In the next example, there are three different indirections directly on addresses. In the first case, the address operation on num results in the address of num. An indirection on that address references an integer at num's memory. The value 5 is assigned to it.

In the second case, the function call to `malloc` results in an address, which is then cast to an integer address. An indirection on this address references the memory at that address as an integer. The value 5 is also assigned to it.

In the third example, a cast operation on the integer 143 results in an address of a `float`. The indirection operation references the memory at address 143 as a `float` variable. The value 7.25 is assigned to it.

```
*(&num) = 5;
*( (int*) malloc(sizeof(int)) ) = 5;
*((float*)143 ) = 7.25;
```

This cast operation can also be written using a define command like that in the previous example.

```
#define FPTR  (float *) 143

    *(FPTR) = 5;
```

There are other kinds of pointer expressions, most notably those used to manage arrays. The basic concept, however, is the same. The pointer expression results in an address that can then be used in an indirection operation to reference an object.

Chapter Summary: Pointers

Pointer variables hold the addresses of objects. These addresses can be used to reference an object. A pointer variable is declared with a data type and a pointer type specifier, the asterisk. Pointers are declared to reference one data type. One can speak of different types of pointers. A pointer to an integer will reference only integers. A pointer to a `float` can only reference `float`s.

Table 5-1: Pointers and Addresses

Pointer Declaration	type * pointer name ;
	`int *numptr;`
	`float *costptr;`

Address Operation	&variable
	`numptr = &num;`
	`*(&num) = 5;`

Allocated Memory	(type *) malloc(sizeof(type)) `numptr = (int*) malloc (sizeof(int));`

Integer Conversion	(type *) integer
	`numptr = (float *) 143;`
	`*((float*) 143) = 7.25;`

An address is always an address of a type of object. It holds not only location information, but also type information. The address of a variable is obtained with the address operation. This address can then be assigned to a pointer variable. An indirection operation can then use this address to reference the variable. An indirection operation on a pointer that holds the address of a variable is just as valid a reference to that variable as the variable's own name. Such an indirection operation can be used anywhere a variable's name can be used, even in an assignment operation.

Addresses can be obtained in several different ways. An address can be obtained from a variable using the address operation. An address can also be obtained from free memory using the `malloc` function. An address can be obtained by converting an integer to an address with a cast operation.

An address is an address of a type of object, not simply a numeric location. An address holds both type and location information. For this reason, the indirection operation works on any address, whether it is held in a pointer variable or is the result of some operation that results in an address. In this sense, an address can be thought of as a pointer itself.

Exercises

1. Modify the following program by adding more variables and pointers to variables. Assign the address of each variable to a pointer. Then use indirection on the pointer in assignment statements. Print out both pointer indirections and addresses in pointers. Print out variables and addresses of variables.

```c
#include <stdio.h>
void  main(void)
     {
     int num;
     int *numptr;

     numptr = &num;
     *numptr = (3 * 5) / 2;

     printf("Indirection = %d, Address = %p\n ",
                        *numptr, numptr);
     printf("Num= %d, Num Address= %p\n ",num,&num);
     }
```

2. Modify the following program by adding pointers of different types. Assign values and print out their addresses. Do not forget to use indirection when you have to.

```c
#include <stdio.h>
#include <stdlib.h>

int main(void)
     {
     int *numptr;

     numptr = malloc(sizeof(int));

     *numptr =  (3 * 5) / 2;
     printf("Numptr Indirection = %d \n", *numptr);
     printf("Num Address = %p\n ", numptr);
     return 0;
     }
```

6

Functions

Definitions and Arguments

6. Functions and Parameters

A program is organized into different tasks. There are two common ways of organizing these tasks: procedures and functions. You use procedures to modularize your program source code. Statements that work together on the same task are placed in their own procedure. You use functions to define new operations. These operations are similar to expressions, performing a calculation and returning a result. In most programming languages, the main difference between a procedure and a function is that a function returns a result, whereas a procedure does not.

   Functions perform a dual role in C. A function can be thought of as a procedure, organizing statements in a program, and a function can be thought of as an operation that defines a new task, returning a result. Many times, the two are the same. In many computer languages, procedures and functions are two different constructs. However, in C, there are no procedures. There are only functions. Functions can be used as if they were procedures, but their underlying structure is that of a function.

   A C program is organized into a set of functions. Each function is defined independently from the others. A program progresses from one function to another through function calls. When called, a function can receive values from other functions through its parameter variables. A function can also return a value to the function that called it.

   In C there is a clear distinction between a function definition and a function declaration. A function definition is the actual writing out of the function with the parameters and statements that make it up. A function declaration specifies only the function name and the data types for its parameters and return value. Function declarations are used to inform calling functions of the type of values a called function can have passed to its parameters and the type of value it will return.

   This chapter will examine function definitions, function calls, return values, and parameters, as well as the role function declarations play in each.

Function Calls

A function consists of a header and a body. The header contains the function name, its return type, and parameter types. If there is no return type or parameter type, the keyword void is used in their place. The body of a function is a block, which usually contains variable declarations and statements. A block begins with an open brace and ends with a close brace. Figure 6-1 contains a sample of a function without the return type and parameters.

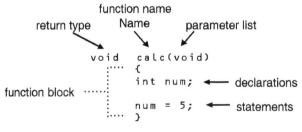

Figure 6-1: Function definition.

The statements in a function are executed when the function is called. A function is called from within another function. A program begins with the function named with the keyword `main`. Beginning with function calls in `main`, control will be transferred from one function to another. A function call is designated by the function name with the function call operator, `()`. Arguments are placed within the operator parenthesis separated by commas. The following example is a function call for the function `printname` with no arguments.

```
printname();
```
\

Once control has been transferred to a given function, statements are executed sequentially. However, if a statement executed is a function itself, control is immediately transferred to that called function. A program progresses by transferring control from one function to another function through function calls.

After all the statements in the function have been executed, control is pulled back automatically to the function from which it was called. Execution of statements in the calling function continues sequentially following the point of the function call.

In the **pname.c** program in LISTING 6-1, the `printname` function call in `main` transfers control to the `printname` function. All statements are executed in printname. Control then returns to `main`. The next statement is then executed in `main`, `printing` out the contents of the variable `i`.

LISTING 6-1:

pname.c

```
#include <stdio.h>

 void   printname(void);

 int main(void)
                {
                int i;

                i = 3;
                printname();
                printf("%d\n", i);
                return 0;
                }

 void printname(void)
                {
                printf("The author's name is Dickens\n");
                }
```

Output for LISTING 6-1:

```
        The author's name is Dickens
        3
```

Function Definitions and Declarations

To use a function, you need first to define it and then declare it. A function definition is not the same as its declaration. A function definition names the function and specifies its variables and statements. When the programmer writes the code for a function, the programmer is defining the function. A function declaration only consists of name and type information. It provides other functions with information about the function's name and the type of values it receives and returns. A function declaration is used to ensure proper communication between functions.

The terms declaration and definition can be confusing. A declaration provides information about an object. A definition actually creates the object. Take, for example, the declaration of a variable. The declaration of a variable requires two elements: a type and a name. The name identifies the variable, and the type determines how the variable is interpreted. However, there is a further process, called a definition, in which actual memory is allocated for the variable. The declaration has only provided information about the variable, whereas the definition has actually established it. In the case of variable declarations, the definition is automatic. A variable declaration will both declare and define a variable (an `extern` declaration is an exception to this rule, as described in Chapter 8). However, in the case of functions, a declaration can be made without a definition. C will include parameter types in a function declaration.

Function Definitions

Each function is defined with a header and a body. The header consists of the function name, return type, and parameter list. These elements are positioned left to right, starting with the return type, the name of the function, and, in parentheses, the list of parameter variable declarations. Unlike functions in other programming languages such as Pascal, in a C function, there is no semicolon after the closing parenthesis at the end of the parameter list. Figure 6-2 shows the syntax of a function header.

return type
function name
(parameter variable declarations)
float calc (int num, float cost)

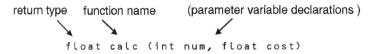

Figure 6-2: Function header.

The body of a function is a block. A block begins with an open brace and ends with a close brace. Variable declarations are placed at the beginning of the block. The declarations are then followed by program statements. Figure 6-3 illustrates the different components of a function block.

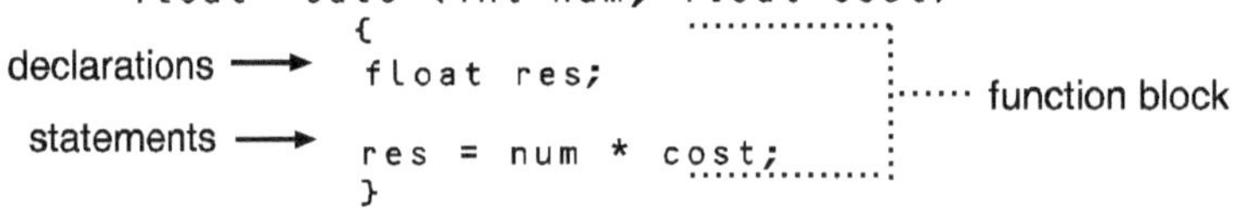

float calc (int num, float cost)
{
declarations
float res;
statements
res = num * cost;
}
function block

Figure 6-3: Function block.

If a function does not have a return value or parameters, the keyword void is used in their place. The `printname` function shown here uses the keyword void to indicate that it has no return type or parameters.

```
void printname(void)
        {
        printf("The author's name is Dickens");
        }
```

You cannot define a function within the block of another function. Each function is its own separate entity. In the **funcname.c** program in LISTING 6-2, the `printname` function is not defined within the braces of the `main` function. It is defined outside of the `main` function. This is different from programming languages such as Pascal or PL/1, but very typical of function-applicative languages such as LISP. In C, functions should be thought of as independent entities. One function cannot exist inside of another.

LISTING 6-2:

funcname.c

```
#include <stdio.h>
 void  printname(void);

int main(void)
        {
        int i;  /*declarations*/

        i = 3;
        printname();   /*function call */
        return 0;
        }
void printname(void)
        {
                printf("The author's name is Dickens");
        }
```

Function Declarations

A declaration requires both name and type information. In the case of a function declaration, the name information is the function name. This name is globally known and therefore must be unique. In a program, you cannot have two functions with the same name.

The type information in a function declaration refers to the types of values received and returned by the function. These types taken together will form the function's type. A function declaration consists of the type of value returned by the function, the name of the function, and the types of values received by the function. The type of value returned is the return type, and the types of values received are the types of the function parameters. An example of a function declaration follows. The function name is `calc`, the return type is `float`, and the parameter types are `int` and `float`.

```
float calc (int , float );
```

A function definition is like a function declaration attached to a block. The block constitutes the body of the function, and the declaration is the header. In the function definition, the parameter list is not simply a set of types; it is a set of actual variable declarations. These are the function's parameter variables.

```
float calc (int num, float cost)
        {
        /* block */
        }
```

Whereas the function definition creates the actual function, the function declaration is used to provide information about a function's return type and parameter types to other functions. A function declaration becomes necessary whenever you call a function. The declaration provides the calling function with type information about the called function.

Often a function will have no return value or parameter variables. In this case, the function returns no value and accepts no arguments. The function definition and the function declaration use the keyword void to indicate that there is no return value or that there are no parameters. Following are both the function declaration and definition for a function called greeting. It has neither a return value nor parameters.

```
void greeting (void);

void greeting (void)
        {
        printf (" Hello\n");
        }
```

In the calc.**c** program in LISTING 6-3 is an example of C function definitions. The function declaration for the calc function is placed at the beginning of the file. Notice how it includes the parameter types.

LISTING 6-3: C Parameters

calc.c
```
#include <stdio.h>

    float calc(int, float);        /* Function declaration*/

    int main(void )
                {
                float rate, res;

                rate = 2.0;
                calc ( 5, rate);        /* Function call*/
                return 0;
                }

    float calc(int num, float calc_rate)
                {
                float cost;

                cost = calc_rate * num;
                }
```

Function Return Values

Functions can pass information back and forth to each other. Information can be passed from a calling function to a called function through arguments. Information can be returned to the calling function through a return value. Let us look first at the return value and then at the parameters.

A function call is an expression itself. The parentheses in a function call form an operator: the function call operator, (). The function call operator operates on the function name and any values listed within the parentheses. Any such listed values are referred to as arguments. The return value of the function is the result of the function call operation. The function call is, in this sense, an expression whose result is the return value of the function.

Within the function, the return value is determined by the `return` statement. The `return` statement includes an expression whose value will be passed back to the calling function.

Depending upon the situation, C may or may not check the types of communicated values. It is the programmer's responsibility to make certain that the types of all values passed back and forth are consistent.

The Return Statement and Function Return Value

The `return` statement consists of the keyword `return`, an expression, and a semicolon. The expression is required unless the return type is void. The `return` statement has two roles: it will end the processing of a function, returning to the calling function, and it will also specify the function's return value. There is a special relationship between the `return` statement's expression and the function's return type. Both are used to determine the return value of the function. Following is the syntax for the `return` statement.

```
return expression ;
```

A function does not necessarily have to finish all its executable statements in order to return to the calling function. The function will forcibly return if a `return` statement is executed. Usually, but not necessarily, the `return` statement is also the last statement in the function. It does exactly what it says. It returns to the calling function. The program **calcret.c** in LISTING 6-4 has a simple `return` statement.

LISTING 6-4:

calcret.c
```c
#include <stdio.h>
void calc(void);
int main(void)
        {
        calc();
        return 0;
        }

void calc(void)
        {
        printf ("price is 3.00");
        return;
        }
```

The `return` statement can also return a value. This value is obtained from an expression following the keyword `return`. Any valid expression is permitted. This return expression's result is used to determine the function's return value. The return value is the value returned by the function's function call. Functions that are declared as having a return type will require a `return` statement with an expression. A simple `return` without an expression should only be used with a function that has a void return type. The following are all valid examples of `return` statement expressions.

return *expression*;	**return *value***
`return 6*3;`	18
`return    i;`	value of i variable
`return    4;`	4
`return (i=7);`	value assigned, 7

The return value of the function is managed by a special temporary variable in which the return expression's result is placed. This temporary variable is generated at the time of the function call. It is inaccessible to the programmer and it is used only to hold the return value.

To accurately understand the process of returning a value, you need to think of the `return` statement as if it were an assignment operation. The two operands of such an assignment operation are the return expression's result and the temporary variable that will hold the return value. The `return` statement assigns the result of its return expression to this temporary variable. The calling function then locates the temporary variable and reads the return value. The value of the `return` statement expression is not passed directly to the calling function. It is relayed through the temporary variable.

```
return type     function name ()
                   {
                   declarations;
                   statements;
                   return expression;
                   }
```

Though the return expression's type does not have to be the same as the function return type, it is always advisable to make it the same type, even if you have to force it with a cast. If the types are different, then conversions may take place, just as they would in assignment operations. It is the programmer's responsibility to make sure that the types match, or at least that they cause no detrimental conversions.

In the next example, the `return` statement evaluates the expression 3.00 * 5.25. The value of the expression is a `float`. This value is assigned to the temporary variable used to hold the function's return value. The type of this variable is that of the function's return type. The expression result in the `return` statement and the function's return type are both the same type. So far, the two types match.

```
float calc(void)
    {
    return (3.00 * 5.25);
    }
```

If the expression in the `return` statement is a variable, care must be taken to match the type of the variable with the function's return type.

```
float   calc(void)
        {
        float cost;

        cost = (3.00 * 5.25);
        return (cost);
        }
```

In the previous example, the `return` statement's expression consists of the variable `cost`. The variable `cost` is a `float`, and its value is a `float`. This matches the return type, which is also a `float`.

variable declaration	**return expression**	**return type**
`float cost`	`return(cost)`	`float calc()`
`15.75`	`15.75`	`15.75`

Function Declaration and Return Value

The calling function receives a value back from the returning function. However, the calling function does not know what kind of value it is receiving, unless it is told. Since each function is independent of the other, the calling function cannot simply look at the returning function and check the type of its return value. The calling function must be informed of the called function's return type. This is the role of a function declaration. A function declaration declares the type of value being returned by that function.

In the **calcdec.c** program in LISTING 6-5, the calling function, `main`, needs to know the type of the return value of `calc`. Is it a `float`, an integer, or some other type? A function declaration for `calc` is placed in the `main` function to inform `main` that `calc` returns a `float`. Figure 6-4 illustrates the return value and its relationship to the calling function.

The function call for `calc` is part of an assignment expression. The return value of `calc` will be assigned to the variable res. If the return type of `calc` is different from the variable to which its return value is assigned, conversions may take place. The programmer now faces the problem of making sure all the types of the values passed between functions match. The return type of the `calc` function declaration in `main` is a `float`. The return type of the `calc` function definition is also a `float`. The declaration and the definition types match. The function declaration of `calc` in `main` tells `main` to expect a floating-point value from `calc`, allowing `main` to correctly perform any needed conversions.

As shown in the next example, the programmer now has several values whose types need to match. The return expression value needs to match the defined return type. The defined return type needs to match the declared return type. The declared return type should match the type of any variable to which the return value is assigned. The next example lists the different components of the **calcdec.c** program whose types you need to keep track of and match. Otherwise, unintended conversions could occur at any point where the types do not match.

Calc *function*			**Main** *function*	
`float cost;`	`return(cost)`	`float calc()`	`calc();`	`float res;`
local	expression	return value	function call	assignment
variable	value	temp var	value	variable
float	float	float	float	float

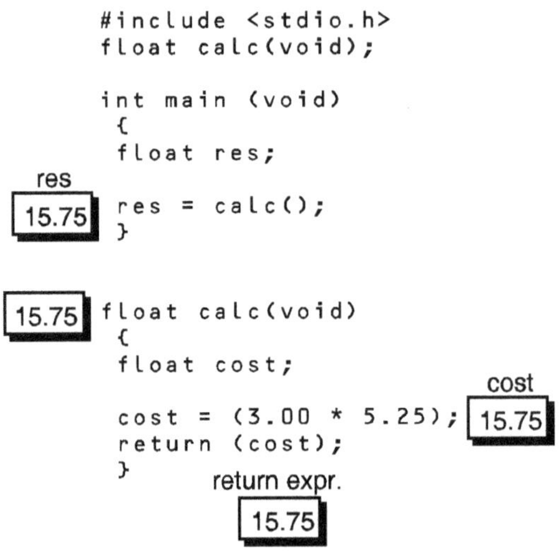

```
                    #include <stdio.h>
                    float calc(void);

                    int main (void)
                     {
                     float res;
       res
     ┌───────┐
     │ 15.75 │      res = calc();
     └───────┘       }


     ┌───────┐  float calc(void)
     │ 15.75 │       {
     └───────┘       float cost;
                                                    cost
                                               ┌───────┐
                     cost = (3.00 * 5.25);      │ 15.75 │
                     return (cost);             └───────┘
                      }           return expr.
                              ┌───────┐
                              │ 15.75 │
                              └───────┘
```

Figure 6-4: Function return value.

LISTING 6-5:

calcdec.c
```c
#include <stdio.h>

int main (void)
        {
        float calc(void); /*function declaration*/
        float res;

        res = calc();
        return 0;
        }

    float calc(void)
        {
        float cost;

        cost = (3.00 * 5.25);
        return (cost);
        }
```

Often in programs, the same function will be called by many different functions. Technically, the function declaration would have to be placed in each calling function. A more convenient and common approach is to declare the function once externally at the head of the program file. A function that is declared externally is known to all functions in the program. In the **calcext.c** program in LISTING 6-6 the `calc` function is declared once, externally, outside of any functions.

LISTING 6-6:

calcext.c

```c
#include <stdio.h>

float calc(void);                /* Function Declaration */

int main(void)
        {
        float result;

        result = calc();
        return 0;
        }

float calc(void)
        {
        float cost;

        cost = (3.00 * 5.25);
        return (cost);
        }
```

Functions as Expressions

A function call can be considered an expression whose result is the function's return value. Expressions are commonly used as the assigned value in an assignment operation. This is also a common use of the return value of a function call. A function call can be combined with an assignment operation into one complex expression. In such an expression, first a function is called. Then the return value of the function call is assigned to a variable. In the **calcexpr.c** program in LISTING 6-7, the return value of the function call to `calc` is assigned to the variable result: `result=calc();`. The type of result is the same as the type of the return value in the function declaration of `calc`.

```c
float result;          float calc();
```

Since a function call is an expression, it can be used anywhere an expression can be used. A function call can be a subexpression in a larger expression, the test expression in a control structure, or part of an assignment expression.

The use of both function calls and assignment operations leads to some complex, yet common expressions. The expression `((result= calc()>10)` in the **calcexp2.c** program in LISTING 6-8 performs three different operations. First, there is a function call whose return value is an operand in an assignment operation. Second, there is an assignment operation whose value assigned is an operand in a relational operation. Third, there is a greater-than relational operation in which one operand is the constant 10. The first operand of the relational operation is the same value as the return value of `calc`.

LISTING 6-7:

calcexpr.c

```
#include <stdio.h>

float calc(void);

int main(void)
          {
          float result;

          result = calc();
          result = 7 + (4 * calc());
          if (calc() > 3)
                  printf ("Calc");
          return 0;
          }

     float calc(void)
          {
          float cost;

          cost = (3.00 * 3.56);
          return (cost);
          }
```

LISTING 6-8:

calcexp2.c

```
#include <stdio.h>

     float calc(void);

     int main(void)
          {
          float result;

          if((result = calc()) > 10)
                  printf ("Calc");
          return 0;
          }

     float calc(void)
          {
          float cost;

          cost = (3.00 * 3.56);
          return (cost);
          }
```

Return Inconsistencies

There are two types of return errors: return value inconsistencies and return type inconsistencies. Return value inconsistencies occur when the return expression has a different type than the function's return type. Return type inconsistencies occur when the return type of a function's declaration is different from the return type specified in its definition.

Return Value Inconsistencies

If the return type of a function is different from the type of the return expression, unintended conversions may result. If the return expression results in a value of a different type than the return type, then it is as if an assignment were taking place with two operands of different types. The assigned value, the return expression's result, will be converted to the return type. If the return type of a function is an integer and the `return` statement expression results in a long, then conversion rules will take effect. The long will be truncated to an integer, possibly losing information.

     In the **numerr.c** program in LISTING 6-9, the value in **res** will be 9464. The value of num is the return expression's value, which is a long, 75000. This value is first assigned to the temporary variable that holds the return value. This temporary variable is of type `int`, the return type of the `getnum` function. Whenever a long is assigned to an integer, the long value is converted by `truncation` to an integer value and then assigned. Truncation of the long value 75000 leaves a 2-byte value whose bits are equivalent to the integer 9464. In `main`, res is assigned the return value of `getnum`. `getnum`'s return value is located in the temporary variable. The value here is 9464. Figure 6-5 shows the value of the return expression and the truncated return value.

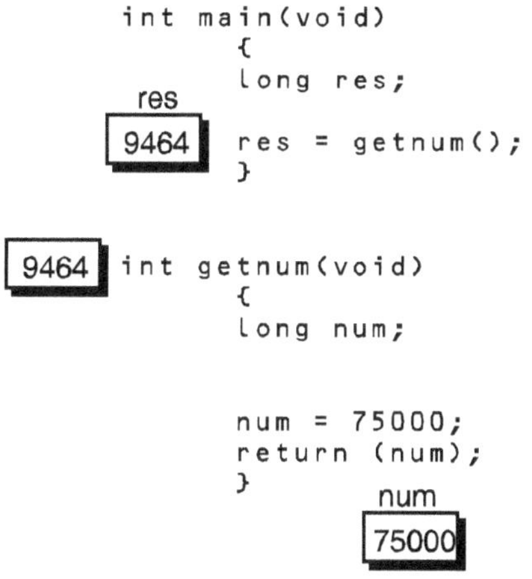

```
int main(void)
     {
     long res;
res
9464  res = getnum();
     }


9464  int getnum(void)
     {
     long num;

     num = 75000;
     return (num);
     }      num
            75000
```

Figure 6-5: Return value conversions.

LISTING 6-9:

numerr.c

```
#include <stdio.h>

        int getnum(void);

int main(void)
            {
            long res;

            res = getnum();
            printf("Res is %ld\n", res);
            return 0;
            }

int getnum(void)
            {
            long num;


            num = 75000;
            printf("Num is %ld\n", num);
            return (num);
            }
```

Output for LISTING 6-9:

```
        Num is 75000
        Res is 9464
```

Return Type Inconsistencies

Return type inconsistencies occur when the return type of a function declaration is different from that of its function definition. This will result in a compiler error.

Parameters and Arguments

Parameters bring information into a function, whereas the return value sends information out of a function. There can be many parameters, but only one return value. Parameters themselves are variables. These variables receive their values from another function. In this way, a function can receive information from another function.

Each function itself can call other functions. When a function calls another function, it transfers control to that function. It can also send information to that function. It does so with a list of expressions placed in the function call. These expressions are referred to as arguments. The values of these argument expressions are then assigned to the parameter variables of the called function.

With arguments and parameters, information can be sent from one function to another. However, there are limitations. You can use arguments and parameters to send information in only one direction, from the calling function to the function called. Furthermore, functions can only receive values from another function. Passing values in a function call is referred to as call-by-value.

Though values can be sent from one function to another, variable references cannot. In many other programming languages, the variables in one function can be modified by parameters in another function. The process by which this is done is referred to as call-by-reference. There is no call-by-reference in C. However, call-by-reference can be simulated using pointers.

The terms parameter and argument are often used in several different ways. Another term for parameters is formal arguments, and a term often used for arguments is actual arguments. Actual arguments are passed to formal arguments. This terminology can be confusing. The C language grammar calls formal arguments parameter declarations. Actual arguments are called argument expressions. For this reason and for the sake of clarity, the terms argument and parameter are used in this text, instead of formal and actual arguments. Arguments are passed to parameters.

Call-by-Value

A function call consists of a function name and a list of arguments placed within parentheses and separated by commas. Each argument is an expression. The argument list is really a list of expressions. Each expression is evaluated, and its resulting value is then passed to the called function. These values are then assigned the function's parameter variables. The passing of arguments to parameters can be thought of as an assignment operation in which the result of an expression is assigned to a variable. The argument is the expression, and the parameter is the variable.

In a function definition, parameters are declared in a parameter list within parentheses next to the function name. The sequence of parameters in the list is important. Values in the argument list will be matched up sequentially to the parameter variables in the parameter list. In LISTING 6-10, the argument list consists of two primary expressions, the constant 5 and the variable rate. These expressions evaluate to the values 5 and 2.0. These values will then be assigned sequentially to **num** and `calc_rate` in the `calc` function's parameter list. 5 will be assigned to num, and 2.0 will be assigned to `calc_rate`. The next example shows the corresponding values between the arguments and parameters. The parameter list contains expressions that are evaluated and whose resulting values are then assigned to corresponding parameter variables. In this example, the argument expressions are primary expressions consisting of a variable and a constant.

argument expression	argument value	parameter variable
5	5	num
rate	2.0	calc_rate

Parameter variables are locally declared variables. They are known only within their own function. They only differ from other local variables in that they receive their initial values from arguments. In LISTING 6-10, the parameter `calc_rate` in the `calc` function operates just like the local variable `cost`.

Using a variable as your argument could give you the impression that somehow a change in the corresponding parameter could change that variable. However, this is not the case. The variable used as an argument is only a primary expression whose value is passed down to the parameter. The parameter operates solely as a local variable. In LISTING 6-10, a change in the contents of the variable `calc_rate` in the `calc` function in no way affects the variable rate in the `main` function. The `calc` function has no idea that the variable rate even exists.

Information can be sent to a function using parameters, and information can be returned from that function using the return value. Often, a function call with arguments is combined with an assignment of the function's return value to a variable. In the **calcres.c** program in LISTING 6-11, the function call to `calc` with the arguments 3 and 3.56 has its return value assigned to the variable result.

LISTING 6-10:

calcparm.c
```c
#include <stdio.h>

        /* Function Declaration*/
        float calc(int, float);

 int main(void )
                {
                float rate;

                rate = 2.0;
                calc ( 5, rate);        /* argument values */
                return 0;
                }

float calc (int num, float calc_rate) /*parameter variables*/
                {
                float cost;

                cost = calc_rate * num;
                }
```

The use of `calc` in LISTING 6-11 is common. Values are passed from the arguments in `main` to the corresponding parameter variables in `calc`. These values in these parameter variables are then used in some local calculation in the `calc` function. A result is then returned to the calling function, `main`, through the return value of `calc`.

LISTING 6-11:

calcres.c
```c
#include <stdio.h>
float calc(int, float);

 int main(void)
                {
                float result;

                result = calc(3, 3.56);
                return 0;
                }

 float calc(int calc_num, float calc_rate)
                {
                float cost;
                cost = (calc_num * calc_rate);
                return (cost);
                }
```

Arguments and Parameters

There is a limited built-in promotion of arguments in function calls. In any expression, the `float` and character operands are always promoted to `doubles` and `ints`. This means that a floating-point expression will always have a result that is a `double`. The floats are first promoted to doubles and then operated on. As expressions, argument expressions will never pass a `float` or `char` value. The `float` or `char` will always be promoted to a `double` or `int`.

Function declarations in C provide information about parameter types to functions making function calls (function declarations are sometimes referred to as prototypes). An example of a function declaration follows.

```
float calc (int rate, float cost);
```

A function declaration tells the calling function the type of values the called function expects for its parameters. This allows the calling function to first check that argument values are consistent with the corresponding parameter variables. If this is not the case, then the calling function will convert its argument values to the appropriate types before sending them over.

A function declaration (prototype) will first specify the return type, then the function name, and, in parentheses, a list of the types of the parameter variables. The names of the parameter variables may be included. However, the names are optional. Only the types are required. In fact, the names are virtually ignored and can be different from the actual parameter variable names. Figure 6-6 illustrates a function declaration (prototype) for the `calc` function.

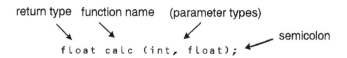

Figure 6-6: Function prototype (function declaration).

In the **calcargs.c** program in LISTING 6-12, `calc` is called with the argument values 10.25 and 32. 10.25 is a `float` and 32 is an integer. Their types do not match the types of their corresponding parameter variables, `rate` and `cost`. `rate` is an integer and the argument 10.25 is a `double`, `cost` is a `double` and the argument 32 is an integer.

```
calc (10.25, 32);
```

In this case, conversions would take place before the arguments are assigned to the parameters. The argument value 10.25 would be converted to the integer 10 from the `float` 10.25. The integer 32 would be converted to the `float` 32.00. Then the values 10 and 32.00 would be passed into the parameter variables rate and `cost`.

LISTING 6-12:

calcargs.c
```
#include <stdio.h>
float calc (int, float);  /* Prototype */

 int main(void)
              {
              float result;

              result = calc(10.25, 32);
              return 0;
              }

 float calc(int rate, float cost)
              {
              float res;

              res = rate * cost;
              return (res);
              }
```

Call-by-Reference: Simulation with Pointers

In a call-by-reference operation, a variable in one function can be modified in another function. Other languages, such as Pascal, have a call-by-reference capability. In call-by-reference, an argument in a function call is a reference to a variable rather than a value resulting from an expression. The reference can then be used to manipulate the variable in the called function. In C, there is no call-by-reference. Instead, a call-by-reference operation needs to be simulated using addresses and pointers.

There are three elements to such a call-by-reference simulation. First, the parameter of the called function must always be a pointer variable. Second, the argument in the function call must be an address of a variable. Third, an indirection operation in the function is used to access the variable whose address was passed.

A pointer variable can access an address of any variable in the program, regardless of where the variable has been declared. All a pointer requires is the variable's address. This means that a pointer variable in a given function has the inherent capability to access a variable in any other function.

How, then, can a pointer variable in one function obtain the address of a variable in another function? A way of communicating information between functions is the call-by-value operation, in which values are sent from one function to another when a function is called. As a value, an address can be passed from one function to the next in a standard call-by-value process. The kind of parameter variable that receives an address is a pointer variable. An argument that is an address has a pointer variable as its corresponding parameter.

How, then, is the address of a variable obtained in the calling function? This is the role of the address operation, &. The result of an address operation is the address of a variable. In Figure 6-7, the address operation, &num, results in the address 546. This is the address of the memory allocated for the variable num.

Figures 6.7, 6.8, and 6.9 show how a call-by-reference operation works. The argument value passed to `calc` is an address. The address is obtained from the address operation on the variable num, &num. This address, 546, is passed to the corresponding parameter in `calc`. The corresponding parameter is the pointer variable, `cptr`. In this way, `cptr` obtains the address of a variable in another function-in this case, the variable num in the `main` function.

Given an address, indirection on a pointer can access the memory at that address, regardless of where that memory is or what it is used for. The indirection operation on `cptr` references the memory at address 546 as an integer. This referenced integer is then changed. In this case, the memory at 546 has been changed from a 7 to an 8. When the `calc` function returns to `main`, the value of the variable num in `main` is now 8.

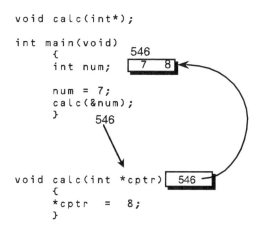

Figure 6-7: Call-by-reference.

```
void calc (int *);

int main(void)
        {
        int num;                    546
                             num[  7  ]    before calc

        num = 7;
        calc ( &num );              &num is 546
        }                           546
                             num[  8  ]    after calc

void calc( int *cptr)
        {                    cptr [ 546 ]
        *cptr = 8;
        }
```

Figure 6-8: Call-by-reference and variable addresses.

cptr is a variable local to and known only to the `calc` function. Similarly, **num** is a variable local to and known only to the `main` function. It is because of the capabilities of the indirection operation that the pointer variable `cptr` is able to change the contents of the variable **num**. In a sense, *cptr and **num** are just two different ways of accessing the same memory. **num** accesses that memory using its variable name, whereas *cptr accesses that memory through an indirection operation.

cptr is only able to change the memory at 546 through an indirection operation, *cptr. Leave out the indirection operator, *, and there is just a simple local variable assignment operation. cptr=8 would simply change the address in cptr from 546 to 8.

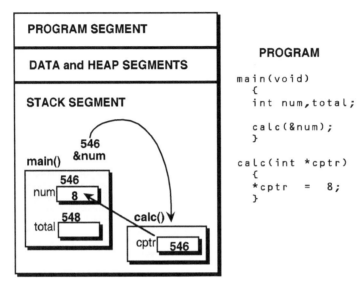

Figure 6-9: Program memory and call-by-reference.

LISTING 6-13:

callref.c

```
#include <stdio.h>

void calc(int *);      /* Function declaration */

int main(void)
      {
      int num;

      num = 7;
      calc (&num);    /* Address as argument */
      return 0;
      }

 void calc(int *cptr) /*Pointer as parameter*/
      {

      *cptr = 8; /* Indirection to access variable */
      }
```

The **callref.c** program in LISTING 6-13 shows the call-by-reference operation described in the previous figures. In the function declaration, the parameter's pointer type is specified, in this case int*. You have already seen call-by-reference operations whenever you used the scanf function. The scanf function uses call-by-reference to assign converted input values to variables. It is passed the addresses of variables, and then uses those addresses to change those variables with the converted input values. For this reason, the arguments for scanf must be addresses. Usually these addresses are obtained from the address operation on variables.

```
scanf ("%d", &num);
```

What if the function calc then passes the address in cptr, which holds the address of num, on to another function? Remember that the argument must be a value and that a value can be obtained from a variable. The value obtained from a pointer variable is an address. Though an address can be obtained from an address operation on a variable, an address may also be obtained from a pointer variable.

In the **parmptrs.c** program in LISTING 6-14, an address is obtained from the pointer variable cptr. In calc, the argument value of the function call to crunch is simply the address obtained from the pointer variable cptr. The parameter crunptr in crunch also has the address of num in main. An address could be passed in this way from one function to the next. An indirection operation at any point will still access num in main. Figures 6.10 and 6.11 illustrate how the address of the variable num in main is passed to the calc function, and from there to the crunch function. Both cptr and crunptr hold the address of num, 546. The indirection on crunptr and the indirection on cptr both reference the variable num in main.

LISTING 6-14:

parmptrs.c
```c
void calc(int*);
void crunch(int*);

#include <stdio.h>

int main(void)
          {
          int num;

          num = 7;
          calc(&num);
          return 0;
          }                              /* num is 2 at this point */

void calc(int *cptr)
          {
          crunch (cptr);
          }

void crunch(int *crunptr)
          {
          *crunptr = 2;
          }
```

int main(void)
{
int num;
546
2
num = 7;
calc(&num);
}
546
void calc(int *cptr)
{
546
crunch (cptr);
}
546
void crunch (int *crunptr)
{
546
*crunptr = 2;
}

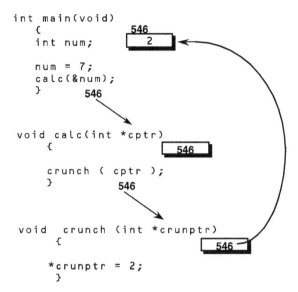

Figure 6-10: Call-by-reference from one pointer to another pointer.

void calc (int*);
void crunch(int*);
int main(void)
{
int num;
546
num 7 before calc
num = 7;
calc(&num);
/* &num is 546 */
}
546
num 2 after calc
void calc(int *cptr)
{
cptr 546
crunch(cptr);
/* cptr is 546 */
}
void crunch(int *crunptr)
{
*crunptr = 2;
crunptr 546
}

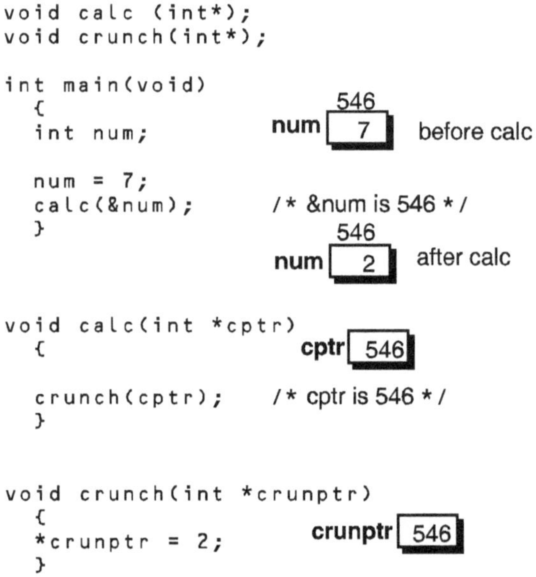

Figure 6-11: Call-by-reference from one pointer to another pointer.

The same kind of process is taking place in the **scanptr.c** program in LISTING 6-15 with `scanf`. Here the address of num has been passed to the input function. The input function, in turn, calls `scanf`. `scanf` operates by call-by-reference. Its parameters are all pointers. It expects to receive addresses. Ordinarily, addresses are obtained by an address operation on a variable. However, `scanf` does not care how an address is obtained. An address can result from an address operation or it can be taken from a pointer variable. In the **scanptr.c** program, the address for **num** is held in the pointer variable `cptr`. The argument for `scanf` is simply this pointer variable.

Table 6-1: Values and Variables, Addresses and Pointers

Call by Reference

Address of Var to Ptr (&)

```
void calc(int*);

int main(void)
    {
    int num = 10;

    calc( &num );
    }


void calc(int *clnumptr)
    {
    *clnumptr = 5;
    scanf("%d",clnumptr);
    printf("%d",*clnumptr);
    }
```

Call by Value

Variable to Variable

```
void calc(int);

int main(void)
    {
    int num = 10;

    calc (num);
    }


void calc(int clnum)
    {
    clnum = 5;
    scanf("%d",&clnum);
    printf("%d",clnum);
    }
```

Pointer to Pointer

```
void calc(int*);


int main(void)
    {
    int *numptr;
    int *numptr;

    numptr = &num;
    calc(numptr);
    }

void calc(int *clnumptr)
    {
    *clnumptr = 5;
    }
```

Ptr Indirection to Var

```
void calc(int);


int main(void)
    {
    int num = 10;
    int num = 10;

    numptr = &num;
    calc(*numptr);
    }

void calc(int clnum)
    {
    clnum = 5;
    }
```

LISTING 6-15:

scanptr.c
```c
#include <stdio.h>
void input(int*);

int main(void)
        {
        int num;
        input (&num); /* address of num passed to cptr*/
        return 0;
        }

void input(int *cptr)
        {
        printf("Please enter value for num: ");
        scanf("%d", cptr );     /*no address operator*/
        }
```

Pointers and Values in Function Calls

In call-by-reference, the parameter variable is always a pointer, and the argument is always an address. The address can be derived from any pointer expression. The most common pointer expressions are address operations and pointer variables.

In call-by-value, the parameter variable is always a variable, and the argument is any value. The value can be derived from any expression. The most common expression is a primary expression consisting of a variable. However, it is important to note that an indirection operation on a pointer is the equivalent of a variable reference. This means that an indirection operation can be used as an argument in a call-by-value operation, just as any variable reference can be used as an argument in a call-by-value operation. Table 6-1 lists the various kinds of argument/parameter arrangements commonly seen in call-by-reference and call-by-value.

Pointers to Functions

When a function name is used in a function call, it is treated as if it were a pointer. The function name represents the address of the function. A function call operator takes the address of a function as its operand. With the address, the function call operator is able to reference and thereby execute the function.

Pointers can be declared to hold the address of a function. Such pointers can then be used as operands in a function call. You declare a pointer to a function using both the pointer and function type specifiers: an asterisk, *, and parentheses, (). The pointer variable will point to a given type of function. This type must be specified in the pointer declaration. A function type consists of the return type and the parameter types enclosed in parentheses. The parentheses, in this case, are actually the function type specifier. A pointer to a function is declared with the pointer specifier and a function type. However, the parentheses used for the function type have a higher precedence than the pointer specifier, the asterisk. Since a pointer is being declared, the asterisk must be evaluated before the parentheses. To do this, the pointer specifier, along with the variable name, is placed within its own parentheses. Figure 6-12 illustrates the syntax for the declaration of a pointer to a function. In this case, the pointer variable `cfunc` is declared as a pointer to a function that returns an integer and takes no arguments.

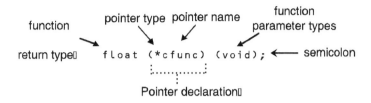

Figure 6-12: Pointer to function declaration.

You need to be careful to distinguish between a pointer to a function and a simple function declaration. The declaration of a pointer to a function appears similar to a function declaration. In the following declarations, `cfunc` is declared as a pointer to a function that returns an integer. If the parentheses are left out, the declaration is a function declaration in which the function return type is a pointer. The next two declarations are simple function declarations. The `calc` declaration declares a function that returns a `float`, and the declaration for getint declares a function that returns a pointer to an `int`.

Declarations	**Objects**	**Data Types**
`float (*cfunc) (void);`	`Pointer`	`float (*)(void)`
`float  calc(void);`	`Function`	`float (void)`
`float *getint(void);`	`Function`	`float* (void)`

The address of a function is represented by the function's name. A pointer can be assigned the address of a function by simply assigning the function name to the pointer. The function name will evaluate to an address, and the address will then be assigned to the pointer. Figure 6-13 illustrates the relationship between a pointer to a function and a function's address. Below, the pointer `cfunc` is assigned the address of the `calc` function.

```
int (*cfunc) (void);
int calc(void);

        cfunc = calc;
```

When the function call operator uses a function address to reference the function, a kind of indirection takes place. The address is used to reference the object pointed to, in this case, a function. When a pointer to a function is used in a function call, the indirection operator is required. Indirection on a pointer to a function again runs into a precedence problem. The parentheses of the function call operation have a higher precedence than the asterisk of the indirection operation. Yet, the function must first be referenced in an indirection operation before it can be called. For this reason, you need to place parentheses around the indirection operator and the pointer name to ensure prior indirection of the pointer.

In the following example, the function `calc` is called twice, first with the function name and then with the pointer `cfunc`, which holds the address of `calc`.

```
float (*cfunc) (void);
float calc(void);

    cfunc = calc;
    calc();
    (*cfunc)();
```

In the **funcptrs.c** program in LISTING 6-16 a pointer to a function is used to reference `calc`. The declaration of the pointer includes prototype information. The type that the pointer references is literally the type used in a function declaration, a return type and list of parameter types. The function declaration for `calc` and the declaration of `cfunc` follow.

```
float calc(int, float);

float (*cfunc) (int, float);
```

In the function call, the arguments are placed with the parentheses of the function call operator, just as they are in any standard function call.

LISTING 6-16:

funcptrs.c
```
#include <stdio.h>
float calc(int, float);

int main(void)
        {
        float result;
        float (*cfunc) (int, float);

        cfunc = calc;
        result = (*cfunc)(3, 5.25);
        printf("Cost = %.2f\n", result);
        return 0;
        }

    float calc(int calc_num, float calc_rate)
        {
        float cost;

        cost = calc_num * calc_rate;
        return (cost);
        }
```

You can use pointers to functions to provide a way of selecting different actions. You can set a pointer to a function to the address of the particular function you want to execute. In LISTING 6-17. the **gretfunc.c** program uses a set of functions and a pointer to a function. `stylefunc` is a pointer to a function. Depending upon the user's choice, it will be assigned an address of one of the functions. `stylefunc` is then used to call the function. A variation of this approach can be implemented with arrays. This will be discussed in Chapter 14.

You can also pass a function name as an argument within a function call's argument list. The corresponding parameter for a function name is a pointer to a function. The function name will evaluate to the addresses of the function. The address will then be passed, and the pointer variable will receive it.

In the **printfun.c** program in LISTING 6-18, the address of the `calc` function is passed to the `prcalc` function. The parameter `pfunc` is a pointer to a function of the same type as `calc`. It receives the `calc` function address and is used to call the `calc` function from within `prcalc`.

LISTING 6-17:

gretfunc.c

```c
#include <stdio.h>

#define FORMAL 1
#define COMMON 2
#define FRIENDLY 3

void printformal(void);
void printcommon(void);
void printfriendly(void);

int main(void)
    {
    int formal;
    void (*stylefunc)(void);

    printf("Enter Greeting Code\n");
    scanf ("%d", &formal);

    switch (formal)
        {
        case FORMAL:
                    stylefunc = printformal;
                    break;
        case COMMON:
                    stylefunc = printcommon;
                    break;
        case FRIENDLY:
                    stylefunc = printfriendly;
                    break;
        }
    (*stylefunc)();/* Function Call with Pointer */
    return 0;
    }

void printformal(void)
        {
        printf("greetings");
        }

void printcommon(void)
        {
        printf("hello");
        }

void printfriendly(void)
        {
        printf("hi");
        }
```

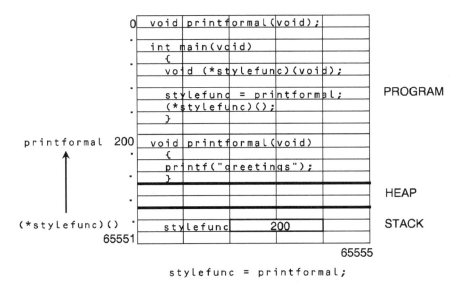

Figure 6-13: Pointer to function.

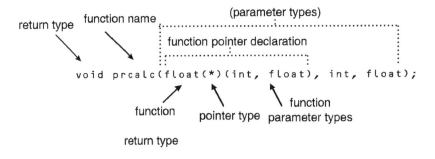

Figure 6-14: Function prototype with parameter as function pointer.

The parameter declaration for a pointer to a function can be disconcerting. The declaration of a pointer to a function will include the function type, which in turn includes the return type and parameter types. Below, pfunc is a parameter declared as a pointer to a function that returns a float and has as its parameters an integer and a float.

```
void prcalc( float (*pfunc)(int, float) )
        {
        }
```

The function prototype can be just as confusing. In Figure 6-14, the function prototype for prcalc specifies that its first argument is a pointer to a function that returns a float and takes as its arguments an integer and a float value. The type of a pointer to a function is literally an asterisk enclosed in parentheses and placed within a function declaration where the function name would be.

Shown here is just the type for a pointer to a function that returns a `float` and has two parameters, an `int` and a `float`. Notice how it is used in the `prcalc` prototype at the head of the **printfunc.c** program.

```
float (*)(int, float)
```

LISTING 6-18:

printfun.c

```
#include <stdio.h>

float calc(int, float);
void prcalc(float(*)(int, float), int, float);

int main(void)
       {
       float rate = 5.25;

       prcalc(calc, 3, rate);
       return 0;
       }

void prcalc(float(*pfunc)(int,float),int num,float rte)
       {
       float result;

       result = (*pfunc)(num,rte);
       printf("Result is %.2f\n", result);
       }

float calc(int calc_num, float calc_rate)
       {
       return (calc_num * calc_rate);
       }
```

In LISTING 6-18, you had to indicate a specific type of function when you declared the pointer to a function, just as you have to indicate a specific data type whenever you declare a pointer to an object. However, it is possible to declare a generic type of pointer using the `void` data type. A pointer to type void can be used to hold pointer values of any type. Normally you cannot assign a pointer to one type of object to a pointer to another type of object. Nor can you pass an argument pointer to a certain type of object to a parameter pointer that points to a different type of object. A pointer to an `int` cannot be passed to a pointer to a `float`. However, with a generic pointer, you can get around this restriction. At one place you could assign a pointer to an `int` to a generic pointer, and then at another place assign a pointer to a `float` to that same generic pointer.

The **maxnum.c** program in LISTING 6-19 makes extensive use of generic pointers. The `maxgen` function determines the maximum of two values. One of its parameters is a function that performs the actual comparison. The comparison of integers is a different operation from the comparison of floats. Two maximum comparison functions are defined, one to compare floats and the other to compare integers. There are then two calls of the `maxgen` function, one with the `maxint` function to compare integers, and one with the `maxfloat` function to compare floats. The first function call includes pointers to integers that reference the values to be compared, and the second function call includes pointers to floats. The `maxgen` parameters are all generic pointers, allowing different types of pointers to be passed to it.

LISTING 6-19:

maxnum.c

```c
#include <stdio.h>

int maxfloat(float*, float*);
int maxint(int*, int*);
int maxgen(int(*)(void*,void*), void*, void*);

int main(void)
        {
        float fnum1, fnum2;
        int Fltres, Intres, num1, num2;

        num1 = 5, num2 = 10;
        Intres = maxgen(maxint, &num1, &num2);

        fnum1 = 2.34, fnum2 = 1.45;
        Fltres = maxgen(maxfloat, &fnum1, &fnum2);
        return 0;
        }

int maxgen(int (*maxfunc)(void*,void*),
                                        void *val1, void *val2)
        {
        if((*maxfunc)(val1, val2) > 0)
                return 1;
        else
                return 0;
        }

int maxfloat(float *fnum1, float *fnum2)
        {
        if(*fnum1 > *fnum2)
                return 1;
        else
                return 0;
        }

int maxint(int *num1, int *num2)
        {
        if (*num1 > *num2)
                return 1;
        else
                return 0;
        }
```

There is extensive use of call-by-reference operations in the **maxnum.c** program. Variables are declared in `main`, and their addresses, along with the address of a function, are passed to `maxgen`. The pointers in `maxgen` are declared as pointers to void. They are still pointers, using the same amount of memory as other pointers. They hold addresses. However, the type of object they reference is unknown. The address of any type can be assigned to a pointer to void. The address held by a pointer to void can, in turn, be assigned to any other type of pointer. That is what is happening in the function calls. In the first function call, addresses of integers are passed to pointers to void. Within `maxgen`, the addresses held in the pointers to void are then passed to pointers to integers.

The same process occurs for the function pointer. The type of the function pointer in `maxgen` is one in which the parameters are pointers to void. The parameters are pointers, but it is not known to what objects they point. This function pointer can receive the address of a function whose parameters are pointers to integers, and it can also receive the address of a function whose parameters are pointers to floats. That is what is happening in the two function calls to `maxgen`. In the first function call, the `maxint` function is passed to `maxfunc`. Then in the second function call, the `maxfloat` function is passed to `maxfunc`.

When you use such generic pointers, your compiler may still balk at the type difference between the function name and the generic function pointer. In that case, you can use a cast in any function calls to change the type of the pointer argument to generic pointer type. In the following example of the `maxgen` function call, there is a cast for the `maxint` function, changing the type of the `maxint` parameters to void pointers.

```
maxgen( (int(*)(void*,void*)) maxint, (void*) &num1, (void*) &num2);
```

Functions with Varying Arguments

It is possible to define a function whose arguments may vary with each function call. `printf` and `scanf` are such functions. In the case of `printf`, with one call you may want to print out three values, so you list four arguments, whereas in another function call to `printf`, you may want to print out five values, so you would list six arguments. The number of arguments is one more than the number of values you want to pass. This is because print also requires you to pass a string that provides information about the number of arguments being passed. In the case of any function with varying arguments, you will need to inform it of the number of arguments being passed with each function call. Usually, this is done in the first argument. The arguments in such a function are divided into two categories, declared arguments and undeclared arguments. Declared arguments are listed first and always need to be provided in every function call. The format string in a `printf` function call is an example of a declared argument. You always have to have it. The undeclared arguments follow the declared ones, and their number may vary from one function call to the next.

Since the number of undeclared arguments is unknown, there are no corresponding parameter declarations for them in the function definition. Instead, there are only the parameter declarations for the declared arguments. One of the declared parameters will be used to determine the number of undeclared argument values passed to the function with each function call.

Though undeclared arguments have no corresponding parameter declaration, their values are still passed to the function. The **stdarg.h** file contains macro operations that allow the user to locate and reference the passed values of these undeclared arguments, treating them as parameter variables. You need to include this header file in your program. These macros look like functions, but should be thought of as expressions. Exactly how they work will be discussed in the chapter on character arrays.

In the next example, the `sumvar` function is a function that takes a varying number of arguments. It sums a varying number of integers and returns the total. The parameter list consists of only one parameter declaration followed by the symbol . . . . This series of dots is called an ellipsis. It indicates that there are a varying number of argument values that can be passed down. The variable declared just before the ellipsis is known as the last declared parameter. There may be other declared parameters, but they must all precede the ellipsis. You also need to include the ellipsis in any function declarations. Figure 6-15 references the different components of the `sumvar` function.

```
int sumvar (int num, ...)
    {
    va_list  parnums;
    int i, total = 0;

    va_start(parnums, num);
    for(i = 0; i < num; i++)
        {
        total = total + va_arg(parnums, int);
        }
    va_end(parnums);
    return total;
    }
```

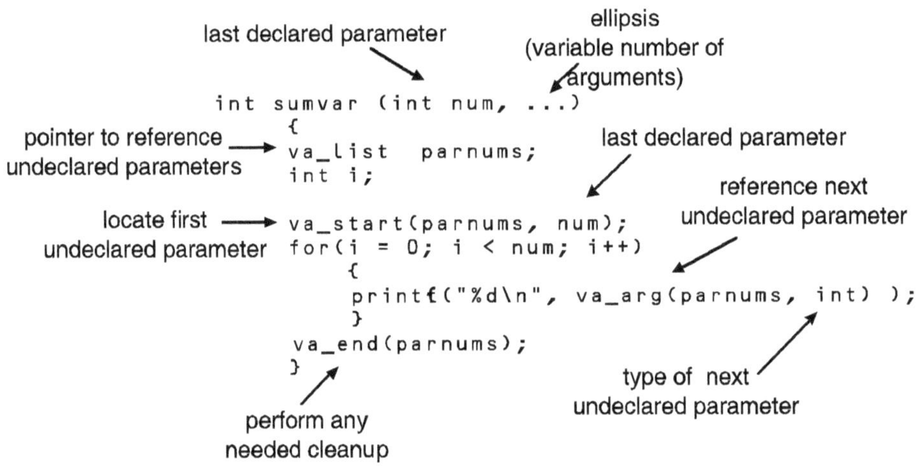

Figure 6-15: Functions with variable numbers of arguments.

You reference the undeclared arguments using a specially declared variable and three special macros defined in the **stdarg.h** header file. First, you need to declare a variable of type `va_list`. In the sumvar function, this is the variable `parnums`. This special variable, together with the macros `va_start`, `va_arg`, and `va_end`, allows you to reference the undeclared arguments. The `va_list` data type is actually a pointer. You will be declaring a pointer with which to reference argument values. The `parnums` variable in the sumvar function is such a pointer. ;

The `va_start` macro initializes the process of referencing the undeclared arguments. `va_start` takes as arguments the `va_list` variable and the name of the last declared object in the parameter list. In the `sumvar` function, the last declared object is num and the `va_list` variable is `parnums`. Recall that the va_list variable is actually a pointer. `va_start` has the effect of pointing the `va_list` pointer to the first undeclared argument following the last declared parameter. In this case, the `parnums` variable will point to the memory just after that used for the num parameter. This is where the values for the undeclared arguments will be located. The va_arg macro will then use `parnums` to consecutively reference each argument value. va_arg requires the type of the argument values being referenced. In the sumvar function, all the arguments are integers, so `va_arg` always uses the int type. Each use of `va_arg` automatically advances `parnums` to the next argument. This means that you only reference the arguments sequentially. You cannot jump from one to another. `va_end` then simply deinitializes the process. It must be called before the function returns. After va_end you can, if you wish, start over with va_start to reference the arguments again.

In the **sumargs.c** program in LISTING 6-20 the sumvar function is called twice, each time with a different number of arguments. The number of undeclared arguments is specified by the first argument. Each time sumvar is called, its first argument must be the number of remaining arguments. This number will be passed to the num parameter. Notice the use of ellipses in both the sumvar function declaration and the function definition. Also, the header file **stdarg.h** is included at the top of the file. **stdarg.h** contains the definitions of va_list, va_start, va_arg, and va_end.

LISTING 6-20:

sumargs.c

```c
#include <stdio.h>
#include <stdarg.h>

int sumvar (int, ...);

int main(void)
        {
        int res;

        res = sumvar(4, 10, 20, 30, 40);

        res = sumvar(2, 6, 4);
        return 0;
        }

int sumvar (int count, ...)
      {
      va_list parnums;        /*pointer to undeclared args*/
      int i, total = 0;

      va_start(parnums, count);     /*set pointer to args*/

      for(i = 0; i < count; i++)
            {
            total = total + va_arg(parnums, int);
            }

      va_end(parnums);        /*end referencing of args*/
      return total;
      }
```

The sumvar example assumes that the variables passed to a function are all of one type. printf is able to take variables of different types through a clever manipulation of a character string. printf and its varying parameters are examined in Chapter 11.

Macros: define with Arguments

A define symbol can be used to represent not only constants, but also expressions and even whole statements. However, the define command does not actually recognize statements or expressions. It only performs a substitution on text, whatever it may be. In the **mult.c** program in

LISTING 6-21, the define symbol `MULT` is replaced by an arithmetic expression. The define symbol `GREETING` is replaced by a `printf` function call.

LISTING 6-21:

mult.c
```
#include <stdio.h>
#define   RATE   0.10
#define   GREETING   printf("Hello\n")
#define   MULT   (4 * 5)

int main(void)
      {
      int res;

      GREETING;
      res = MULT;
      printf("Rate is %f, Res = %d\n", RATE, res);
      return 0;
      }
```

The preprocessor will generate the following code based on the **mult.c** program in LISTING 6-21. This is what the compiler actually receives:

```
int main(void)
         {
         int res;

         printf("Hello\n");
         res = (4 * 5);
         printf("Rate is %f, Res = %d\n", 0.10, res);
         }
```

It makes sense to give the `MULT` symbol arguments so that it could generate the symbols for multiplication operands other than 4 and 5. The define command has this capability. However, the term "arguments" is misleading. A define symbol with arguments looks similar to the code for a function definition. It is not. It is really a text substitution operation. The define symbol will expand to replacement text specified in its define command. In this sense, a define symbol with arguments can best be described as a macro. The next example defines the `mult` macro using arguments x and y.

```
#define mult(x,y)   x * y
```

A define symbol with arguments is usually written in lowercase. It is important that there be no spaces between the symbol name and the arguments. The name must be right next to the opening parenthesis for the arguments. Figure 6-16 illustrates the syntax for the define command with arguments.

The define symbol has arguments that appear to form a parameter list. However, the x and y in the parameter positions (x, y) are not parameter variables. They can be thought of more as substitution markers. This is strictly a word-processing-like operation. Whatever text is in the x position will be substituted for all the x positions in the replacement text.

The arguments are only text substitution directives. Whatever text is found in the argument position is mapped into the replacement text. The macro `mult` replaces the x and y positions in the replacement text with the text found in the respective x and y argument positions (5, 4). The text found in the x's position will be placed wherever the x occurs in the replacement text. The final constructed text is then sent to the compiler. The text does not necessarily have to make sense. Several examples follow that illustrate the literal substitution operation of macros.

```
mult(5,4)         is replaced by          5 * 4
mult(john,53)     is replaced by          john * 53
mult(7&0%,yl!)    is replaced by          7&0% * yl!
```

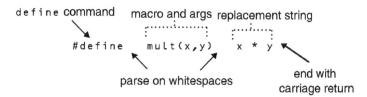

Figure 6-16: define macro with arguments.

In the **multmac.c** program in LISTING 6-22, the define macro, `mult`, will take the symbols in its parameter positions, 4 and 5, and replace them for every x and y in the replacement text. It is a simple text substitution.

LISTING 6-22:

multmac.c

```
#define mult(x,y)   x * y

int main(void)
        {
        int res;
        res = mult(4,5);
        return 0;
        }
```

After the preprocessor has executed, this is what the compiler will receive:

```
int main(void)
        {
        int res;
        res = 4 * 5;
        }
```

The use of the `mult` define symbol with arguments looks exactly like a function call. It is not, and should never be thought of as one. A macro should be thought of as another way of writing an expression, not a function. Just as the define command is used to define constants, a macro can be thought of as defining an expression. The `mult` macro expands to inline code, in this case, an arithmetic expression.

A macro has a performance advantage over a function in the same way that expressions have a performance advantage over functions. There are functions that can be written easily as expressions. Functions that can be written as single expressions could be replaced by a macro that will expand to an expression. In the next example, a greater-than comparison is defined with a macro.

```
#define   max(x,y)    ((x > y) ? x : y)
```

As with constants, a macro has the advantage of defining an expression only once and then using it many times throughout the program. If the expression ever needs to be changed, you only need to modify the define macro.

define Macro Errors

Once you start thinking of a macro as an expression, you realize that the same kinds of problems found in expressions are also found in macros. Like expressions, macros must deal with problems of associativity, precedence, and side effects. Precedence and associativity problems can occur when a macro is combined with other expressions, and when a macro's arguments are themselves expressions.

When a macro is combined with other expressions, precedence and associativity rules can cause unintended results. The mult macro, as it is written, is prone to such problems. In the following example, the division and multiplication operators associate from left to right. The division is performed first, instead of multiplication.

```
     21 / mult(4,5)      is     21 / 4* 5
                                (21/4) * 5
```

Precedence and associativity can always be overcome by using parentheses. That is the solution here. A define macro should always have a set of parentheses placed at the beginning and end of its replacement text. In the next example, the replacement text of the mult macro now includes enclosing parentheses.

```
#define mult(x,y) (x * y)
```

```
     21 / mult(4,5)      is     21 / (4 * 5)
```

Another problem occurs when the replacement text in a macro's argument is an expression itself. In that case precedence and associativity problems can arise within the macro's expression. In the next example, the $4 + 2$ in the macro argument is clearly intended to be executed before the multiplication by 5. However, the substitution gives us one expression, $4 + 2 * 5$, in which multiplication takes precedence. This expression first multiplies $2 * 5$ and then adds 4 to the result.

```
     mult(4+2,5)        is     4 +  2 * 5
                                4 + (2 * 5)
```

Again, the solution is parentheses, but this time the parentheses are placed around the argument symbols in the replacement text. Now the substitution includes parentheses that preclude any precedence problems. The $4 + 2$ argument is enclosed in its own parentheses and so is executed first, before the multiplication.

```
#define mult(x,y)  ( (x) * (y))
```

```
        mult(4+2,5)              is      ((4 +  2) * 5)
```

Another serious problem can occur if you use an increment as a macro argument. A macro whose argument is an increment may generate an expression with multiple increments on the same variable. Multiple increment operations on the same variable are to be avoided in expressions. In the next example, the user defines the `square` macro, then multiplies a value by itself. The user then makes the mistake of using an increment of `i` as a macro argument.

```
#define square(x)   x * x
```

```
        square(i++)              is      i++ * i++
```

If the `square` macro is thought of as a function call, the `square` macro looks as if it is incrementing `i` only once. In fact, it generates an expression in which `i` is incremented twice.

Program Examples

In this section, there are examples of functions using return values, parameters, and pointers. The first example shows how a function's return value can be used. The second example focuses on parameters. The same program is written first with call-by-value operations and then with call-by-reference operations.

Example: Functions and Return Values

The **price.c** program in LISTING 6-23 asks the user to enter a cost. It then determines the price and calculates a profit. It is written with four functions: `main`, `calc`, `user_input`, and user_response. The return values of those functions pass information back to `main`. The function `user_input` allows the user to input the cost. The prompt and `scanf` are placed in this function. In `main`, the return value of `user_input` is assigned to `cost`. The function `calc` allows the user to input the wholesale price. In `main`, the return value of `calc` is assigned to `price`. In the `main` function, the entire process is placed within a loop, which then asks the user whether or not to continue. If the user says no, then the loop ceases.

LISTING 6-23:

price.c

```
/* RETURN VALUES */

#include <stdio.h>
#define MARGIN  0.05

double calc(void);
double user_input(void);
int user_response(void);

int main(void)
        {
        double price, cost, profit;
        int response = 'y';

        while (response != 'n')
                {
                cost = user_input();
                price = calc();
                profit = price - cost;
                printf("Profit = %.2f\n", profit);
                while (getchar() != '\n');
                response = user_response();
                }
        return 0;
        }

double user_input(void)
        {
        double  user_cost;

        printf("\nPlease enter cost: ");
        scanf ("%lf", &user_cost);
        return (user_cost);
        }

double calc(void)
        {
        double w_price, calc_price;

        printf("\nPlease enter wholesale price: ");
        scanf ("%lf", &w_price);
        calc_price = w_price + (w_price * MARGIN);
        return (calc_price);
        }

  int user_response(void)
        {
        int res;

        printf ("\nDo you wish to continue ? ");
        res = getchar();
        return (res);
        }
```

Example: Functions and Parameters

The **pricearg.c** program in LISTING 6-24 is written with five functions: `main`, `calc_price`, `calc_profit`, `input_cost`, and `input_wholesale`. The return values of those functions are used to pass information back to `main`.

A.   The function `input_cost` allows the user to input the cost. The prompt and `scanf` are placed in this function. In `main`, the return value of `input_cost` is assigned to `cost`.

B.   The function `input_wholesale` allows the user to input the wholesale price. In `main`, the return value of `input_wholesale` is assigned to wholesale_price.

C.   The function `calc_price` has one parameter, `wholesale_price`. The price is calculated by price = (wholesale_price * MARGIN). In `main`, `calc_price` is called with the arguments `cost` and `wholesale_price`. In `main`, the return value of `calc_price` is assigned to price.

D.   The function `calc_profit` has two parameters: `cost` and `price`. The profit is calculated by `profit = (price - cost)`. In `main`, `calc_profit` is called with the arguments `cost` and `price`. In `main`, the return value of `calc_profit` is assigned to `profit`.

LISTING 6-24: PARAMETERS AND RETURN VALUES

pricearg.c

```c
#include <stdio.h>
#define MARGIN 0.05

/* Function Declarations */
double input_cost(void);
double input_wholesale(void);
double calc_price(double);
double calc_profit(double, double);

int main(void)
    {
    double price, cost, profit, wholesale_price;
    char response = 'y';

    while (response != 'n'){
        cost = input_cost();
        wholesale_price = input_wholesale();
        price = calc_price( wholesale_price );
        profit = calc_profit( cost, price );
        printf("Profit = %.2f\n", profit);
        printf("Do you wish to continue:");
        while (getchar() != '\n');
        response = getchar();
        }
    return 0;
    }

double input_cost(void)
    {
    double  user_cost;
    printf("\nPlease enter cost: ");
    scanf ("%lf", &user_cost);
    return (user_cost);
    }

double input_wholesale(void)
    {
    double  user_wholesale;
    printf("\nPlease enter wholesale price: ");
    scanf ("%lf", &user_wholesale);
    return (user_wholesale);
    }

double calc_price (double w_price)
    {
    double  calc_price;
    calc_price = w_price + (w_price * MARGIN);
    return (calc_price);
    }

double calc_profit (double cost, double price)
    {
    return (price - cost);
    }
```

In the **priceptr.c** program in LISTING 6-25, the **pricearg.c** program in LISTING 6-24 has been modified to use call-by-reference. Pointers are used instead of return values for all functions. The functions input_cost and input_price are combined into one function, user_input. user_input has two pointer parameters, costptr and wholesaleptr. In the user_input function, the parameters will become pointers. scanf will not need an ampersand. Why?

LISTING 6-25: PARAMETERS AND POINTERS

priceptr.c

```c
#include <stdio.h>
#define MARGIN 0.05

/* Function Declarations */
void user_input(double*, double* );
void calc_price( double, double* );
void calc_profit( double, double, double* );


int main(void)
        {
        double price, cost, profit, wholesale_price;
        int response = 'y';

        while (response != 'n'){
                user_input(&cost, &wholesale_price);
                calc_price(wholesale_price, &price);
                calc_profit(cost, price, &profit);
                printf("Profit = %.2f\n", profit);
                printf("Do you wish to continue:");
                response = getchar();
                }
        return 0;
        }

void user_input(double *costptr,double *wh_ptr)
        {
        printf("\nPlease enter cost: ");
        scanf ("%lf", costptr);
        printf("\nPlease enter wholesale price: ");
        scanf ("%lf", wh_ptr);
        while (getchar() !='\n');
        }

void calc_price (double w_price,double *priceptr )
        {
        *priceptr = w_price + (w_price * MARGIN);
        }

void calc_profit(double cost, double price,
            double *profitptr)
        {
        *profitptr = (price - cost);
        }
```

Chapter Summary: Functions

Functions in C perform a dual role. They operate as procedures, organizing a program, and they also operate as functions, defining new operations. A program progresses through function calls. The program always begins with a function named with the keyword `main`.

The definition of a function consists of a return type, a name, a parameter list, and a function block. In C, the parameter declarations are included in the parameter list. If a function returns no value or has no parameters, the void type is used for the return type or parameter list.

A function declaration conveys name and type information about the function. The type of a function consists of its return type and the types of its parameters. A function declaration includes the name of the function, its return type, and parameter types. In C, the function declaration is referred to as a prototype. Figure 6-17 shows the different components of a function declaration and definition.

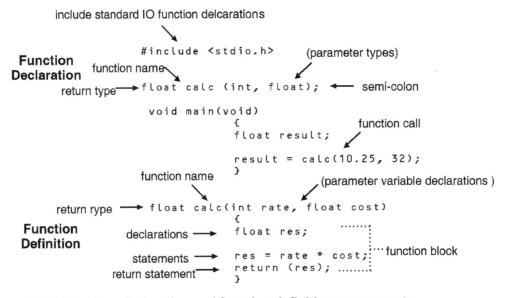

Figure 6-17: Function declaration and function definition components.

Information can be passed back and forth between functions using the return value and the function parameters. To ensure correct communication, function declarations must be used. Information is passed out of a function by using the `return` statement. The `return` statement is used to return a value. Care must be taken to ensure that the types of the `return` statement's expression and the function's return type match. If not, unintended conversions may result.

Information is passed into a function using arguments and parameters. This is a call-by-value operation, in which the arguments are expressions whose values are passed to parameter variables. Parameter variables only receive values from the calling function. Parameter variables themselves are locally declared variables known only to their own function.

Function calls can be thought of as user-defined expressions. The function name is the operator. The parameters are the operands, and the return value is the result of the expression. Function calls can be combined in other expressions, such as the assignment expression. The result of a function call can be assigned to a variable. Function calls can even be used as argument expressions in other function calls.

In the **square.c** program in LISTING 6-26 the value 7 is passed to the function `sqnum`. It is assigned to the parameter variable `snum`. `snum` is then squared. This value is returned in a `return` statement. This result of the function call is then assigned to res in `main`. A function declaration of `sqnum` placed before `main` informs `main` of the type of value it must send and receive from `sqnum`.

LISTING 6-26:

square.c

```
#include <stdio.h>

int sqnum(int);        /* Function Declaration */

int main(void)
        {
        int res;

        res = sqnum(7);    /* Function Call */
        return 0;
        }


int sqnum(int num)    /* Function Parameter */
        {
        return (num * num);   /* Return Statement */
        }
```

Pointers are used to simulate call-by-reference operations. In a call-by-reference operation, a variable in a calling function is referenced from within a called function. The address of a variable is passed to a parameter, which is a pointer variable. Indirection on the pointer references the variable whose address was passed.

You can also define pointers to functions. A pointer to a function holds the address of a function. The address of a function is obtained from a function name. Indirection on a pointer to a function will reference and execute the function at that address.

You can also define functions that have varying parameters. This requires a special set of macros that provide the addresses of varied arguments. You then need to use pointer operations to access these arguments.

The define macro appears similar to a function call. It is, however, simply an expression. You need to be careful that the expression generated by a define macro is arranged correctly.

Exercises

In this section there are three small exercises followed by one larger project. The larger project is based on the program examples in the preceding section.

1. Write a program consisting of two functions, `main` and `printname`. The function `printname` takes one parameter: the number of times the user wants to print out a name. To specify the name, simply

place your name in a `printf` function call. In `main`, the user is allowed to enter in the number of times that the name is to be printed. The user is also allowed to do it again.

2. Write a program consisting of two functions, `main` and `multable`. The `multable` function prints out a multiplication table. It takes two parameters: the first specifies the lower boundary of the table, and the second specifies the top boundary of the table. To print out a multiplication table starting from 25 and ending at 130, `multable` would be called with the parameters 25 and 130, `multable(25, 130);`.

      In the `main` function, the user will be allowed to enter the boundaries of the table. `multable` will then be called. The user should be allowed to enter in another set of boundaries.

3. Write a program with two functions, `square` and `min`. `square` will square a number, and `min` will return the minimum of two numbers. In the `main` function, the user enters two numbers. One is squared using the `square` function. Its squared value is then used in a function call to `min`. `min` takes two arguments: the squared number and the other number entered. It returns the minimum value. Print out the numbers, the result of `square`, and the result of `min`.

      Rewrite the program using only define macros for `square` and `min`.

4. Project for functions and parameters:

      Our company wants to calculate the price of a product based on its cost and the markup percentage. The markup percentage is determined by the product number. Write a program with four functions: `main`, `user_input`, markup, and `calc`.

The product number and cost are obtained by asking the user for them. Place the statements asking the user to input the cost and product number in a separate function called `user_input`. The two parameters for this function should be pointers. This is a call-by-reference situation.

      In a function called markup, use the product number to determine the markup percentage. Markup percentage is determined by the product number. There is a predetermined cutoff point of 10. Product numbers below 10 will have a markup percentage of 0.05. A product number above or equal to 10 will have a markup percentage of 0.10. Determine which particular markup percentage to use. Use symbolic constants for the two markup percentages and the cutoff (preprocessor define commands). The markup percentage and the cost are passed to the function `calc`, which will calculate the price. The `calc` function calculates the price by using the markup percentage and the cost. The formula is `price = (cost + (cost * markup_percent).`

      The whole process should be in a loop that will permit the user to decide whether or not to do it again. As each entry is processed, a total of all the prices should be kept. After the user quits, the total is printed out.

Structures

Members and Pointers

7. Structures

A structure consists of a set of data objects that can be referenced as one object. Such data objects are referred to as members of a structure. This chapter will focus exclusively on structures and their members. Structure type declarations, as well as pointers to structures, will be explored extensively. However, arrays of structures and structure member arrays will be covered in Chapter 12.

Structure Type Declarations

In C, the term structure declaration is used in two different ways. In one way, the term structure declaration refers to the declaration of a structure variable. This is like any other variable declaration. This sense of the term will be referred to as a structure variable declaration. In another way, the term structure declaration refers to the definition of a structure's type. This use of the term will be referred to as a structure type declaration. Technically, both are declarations. However, a structure type declaration defines a structure type, whereas a structure variable declaration declares a structure variable. Table 7-1 shows the various forms of structure type declarations and structure variable declarations.

The declaration of a structure's type consists of the keyword struct and a list of declarations contained within opening and a closing braces. The set of declarations defines the structure type. These declarations are referred to as the members of the structure. Shown here is a definition of a structure type consisting of two members, the variables `id` and `salary`.

```
struct {
        int id;
        float salary;
        }
```

The member declarations are only declarations. They are not definitions. No actual variables have been created. A declaration provides type and name information about a variable. It does not necessarily define the variable. The declaration of the structure type is itself only a declaration in that it, too, only defines a type of structure. No actual structure variables are defined.

The `struct` type is an incomplete type. It must be completed by the programmer, who must specify a list of members. You can declare many different kinds of structure types. Each defines a new type of structure. Structures with a different set of members are different types of structures. They have different structure type declarations. The two structures that follow are two different types of structures because they have different sets of members. One has as its member the integer `id`. The other has as its member the float cost.

```
struct {                          struct{
        int id;                           float cost;
        float salary;                     float salary;
        }                                         }
```

The list of declarations within a structure type describes the possible members of a structure variable. This declaration of a structure type with its list of declarations is often referred to as a template. It is a plan as to how a structure variable should be set up.

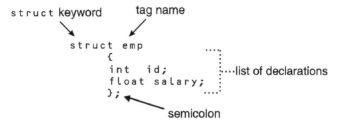

Figure 7-1: Structure type declaration using tag.

For reasons described in the next section, you will find it helpful to place a tag in a structure type declaration. A tag is a name you use to label a given structure type declaration. In the structure type declaration, the keyword `struct` may be followed with a tag placed before the opening brace of the declaration list. The tag may be any word you choose. It may also be the same word as that used for a variable. In Figure 7-1, the structure type declaration is specified with the tag name `emp`. The `emp` tag can then be used to reference this structure type declaration. You can then speak of a structure variable of type emp. Table 7-1 shows the syntax and use of a tag in structure type and variable declarations.

Structure Variable Declarations

A structure type declaration is the type used in a structure variable declaration. In the next example, a structure variable is declared using a structure type consisting of the members `id` and `salary`. The structure variable declaration will define a structure variable. Actual memory will be set aside for the structure variable. employee is a structure variable that consists of a set of two variables named `id` and `salary`. The definition of the structure variable defines its members. `id` and `salary` now exist as part of employee, as shown in Figure 7-2.

```
int count;
struct {
        int id;
        float salary;
        } employee;
int i, j;
```

Figure 7-2: employee structure variable.

If a structure type declaration includes a tag, the tag can be used in a structure variable declaration in place of the full structure type declaration. In the structure variable declaration, the tag can be thought of as a macro, inserting the structure type declaration wherever the tag is found. The programmer uses the tag in a structure variable declaration as part of the structure variable's type. In the declaration, the type is specified with the keyword struct, which specifies that this variable is a structure. It is followed by the user-given tag name, which, in effect, labels what kind of structure type is being used. Figure 7-3 show the syntax for a structure variable declaration using a tag.

Figure 7-3: Structure variable declaration using tag.

In the next example, the declaration of the structure variable employee is specified with the keyword struct and the tag emp. The variable declaration creates a variable that is of type struct. The type of structure is emp. This defines a structure variable named employee whose members will be two variables, id and salary.

```
struct emp{
            int   id;
            float salary;
            };

int main(void)

            {
            int count;
            struct emp employee;
            int i, j;

            }
```

Using the same tag, you can declare several structure variables of the same type. In the next example, two structure variables are declared, both of the same structure type, struct emp. Figure 7-4 displays the structure variables declared in this example.

```
struct   emp {
            int   id;
            float salary;
            };

int main(void)

            {
            struct emp  employee;
            struct emp  trainee;

            }
```

Figure 7-4: Multiple structure variables.

In a structure variable's declaration, you can initialize the structure variable by listing a set of values, each one corresponding to a member. The values are placed within braces and separated by commas. Taken together, these values constitute the value of the structure.

The value of the employee structure variable consists of the values of its members, `id` and `salary`. In the next example, values are assigned to the structure variable employee using the initialization procedure. The value of `employee` consists of the integer 83 and the float 2000.00. This set of member values makes up the value of the structure variable employee.

```
typedef struct emp{
                    int id;
                    float salary;
                    } EMP;

EMP employee = { 83, 2000.00 };
```

Typedef and Structure Types

A `typedef` is used to allow the programmer to give another name to a type. In the next example, the `int` type has been given the name integer. Both `int` and `integer` can be used as the type in integer declarations. In fact, the word integer can be thought of as being replaced by the `int` type. The `typedef` makes the `name` integer just another name for int. Following is the syntax required when using a `typedef`..

```
typedef type  NAME;

typedef int integer;

integer id;    is really int id;
```

The type specified in the `typedef` is literally a type. It is not simply a word. Though a `typedef` may appear similar to a define command, it is not the same. A define command is merely a word-processing-like substitution of symbols, whereas a `typedef` is managed by the compiler itself. The type in a `typedef` must be a valid C type. The type may be a simple data type, as in the example just shown, or it may include type modifiers, such as the asterisk used in the pointer type. The `typedef`s shown here are all valid.

```
typedef char* CHARPTR;

typedef int FUNCINT();

CHARPTR ptr;                        char *ptr;

FUNCINT calc;                       int calc()
```

The `typedef` CHARPTR is a new name for a pointer to a char type. `ptr` is declared as a pointer to a char. The `typedef` for FUNCINT is a new name for the type for a function declaration. `calc` is declared as a function that returns an int. In the case of FUNCINT, the `typedef` name is placed where the variable name would occur in an actual declaration.

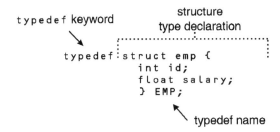

Figure 7-5: Typedef and structure type declaration.

Typedefs are used extensively with structure types. In Figure 7-5, a `typedef` operation gives the name EMP to the `struct` emp structure type. Notice how the structure type declaration is embedded within the `typedef`. When used for a structure type, a `typedef` name eliminates the need for a struct-tag format in a structure variable declaration. A structure variable can then be declared with the `typedef` name alone, instead of the keyword `struct` and tag name. Table 7-1 and the following example both show the use of a `typedef` in structure type declarations.

```
typedef struct {
            int id;
            float salary;
            }      EMP;

int main(void)
            {
            EMP employee;
            EMP trainee;

            }
```

The use of a `typedef` with a structure type declaration does not preclude the use of a tag. In the next example, the tag is used in the structure type definition. It is also used in a variable declaration. A `typedef` of a structure can also be performed using only the structure's tag. The next example contains two `typedef`s, one on the structure definition and the other on the structure tag. Both are valid. All the structure variables declared here have the same structure type.

```
typedef struct emp {
            int id;
            float salary;
            } EMP;

typedef struct emp EMPLOYEE;

int main(void)
        {
        EMP employee;
        EMPLOYEE trainee;
        struct emp newemp;

        }
```

Table 7-1: Structure Type Declarations: Tag and Typedef

Tag:

```
struct tag {
            data type   member name;
            };
```

Structure type declaration with tag:

```
struct emp {
            int id;
            float salary;
            };
```

Structure variable declaration with tag:

```
struct emp employee;
```

Typedef:

```
typedef struct tag {
            data type   member name;
            } typedef name;
```

Typedef with structure type declaration:

```
typedef  struct emp {
            int id;
            float salary;
            } EMP;
```

Typedef with structure tag:

```
typedef  struct tag  EMP;
```

Structure variable declaration with typedef name:

```
EMP employee;
```

Structure Variables and Structure Members

Structure variables are variables. To a great extent they function like other kinds of variables. The values of structure variables can be assigned to other structure variables. Their values can be passed in a function call to corresponding parameter structure variables. A structure's value can be returned by functions as a return value.

Each member of a structure can be referenced and used according to its declared type. Members can be variables, arrays, and even other structures. When the member of a structure is another structure, the structures are said to be nested, one within the other.

Structure Values

A structure variable has a value. This value is composed of all the respective values of its members. However, this entire value of a structure variable is not a single value that can be used in expressions, such as arithmetic expressions. For this reason, structure variables cannot be used as operands in any comparison or arithmetic expressions. For example, a structure variable cannot be tested for truth or falsity. Nor can it be added or multiplied. The only kind of expression in which a structure as a whole can be used is an assignment expression. You can assign the entire value of one structure variable to another structure variable of the same type.

Because structures have a value, C allows the use of a structure in an assignment operation. However, the right-hand side of the assignment operation must be a structure value. In LISTING 7-1, a structure variable is assigned the value of another structure variable. In this case, the structure value is obtained from the structure variable trainee. In later sections, it will be shown how a structure value can be the return value of a function call. Structure values are used mainly in assignment operations and function calls.

LISTING 7-1:

```
#include <stdio.h>

    typedef struct emp{
                                int id;
                                float salary;
                                } EMP;

    int main(void)
        {
        EMP trainee = {83, 2000.00};
        EMP employee;

        employee = trainee;

        return 0;
        }
```

Structure Members: The Member Operator

Members within a structure variable are referenced with the member operator. The member operator is a period, ., and is sometimes referred to as the dot operator. To reference a particular member, the name of the structure variable is placed before the member operator, and the name of the member is placed after the member operator. In the next example, the salary member of the employee structure is referenced by the member operation employee.salary.

```
    employee.id              references     id
    employee.salary          references     salary

    employee.id = 7;
    printf ("%f", employee.salary);
```

In the **empmem.c** program in LISTING 7-2, values are assigned to members within the employee structure variable. The values in those members are then printed out. Each member is referenced using the member operator. Figure 7-6 illustrates the member operation.

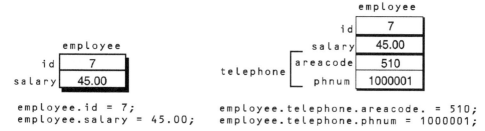

employee.id = 7;   employee.telephone.areacode. = 510;
employee.salary = 45.00;   employee.telephone.phnum = 1000001;

Figure 7-6: Member operation.

LISTING 7-2:

empmem.c

```
#include <stdio.h>

typedef struct emp{
                int id;
                float salary;
                } EMP;

int main(void)
     {
     EMP employee;

     employee.id = 7;
     employee.salary = 45.00;

     if (employee.id > 5)
            {
            printf("ID: %d\n", employee.id);
            printf("Salary: %.2f\n", employee.salary);
            }
     return 0;
     }
```

Nested Structures

A member of a structure can itself be another structure, in that case, one structure is nested within the other. However, the structure type declarations are not nested. Each structure type is independently declared and defined.

The member operator must be used for each nested structure. In the **emptel.c** program in LISTING 7-3, the PHONE structure type is the type of the telephone structure declared as a member of EMP. To access the areacode member of the telephone structure, two member operations are required. The first references the telephone member in the employee structure. The second member operation references the areacode member in the telephone structure. Figure 7-7 illustrates a nested structure.

There is no limit to this nesting. However, the structure types for each structure must be hierarchical. No structure can have as one of its members a structure of its own type. Nor can any of the nested structures have a member whose structure type is the same as one of structures within which it is nested. To do so would be like having a dog that forever chases its own tail.

It is valid, however, for a structure to have as one of its members a pointer to a structure of its own type. This is known as a self-referential structure and is used extensively to implement data structures. Self-referential structures are discussed in the chapter on data structures.

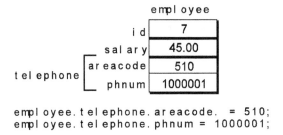

```
employee.telephone.areacode.  = 510;
employee.telephone.phnum = 1000001;
```

Figure 7-7: Nested structures.

LISTING 7-3:

emptel.c
```c
#include <stdio.h>

typedef struct phone{
                int areacode;
                long phnum;
                }  PHONE;

typedef struct emp{
                int id;
                float salary;
                struct phone telephone;
                }  EMP;

 int main(void)
      {
      EMP employee;

      employee.id = 7;
      employee.salary = 45.00;
      employee.telephone.phnum = 1000001;
      employee.telephone.areacode = 510;

      if (employee.telephone.areacode == 510)
            {
            printf("ID: %d\n", employee.id);
            printf("Salary: %.2f\n", employee.salary);
            printf("Phone:%ld\n",employee.telephone.phnum);
            }
      return 0;
      }
```

Pointers to Structure Variables

You can use pointers with structures in a variety of different ways. You can have pointers to structures, pointers as members of structures, pointers to structure members, or pointers to member pointers. All use the same indirection operation described in Chapter 5 to reference objects, though in the case of pointers used with structures you will often need to combine the indirection operation with a member operation. Table 7-2 lists the different ways you use pointers with structures.

You can define a pointer to a structure and use it to reference an entire structure variable. In the next example, numptr is declared as a pointer to an integer, whereas emptr is declared as a pointer to a structure of type EMP. Notice the use of the `typedef` in the declaration of emptr. You could just as easily use the struct-tag format as in `struct emp *emptr.`.

```
int *numptr;
EMP *emptr;
```

A pointer to a structure operates just like a pointer to any other kind of variable. Just as you can use a pointer to reference a variable, so also you can use a pointer to a structure to reference a structure. You can obtain the address of a structure variable with the address operation, and then assign that address to a pointer. An indirection on that pointer will then reference the structure variable.

In the **empref.c** program in LISTING 7-4, the address of the structure variable `employee` is obtained with the address operation. This address is then assigned to `emptr`. `emptr` is a pointer variable that points to a structure of type `EMP`. A pointer indirection on `emptr` will reference a structure variable of type `EMP`. Since `emptr` holds the address of the employee structure variable, the indirection operation on `emptr` references the employee structure (see Figure 7-8). The indirection on `emptr` takes place in an assignment operation. The values of the structure variable referenced by the indirection on emptr, in this case employee, are assigned to the trainee structure variable.

LISTING 7-4:

empref.c

```c
#include <stdio.h>

typedef struct emp{
                            int id;
                            float salary;
                            } EMP;

 int main(void)
      {
      EMP trainee;
      EMP employee;
      EMP *emptr;

      emptr = &employee;
      trainee = *emptr;

      return 0;
      }
```

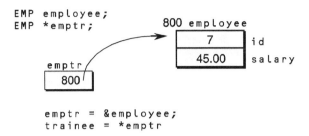

Figure 7-8: Pointer to structure.

Pointers to Structures and Members

Not only can you use a pointer to reference a structure, but you can also use a pointer to a structure to reference a member of that structure. Referencing a member with a pointer requires a combination of indirection and member operations. The pointer indirection on a pointer to a structure only references the structure variable itself. You then need to use a member operation to reference a member within the structure. In the next example, the pointer emptr points to the employee structure variable. Indirection and member operations reference the member variable salary. First indirection on emptr references the employee structure, and then the member operation references the salary member of the employee structure.

```
EMP employee;
EMP *emptr = &employee;

(*emptr).salary
```

Parentheses are placed around the pointer indirection operation on emptr. In the expression (*emptr).salary, the parentheses around the indirection operation on emptr, (*emptr), force the execution of the pointer indirection first. emptr is treated as a pointer variable. The pointer indirection, *, references a structure variable of type EMP. Having done this, the pointer indirection part of the expression is finished. The member operation to access the structure variable salary then commences.

If the parentheses are absent, the indirection operation will fail. The member operator, ., has a higher precedence than an indirection operator, *. *emptr.salary is really the expression *(emptr.salary). This expression first references a structure member, salary, followed by a pointer indirection that treats salary as a pointer variable *salary. emptr is treated as if it were a structure variable of type EMP, when in fact it is only a pointer variable. The operation fails.

The required parentheses make this operation awkward to program. It is easy to forget or misplace the parentheses. For this reason, there is an alternative way of writing this operation that is commonly used instead. This combined pointer indirection and member operation can be written using only the structure pointer operator, an arrow. This arrow is used in place of the parentheses, the asterisk, and the dot. The structure pointer operator is represented by a dash followed by a greater-than symbol, looking approximately like an arrow, ->. The structure pointer operator (->) substitutes for both the indirection operator, *, and the member operator, .. It replaces the format (*ptr).member with ptr->member. The two following indirection and member operations are equivalent.

```
(*emptr).salary
emptr->salary
```

In the **emparrow.c** program in LISTING 7-5, the members of `employee` are referenced through `emptr`. The combined indirection and member operation, as well as the structure pointer operation, is used to reference the members. Figure 7-9 illustrates these two methods.

LISTING 7-5:

emparrow.c

```c
#include <stdio.h>

typedef struct emp{
            int id;
            float salary;
            } EMP;

int main(void)
    {
    EMP employee;
    EMP *emptr;

    emptr = &employee;
    (*emptr).id = 7;

    emptr->id = 3;
    emptr->salary = 100.00;

    return 0;
    }
```

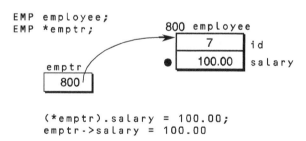

```
(*emptr).salary = 100.00;
emptr->salary = 100.00
```

Figure 7-9: Indirection and member operation.

Pointers to Structures and Pointer Members

A member of a structure can be any type of object, including a pointer. You can declare a pointer as a member of a structure. Performing pointer operations on such a member can lead to odd-looking combinations of the indirection and member operators, some of which are similar to the indirection and member operations performed on pointers to structures. Sometimes it may be difficult to tell when you are dealing with a pointer to structures or a pointer member of a structure. The situation becomes even more complex when you use a pointer to a structure to reference a pointer member in that structure.

In the next example, a new member has been added to the EMP structure, numptr. numptr is a pointer variable that points to an integer. This member is referenced with the member operation, just like any other member. Once referenced, numptr can be used like any other pointer variable. As shown here, an indirection operation can be performed on it.

```
typedef struct emp{
            int id;
            float salary;
            int * numptr;
            } EMP;

EMP employee;

*(employee.numptr)
```

Since the member operator has precedence over the indirection operator, the parentheses can be left out.

```
*employee.numptr
```

In the program **empnum.c** in LISTING 7-6, the member numptr is assigned the address of an integer variable. A combined member and indirection operation is then performed on numptr to reference that integer.

LISTING 7-6:

empnum.c

```
#include <stdio.h>

typedef struct emp {
            int id;
            float salary;
            int *numptr;
            } EMP;

 int main(void)
      {
      EMP employee;
      int mynum;

      employee.numptr = &mynum;
      *employee.numptr= 7;

      printf("Mynum= %d and %d\n",*employee.numptr,mynum);

      return 0;
      }
```

A pointer to a structure can also be used to reference a member that is a pointer itself. Remember that an indirection on a pointer to a structure, combined with a member operation, will reference members of a structure. This indirection operation on a pointer to a structure, when combined with the member operation, requires either the use of parentheses or the use of the structure pointer operator (->). In the next example, `emptr` is a pointer to a structure of type `EMP`. An indirection is first performed on `emptr`. Then a member operation references the `numptr` member. An indirection is then performed on `numptr`. Notice the nested parentheses. The inner parentheses force execution of the indirection operation on `emptr` first, referencing the employee structure. The outer parentheses then force execution of the member operation, referencing the `numptr` pointer. Then indirection takes place on `numptr`.

```
* ((*emptr).numptr)
```

If the structure pointer operator is used, then parentheses can be dispensed with altogether. The structure pointer operator (->) has higher precedence than the indirection operator. The structure pointer operator is evaluated first, in this case, referencing the `numptr` member variable.

```
*emptr->numptr
```

In the **empind.c** program in LISTING 7-7, a pointer to a structure is used to reference a member that is also a pointer. Assignment and indirection are performed on the pointer member using both parentheses and the structure pointer operator. Figure 7-10 illustrates indirection on a structure member. The structure has first been referenced by an indirection on a pointer to a structure.

LISTING 7-7:

empind.c

```c
#include <stdio.h>

typedef struct emp{
                    int id;
                    float salary;
                    int *numptr;
                    } EMP;

 int main(void)
        {
        EMP employee;
        EMP *emptr;
        int mynum;

        emptr = &employee;

        (*emptr).numptr = &mynum;
        *(*emptr).numptr= 24;

        emptr->numptr = &mynum;
        *emptr->numptr= 24;

        printf("Mynum=%d and %d\n",mynum,*emptr->numptr);

        return 0;
        }
```

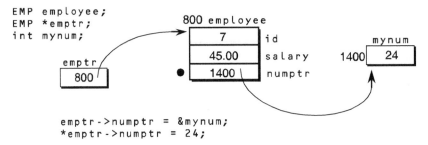

emptr->numptr = &mynum;
*emptr->numptr = 24;

Figure 7-10: Pointer to structure and member pointer.

Table 7-2: Structures and Pointers

`struct emp *emptr;` `EMP *emptr;`	Declaration of pointer to a structure
`&employee`	Address of structure
`*emptr`	Indirection on pointer to structure
`(*emptr).id` `emptr->id`	Indirection and member operation
`&employee.id`	Address of member of structure
`&emptr->id`	Address of member through pointer to structure
`*employee.numptr` `*emptr->numptr`	Member of structure as pointer.

Address Operation and Members

Just as a structure variable has its own address, members within a structure also have their own addresses. In the next example, the structure variable employee has the address 800. The `salary` variable in `employee` has the address 802. The address of employee and the address of the `id` within employee are the same. The structure variable and the first member in that structure will have the same address.

```
employee     800    id
             802    salary
```

You can use the address operation to obtain the address of any member variable within a structure. However, you first need to reference the member variable using the member operation. Once referenced, the member variable's address can be obtained through the address operation. In the next example, the member operation first references the `id` member of the employee structure, and then the address operation obtains the `id` member's address.

```
&(employee.id)
```

Because the member operator has a higher precedence than the address operator, you can leave the parentheses out. In the next example, the member operation is executed first, referencing the variable `id`. Then the address operation executes, obtaining the address of `id`.

```
&employee.id
```

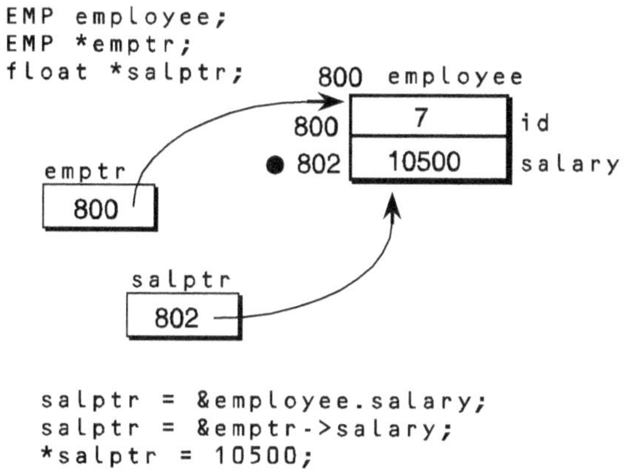

```
EMP employee;
EMP *emptr;
float *salptr;            800  employee
                   800  ┌─────────┐
                        │    7    │ id
            emptr  ● 802 │  10500  │ salary
          ┌─────┐       └─────────┘
          │ 800 │
          └─────┘
            salptr
          ┌─────┐
          │ 802 │
          └─────┘

salptr = &employee.salary;
salptr = &emptr->salary;
*salptr = 10500;
```

Figure 7-11: Address of Member.

The address resulting from the address operation in the previous example is an address of an integer, not a structure. In the **idref.c** program in LISTING 7-8, the result of the address operation on `employee.id` is assigned to the pointer variable `idptr`. `idptr` is a pointer to an integer.

```
&(*emptr).id
```

The address of a member variable within a structure can also be obtained using a pointer to that structure, instead of the structure variable's name. An indirection on such a pointer, followed by a member operation, references a member variable within that structure. Once that member variable is referenced, the address operation can obtain its address.

In the following example, `emptr` is a pointer to the structure variable employee. An indirection operation on `emptr` references the `employee` structure, and then a member operation references the `id` member in that structure. Once the `id` member has been referenced, its address can be taken.

The previous example can be written in a simple way using the structure pointer operator. Recall that the structure pointer operator represents a combined indirection and member operation. The address operation `&(*emptr).id` is equivalent to `&emptr->id`. As shown in the next example, the address operation on a member reference through a structure pointer can be very elegantly written using just the structure pointer operator and the address operator.

```
&emptr->id
```

LISTING 7-8:

idref.c
```c
#include <stdio.h>

typedef struct emp{
                    int id;
                    float salary;
                    } EMP;

 int main(void)
       {
       EMP employee;
       int *idptr;

       idptr = &employee.id;
       *idptr = 7;

       return 0;
       }
```

The program **memrefs.c** in LISTING 7-9 shows two uses of member addresses. First the address of the `salary` member is obtained and assigned to the `salptr` pointer variable. `salptr` is then used to directly change the value of the `salary` member. In the `scanf` function call, its argument is the address of the `id` member. Remember that `scanf` requires the address of a variable. In this case, the variable is the `id` member in the structure pointed to by `emptr`. The indirection and member operation references the `id` member. But `scanf` requires the address of that variable. The address operation is then applied to the member referenced by the indirection and member operation, as shown in Figure 7-11.

```c
       scanf("%d", &emptr->id);
```

LISTING 7-9:

memrefs.c
```c
#include <stdio.h>
typedef struct emp{
                    int id;
                    float salary;
                    } EMP;
 int main(void)
       {
       EMP employee;
       EMP *emptr;
       float *salptr;

       emptr = &employee;

       salptr = &(*emptr).salary;
       salptr = &emptr->salary;
       *salptr = 10500;

       printf("Please enter employee id: ");
       scanf("%d", &emptr->id);

       return 0;
       }
```

Functions and Structures: Return Values and Parameters

Functions treat structures just like any other variable. For instance, a function can return a structure value. A structure can also be a parameter variable, and you can use structure variables as arguments in function calls. In such a case, the structure's value will be passed into corresponding parameter structures.

You can use pointers to structures to implement a call-by-reference process for a structure. The address of a structure can be passed to a parameter that is pointer to a structure. Functions can even return addresses of structures.

Return Values and Structure Variables

A function can be defined to return the value of a specific structure type. The return type of such a function will be the type of that specific structure. In both the function definition and any function declarations, you would need to specify the structure type as the type of the return value. In the **empfill.c** program in LISTING 7-10, the function `fillrec` is defined to return a structure value of type `EMP`. The return type of the function declaration of `fillrec` is also a structure of type `EMP`.

In the **empfill.c** program, `emprec` is a locally declared structure variable in the `fillrec` function. Its members are assigned values. In the return statement, the values of the emprec variable become the return value of the `fillrec` function. This structure value is then assigned to the structure variable `employee` declared in main.

LISTING 7-10:

empfill.c
```c
#include <stdio.h>
typedef struct emp{
                        int id;
                        float salary;
                        } EMP;
EMP fillrec( void);

 int main(void)
        {
        EMP employee;

        employee = fillrec();

        return 0;
        }

EMP fillrec(void)
        {
        EMP emprec;
        emprec.id = 4;
        emprec.salary = 45.00;
        return emprec;

        }
```

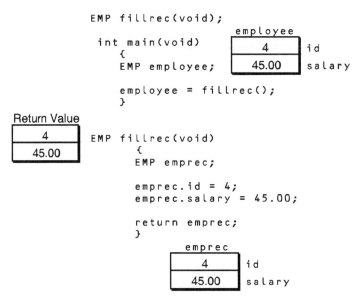

Figure 7-12: Function return value.

LISTING 7-11:

fillptr.c
```c
#include <stdio.h>
     typedef struct emp{
                    int id;
                    float salary;
                    } EMP;

    EMP *fillrec(void);
    EMP employee;

    int main(void)
          {
          EMP *emptr;

          emptr = fillrec();

          return 0;
          }

    EMP *fillrec(void)
          {
          EMP *empfptr;

          empfptr = &employee;
          empfptr->id = 4;
          return(empfptr);
          }
```

In the **empfill.c** program, memory must be set aside for three structures of type EMP. There are the two structure variables, employee and emprec. Then there is the return value of fillrec, which is also of type EMP (see Figure 7-12). If the structure has many members, such an operation can require a great deal of space. A lot of work must also be performed. All the values of the members in `emprec` must be copied to the return value of `fillrec`. Then all the values in the members of the return value structure must be copied to the employee structure.

In applications with large structures, it is advisable to return a pointer to a structure, instead of returning the value of a whole structure. For such a purpose, a function can be defined and declared to return a pointer to a structure. In the **fillptr.c** program in LISTING 7-11, `fillrec` returns a pointer to a structure variable of type EMP. The declaration of the fillrec function specifies that it returns a pointer to EMP, `EMP *fillrec`.

The **fillptr.c** program in LISTING 7-11 is somewhat contrived. Care must be taken to make sure that the address returned by a function is not an address of a locally declared structure variable. Locally declared variables exist only during the execution of the function. After execution of a function, a locally declared structure variable will cease to exist, and its address will no longer be valid. In the **fillptr.c** program, employee is declared once as an external variable and, as an external variable, will exist throughout the run of the program. In `fillrec`, pointers are used on employee in order to demonstrate how a function can return a pointer. Figure 7-13 shows the effect of returning a pointer to a structure.

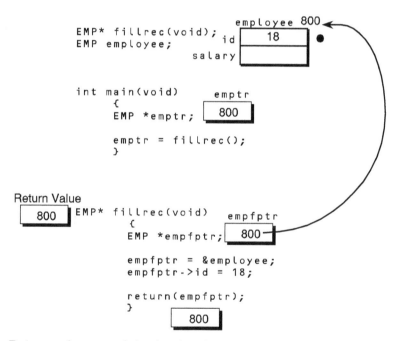

Figure 7-13: Return value as pointer to structure.

Parameters and Structure Variables

Structure variables can be passed to functions using either call-by-value or call-by-reference operations. Call-by-value and call-by-reference operate on structure variables in the same way they operate on other kinds of variables. In call-by-value, the structure's value is passed to a parameter that is a structure variable itself. In call-by-reference, the address of the structure variable is passed to a parameter that is a pointer to a structure.

Structure Variables and Call-by-Value

Structures are variables and can be declared as parameter variables in a function definition. When such a function is called, the corresponding argument can be a primary expression consisting of a single structure variable. The value of that structure variable is then passed to the parameter structure variable defined in the function.

LISTING 7-12:

printemp.c
```c
#include <stdio.h>
typedef struct emp{
                    int id;
                    float salary;
                    } EMP;
 void addrec (EMP);
 void printrec (EMP);

 int main(void)
      {
      EMP employee;
      employee.id = 8;
      employee.salary = 2000.00;
      printrec(employee);
      return 0;
      }

 void printrec (EMP emprec)
      {
      printf("\n\n Employee Record \n");
      printf("\n\t ID    :%d \n", emprec.id);
      printf("\n\t SALARY:%.2f \n\n", emprec.salary);
      }
```

A call-by-value operation is often used for tasks in which members of a structure variable need not be changed. In the **printemp.c** program in LISTING 7-12, the function `printrec` simply prints out the values in the members of a structure.

A call-by-value operation can be combined with a return value assignment to effect a change in the members of a structure in the calling function (see Figure 7-14). In the **empadd.c** program in LISTING 7-13, the values of the structure variable employee are passed to the parameter variable `emprec`. Both employee and `emprec` are structure variables of type `EMP`. At the time of the function call, the members of `emprec` will be given the corresponding values of the members of employee. Operations on the members of `emprec` will in no way affect those of employee. They are two separate structure variables.

In the function `addrec`, values of the structure variable `emprec` become the return value of the function. The function is defined as returning a value of type `EMP`. In main, this return value is then assigned to `employee`. This has the effect of assigning the member values of `emprec` to the members of employee.

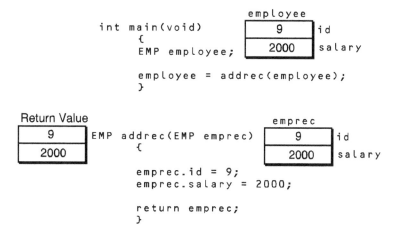

Figure 7-14: Structure parameters and return value.

LISTING 7-13:

empadd.c

```c
#include <stdio.h>
    typedef struct emp{
                int id;
                float salary;
                } EMP;
    EMP addrec(EMP);

    int main(void)
        {
        EMP employee;
        employee.id = 8;
        employee = addrec(employee);
        printf("%d",employee.id);
        return 0;
        }

    EMP addrec(EMP emprec)
        {
        emprec.id = 9;
        emprec.salary = 2000;
        return emprec;
        }
```

If you use this technique, bear in mind that it should only be used for small structures. Very large structures may overflow your stack, the memory reserved for your parameter variables. In LISTING 7-14, the **book.c** program uses call-by-value and return values to effect changes in a structure. Each function has its own locally declared structure variable of type BOOKREC. The return values of the input_rec and calc_price functions are then assigned to the structure variable book.

LISTING 7-14:

book.c
```
#include <stdio.h>
#define   YEAR  1980

typedef struct bookrec {   /* Book structure */
                        int   year;
                        float price;
                        } BOOKREC;

 BOOKREC input_rec(void);
 BOOKREC calc_price(BOOKREC);
 void output_rec(BOOKREC);

 int main(void)
      {
      BOOKREC book;

      book = input_rec();
      book = calc_price(book);
      output_rec(book);
      return 0;
      }

 BOOKREC input_rec(void)
      {
      BOOKREC book;
      printf("\nplease enter book price: ");
      scanf("%f", &book.price);
      printf("\nplease enter year published: ");
      scanf("%d", &book.year);
      return book;
      }

 BOOKREC calc_price( BOOKREC book)
      {
      if (book.year < YEAR)
            book.price *= 0.5;
      return book;
      }

 void output_rec(BOOKREC book)
      {
      printf("\n\n Book Record \n");
      printf("\n\t YEAR : %d \n", book.year);
      printf("\n\t PRICE: %f \n\n", book.price);
      }
```

Pointers to Structures and Call-by-Reference

In call-by-reference, a structure in one function can have its members changed in another function. Pointers to structures are used to simulate call-by-reference operations for structure variables. In such a call-by-reference operation, the parameter variable needs to be a pointer to a structure. The argument is the address of a structure variable. An indirection and member operation on the parameter structure pointer references members of the structure back in the calling function (see Figure 7-15).

In the **recref.c** program in LISTING 7-15, the address of the structure variable employee is passed to the structure pointer `emptr`. employee is declared as a structure variable of type EMP, and `emptr` is declared as a pointer to a structure of type `EMP`. An indirection and member operation is then performed on `emptr` to reference the `id` member of employee. The structure pointer operator is used to indicate the indirection and member operation. As a result of the call-by-reference operation, the `id` member of employee is changed to 5 by the assignment in `addrec`. Notice that `emptr->id` is the same as `(*emptr).id`.

LISTING 7-15:

recref.c

```
#include <stdio.h>

        typedef struct emp{
                        int id;
                        float salary;
                        } EMP;

        void addrec(EMP *);

        int main(void)
            {
            EMP employee;

            addrec(&employee);
            return 0;
            }

        void addrec(EMP *emptr)
            {
            emptr->id = 5;  /*same as (*emptr).id */
            }
```

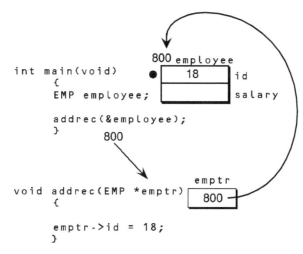

Figure 7-15 Call-by -reference and a pointer to a structure.

A structure is often used as a record whose fields are the structure's members. In this case, a function may be needed for entering data into the fields. Still other kinds of functions may be needed in which several fields of a record are used in some kind of calculation. The result may, in turn, be stored in another field within the record. Such tasks may best be dealt with using call-by-reference operations.

LISTING 7-16:

bookref.c

```c
#include <stdio.h>

#define  YEAR  1980

typedef  struct bookrec {      /* Book structure */
                    int  year;
                    float price;
                    } BOOKREC;

void input_rec(BOOKREC *);
void calc_price(BOOKREC *);
void output_rec(BOOKREC *);

int main(void)
      {
      BOOKREC book;

      input_rec(&book);
      calc_price(&book);
      output_rec(&book);
      return 0;
      }

void input_rec(BOOKREC *bookptr)
      {
      printf("\nPlease enter year published: ");
      scanf("%d", &bookptr->year);
      printf("\nPlease enter book price: ");
      scanf("%f", &bookptr->price);
      }

void calc_price(BOOKREC *bookptr)
      {
      if (bookptr->year < YEAR)
            bookptr->price *= 0.5;
      }

void output_rec(BOOKREC *bookptr)
      {
      printf("\n\n Book Record \n");
      printf("\n\t YEAR  : %d \n", bookptr->year);
      printf("\n\t PRICE:%.2f \n\n", bookptr->price);
      }
```

In LISTING 7-16, the **bookref.c** program is a rewritten **book.c** program using call-by-reference operations. There is only one structure variable, the book structure, declared in main. The book variable is used in call-by-reference operations to fill its fields and to perform a calculation on the price fields. A call-by-reference operation is also used to print the record out.

LISTING 7-17:

bookptr.c
```
#include <stdio.h>
#define  YEAR  1980
typedef  struct bookrec{        /* Book structure */
                        int year;
                        float price;
                        } BOOKREC;
void input_rec(BOOKREC *);
void output_rec(BOOKREC *);
BOOKREC* choose_book(BOOKREC*, BOOKREC*);

int main(void)
      {
      BOOKREC firstbook;
      BOOKREC secondbook;
      BOOKREC *bookptr;

      input_rec(&firstbook);
      input_rec(&secondbook);
      bookptr = choose_book(&firstbook, &secondbook);
      output_rec(bookptr);

      return 0;
      }

 void input_rec( BOOKREC *bookptr)
      {
      printf("\nPlease enter year published: ");
      scanf("%d", &bookptr->year);
      printf("\nPlease enter book price: ");
      scanf("%f", &bookptr->price);
      }

 BOOKREC* choose_book(BOOKREC *fbkptr, BOOKREC *sbkptr)
      {
      BOOKREC *bkptr;
      if (fbkptr->year > sbkptr->year)
            bkptr = fbkptr;
        else
            bkptr = sbkptr;
      return bkptr;
      }

 void output_rec(BOOKREC *bookptr)
      {
      printf("\n\n Book Record \n");
      printf("\n\t YEAR  :  %d \n", bookptr->year);
      printf("\n\t PRICE:%.2f \n\n", bookptr->price);
      }
```

In each function call, the address operation on book obtains its address. This address is then passed to a pointer variable that is a pointer to a structure. Structure pointer operators (->) then perform indirection and member operations to reference particular members in the book structure.

The **bookptr.c** program in LISTING 7-17 explores how a pointer to a structure could be used not only as a parameter, but also as a return value. **bookptr.c** is a modified version of **bookref.c**. In **bookptr.c**, the original program has been modified to receive information on two books and then print out the one most recently published. A new function called `choose_book` has two pointers as its parameters. It then chooses the most recently published book and returns a pointer to that structure.

Unions

A union is a single variable that can be referenced as different data types. The possible set of data types available for a union is declared in a union type declaration. The programmer may declare different types of unions. The type of a union defines the set of possible data types available to a union variable. Each type is declared with its own name. These declarations appear to be members, much like the members in a structure. However, while the declarations in a structure are all separate members, the declarations in a union only refer to different data types with which to interpret the one union variable. In this respect, unions are different from structures.

A union type declaration begins with the keyword union, followed by a tag and a block of declarations. Except for the keyword union, the type declaration is similar to a structure type declaration. A union variable is declared with the keyword union and the tag placed before the union variable's name. To reference the union variable as a specific type of object, the member operator is placed between the union variable's name and the name of the declaration with the type to be used. Again, this appears to be the same as the structure member operation.

LISTING 7-18:

totypes.c
```c
#include <stdio.h>
        union totype   {
                        int totint;
                        float totfl;
                        } ;

int main (void)
        {
        union totype mytotal;

        mytotal.totfl = 37.54;
        printf ("Total = %f \n", mytotal.totfl);

        mytotal.totint = 120;
        printf ("Total = %d \n", mytotal.totint);

        return 0;
        }
```

In the **totypes.c** program in LISTING 7-18, a union type is declared with the tag `totype`. A union variable is then declared with the name `mytotal`. At this point there is only one variable, `mytotal`. In the first statement, `mytotal` is used as an integer variable. In the second `statement`, `mytotal` is used as a floating-point variable. It is important to be consistent in one's use of a union variable. Suddenly referencing a union variable as a different type of object may lead to errors. In the two `printf` statements, the union variable is printed out as both a float and an integer. However, `mytotal` was last used as a float. The value it holds is a floating-point value and will remain one until `mytotal` is referenced as an integer and assigned an integer value. The actual number of bytes allocated for a union variable is the size of the largest type declared in its type declaration. The size of the `mytotal` union variable is the size of a float. However, as an integer, it will use only two of those bytes, the size of an integer.

Chapter Summary: Structures

A structure is an object that consists of different types of objects. There may be many different types of structures, each made up of a different set of objects. These objects are called members of the structure.

Table 7-4: Structures and Pointers

struct emp *emptr; EMP *emptr;	Declaration of pointer to a structure
&employee	Address of structure
*emptr	Indirection on pointer to structure
(*emptr).id emptr->id	Indirection and member operation
&employee.id	Address of member of structure
&emptr->id	Address of member through pointer to structure
*employee.numptr *emptr->numptr	Member of structure as pointer.

A structure type is defined by the programmer with a structure type declaration. A structure type declaration may include a tag with which to identify the structure type. The syntax for a structure type declaration is the keyword `struct` followed by both a tag name and a set of declarations within braces. A semicolon is placed after the closing brace. A structure type declaration can be given another name using a `typedef` operation. Usually the new name is written in uppercase. Table 7-3 shows the use of both tag and `typedef` in structure type declarations.

A structure variable is declared using the `typedef` name of a structure type declaration, or the keyword `struct` and the tag name. A structure variable has a value that consists of all the values of its members. This value can be assigned to other structure variables of the same type. A structure variable can also be returned by a function or passed to a function.

A member of a structure is referenced with the member operator. The left operand is usually a structure variable's name. The right operand is the name of the member to be referenced. A pointer to a structure variable can be used to access a member. Indirection on the pointer references the structure variable. Then the member operation works on that referenced structure. This combination of the indirection and member operations can be written using the structure pointer operator (`->`).

Pointers to structures are used to implement call-by-reference operations on structures. The address of a structure variable is passed to a pointer to a structure. The structure pointer operation (`->`)

then references members in that structure variable. Table 7-4 shows the various forms of pointer and structure operations.

If a member of a structure is a pointer itself, it can first be referenced by a member operation, and then an indirection can be performed on it. Using a pointer to a structure to reference a member is different from using a member operation to reference a member that is a pointer and then using that pointer to reference some other variable. You need to be aware of the differences between pointer operations on pointers to structures and pointers that are members of structures, pointer members.

Table 7-3: Structure Type Declarations: Tag and Typedef

Tag:

```
struct tag {
            data type   member name;
            };
```

Structure type declaration with tag:

```
struct emp {
            int id;
            float salary;
            };
```

Structure variable declaration with tag:

```
struct emp employee;
```

Typedef:

```
typedef struct tag {
            data type   member name;
            } typedef name;
```

Typedef with structure type declaration:

```
typedef  struct emp {
            int id;
            float salary;
            }  EMP;
```

Typedef with structure tag:

```
typedef  struct tag  EMP;
```

Structure variable declaration with typedef name:

```
EMP employee;
```

Exercises

1. Modify the following program, separating processes into different functions. Use the return value of those functions to pass whole structures back to the main function.

   1. Modify the program to use a function called `calc_sal`, which takes years as its parameter and returns a value to `employee.salary`.
   2. Place the prompts and user inputs in their own function, `input_rec`. Have those values assigned to a local structure variable of the same type as `employee` `(EMP)`. `calc_sal` should now be called within this new input function. Have the function itself return as its value a structure variable of type `EMP`. In main, have the return value of that function assigned to employee.
   3. Place the `printf` statements for printing out a record in their own function. Pass employee as an argument to the function. The function will have its own local parameter variable of type `EMP`. At the function call, the values of the employee record will be copied into the local parameter variable. Be careful to use function declarations.

2. Rewrite the program using call-by-reference. Pass the addresses of structure variables to parameters that are pointers to structures. In the `input_rec` function, the parameter structure variable will become a pointer. However, `scanf` will still need an ampersand when accessing a variable in the structure. Why?

```
typedef  struct emp { /* EMP structure */
            int  id;
            float salary;
            } EMP;

int main(void)
      {
      EMP employee;
      int years;

      printf("\nplease enter employee id: ");
      scanf("%d", &employee.id);
      printf("\nplease enter years experience: ");
      scanf("%d", &years);
      employee.salary = years * 10000.00;
      printf("\n\n Employee Record \n");
      printf("\n\t ID: %d \n", employee.id);
      printf("\n\t SALARY:%f\n\n", employee.salary);
      }
```

Storage Classes
and
Scope Rules

Internal Variables

External Variables: **extern**

Type Qualifiers: **const** and **volatile**

Inner and Outer Blocks

Source FIles and External Variables

8. Storage Classes and Scope Rules

Variables can be declared within a function or outside of any function. Variables declared within a function are referred to as local or internal variables. Variables declared outside of any function are referred to as global or external variables. Internal variables can be further scoped within blocks., and external variables can be scoped within source code files. Each has different scoping rules and storage features.

The C programming language has a set of storage classes that allow you to use variables in different ways. A variable can have automatic, register, static storage. An externally stored variable can be referenced with the `extern` declaration. automatic and register storage classes are restricted to use by internal variables. The static storage classes can be used for both internal and external variables, but has different effects on each. In addition, there are type qualifiers that restrict how a variable can be managed. First, each storage class will be discussed. Then the scoping rules for internal and external variables will be examined.

Storage Classes

A particular storage class is indicated in a variable declaration with a storage class specifier. A storage class specifier is placed before the variable type in the variable declaration. There are four storage class specifiers:

```
auto    static  register        extern
```

The first three storage specifiers actually affect storage. The last, `extern`, simply references an external variable. `auto` and `register` are storage specifiers for internal variables only. `static` is a storage specifier for both internal and external variables, but affects each differently. Here are examples of the use of the `auto`, `register`, and `static` storage specifiers in variable declarations.

```
auto float cost;
register char letter;
static int num;
```

The `extern` specifier is a special case. When an `extern` specifier is used in a variable declaration, no definition takes place. A variable declaration with the keyword `extern` is only a declaration, not a definition. The `extern` storage specifier only conveys name and type information about a variable. An example of the `extern` declaration follows.

```
extern double total;
```

Storage Classes for Internal Variables

The storage specifiers for internal variables are `auto`, `register`, and `static`. The default specifier is `auto`. This means that if you declare a variable without a storage specifier, then, by default the variable's storage specifier will be `auto`.

Automatic Storage: auto

The automatic storage class automatically re-defines a variable each time its function is called. In a sense, the variable is recreated with each function call. Automatic variables are placed on the stack. The stack is in a constant state of change as functions are called, executed, and then returned. When a function is called, a function uses storage on the stack. When the function is finished and returns, that storage is released for use by the next function called. Part of the storage that a function uses when it executes is set aside for its automatic variables. When the function is finished, the storage for these automatic variables is freed. Because `auto` is the default specifier, both **num** and `count` shown here have the same storage specifier, `auto`.

```
auto int num;
int count;
```

Register Storage: register

Register storage differs from automatic storage in that it allows a register to be appropriated for use as a variable. The declaration of a `register` precedes the variable type with the keyword `register`.

```
register int num;
```

Whether or not a register can actually be appropriated is system-dependent. Many systems have unused registers that can be used by applications. Many do not. The `register` specifier does not guarantee that a register will be used. It only tells the compiler to use a register if it is at all possible to do so.

A `register` variable is used for speed. Each time a variable is used in a program, its memory must first be referenced. Using a variable many times in a function will require a corresponding number of memory references. A register, however, will not require memory references. For this reason, use of a register may increase the overall performance speed of the program. In the **maxnums.c** program in LISTING 8-1, the integer `num` is used 600 times (3 times in each loop), whereas max is used far less. For this reason `num` is declared with the `register` storage specifier, whereas max has the usual `auto` specifier, by default.

LISTING 8-1:

maxnums.c

```
#include <stdio.h>

 int main(void)
        {
        register int num;      /* register declaration */
        int max = 200;     /* automatic declaration */

        for (num = 0; num < max; num++)
             printf ("%d\n", num);

        return 0;
        }
```

Since a register is not actually part of memory, it does not have an address. The address operation cannot be performed on a `register` variable. An address operation on the register `num` would be invalid.

In all other respects, registers operate like automatic variables. The register is released when a function is finished executing. Each time a function with a register is called, a new register is appropriated for use. If no register is available, then automatic storage is provided. In that case, the `register` specifier is ignored, and an automatic variable is created in its place. In LISTING 8-1, if there was no register available when the **maxnums.c** program was run, the register **num** would actually be an automatic variable.

Static Storage: static

The `static` storage specifier allocates static storage for a variable. The declaration of a static variable places the keyword `static` before the variable's type.

```
static int num;
```

Static storage is different from storage used by automatic variables. The storage for a static variable is allocated when the program is loaded, just before it runs. This originally allocated storage remains in place throughout the duration of the program. In subsequent function calls, a static variable will use its previously allocated storage. This has the effect of allowing a static variable to retain its value across function calls. Unlike automatic variables, a static variable is not re-defined with each function call. It is defined only once. In this sense, the same static variable is used in each function call.

LISTING 8-2:

statnum.c

```c
#include <stdio.h>

 void printstat(void);

 int main(void)
            {
            printstat();
            printstat();
            printstat();
            return 0;
            }

 void printstat(void)
            {
            int count = 1;
            static int num = 1;      /* static variable */

            printf("Count = %d,Num = %d\n",count,num);
            num++;
            }
```

Output for LISTING 8-2

```
Count = 1, Num = 1
Count = 1, Num = 2
Count = 1, Num = 3
```

The initializations of automatic and static variables have different overall effects. In the **statnum.c** program in LISTING 8-2, `count` is an automatic variable. Its memory is re-allocated with each function call to `printstat`. In this sense, `count` is defined with each function call. Included with the `count` declaration is an initialization. This initialization is performed with each definition. The function `printstat` is called three times. There are three definitions and initializations of `count`. In this sense, there is an initialization for `count` each time the function is called.

num, on the other hand, is a static variable. Its memory is allocated once. It is defined only once, and as such there is only one initialization. This initialization takes place when the function is called the first time. Unlike the case with `count`, there are no subsequent initializations of **num** in the later function calls.

Throughout the later function calls, **num** will retain its original definition. Its value will be retained across function calls. The increment of **num** will be working on this original variable. The first call to `printstat` will initialize num to 1, print it, and then increment it to 2. The second function call will print num and then simply increment it to 3. There will be no initializations after the first function call.

Storage Class for External Variables: extern

An external variable is a variable declared outside of any function. It has the same syntax as any other variable declaration, with the exception that it cannot have an `auto` or `register` storage specifier. An external variable is defined when the program is loaded and exists for the entire run of the program. External variables have the same role as global variables in other languages. Their relationship with other variables is determined by scope rules. In the next example, result and total are external variables. `count` is an internal automatic variable.

```
int result;
int total = 2;

int main(void)
            {
        int count;

            }
```

All external variables are initialized. They can be initialized with an explicit initialization, as in the case of total. If not explicitly initialized, they will be initialized by default to zero. In the previous example, result will be initialized to zero by default. The initialization takes place once, when the program is loaded. In this respect, external variables are similar to static variables. Though you shall see that external and static variables differ in terms of scope.

An external variable may be any type of variable. For example, an external structure variable declaration declares a structure variable known to all functions. More than one external structure variable of the same type can be declared by simply using the comma operator to attach more variable names. In the **extstruc.c** program in LISTING 8-3, two external structure variables have been declared, employee and `newemp`. In the case of external structure variables, a structure tag or `typedef` may be unnecessary, though it will not hurt.

LISTING 8-3:

extstruc.c

```
#include <stdio.h>

        struct {              /* external structure variables */
                int id;
                float salary;
                } employee, newemp;

 int main(void)
                {
                employee.id = 4;
                newemp.salary = 7.60;
                return 0;
                }
```

An external variable can be defined only once. But it can be declared many times using the `extern` keyword. A declaration is not necessarily the same as a definition. Usually when variables are declared, they are also defined. However, when a declaration of an external variable is preceded with the `extern` keyword, the declaration does not include a definition. It is only a declaration in a very restricted sense of the term. The `extern` declaration only conveys type and name information about the variable. The `extern` declaration simply states that there exists an external variable of a given type and name that has been defined somewhere in the program. In the next example, the `extern` declaration of result in main is only a declaration. It conveys type and name information about the external variable to main.

```
        int result;

        int main(void)
            {
            int count;
            extern int result;

            }
```

Since the `extern` declaration of result is only a declaration, and not a definition, there can be no initialization. The initialization can operate only on a variable's definition. The definition allocates storage. If there is no storage, there is nothing to initialize. The following initialization is invalid:
`extern int result = 1.`

Type Qualifiers: const and volatile

The type qualifiers restrict the way in which variables can be managed. The `const` qualifier effectively treats a variable as if it were a constant. It prevents any change of a variable's value after its initialization. Externally declared constant variables can function as symbolic constants. They are an alternative to the define symbols currently used. The `const` qualifier is also used in parameter declarations for parameter variables whose value should not be changed. In effect, this allows the value of a symbolic constant to be passed to a parameter and have the value still treated as a constant.

In the **rate.c** program in LISTING 8-4, rate is declared as an external constant variable and initialized with the value 0.10. `rate` is then externally referenced in main as an argument in the `calc` function call. Its value is passed to `myrate`, which is also a constant variable. Since `myrate` is declared with the `const` qualifier, its value cannot be changed.

LISTING 8-4:

rate.c

```
#include <stdio.h>

 float calc(float, const float);

 const float rate = 0.10;        /* external constant */

 int main(void)
              {
              float result, cost = 25.00;

              result = calc(cost, rate);
              return 0;
              }

 float calc(float mycost, const float myrate)
              {
              float myres;

              myres = mycost * myrate;
              return myres;
              }
```

The `volatile` type qualifier specifies that a declared variable is to be defined and referenced even if it is not explicitly used in program statements. The `volatile` type qualifier was designed to prevent a compiler's optimization capabilities from interfering with the definition and reference of declared variables. A compiler's optimizing strategies could prevent access to a variable's actual memory. For example, if a variable is not explicitly used in any statement in a program, the compiler may simply eliminate the variable. If a variable's value is used often, and the value is not explicitly changed, the compiler may simply place its value in an easily accessed register. A reference to the variable would access the register instead of the variable's memory. A problem occurs when a variable that is declared is accessed and changed by utilities outside the program. An operating system utility may change the variable through an interrupt of its own. For example, data communications utilities may store data in a variable without explicit program instructions. The `volatile` type qualifier guarantees that the variable will be defined as declared and its memory accessed whenever it is referenced.

```
        volatile int iodata;
```

The `volatile` type qualifier is useful when working with system interfaces or device drivers. Values may be assigned by the operating system to specific locations in memory. Such memory could be directly referenced by pointers in a program. The `volatile` type qualifier used for the data type in a pointer declaration ensures that if an indirection operation is coded in the program, the indirection will take place, accessing the memory the pointer references.

```
volatile int* ioptr;
```

Scope Rules

In C, variables are scoped in terms of three different structures. These three structures are functions, blocks, and source code files. The first of these, functions, defines the most familiar kind of scoping - external, as opposed to internal variables. The terms internal and external also go by the names local and global. The last structure, the source code file, is a new and often unfamiliar kind of scoping in which the physical file itself is considered a kind of scoping boundary.

Functions: External and Internal Variables

Internal variables are those variables declared and defined within a function. External variables are those variables declared and defined outside of a function. Automatic and `register` variables can only be declared as internal variables. Conversely, an external variable can be neither an automatic nor a `register` variable. Both external and internal variables can be static. However, an internal static variable has a different role than that of an external static variable.

Internal variables are scoped to the functions in which they are declared. They cannot be referenced outside of their functions. Automatic and `register` variables literally exist only during a given function's function call. A static variable declared within a function will exist across function calls, but cannot be referenced outside of their functions.

LISTING 8-5:

numscope.c

```
#include <stdio.h>

void calc(void);

int result;          /* external variable definition */

int main(void)
        {
        int count = 10;
        extern int result;    /* external declaration */

        result = count * 2;
        calc();
        return 0;
        }

void calc(void)
        {
        int num = 2;
        extern int result;    /* external declaration */

        result = num / 2;
        }
```

External variables, on the other hand, can be referenced by many different functions. Technically, a function can only use variables that have been declared within the function. It does not have to be defined, but it must be declared. The `extern` declaration is used to declare an external variable within a function. The `extern` declaration is only a declaration conveying type and name information about the external variable. It is a declaration within a function that references an external variable defined outside the function.

In the program **numscope.c** in LISTING 8-5, result is an external variable known to all functions. In each function, there is an `extern` declaration of result. `count` and **num** are internal variables. `count` is known only to main, and `num` is known only to `calc`.

The `extern` declaration of an external variable within a function is a default. It can be left out, and the compiler will assume the `extern` declaration. In the **resdeflt.c** program in LISTING 8-6, the `extern` declarations for result have been left out.

LISTING 8-6:

resdeflt.c

```c
#include <stdio.h>

void calc(void);
int result;        /* external definition of result */

int main(void)
        {
        int count = 10;

                        /* assumed extern declaration */
        result = count * 2;
        calc();
        return 0;
        }

void calc(void)
        {
        int num = 2;

                        /* assumed extern declaration */
        result = num / 2;
        }
```

An external and an internal variable can have the same name. If, within a function, an internal function variable has the same name as an external variable, the internal variable takes precedence. The name will reference the internal variable, not the external variable. In the **reslocal.c** program in LISTING 8-7, there are two variables with the name, result. One is an external variable, and the other is the internal variable declared in `calc`. The use of the name result in main will always reference its own internal variable. In this sense, the external variable result is excluded from the main function. In `calc`, result is declared as an `extern` referring to the external variable result. Any use of result within `calc` uses the external variable.

The placement of an external variable's declaration within the source code file will determine the default scope of that variable. In the previous program examples, the declaration of external variables was placed at the head of the file. Technically, an external variable is known to all functions following its definition. If an external variable declaration were placed in the middle of a source code file, only the functions following it would automatically be able to reference it. In the **resfuncs.c** program in LISTING 8-8, result is now declared after main. result cannot be automatically referenced within the main function.

LISTING 8-7:

reslocal.c
```
#include <stdio.h>

void calc(void);
int result;       /* external definition of result */

int main(void)
         {
         int count = 10;
         int result;           /* local declaration */

         result = count * 2;
         calc();
         return 0;
         }

void calc(void)
         {
         int num = 2;
         extern int result;     /* extern declaration */

         result = num / 2;
         }
```

LISTING 8-8:

resfuncs.c

```
#include <stdio.h>

void calc(void);

int main(void)
         {
         int count = 10;
         int myres;

         myres = count * 2;
         calc();
         return 0;
         }

int result;       /* external definition of result  */

void calc(void)
         {
         int num = 2;

         result = num / 2;
         }
```

Inner and Outer Blocks

A block is a compound statement with variable declarations. A compound statement is a statement that consists of other statements encased within braces. After the opening brace, variables may be declared. If variables are declared, the compound statement is considered to be a block. In fact, the body of a function is a block, a compound statement with variable declarations.

Since the block is a compound statement, it can be placed where any statement can be placed. You can even place a compound statement within another compound statement. The same is true of blocks. You can place a block within another block, creating nested blocks.

The variables declared within a block are internal to the block. They are known only within the block. Automatic variables within a block are redefined each time the block is entered. They exist only when the block is executed.

Though rarely used, blocks are useful for generating temporary variables. There may be cases in which a variable may only be needed for a simple task within the function and then could be discarded. This has the advantage of not having variables that are no longer needed hanging around.

LISTING 8-9:

iblock.c

```
#include <stdio.h>

int main(void)
        {
        int res = 0;

            {
            int i;     /* variable declared within a block */
            for (i = 0; i < 3; i++)
                    {
                    res +=  i;
                    }
            }
        return 0;
        }
```

In the **iblock.c** program in LISTING 8-9, the variable i has been declared within its own block. When the block is exited, the i variable disappears. This technique is useful when the name i is being used in different tasks. Figure 8-1 shows the different i variables and their values. In the **dualblck.c** program in LISTING 8-10, there are two different variables named i. Each loop has its own private i variable.

In both LISTINGs 8.9 and 8.10, the variable res can be used within each block. Variables declared in outer blocks are known and can be referenced within inner blocks. The one exception is when two variables have the same name. In this case, the inner variable takes precedence.

In **nestblck.c** program in LISTING 8-11, the compound statement of the for loop has become a block with the declaration of num. num is created each time the block is entered, which is each time the loop is executed. Within this block, the i used in the printf is the i declared in the next outer block. This is the same i used to control the for loop.

The i used in the for loop is the i declared in the first block within the function. It is not the i declared in the function block itself. The i declared in the function block is precluded by the i in the inner block.

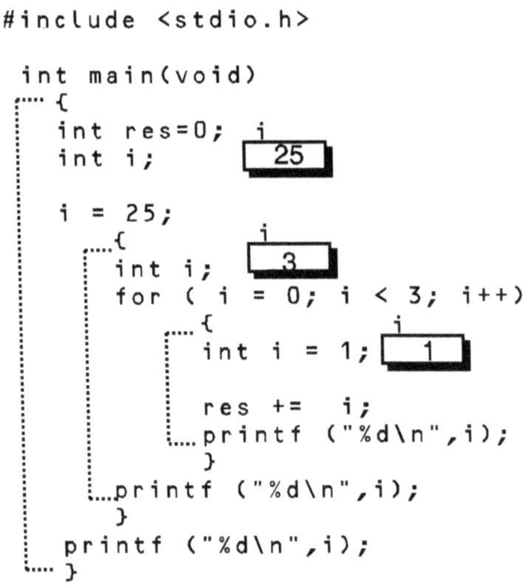

```
#include <stdio.h>

int main(void)
{
  int res=0;      i
  int i;         25

  i = 25;
    {           i
    int i;      3
    for ( i = 0; i < 3; i++)
      {           i
      int i = 1;  1

      res +=  i;
      printf ("%d\n",i);
      }
    printf ("%d\n",i);
    }
  printf ("%d\n",i);
}
```

Figure 8-1: Scope of blocks.

LISTING 8-10:

dualblck.c

```
#include <stdio.h>

int main(void)
        {
        int res = 0;

            {
            int i;
            for ( i = 0; i < 3; i++)
                {
                res +=  i;
                }
            }

            {
            int i = 0;
            while ( i < 5)
                {
                printf ("%d\n",i);
                i++;
                }
            }
        return 0;
        }
```

LISTING 8-11:

nestblck.c

```c
#include <stdio.h>

int main(void)
        {
        int res = 0;
        int i;          /* outer block declaration of i */

        i = 25;
            {
            int i;    /* inner block declaration of i */
            for ( i = 0; i < 3; i++)
                {
                int num = 1;

                res +=  i;
                printf ("%d %d\n", i, num);
                }
            printf ("%d\n",i);
            }
        printf ("%d\n",i);
        return 0;
        }
```

Output Values for LISTING 8-11:

```
inner i num
        0       1
        1       1
        2       1
        3
outer i
        25
```

Files and External Variables: extern and static

A C program can be separated into several different C source code files. Each file is separately and individually compiled. This has no effect on internal variables. But it does have an effect on external variables.

For an external variable to be known globally to all functions in a program, it must be declared in all source code files. However, as a variable, the external variable can only be defined once. Again, this problem is solved by the `extern` declaration. For an external variable to be known by functions in another source code file, that other file must contain an `extern` declaration of the variable. If the `extern` declaration is missing, the compiler will not know what the name refers to. Any use of the name will be classified as an unknown identifier.

In LISTING 8-12, the function `calc` has been placed in its own source code file. For `calc` to know what the name result refers to, result must be declared in the same file, **calcfile.c**. However, result can only be defined once. This is done in **main.c**. All other declarations of result can only be `extern` declarations. If another result were defined, the compiler would think that the programmer was attempting to give the same name to two variables.

LISTING 8-12:

main.c
```
void calc(void);
 int result;         /* definition of result variable */

 int main(void)
            {
            int count = 10;

            result = count * 2;
            calc();
            return 0;
            }
```

calcfile.c
```
extern int result;   /* extern declaration of result */

 void calc(void)
            {
            int num = 2;

            result = num / 2;
            }
```

LISTING 8-13:

main.c
```
 void calc(void);

 int result;

 int main(void)
            {
            int count = 10;

            result = count * 2;
            calc();
            return 0;
            }
```

calcfile.c
```
      extern int result;

      static int num;     /*static external declaration */

 void calc(void)
            {

            result = num / 2;
            }
```

    While the `extern` declaration extends the scope of an external variable across source code files, the `static` storage class will limit the scope of an external variable to its own source code file. A static external variable is known only to functions in its own source code file. In a sense, the `static` modifier makes the external variable internal to its file. A static external variable is not known to functions outside its file. In LISTING 8-13, `num` is an external variable known to all functions defined in **calcfile.c**. However, `num` is not known to functions in **main.c**.

    Static external variables are often used to protect data from accidental access by unrelated functions. In LISTING 8-14, the style program has been divided into two source code files. The variable style is a static external variable. It is known to all functions in the file **style.c**. But it is unknown to any functions in **main.c**. The external variable style is thereby protected from use by any other function defined outside of the **style.c** source file.

    A call to `setstyle` will set the style variable in **style.c** to a certain value. Subsequent function calls to `printintro` and `printexit` will print out the greeting or farewell in the appropriate style. Notice that style is defaulted to 1.

LISTING 8-14:

main.c

```
#include <stdio.h>

void setstyle(int);
void printintro(void);
void printexit(void);

int main(void)
         {
         int i;

         setstyle(2);

         for (i = 0; i < 3; i++)
             {
             if (i == 0)
             printintro();
             printf ("\nNumber %d\n", i);
             if (i == 2)
             printexit();
             }
         return 0;
         }
```

style.c

```
#include <stdio.h>

 static int style = 1;     /* static external variable */

 void setstyle(int mystyle)
            {
            style = mystyle;
            }

 void printintro(void)
            {
            switch (style)
                {
                case 1:
                printf("greetings");
                      break;
                case 2:
                printf("hello");
                      break;
                }
            }

 void printexit(void)
            {
            switch (style)
                {
                case 1:
                printf("farewell");
                      break;
                case 2:
                printf("goodbye");
                      break;
                }
            }
```

Output for LISTING 8-14:

```
            hello
            Number 0
            Number 1
            Number 2
            goodbye
```

It is also possible to declare a function as static. In this case the function is known only within its own source code file. The function can only be called by functions defined within that same source code file.

There are situations in which tasks, as well as data, need to be protected. In this case, functions that perform such tasks can be declared as static and thereby scoped within their source code file. No function outside the source file will be able to call these static functions. In LISTING 8-15, getstyle is an example of a static function. In **main.c**, setstyle is now called with no arguments. The style is received from the user in a call to getstyle from within setstyle. The way in which setstyle obtains its style is completely hidden from the rest of the program.

Figure 8-2 illustrates the scope of external , external static, and internal variables; as well as the scope of static functions. The variable result is an external variable known throughout the program. The variable style is an external static variable known only to functions in the **style.c** file. The variable i and `mystyle` are internal variables known only within their respective functions. In addition, the function `getstyle` is defined as `static`. It can be called only by functions defined within the **style.c** file.

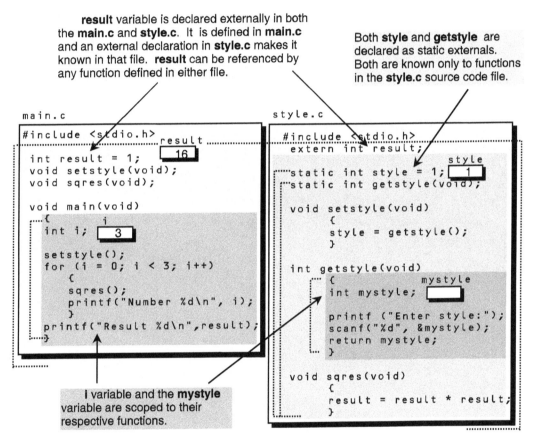

Figure 8-2: Scope of static external variables.

LISTING 8-15:

main.c

```
#include <stdio.h>

void setstyle(void);
void printintro(void);
void printexit(void);

int main(void)
          {
          int i;

          setstyle();

          for (i = 0; i < 3; i++)
               {
               if (i == 0)
               printintro();
               printf ("\nNumber %d\n", i);
               if (i == 2)
               printexit();
               }
          return 0;
          }
```

style.c

```
#include <stdio.h>

        static int style = 1; /* static external variable */

        static int getstyle(void);  /* static function */

 void setstyle(void)
                {
                style = getstyle();
                }

 static int getstyle(void)
                {
                int mystyle;
                printf ("Please enter style:");
                scanf("%d", &mystyle);
                return mystyle;
                }

 void printintro(void) {
                switch (style)
                        {
                        case 1:
                        printf("greetings");
                                break;
                        case 2:
                        printf("hello");
                                break;
                        }
                }

void printexit(void) {
                switch (style)
                        {
                        case 1:
                        printf("farewell");
                                break;
                        case 2:
                        printf("goodbye");
                                break;
                        }
                }
```

Output for LISTING 8-15:

```
        Please enter style: 1
        greetings
        Number 0

        Number 1

        Number 2
        farewell
```

Chapter Summary: Storage Classes and Scope Rules

There are four types of storage classes: `auto`, `register`, `static`, and external. Variables declared within functions are automatic by default. They are redefined each time the function is called. If a variable is declared as `static` within a function, it is defined and initialized once. A static variable exists across function calls.

External variables are declared external to any function. External variables can be referenced by default within any function following the external variable's definition. Usually the external variable's definition is placed at the head of a file, making it known by default to all functions in the file. You can declare an external variable within a function using the `extern` declaration. However, an `extern` declaration is a restricted declaration, providing only type and name information. It is not a definition.

Variables are scoped within functions, blocks, and source code files. Variables declared within a function are known only within that function. Variables declared within a block are known only within that block.

If an external variable is declared as `static`, it is known only to the functions defined within its source code file. Similarly, if a function is declared as `static`, it can only be called by functions within its source code file. This has the advantage of allowing you to hide data or operations from other functions in the program.

Exercises

1. Write a function that increments a variable 10,000 times. Write the function first using automatic variables and then using register variables.

2. Write a program which uses blocks to declare temporary variables used in loops.

3. Write a program in which a static variable is declared within a function.

9

Program Organization

Source Code Files, Header Files, and Make

Source, Object, and Executable Files

extern Declarations

Header Files

Make

Program Examples

9. Program Organization

C programs involve the use of many different kinds of files. A program itself is usually organized into separate source code files. Type information such as extern declarations and structure type declarations may be placed in header files and incorporated into the source files with preprocessor include commands. The C compiler will generate both corresponding object code files for the source code files and one executable file combining them all. The compilation of all the source code files can be controlled through a MAKE utility, which uses its own file called **makefile**. The program itself may create new data files. There are six kinds of files the programmer may be dealing with, many of which have their own extension: source code files (**.c**), object code files (**.o**), executable files (**a.out** or .exe), header files (**.h**), make files (**makefile**), and data files (any name). This chapter will cover all of these different kinds of files, except data files. Data files are handled in chapters 16 and 17.

Source, Object, and Executable Files

A C program can be organized into many different source code files. All of these source code files will have the **extension .c**. Distributing a program over several source code files provides organizational advantages. Functions can be categorized and a file set up for each category. Functions belonging to a category can then be placed in the same file. For example, in a database program, all the functions for searching records could be in one file and all the functions for adding records in another file. By convention, the main function is usually placed in a file by itself, sometimes called **main.c**.

LISTING 9-1 is a small example of a multiple file program. The main function is in its own file, and the calc function is in another file, **calc.c**.

LISTING 9-1:

main.c

```
float calc(int , int );

int main(void)
            {
            float res;

            res = calc(4,5);

            return 0;
            }
```

calc.c

```
float calc(int x, int y)
            {
            return (x * y);
            }
```

It is important to keep in mind that source code files are compiled separately. Each source code file will generate its own separate object code file. Object code files have the extension .o in Unix and Linux. For the program in LISTING 9-1, the compiler will generate object code for the **main.c** file and place it in a new file, **main.o**. The same will happen for the **calc.c** file. Its object code file will be

calc.o. There are now four files: **main.c**, **calc.c**, **main.o**, and **calc.o**. At this point the compiler has finished its work. It has generated the object code for the source code files. But there is still no runnable program. This is the job of the linker.

After the compilation of all source code files (**.c**), which creates the object files (**.o**), the object files are then used by the linker to generate a file of executable code. The linker copies all object code into the executable file and then links all external references. The function call of calc in **main.c** is linked to the function calc in **calc.c**.

Compiling and linking multiple file programs is as simple as listing the source code files which make up a program. In Unix, a program is compiled and linked by an invocation of the cc command. Multiple file programs are compiled simply by listing the source code files after the cc command.

```
cc  main.c  calc.c
```

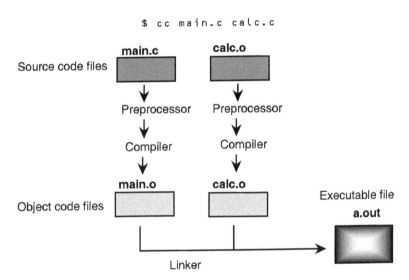

Figure 9-1: Compiling program with multiple source code files.

The default name for executable code is different depending upon the system and the compiler used. In Unix, the executable file will be given, by default, the name **a.out**. In MS WINDOWS, it will be given the name of the first source code file but with the extension .exe. Almost all compilers have an option to change the name of the executable file from the default to one chosen by the user. The option for this is 'o' and is indicated by a -o. You can then change the name of the executable file from the default name to one of your own choosing. To specify the name of an executable file to be **mycalc** instead of **a.out**, you place the -o option in the cc command, followed by this new name.

```
cc  main.c  calc.c  -o  calc
```

The command that you use to compile your program is actually a small management utility that contains three separate operations: preprocessing, compiling, and linking. In Unix, the cc is a small management utility that calls the preprocessor, the compiler, and then the linker. The preprocessor executes any preprocessing commands, performing any specified in-line substitution like replacing a symbolic constant with its equivalent value. The compiler actually generates the object code files from the source code files. And the linker combines the object code files into one executable file. If any one of these steps fails, the management utility will stop and issue error messages.

The cc management utility will check the extensions of all the files you invoke it with to see if they are source code or object code files. If cc is given an object code file, it will skip the preprocessor and compilation phases for that file. A new object code file will not be generated. The original object code file will then be used by the linker in the creation of a new executable file.

This has the advantage of allowing you to compile only those files in which you have made changes. If you made changes in **main.c**, but not in **calc.c**, then you would not have to compile **calc.c**. You could then specify **calc.o** instead of **calc.c** when you invoke cc. In the next example, **calc.o** will not be compiled, only linked, whereas **main.c** will be both compiled and linked.

```
cc    main.c calc.o
```

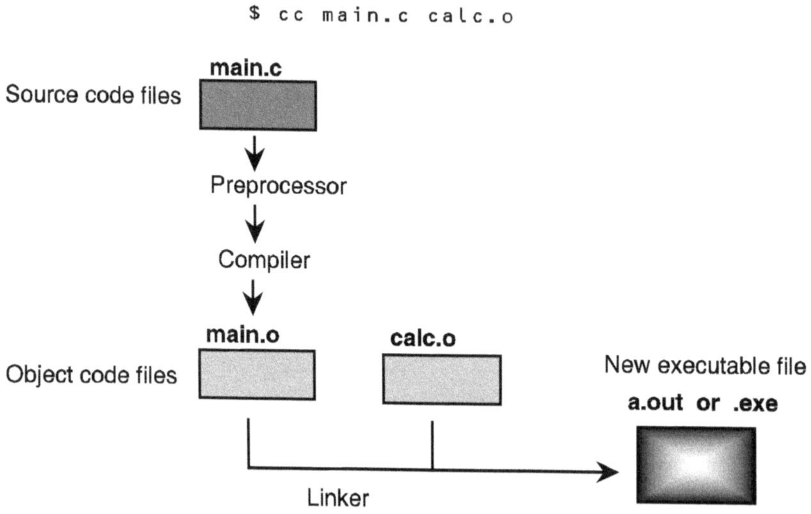

Figure 9-2: Compiling some source code files, but linking all object code files into a new executable file, cc main.c calc.o

extern Declarations: Functions, Variables, and Structures

The linker resolves all differences between the files. This means that it is very possible for all the source code files to individually compile correctly, while the overall linking process may fail. This gives rise to a different kind of error: the link error.

Since source code files are compiled separately, the compiler only knows what exists in that file. It has no idea what may exist in other source code files. In LISTING 9-2, the compiler will first compile **main.c**, and then **calc.c**. While it is compiling **main.c** it does not know that the calc function really exists. It believes that there is a calc function somewhere in another file, but it does not know for certain.

In LISTING 9-2, the source code files both compile accurately, but the linker fails. This is because the linker cannot find the calc function, which was referenced in **main.c**. In **calc.c** there is a mult function, but there is no calc function. The linker simply returns an error saying `calc` is undefined.

LISTING 9-2:

main.c

```
float calc(int, int);

int main(void)
        {
        float res;

        res = calc(4,5);
        return 0;
        }
```

calc.c

```
float mult(int x, int y)
        {
        return (x * y);
        }
```

When a function is used in one file and defined in another, function declarations become crucial. A function declaration will convey type information about the function to the source code file it is used in. A function declaration will inform the compiler what the return value of a function is supposed to be. Whenever you have a function call for a function that is defined in another file, you need to declare that function in your file. Recall that a function declaration only specifies the name and return type, as well as parameter types used in a function. It does not define the function.

Function declaration placed outside of any function are external declarations. External function declarations are known to all functions. You can precede such an external function declaration with the keyword extern. The extern keyword is a default. If it is left out, the compiler will assume it. Both examples shown here are valid declarations for the calc function.

```
        extern float calc(int, int);
        float calc(int, int);
```

In LISTING 9-3, the function declaration for calc is now placed in the **main.c** file. When main is compiled separately, the extern declaration of calc tells the compiler to expect a float value returned from calc. Everything is in sync.

The extern declaration is also used for external variables. Since each file is compiled separately, an extern declaration of an external variable must be placed in each file where that variable is used. Without the extern declaration, the compiler has no idea what the variable name refers to. Unlike normal variable declaration, the extern variable declaration does not define a variable. Like a function declaration, an extern declaration only specifies name and type of a variable, whereas a standard variable declaration defines the variable as well as declares the variable's name and type. The extern declaration is used only to convey to functions in a given source code file, the name and type information about a variable defined in another file. In LISTING 9-4, `calcres` is external to functions in both **calc.c** and **main.c**. External variables: scope.

LISTING 9-3:

main.c

```
extern float calc(int, int);

int main(void)
        {
        float res;

        res = calc(4,5);
        return 0;
        }
```

calc.c

```
float calc(int x, int y)
        {
        float calcres;
        calcres = (x * y) * 0.05;
        return (calcres);
        }
```

LISTING 9-4:

main.c

```
extern float calc(int, int);
extern float add(int, int);

extern float calcres;          /* extern declaration */

int main(void)
        {
        float res;

        res = calc(4,5);
        return 0;
        }
```

calc.c

```
float calcres;          /* external variable definition */

float calc(int x, int y)
        {
        calcres = (x * y) * 0.05;
        return (calcres);
        }

float add(int x, int y)
        {
        calcres = x + y;
        return (calcres);
        }
```

Though an external variable must be declared with an extern declaration in each file, it can only be defined once. `calcres` is declared in **main.c** but defined once in **calc.c**. However, an external variable may have both an extern declaration and a definition in the same file. The extern declaration is only a declaration specifying name and type information, not an object definition.

LISTING 9-5:

main.c

```
        struct emp {         /* structure type declaration */
                int id;
                float salary;
                } ;

        float calc(int, int);

        struct emp employee;   /* definition of external
                                  structure variable */

 int main(void)
                {

                employee.salary = calc(4,5);
                return 0;
                }
```

empcalc.c

```
        struct emp {         /* structure type declaration */
                int id;
                float salary;
                } ;

        extern struct emp employee;
                                /* extern declaration */
 float calc(int x, int y)
                {
                float calcres;

                calcres = (x * y) * employee.id;
                return (calcres);
                }
```

.External structure variable declarations have a special added requirement. When you use an external structure declaration, you need to also include that structure's type declaration. Structures have user-defined types specified in structure type declarations. When you use an extern structure declaration you need to spell out its specific structure type. Otherwise the functions in a given file have no idea what type of structure they are dealing with.

As with ordinary external variables, an external structure variable is defined only once. extern declarations of the structure variable can then be placed in each source code file. The structure type declaration must be included within each source code file that has the extern structure declaration.

In LISTING 9-5, the structure variable employee is declared as an external variable. In the **empcalc.c** file, employee is declared with an extern declaration. Even the extern declaration requires a structure type declaration. The structure type declaration for struct emp is repeated in both the **main.c** and **empcalc.c** files.

LISTING 9-6:

funcs.h

```
float calc(int, int);
float add(int, int);
extern float calcres;
```

main.c

```
#include "funcs.h"        /* include funcs.h file */

int main(void)
        {
        float res;

        res = calc(4,5);
        return 0;
        }
```

calc.c

```
        float calcres;     /* external variable definition */

        float calc(int x, int y)
            {
            calcres = (x * y) * 0.05;
            return (calcres);
            }

        float add(int x, int y)
            {
            calcres = x + y;
            return (calcres);
            }
```

Header Files: extern Declarations

Often extern declarations are used in many different files throughout the program. Instead of being retyped in each file, they can be placed in a header file and simply included. This makes maintenance of extern declarations very manageable. By convention, the extension of a header file is **.h**. To include the header file into your source code file, you need to enter in a preprocessor include command at the beginning of your source code file. The preprocessor include command is the same as that used for **stdio.h** in all previous program examples, with one exception. The file name is enclosed in double quotes, rather than less-then and greater-than signs, "funcs.h". The double quotes indicates that this file is to be found with your other source code files, not among the special compiler header files such as **stdio.h**. An example of such an include command follows.

```
        #include "funcs.h"
```

In LISTING 9-6, the function declarations and extern declaration are placed in the header file **funcs.h**. The preprocessor include command for **funcs.h** is placed in the **main.c** file. The preprocessor will include the contents of the **funcs.h** file in the **main.c** files before it is compiled.

LISTING 9-7:

types.h

```
typedef struct {
        int id;
        float salary;
        } EMP;

float empcalc(EMP*, int);
```

main.c

```
#include "types.h"

int main(void)
        {
        EMP employee;

        employee.id = 3000;
        employee.salary = empcalc(&employee,5);
        return 0;
        }
```

empcalc.c

```
#include "types.h"

    float empcalc(EMP *emptr, int num)
        {
        float calcres;

        calcres = num * emptr->id;
        return calcres;
        }
```

Header files are often used for structure type declarations. A structure's type is user defined. The compiler must be told what it is. Since each file is compiled separately, the structure type declaration must be provided in each source code file that uses structures of that type. A simple way to deal with this problem is to place the structure type declaration in a header file and place an include command for this header file in those source code files. First enter the structure type declaration into a **.h** file. Then include that .h file into the source code files using preprocessor include commands. **.h** files;

In the program in LISTING 9-7, the structure type declaration is placed in a file called **types.h**. The **types.h** file is then included into the many different files which make up the program. This means that the structure type is keyed in by the programmer in one place only, a **.h** file. Changes to it need be made only in one place, that **one .h** file. Figure 9-3 show the relationship between a header file and different source code files.

LISTING 9-8:

emp.h

```
typedef struct {
        int id;
        float salary;
        } EMP;
```

funcs.h

```
float salcalc(int, int);
```

main.c

```
#include <stdio.h>
#include "emp.h"
#include "funcs.h"

int main(void)
        {
        EMP employee;

        employee.id = 3000;
        employee.salary = salcalc(employee.id,5);
        printf ("%.2f", employee.salary);
        return 0;
        }
```

salcalc.c

```
float salcalc (int id, int num)
        {
        return (num * id);
        }
```

You can combine your extern declarations into one header file, or, if you wish, put them into separate header files, and include each into a file separately. LISTING 9-9 is a rewrite of LISTING 9-8 using two different header files, **emp.h** for the structure type declarations and **funcs.h** for the function declarations.

The salcalc functions is defined to take just integers. It does not operate on an emp structure as the empcalc function does in LISTING 9-7. Since the salcalc function is now more generalized, it makes sense to treat it separately from the emp structure type declaration. This is not the case for LISTING 9-8 where empcalc references the emp structure type. In such a situation where functions reference structures, you would want to keep those function declarations together with the structure type declarations in the same header file as in done in **types.h**.

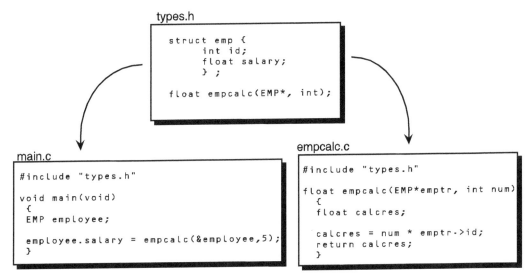

Figure 9-3: Header file and source code files with include command.

Program Example

In the example in LISTING 9-9, the program from LISTING 6-27 in Chapter 6 has been organized into two different source code files and one header file. The header file, **protos.h**, contains the function declarations (prototypes) and the define commands. **protos.h** is then included into the **main.c** source code file with the preprocessor include command. The source code files are organized to hold different categories of functions. The file **main.c** holds only the main function. The **input.c** file contains all the input function, and the **calc.c** file contains all the calculation functions.

LISTING 9-9:

protos.h

```
#define MARGIN 0.05
double input_cost(void);
double input_wholesale(void);
double calc_price(double);
double calc_profit(double, double);
```

calc.c
```
#include <stdio.h>
#include "protos.h"
double calc_price ( double w_price )
      {
      double  calc_price;
      calc_price = w_price + (w_price * MARGIN);
      return (calc_price);
      }
double calc_profit(double cost, double price)
      {
      return (price - cost);
      }
```

input.c

```c
#include <stdio.h>

double input_cost(void)
        {
        double  user_cost;

        printf("\nPlease enter cost: ");
        scanf ("%lf", &user_cost);
        return (user_cost);
        }

double input_wholesale(void)
        {
        double  user_wholesale;

        printf("\nPlease enter wholesale price: ");
        scanf ("%lf", &user_wholesale);
        return (user_wholesale);
        }
```

main.c

```c
#include <stdio.h>
#include "protos.h"

int main(void)
        {
        double price, cost, profit, wholesale_price;
        char response = 'y';

        while (response != 'n')
                {
                cost = input_cost();
                wholesale_price = input_wholesale();
                price = calc_price( wholesale_price );
                profit = calc_profit( cost,price);
                printf("Profit = %.2lf\n", profit);
                printf("Do you wish to continue:");
                while (getchar() != '\n');
                response = getchar();
                }
        return 0;
        }
```

The MAKE Utility

You will often be working with a program that has many source code files. As you develop the program, making modifications, you will need to compile the program over and over again. However you need only compile those source code files in which you made changes. The linker then links the newly generated object code files with previously compiled object code files creating a new executable file. The fact that only a few of your source files are actually compiled, drastically cuts down on the work of the compiler. Each time you need a new executable program you do not need to recompile each source code file.

It can be difficult in large programs with many source code files to keep track of which files have been changed and need to be compiled, and which files need only to be linked. A utility called the Make utility will do this for you. Make was designed for a development environment in which different source code files in a program are constantly being modified. Make keeps track of which source files have been changed and which have not. It then recompiles only those that have been changed, linking them with the rest of the object code files to create a new executable file. Different features and options of the Make utility are described in Table 9-1.

Most C compilers will include a Make utility with which you can manage your programs. Though the actual implementation of Make may differ depending upon the compiler you use or the operating system you are working on, all use the same basic structure originally designed for the UNIX Make utility. Make was originally a UNIX utility that was later transported to other systems. The following examples of Make are based on the UNIX Make utility since the UNIX version remains a simple and easy to understand implementation of Make. In the next example, the user enters the command make on the command line to invoke the Make utility. Make then compiles those files that have recently been modified and creates a new executable file. Make displays each Unix command it executes, in this case, compiler commands to compile a program.

```
$ make
cc -c main.c
cc -c io.c
cc main.o io.o
$
```

If all the files in your program are up to date, then the Make utility only returns a messages telling you so.

```
$ make
'a.out' is up to date.
$
```

To understand how the Make utility works, you need to realize that it uses a source code file's time stamp to determine whether or not it should be compiled. Whenever a file is created, re-created, or modified in any way, a new time stamp is placed on it by your operating system. If you create a file at 1:00 that file is stamped with the time 1:00. If you then change the file at 6:00, the file is re-stamped with the time 6:00. When compiling a program, only those source code files that have been changed need to be recompiled. Since the change of any file changes the time stamp, the time stamp can be used to determine which files need to be compiled. In this way, Make knows which files need to be compiled and actually selects the files to be compiled for the programmer.

In the next example, the user manages a program consisting of two source code files: **main.c** and **io.c**. Both files have corresponding object code files: **main.o** and **io.o**. These are used to create an executable file called **a.out**. If either **main.c** or **io.c** have been modified since **a.out** was last created, then make will again compile the modified source code file, generating a new object code file and then create a new executable file. Shown here is a Unix listing of all files that specifies the time the file was last modified just before the name of the file at the end of the line. All files, except for **main.c**, have times earlier than the executable file **a.out**.

```
$ ls -l
total 56
-rwxr-xr-x  1 chris    48728 Nov  3 04:31 a.out
```

```
-rw-r--r--  1 chris      256 Nov  3 04:30 io.c
-rw-r--r--  1 chris     2080 Nov  3 04:30 io.o
-rw-r--r--  1 chris      136 Nov  3 05:05 main.c
-rw-r--r--  1 chris      604 Nov  3 04:30 main.o
-rw-r--r--  1 chris       66 Nov  3 03:00 types.h
```

The user then executes the make command. Make finds that **main.c** was changed more recently than **a.out**, so **main.c** is compiled creating a new **main.o** file. Both the new **main.o** and the old **io.o** file are then used to create a new **a.out** file. The following file listing shows that the times for **main.o** and **a.out** are now more recent than **main.c**.

```
$ make
cc -c main.c
cc main.o io.o
$ ls -l
total 56
-rwxr-xr-x  1 chris    48728 Nov  3 05:06 a.out
-rw-r--r--  1 chris      256 Nov  3 04:30 io.c
-rw-r--r--  1 chris     2080 Nov  3 04:30 io.o
-rw-r--r--  1 chris      136 Nov  3 05:00 main.c
-rw-r--r--  1 chris      604 Nov  3 05:05 main.o
-rw-r--r--  1 chris       66 Nov  3 03:00 types.h
$
```

Make does not automatically compile any source code file that has been changed. You need to first provide the Make utility with a coded set of instructions that tells Make how to determine what files are to be compiled. These instructions are often referred to as dependency lines and are placed in a file called **makefile**. Make will automatically read and execute the dependency lines that it finds in the **makefile**.

By default, Make will look for a file called **makefile** in your current working directory in your operating system. Each directory can have its own file called **makefile**. Suppose, however, that you needed to have more than one **makefile** in your current directory. Using the -f option, Make can read a file that contains dependency lines, but has a name other than "**makefile**". In the next example, the user reads dependency lines from a file called prog.mak. By convention, such files often have the extension **.mak**. However, this extension is not required. Other UNIX Make options are listed in Table 9-1, and are commonly found in Make utilities used on other systems.

```
$ make -f prog.mak
cc -c io.c
cc main.o io.o
$
```

Another Make option that you may find helpful as you learn Make, is the -n option. With this options, Make does not execute any actual commands. Instead it only displays those commands that would be executed by Make. In this way you can see how your Make instructions are operating, and if they are performing as you want them to. In the next example, the make command does not actually compile the program. It only displays the cc commands that Make would execute.

```
$ make -n
cc -c io.c
cc main.o io.o
```

The makefile: dependency Lines

The Make utility works on a file called **makefile** which consists of Make commands. Such Make commands are made up of dependency lines followed by operations to be executed. Let us first take a look at the concept of dependency as it is used in Make.

A dependency line specifies a dependency relationship between files. Make operates in terms of dependencies. A source code file is used to create an object code file which in turn is used to create a runnable program. The program can be said to be dependent on the object code file which in turn is dependent on the source code file. You need to specify the dependency relationship between a source code file and an object code file in a dependency line. In another dependency line you need to specify the dependency relationship between an executable file and all its object code files.

A dependency line can be thought of as a kind of conditional statement. The dependency relationship is its test condition. If an object code file depends on a source code file and the source code file has been recently modified, then the test condition is true and the file is then recompiled. However, the syntax for a dependency line is a bit more complex than a standard conditional statement. A dependency line consists of three components: a target file, a list of dependency files, and a command. If any of the dependency files have been modified more recently than the target file, then the command is executed. The target file and the dependent files are written on the same line, separated by a colon. You can either place the command on the same line, separated from the dependent files by a semicolon, or you can place the command on the next line preceded by a tab. You can list more than one command if you wish. When entered on the same line you separate Unix commands with semicolons. On separate lines, each command has to be preceded by a tab. The dependency line ends with a following empty line. In these examples the command is an invocation of the cc compiler, compiling a source code file or linking object code files. The syntax for a dependency line is as follows:

```
target file : dependent files ; command
empty line

target file : dependent files
tab    command
empty line
```

The following **makefile** lists the dependency lines for a C program consisting of two source code files: **main.c** and **io.c**. In such a two-file program there are really five files to manage. For each .c file there is a corresponding .o file. There is the executable file, **a.out**. You need to set up your **makefile** with dependency lines to manage all of these files, specifying dependencies for each. An object code file (**.o**) is dependent on a source code (**.c**) file. An executable file, **a.out**, is dependent on several object code files (**.o**). In this example, **a.out** is dependent on (made up of) the two object code files **main.o** and **io.o**. Each object code file is, in turn, dependent on their respective source code files; **main.o** on **main.c** , and **io.o** on **io.c** (see Figure 9-4).

In the **makefile**, three dependency lines are needed for the **a.out**, **main.o**, and **io.o** files respectively. The linking and compilation of the program are split up among the different dependency lines. The compiler command for the **a.out** target only links the two object code files, creating a new executable file. It invokes cc with only object code files (.o), causing only the linker to be invoked. The compiler commands for the **main.o** and **io.o** targets only compile, creating .o object files. The -c option used with cc means that no linking is done, only compilation, generating the object code file for this source code file.

makefile

```
a.out : main.o io.o
        cc main.o io.o

main.o : main.c
        cc -c main.c

io.o : io.c
        cc -c io.c
```

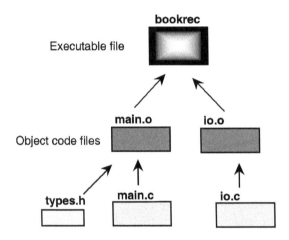

Source code files and header files

Figure 9-4: Dependency diagram. bookrec depends on both main.o **and** io.o. main.o **depends on both** main.c **and** types.h. io.o **depends only on** io.c.

The flow of control for a dependency line operates somewhat like a series of function or procedure calls. Control is transferred from one dependency line to another, each time checking the time stamps of files in the list of dependent files. The flow of control operates according to three basic rules applied to each dependency line.

1. Start checking the list of dependent files. Take the first dependent file and check to see if it is itself a target file in another dependency line. If it is, then suspend operation on the current dependency line and transfer control to that other dependency line. This operation is similar to a function call, where control is transferred from one part of the program to another. The target files form a left hand column on the left edge of the file.

2. When control has returned to the dependency line after another dependency line has finished, or if the dependent file is not itself a target file , then continue on to the next dependent file in the list of dependent files. Check, in turn, to see if this next dependent file is itself a target file in another dependency line. If so transfer control.

3. After all the dependent files have been processed, Make then checks if any of the time stamps for the dependent files is more recent than that of the target file. If so, the dependency line executes the compiler command. If not, the compiler command is not executed.

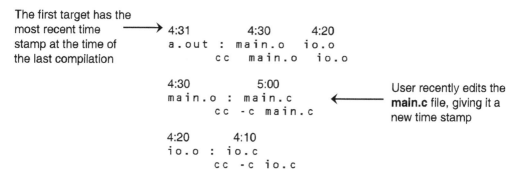

The first target has the most recent time stamp at the time of the last compilation →

```
4:31          4:30      4:20
a.out : main.o   io.o
          cc   main.o   io.o

4:30          5:00
main.o : main.c          ← User recently edits the
          cc -c main.c       main.c file, giving it a
                             new time stamp

4:20      4:10
io.o : io.c
          cc -c io.c
```

Figure 9-5 dependency lines with time stamps illustrated before executing the make utility and after changing the main.c **file.**

Figure 9-5 is an example of **makefile** dependency lines with time stamps added in. Suppose you modify **main.c**, saving it at 5:00. When you do so, your operating system gives **main.c** a new time stamp of 5:00. Then you execute the make command to update your program, incorporating the changes you just made. The Make utility reads the dependency lines in your **makefile**. Make then starts at the first dependency line which happens to have target file **a.out**. It then starts on the first dependent file in that line: **main.o**. Is **main.o** itself a target file in another dependency line? It is. Control is transferred to that line. Make then examines the first dependent file in the **main.o** dependency line. It is **main.c**. Is **main.c** itself a target file? It is not. This is the only dependent file for **main.o**. The next step is to check if the timestamp of any of the dependent files is more recent than the target file, **main.o**. There is only one dependent file, **main.c**, and its time stamp is more recent than that of **main.o**. The time stamp for **main.c** is 5:00 than the time stamp for **main.o** is 4:30. The compiler command for the **main.o** dependency line, is then executed. The compiler command is a cc command with a -c option to recompile **main.c**. The recompilation of **main.c** creates a new **main.o** file with a new time stamp. The time stamp of **main.o** is now 5:05. The dependency line ends and returns control to the dependency line it came from, **a.out**. Figure 9-6 points out the different time changes to files in the **main.o** and **a.out** dependency lines.

Once back at the **a.out** dependency line, Make continues down the list of dependent files. It finds **io.o**. It then asks if **io.o** is itself a target in another dependency line. It is. Control is transferred to that dependency line. In the **io.o** dependency line, Make examines files in the dependency list. The only dependent file is **io.c** which is not itself a target file. Nor is its timestamp more recent than the target file, **io.o**. So the compiler command for the **io.o** dependency line is not executed, and control returns to the dependency line it came from, **a.out**.

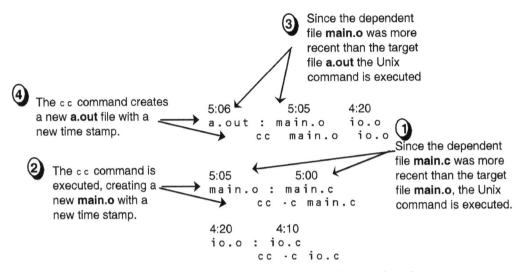

Figure 9-6: Make utility executing dependency lines and changing time stamps

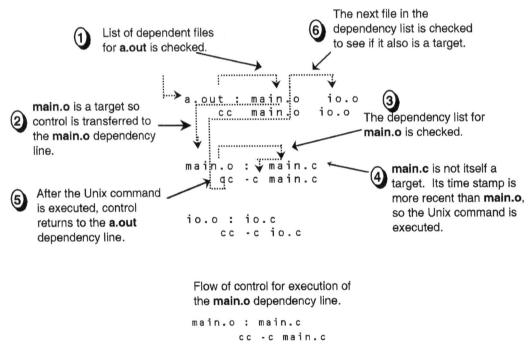

Figure 9-7: Makefile flow of control for lib.o **dependency lines.**

Again back at the **a.out** dependency line, Make has now finished processing a.out's list of dependent files. It then checks if there any dependent files whose timestamp is more recent than the timestamps of the target file. There is one. The time stamp for **main.o**, 5:05 is now more recent than the time stamp for **a.out**, 4:31. So the compiler command for the **a.out** dependency line is executed. The compiler command is a cc command that links the .o files into a new **a.out** file. Since only object code files are provided to the cc command, only linking is performed, not compiling. This operation will create a new **a.out** file with a new time stamp, in this case 5:06. Notice that 5:06 is more recent than all the other files in the dependency lines. Figure 9-7 illustrates the flow of control from one dependency line to another and back again.

Header Files

Dependency relationships can be set up between files of any type, not just source code and object code files. For example, you can set up a dependency relationship between an object code file and a header file. A header file is a text file that contains segments of source code that are inserted into your main source code files by your compiler. They become an actual part of the program. In this respect, an object code file may not only be dependent on a source code file, but also a particular header file.

In the next example, the **main.o** file depends on the both the **main.c** source code file and the **types.h** header file. Should you make changes to the **types.h** file, you would want to have Make generate a new **main.o** file. To do this, you need to place **types.h** as a dependent file in the **main.o** dependency line. If there are any changes to either **main.c** or to **types.h** header file, then **main.c** will be recompiled.

makefile

```
a.out : main.o io.o
        cc main.o io.o

main.o : main.c types.h
        cc -c main.c

io.o : io.c
        cc -c io.c
```

Implied Make Dependencies

The Make utility has a set of implied dependency relationships that it automatically applies to source code and object code files. Though these implied dependencies were originally defined for use in Unix, many have been carried over to other operating systems. In Unix, the source code file for any given programming language must contain a specific suffix. C source code files require .c suffixes. Fortran files require a .f suffix. .s is used for assembler source code files. Make will examine the source code file suffix of a corresponding object code file in a dependency list, and automatically invoke the appropriate compiler for that source code file. This means that, using implied dependencies, you can dispense with the dependency lines for compiling source code files. You can then reduce your **makefile** to one compiler command, the command to link files.

Exactly how Make implements implied dependencies is discussed later during the examination of suffix rules. Using such rules you will learn how to create your own implied dependencies. For now it is enough to know that you can drastically reduce the number of dependency lines in your **makefile** if you wish to do so.

In the next example, by relying on implied dependencies, the **makefile** for the `bookrecs` program only needs two dependency lines. When examining the dependency list for the `bookrecs` dependency line, Make will look for corresponding source code files in the current directory. It will find **main.c** and **io.c**. Since these files have a .c extension, the dependency line would recognize these as C source codes and would invoke the cc compiler if necessary. Suppose the user recently modified **io.c**. Then Make would know to compile **io.c** with the C compiler, `cc -c`.

makefile

```
bookrecs : main.o io.o
        cc main.o io.o -o bookrecs
```

```
$ ls *.c
main.c io.c
$ make
cc -c io.c
cc main.o io.o -o bookrecs
$
```

To denote the dependency of header files on an object code file, you need to add a dependency line but without a following compiler command. Make will locate the source code file and compile it to create the object code file. In the next **makefile** example, another dependency line is added for the **main.o** and **types.h** dependency.

makefile

```
bookrecs : main.o io.o
        cc main.o io.o -o bookrecs

main.o: types.h
```

Make Variables

You may often need to use a list of filenames in more than one place in a **makefile**. Instead of retyping the list in each dependency line in which you use it, you could assign the list to a variable and use the variable in its place. In your **makefile** you can define variables and assign values to them. You can then evaluate the variables in different dependency lines throughout the **makefile**. To evaluate a Make variable you first encase the variable name within parentheses, and then precede the parentheses with a dollar sign, $. For example, if you assign a variable a list of filename, then, when you evaluate that variable, the list of filenames that it holds will be substituted for the variable name.

In the next **makefile** example, a list of object code files is assigned to a variable called `OBJECTS`. In previous **makefile** examples, the `bookrecs` dependency line required that you enter in the list of object code files both in the list of dependent files and also in the cc command to link those files. In this **makefile**, you simply enter in an evaluation of the `OBJECTS` variable in both places., `$(OBJECTS)`.

makefile

```
OBJECTS = main.o io.o

bookrecs : $(OBJECTS)
        cc $(OBJECTS) -o bookrecs

main.o : main.c
        cc -c main.c

io.o : io.c
        cc -c io.c
```

The list of filenames assigned to a variable is really just a string. Just as you can assign filenames to a variable, you can also assign compiler options. The options are really just strings as far as the variable is concerned. Options are represented with a dash followed by a letter code and sometimes an argument. In the next make example the variable LINKFLAGS holds the linker option -o followed by a filename. This option allows you to specify another name for the executable file, in this case bookrecs.

makefile

```
OBJECTS = main.o io.o
LINKFLAGS = -g -o bookrecs

bookrecs : $(OBJECTS)
        cc $(LINKFLAGS) $(OBJECTS)

main.o : main.c
        cc -c main.c

io.o : io.c
        cc -c io.c
```

Suffix Rules

A suffix rule is a special dependency that specifies how files with different suffixes depend on each other. For example, the **main.c** file and the **main.o** file have same name but different suffixes: **.c** and **.o**. A suffix rule for files ending in **.c** and **.o** would show how a **main.o** file depends on a **main.c** file. In other words, how you would use a **main.c** file to create a **main.o** file.

Suffix rules provide generality to the dependency line. Instead of applying to one specific set of files, a suffix rule applies to whole categories of files. The categories are determines by the suffixes. For example, you can write a suffix rule that applies to all files ending in .o and those ending in **.c**. Because of this generality, suffix rules can drastically reduce the number of dependency lines you may need in your make file. This is particularly true of dependency lines are perform the same actions and differ only according to the name of the files specified. In previous **makefile** examples, the **main.o** and **io.o** dependency lines are identical in every respect except for the names of their files. Both perform the same action, specifying how a .o file depends on a .c file and how the cc command create the .o file. You can replace both of these dependency lines with one suffix rule that specifies the dependency of **.o** and **.c** files. Moreover, this suffix rule would apply to all files you may later add that end in **.c** and **.o**. You would not have to add any new dependency lines for them.

The target of a suffix rule consists of a sequence of two suffixes, each beginning with a period. The second suffix depends on the first suffix. The target for a suffix rule for **.c** and **.o** files, would consist of the suffix **.c** followed by **.o**: **.c.o**. A **.o** file depends on a **.c** file. The syntax for a suffix rule follows.

```
.suf1.suf2:
        command
```

The suffix rule has no list of dependent files following the colon. In a sense, the dependent files are those specified by the first suffix in the target, and the target file is the one specified by the second suffix. In the case of a **.c** and b dependency, if you change a **.c** file and then execute Make, the .c.o suffix rule would be activated and its compiler command executed. The .c.o suffix rule will be activated for each .c file that has been recently changed. Each time you activate the rule, in the compiler command you need to be able to reference the particular .c file you are dealing with at the time. When the .c.o suffix rule is invoked for say the **main.c** file, you need to be able to reference the **main.c** file in the compiler command. The $< special variable evaluates to the name of the current dependent file that is causing the suffix rule to activate. For example, if you change your **main.c** file, then, in the .c.o suffix rule, $< will be set to **main.c**. If you change several **.c** files, then $< will be set in turn to each one as the suffix rule is invoked for them.

You can now construct a suffice rule for the source code files and their object code files. The target consists of the suffixes .c.o and the compiler command consists of the cc -c command with the $< special variable.

```
.c.o:
        cc -c $<
```

In the next **makefile** example, the dependency lines for the **main.o** and **io.o** files are now replaced by the .c.o suffix rule. Should you have a program consisting of many source code files, you now only need one suffix rule to cover them all, instead of a dependency line for each one.

makefile

```
bookrecs : main.o io.o
        cc main.o io.o -o bookrecs

.c.o:
        cc -c $<


        $ make
        cc -c main.c
        cc -c io.c
        cc main.o io.o -o bookrecs
```

A makefile Example

Bringing together all these features, you can now create a powerful **makefile**. In the next **makefile** example, the user first defines variables to hold different lists of filenames and compiler options. The different variables are then used throughout the dependency lines.

A suffix rule follows for creating object code files from C source code files. The target for the object code files is `.c.o`. The `$<` variable holds the name of the C source code file that needs to be compiled. The out of date member's C source code file is compiled, creating a new object code file. The `$<` holds the name of the member's C source code file, such as **print.c**. You can, of course, do away with the suffix rule listed here, and rely on the standard suffix rules to determine how to update object code files.

The dependency lines follow beginning with the bookrecs dependency line. In this line, object code files form the list of dependent files. Its compiler command uses the cc compiler to create an executable program called bookrecs. The `$@` holds the name of the target, in this case, `bookrecs`. The CC variable is a built-in variable that holds the name of the compiler command, `cc`. The next two dependency lines lack any commands. They will rely on suffix rules to update their targets. If **types.h** is out of date, then its target, **main.o**, needs to be updated and will make use of the suffix rule for updating `.o` files.

makefile

```
CFILES = main.c input.c print.c
OBJECTS = main.o
CFLAGS = -g -O

.c.o:
        $(CC) $(CFLAGS) -c $<

bookrecs : $(OBJECTS) $(LIBS)
        $(CC) $(CFLAGS) $(OBJECTS) -o $@

main.o: types.h


        $ make
        cc -O -c main.c
        cc -g -O main.o iolib.a -o bookrecs
        $
```

Chapter Summary: Program Organization

A C program is usually organized into several different source code files. Each file is compiled separately, generating its own object code file. The linker then links these object code files into an executable file.

If a function is defined in one file and called in another file, the function must be declared in that file. Function declarations must be placed in each file in which the function is called. Similarly, if external variables are defined in one file and used in another, that variable must be declared with an extern declaration in that other file. In the same way, a structure type declaration must be placed in each file in which structures of that type are used or declared.

Table 9-1: The make Utility: managing programs

Make

The make utility manages programs, keeping track of what source code files have been changed and compiling only those files when creating a new executable file. Below is an example of make.

```
$ make
cc -c io.c
cc main.o io.o -o bookrecs
$
```

make updates programs by reading dependency lines from a file. These dependency lines instruct make on dependencies between files. You enter these files in a file called **makefile**. You can specify your own file with the -f option and the filename. Below is the syntax for a dependency line.

```
target file :  dependent files ; command
```

```
target file : dependent files
tab      compiler command
empty line
```

A dependency line without a dependency list will always execute its command.

```
target file :
tab      command
empty line
```

You can define variables in the **makefile** in the same way that you define shell variables. The evaluation is different. To evaluate a variable you need to encase it in parentheses first and then precede it with a $ sign.

```
variable-name = string
$(variable-name)
        CFILES = main.c io.c
        $(CFILES)
```

You define suffix rules using as a target two suffixes. The first is used to make the second. A suffix rule is applied if there is no dependency line with which to make a target. The $< special variable is used in suffix rule to hold the name of the out-of-date file. $* holds the name of the target without its suffix.

```
.c.o:
        cc -c $<
```

Options

-f *filename*	This option allows you to specify your own **makefile** that has the name filename. The default name is **makefile**.
	`$ make -f disp.mak`
-n	This option only displays the commands that make would currently execute. It does not actually execute the commands.
-t	This option by itself updates the time stamp of all the target files. No commands are executed.

Function declarations, extern variable declarations, and structure type declarations are usually placed in a header file. A header file has the extension .h. This header file is then inserted into each source code file with a preprocessor include command. This strategy allows the function declaration, extern variable declarations, and structure type declarations all to be placed in one file. Any changes need be made only once, in the header file.

You can use the Make utility to manage your different source code files. Make keeps track of source code files that have been changed. When invoked, Make compiles only those files that have been changed. The remaining files are linked using their current object code files.

Exercises

1. Take Exercise 1 from Chapter 6 and rewrite it using a different source code file. Add a new function that makes the CUTOFF a static variable in a source code file other than **main.c**. Set up an access function to allow the user to change the cutoff. Pass as its argument the new value for the cutoff.

2. Take Exercise 2 from Chapter 7 and rewrite it using a different source code file.
    A. Place the functions into four different source files: **main.c**, **input.c**, **output.c** and **io.c**. Be sure to use extern function declarations. Place the typedef statement, EMP, in its own file, **types.h**. Include this file with the include statement into each source file that needs it.

    B. Implement a menu for the program in which the user is given the options to input a record, print a record, or quit. Place the menu in a loop. Use the user_input function in the **io.c** file. In main, have the return value of that function assigned to response. Be sure to include **io.c** in your link.

Part 2

Arrays
and
Pointers

Arrays and Pointers

Offset Expressions, Increments, and Indexes

Part 2: Arrays and Pointers

10. Arrays and Pointers

An array is a collection of objects, all of the same data type. Any one data type can be used in an array. You can declare an array of integers, an array of characters, an array of structures, and even an array of pointers. Though an array may contain objects, an array is not an object itself. The declaration of an array reserves memory, which is then managed by pointers. Array objects themselves are actually referenced through pointer indirections. In this respect, there is a special relationship between arrays and pointers. That relationship will be carefully explored throughout this chapter.

There are the three pointer operations designed specifically to manage arrays. They are described in this text as the offset, increment, and index operations. The offset operation references an object in an array. The increment operation advances sequentially from one object to the next. The index operation provides the position of an object in an array.

An array object can also be referenced using array subscripts. An array subscript is a notation consists of a set of brackets and the index of an object. Array subscripts looks much like array references in other languages. It is often clearer and more elegant to use. An array subscript is equivalent to the pointer offset operation. It is, in fact, just another way of writing a pointer offset operation.

Array Declarations and Initializations

An array declaration consists of four parts: the object data type, the array name, the array data type, and the number of objects in the array. The array data type is represented with opening and closing brackets, `[]`. An integer value is placed within the brackets to specify the number of objects being declared. Figure 10-1 describes the different components of an array declaration. The declaration shown here declares an array of 5 integers. The array name is `mynums`.

```
int mynums[5];
```

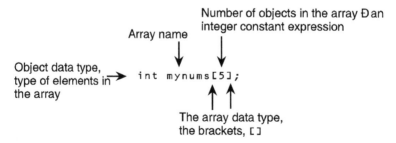

Figure 10-1: Array Declaration.

The number of objects in an array is determined by an integer constant expression. In the declarations that follow, the number of objects for `mynums` is determined by the constant 5. The number of objects in the array totals is determined by a constant arithmetic expression, 3 * 5.

```
int totals [3*5];

int main(void)
        {
        int nums [5];

        }
```

You can declare many different kinds of arrays, each having its own data type and number of objects. In the next example, the arrays mynums and name have the same number of objects, 5, but different types. mynums is an array of integers, and name is an array of characters. Though the arrays mynums and totals have the same type of objects, they have a different number of objects. mynums has 5 objects, and totals has 10 objects.

```
int mynums [5];
int totals [10];
char name[5];
```

You can think of the objects in an array as being numbered sequentially. The numbering begins with zero and ends with one less than the number of objects in the array. The array mynums is an array of 5 integers, each numbered sequentially from 0 to 4 (see Figure 10-2).

Figure 10-2: Array elements numbered from 0.

The array itself is identified by its array name. Each object in the array is referenced through the array name. The number of an object's place in the sequence, together with the array name, is used to reference the object.

Array Initialization

Recall that when you declare a variable you can also initialize it with a value. In the declaration char mychar='E', the variable mychar is initialized with the character value 'E'. In much the same way, when you declare an array, you can also initialize its elements. You list the initialization values within a set of braces and separate them sequentially by commas. The first value will be assigned to the first element, the second value to the second element, and so on. In the next example, the mynums array is declared as an array of five integer objects, each initialized by a value in the initialization list. The first object is assigned the first value in the initialization list, in this case 3. The second object is assigned the second value, 4, and so on.

```
int mynums[5] = { 3,4,5,6,7 };
```

You can even use the initialization part of the array declaration to specify the actual number of objects in the array. To do so, you simply leave out the number that you would usually place within the brackets to specify the number of objects in the array, leaving you with a set of empty brackets followed by a list of initialization values. The number of objects in the array will then be determined by the number of values in the initialization list. In the next example, the myletters array is declared as an array of three integers. Notice the empty brackets. The number of objects in the array is determined the number of values in the initialization list, in this case three.

```
int myletters[] = { C,D,E };
```

In the **arinit.c** program in LISTING 10-1, both the arrays letters and totals use this form of array declaration. myletters is declared as an array of three characters. The array declaration uses empty brackets and has three values in its initialization list. totals is declared as an array of four integers, having four values in its initialization list.

LISTING 10-1

arinit.c

```
#include <stdio.h>

int main(void)
        {
        char myletters[] = {'C','D','E'};
        int totals[] = {23, 8, 11, 31};

        putchar (myletters[1]);

        return 0;
        }
```

There are variations on array initialization which are unique to the type of arrays declared. Arrays of characters allow certain kinds of initialization using string constants, as do arrays of pointers to characters. Arrays of arrays and arrays of structures use nested lists of array values. Each variation will be presented when those types of arrays are discussed.

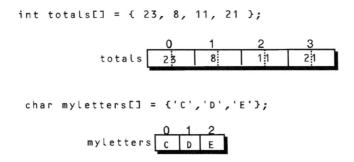

Figure 10-3: Array initialization using empty brackets.

Array References and Array Subscripts

Once you have declared an array, you can reference its objects, and then use those objects in expressions. To reference an array object, you need to specify its position in the array. As previously noted, objects in an array are arranged in sequence, starting from zero. In this sense, objects are numbered according to their position in that sequence. You can then use this numbering to reference individual objects in the array. You can reference an object in the third position using the number 2. The object in the second position is reference using the number 1. Remember that the numbering starts from 0, not 1, so that the first object is referenced using the number 0 (not 1). The number of an object's place in an array sequence is often referred to as either the object's index or subscript.

You reference an array object by using a combination of the array name together with the position of that object in the array. The actual reference can take two different forms: that of array subscripts or of a pointer offset operation (the pointer offset operation is discussed later in this chapter.) An array subscript is similar to the way in which arrays are referenced in other programming languages. With an array subscript, a particular object in an array is referenced with its array name and the number of the object's position in the array, which is placed within brackets. `mynums[2]` refers to the third object in the `mynums` array; `mynums[0]` refers to the first object. The numbering always begins with 0.

```
mynums[0]            /*first object */
mynums[2]            /*third object */
mynums[4]            /*fifth object */
```

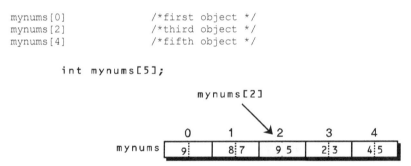

Figure 10-4: Referencing array elements.

Once you have referenced an object, you can use it as you would any other object of that type. An integer object can be used like any integer variable. You can think of a reference of an object in an array of integers, as a reference an integer variable. Just as variables can be assigned values, each object of an array can be assigned a value. You can use an array reference to an integer object in an arithmetic expression, just as you would use an integer variable. In the next example the fourth object in the `mynums` array is first assigned a value, and then used in an addition operation, assigning the result to the first object.

```
int mynums[5];

mynums[3] = 23

mynums[0] = ( 2 * mynums[3]);
```

The term element is often used to refer to an object in an array. In an array of integers, the integer objects making up the array are referred to as elements of the array. `mynums[2]` references the third element in the `mynums` array (see Figure 10-4). The term element can be misleading. An element is an object itself, not merely a piece of a larger construct. A reference of an element in an array of integers references an integer variable. In LISTING 10-2, each element of the `mynums` array is referenced and used in an assignment operation. Figure 10-4 shows the `mynums` array with its assigned values.

LISTING 10-2:

element.c

```
#include <stdio.h>

int main(void)
        {
        int mynums[5];

        mynums[0] = 9;
        mynums[1] = 87;
        mynums[2] = 95;
        mynums[3] = 23;
        mynums[4] = 45;

        return 0;
        }
```

Array Management and Loops

An array is only a collection of objects. It is not an object itself. This means that you cannot perform an operation on an array as a whole. Instead, you need to perform a separate operation on each individual element, dealing with them one by one. For example, to assign a set of values to an array, you need to reference and assign a value to each individual element of the array.

In this respect, an array initialization can appear misleading. The format of an array initialization looks like a single assignment operation as it is written. This may wrongly lead you to infer that the array is being treated as a whole   It is not. In fact, each element of the array is initialized its own value. For example, the array initialization shown in LISTING 10-3 may appear to be a single operation on the array `mynums`, but it is not. You should think of the array initialization:

```
int mynums[3]={12, 5, 27};
```

as if it were three separate assignment operations, one for each element of the 3 element `mynums` array:

```
mynums[0]= 12
mynums[1]= 5
mynums[2]= 27
```

Often you will have a task in which you need to reference all elements in an array, performing the same operation on each element. Simply printing out an array is an example of such a situation. Each element is referenced and printed out. You could write a print statement for each individual element, but it is far more practical to simply use a loop control structure such as a while or for. Inside the loop you would then need only one print statement, and each time through the loop the next element would be printed, progressing from one element to the next. The integer variable used to control the count of the loop would also be used to index and reference each array element in turn.

LISTING 10-3:

mynums.c

```c
#include <stdio.h>

int main(void)
        {
        int mynums[3]={12, 5, 27};
        int i;

        for (i = 0; i < 3; i++)
                {
                printf("%d \n", mynums[i]);
                }

        return 0;
        }
```

In the **mynums.c** program in LISTING 10-3, a for loop is used to print out all the values in an array. Within the loop each element is individually referenced and printed out. Since arrays are numbered from 0, care is taken to initialize the counting variable i to 0. The index of the last element of the letters array is 2. The loop must cut out after 2, before 3. For this reason, the test is (i<3). It could just as easily have been (i<=2).

A common rule of thumb is that the test for the end of an array consists of the less-than operator, <, tested against the number of objects declared in the array. If you declare an array to have 3 objects, then, in a loop, you will test against 3, (i<3). To ensure this fact, it is a common practice to define a symbolic constant that represents the number of elements in a given array. You could then use this same symbol in loop control structures as the cutoff in the loop's test. In the **maxnums.c** program in LISTING 10-4, the same symbolic constant, MAX, is used in both the array declaration and the test for the last array object in the for loop. Such a strategy has the distinct advantage of letting you easily change the size of an array. Just change the number specified for the symbolic constant.

LISTING 10-4:

maxnums.c

```c
#include <stdio.h>
#define MAX 3

int main(void)
        {
        int mynums[MAX]={12, 5, 27};
        int i;

        for (i = 0; i < MAX; i++)
                {
                printf("%d ", mynums[i]);
                }

        return 0;
        }
```

You can also use loops to perform operations such as copying one array to another. Copying an array requires that you individually reference the value of each element and assign it to an element in another array. The **copynums.c** program in LISTING 10-5 uses a for loop to copy the `mynums` array to the **newnums** array by individually copying each elements, one by one.

LISTING 10-5:

copynums.c

```
#include <stdio.h>
#define MAX 3

int main(void)
    {
    int mynums[MAX]={12, 5, 27};
    int newnums[MAX];
    int i;

    for (i = 0; i < MAX; i++)
        {
        newnums[i] = mynums[i];
        }

    return 0;
    }
```

Array References and Pointer Operations

An array subscript allows you to write a reference to an array element in much the same way as you would write a simple variable reference. A variable is reference by its name, and an array element is referenced by the array name and an index (an integer representing the position of the element in that array). You can use such array subscripts references in the same way as you would use any variable reference. The array subscript reference of an element only appears similar to that of a variable. In fact, an array subscript is merely a notation, hiding the true underlying operation taking place, a pointer operation. Arrays are actually managed entirely by pointers. What appears to be a simple variable-like array element reference, is actually a pointer operations using a pointer and indirection. To truly understand how arrays work in C, you need to know the pointer operations that actually manage them. There are three pointer operations used to manage arrays: the offset, increment, and index operations. Array subscript is actually translated into a pointer offset and indirection operation.

So far you have only examined how you can use pointers to reference a variable (as noted in Chapters 5, 6, and 7). You can reference a variable either with its name or with an indirection operation on a pointer that holds the address of that variable. Array elements are not themselves variables, and the pointer operations on arrays are not quite the same as those used on variables. To understand the differences, it is important to remember that the indirection operation does not require that pointer's address be the address of a variable. The indirection operation references the memory at any address as if it were a variable. An indirection operation on a pointer to an integer references memory as if it were reserved for an integer variable. Remember how the function malloc works with pointers. In the example discussed in Chapter 5, the function malloc set aside memory in the heap and returned its address. There was no variable declaration. The address was assigned to a pointer to an integer. Indirection on that pointer referenced that memory in the heap as if it were the memory of an integer variable. A variable requires a type, an address, and memory reserved at that address. The pointer provided the type and address. malloc provided the reserved memory.

A similar process takes place for arrays. An array declaration reserves memory. The array name used in the declaration then functions as a pointer holding type and address information. In this respect, an array name radically differs from variable names,. It is, in fact, a pointer. The array name itself is the address of the first byte in that memory. Indirection operations can reference different parts of that memory as if they were different variables. In this sense, an array declaration does not actually create objects. Though you can treat array elements as variables, they are actually referenced through pointer operations on the array's memory.

An array declaration reserves enough memory for the number of elements declared. An array of 10 integers will reserve 20 bytes, 2 to an integer. An array of 5 characters will reserve 5 bytes, one for each character. You then use an indirection operation to reference each element. Before you can reference a particular element in an array, you need to first calculate the address of that element's memory. The offset and increment pointer operations can calculate the address of an array element. Once calculated, an indirection operation can then reference the element. The index operation allows you to use two addresses to calculate an element's index, its position in an array.

The pointer operations were designed specifically to work on arrays. It is possible for them to work on any chunk of memory. However, they only make sense when applied to arrays.

The Array Name as Pointer

The use of an array name in an array's declaration can be misleading. An array declaration is made using the array name and the array data type, []. There is no specific pointer type in the declaration, *. When an array name is used in an expression, its type is that of a pointer. In expressions, the array name becomes a pointer that holds the address of the first element in the array. Any operations using the array name, including array subscript references, are really pointer operations. In Figure 10-5, the mynums array declaration defines an array of five character bytes that are consecutively set aside together in memory. In any expressions, the array name mynums is a pointer representing the address of the first byte.

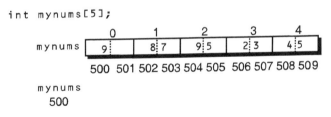

Figure 10-5: Arrays and address.

An array name, when used in expressions, operates like of a pointer constant. You can think of it as a symbolic constant that represents the address of the first array element. An array name cannot have its address changed. It is not a pointer variable. Nor can the address operator operate on it. The address operation &mynums is invalid.

You can use an array name as the pointer operand in an indirection operation, just like a pointer variable. Indirection on the array name itself references the first element in the array, as shown in Figure 10-6. The indirection operation below references the first element in the mynums array.

```
*mynums
```

In the following statement, the call to `printf` prints out the contents of the first integer element in the `mynums` array, in this case 9.

```
printf("%d",*mynums);
```

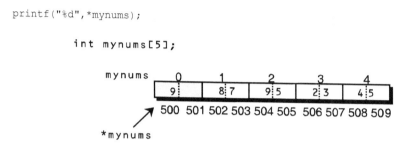

Figure 10-6: Using indirection on an array name to reference the first element in the array.

Though, in almost every expression, an array name is a pointer, there is one important exception. As an operand of the sizeof operator, the array name does not function as a pointer. Instead it maintains the original array data type defined in its array declaration. The array data type will specify the type of object and number of objects in the array. The sizeof operator will result in the total number of bytes in the array. sizeof calculates the size by multiplying the size of the type of object in the array by the number of objects. In the **sizenums.c** program in LISTING 10-6, the size of the `mynums` array is 6, and the size of the last array is 5.

LISTING 10-6:

sizenums.c
```c
#include <stdio.h>

int main(void)
        {
        char last[5] = {'R','I','C','H','\0'};
        int mynums[3] = {12, 5, 27};
        int numsize, lastsize;

        numsize = sizeof mynums;
        lastsize = sizeof last;
        printf ("Size of mynums is %d\n", numsize);
        printf ("Size of last is %d\n", lastsize);

        return 0;
        }

        Size of mynums is 6
        Size of last is 5
```

Pointer Offset Expressions

A pointer expression is an operation that results in an address. A pointer expression can be a primary expression consisting of a pointer variable or a pointer constant. A pointer expression can also be a function call, such as `malloc`, that returns an address. A pointer expression can even be an assignment operation, in which an address is assigned to a pointer variable. The address assigned is the resulting value of the expression.

There is another pointer operation, which is technically referred to as a pointer arithmetic operation. It appears similar to an arithmetic additive operation. It is not a simple arithmetic process. It is designed to calculate the addresses of array objects. A better name for it may be the pointer offset operation. It uses an offset to calculate an object's address in an array.

The pointer offset expression consists of two operands: a pointer and an integer. The integer is added to (or subtracted from) the pointer, resulting in a new address. This integer will be referred to here as the offset. The pointer operand is any pointer expression. It can be a pointer variable, an array name, a pointer assignment expression, or even another pointer offset expression.

```
(pointer +  integer )
```

The offset in the pointer offset expression actually refers to the number of objects, not the number of bytes. If an offset of 1 is added to an initial address, the address of the next object in the array will be referenced. It is tempting to think of a pointer offset operation as adding the offset to the pointer address. The offset is not added directly to the address. In pointer offset expressions, there is a further hidden, implied calculation using the pointer's data type. The offset is always multiplied by the size of the pointer's data type. The result of this calculation is the number that is then added to the pointer address. In Figure 10-7 an offset of 3 is added to the array name `mynums`. The integer 3 will be used to calculate an offset of 3 integers from the base address. The pointer's data type is an integer, and the size of an integer is 2 bytes. An offset of 3 on an integer array actually adds 6, (3 * 2). In the expression `(mynums+3 )`, the hidden multiplication by the size of the integer type results in the address of the fourth element, 506.

```
(mynums + 3)
```

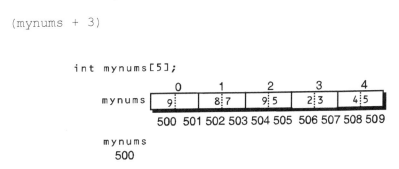

Figure 10-7: Pointer offset expression.

The address that results from the pointer offset expression can then be used in an indirection operation to reference the object at that address. Remember that an address is not merely an address, but an address of a type of object. In this sense, an address can be thought of as a pointer itself. An address of an array element calculated by the pointer offset operations, will hold the data type of that element. An indirection operation on the address of an array element can then reference that element.

```
(mynums + 3)    is          506
                            (500 + (3 * 2) );
                            (500 + 6)  is 506
```

You can apply the indirection operator directly to a pointer offset operation. Using an array name as the pointer operand in an offset operation, a combined pointer offset and indirection operation can reference a particular element in the array. For example, the combined expression * (mynums+2) first calculates the address of the third object in the array and then references that object with an indirection operation.

```
* (mynums + 2)
```

the integer used in the pointer offset operation is the index of the object referenced. Figure 10-8, shows how a pointer offset operation derives the address of an array element, and how an indirection operation on this address references the element.

In the program **offnums.c** in LISTING 10-7, the programs presented in LISTINGs 10.5 and 10.6 are combined and implemented using combined pointer offset and indirection operations, instead of array subscripts. Notice how the integer used in the pointer offset expressions is derived from a pointer variable, i, not a constant.

LISTING 10-7:

offnums.c

```c
#include <stdio.h>
#define MAX 3

int main(void)
        {
        int mynums[MAX]={12, 5, 27};
        int newnums[MAX];
        int i;

        for (i = 0; i < MAX; i++)
                {
                printf("%d\n", *(mynums + i) );
                }

        for (i = 0; i < MAX; i++)
                {
                *(newnums + i) = *(mynums + i);
                }

        return 0;
        }
```

The integer in the pointer offset expression need not be a constant. The integer is literally derived from an integer expression, which could just as easily be a variable, an arithmetic expression, or a function call returning an integer. In the program **offsets.c** in LISTING 10-8, there are several ways in which the integer of the pointer offset expression is calculated. All these offset operations reference the fifth object. In the last statement the integer is obtained from an integer variable referenced through a pointer.

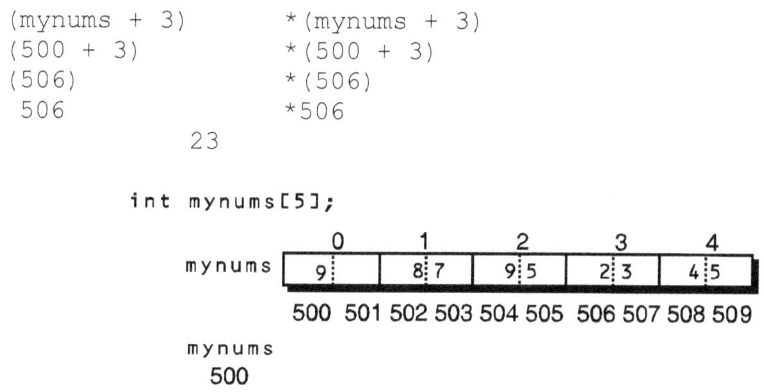

```
(mynums + 3)          *(mynums + 3)
(500 + 3)             *(500 + 3)
(506)                 *(506)
 506                  *506
              23
```

```
int mynums[5];
```

Figure 10-8 Pointer offset and indirection to reference array element.

LISTING 10-8:

offsets.c

```c
#include <stdio.h>

int square(int);

int main(void)
        {
        char mynums[13];
        int myoffset;
        int square(int);
        int *ptr;

        myoffset = 4;
        *(mynums + myoffset);

        *(mynums + (2 * 2));
        *(mynums + (8 / ((int) 2.786)) );

        *(mynums + square(2) );

        ptr = &myoffset;
        *(mynums + *ptr);

        return 0;
        }

int square(int num)
        {
        return (num * num);
        }
```

Array Subscripts as Pointer Offsets

As previously noted, array subscripts consist of brackets enclosing an index and placed next to an array name. The brackets used in a declaration have a different meaning than those used in array subscripts. The brackets in an array declaration represent the array data type. In array subscripts, the brackets are only a convenient and optional representation of a combined pointer offset and indirection operation. In fact, your compiler will strip away brackets used in an array subscripts and replace them by an offset and indirection operation. The array subscript `mynums[i]` actually represents the offset and indirection operation `*(mynums+i)`. For example, the programs in LISTING 10-9 are exactly of equivalent. The **poffset.c** program in LISTING 10-9A uses array subscripts, whereas the **notation.c** program in LISTING 10-9B uses the combined offset and indirection operations.

LISTING 10-9A: LISTING 10-9B:

poffset.c	notation.c

```
poffset.c
#include <stdio.h>

int main(void)
{
int i;
int mynums[2] = {12,44};


i = 0;
while(i < 2)
        {
        printf("%d",*(mynums+i));
        i++;
        }
}
```

```
notation.c
#include <stdio.h>

int main(void)
    {
    int i;
    int mynums[2] = {12,44};


    i = 0;
    while(i < 2)
        {
        printf("%d ",mynums[i]);
        i++;
        }
    }
```

LISTING 10-10A: LISTING 10-10B:

ptr_off.c	ptr_note.c

```
ptr_off.c
#include <stdio.h>


int main(void)
{
int mynums[2] = {12,44};
int *numptr;
int i;


numptr = mynums;
i = 0;
while(i < 2)
        {
        printf("%d",*(numptr+i));
        i++;
        }
}
```

```
ptr_note.c
#include <stdio.h>


int main(void)
    {
    int mynums[2] ={12,44};
    int *numptr;
    int i;


    numptr = mynums;
    i = 0;
    while(i < 2)
        {
        printf("%d ",numptr[i]);
        i++;
        }
    }
```

One often confusing feature of array subscripts is that it does not have to be used with just array names. It can also be used with regular pointer variables. Array subscripts works equally well for both pointer variables and array names. Since array subscript is really a pointer offset expression, the address used in the offset expression can just as easily be obtained from a pointer variable as from an array name. In LISTING 10-10 there are two versions of the same program. Both use a pointer variable. The pointer variable, `numptr`, is first assigned the beginning address of the `mynums` array, `numptr = mynums`. The array name `mynums` evaluates to the beginning address of the array. The **ptr_off.c** version in LISTING 10-10A uses the standard pointer offset operation. The **ptr_note.c** version in LISTING 10-10B uses array subscripts with a pointer variable.

Pointer Arithmetic

Kernighan and Ritchie describe a set of pointer expressions by the term pointer arithmetic, which can be misleading. Arithmetic operations, as such, cannot be performed on pointers (see Kernighan, B. and D. Ritchie, "The C Programming Language. (2nd Edition.)", pp.100-103). You cannot divide, multiply, or add pointers. Technically, you can subtract pointers. But even pointer subtraction is not the same as arithmetic subtraction, and is more accurately referred to a pointer difference operation.

Though a pointer cannot be added to another pointer, a pointer can be added to an integer. An integer can also be subtracted from a pointer. Other types, such as floats, doubles, and longs, cannot be added to or subtracted from a pointer. Furthermore, pointers cannot be multiplied or divided by integers. Multiplication or division of any kind is strictly prohibited with pointers. These restrictions eliminate most arithmetic operations. Only the following two operations are permitted:

1. The addition or subtraction of an integer to a pointer.
2. The subtraction of a pointer from another pointer.

The addition or subtraction of an integer to a pointer is referred to here as the pointer offset operation. This operation is used almost exclusively to reference objects in an array. The subtraction of one pointer from another is usually used to determine the integer index of an object in an array. For that reason it is referred to here as the index operation.

Increments: Pointer Assignments

You may recall the increment operator, ++, and its corresponding decrement operator, --, as described in Chapter 3. When applied to an integer variable, the increment operator increments the integer variable by 1, performing a combined addition and assignment operation. Remember that:

`i++`   is equivalent to   `i=i+1`

The decrement operator would decrement the integer by 1, performing a subtraction instead of an addition. i-- is equivalent to i=i-1.

In much that same way, you can also apply the increment and decrement operators to pointer variables. But in this case, the increment and decrement operations are equivalent to pointer expressions, not simple addition and subtraction. When you use an increment operator, ++, on a pointer variable, the increment operation can be thought of as incrementing the pointer variable's address. This pointer increment operation is the equivalent of a combined pointer offset and pointer assignment operation. In the pointer offset operation, the pointer operand is the pointer variable, and the integer is the constant 1, which is added to the address held by the pointer variable. The resulting address is then assigned back to the same pointer variable.

`numptr++`   is equivalent to `numptr=numptr+1`

It is important to realize that an offset of 1 includes a hidden multiplication by the size of the pointer's data type. In Figure 10-9, an increment of `numptr` increments by the size of an integer, 2 bytes. Given this fact, you can now see how such pointer increments can be useful in referencing array elements. If a pointer variable holds the address of an array element, then an increment operation on that pointer will give it the address of the next element in the array, effectively moving from one element to the next. An increment of such a pointer is always an increment of the pointer to the address of the next element in the array.

```
numptr++    is              502
                            (500 +  (1 * sizeof(int)))
                            (500 + (1 * 2) );
                            (500 + 2)  is 502
```

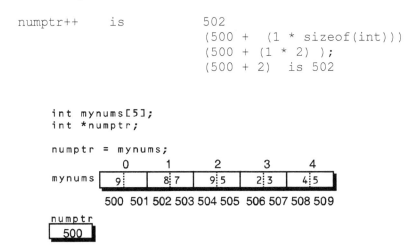

Figure 10-9: Increment on pointer variable, referencing array elements.

Once the increment operation changes the pointer variable to the address of the next array element, then you can reference that element by performing an indirection operation on that pointer. For example, as shown in Figure 10-9, the increment of the `numptr` variable changed the address it held to 502, the address of the second element. An indirection operation on `numptr` will then reference that second element, `*numptr`. In this case, the following `printf` out display the value of the second element in the `mynums` array, 87.

```
printf("%d\n",*numptr);
```

The increment operation applied to a pointer variable is often used to advance down an array, element by element. Such a pointer variable is often referred to either as a working pointer or as a temporary pointer. The pointer variable is first assigned the beginning address of the array, the address of the first element. Then subsequent increment operations will move the pointer from one element's address to the next. A indirection operation on that address will reference that element. In the program **ar_inc.c** in LISTING 10-11, `numptr` is an example of such a working pointer. `numptr` is used to advance down the `mynums` array. Each integer in the `mynums` array is printed out using a pointer, `numptr`. `numptr` is incremented by the size of an integer. It is consecutively set to the address of each integer element in the array (see Figure 10-10).

LISTING 10-11:

ar_inc.c

```
#include <stdio.h>

int main(void)
    {
    int i = 0;
    int mynums[5] = { 9, 87, 95, 23, 45 };
    int *numptr;

    numptr = mynums;
    while (i < 5)
        {
        printf("%d %d %p \n", i, *numptr, numptr);
        numptr++;
        i++;
        }

    return 0;
    }
```

Assuming that the address of the `mynums` array in LISTING 10-11 is 500, the program would print out:

0	9	500
1	87	502
2	95	504
3	23	506
4	45	508

In the **ar_inc.c** program in LISTING 10-11, a counter, i, had to be tested against the number of objects in the array, 5, in order to detect the end of the array. The counter is not needed for anything else. There is a way to do away with this overhead, and use the pointer variable instead of an integer counter to detect the end of the array. To do so you need to determine the end address of the array The working pointer can then be tested against this end address. You can easily determine the end address of an array by a pointer offset operation in which the number of objects in an array is added to the array name. For example, given the declaration `mynums[5]`, you can calculate the end address of the `mynums` array with the offset expression `mynums+5`. Assuming that the `mynums` array name is the address 500, `mynums+5` will result in the address 510. You could then test a working pointer against this address to detect the end of the array. In LISTING 10-12, `numptr` tests for the end of the array with the expression `numptr<(mynums+5)`. There is now no longer any need for a counter variable. The entire loop is managed using pointers and pointer operations such as offsets, increments, and indirections.

Remember that `mynums` as an array name is a pointer, and that `mynums+5` is a standard pointer offset operation. As such there is a hidden multiplication by the size of the pointer data type, in this case an integer. Assuming that an integer is 2 bytes, the `mynums+5` is equivalent to `mynums + (5*2)`. If `mynums` is 500, this gives us 500 + 10, 510, the end address of the array.

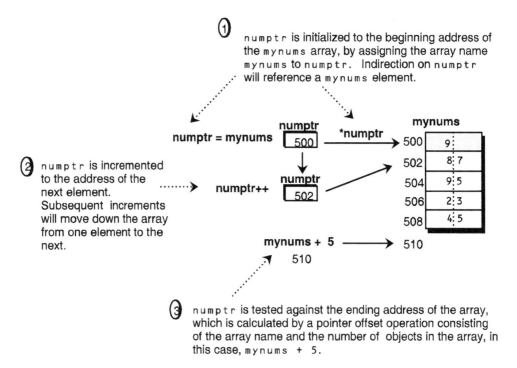

Figure 10-10: Using working pointers on an array.

LISTING 10-12:

ptrinc.c

```
#include <stdio.h>

int main(void)
        {
        int mynums[5] = { 9, 87, 95, 23, 45 };
        int *numptr;

        numptr = mynums;
        while (numptr < (mynums + 5))
                {
                printf("%d   %p \n", *numptr, numptr);
                numptr++;
                }

        return 0;
        }
```

A decrement operator performs the same kind of operation, except that a pointer is decremented to the address of the previous object. The decrement is actually a combination of the subtraction and assignment operations.

```
numptr--        is equivalent to    numptr=numptr-1
```

Like the increment operation, the decrement contains a hidden multiplication by the size of the pointer data type. The result is the subtracted from the pointer variable. Using the `mynums` array in Figure 10-9 as an example, if `numptr` is set to 508, then `numptr--` will set `numptr` to 506. Since `numptr` is a pointer to an integer, there is a hidden multiplication by the size of an integer, 2.

```
int *numptr;
numptr--        evaluates to              numptr = numptr - (1 * 2)
```

In the **ptrdec.c** program in LISTING 10-13, the `mynums` array is printed out in reverse using the decrement operator. Notice how `numptr` is initialized to the last object in the array. The offset of the last object is always the number of objects in the array minus 1.

LISTING 10-13:

ptrdec.c

```c
#include <stdio.h>
#define MAX 5

int main(void)
        {
        int mynums[MAX] = { 9, 87, 95, 23, 45 };
        int *numptr;

        numptr = mynums + (MAX - 1);
        while (numptr >= mynums)
                {
                printf("%d  %p \n", *numptr, numptr);
                numptr--;
                }

        return 0;
        }
```

You can, if you wish, combine the pointer increment and indirection operations. Such combinations can be difficult to interpret so you may want to avoid them. They do allow the development of very compact code. One key point to remember in such combination is that the increment can be either a postfix or prefix operator. When placed before a variable it is prefix operation, being performed before any other operation in the expression. When placed after the variable, it is a postfix operator and is only performed after all other operations in the expression. Commonly the increment is combined with indirection as a postfix operation. The indirection operator is placed before the pointer variable and the increment operator after it.

```
*numptr++
```

The other key point in such combinations is to keep in mind that the increment operation can operate either on the pointer or on the object pointed to by the pointer. This all depends upon which operation is evaluated first. If the increment is evaluated first, then the pointer is incremented. But if the indirection is evaluate first, then the increment operates on the object referenced by that indirection.

You should think of `*numptr++` as actually two operations in one, `*numptr` and `numptr++`. Since both the indirection and increment operators have the same precedence, their associativity will determine the order in which they are evaluated. This means that where you position the increment and indirection operators is crucial. The indirection and increment operators associate from right to left. The right-most operator will be evaluated first. In the case of `*numptr++`, the increment, `++`, is first evaluated and applied to the variable `numptr`. This means that the address in `numptr` will be incremented. Incrementation, in this case, applies to the pointer variable. The increment operator is placed after the pointer, making it a postfix operation. The increment will be performed after all other operations in the expressions, including the indirection operation. Then the indirection operation is evaluated. Since the incrementation is postfix, the indirection operation is performed before the address is incremented.

In the following example, the combined indirection and increment operations are broken down into their equivalent statements. Doing this can often help you keep straight what is being incremented and when.

```
*numptr++;              *numptr;
                        numptr = numptr + 1;
```

The differences become a bit clearer when you use the combination as part of a larger expression.

```
*numptr++ = 5;          *numptr = 5;
                        numptr = numptr + 1;
```

To clarify such operations, it is advisable to use parenthesis to determine the sequence of evaluation, instead of relying on associativity. Parenthesis will force the evaluation of one operation before another. In the next example, parenthesis around the indirection operation clearly indicate that the indirection will be performed before the increment.

```
(*numptr)++ = 5;
```

If you place the increment before the pointer variable, it becomes a prefix operation. In this case it is executed before any other operations in the expression. In the following example, the pointer variable is incremented first. Indirection will then operate on the new address. though the increment is placed before the variable, it still comes after the increment operator, `*++numptr`. The right to left associativity will still evaluate the increment operation first, making the increment an operation on the pointer variable.

```
*++numptr;              numptr = numptr + 1
                        *numptr;
```

Again, use of parenthesis will clarify the sequence of operations.

```
*(++numptr);
```

In LISTING 10-14, there are two examples of this combination of indirection and postfix increment of a pointer. The increment and indirection on `numptr` now both take place in the `printf` statement. In the **postinc.c** program in LISTING 10-14A, the increment is a postfix operation, and in the **preinc.c** program in LISTING 10-14B, the increment is a prefix operation. In LISTING 10-14B, the increment takes place before the first element is printed out. The first element is never printed.

LISTING 10-14A: **LISTING 10-14B:**

postinc.c   **preinc.c**

```
#include <stdio.h>                   #include <stdio.h>

int main(void)                       int main(void)
{                                        {
int mynums[2] = {12,44};                 int mynums[2] = {12,44};
int *numptr;                             int *numptr;


numptr = mynums;                         numptr = mynums;
while(numptr<(mynums+2))                 while(numptr<(mynums+2))
      {                                        {
      printf("%d",*numptr++);                  printf("%d",*++numptr);
      }                                        }
}                                        }
```

If you should place the increment operator to the left of the indirection operator, the element referenced is incremented instead of the pointer variable. The right to left associativity will the first evaluate the indirection operation, referencing the object. The variable pointed to is referenced. The increment operation is then evaluated and operates on the referenced object. That variable is then incremented. In the next example, the integer variable referenced by numptr, not the address in numptr, is incremented.

    ++*numptr;   is equivalent to   (*numptr) = (*numptr) + 1;

The same kind of combinations can work for decrements. For example:

```
      *numptr--;              *numptr;
                              numptr = numptr - 1;
```

Like the increment operator, the decrement can be either a postfix or prefix operation. Here is an example of the prefix decrement operation.

```
      *--numptr;              numptr = numptr - 1
                              *numptr;
```

If you should place the decrement operator before the indirection operator, then the object pointed to is decremented, not the pointer.

    --*numptr;   is equivalent to   (*numptr) = (*numptr) - 1;

Using parenthesis will clarify the sequence.

```
      --(*numptr);
```

In the **predec.c** program in LISTING 10-15, a combined decrement an indirection operation is used in the `printf` statement to both move to the previous element in the array and to reference that element, `*--numptr`. Notice, that, unlike LISTING 10-14, `numptr` is set to the end address of the array, not the address of the last element. This can be done because the decrement is a prefix operation taking effect before the first indirection. `numptr` is first decremented back to the address of the last array element and only then does indirection references that element. Using the `mynums` example in Figure 10-9, `numptr` is set to 510, then decremented to 508 (the address of the last element), before the indirection takes place.

Notice also that the test for the beginning of the array uses only a > operator instead of a >= operator in LISTING 10-14. With postfix and prefix operations you need to be careful to not to either stop too soon or stop too late at the end of the array.

LISTING 10-15:

predec.c

```c
#include <stdio.h>
#define MAX 5

int main(void)
        {
        int mynums[MAX] = { 9, 87, 95, 23, 45 };
        int *numptr;

        numptr = mynums + MAX;
        while (numptr > mynums)
                {
                printf("%d\n", *--numptr);
                }

        return 0;
        }
```

Indexes: Pointer Differences

An index is the position of an element in an array. In C, array elements are indexed from zero. For example, the third element of an array has an index of 2, and the first element has an index of 0. You could find yourself in a situation in which you have the address of an element, but not its index. In such a case you can use the pointer difference operation to calculate that element's index. In a pointer difference operation one pointer is subtracted from another. The subtraction results in an integer value that is the difference between two pointers. It does not result in an address. Technically, this integer value is the number of objects between two addresses. Though pointer difference can operate between any two addresses, it was designed to operate on arrays, determining the index of an element given only its address. To do so the array name is used as one operand and the element address as the other. The array name is then subtracted from the address of an element. The result is the index of that element in the array.

        working_pointer – array name

Usually you will have a working pointer that holds the address of the element. You then subtract the array name from the working pointer. In the next example, the index is calculated by subtracting the array name `mynums` from the pointer variable `numptr`. The result is an integer and this value is assigned to the integer variable rindex.

```
rindex = numpter - mynums;
```

The **index.c** program in LISTING 10-16 performs the same calculation. First, the pointer variable `numptr` is assigned the address of the fourth element, `mynums[3]`. The index of the element is then determined by a subtraction of `mynums` from `numptr`. This index result is assigned to the integer rindex. which is then used to in array subscripts to reference and print out the fourth element. Notice that rindex is declared as an integer, not a pointer. The result of a pointer difference expression is an integer, not a pointer value.

LISTING 10-16:

index.c
```c
#include <stdio.h>

int main(void)
        {
        int mynums[5] = { 9, 87, 95, 23, 45 };
        int rindex;
        int *numptr;

        numptr = mynums + 3;

        rindex = numptr - mynums;

        printf("%d %d\n", mynums[rindex] ,mynums[3]);

        printf("%d %d\n", *(mynums+rindex), *(mynums+3));

        return 0;
        }
```

Assuming the `mynums` array as depicted in Figure 10-11, the **index.c** program in LISTING 10-16 would print out the value of the fourth array element.

```
23      23
23      23
```

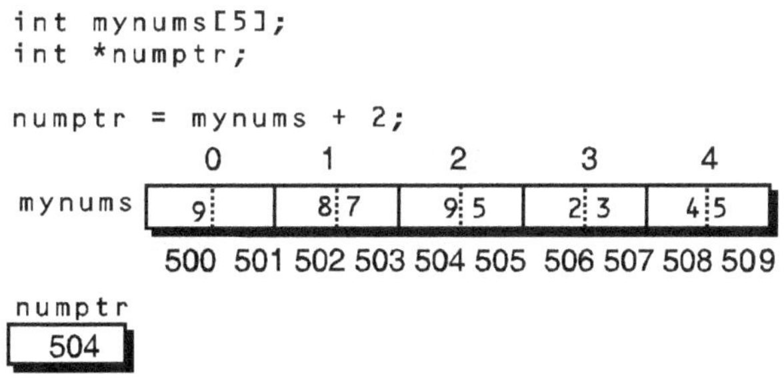

Figure 10-11: The index operation, pointer difference.

The offset expression `mynums+3` assigns the address 506 to `numptr`. 506 is the address of the fourth element in the `mynums` array. The pointer subtraction of the array name `mynums` from `numptr` results in the integer value 3, which is the offset and the index for the fourth element of the `mynums` array. In this situation, `mynums[rindex]`, `mynums[3]`, `*(mynums+rindex)`, `*(mynums+3)`, and `*numptr` all reference the same array element.

In a pointer difference operation, it is important to realize that there is a hidden division by the size of the pointer's data type. In Figure 10-11, a subtraction of `mynums` from `numptr` further divides the difference by the size of an integer, 2 bytes. In this sense, pointer difference always results in the number of elements between two addresses, not the number of bytes. As shown in Figure 10-11, the subtraction of `mynums` from `numptr` results in the integer value 2.

```
(numptr - mynums) is          2
                              (504 - 500) / sizeof(int)
                              4 / sizeof(int);
                              4 / 2 is 2
```

The **numidx.c** program in LISTING 10-17 uses pointer difference to calculate each array index and then uses that index to reference and print out each element in the `mynums` array. The address of each element is held by the pointer `numptr`. `mynums` is then subtracted from `numptr`, and the result is used as an array index. The array index is used with pointer notation to print out an element of the array.

LISTING 10-17:

numidx.c

```c
#include <stdio.h>

int main(void){
        int i = 0;
        int mynums[5] = { 9, 87, 95, 23, 45 };
        int *numptr;
        int index;

        numptr = mynums;

        while (numptr < (mynums + 5))
                {
                index = numptr - mynums;
                printf("%d %d %p %p\n",
                        index, mynums[index], numptr, mynums);
                numptr++;
                }

        return 0;
        }
```

Assuming that the address of the `mynums` array is 500, the **numidx.c** program in LISTING 10-17 would print out:

```
0       9       500     500
1       87      502     500
2       95      504     500
3       23      506     500
4       45      508     500
```

Table 10-1: OFFSETS, INCREMENTS, and INDEXES

OFFSETS
Addition or subtraction of pointer with arithmetic integer value. Implied multiplication by `sizeof(type)` of arithmetic value.

pointer + integer
pointer – integer

```
(numptr + 2)  numptr + (2 * sizeof(int))
(numptr - 2)  numptr - (2 * sizeof(int))
```

INCREMENTS AND DECREMENTS
Addition or Subtraction of 1 multiplied by `sizeof(type)`. Increment to next element in array, or decrement to previous element. Actual increment or decrement by size of type.
pointer_variable++
pointer_variable--

```
numptr++;     numptr = numptr + sizeof(int);
numptr--;     numptr = numptr - sizeof(int);
```

INDEXES
Difference of two pointers or pointer values. Implied division by `sizeof(type)`. Subtract a array name from working pointer to obtain index of an element.
working_pointer – array name
pointer expression – pointer expression

```
(numptr - mynums)    (numptr - mynums) / sizeof(int)
(numptr-(mynums+2))
(numptr - (mynums + (2 * sizeof (int))) / sizeof(int)
```

Pointer difference is not limited to using array names to calculate indexes. The addresses used in the pointer difference operation can be derived from any pointer expression. There is one important limitation. The pointers used as operands in a pointer difference operation must have the same data type. You could not subtract the address of an integer from the address of a float. In the **indexop.c** program in LISTING 10-18, several different pointer expression are used as operands in a pointer difference operation. The result assigned to `rindex` is always 4. First an array name is subtracted from a pointer variable, then a pointer variable is subtracted from another pointer variable, and finally an array name is subtracted from the address resulting from a pointer offset expression.

LISTING 10-18:

indexop.c

```
#include <stdio.h>

int main(void)
    {
    int mynums[5] = { 9, 87, 95, 23, 45 };
    int *lastptr;
    int *firstptr;
    int rindex;

    lastptr = (mynums + 4);
    rindex = lastptr - mynums;
    firstptr = mynums;
    rindex = lastptr - firstptr;
    rindex = (mynums + 4) - mynums;

    return 0;
    }
```

Arrays and Functions

Often you will want to pass an array from one function to another, either to reference its values or to work on its elements. However arrays cannot be passed from one function to another as variables are. The values of an array as a whole cannot be passed to a function. Arrays are not variables. This means that call-by-value operations cannot be performed on an array as a whole. Call-by-value assumes that there is a corresponding parameter variable in which to place the argument's values. The array name is only an address, it is not a variable (see Figure 10-12).

Any function could access elements in an array using pointer offset operations if the beginning address is known. The array name is that beginning address. You can pass this beginning address into a function that has a parameter declared as a pointer variable. This effectively implements a call-by-reference operation for the array, passing the address of the array from one function to another.

When an array name is used as an argument, it is passing a reference for the array. It is not passing a value. This means that a parameter can never be declared as an array. This fact is confused by the fact that there is an array subscript that is often used in parameter declarations. You can declare a parameter using a set of empty brackets. But this notation is simply translated into a pointer declaration. Through this pointer, you can then reference the elements of the array in the calling function.

        `int parray[]` is equivalent to `int *parray`

In the **printnum.c** program in LISTING 10-19, the array name `mynums` is an argument in the function call to **printarray**. The array name is the address of the `mynums` array. This address is passed to **parray**, which is a pointer variable. Here, the array subscript is used to declare the pointer variable. Array subscript is then used in the function to reference elements of the `mynums` array.

LISTING 10-19:

printnum.c

```c
#include <stdio.h>
#define MAX 3

void printarray(int[], int);

int main(void)
      {
      int mynums[MAX] = {12, 5, 27};

      printarray(mynums, MAX);

      return 0;
      }

void printarray(int parray[], int max)
      {
      int i;

      for (i = 0; i < max; i++){
            printf("%d\n", parray[i]);
            }
      }
```

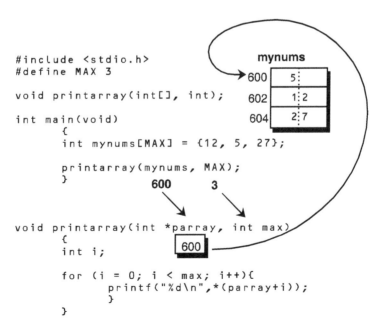

Figure 10-12: Arrays and Functions, passing an address of an array to a function.

The array subscript used in parameter declarations is only a notation. It is really only an alternative way of writing the declaration of a pointer variable. Array subscript and pointer offset operations can be applied interchangeably to a pointer declared in either form. In LISTING 10-20, an array name is passed to a parameter pointer. In the **parptr.c** program in LISTING 10-20A the parameter variable is declared using the pointer type. In the **parnote.c** program in LISTING 10-20B, the parameter variable is declared using the array subscript. Offset operations and array subscripts are used in each case to reference array elements.

LISTING 10-20A:

parptr.c

```
#include <stdio.h>

void add (int*);

int main(void)
        {
        int mynums[5];

        add(mynums);
        }

void add (int *numptr)
        {
        *(numptr + 2) = 35;
        numptr[2] = 35;
        }
```

LISTING 10-20B:

parnote.c

```
#include <stdio.h>

void add(int[]);

int main(void)
        {
        int mynums[5];

        add(mynums);
        }

void add(int numptr[])
        {
        numptr[2] = 35;
        *(numptr + 2) = 35;
        }
```

In the **ptrprint.c** program LISTING 10-21, the program in LISTING 10-19 is rewritten using a pointer type for the parameter declaration instead of array subscripts. Elements of the array are referenced with a combined offset and indirection operation.

The pointer declared as a parameter is a variable itself. As a variable, its values can be changed. In several situations you can use the parameter pointer that references an array as a working pointer to advance down the array from one element to the next. The parameter pointer will be incremented using the increment operator. Of course, the original beginning address of the array is lost. If the function only requires a single sequential use of the array elements, it will not matter if the beginning address is lost. On the other hand, in most situations the beginning address should be preserved. In the **incprint.c** program in LISTING 10-22, the parray pointer is incremented as a working pointer advancing from one element to the next.

In the **constprt.c** program in LISTING 10-23, the address in the parameter pointer is preserved, and a separate working pointer that will advance through the array is declared. The parameter pointer is declared with the const qualifier. This prevents the writing of any code that attempts to modify the parameter pointer. It becomes a constant pointer. The const qualifier is placed after the pointer's data type and before the pointer type, *. This indicates that the pointer, not the object it points to, is being qualified. The address in the pointer itself cannot be changed, not the object it points to.

LISTING 10-21:

ptrprint.c

```c
#include <stdio.h>
#define MAX 3

void printarray(int[], int);

int main(void)
        {
        int mynums[MAX] = {12, 5, 27};

        printarray(mynums, MAX);

        return 0;
        }

void printarray(int *parray, int max)
        {
        int i;

        for (i = 0; i < max; i++){
                printf("%d\n",*(parray+i));
                }
        }
```

LISTING 10-22:

incprint.c

```c
#include <stdio.h>
#define MAX 3

void printarray(int[], int);

int main(void)
        {
        int mynums[MAX] = {12, 5, 27};

        printarray(mynums, MAX);

        return 0;
        }

void printarray(int *parray, int max)
        {
        int i;

        for(i=0; i < max; i++)
                {
                printf("%d\n",*parray);
                parray++;
                }
        }
```

326 Part 2: Arrays and Pointers

LISTING 10-23:

constprt.c

```
#include <stdio.h>
#define MAX 3

void printarray(int const*, int);

int main(void)
        {
        int mynums[MAX] = {12, 5, 27};

        printarray(mynums, MAX);

        return 0;
        }

void printarray(int const *parray, int max)
        {
        int *wkptr;

        for(wkptr=(int*)parray; wkptr<(parray+max); wkptr++)
                {
                printf("%d\n",*wkptr);
                }
        }
```

Controlling modification of Arrays: const

Because you can only pass the address of an array, not its values, an array is open to modification by any function given that address. An array's call-by-reference operation allows a programmer to the write code that modifies it, in any function it is passed to. Sometimes the array elements need to be changed, as in the case of the copy program in LISTING 10-24. The elements of the array **copynums** in main will have their values changed through pointer references in the function **copyarray**.

there are situations in which the elements of an array should not be changed in a function. In the copy program, code that changes the elements of the source array, in this case mynums, should never be written. You can forcibly prevent such modification by qualifying the parameter pointer declaration with the const type qualifier. The const type qualifies a variable as a constant, preventing its value from being changed. It can easily be applied to array elements. In the **constcpy.c** program in LISTING 10-24, the const modifier is used to prevent the sarray pointer from ever changing the source array. In effect, only the value of the source array, mynums, can be referenced.

The const qualifier can be used in two different ways: one to qualify the pointer itself, and the other to qualify the object pointed to.

`const int *sptr;`	Pointed-to object cannot change, but pointer can change
`int const *sptr;`	Pointed-to object can change, but pointer cannot
`const int const *ptr`	Neither pointed-to object nor pointer can change

LISTING 10-24:

constcpy.c

```
#include <stdio.h>
#define MAX 3

void copyarray(int [], const int [], int);

 int main(void)
        {
        int mynums[MAX] = {12, 5, 27};
        int copynums[MAX];

        copyarray (copynums, mynums, MAX);

        return 0;
        }

 void copyarray(int tarray[],const int sarray[],int num)
        {
        int i;
        for (i = 0; i < num; i++)
                {
                tarray[i] = sarray[i];
                }
        }
```

LISTING 10-25:

constsrc.c
```
#include <stdio.h>
#define MAX 3
void copyarray(int*, const int*, int);

 int main(void)
        {
        int mynums[MAX] = {12, 5, 27};
        int copynums[MAX];

        copyarray (copynums, mynums, MAX);

        return 0;
        }

void copyarray(int *tarray, const int *sarray, int num)
        {
        int i;
        for (i = 0; i < num; i++)
                {
                tarray[i] = sarray[i];
                }
        }
```

In the **constsrc.c** program in LISTING 10-25, the program in LISTING 10-24 is rewritten using pointer declarations for the parameters in the definition of `copyarray`. In the declaration of `sarray`, the const modifier affects the elements referenced, not sarray itself. The source array is referenced by the pointer `sarray`. The `const` qualifier placed before the pointer's data type will prevent the pointer from modifying the object it points to. `sarray` can change its value. It can be set to another address. The elements it references through indirection cannot be changed. The expression `*sarray = 10`; is not allowed.

Passing Array Elements: call-by-value and call-by-reference

Though the values of an array as a whole cannot be passed, you can pass the values of individual array elements. In a one-dimensional array, the reference of an array element is equivalent to a variable reference. When used as an argument, the value of the referenced element is passed. In this case, the corresponding parameter is a variable with the same data type as that of the element. In the **printele.c** program in LISTING 10-26, an element of an array is used as an argument. The value of the first element, 12, is passed into an integer parameter variable (see Figure 10-13).

LISTING 10-26:

printele.c

```
#include <stdio.h>

#define MAX 3

void printnum(int);

int main(void)
        {
        int mynums[MAX] = {12, 5, 27};

        printnum(mynums[1]);

        return 0;
        }
void printnum(int num)
                {
                printf("%d ", num);
                }
```

There may be situations in which you may need to modify an array element. In this case, you would have to perform a call-by-reference operation on the array element, passing its address to a pointer variable. You can obtain the address of an element by applying the address operation to a reference of the element. Usually you only need to place the address operator before an array subscript reference of the element. The following example obtains the address of the third element in the `mynums` array.

```
&mynums[2]
```

In the program **getnums.c** in LISTING 10-27, the user is allowed to enter in the values for the `mynums` array. This requires a call to scanf. However, scanf always requires the address of an object. In this case, the object is first referenced with array subscript, and then its address is obtained with the address operator.

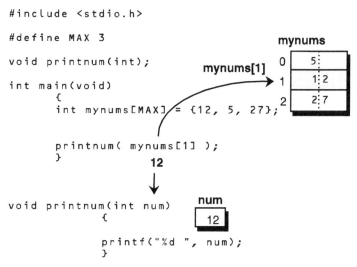

Figure 10-13: Array elements as arguments.

LISTING 10-27:

getnums.c

```
#include <stdio.h>

int main(void)
        {
        int mynums[5];
        int i;

        for (i = 0; i < 5; i++)
                {
                printf("Enter number :");
                scanf("%d", &mynums[i]);
                }

        for (i = 0; i < 5; i++)
                {
                printf("%d \n", mynums[i]);
                }

        return 0;
        }
```

There is, of course a shortcut version of this process. Array subscripts is really equivalent to a pointer offset and indirection operation. In the program **getnoff.c** in LISTING 10-28, the previous program is written with the pointer offset mynums+i rather than with the array subscript and address operation &num[i]. The offset operation mynums+i results in the address of that element. scanf only requires the address. It does not matter how the address is obtained.

num[i]   is equivalent to   *(mynums + i)

&num[i]   is equivalent to   &(*(mynums + i))

&(*(mynums+i))   is equivalent to   (mynums + i)

LISTING 10-28:

getnoff.c
```
#include <stdio.h>

int main(void)
    {
    int mynums[5];
    int i;

    for (i = 0; i < 5; i++)
            {
            printf("Enter number :");
            scanf("%d", (mynums + i));
            }

    for (i = 0; i < 5; i++)
            {
            printf("%d \n",  *(mynums + i));
            }

    return 0;
    }
```

Chapter Summary: Arrays and Pointers

An array is a collection of objects, but it is not an object itself. The objects in an array are referred to as elements. Elements are numbered starting from zero. An array of five elements is numbered 0 to 4. Each element is referenced according to its position in the array. An element can be referenced using array subscripts, which consists of the array name and the position of the element enclosed in brackets.

An array is declared with a data type, an array name, the array data type, and the number of objects in the array. The array data type is a set of brackets. Brackets mean different things depending upon where they are used. Brackets are used in declarations, statements, and parameter declarations. In each situation, brackets have a different meaning. In declarations, brackets denote the array data type used to declare an array. In statements, brackets constitute an array subscript that represents a pointer offset and indirection operation. In parameter declarations, the array declaration is converted to a pointer declaration.

The array name itself is an address of the first element in the array. The array name can be thought of as a pointer constant. You use the array name in pointer operations to reference objects in the array.

Pointer offsets and indexes were designed to work on arrays. An offset is an expression in which an integer is either added to or subtracted from a pointer. The increment operation advances a pointer from one element to the next in an array. An increment simply consist of resetting a pointer to itself with an offset of 1. Indexes are derived by subtracting one pointer from another. The result is the difference, in terms of the number of elements between the two pointers.

The increment operation is often used for a working pointer that advances down the array from one object to the next. The end address of the array can be calculated with an offset expression consisting of the array name and the number of objects in the array. The end address of the array declared as `int mynums[5]` is `mynums + 5`. The working pointer can be tested against this end address as it advances down the array.

Arrays can only be passed to functions in a call-by-reference operation. You can use the const qualifier to either protect the parameter pointer that holds the beginning address or to protect the array in the calling function whose address was passed.

Exercises

Using the program that follows, replace the variable i altogether. Instead of comparing i to 10, compare `numptr` to a pointer offset operation that yields the last address in the array. The first address in the array is `mynums`. The last is `mynums` plus an offset of 10. Also, implement the increment of `numptr` with the increment operator, ++.

Offsets can be negative as well as positive. Rewrite the program, filling up the array in reverse order (decrement from 9 to 0). Use the decrement operator, --.

Add a search process which requests a number to be searched and then prints out the index of that number in the array. Remember that the subtraction of two pointers will result in an index to an array. The address of the array is subtracted from the address of an element in the array. If `numptr` is pointing to the third element, then the expression (`numptr-mynums`) results in the integer 2. This is often helpful in a search.

```
#include <stdio.h>

int main(void)
      {
      int mynums[10], i = 0;
      int * numptr;

      numptr = mynums;
      while (i < 10)
            {
            printf("Enter number :");
            scanf("%d", numptr);
            numptr = numptr + 1;
            i++;
            }

      for(numptr=mynums,i=0;i<10;numptr=numptr+1,i++)
            {
            printf("%d \n", *numptr);
            }

      return 0;
      }
```

Arrays of Characters

String Functions, Constants, & Conversions

11. Arrays of Characters

In C, a character string is implemented as an array of characters. By convention, the end of a string is signified by a null character. A string is manipulated using loops to access each character. A character array, a null character, and a loop are the three elements used to implement and manage strings.

There are standard operations that you will need to perform on strings, such as copying or comparing strings. Many of these operations are already implemented in a set of string function contained in the standard library. String functions in this library are automatically linked to your program when you compile. You can just as easily write your own string functions, creating customized version of standard operations. You can even write your own functions to copy or compare strings.

There is also a special type of string called a string constant. A string constant is a character array whose elements are not meant to be changed. A string constant is not declared and has no array name. You can define them anywhere in your program by simply enclosing characters within two double quotes.

Strings

In C, unlike other languages, there is no string data type. Instead, a string is simulated using an array of characters, a null character, and loops that manage it. The declaration of an array of characters is no different from the declaration of any other kind of array. Assignments can be made much in the same way. The following are declarations of an array of integers and an array of characters, as well as assignments to an element of each.

```
int   num[5];
char  name[5];

    num[2] = 6;
    name[2] = 'T';
```

The end-of-string terminator must be explicitly specified by the programmer. By convention, the end-of-string terminator is the null character, '\0'. The null character is placed at the end of a string. Any time a string is manipulated, the programmer must always be sure to check for the null character in order to know where the string ends. The null character is the equivalent of an integer value of zero. All the bits are zero. You need to be careful not to confuse the null character with the zero numeric character, '0'.

String Initialization

You can initialize strings in the same way that you would initialize any array. You place a set of values within brackets and separate them by commas. In the case of strings, the values are character constants. Care must be taken to make the last constant a null character. If you do not specify the number of elements in an array declaration, then the number of elements in the array will be determined by the number of values specified in the initialization. In the next example, the character array game is declared and initialized with 5 characters, including the null character.

```
char game[] = {'c', 'a', 'r','d','\0'};
```

In the program **arinit.c** in LISTING 11-1, two character strings are declared and initialized, game and sport. Notice that game has no specified number of elements in its declaration. In this case the size of the array is determined by the number of values in the initialization block, 5. sport is declared with 10 characters, but it only actually uses 7. A string can be shorter than the number of elements in its array.

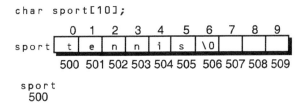

Figure 11-1: Character String.

LISTING 11-1:

arinit.c

```
#include <stdio.h>

        char game[] = {'c', 'a', 'r','d','\0'};

int main(void)
        {
        char sport[10]={'t','e','n','n','i','s','\0'};

        printf("Game is %s, Sport is %s\n",game,sport);

        return 0;
        }
```

LISTING 11-2:

arconst.c

```
#include <stdio.h>

        char game[] = "card";

int main(void)
        {
        char sport[10] = "tennis";

        printf("Game is %s, Sport is %s\n",game,sport);

        return 0;
        }
```

In C, there is an alternative and popular way to specify the values used for the initialization of a string array. Instead of the block of individual character constants, you can use a string constant. A string constant is denoted by a set of double quotes. Characters placed within the double quotes constitute a string. When you use a string constant for an array initialization, the characters in the string constant are assigned one by one to the elements of that declared array. The null character need not be specified. A string constant will automatically add one.

In the **arconst.c** program in LISTING 11-2, the **arinit.c** program from LISTING 11-1 is rewritten to use string constants in the array initializations. The initialization block for both the game and sport array have been replace by a string constant. The null character need not be specified.

This kind of operation works only for the initialization of character arrays. Strings constants cannot be assigned this way to arrays in assignment expressions. The use of string constants in character array initialization should be thought of as an exception. You shall see later that a string constant actually defines its own array and evaluates to that array's address.

String Management: loops

Strings are managed character by character, often doing the same thing to each character. A string is literally an array of characters, whose elements are operated on one by one. The ideal control structure for managing elements of an array is the loop. Each execution of a loop can operate on an element of an array and then advance to the next element. Whereas usually a loop will test for the end of an array, in the case of strings, a loop tests for the end-of-string terminator, the null character. Remember that the string itself is only the set of character values making it up, and is often smaller that the array that contains it. Loops that operate on string arrays always test for the null character, the end of the string, not the end of the array.v

In the **sport.c** program in LISTING 11-3, the sport string is printed out. Since the string is an array of characters, a loop is used to print out each character element, one by one. A test for the null character will stop the loop at the end of the string, not the end of the array. The loop's test expression will be true as long as the value of the current element is not a null character. If the current element's value is a null character, the end of the string has been reached. For the sport string, the end of the string is reached with the sixth element. The sport string is seven characters long, including the null character.

LISTING 11-3:

sport.c

```
#include <stdio.h>

int main(void)
    {
    char sport[10]={'t','e','n','n','i','s','\0'};
    int i;

    i = 0;
    while ( sport[i] != '\0')
        {
        putchar(sport[i]);
        i++;
        }

    return 0;
    }
```

You can also use loops to enter values into strings. In such a case you need to be careful to enter in the final null character. Without the null character, you do not have a string, only an array of character values. In the **getsport.c** program in LISTING 11-4, a loop is used to get input from the user until the user hits the return key. Each character receives its place, one by one, in the array. The loop continues until the newline character, the carriage return, is input. At that point the loop stops. The null character is then assigned to the end of the string. The character array element that was assigned the newline character, is then assigned a null character.

LISTING 11-4:

getsport.c

```
#include <stdio.h>

int main(void)
        {
        char sport[10];
        int i;

        i = 0;
        sport[i] = getchar();
        while (sport[i] != '\n')
                {
                i++;
                sport[i] = getchar();
                }
        sport[i] = '\0';

        return 0;
        }
```

Often loops that manage arrays can be written in using compact code, combining several operations into the loop's test expression. In the program **gsport.c** in LISTING 11-5, the test for the while loop incorporates an assignment statement with a function call and a comparison. First, getchar returns a character from the keyboard. This character is then assigned to the sport[i] element. The value of the assignment is then compared to the character constant '\n', the newline.

LISTING 11-5:

gsport.c

```
#include <stdio.h>

int main(void)
        {
        char sport[10];
        int i = 0;

        while ( (sport[i] = getchar()) != '\n')
                {
                i++;
                }
        sport[i] = '\0';

        return 0;
        }
```

If the null character assignment is left out, there is no string. There is only a collection of characters that never ends. If such a character array is printed out, a strange effect will result. The loop test expression for printing a string will stop when a null character is reached. If there is no null character to begin with, the loop may never stop. The string will be printed, followed by all the bytes of remaining computer memory, until a null character somewhere is reached. If no null character is ever reached, you may end up printing all the bytes in memory, though most likely your program will crash with a segmentation fault when it tries to access a memory protected by the operating system. It is up to you to make sure each string has the null character placed in it.

String Functions and the Standard Library

Often you will need to perform the same string operations over and over again. You may need to print strings, copy them, or even compare them. Instead of writing a loop each time you need to perform such an operation, you could simply place the code in a function, and then call the function when needed. For example, the loops used in LISTING 11-4 for printing and LISTING 11-5 for input can be placed within their own functions. In LISTING 11-6, the printing loop has been placed in a function called `myputs`, and the input loop has been placed in a function called `mygets`. Each time to need to print out an array, you simply call the `myputs` function.

Simple functions such as `myputs` are the kind that you would use in many different programs. Instead of rewriting them for each program, you can place them in their own source code file and just link them into different programs as needed. You can then build up a library of functions that deal with strings. This is a common practice, especially for string functions. It is for this very reason that the `myputs` and `mygets` functions in LISTING 11-6 are placed in a separate file called **lib.c**.

There are certain string functions that are considered such essential and basic operations that they have been incorporated as a standard extensions of the C programming language. This standard set of string functions is provided in a file known as the standard library. The standard library is not a part of the compiler. It is, instead, a file of commonly used functions which are incorporated into your program by the linker. Though the standard library is not a part of the compiler, the functions in it are standard accepted functions. All C compilers have the same functions in the standard library, and they all operate in the same way.

The `myputs` and `mygets` functions are actually variations of two common standard library functions, puts and gets. These functions are designed to input and output strings. There are other functions that perform other string operations. Three of the most common string functions are `strcpy`, `strlen`, and `strcmp`. All are in the standard library. A distinction is made between those functions that handle input and output and those that handle strings. The function declarations for the string management functions are found in the file **string.h**, whereas the input/output function declarations are in **stdio.h**. The **string.h** file should be included whenever string handling functions are used.

The simplest of these functions is `strlen`. It operates much in the same way that puts does. All `strlen` does is count the number of characters in the string. It then returns this count.

```
int strlen(char str[])
        {
        int count;

        count = 0;
        while (str[count] != '\0')
                    ++count;
        return(count);
        }
```

LISTING 11-6:

main.c

```
#include <stdio.h>

void mygets(char str[]);
void myputs(char str[]);

int main(void)
        {
        char name[30];

        mygets(name);
        myputs (name);

        return 0;
        }
```

lib.c

```
#include <stdio.h>

void mygets (char str[])
        {
        int i = 0;

        while((str[i] = getchar()) != '\n')
                {
                i++;
                }
        str[i] = '\0';
        }

void myputs(char str[])
        {
        int i;

        i = 0;
        while(str[i] != '\0')
                {
                putchar(str[i]);
                i++;
                }
        }
```

strcpy and strcat Functions

Though you cannot assign one string to another, you can assign its elements one by one. In effect you can copy one string onto another string using a string function. The strcpy standard library function performs this basic string copy operation. strcat is a variation on strcpy. strcat appends one string to another. Both functions take two string arguments. The first argument is the target string, and the second argument is the source string. In the case of strcpy, the source string is copied to the target string. strcpy literally handles the string one character at a time, much in the same way mygets does.

The **copystr.c** program in LISTING 11-7 contains a simplified version of `strcpy` called mystrcpy. In **mystrcpy** the test for the loop is the null character. If, for some reason, there is no null character in the original string, the loop will continue on past the string. Assignments will continue on through memory, destroying everything in its path. This makes `strcpy` one of the most dangerous functions used in C.

LISTING 11-7:

copystr.c

```
#include <stdio.h>
#include <string.h>

void mystrcpy(char [], char []);

int main(void)
        {
        char originalstring[10];
        char copystring[10];

        gets(originalstring);

        mystrcpy(copystring, originalstring);
                        /*      left           right   */
                        /*      target         source  */

        return 0;
        }

void mystrcpy(char targetstr[], char sourcestr[])
                {
                int i = 0;

                while(sourcestr[i] != '\0') {
                        targetstr[i] = sourcestr[i];
                        i++;
                        }
                targetstr[i] = '\0';
                }
```

A subtle runtime bug occurs when the copy string is smaller than the original string. Damage is limited, but still critical. In this case, assignments will continue off the array into adjacent memory. A basic rule to follow is that the copy string must be as large, if not larger, than the original string. Always leave an extra element for the null character.

The **copyerr.c** program in LISTING 11-8 contains such a subtle error. The loop here is never executed. After the `strcpy` operation, the value of the variable num is zero, so you never enter the loop. The problem is that the string `originstr` is larger than `copystr`, to which it is being copied. The string originstr is declared with six elements, `copystr` only has five. `strcpy` stops at the null character in the source string, which, in this case, is `originstr`. The first five characters are assigned to `copystr`. Then the null character is assigned to the byte following the `copystr` array. This byte happens to be part of the memory designated for the num integer variable. The value of the null character is zero. The value of num after the assignment will be zero, not five to which it was originally initialized. Figure 11-2 illustrates the effect of this error.

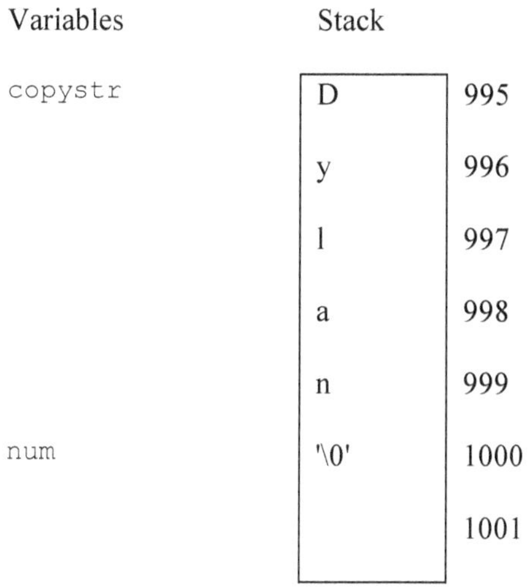

Variables | Stack

copystr

D	995
y	996
l	997
a	998
n	999

num   '\0'   1000

1001

Figure 11-2: Result of copy string smaller than original string.

LISTING 11-8:

copyerr.c

```c
#include <stdio.h>
#include <string.h>

int main(void)
     {
     int num = 5;    /* value of num is 5 */
     char copystr[5];
     int i = 0;
     char originstr[6] = {'D','y','l','a','n','\0'};

     strcpy(copystr, originstr);

     while (i < num)        /* value of num is 0 */
          {
          putchar(copystr[i]);
          i++;
          }

     return 0;
     }
```

The `strcat` function copies a string to the end of another string. In the **copycat.c** program in LISTING 11-9, an extension is attached to the name variable. When the name array is printed out, the extension will now be part of the array: George Jr.. The target string must be declared large enough to hold both its current string and the appended string.

LISTING 11-9:

copycat.c

```
#include <stdio.h>
#include <string.h>

int main(void)
    {
    char name[12] = {'G','e','o','r','g','e','\0'};
    char ext[5] = " Jr.";

    strcat(name, ext);
    puts(name);

    return 0;
    }
```

Output for LISTING 11-9:

```
                          George Jr.
```

strcmp Function

Just as you cannot assign strings directly, you cannot compare them. Instead you need to compare their elements one by one in a string functions. The standard library `strcmp` function performs this task, comparing the values of two strings. Because character values are alphabetically ordered, you can use `strcmp` to arrange strings alphabetically. In this sense, you can test if one string is greater than the other. In fact, all the relational and equality comparisons can, in effect, be made: <, >, ==, !=, <= , and >=. To understand how this works, you need to take a close look at how `strcmp` compares two strings.

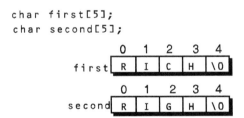

Figure 11-3: Comparison of two strings.

The `strcmp` function operates by comparing sequentially each letter in both strings. It continues these comparisons one by one until it finds a discrepancy. If it finds a discrepancy, processing stops. In Figure 11-3, the first letters in both strings were compared. They were found to be the same, 'R'. So the next letters in both strings were compared. They too were found to be the same, 'I'. So the next letters in both strings were compared. These were found to be different, 'C' and 'G'. At this point, processing stopped, and the two different characters were subtracted, one from the other. Since 'C' is less than 'G' `strcmp` would return a minus value indicating that the first string is less than the second string. The resulting difference is returned by the `strcmp` function. If no discrepancies should be found, processing would continue until the last letter in the source string is reached. Listed here is the code for one version of strcmp.

```
int strcmp(char str1[], char str2[])
       {
       int i, res;

       i = 0;
       while((str1[i] == str2[i]) && (str1[i] != '\0'))
             i++;
       res = str1[i] - str2[i];
       return(res);
       }
```

The two strings in Figure 11-3 are the same until they reach the third letters, 'C' and 'G'. 'G' has a greater value than 'C'. For this reason the second string is considered greater than the first string. In many C compilers, strcmp will return the difference between the values of the two differing characters. If first is compared against second, the value of 'C' would be subtracted from the value of 'G'. strcmp returns the result of this subtraction. A minus value indicates the string is less than the other string. In this case, using an ASCII character set, strcmp would return a -4. c - g is 99 - 103 = -4. Some systems do not return the difference between the characters. Instead they simply return a +1 for a greater-than difference and a -1 for a less-than difference.

Comparisons stop at the first discrepancy. In Figure 11-4, there is a discrepancy right off in the first letters, 'R' and 'F'. The value of 'R' is greater than 'F', so the first string is greater than the second. R-F is 114 - 102 = 12. The next discrepancy between 'I' and 'R' is never reached.

```
       0   1   2   3   4
first  R | I | T | A | \0

       0   1   2   3   4
second F | R | E | D | \0
```

Figure 11-4: Comparison on first letter.

A shorter string is valued lesser than a longer string. In Figure 11-5, both strings share the same first three characters, except that one string is shorter than the other. strcmp detects a discrepancy. Remember that the null character is a valid character value. As such, it can be compared to any other character. In this case there is a discrepancy between the fourth letters, the null character, '\0', and 'H'. The value of the null character is zero and therefore less than 'H'. The first string is less than the second string. '\0'-H is 0 -104 = -104.

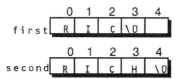

```
       0   1   2   3   4
first  R | I | C | \0 |

       0   1   2   3   4
second R | I | C | H | \0
```

Figure 11-5: Comparing strings of different lengths.

Strings with the same characters return a value of zero. In Figure 11-6, there are no discrepancies at all. The difference between each matching pair of letters is zero. strcmp has continued comparing until it reaches the end of the string. It subtracts the last two letters, which are both null characters. '\0'-'\0' is 0 - 0 = 0. If a zero value is returned by strcmp, it means that the two strings are equal.

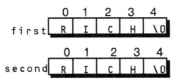

Figure 11-6: Comparing equal strings.

Now that you can see how strcmp works, it is easy to understand how it is used and abused. The use of strcmp depends on its return value. There are three possibilities:

1. str1 > str2   return value is positive   +
2. str1 < str2   return value is negative   -
3. str1 == str2   return value is zero   0

You can set up clear and understandable strcmp test by testing its return value against zero. With such a structure you can easily code common relational comparisons checking to see if a string is less than or greater than another. For example, a test to check if str1 is greater than str2 is essentially a test to check if the return value from strcmp was positive, greater than zero. A test to check if str1 is less than str2 is a test to check if the return value of strcmp is less than zero.

```
(strcmp(str1, str2) > 0)
(strcmp(str1, str2) < 0)
```

A test to check if str1 is equal to str2 is a test to check if the return value of strcmp is actually zero. To check if they are not equal you can simply test to see if the return value is not equal to zero, !=.

```
(strcmp(str1, str2) == 0)
(strcmp(str1, str2) != 0)
```

Similarly, a test to check if str1 is less than or equal to str2 is a test to check if the return value of strcmp is less than or equal to zero. The same is true for a greater-than test.

```
(strcmp(str1, str2) >= 0)
(strcmp(str1, str2) <= 0)
```

The comparison of the return value of strcmp to zero is the clearest way to configure such tests. There are clever and non-intuitive ways that are commonly used. Remember that the truth or falsehood of a test expression depends on whether its result is a numeric zero or some other value. A false test expression is a zero value. A true test is any other positive or negative value. Sometimes, overly clever programmers will make use this fact in tests for the equality or inequality of strings using strcmp. In the next example, the strcmp function call is placed by itself in a test expression. The strcmp function call by itself is actually a test for inequality. The test is true if the result of the test expression is non-zero. strcmp returns a non-zero value if the two strings are not equal. If the strings are equal, the test is false, since strcmp returns a zero if the strings are equal. Often a beginner looks at this code and thinks that equality will evaluate to a true value for the test. In fact, this is equivalent to a test for inequality.

```
if (strcmp(str1, str2)
        printf("str1 is not equal to str2");

if(strcmp(str1, str2) != 0)
        printf("str1 is not equal to str2");
```

The test for equality is even more counter-intuitive. The not operator, !, would seem to indicate a test for inequality. In fact, the not operator has the effect of taking the zero returned by strcmp if the strings are equal and turning the test into true. This is a test for the equality of two strings.

```
if ( !(strcmp(str1, str2))
        printf("str1 is equal to str2");

if(strcmp(str1, str2) == 0)
        printf("str1 is equal to str2");
```

String Functions and Character Pointers

Instead of using array subscripts in your string functions, you can use the pointer operations such as indirection, increments, and indexing. The beginning address of the string passed to a string function is held in a pointer variable. Remember that the parameter to which an array's beginning address is passed to is always a pointer variable. In the case of strings, the parameter is a pointer to a character. Taking this fact into consideration, you can easily design string functions using pointers and pointer operations. A working pointer can increment through the character array, element by element. It would stop at the end of the string, rather than the end of the array. The test expression would include an indirection operation on the working pointer, comparing the value of the element to a null character.

When using pointers this way, you need be sure of when to use indirection and when not to. Indirection is required in the test expression, but not when the pointer is initialized or incremented. The **getstr.c** program in LISTING 11-10 illustrates how you would use a character pointer to manage an array. The character array myname is filled using the working pointer, chptr. chptr is incremented along the array, from one character to the next. The indirection operation is used on chptr both in the test expression and in the assignment of the result of getchar. In both cases, the element referenced by chptr is needed, not chptr itself. The element's value is tested for the newline, and the element is assigned a value. In the initialization and the increment, there is no indirection. The initialization assigns the beginning address of the character array to the pointer variable chptr. The increment increments the address that the pointer holds.

LISTING 11-10:

getstr.c

```
#include <stdio.h>

int main(void)
        {
        char myname[10];
        char *chptr;

        chptr = myname;
        *chptr = getchar();
        while (*chptr != '\n')
                {
                chptr++;
                *chptr = getchar();
                }
        *chptr = '\0';

        return 0;
        }
```

The next example contains string functions rewritten using working pointers. The indirection operation is used in the test to reference a character element in the array. The postfix increment operation is used to advance the pointer to the next character by incrementing the pointer's address. The base address of the array has been passed to the parameter variable. The parameter variable is a variable local to its own function. As a pointer variable it can be used as a working pointer to move along the array. This strategy works if the base address is not needed. In some string functions the array is only traversed once. The end of the string is detected by a test for the null character. There usually is no bounds checking. In the case of puts, the str parameter variable will hold the base address of the array. str is then used as a working pointer to advance down the array, element by element. Indirection is used to reference an element. The increment operation changes the address of the pointer to that of the next element. Notice also the use of indirection in the `strcmp` function. It is important to note that the two elements referenced by the pointers, not the pointers themselves, are subtracted.

So far you have seen how indirection and increments can be used in string functions. There are also situations in which you would need to use the pointer index operation. The index operation is the subtraction of two pointer to obtain the index of an element in an array. String functions that return the position of an element in an array would need to make use of just such an operation. Such functions return the position of an element in an array. If the function is using only working pointers to reference elements, the index operation is used to determine the position of the element.

strchr is an example of such a function. The function strchr uses a pointer to locate a particular character in an array of characters. It then returns as its value the index of that character in the array. If the character is not found strchr returns a -1.

```
void puts(char *str)
            {
            while (*str != '\0') {
                    putchar(*str);
                    str++;
                    }
            }

void strcpy(char *copystr, char *originalstr)
            {
            while(*originalstr != '\0'){
                    *copystr = *originalstr;
                    copystr++;
                    originalstr++;
                    }
            }

int strcmp(char *str1, char *str2)
            {
            while((*str1 == *str2) && (*str1 != '\0'))
                    {
                    str1++;
                    str2++;
                    }
            return(*str1 - *str2);
            }
```

In the **searchst.c** program in LISTING 11-11 the mystrchar function is a version of strchar that only uses pointers. The array myname is initialized to the string RICH. myname and the character 'C' are then passed to mystrchar . In this case the base address of the array needs to be preserved in order to calculate the index later on. A working pointer, cptr, is declared and assigned the base address held by str. cptr then advances through the array, searching for an element with the same value as that of the parameter letter, 'C'. If a match is found then str is subtracted from cptr giving the integer index of the element. As shown in Figure 11-7, when cptr finds the letter 'C', its address is 802, the address of the third element. str holds the base address of the array myname, 800. A pointer subtraction of str from cptr results in the index of that third element, 2.

```
cptr-str              is    2
                            (802 - 800) / sizeof(byte);
                            2 / sizeof(byte)
                            2 / 1 = 2
```

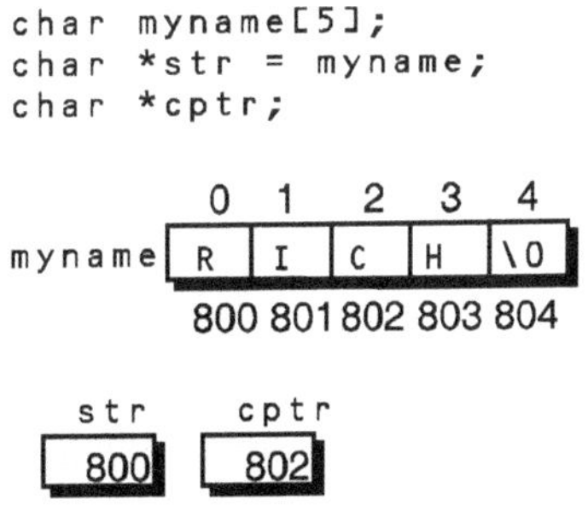

```
char myname[5];
char *str = myname;
char *cptr;
```

```
             0  1  2  3  4
myname   R  I  C  H  \0
           800 801 802 803 804
```

```
     str    cptr
     800    802
```

Figure 11-7: Indexing a character array with pointers.

LISTING 11-11:

searchst.c

```
#include <stdio.h>

 int mystrchr(char*, char);

int main(void)
       {
       char myname[5] = { 'R', 'I', 'C', 'H', '\0' };
       int res;

       res = mystrchr(myname, 'C');
       if (res  < 0 )
              printf("letter not found \n");
       else
              printf("letter is at index %d \n", res);

       return 0;
       }

 int mystrchr( char *str, char letter)
       {
       char *cptr;
       int index;

       cptr = str;
       while((*cptr != letter) && (*cptr != '\0'))
              {
              cptr++;
              }

       if (*cptr != '\0')     /*if end not reached*/
              index = cptr - str;    /*letter is found */
       else
              index = -1;
              return (index);
       }
```

Compact Code using Character Pointers

You can combine the postfix increment operation with the indirection operation to produce more compact code. LISTING 11-12 contains two programs that print out an array. In LISTING 11-12A, the increment operation and the indirection operation are combined. In the `putchar` argument, `*chptr++`, the indirection operation first references the element. After the `putchar` function call, the pointer is incremented. The increment is a postfix operation and will take effect after it has been used. You still need to be careful where you place your increment operation. Unintended errors can result. In 11.12B, the increment operation is combined with `chptr` in the test expression. `chptr` is incremented right after the test, before it is used in `putchar`. The first element is never printed out.

LISTING 11-12A:

```
#include <stdio.h>

int main(void)
{
char myname[5]={"Mark"};
char *chptr;


chptr = myname;
while(*chptr !='\0')
        {
        putchar(*chptr++);
        }
}
```

LISTING 11-12B:

```
#include <stdio.h>

int main(void)
        {
char myname[5]={"Mark"};
char *chptr;

chptr = myname;
while(*chptr++!='\0')
        {
        putchar(*chptr);
        }
}
```

You can develop even more compact code based on the fact that the end of string terminator and the value for falsehood in a test expression are the same, 0. The null character is the equivalent of an integer value of 0. Remember that any test expression that results in a zero value is false. The test expression itself can be a primary expression, which can consist of a single variable or an indirection operation that references a variable. This means that when managing strings, the inequality test for the null character in the test expression can be dropped. When indirection operation reference the element with the null character. This primary expression has a resulting value of 0, rendering the test expression false.

```
while(*chptr)
```
is equivalent to `while(*chptr!='\0')`

For example, the puts function can be written without an inequality test. The increment can then be combined with the indirection in the putchar argument. It would be a mistake to place the increment in the test expression. The pointer would be incremented before the first element is referenced for putchar.

```
void puts(char *str)
        {
        while (*str)
                putchar(*str++);
        }
```

If a null character is the assigned value in an assignment operation, then the result of the assignment expression is 0. You can use this fact to reduce the `strcpy` function to a single while test expression. In the next example, the test expression is doing all the work. In the test expression, three operations are happening at once. First, there are two indirection operations taking place on their respective pointers. Second an assignment operation is taking place. The result of the assignment is the value assigned. If the value assigned is a null character, '\0', then the result of the assignment expression is 0. This will stop the loop. If any other character value is assigned, the assignment expression will be true, and the loop will continue. Third, the postfix increment operations are executed, advancing the pointers to the next characters in their arrays. Since increments are postfix, they execute after the assignment. Since they are placed to the right of the indirection operator, they are evaluated first, before the indirection operator. This means that the postfix operators operate on the pointers, not the characters referenced in the indirection operations.

```
void strcpy(char *copystr, char *originalstr)
           {
           while(*copystr++ = *originalstr++);
           }
```

You can even significantly reduce the `strcmp` function. In this case, the end of the string is tested for using the same indirection operation used in **puts**, and the comparison operation is combined with the increments similar to the `strcpy` combination. When constructing such compact code, you need to be careful how you place the components. The test for the end of the string, (`*str1`), is placed before the comparison. This placement takes advantage of the fact that a logical AND expression always evaluates from left to right. This ensures that `str1` will first be tested for a null value before it is incremented in the next expression. If the placement were reversed, then, in the case of equal strings, the pointer would increment one character beyond the end of their respective strings.

```
int strcmp(char *str1, char *str2)
          {
          while((*str1) && (*str1++ == *str2++));
          return(*str1 - *str2);
          }
```

Compact code may or may not result in more efficient processing, depending on the optimizing strategies used by a given compiler. Yet it is often hard for programmers to resist. There are serious drawbacks to compact code in that it tends to be difficult to read and dangerous to modify. Unless efficiency is a top priority, it may be best to let the compiler do the optimizing. Most compilers these days may do a far better job of optimizing code than programming efforts could accomplish. Clear code is far more important than obscure "optimizations."

String Constants

A string constant is an array of characters initialized with a given set of values that are not meant to be changed. A string constant is specified by a set of double quotes. Any letters within the double quotes are values with which to initialize the array. The size of the array is the number of letters within the quotes plus one for the null character. The string constant will automatically add the null character. Each string constant has its own array with its own address. When the compiler detects a string constant, it sets aside memory for the array, fills the array with the characters within the double quotes, and returns, at that point in the program, the address of that array. The following are all examples of string constants.

```
"Greetings";
"Does not compute";
"1st string is %s\n"
```

In a sense, the double quotes can be thought of as defining and initializing an array, but not declaring it. Memory for an array is allocated. Its elements are initialized with a set of values. The result of the definition is an address, the address of the array. All these actions take place only once, when the program is loaded. String constants are placed in external storage. They endure for the entire run of the program. Their addresses are available only at the place they are defined in the program.

In LISTING 11-13, two string constants are defined. Their definitions evaluate to the addresses of their respective arrays. Each definition generates a different string constant. The first is printed out, and the second has only its address printed out.

LISTING 11-13:

```
#include <stdio.h>

int main(void)
    {
    printf("1st string is %s\n", "hello");
    printf("2nd string's address =% p","goodbye");
    return 0;
    }
```

Like an array name, the definition of the string constant evaluates to the address of its array. When a string constant is used in an expression, it is the string's address which is actually being specified. The string constant array has already been allocated and initialized. Its address is then used in whatever expression the string constant has been written. When a string constant is used as an argument in a function call, the argument is actually the address of the string constant array. This address is then passed to the function. String constants have already been used as arguments in printf function. They can also be used as arguments in other functions.

```
strcmp(game, "card");
strcpy(sport, "tennis");
strlen("baseball");
```

The use of `strcpy` with string constants can lead to subtle errors. The **strerror.c** program in LISTING 11-14 fails, and it fails for the most common reason. The size of the name array is 5 elements, for 5 characters. The string constant has 5 characters. But there is an extra element for the null character. So the string constant "hello" requires an array of 6 elements. `strcpy`, as it exists in the standard library, does not check for such discrepancies. The memory used for the variable next to the name array ends up getting the extra characters. In this case, the variable count gets the null character. When the program is run, 0 is printed out for the value of count. Figure 11-8 illustrates this error.

LISTING 11-14:

strerror.c
```
#include <stdio.h>
#include <string.h>

int main(void)
    {
    int count;
    char name[5];

    count = 7;
    strcpy(name, "hello");
    printf("The value of count is %d.", count);
    return 0;
    }
```

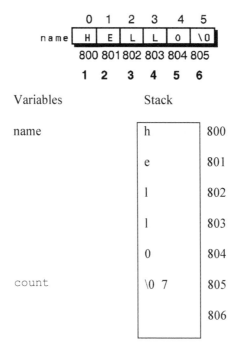

Figure 11-8: String constant run-time error.

Though the string constant's address is only available where it is defined, you can use a pointer to reference the string constant itself from anywhere. You can assign the address of a string constant to a pointer at the place of its definition. This is why character pointers often work hand-in-hand with string constants. In the case of the function calls above, the addresses of the string constants were passed into parameter pointer variables. Elements in the constant array were then referenced by the pointers. In LISTING 11-15 the address of a string constant is assigned to a character pointer. The character pointer then holds the address of the string constant's array. The pointer can then be used to reference the string array in many different expressions. Figure 11-9 shows the respective values of the pointer variable `strptr` and the string constant "hello".

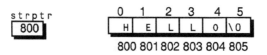

Figure 11-9: String constant and pointer variable.

LISTING 11-15:

```
#include <stdio.h>

int main(void)
        {
        char *strptr;

        strptr = "hello";
        puts(strptr);
        printf("%s\n", strptr);
        return 0;
        }
```

Often you will see code in which the assignment of a string constant's address to a pointer is combined with the pointer's declaration. In this case, the pointer is initialized with the address of the string constant. This may appear similar to the use of string constants in array initializations. It is not the same. In the program **message.c** in LISTING 11-16, message1 is declared as a single pointer variable initialized with the address of the string constant array "Does not compute". message1 is not an array itself.

LISTING 11-16:

message.c

```
#include <stdio.h>

        char *message1 = "Does not compute\n";
        char *message2 = "Need help now\n";

int main(void)
        {
        int i;

        scanf("%d", &i);
        if (i == 1)
                printf(message1);
         else
                printf(message2);

        return 0;
        }
```

Be careful not to confuse the string constant used in an array declaration with a string constant whose address is assigned to a pointer variable. In the following example, game is an array, whereas message is a pointer variable.

```
        char game[] = "tennis";
        char *message = "We play today";
```

Though a string constant can be used in an array initialization, a string constant cannot be assigned to an array name. In the next example, an attempt is made to assign the address of the character constant to an array name. An array name is not a variable. It is an address. This is an attempt to assign an address to an address, a value to a value.

```
        char name[5];
        name = "hello";            /* Invalid*/
```

In order to copy the characters in the string constant array to the name array, you have to use strcpy. In other words, you have to think of the string constant as another array, just like the name array.

```
        char name[6];
        strcpy(name, "hello");
```

In the **strconst.c** program in LISTING 11-17, string constants are used in a variety of ways. "Greetings" has its address assigned to the pointer variable message. "Chris" and "Larisa" are used simply for the array initializations of myname and lname. " Jr." has its address passed to the function strcat, which then copies it to the end of myname. "Aleina" has its address passed to strcpy, which then uses it to copy "Aleina" to the **aname** array. The address of "Greetings", held by the pointer message, is then passed to printf. "Greetings" is printed out.

LISTING 11-17:

strconst.c

```
#include <stdio.h>
#include <string.h>

        char *message = "Greetings\n";

int main(void)
        {
        char myname[10] = "Chris";
        char aname[10];
        char lname[] = "Larisa";

        strcat(myname, " Jr.");
        strcpy(aname, "Aleina");
        printf("%s %s", message, myname);

        return 0;
        }
```

Variable Length Arguments of Different Types: printf

As explained in Chapter 6, you can define a function to take a varying number of arguments. The parameters remain undeclared. What was not explained was how arguments of different types could be passed to and referenced within the function. To enable a function to accept a varying number of different types of objects, you need a format string. A format string is a string that contains codes designating the types of the arguments passed.

Let's take the example of printf. printf is a function that takes a varying number of different types of arguments. In the printf function, the first parameter variable is declared as a pointer to a character. This is because the first argument is always a string constant. The address of the string constant is passed to the pointer. Within the string constant there are code symbols that specify the types of the other arguments passed. These symbols are the conversion specifiers. A conversion specifier consists of the percent sign, %, followed by a predetermined code letter. For example, %d indicates that an argument is an integer, and %f indicates that it is a floating point value.

LISTING 11-18:

myprint.c
```c
#include <stdio.h>
#include <stdarg.h>

void myprintf(char *str, ...);

int main(void)
      {
      int num = 23;
      float cost = 4.50;

      myprintf("Cost is %f, Num is %d\n", cost, num);

      return 0;
      }
void myprintf(char *str, ...)
      {
      char *chptr;
      va_list parptr;

      va_start(parptr, str);
      chptr = str;
      while(*chptr != '\0')
            {
            if(*chptr == '%')
                  {
                  chptr++;
                  switch(*chptr)
                        {
                        case 'd':
                        printf("%d", va_arg(parptr, int));
                                    break;
                        case 'f':
                        printf("%f", va_arg(parptr, double));
                                    break;
                        case 'c':
                              putchar(va_arg(parptr, char));
                                    break;
                        default:
                                    putchar(*chptr);
                        }
                  }
            else
                  putchar(*chptr);
            chptr++;
            }
      va_end(parptr);
      }
```

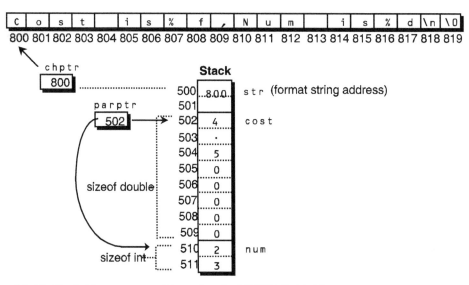

Figure 11-10: Variable argument function in LISTING 11.18.

A character pointer is assigned the base address of this string constant and advances through the array searching for the percent symbol. When one is found, the letter following it is read. Depending on that letter, a parameter will be accessed as a certain type. In the **myprint.c** program in LISTING 11-18 the function `myprintf` is a short version of `printf`. All it does is print out the arguments passed. As in Chapter 6, the macros `va_list`, `va_start`, `va_arg`, and `va_end` are used.

Now let us take a closer look at how the macros for managing the variable arguments are implemented. The macros are only pointers that progress along the stack. The stack can be thought of as an array whose elements are of different types. In order to progress from one to the next, a pointer is incremented by the size of that type. There is no standard required code for these macros, and they may differ depending upon the compiler you have. Shown here is a set of possible versions.

```
typedef void *va_list;
#define va_start(ap,param) ap=&param+sizeof(param)
#define va_arg(ap,type)    ((*(type*)(ap)),ap=ap+ sizeof(type))
```

`va_list` is another name for a pointer to a void type. Given the typedef and define macros above, the declaration of `parptr` with the data type of `va_list` in LISTING 11-18, simply declares `parptr` as a pointer to char. `va_start` assigns to `parptr` the address of the first undeclared parameter. It takes the first parameter, in this case `strptr`, and takes its address. It then increments that address by the size of `strptr`. `strptr` is a pointer variable, so `parptr` will be incremented the size of a pointer variable. The macro `va_arg` simply casts `parptr` to a type of object. An indirection on the casted parptr then references that object. A size of that object's type is then added to `parptr`. This advances the pointer by the size of that type, onto the next object. In the **myprint.c** program, `parptr` is first cast to an integer. Indirection on `parptr` references the integer. The size of an integer is then added to `parptr`, advancing it beyond the integer to the next object.

LISTING 11-19:

myprtptr.c

```
#include <stdio.h>

void myprintf(char *str, ...);

int main(void)
    {
    int num = 23;
    float cost= 4.50;

    myprintf("Cost is %f, Num is %d\n", cost, num);

    return 0;
    }

void myprintf(char *str, ...)
    {
    char *chptr;
    char *parptr;

    parptr = ((char*)&str) + sizeof(str);
    chptr = str;
    while(*chptr != '\0')
        {
        if(*chptr == '%')
            {
            chptr++;
            switch(*chptr)
                {
                case 'd':
                    printf("%d", *((int*)parptr) );
                    parptr = parptr + sizeof(int);
                    break;
                case 'f':
                    printf("%f", *((double*)parptr));
                    parptr = parptr + sizeof(double);
                    break;
                case 'c':
                    putchar(*((char*)parptr));
                    parptr = parptr + sizeof(char);
                    break;
                }
            }
        else
            putchar(*chptr);
        chptr++;
        }
    }
```

You do not necessarily need to use the va_list macros. In the **myprtptr.c** program in LISTING 11-19, the **myprint.c** program in LISTING 11-18 has been rewritten without the macros. A floating point is treated as a double. An floating point parameter whose type is not specified as float in a prototype, will automatically be promoted to a double. Though the argument passed to myprintf is a float, it is promoted and placed on the stack as a double. For this reason, parptr needs to treat the floating point argument as a double. Figure 11-10 shows how the different arguments are referenced on the stack. parptr is a pointer to char that is cast to different pointer types. chptr is a pointer to a string constant and is the last declared parameter for the function. `parptr` is set to the address of the first undeclared argument. `parptr` is then cast to point to a double. It is then incremented by the size of a double, and then cast to point to an integer.

The actual implementation of stack arguments may vary from system to system. The `va_list` macros will always reflect these differences. It is safer to use them. It is also possible to have more than one named parameter in a function with a varying number of parameters. In this case the processing begins with the last named parameter. **.h**;

String Conversion Functions: atoi, atof, sprintf and sscanf

There are several standard conversion functions that convert strings to arithmetic values and back again. Two functions, `sscanf` and `sprintf` operate much like `printf` and `scanf` except that they convert strings. Otherwise the syntax is exactly the same.

```
sscanf(string, "format string", list of addresses);
sprintf(string, "format string", list of values);
```

Another set of string conversion functions returns one type of arithmetic value. The function `atoi` takes a string and converts it to an integer. `atof` converts a string to a float. `atol` converts a string to a long. Some compilers will include the corresponding functions to convert arithmetic values into strings. `itoa` converts a string to an integer. `ftoa` converts a float into a string.

LISTING 11-20:

strconv.c
```c
#include <stdio.h>
#include <stdlib.h>

int main(void)
        {
        int num;
        float cost;
        char str[80];

        cost = atof("35.74");
        num = atoi("256");

        sscanf("4500", "%d", &num);
        sprintf(str, "%f", 2000.50);

        printf("Please enter a cost\n");
        gets(str);
        cost = atof(str);

        printf("Please enter a num\n");
        gets(str);
        sscanf(str, "%d", &num);

        return 0;
        }
```

The string conversion functions are useful for receiving input from user interfaces, such as window-based systems. Often such systems process all input from the user and send the program a string. The string is in the appropriate format for either integer or float values, but it is still a string. It must be converted before it can be used.

The **strconv.c** program in LISTING 11-20, shows several uses of the string conversion functions. The function declarations for the string conversion functions are found in **stdlib.h**. The character I/O functions such as `getchar` and `putchar` are in **stdio.h**. Notice that `sscanf` performs the same type of conversions as `atoi` and `atof`. In the last statements, input is brought in as a string with `gets`. The string is then converted to a float using `atof`. With the string conversion functions, you need no longer be completely dependent on `scanf` for input conversions.

Character Test Operations: ctype.h

Character test operations test a single character for certain features. For example, the `isdigit` operation tests a character to see if it represents a digit, '0' through '9'. If the character is a digit the operation returns a non-zero value. If the character is not a digit the operations will return a 0 value. Another example is the `islower` operation. It tests to see if a character is lower case or not.

Unlike the other character test operations, the `tolower` and `toupper` operations return a character value instead of a 1 or 0. They are used to change the value of a character. The `tolower` operation changes a character value from upper case to lower case and then returns the lower case value. The `toupper` operations return the upper case of a lower case value.

Table 11-1: Character Test Functions: ctype.h

isalnum(char c)	Letter or digit
isalpha(char c)	Letter
iscntrl(char c)	A control character
isdigit(char c)	Digit
isgraph(char c)	Printable character, except space
islower(char c)	Lower case character
isprint(char c)	Printable character including space
ispunct(char c)	Printable character, except space, letter, or number
isspace(char c)	Whitespace character, \f, \n, \t, \v, \r ,space
isupper(char c)	Upper case character
isxdigit(char c)	Hexadecimal digit
int tolower(int)	Change upper case character to lower case and return the lower case value
int toupper(int)	Change lower case character to upper case and return the upper case value

The character test operations are actually define macros contained in the **ctype.h** header file. They take as their argument an integer and return an integer. The integer argument is used to hold a character value. You need to include this header file in order to use these operations. The character test operations are listed in Table 11-1.

In the **charfunc.c** program in LISTING 11-21, each character in a string is tested for upper case, lower case, a white space, and a digit. The count of each is then printed out. If a character is lower case, it is changed to upper case by assigning the result of the `toupper` operation to its element. Notice the inclusion of the **ctype.h** file.

LISTING 11-21:

charfunc.c

```
#include <stdio.h>
#include <ctype.h>

int main(void)
    {
    int i,countup,countlow;
    int countspace,countdigit;
    char str[80]="Dickens, Virgil, and Poe wrote before 1900";

    i=countup=countlow=countspace=countdigit=0;

    while(str[i] !='\0')
        {
        if(isdigit(str[i]))
            countdigit++;
        if(isspace(str[i]))
            countspace++;
        if(isupper(str[i]))
            countup++;
        if(islower(str[i]))
            {
            countlow++;
            str[i] = toupper(str[i]);
            }
        i++;
        }

    printf("The number of digits = %d\n",countdigit);
    printf("The number of spaces = %d\n",countspace);
    printf("Upper case letters = %d\n", countup);
    printf("Lower case letters = %d\n", countlow);
    printf("%s\n", str);

    return 0;
    }
```

Output for LISTING 11-21:

```
The number of digits = 4
The number of spaces = 6
Upper case letters = 3
Lower case letters = 27
DICKENS, VIRGIL, AND POE WROTE BEFORE 1900
```

Chapter Summary: Arrays of Characters: Strings

An array of characters is used to implement a string. The end of the string is marked with a null character. Loops are used to manage the string, one character at a time. A test for the null character detects the end of the string.

A set of functions in the standard library is designed to perform common operations on strings. `strlen` finds the length of a string. `strcpy` copies a string. `strcmp` compares two strings. These functions can be written in very compact code by using pointers.

A string constant is specified by a set of double quotes. This string constant definition evaluates to the address of the string. A string constant has no array name. Its address can only be accessed where the string is defined. The string's address can be assigned to a pointer. Through the pointer, the string can be accessed anywhere.

A format string enables a function defined with varying arguments to accept different types of arguments. The `va_list` macros can be used to reference each object. These macros essentially manage a pointer that advances along the stack. The stack is treated like an array of different types of objects. Though you can define your own pointers to reference the objects, it is always safer to use the `va_list` macros.

Exercises

1. Write a mygets function, using only pointers. `mygets` is your own version of gets.

2. Write a `stringcat` and a `stringlen` function.
      Use only pointers. These are your own versions of `strcat` and `strcat`.

3. Modify the program in LISTING 11-22 to use pointers only.
      Currently, the program already reads a string using gets. It first gets a pattern for which to search from the user. It then reads a line from the user. It then searches each line for the presence of the pattern. If it finds the pattern in that line, it prints out the line. If not, it prints out a message saying the pattern was not found. gets reads a line in from the user. It then places it into the character array, here called buffer, and places a NULL at the end to make it a genuine string. If the user enters nothing but a carriage return, the loop will stop. The function used to search a line for a pattern is the `index_str` function. It works on a string, in this case pattern. It works on the arrays pattern and str element by element.

Modify the program as follows:

A. Rewrite index_str using pointers.
      Treat str and pattern as pointers to character strings (`char *str_ptr, *pattern_ptr;`). Instead of having integer indexes to arrays such as i, j, and k (pattern`[k]`), use three or more pointers to characters. You will need at least three. They will operate somewhat the same way as the indexes but with significant differences. You will need a pointer to take the place of the i index to move along the str character string. You will need a pointer to take the place of the j index to move along the str character string when comparing with the pattern character string. You will need a pointer to take the

place of the k index to move along the pattern string. Instead of initializing to zero as with the integer indexes, you initialize to the beginning address of the string (i_ptr = str_ptr).

```
int index_str(char *str_ptr, char *pattern_ptr)
```

B. Keep a count of each instance of a pattern in all the lines entered.

Print out the count at the end of the program. To do this you must modify the program to search for multiple instances of a pattern in the line. Use a pointer (lineptr) to move through the line. This will require an inner while loop. The outer while is for the lines in the file, line by line. The inner while is for the instances of the pattern in a particular line. If index_str returns < 0, you know there are no more patterns in that line. If it returns >=0, there may be more patterns.

How do you know where the rest of the line starts? You know that index_str returns the beginning index of the pattern in the character array. That, plus the length of the pattern, puts us at the beginning of the remainder of the line to be searched. Do something like: lineptr + pos + strlen(*pattern*).

C. Modify your program by adding a function that will print out a ^ underneath the beginning of the instance just found.

LISTING 11-22: Program for Exercise 3

main.c

```c
#include <stdio.h>

#define MAXLINE  80
#define USERMAX 20

int index_str(char*, char*);

int main(void)
        {
        int pos;
        char buffer[MAXLINE];
        char pattern[USERMAX];

        printf("\nplease enter pattern: ");
        gets(pattern);
        printf("\nEnter string to be searched:");
        gets(buffer);
        while (buffer[0] != '\0')
                {
                if((pos = index_str(buffer, pattern)) >= 0)
                        {
                        printf ("\n%s\n",buffer);
                        }
                else
                        printf("\nPattern not found\n");
                printf("\nEnter string to be searched:");
                gets(buffer);
                }
        return 0;
        }
```

lib.c

```
int index_str (char str[], char pat[])
        {
        int i, j, k;

        for ( i = 0; str[i] != '\0' ; i++)
                {
                for(j=i,k=0; (pat[k]!='\0')&&(str[j]==pat[k]); j++,k++);
                if (pat[k] == '\0')
                        return (i);
                }
        return(-1);
        }
```

Arrays of Structures

Members, Pointers, and Functions

Arrays as Structure Members

Arrays of Structures

Pointers and Structure Elements

Arrays of Structures and Functions

Program Examples

12. Arrays of Structures

Arrays of structures combine two aggregate data types, arrays and structures. An array consists of many objects of the same type, whereas a structure consists of several objects of different data types. Structures themselves are objects. You reference members of a structure through the member operation. However, arrays are not objects. You can only reference elements in an array through pointer operations. In an array of structures, the elements of the array are structures. To reference a member within a structure element in an array, you need to combine a pointer operation with the member operation. The pointer operation first references the element, and then a member operation references the member.

The array name in any array declaration is used as a pointer. It points to the first element in the array. In the case of an array of structures, the array name is a pointer to a structure. The pointer operations on an array of structures operate much like any pointer to a structure. Elements in an array of structures are referenced using a pointer offset operation. As an alternative to an explicit pointer operation, you can use array subscripts to reference a structure element in an array. Array subscripts is just another way of writing the pointer offset operation.

Arrays can themselves be members of a structure. Such arrays are first referenced with a member operation, and then elements in the array are referenced with pointer operations. This chapter will first examine arrays that are structure members, and then discuss arrays of structures.

Arrays as Structure Members

You can declare an array as a member of a structure, just as you can declare variables as members. An array that is a member of a structure, once referenced, operates like any other array. The same pointer operations such as offsets, increments, and indexes, as well as array subscripts, all apply. Table 12-1 list various operations on array members. In Figure 12-1, the type EMP has been defined with a member that is an array: name. When the member operator references name, it will reference an address, not a variable. Arrays are not objects. An array is memory referenced using pointers and addresses. When the member operation references name, it is referencing an array name, the beginning address of the array. It is not referencing a variable. In the following example, the argument for scanf function, employee.name, does not have an address operator before it, as a variable would. The address operator is not applied to the name member because name is an array name. It is already an address.

```
scanf("%s", employee.name);
```

Since the name member is an array name, an offset operation can be performed on it to reference elements in that array. The offset operation can take the form of either array subscript or a pointer offset operation. In the **member.c** program in LISTING 12-1, each element of the array is filled using array subscripts. Each element is then printed out using pointer offset operations. Parentheses are not needed to separate the member operation from the offset operation. The member operator takes precedence over the addition operator. s

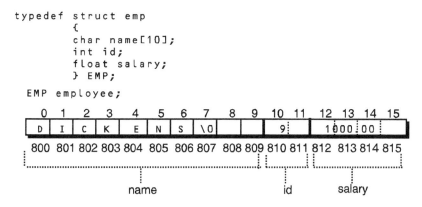

Figure 12-1: Structure member as an array.

LISTING 12-1:

member.c

```c
#include <stdio.h>

        typedef struct emp
                {
                char name[10];        /* structure member array */
                int id;
                float salary;
                } EMP;

 int main(void)
        {
        EMP employee;
        int i;

        employee.id = 9;
        employee.salary = 1000.00;

        i = 0;
        while ((employee.name[i] = getchar()) != '\n')
                {
                i++;
                }
        employee.name[i] = '\0';

        i = 0;
        while ( *(employee.name + i) != '\0')
                {
                putchar(*(employee.name + i));
                i++;
                }

        return 0;
        }
```

Within the structure's initialization, you can initialize member arrays using a nested set of braces. In the case of a character array, you can use a string constant in the place of a nested set of braces. In the **offmemb.c** program in LISTING 12-2, a string constant is used to initialize the name array, and a nested set of braces is used to initialize the accounts array. Remember that the initialization is done when the structure variable is defined, not when the structure type is declared. Figure 12-2 shows the values of the `employee` structure upon initialization.

You can also use a pointer to a structure to reference an element in the member array. In LISTING 12-.2, pointers to structures are used to print out each member array. The arrow notation denotes the pointer to a structure. Again, parentheses are not required since the arrow operator takes precedence over the addition operator. However, the arrow notation is really an indirection and member operation. If you were to use the indirection and member operations instead of the arrow operator, the indirection operation would require its own set of parentheses. The following examples are three equivalent operations. Each assigns 'C' to the third element of the name array.

```
*((*emptr).name + 3) = 'C';
*(emptr->name + 3) = 'C';
emptr->name[3] = 'C';
```

LISTING 12-2:

offmemb.c

```c
#include <stdio.h>

        typedef struct emp{
                char name[100];
                int accounts[3];
                int id;
                float salary;
                } EMP;

 int main(void)
        {
        EMP employee={"DICKENS",{10,2,8},9,1000};
        int i;
        EMP *emptr;

        emptr = &employee;
        i = 0;
        while(*(emptr->name + i) != '\0')
                {
                putchar(*(emptr->name + i));
                i++;
                }

        i = 0;
        while ( i < 3)
                {
                printf("%d \n",*(emptr->accounts + i));
                i++;
                }

        return 0;
        }
```

```
typedef struct emp
        {
        char name[10];
        int accounts[3];
        int id;
        float salary;
        } EMP;
```

EMP employee = {"Dickens", {10,2,8}, 9, 1000};

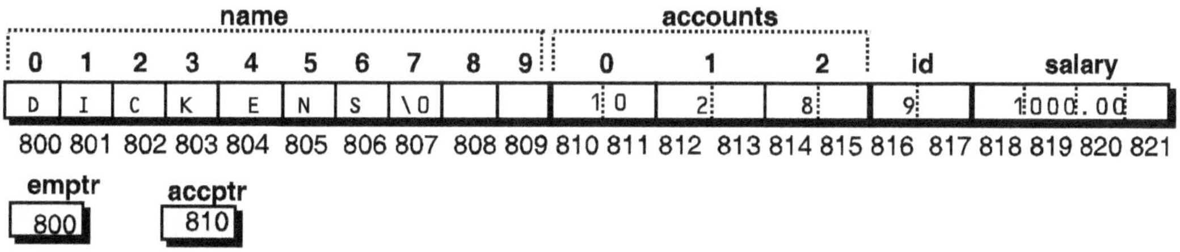

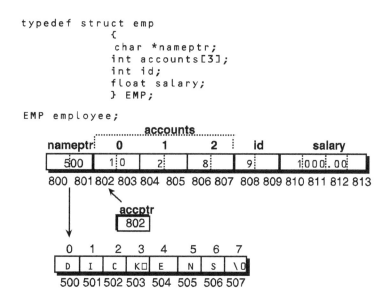

Figure 12-2: Arrays as structure members.

```
typedef struct emp
        {
        char *nameptr;
        int accounts[3];
        int id;
        float salary;
        } EMP;
```

EMP employee;

Figure 12-3: Pointers referencing arrays as members in structures.

LISTING 12-3:

ptrmemb.c

```c
#include <stdio.h>

        typedef struct emp
                {
                char *nameptr;
                int accounts[3];
                int id;
                float salary;
                } EMP;

 int main(void)
        {
        EMP employee = {0,{10,2,8},9,1000};
        int i;
        EMP *emptr;
        int *accptr;

        employee.nameptr = "DICKENS";
        accptr = employee.accounts;
        emptr = &employee;

        i = 0;
        while( employee.nameptr[i] != '\0')
                {
                putchar(*(emptr->nameptr + i));
                i++;
                }

        while( accptr < (employee.accounts + 3))
                {
                printf("%d \n",*accptr);
                accptr++;
                }

        return 0;
        }
```

You can manage member arrays just as you would any other array. You can calculate their end address and have working pointers advance through them. In the **ptrmemb.c** program in LISTING 12-3, the pointer variable accptr is used as a working pointer for accounts member array. accptr is first assigned the address of the accounts array. accptr then progresses along the array. The end of the array is calculated using the array name accounts and the offset of the number of elements in accounts. Figure 12-3 shows a working pointer, accptr, and a member array, accounts.

A member of a structure could just as easily be a pointer to a separately defined array. In LISTING 12-3, nameptr is declared as a pointer to a character and assigned the address of a string constant. The string constant could be placed in the array initialization, as was done in LISTING 12-2. Here the string constant is explicitly assigned in a statement for the sake of emphasis. The string constant is a separate array unto itself. The nameptr member is only a pointer variable that holds the address of the string constant's first element. Figure 12-3 shows both a pointer as a member of a structure, nameptr, and the string array it points to.

Table 12-1: Arrays as Members of Structures

employee.name[1]	Reference of an element of an array that is a member of a structure.
emptr->name[1]	Reference of an element of an array that is a member of a structure using a pointer to a structure.
emprecs[2].name[1]	Reference of an element of an array that is a member of a structure element.
(emprecs+2)->name[1]	Reference of an element of an array that is a member of a structure element. The structure element is first referenced with the pointer structure operator.
(*(emprecs+2)).(*(name+1))	Pointer offset and indirection operations to reference both a structure element in an array of structures and an array element of an array that is member of a structure.

Arrays of Structures

Array subscripts: structure elements;Array of structures: members of structure elements;
You declare an array of structures by specifying the structure type, an array name, and a set of brackets containing the number of elements in the array. Its format is the same as any other type of array declaration. The only difference is that the data type is a structure type. In the following examples, the structure type is referenced by a typedef, in this case EMP (see Figure 12-4)>

```
EMP emprecs[3];
```

It is important to note that the name used in the array declaration is an array name, not the name of a structure variable. The array name is the address of the first element in the array. In the previous example, emprecs is an address, not a variable.

Should you want to, you can initialize each structure in an array of structures. You enter the values for each structure within its own set of braces, all of which are then enclosed within an outer set of braces. In the **struct.c** program in LISTING 12-4, the emprecs array is initialized with a set of values. Figure 12-5 illustrates this array showing each structure, its members, and their values.

As with any array, you need to use pointer operations to reference array elements. The elements in this case are structures. A combined pointer offset and indirection operation will reference a particular structure element. At the same time, each structure element within an array of structures has its own members. To further reference a member within a particular structure element, you need to combine the offset and indirection operations together with a member operation.

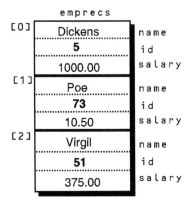

Figure 12-4 Array of structures.

LISTING 12-4:

struct.c

```c
#include <stdio.h>
#define MAX 3

        typedef struct emp{
                char name[10];
                int id;
                float salary;
                } EMP;

 int main(void)
        {
        int i;
        EMP emprecs[MAX] = {   {"Dickens", 5, 1000},
                               {"Poe", 73, 10.50},
                               {"Virgil", 51, 375.00} };

        i = 0;
        while (i < MAX)
                {
                printf("\nName is %s\n", emprecs[i].name);
                printf("id is %d\n", emprecs[i].id);
                printf("Salary is %.2f\n",emprecs[i].salary);
                i++;
                }

        return 0;
        }
```

Recall that you can use array subscripts to represent the combined offset and indirection operation. In array subscripts, the index of an array element is placed in brackets next to the array name. This will effectively reference a structure element in the array. Figure 12-5 illustrates the emprecs array and the array subscript used to reference each element.

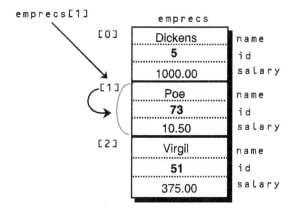

Figure 12-5 Referencing and structure element in an array of structures.

Once a structure is referenced, you can then use a member operation to access one of that structure's members. The next example and in LISTING 12-4, and array called `emprecs` is declared whose elements are `EMP` structures. The last structure in the array is referenced using the array index, `[2]`. The id member of that structure is then referenced using the member operator, .id. The value 51 is then assigned to the id member of the third structure in the `emprecs` array. Figure 12-6 illustrates this structure reference and member operation.

```
EMP emprecs[3];
emprecs[2].id = 51;
```

When working with members of a structure element within an array of structures, some operations may appear confusing. One such case is when you need to obtain the address of a member within a structure element. In the following example, the address operator takes the address of the id member of the second structure element in the `emprecs` array. The address operator is placed before the array name, not the member. This may appear as though the address operator is being applied to the array name, but its not. Precedence is actually allowing the address operator to apply to the member. Both the brackets and the member operator have a higher precedence than the address operator, so they will be evaluated first, before the address operator. First the brackets reference the structure, and then the member operation references the structure member, and finally the address operator obtains the address from that member. (see Figure 12-7).

```
&emprecs[1].id
```

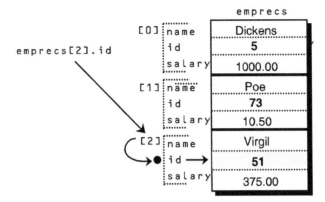

Figure 12-6: Members of structure elements.

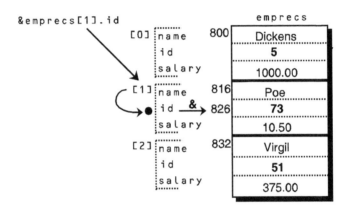

Figure 12-7: Addresses of structure element members .

In the **inputstr.c** program in LISTING 12-5, a series of `scanf` operations is used to input values into each element of the array. The `scanf` function will require the address of a member for its argument so that it can directly reference and assign values to those members. The address operator is applied to structure members to obtain their addresses. However, the address operator works only on members that are variables, not on members that are themselves arrays. In the case of a member array, the array name is already an address, and so the address operator is not needed. For example the name member argument for `scanf` does not have an address operator. `name` is an array name and so is already an address.

```
scanf("%d", &emprecs[i].id);
scanf("%s", emprecs[1].name);
```

In these programs, the `scanf` function for the name member uses a version of the `[]` conversion specifier that allows you to enter in several words for the name - `%[^\n]s`. It literally reads anything you type into the string array up until you press the ENTER key. The \n represents the newline character - the ENTER key. The conversion specifier is preceded by a `*` field skipper applied to another `[]` conversion specifier that skips over any preceding whitespaces (newline, tab, or space) in the input - `%*[\n\t ]`. The `[]` conversion specifier and the `*` field skipper are discussed in detail in Chapter 25.

```
scanf("%*[\n\t ]%[^\n]s", emprecs[1].name);
```

LISTING 12-5:

inputstr.c

```c
#include <stdio.h>

#define MAX 3
    typedef struct emp{
        char name[100];
        int id;
        float salary;
        } EMP;

int main(void)
    {
    EMP emprecs[MAX];
    int i;

    i = 0;
    while (i < MAX)
        {
        printf("\nEnter Name:");
        scanf("%*[\n\t ]%[^\n]s", emprecs[i].name);
        printf("\nEnter Id:");
        scanf("%d", &emprecs[i].id);
        printf("\nEnter Salary:");
        scanf("%f", &emprecs[i].salary);
        i++;
        }

    i = 0;
    while (i < MAX)
        {
        printf("\nName is %s\n", emprecs[i].name);
        printf("id is %d\n", emprecs[i].id);
        printf("Salary is %.2f\n",emprecs[i].salary);
        i++;
        }

    return 0;
    }
```

Arrays of structures tend to use a great deal of memory. In some systems the default configurations for the stack or data segments may not be capable of holding large arrays. The segments may have to be expanded before a large array of structures can be declared safely.

As an alternative, you may want to dynamically allocate memory for your structure array. In this case you would only declared a pointer to a structure, not an array of structures. You could then use an allocation function such as `calloc` to allocate the memory you need and then assign the address of that memory to your structure pointer. Remember that arrays are managed using only addresses and pointer operations performed on allocated memory. Whether the memory is allocated in an array declaration or by an allocation function like `calloc`, does not really matter. You can also just as easily use a pointer variable to perform array operations, instead of an array name. The same pointer operations, offsets, increments, indexes, as well as array subscripts, apply. The following example shows how you would use a pointer and allocated memory in place of an array declaration.

```
EMP *empallptr;

empallptr = (EMP*) calloc(3, sizeof(EMP));
```

The `calloc` function takes two arguments, the number of objects and the size of an object. Though `calloc` is only allocating a chunk of memory, its arguments are designed to allow you to easily allocate memory to be used for an array. You can think of the first argument as the number of elements in your array, and the second argument as the size of those elements. In this case, the `sizeof` operation was used to obtain the actual number of bytes used for an `EMP` structure. If the size of a structure is 16 bytes, then `calloc`, in this example, will allocate 48 bytes (3 * 16). The beginning address of this memory is assigned to `empallptr` which you can then use as you would an array name, a pointer holding the beginning address of an array. To reference an element you need only use array subscripts on `empallptr`. And to reference a member, just use array subscript with the member operation.

```
empallptr[2]
empallptr[2].id
```

Pointers and Structure Elements

Like any other array name, the array name declared for an array of structures is a pointer. The elements in the array are referenced by offset and indirection pointer operations. Table 12-2 lists different pointer operations on structure elements. Figure 12-8 shows how a structure in the array can be referenced with a pointer offset and indirection operation. The array name and the offset gives you the address of a structure. Then an indirection on that address references the structure itself. The next example references the second element in the array using an offset of 1 on the array name, and an indirection on the resulting address.

```
*(emprecs + 1)
```

To reference a member of a structure in an array, you need to combine the offset and indirection operations with the member operation. Two sets of parentheses are required for such a combination. First, because the addition operator has a lower precedence than the indirection operator, parentheses are needed around the addition operator. This way the pointer offset calculation will be performed before the indirection. Second, because the member operator has a higher precedence than the indirection operator, parentheses are required around the indirection operator. This forces the indirection operation to take place first before the member operation. The address of the structure is calculated, and then the indirection is performed on that address, not on the member. The structure element is first referenced, and then the member is accessed.

In the next example, the array name `emprecs` is offset by 1, resulting in the address of the second structure element. An indirection is then performed on the address of the second structure element. Then the id member of that structure element is referenced. Figure 12-9 illustrates this combined offset, indirection, and member operation.

```
(*(emprecs + 1)).id
```

The **inputoff.c** program in LISTING 12-6 is a rewritten version of the **inputstr.c** program in LISTING 12-5, using pointer operations. Again, since the member operation has higher precedence than the address operator, no added parentheses are needed.

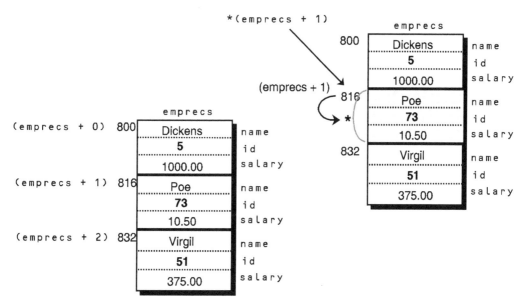

Figure 12-8: Pointer offsets and structure elements.

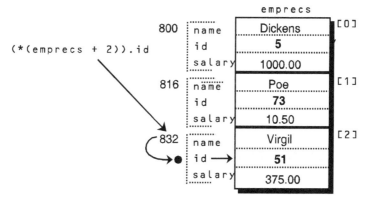

Figure 12-9: Pointer offsets and structure element members.

LISTING 12-6:

inputoff.c

```
#include <stdio.h>

#define MAX 3

        typedef struct emp{
                char name[100];
                int id;
                float salary;
                } EMP;

 int main(void)
        {
        EMP emprecs[MAX];
        int i;

        i = 0;
        while (i < MAX)
                {
                printf("\nEnter Name:");
                scanf("%*[\n\t ]%[^\n]s",(*(emprecs + i)).name);
                printf("\nEnter Id:");
                scanf("%d", &(*(emprecs + i)).id);
                printf("\nEnter Salary:");
                scanf("%f", &(*(emprecs + i)).salary);
                i++;
                }

        i = 0;
        while (i < MAX)
                {
                printf("\nName is %s\n",(*(emprecs + i)).name);
                printf("id is %d\n", (*(emprecs + i)).id);
                printf("Salary %.2f\n",(*(emprecs + i)).salary);
                i++;
                }

        return 0;
        }
```

As with any array name, the array name for an array of structures is a pointer to the type elements in the array. In this case, the type of element is a structure. The array name is actually a pointer to a structure. For example, emprecs is a pointer to an object of type EMP. Remember that pointer operations such as offsets, increments, and indexes, take into account the type of object pointed to. The pointer offset operation performs an implied multiplication of the offset by the size of the object the pointer points to. In the case of pointers to structures, a pointer offset operation will multiply the size of the structure. For emprecs, the multiplication is by the size of an EMP structure. The offset operation emprecs+2 is really emprecs+(2*sizeof(EMP)). If the size of an EMP structure is approximately 16 bytes (char[10], int = 2, float = 4). The sizeof operator would give an accurate count. Each element in the emprecs array would be laid out in multiples of 16. If the base address was 800, then the second element would be at address 816. Its offset would be emprecs + 1. The next address would be at 832. In these programs, the size of the EMP structure is actually 106 with

100 bytes for the name array. In this case, if the base address was 800, then the second element would be at address 906.

```
EMP emprecs;
EMP *emptr;
```

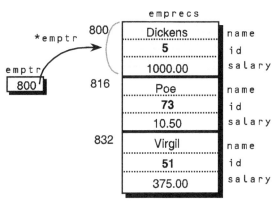

Figure 12-10: Pointer to structure element.

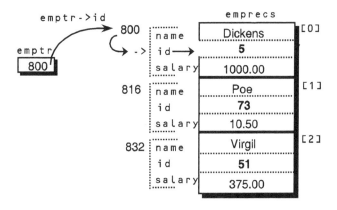

Figure 12-11: Using the structure pointer operation, ->, to reference a member of a structure element with just a pointer.

Just as you can use a pointer variable to reference elements in an array, you can also use a pointer to a structure to reference a structure in an array of structures. You can declare a pointer to a structure, assign it the address of a structure in the array, and then use that pointer to directly reference that structure element. In Figure 12-10, the pointer variable `emptr` is assigned the address of the first structure in `emprecs`.

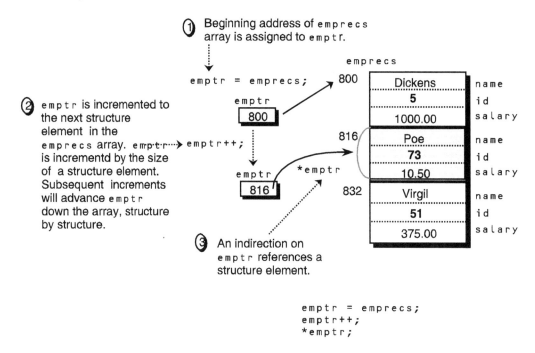

Figure 12-12: Incrementing pointer to structure element. A working pointer that advances down an array of structures, structure by structure.

Recall how you can use a structure pointer operation, the arrow, `->`, to reference a member of structure through a pointer to that structure. The structure pointer operation is a short-hand for the combined indirection and member operation. `emptr->id` is just another way of writing `(*emptr).id`. You use the `->` operation to reference a member of a structure element, using just a pointer to that structure. In the next example, the `->` operation is applied to `emptr` to reference the id member of the first element. The operation is illustrated in Figure 12-11.

Recall how the increment operation works with working pointers to advance down an array, from one element the next. This operation works very effectively with arrays of structures. You can declare a pointer to a structure and use a working pointer to advance from one structure to another in the array of structures. The pointer to a structure is incremented from the address of one element to the next. Remember that the increment operation on a pointer is equivalent to an offset of 1. This means that there is a hidden multiplication by the size of the structure, allowing for a very neat advancement from one structure to the beginning of the next. In Figure 12-12, `emptr++` is the same as `emptr=emptr+1`. Given that the size of an `EMP` structure is 16 bytes, an increment of `emptr` will increment its address by 16, if the size of the structure is 106 then `emptr` is incremented by 106.

When using such a working pointer, you will only need an indirection and member operation to reference a structure's member. You do not need the pointer offset operation. The working pointer is only a simple pointer to a structure. It holds the address of the structure element, and can thereby reference the structure directly. In fact, the working pointer will reference the structure element as if it were a structure variable. The indirection and member operations on such a working pointer are easily represented with the structure pointer operator, the arrow.

```
EMP *emptr;
emptr++ is equivalent to      emptr = emptr + 1;
```

In LISTING 12-7, the **inputoff.c** program in LISTING 12-6 is rewritten using a working pointer. `emptr` is initialized to the array name `emprecs`. `emptr` is then incremented to advance from one element to the next. The test for the end of the array is the offset of the array name and the number of elements in the array. The end address of the `emprecs` array is given by the offset, `emprecs+MAX`. If emprecs is 800 and the `EMP` structure has a size of 16 bytes, then `emprecs+3` will be 848. With a size of 106, `emprecs+3` will be 1118.

LISTING 12-7:

inputptr.c

```c
#include <stdio.h>

#define MAX 3

        typedef struct emp{
                char name[100];
                int id;
                float salary;
                } EMP;

 int main(void)
        {
        EMP emprecs[MAX];
        EMP *emptr;

        emptr = emprecs;
        while (emptr < (emprecs+MAX))
                {
                printf("\nEnter Name:");
                scanf("%*[\n\t ]%[^\n]s", emptr->name);
                printf("\nEnter Id:");
                scanf("%d", &emptr->id);
                printf("\nEnter Salary:");
                scanf("%f", &emptr->salary);
                emptr++;
                }

        for(emptr=emprecs; emptr<(emprecs+MAX);emptr++)
                {
                printf("\nName is %s\n", emptr->name);
                printf("id is %d\n", emptr->id);
                printf("Salary is %.2f\n",emptr->salary);
                }

        return 0;
        }
```

Though the structure pointer operator, ->, is usually used with a pointer to a structure to reference a structure member, you can also use it in a combined pointer offset and member operation. If you use a pointer offset operation to access a structure member, you need the double set of parentheses as well as the indirection and member operators. For example: `(*(emprecs+2)).id`. A combination the pointer offset and structure pointer operator will give a more simplified version. Recall that the structure pointer operator, ->, substitutes for the indirection and member operation, `(*)`.. `(*emptr).id` is equivalent to `emptr->id`. In the case of the combined pointer offset and member operation, the structure pointer operator will replace the indirection and member operator, leaving the addition segment of pointer offset operation. `(*(emprecs+2)).id` becomes `(emprecs+2)->id` Figure 12-13 illustrates this use of the structure pointer operator with pointer offset operations.

```
(emprecs + 2)->id        is equivalent to   (*(emprecs+2)).id
                                 and    emprecs[2].id
```

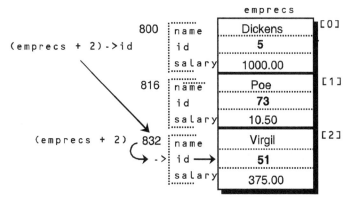

Figure 12-13: Pointer offset and structure pointer operator.

The loop to print out the `emprecs` array in the **inputoff.c** program in LISTING 12-6 is rewritten here using structure pointer operators.

```
i = 0;
while(i < MAX)
        {
        printf("\nName is %s\n", (emprecs+i)->name);
        printf("id is %d\n", (emprecs+i)->id);
        printf("Salary is %.2f\n",(emprecs+i)->salary);
        i++;
        }
```

In most cases, it is easier and clearer to use a working pointer to advance through array elements instead of using complex offset operations.

Table 12-2: Structure Elements and Pointers

`EMP *emptr;`	Pointer to structure element (pointer to structure)
`emptr++`	Increment pointer to a structure to the address of the next structure element in the array.
`(*emptr).id`	Reference member of structure element with indirection on a pointer to a structure and a member operation.
`emptr->id`	Reference member of structure element with a pointer to structure, using a structure pointer operator and a member operation.
`&emptr->id`	Address of member of structure a structure element referenced with pointer to a structure and structure pointer operator.

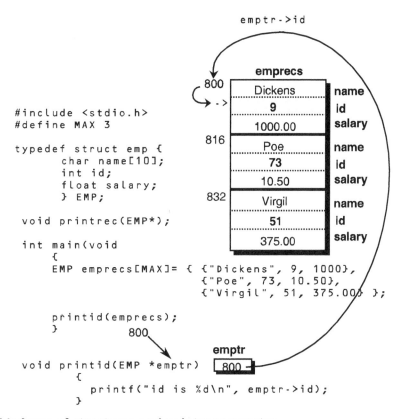

Figure 12-14: Array of structures and pointer parameter.

Arrays of Structures and Functions

Remember that an array name evaluates the address of an array. When you use an array name as an argument in a function call, the address of the array is passed to a pointer in the called function. Indirection operations on that pointer can then reference each element in the array from within the function. The same is true for arrays of structures. The array name for the array of structures is the address of the array. When an array name is used in a function call, the address of the first structure element is passed. The corresponding parameter for the address of a structure is a pointer to a structure. In Figure 12-14 the address of the emprecs array is passed to the parameter variable emptr. emptr is a pointer to a structure of type EMP.

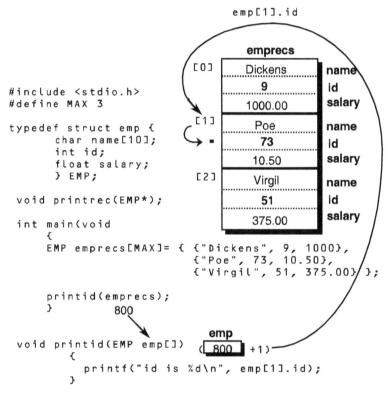

Figure 12-15: Array subscripts and Array of structures.

Within the function you can use either array subscript or pointer offset operations on the parameter pointer to reference array elements. Figure 12-15 shows how array subscripts references structure elements in the calling function. In the **funcstru.c** program in LISTING 12-8, the loop for inputting values into the array is placed within the function inputrecs. Array subscript is used to reference each member. The loop for printing out the array has been placed in the function outputrecs. Pointer offset operations are then used to reference structure members. Note that in the outputrecs function, the indirection and member operations are specified with the structure pointer operator, ->. Figure 12-14 shows how structure pointer operation references structure elements in the calling function.

LISTING 12-8:

funcstru.c

```c
#include <stdio.h>

#define MAX 3

        typedef struct emp{
                char name[100];
                int id;
                float salary;
                } EMP;

void inputrecs(EMP[]);
void outputrecs(EMP*);

 int main(void)
        {
        EMP emprecs[MAX];

        inputrecs(emprecs);
        outputrecs(emprecs);

        return 0;
        }

 void inputrecs(EMP emps[])
        {
        int i;

        i = 0;
        while (i < MAX)
                {
                printf("\nEnter Name:");
                scanf("%*[\n\t ]%[^\n]s", emps[i].name);
                printf("\nEnter Id:");
                scanf("%d", &emps[i].id);
                printf("\nEnter Salary:");
                scanf("%f", &emps[i].salary);
                i++;
                }
        }

 void outputrecs(EMP *emps)
        {
        int i;

        i = 0;
        while (i < MAX)
                {
                printf("\nName is %s\n", (emps+i)->name);
                printf("id is %d\n", (emps+i)->id);
                printf("Salary is %.2f\n",(emps+i)->salary);
                i++;
                }
        }
```

The functions in LISTING 12-8 are written to reference an entire array. There may be times when you only need to pass single elements of an array to a function. In an array of structures, each element of the array is a structure object in its own right, and can be referenced as a single structure variable. As such you can pass single structure elements as you would any variable. You can perform either call-by-value or call-by-reference operations. You can use the value of a single structure in the array as an argument in a call-by-value operation. In this case, the corresponding parameter in the called function is a structure variable. You can also use the address of a single structure in the array as an argument in a call-by-reference operation. In this case, the corresponding parameter is a pointer to a structure variable.

The `fillrec` and `printrec` functions in the **funcelem.c** program in LISTING 12-9 handle only a single structure element at a time. The loops to traverse the array have been placed in the main function. The `fillrec` function implements a call-by-reference operation on a single structure element. This requires that the address of the structure element is passed. There are two ways to do this. The element could be referenced and then its address obtained with the address operator. Or the address could simply be calculated with the offset operation alone. For the sake of clarity, the address operator is used here.

```
&emprecs[2]  is equivalent to  emprecs + 2
```

Besides outputting and getting input, one common task performed on arrays is to search them for specified values. This is particularly true for arrays of structures. You may need to search through an array of structures, searching for a particular value in a structure' member. In this respect, you can think of a structure as a record, and its members as fields. You would search through records for a certain value in a type field. The type of field searched is commonly referred to as a key. For example, you might search the name member of each structure looking for a person's name. Once found, you have located that person's record. The name is the key for that search.

You can design functions to perform such searches on an array of structures. The address of the first element represented by the array name is passed to the function and pointer operations are then used to search each structure. The programs in LISTING 12-10 and LISTING 12-11 perform sequential searches of an array of structures. The key for the search is an id value. The user enters an id and the `findrec` function searches for a structure with that id. for the structure with a given id.

The **indexsr.c** program, in LISTING 12-10, has been written using array subscripts. The `findrec` function returns the index of the structure located. Notice how the entire search is performed by a single for loop with only a null statement. All the work for the search is performed in the for loop expressions. The value of i after the loop ceases will be either the index of the element with the searched-for id or the same value as `MAX`, the number of elements in the array.

In LISTING 12-11, the **ptrsear.c** program in LISTING 12-10 is rewritten using pointers instead of array subscripts. The loop in the `findrec` function is now managed with working pointers. The `findrec` function is defined as returning a pointer to a structure. The `findrec` function returns the address of the structure element found, not an integer index. Since a zero address is always invalid, a test for 0 will determine if a structure with the correct id was located. Figure 12-16 shows the respective values of pointers used to manage the search of the `emprecs` array.

LISTING 12-9:

funcelem.c

```c
#include <stdio.h>
#define MAX 3

        typedef struct emp{
                char name[100];
                int id;
                float salary;
                } EMP;

void fillrec(EMP*);
void printrec(EMP);

 int main(void)
        {
        EMP emprecs[MAX];
        int i;

        for(i = 0; i < MAX; i++)
                {
                fillrec(&emprecs[i]);
                }

        for(i = 0; i < MAX; i++)
                {
                printrec(emprecs[i]);
                }

        return 0;
        }

 void fillrec(EMP *emptr)
        {
        printf("\nEnter Name:");
        scanf("%*[\n\t ]%[^\n]s", emptr->name);
        printf("\nEnter Id:");
        scanf("%d", &emptr->id);
        printf("\nEnter Salary:");
        scanf("%f", &emptr->salary);
        }

 void printrec(EMP employee)
        {
        printf("\nName is %s\n", employee.name);
        printf("id is %d\n", employee.id);
        printf("Salary is %.2f\n",employee.salary);
        }
```

LISTING 12-10:

indexsr.c

```c
#include <stdio.h>
#define MAX 3

        typedef struct emp
                {
                char name[100];
                int id;
                float salary;
                } EMP;

int findrec (EMP[], int);
void printrec(EMP);

int main(void)
        {
        int empid, recno;
        EMP emprecs[MAX]= { {"Dickens", 9, 1000},
                                    {"Poe", 73, 10.50},
                                    {"Virgil", 51, 375.00} };


        printf("\nPlease enter employee id: ");
        scanf("%d", &empid);

        recno = findrec(emprecs, empid);
        if (recno > -1)
                printrec(emprecs[recno]);

        return 0;
        }

int findrec (EMP emps[], int empid)
        {
        int i;

        for(i=0; (emps[i].id != empid) && (i < MAX); i++);

        if((i<MAX) && (emps[i].id == empid))
                return (i);
         else
                return ( -1 );
        }

void printrec(EMP employee)
        {
        printf("\nName is %s\n", employee.name);
        printf("id is %d\n", employee.id);
        printf("Salary is %.2f\n", employee.salary);
        }
```

LISTING 12-11:

ptrsear.c

```c
#include <stdio.h>
#define MAX 3

        typedef struct emp_type{
                char name[100];
                int id;
                float salary;
                } EMP;

 EMP *findrec(EMP*, int);
 void printrec(EMP *);

 int main(void)
        {
        EMP *recptr;
        int employeeid;
        EMP emprecs[MAX] = { {"Dickens", 9, 1000},
                                            {"Poe", 73, 10.50},
                                            {"Virgil", 51, 375.00} };

        printf("\nPlease enter employee id: ");
        scanf("%d", &employeeid);

        recptr = findrec(emprecs, employeeid);
        if (recptr != 0)
                printrec(recptr);

        return 0;
        }

 EMP *findrec (EMP *emps, int empid)
        {
        EMP *emptr;

        emptr = emps;
        while( (emptr->id != empid) && (emptr < (emps+MAX)))
                {
                emptr++;
                }
        if((emptr < (emps+MAX)) && (emptr->id == empid))
                return emptr;
         else
                return 0;
        }

 void printrec(EMP *emptr)
        {
        printf("\nName is %s\n", emptr->name);
        printf("id is %d\n", emptr->id);
        printf("Salary is %.2f\n", emptr->salary);
        }
```

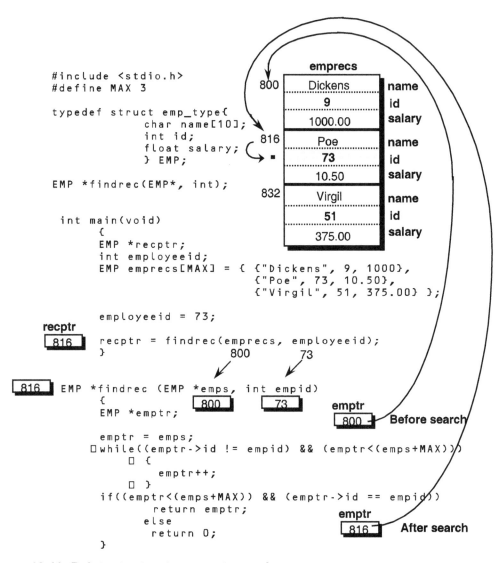

Figure 12-16: Pointer to structure as return value.

Program Examples

In LISTING 12-12, all the features previously described are brought together in a program to input
`employee` records and print the records out. The records are implemented as an array of `employee`
structures. Two versions of the program are presented, one with array subscripts and the other with
pointer operations.

For the pointer version of the program the **io.c** file is changed. The **main.c** file remains the
same. The **types.h** file will include prototypes for the functions in **io.c**. A pointer offset operation is
used in the function call to `fillrec` in order to determine the address of the next empty structure.

`outputrecs` calls the function `printrec` to actually print a record. This separates the display of a record from the actual array references performed by `outputrecs`.

LISTING 12-12

types.h
```
typedef  struct emp {
                char name[100];
                int  id;
                float salary;
                } EMP;

void outputrecs(EMP []);
void printrec(EMP );
EMP fillrec(void);
void add_rec(EMP []);
void menu(void);
```

main.c
```
#include  <stdio.h>
#include  "types.h"

int main(void)
      {
      EMP emprecs[30];
      int more = 0;
      char response[2];

      while (more == 0)
            {
            menu();
            scanf("%s",response);

            switch(response[0])
                  {
                  case 'a':
                        add_rec(emprecs);
                        break;
                  case 'p':
                        outputrecs(emprecs);
                        break;
                  case 'q':
                        more = 1;
                        break;
                  default:
                        printf("invalid input\n");
                  }
            }

      return 0;
      }

void menu(void)
      {
      printf("\na = add a record\n");
      printf("p = print records\n");
      printf("q = quit program\n\n");
      }
```

io.c

```
#include   <stdio.h>
#include   "types.h"

static int avail = 0;

void add_rec(EMP emps[])
        {

        emps[avail] = fillrec();
        avail++;
        }

EMP fillrec(void)
        {
        EMP employee;

        printf("\nEnter Name:");
        scanf("%*[\n\t ]%[^\n]s", employee.name);
        printf("\nEnter Id:");
        scanf("%d", &employee.id);
        printf("\nEnter Salary:");
        scanf("%f", &employee.salary);
        return(employee);
        }

void outputrecs(EMP emps[])
        {
        int i;

        for (i = 0; i < avail; i++)
                {
                printrec(emps[i]);
                }
        }

void printrec(EMP out_emp)
        {
        printf("\n\n Employee Record \n");
        printf("\t NAME  : %s\n", out_emp.name);
        printf("\t ID    : %d\n", out_emp.id);
        printf("\t SALARY: %.2f\n", out_emp.salary);
        }
```

In LISTING 12-13, a new management strategy is added to the program depicted in previous listings. Instead of sequentially filling up the array and printing it all out, the user can now either enter a new record or print out those entered so far. The user is given a menu from which to choose to add a record or to print the records already entered. This design requires that you keep, a count of the number of records entered. In this program, the count is held in a variable called avail in the **io.c** source file. avail is declared static in order to hide it from functions in other source code files that may make up the program. `avail` is a critical piece of data management information. Declaring it static has hidden it within the **io.c** file and makes it known only to the functions in that file.

LISTING 12-13:

types.h

```
typedef  struct emp {
               char name[100];
               int  id;
               float salary;
               } EMP;

void outputrecs(EMP *);
void printrec(EMP*);
void add_rec(EMP*);
void fillrec(EMP*);
void menu(void);
```

io.c
```
#include  <stdio.h>
#include  "types.h"
static int avail = 0;                   /* Scoped to io.c file */

void add_rec(EMP *emptr)
       {

       fillrec(emptr + avail);
       avail++;
       }

void fillrec(EMP *emptr)
       {
       printf("\nEnter Name:");
       scanf("%*[\n\t ]%[^\n]s", emptr->name);
       printf("\nEnter Id:");
       scanf("%d", &emptr->id);
       printf("\nEnter Salary:");
       scanf("%f", &emptr->salary);
       }

void outputrecs(EMP *emps)
       {
       EMP *emptr;

       for(emptr = emps; emptr < (emps+avail); emptr++)
             {
             printrec(emptr);
             }
       }

void printrec(EMP *pemptr)
       {
       printf("\n\n Employee Record \n");
       printf("\t NAME  : %s\n", pemptr->name);
       printf("\t ID    : %d\n", pemptr->id);
       printf("\t SALARY: %.2f\n", pemptr->salary);
       }
```

Chapter Summary: Arrays of Structures

An array of structures combines two aggregate data types. While a structure is an object, an array is not. Members of a structure are referenced with the member operation, whereas elements of an array are referenced through pointer operations. Table 12-3 describes these pointer operations.

Table 12-3: Arrays of Structures and Pointer Operations

`EMP emprecs[3];`	Declaration of an array of structures.
`emprecs`	Array name is address of first structure element.
`emprecs[2]`	Reference structure element with array subscripts.
`*(emprecs + 2)`	Reference structure element with pointer offset and indirection operations.
`&emprecs[2]`	Address of structure element in array obtained with array subscripts and address operation.
`emprecs + 2`	Address of structure element in array obtained with pointer offset operation.
`emprecs[2].id`	Reference member of structure element with array subscripts and member operation.
`(*(emprecs+2)).id`	Reference member of structure element with pointer offset, indirection, and member operations.
`(emprecs+2)->id`	Reference member of structure element with structure pointer operator and member operation.
`&employee[2].id` `&(*(employee+2)).id`	Address of member of a structure element. Address of member of a structure element referenced with offset and indirection operations.
`&(employee+2)->id`	Address of member of a structure element referenced with offset and pointer structure operator.

    The array name for an array of structures is a pointer to a structure. A combination of offset, indirection, and member operations references a member of a structure element. You can use a working pointer to advance down the array, moving from one structure to the next. An increment of a pointer to a structure will increment the pointer by the size of the structure, advancing it to the next structure in the array. Table 12-4 describes different operations on pointers to elements of an array.

    A member of a structure can be an array itself. A member operation that references such a member array will reference the address of the array. Normal pointer operations can be performed on the member array. Table 12-5 describes various operations on member arrays.

Table 12-4: Structure Elements and Pointers

`EMP *emptr;`	Pointer to structure element(pointer to structure)
`emptr++`	Increment pointer to a structure to the address of the next structure element in the array.
`(*emptr).id`	Reference member of structure element with indirection on a pointer to a structure and a member operation.
`emptr->id`	Reference member of structure element with a pointer to structure, using a structure pointer operator and a member operation.
`&emptr->id`	Address of member of structure a structure element referenced with pointer to a structure and structure pointer operator.

Table 12-5: Arrays as Members of Structures

`employee.name[1]`	Reference of an element of an array that is a member of a structure.
`emptr->name[1]`	Reference of an element of an array that is a member of a structure using a pointer to a structure.
`emprecs[2].name[1]`	Reference of an element of an array that is a member of a structure element.
`(emprecs+2)->name[1]`	Reference of an element of an array that is a member of a structure element. The structure element is first referenced with the pointer structure operator.
`(*(emprecs+2)).(*(name+1))`	Pointer offset and indirection operations to reference both a structure element in an array of structures and an array element of an array that is member of a structure.

Exercises

The program in LISTING 12-14 has three primary functions. The first function enters employee information into an array of structures, one structure per employee. A count is kept of how many structures in the array are actually used. There are three fields in the structure: 1) the employee's name, name, 2); the store's id where the employee works, store_id; 3) the dollar amount of sales the employee has made, sales. The structure is typedef in the types.h file as `EMP`. Consequently, the structure type is referred to as `EMP` in the declarations. The array of `EMP` structures is declared in main as `EMP emprecs[MAXEMPLOYEES];`.

The second function is a report of the cumulative totals of sales in each store. There is a separate array of doubles used to hold the information on the stores, `store_rep`. Once the information is gathered, this array is printed out.

Modify the program in the following ways:

Modify the `add_employees` and `fillemprec` functions to take as a parameter a pointer to `EMP`. `add_employees` then returns the address of the last-used `EMP` structure. `fillemprec` is passed only the pointer to the current `EMP` structure. In main, the variable used to receive the return value of `add_employees` is a pointer. The arguments for the function calls for `outputrecs` and store_report will all be pointers.

Program your own `outputrecs` function. It will take two parameters: the pointer to the first structure and the pointer to the last structure used (this was received from `add_employee`).

Modify `store_report` to use pointers. Again you will need two parameters: the address of the beginning structure and the address of the last structure.

Replace your array declaration with a pointer variable and dynamically allocated memory using `calloc`.

An example of the output follows. The changes made with pointers to the functions should not make a difference in the output.

```
Please enter  name : Marylou
Please enter store id : 2
Please enter sales : 5.50
Again (y/n) ? :y
Please enter name : George
Please enter store id : 2
Please enter sales : 6.50
Again (y/n) ? :y
Please enter name : Valerie
Please enter store id : 1
Please enter sales : 23.40
Again (y/n) ? :y
Please enter name : Robert
Please enter store id : 0
Please enter sales : 3.45
Again (y/n) ? :y
Please enter name : Dylan
Please enter store id : 4
Please enter sales : 2.50
Again (y/n) ? :y
Please enter name : Cecelia
Please enter store id : 4
Please enter sales : 17.60
Again (y/n) ? n

THE LIST OF EMPLOYEES
Name = Marylou, Store id = 2, Sales = 5.50.
Name = George, Store id = 2, Sales = 6.50.
Name = Valerie, Store id = 1, Sales = 23.40.
Name = Robert, Store id = 0, Sales = 3.45.
Name = Dylan, Store id = 4, Sales = 2.50
Name = Cecelia, Store id = 4, Sales = 17.60.
REPORT OF STORE SALES TOTALS
0 3.45
1 23.40
2 12.00
3 0.00
4 20.10
```

LISTING 12-14:

types.h

```
#define MAX_FIELD_LEN 100
#define MAXEMPS 20
#define STORE_COUNT  5

        typedef  struct emp_type {
                char name[MAX_FIELD_LEN];
                int store_id;
                double sales;
                } EMP;

int add_employees (EMP []);
void fillemprec (EMP [], int);
void store_report (EMP [], int);
int get_user_ok(void);
```

add.c

```
#include <stdio.h>
#include  "types.h"

int add_employees (EMP emp_recs[])
        {
        int rec_count = 0, more = 1;

        while((more == 1) && (rec_count < MAXEMPS))
                {
                fillemprec (emp_recs,rec_count);
                rec_count++;
                more = get_user_ok();
                }
        rec_count--;
        return rec_count;
        }

void fillemprec (EMP emp_recs[], int rec_num)
        {
        printf("Please enter name : ");
        scanf("%*[\n\t ]%[^\n]s",emp_recs[rec_num].name);
        printf("Please enter store id : ");
        scanf("%d",&emp_recs[rec_num].store_id);
        printf("Please enter sales : ");
        scanf("%lf",&emp_recs[rec_num].sales);
        }

int get_user_ok(void)
        {
        char response[2];
        printf("Do you wish to enter another record?");
        scanf("%s", response);
        if(response[0] =='y')
                return 1;
        else
                return 0;
        }
```

report.c

```
#include <stdio.h>
#include "types.h"

void store_report (EMP emp_recs[], int rec_count)
        {
        int i;
        double store_rep [STORE_COUNT];

        for  (i = 0; i < STORE_COUNT; i++)
              store_rep[i] = 0.00 ;

        for (i = 0; i <= rec_count; i++)
        {
        store_rep[emp_recs[i].store_id]+=emp_recs[i].sales;
        }

        printf ("\n\tREPORT OF STORE TOTALS \n\n");

        for (i = 0; i < STORE_COUNT; i++)
              printf ("\t\t%d %.2f\n", i, store_rep[i]);

        }
```

main.c

```
#include "types.h"

EMP emprecs[MAXEMPS];  /* Array declared external to
        avoid any stack storage problems */

int main(void)
        {
        int count;     /* count of used structures */

        count = add_employees (emprecs);
        store_report (emprecs, count);

        return 0;
        }
```

Arrays of Arrays

Pointers to Arrays and Double Indirection

Declaration of Array of Arrays

Initialization of Arrays of Arrays

Pointer to an Array

Nested Pointer Expressions

Pointers to Arrays and Functions

13. Arrays of Arrays

In array of arrays is the C term for what other programming languages refer to as a multidimensional array. The term array of arrays was very carefully chosen. It more accurately describes of how multidimensional arrays in C are organized. You can, in fact, think of a multidimensional array as a way of grouping together arrays of the same type. For example, in other computer languages, a two-dimensional array of integers generates several integer arrays and treats them as part of one entity. In C, a two-dimensional array of integers generates integer arrays that are then group together as elements of yet another array. You now have an array whose elements are themselves arrays. In C, a two-dimensional array is really an array whose elements happen to be arrays, an array of arrays.

Pointer operations on arrays of arrays can result in very complicated code. In most cases, you only need to use array subscript versions of the pointer operation. Array subscripts for arrays of arrays is very simple and easy to understand. By contrast, the code for corresponding pointer offset operations can be very confusing, involving nested offset and indirection operations.

Perhaps the most confusing aspect of arrays of arrays is the fact that they use a new kind of pointer, a pointer to an array. A pointer to an array references a whole array, rather than just the first object in it as array names do. With a pointer to an array you are able to perform pointer operations on an array whose elements are themselves arrays, an array of arrays.

In this chapter, arrays of arrays will first be examined using array subscripts. Then the more difficult concept of pointers to arrays will be presented. As with single-dimensional arrays, array subscripts is clearer and easier to use. However, arrays of arrays are actually managed by the same pointer operations that manage single-dimensional arrays. An understanding of how these pointer operations affect arrays of arrays is crucial to detecting possible errors that may occur.

Declarations and Initialization

You declare multi-dimensional arrays by specifying each outer array within its own brackets. Each outer dimension is considered to be its own array whose elements are themselves arrays, an array of arrays. You can specify as many arrays of arrays as want, in effect, specifying how many dimensions you want. In this respect, the term multi-dimensional array is misleading in C. You do not speak of a single array with several dimensions. Instead you can have aggregate constructs that combined several arrays of arrays. You declare the equivalent of a multi-dimensional array by combining series of array of arrays declaration types into one declaration. Recall that the array type consists of two brackets that may enclose the number of elements. Each array of arrays is specified by its own array type, its own brackets enclosing the number of elements. A series of these array types in an array declaration defines the equivalent of a multi-dimensional array.. The next example is a declaration of the equivalent of a three dimension array.

```
double forecasts[4][3][7];
```

To better understand how an array of arrays declaration works, you need to distinguish between an array of arrays and an array of objects. An array of objects is an ordinary single dimensional array such as an array of integers or an array of characters, even an array of structures. You can think of an object as anything you can declare as a variable. Arrays, however, are not objects, they are memory managed by pointer operations. An array of arrays has as its elements other arrays, not objects.

Take the example of a two-dimensional array, an array of an array. First you have the declaration of an array of objects, just as you would declare a single dimensional array. This consists of the type of object, and the number of objects enclosed in brackets. Then, inserted to the left of the brackets for the array of objects, you then have the declaration of the array of arrays. This consist of just a set of brackets enclosing the number of elements in this array. In this case the elements are the just specified arrays of objects. You then place the array name to the left of the declaration of an array of arrays. The array name in this declaration is a pointer to a array, not a pointer to an object.

A simple rule to followed is that brackets for each array of arrays are placed to the left of the array of objects. You can think of the array of objects as the innermost dimension of a multidimensional array. The arrays of arrays are the progressively outer dimensions moving from right to left toward the array name. You can think of the array of arrays whose brackets are placed next to the array name as the outermost dimension of a multidimensional array.

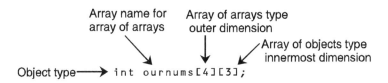

Figure 13-1: Array of arrays declaration.

In the next example, you can think of the declaration of the array `ournums` as declaring five arrays (see Figure 13-1). The first array is specified by the first set of brackets, [4]. `ournums` is declared as an array of four elements. Each of these elements is an array itself. `ournums` is an array of arrays. The next four arrays are these elements. Unlike the first array, they are arrays of objects. Each is an array of three integers. Their array type is specified by the second set of brackets, [3]. `ournums` is an array of arrays whose elements are arrays of three integers.

```
int  ournums[4][3];
```

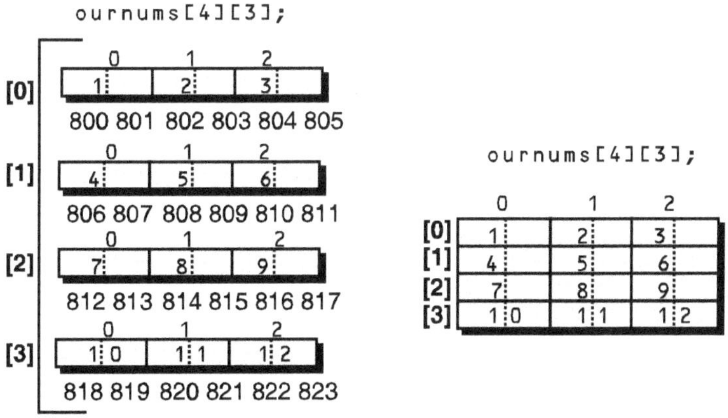

Figure 13-2: Array of arrays and multidimensional arrays.

It is conceptually clearer to think of an array of arrays as a multidimensional array. In the case of a two-dimensional array, the array of arrays is the outer dimension, and the arrays of integers are the inner dimension. The first dimension can be thought of as rows, and the second dimension can be thought of as columns. Figure 13-2 illustrates these two dimensions. To reference a particular element in the two-dimensional array, indicate first its row and then its column. The element in the third row and second column is referenced by `ournums[2][1]`. Both dimensions number from zero. The first row is row 0, and the second column is column 1.

```
ournums[2][1] = 8;
```

As with single-dimensional arrays, brackets have two very different meanings when used in an array declaration and in the reference of an array element. In an array declaration, a set of brackets represents the array data type. When used to reference an element in an array, brackets constitute a special kind of notation called array subscripts. Array subscripts represents a combined pointer offset and indirection operation. As with single-dimensional arrays, multi-dimensional arrays are actually managed by pointer operations.

It is always clearer, simpler, easier, and more practical to use array subscripts to reference elements in multidimensional arrays. In LISTING 13-1, the array `ournums` is printed out using array subscripts. The first index references a row in the two-dimensional array. The second index references a particular integer element in the row. In actuality, the first index references an array of integers within the array of arrays. The second index references a particular integer element in that array of integers.

Initialization of a two-dimensional array is similar to the initialization of a single dimensional array. An array of arrays is initialized by a set of comma-delimited sets of braces. Within the braces are the comma-delimited values for an inner array. In the next example, all four arrays in the `ournums` array are initialized with four sets of values, each enclosed within its own braces.Initializations: array of arrays;

```
int ournums[4][3] = {{1, 2, 3 },
                     {4, 5, 6 },
                     {7, 8, 9 },
                     {10, 11, 12}};
```

You use loops to manage multi-dimensional arrays, much as you do on simple arrays. For arrays of arrays, you need a loop for each outer array. For example, a nested for loop will effect an operation on all the elements of a two-dimensional array. The outer for loop references rows, and the inner for loop references columns, elements in the rows.

In the **table.c** program in LISTING 13-1, an array of arrays is declared that has the equivalent of two dimensions. Each array in this array of arrays is initialized with a set of integer values. Notice the use of symbolic constants for number of objects in each type of array. The terms ROW and COL provide a conceptual framework like that of a two-dimensional array. The `ournums` array is then printed out using nested for loops. The outer loop references each array in the array arrays, in other words, the outermost dimension, the rows. The inner loop reference each integer object in a particular array of integers, in other words, the inner dimension.

LISTING 13-1:

table.c

```
#include <stdio.h>

#define ROW 4
#define COL 3

int main(void)
    {
    int ournums[4][3] = { {1, 2, 3 },
                          {4, 5, 6 },
                          {7, 8, 9 },
                          {10, 11, 12}};
    int i, j;

    for (i = 0; i < ROW; i++)
        {
        for (j = 0; j < COL; j++)
            {
            printf("%d ", ournums[i][j]);
            }
        }

    return 0;
    }
```

Pointer to an Array

It is difficult, at first, to understand the pointer offset and indirection operations that actually reference elements in an array of arrays. They will appear to you at first to be very confusing. It is helpful to first examine how pointers to arrays operate. Once you understand pointers to arrays, you will find it easier to see how pointer operations work on multi-dimensional arrays. You will start off with an examination of how a working pointer references an array of arrays. The **ptrarray.c** program in LISTING 13-2 is an example of how you would use pointers to print out a two-dimensional array. It is a rewritten version of 13.1 using only pointers.

To see how pointers operate on multi-dimensional arrays, you first have to know that a multi-dimensional array is placed in consecutive memory, as shown in Figure 13-3. For example, the ournums array of 4 three integer arrays is placed in memory in 24 consecutive bytes. Pointer operations take advantage of this fact to accurately locate an reference arrays and objects in an array of arrays.

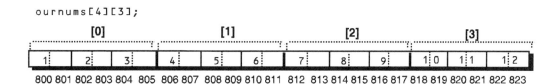

Figure 13-3: Two-dimensional array arranged in consecutive memory.

You can declare a pointer variable that points to an array as a whole, not just to an element in it. In this case, the pointer is not a pointer to an object, a variable, but a pointer to an array. In the next example, there are three different declarations: an array of arrays, a pointer to a variable, and a pointer to an array. `rowptr` is a pointer to an array. `intptr` is a pointer to an integer variable. An indirection on `intptr` will reference an integer variable, whereas an indirection on `rowptr` will reference an array. The array name `ournums` is also a pointer to an array. An array name is a pointer to the first element in its array. The elements in an array of arrays are also arrays, making `ournums` also a pointer to an array.

```
int ournums[4][3];
int (*rowptr)[3];
int *intptr;
```

In the declaration of `rowptr`, the pointer type (the asterisk) is placed within parentheses because of precedence. The brackets, `[]`, have greater precedence than the asterisk, `*`. Without the parentheses to force precedence, the brackets would be evaluated first. You would then have an array of pointers instead of a pointer to an array.

You can use a pointer to an array to reference the rows of a two-dimensional array. Each row is an array itself. In LISTING 13-2, `rowptr` is a pointer to a row of integers in the two-dimensional array `ournums`. The rows themselves are elements in the array of arrays. `rowptr` can be advanced from one element of the array of arrays to the next. It can be positioned to the address of one array after another. A pointer to an array advances down an array of arrays in the same way that a pointer to an integer can advance down an array of integers. The pointer is simply incremented. Recall that an increment of a pointer increments by the size of the data type it points to. Since `rowptr` points to an array of three integers, an increment of `rowptr` increments its address by the size of an array of three integers. Effectively, an increment of `rowptr` moves from one row to the next.

```
rowptr++;  is really    rowptr + (1 * sizeof(int[3]))
                         rowptr + (1 * (3 * 2))
```

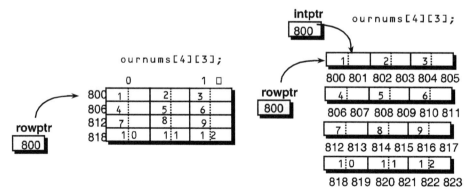

Figure 13-4: Pointer to an array.

The array name `ournums` is a pointer to the first element in its array. The elements in this array are arrays of three integers themselves. Both `rowptr` and `ournums` are pointers to arrays of three integers. Since both `ournums` and `rowptr` are pointers to the same data type, you can assign `ournums` to `rowptr`, `rowptr = ournums`. Figure 13-4 illustrates how a pointer to an array works.

LISTING 13-2:

ptrarray.c

```
/* Print rows of a two dimension array of integers */

#include <stdio.h>

int main(void)
        {
        int ournums[4][3]= {   {1, 2, 3 },
                               {4, 5, 6 },
                               {7, 8, 9 },
                               {10, 11, 12}};
        int (*rowptr)[3];
        int *intptr;

        rowptr = ournums;
        while (rowptr < (ournums + 4))
              {
              intptr = *rowptr;
              while (intptr < (*rowptr + 3))
                      {
                      printf("%d ", *intptr);
                      intptr++;
                      }
              rowptr++;
              }

        return 0;
        }
```

In the **ptrarray.c** program LISTING 13-2, `intptr` is assigned the result of an indirection operation on `rowptr`. `rowptr` is a pointer to an array. This indirection operation is an indirection on a pointer to an array. The indirection operation on a pointer to an array references an array.

```
        intptr = *rowptr;
```

An indirection operation on a pointer to an array can be very confusing. In most cases, the indirection operation on a pointer references a variable. This is because most pointers are actually declared and used as pointers to variables. However, `rowptr` is a pointer to an array. ARRAYS ARE NOT VARIABLES. This is a crucial point. Arrays are referenced as addresses, not as variables. Whereas an indirection on a pointer to a variable references a variable, an indirection on a pointer to an array references an address. This address is not a pointer to an array, but a pointer to the first element in the array. While an integer is referenced as a variable, an array of integers is referenced as the address of the first element. So an indirection operation on a pointer to an integer references an integer variable, whereas an indirection operation on a pointer to an array of integers references the address of the first integer.

You can apply yet a further indirection on an indirection on a pointer to an array. An indirection on a pointer to an array references an address. This address is the address of the first element in the array. A further indirection, in turn, on this address references the first object in this array. For example, an indirection on a pointer to an array of integers references the address of the first integer in the array. Then, an indirection on this address references the first integer variable itself. This kind of double indirection on a pointer to an array is written by placing two indirection operators before the pointer. The second indirection is operating on the address referenced by the first indirection.

```
*(*rowptr)                    **rowptr
```

In the **doublind.c** program LISTING 13-3, the indirection on `intptr` and the double indirection on `rowptr` print out the same value. Both reference the first integer variable in the array. However, an increment on `intptr` only progresses to the next integer variable. An increment on `rowptr` progresses to the next array of integers, the next row.

The double indirection on `rowptr` is used as an integer variable in an assignment expression. Although the first indirection only references an address, the second indirection references a variable and can be used as such. However, an attempt to use only a single indirection on `rowptr` in an assignment expression is invalid. Only variables, not addresses, can be assigned values.

LISTING 13-3:

doublind.c

```c
#include <stdio.h>

int main(void)
{
int ournums[4][3] = { {1, 2, 3 },
                      {4, 5, 6 },
                      {7, 8, 9 },
                      {10, 11, 12}};
int (*rowptr)[3];
int *intptr;

rowptr = ournums;

intptr = *rowptr;
printf("%d %d %d\n",ournums[0][0],*intptr,**rowptr);

*intptr = 83;
printf("%d %d %d\n",ournums[0][0], *intptr,**rowptr);

**rowptr = 7;          /* *rowptr = 6 is invalid */
printf("%d %d %d\n",ournums[0][0],*intptr,**rowptr);

intptr++;
rowptr++;
printf("%d %d %d\n",ournums[0][0],*intptr,**rowptr);

return 0;
}
```

Output for LISTING 13-3:

```
   1        1       1
  83       83      83
   7        7       7
   7        2       4
```

The **firstcol.c** program in LISTING 13-4 uses double indirection to print out the first column of an array. The first integer element of each array is accessed through a double indirection operation on `rowptr`, `**rowptr`. `rowptr` is a pointer to an array. The first indirection references an array. An array is referenced as the address of its first element. The first indirection on `rowptr` references the address of the first integer variable in the array. The second indirection then operates on this address, referencing the first integer variable. Figure 13-5 illustrates this double indirection.

LISTING 13-4:

firstcol.c

```c
/* Print first column only of a two-dimensional array */

#include <stdio.h>

int main(void)
     {
     int ournums[4][3]= {   {1, 2, 3 },
                            {4, 5, 6 },
                            {7, 8, 9 },
                            {10, 11, 12}};
     int (*rowptr)[3];

     rowptr = ournums;
     while (rowptr < (ournums + 4))
           {
           printf("%d ", **rowptr);
           rowptr++;
           }

     return 0;
     }
```

You can also use double indirection and increments of pointers to arrays to reference elements by column. Figure 13-6 illustrates such a task. In the **colptr.c** program in LISTING 13-5, a two-dimensional array is printed out by columns instead of rows. The integer pointer `colptr` is initialized to the address of the first row. In the outer loop it advances from one integer to another, specifying the beginning of each column. `colptr` must receive the address of the first array from `ournums`. However, their types do not match. `colptr` is a pointer to an integer. The array name `ournums` is a pointer to an array of three integers. By performing an indirection on `ournums` you reference that array of integers. An array of integers is referenced with the address of the first integer element. The types now match. `colptr` is a pointer to an integer, and an indirection on `ournums` evaluates to the address of an integer. `colptr` is then assigned the result of an indirection on `ournums`, the address of the first integer variable in the first row.

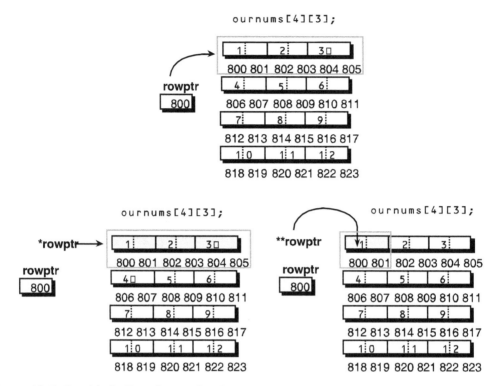

Figure 13-5: Double indirection and pointer to array.

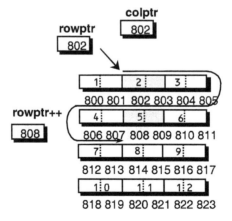

Figure 13-6: Pointer to array and columns.

The next integer in a column is reached by offsetting by the size of a row (see Figure 13-6). A pointer to an array of three integers will offset by the size of a row when incremented. `rowptr` is used for this purpose. It is assigned its initial address by `colptr`. The pointer types of `colptr` and `rowptr` do not match. `colptr` is a pointer to an integer. `rowptr` is a pointer to an array. The address of `colptr` must be cast as a pointer to an array to allow it to be assigned to `rowptr`. The type for any given pointer to an array is the same as the type specified in its declaration. Simply leave out the name and you have the type. `rowptr`'s type is a pointer to an array of three integers, `int(*)[3]`. This is used as the type in a cast operation on the address held by `colptr`.

You have already seen how a single-integer element can be referenced by a double indirection on `rowptr`. The first indirection references an address of an integer, and the second indirection references the integer variable itself. A double indirection on `rowptr` is used in the `printf` operation to reference a particular integer element.

LISTING 13-5:

colptr.c

```
/* Program to print columns in a two dimension array */

 #include <stdio.h>

int main(void)
        {
        int (*rowptr)[3];
        int *colptr;
        int ournums[4][3]= {   {1, 2, 3 },
                                {4, 5, 6 },
                                {7, 8, 9 },
                                {10, 11, 12}};

        colptr = *ournums;
        while (colptr < (*ournums + 3))
                {
                rowptr = (int(*)[3]) colptr;
                while (rowptr < (ournums+4))
                        {
                        printf("%d ", **rowptr);
                        rowptr++;
                        }
                colptr++;
                }

        return 0;
        }
```

Pointer Expressions

You can now begin to see how the pointer operations that reference multi-dimensional arrays actually work. As in single-dimensional arrays, objects in a multidimensional array are referenced using a combined pointer offset and indirection operation. Using pointers to reference elements in a multidimensional array requires a set of nested offset expressions, each with its own indirection operation. In the case of two-dimensional arrays, the pointer offset operation for the outer dimension is nested inside the pointer offset operation for the inner dimension.

$$*(\ (*(ournums + 2))\ + 1)$$

What is taking place here is a double indirection. The first offset operation results in the address of an array. This address is equivalent to a pointer to an array. The indirection operation on a pointer to an array references an array. An array is referenced with the address of the first element. The result of the first indirection is the address of the first element in an array. The next example references the third array in the ournums array of arrays. It results in the address of the first element of that array - the address of the first integer in the third array.

```
*(ournums + 2)
```

Recall that in a pointer offset operation, there is an implied multiplication by the size of the type pointed to. The array name ournums is a pointer to an array. The size of an array is the number of elements in the array times the size of those elements. An element of the ournums array is an array of 3 integers. The size of an array of 3 integers is 3 times the size of an integer: 3 * sizeof(int). Given an integer size of 2 bytes, the size of a 3-integer array is 6 bytes. An offset of 1 on ournums results in an implied multiplication by the size of an array of 3 integers. An offset of 2 on ournums results multiply 2 by the size of an array of 3 integers (2 * (3 *2)) = 12), referencing the third array.

```
(ournums + 2)
(ournums + (2 * (3 * sizeof(int))))
(ournums + 12)
```

In array subscripts, you could use just one index to write the above indirection and offset operations. When an array of arrays is written with one index, it references one of its arrays. You can reference each array in an array of arrays by sequentially indexing each one in array subscripts. The next example is the equivalent of the just shown indirection and offset operation. Both reference ournums' third array.

```
ournums[2]
```

Given the base address of any array, you can use a pointer offset operation to calculate the address of any element. In an array of arrays, once you have referenced a particular array, you can then use the pointer offset operation to calculate one of its elements. In the next example, the address of the second integer element in the third array is calculated with an offset of 1 on the array's base address. The base address is first determined by referencing the third array with an indirection and offset operation of 2 on ournums.

```
(*(ournums+2)) + 1
```

Once you have calculated the address of an array element, you can use indirection the element to reference it. In the next example, once the address of the second integer element has been calculated, an indirection on that address references the integer element. The first indirection operation on the ournums array may appear confusing. The array name ournums, when used in an expression, is a pointer. It points to the type of elements in its array. The type of elements in the ournums array is an array. ournums is actually a pointer to an array. Indirection on a pointer to an array references an array. Whereas a reference to a variable provides a variable object, a reference to an array only provides an address, the address of the first element.

```
*(*(ournums+2)) + 1
```

Once referenced, the integer element can then be used like any integer variable. In the next example, it is assigned the value of 5. The nested indirection and offset expressions are equivalent to two array subscript indexes.

```
*((*(ournums+2)) + 1) = 5;
```

In the next example, the implied multiplication for each offset has been added in to show how the address is actually being calculated.

```
*((*(ournums+(2*(3*sizeof(int))))))+(1*sizeof(int)))
```

The nested combined pointer offset and indirections operations can more clearly be represented using array subscripts. Remember that array subscript is just another way of writing a combined pointer offset and Indirection operation. In the next example, ournums[2][1] is equivalent to *((*(ournums+2))+1). ournums[2] represents the nested pointer offset and indirection operation, *(ournums+2), and then [1] represents the next outer pointer offset and indirection operations, *(()+1).

```
ournums[2][1]  is equivalent to  *((*(ournums+2))+1)
```

In the **indoffs.c** program in LISTING 13-6, the two-dimensional array is printed out using nested pointer offset and indirection operations, instead of array subscripts.

LISTING 13-6:

indoffs.c

```
#include <stdio.h>

int main(void)
    {
    int ournums[4][3]= {   {1, 2, 3 },
                           {4, 5, 6 },
                           {7, 8, 9 },
                           {10, 11, 12}};
    int i, j;

    for (i = 0; i < 4; i++)
        {
        for (j = 0; j < 3; j++)
            {
            printf("%d ", *((*(ournums+i)) +j));
            }
        }

    return 0;
    }
```

Pointers to Arrays and Functions

When working with multidimensional arrays, you will often have to pass them to functions. This involves passing an address to a corresponding parameter variable that has been declared as a pointer.

The pointer data type of the parameter and the address need to match. They have to point to the same type of object. The address of an integer is passed to a parameter declared as a pointer to an integer. In the same way, the address of a whole array is passed to a parameter declared as a pointer to an array.

The array name for a two-dimensional array is a pointer to an array. When a two-dimensional array name is the argument in a function call, the corresponding parameter within the function must also be a pointer to an array. In the **printptr.c** program LISTING 13-7, the array name ournums is a pointer to an array of three characters. ournums is used as an argument in the function call of printarray. The address represented by ournums is passed to its corresponding parameter, parray. parray is also a pointer to an array - a pointer to an array of three characters (see Figure 13-7).

An important point to remember when dealing with parameters that are pointers to arrays, is that the number of elements in the pointed to array is an integral part of the type. An array of 3 integers is a different type from that of an array of 4 integers. For pointers to arrays to match, they not only need to reference arrays of the same type of object, but also of the same number of objects. So if an array name of a two-dimensional array points to an array of 3 integers, its corresponding parameter must also be a pointer to an array of 3 integers, not 2 or 4 integers.

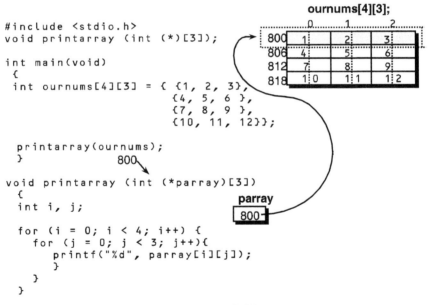

Figure 13-7: Pointer to array as parameter variable.

LISTING 13-7:

printptr.c

```c
#include <stdio.h>

void printarray (int (*)[3]);

int main(void)
        {
        int ournums[4][3] = {  {1, 2, 3 },
                               {4, 5, 6 },
                               {7, 8, 9 },
                               {10, 11, 12}};
        printarray(ournums);

        return 0;
        }

void printarray (int (*parray)[3])
        {
        int i, j;
        for (i = 0; i < 4; i++)
                {
                for (j = 0; j < 3; j++)
                        {
                        printf("%d ", parray[i][j]);
                        }
                }
        }
```

It is also important to remember to enclose the pointer type, the asterisk, and the parameter name within parenthesis. If you leave the parenthesis out, then you actually have an array declaration, not a pointer variable declaration (see chapter 14). There is another simpler way to declare a parameter as a pointer to an array. Recall that any parameter pointer variable can be written in array subscript using a set of empty brackets. This only applies to pointer variables that are parameters. You can apply this same representation to parameters that are pointer to arrays. Instead of an asterisk and parenthesis, you can simply have an initial set of empty brackets followed by the type of array pointed to - another set of brackets with the number of objects. The type is still the same, a pointer to an array. This representation is used in the **prntnote.c** program in LISTING 13-8. In the next example, both forms of parameter pointer to array declarations are shown.

```c
        void printarray (int parray[][3] )
        {
                        is equivalent to
        void printarray (int (*parray)[3] )
        {
```

LISTING 13-8:

prntnote.c

```c
#include <stdio.h>

void printarray (int [][3]);

int main(void)
        {
        int ournums[4][3] = {  {1, 2, 3 },
                               {4, 5, 6 },
                               {7, 8, 9 },
                               {10, 11, 12}};
        printarray(ournums);

        return 0;
        }

void printarray (int parray[][3])
        {
        int i, j;
        for (i = 0; i < 4; i++)
                {
                for (j = 0; j < 3; j++)
                        {
                        printf("%d ", parray[i][j]);
                        }
                }
        }
```

Passing Arrays of Objects to Functions

There will be situations in which you will only want to pass to a function a reference to a single dimensional array that is itself part of a multi-dimensional array. A single dimensional array is an array of objects, and many functions, such as string functions, are designed to operate on just an array of objects. In LISTING 13-9, the **printints** function prints out an array of integer objects. When working with an array of arrays, you can take advantage of such functions by passing to them a reference to one of the arrays of objects within your array of arrays. Again in LISTING 13-9, each array of integers in the ournums array is passed, in turn, to the **printints** function to be printed out.

The argument to such a function call needs to be a reference to an array within the array of arrays. The simplest way to reference such an array is to use array subscripts with a single index. The single index will reference only the array, not an object in it. In the **prtarray.c** program in LISTING 13-9, the beginning address of each array in ournums is passed to a function that prints out an array of integers. The corresponding parameter variable, iptr, is simply a pointer to an integer, not a pointer to an array (see Figure 13-8).

This situation commonly occurs with strings. For example, you could have a two-dimensional array made up of arrays of characters, an array of arrays of characters. Each character array could be implemented as a string with a terminating null character. To print out one of these strings, you just pass a reference to that array of characters to a string function such as printf.

LISTING 13-9:

prtarrays.c

```
#include <stdio.h>

void printints (int []);

int main(void)
     {
     int i;
     int ournums[4][3] = {  {1, 2, 3 },
                            {4, 5, 6 },
                            {7, 8, 9 },
                            {10, 11, 12}};
     for (i = 0; i < 4; i++)
             printints(ournums[i]);

     return 0;
     }

void printints (int *iptr)
     {
     int i;

     for (i = 0; i < 3; i++)
                   printf("%d ", iptr[i]);
     }
```

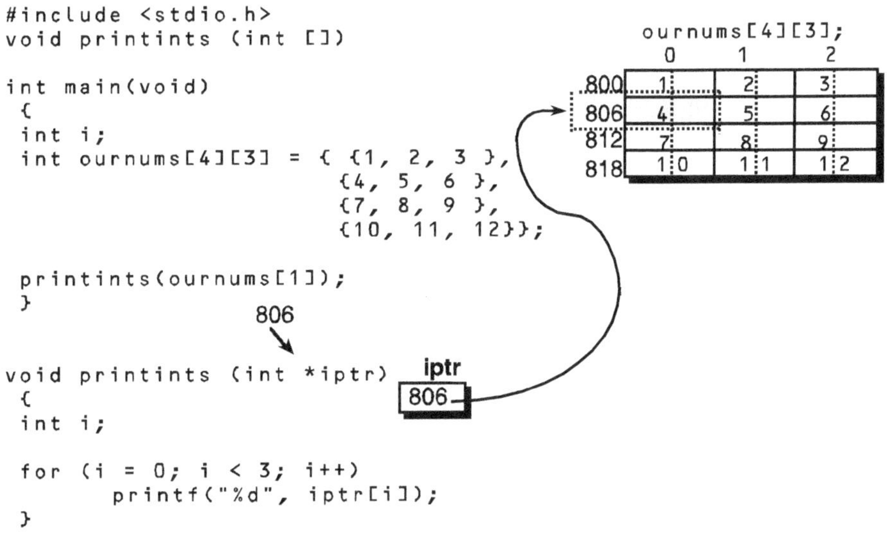

Figure 13-8: Array as element of array of arrays.

Chapter Summary: Arrays of Arrays

An array of arrays is the equivalent of a multidimensional array. Literally, an array of arrays is a single array whose elements are arrays themselves. Array subscripts can be used to reference elements in the array, but in actuality, pointer operations are performed. The pointer operations to reference elements in an array of arrays can become very complex. It is always easier and clearer to use array subscripts when dealing with multidimensional arrays. Table 13-1 lists the different pointer operations for arrays of arrays.

Table 13-1: Array of Array Pointer Operations

`int ournums[4][3];`	Array of arrays, Array of 4 arrays of 3 integers
`int (*rowptr)[3];`	Pointer to an Array, a pointer to an array of 3 integers
`int parray[][3]`	Declaration of a parameter for a function as a Pointer to an Array, a pointer to an array of 3 integers
`*rowptr`	Indirection on a pointer to an array references the array, the address of the first element in that array.
`**rowptr`	Double indirection on a pointer to an array references the first element in that array.
`ournums[1][2]`	You can use array subscripts to reference elements in a multidimensional array.
`*( (*(ournums+1)) +2)`	Nested pointer offset and indirection operations reference elements in a multidimensional array. Array subscripts is really just another way of writing these nested pointer operations.
`ournums[1]`	Using only a single set of brackets for an array subscript reference, will reference one of the arrays making up the array of arrays. This reference an array giving the address of the first element in that array.
`*(ournums + 1)`	A single pointer reference and indirection operation on an array of arrays will reference one of the arrays, giving the address of the first element in that array. The indirection operation changes the data type of the address provided by the pointer offset operation.
`ournums + 1`	Data type of address is a pointer to an array.
`*(ournums + 1)`	Data type of address is a pointer to an integer object

The array name declared for an array of arrays is a pointer to an array. A working pointer declared to point to elements of an array of arrays is also a pointer to an array. A pointer to an array is not the same as a pointer to a variable. Whereas indirection on a pointer to a variable references a variable, indirection on a pointer to an array references an array - the address of the first element. In the case of a two-dimensional array, a double indirection on a pointer to an array references an object. The first indirection references the address of the array. The second indirection references the object at that address. Incrementing a pointer to an array increments its address by the size of that array, effectively using the pointer to an array to advances from one array to the next.

In functions, the appropriate parameter for an array of arrays is a pointer to an array. A pointer to an array requires parentheses placed around the pointer name and pointer type, though you can use array subscripts.

Exercises

1. Write a function, called strfind, that searches for a string in an array of strings. The function has two parameters: the array of strings and the string to be searched for.

Return a 1 if the string is found in the array.
Return a 0 is the string is not found in the array.

Only use pointers. Do not use array subscripts.

The array of strings is implemented as a two-dimensional array of characters. The first dimension is 10, the second is 40. The search ends if a match is found or the end of the array is reached. The end of the array is indicated by the offset 10 with the beginning address of the array. A match is determined by a call to strcmp which returns a value which indicates equality of two strings.

Arrays of Pointers

Pointers to Pointers, Data Indexes, and argv

14. Array of Pointers

An array of pointers is an array of pointer variables. The pointer variables in such an array are all pointers of the same type. For example you can declare an array of pointers to characters or an array of pointers to integers, even an array of pointers to functions. The pointers can hold the addresses of variables or the address of the first element in an array. Arrays of pointers are often used to reference a set of character arrays.

Pointers in an array of pointers are referenced using the same pointer operation used to reference elements in any array. Array subscript references a particular pointer in the array. You can declare a working pointer that advances down an array of pointers and references each element. Such a working pointer is declared as a pointer to a pointer. The type of object it references is itself a pointer.

A pointer to a pointer is also used as a parameter in functions when the corresponding argument is an array of pointers. In declaring parameters, you need to take care not to confuse a pointer to a pointer with a pointer to an array. Their declarations are similar, but they are two very different types of pointers. The most noted pointer to a pointer is `argv`. `argv` is a special parameter used for a program's main function to reference arguments from the command line when the program is invoked.

Arrays of pointers have various applications. A common application is that of a sorted index for a set of data. For example, an array of pointers that hold the addresses of a set of character arrays, can function as a sorted index for those character arrays. The pointers are sorted according to the alphabetic order of the character strings. You can then use the array of pointers to print out an ordered list of the character strings.

Array of Pointers

You define an array of pointers to point to a specific data type. You can have an array of pointers to integers, or an array of pointers to floats, and even an array of pointers to strings. Each element in that array is itself a pointer to an object of that data type. In an array of pointers to integers, each element is a pointer to an integer.

Though different arrays of pointers may point to different types, they all have the same structure. They are all arrays whose elements are pointers. Still, the way they are used will differ depending upon what they point to. In this respect, arrays of pointers can be said to breakdown into two general categories. There are arrays of pointer that point to objects such as array of pointers to integers, and there are arrays of pointers that point to arrays, such as an array of pointers to strings. Recall that references to objects differ from references to arrays. A object is referenced as a variable, whereas an array is referenced with its beginning address. To use a pointer to reference an object you need to perform indirection. To use a pointer to reference an array, you only need the address that the pointer holds. These differences are reflected in how arrays of pointers to objects and arrays of pointers to arrays are used. Both categories will be discussed in detail beginning with arrays of pointers to objects.

Array of Pointers to Objects

To understand how arrays of pointers to objects works, you first need to take a closer look at how pointer variables operate. A pointer variable can be used to hold the address of another object. You can use the address operator to obtain the address of a variable and then assign that address to a pointer. In the following example, the first three declarations are integer variables. The pointer variable, `myptr`, is

a pointer variable, a pointer to an integer. The address operator is used to obtain the address of the
mynum variable and then assign that address to myptr.

```
int mynum = 9;
int yournum = 80;
int ournum = 43;

int *myptr;

        myptr = &mynum;
```

An indirection operation on a pointer variable then references the object pointed to. In the
next example, both printf operations print the value of mynum. In the second printf, an indirection
on the myptr pointer references the mynum variable.

```
        printf("%d", mynum);
        printf("%d", *myptr);
```

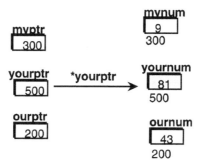

Figure 14-1: Pointers and variables.

Other pointer variables can be declared and then assigned the addresses of the other variables.
The assignments shown here result in the pointers and integers illustrated in Figure 14-1.

```
int mynum = 9;
int yournum = 80;
int ournum = 43;

int *myptr;
int *yourptr;
int *ourptr;

        myptr= &mynum;
        yourptr= &yournum;
        ourptr= &ournum;
```

There are now three pointer variables, each pointing to the same kind of object. Each pointer
is a pointer to int. Now, if you ever need several objects of the same type, you can much more easily
declare these objects as elements in an array. For example, should you need three floats, you could
declare an array of three floats. Similarly, if you need three pointers to int, you can simply declare an

array of three pointers to int. Next is an example of such a declaration. `numptrs` is an array whose elements are pointers variables.

```
int *numptrs[3];
```

Precedence is important in this declaration. According to precedence, the pointer type - the asterisk, *, has a lower precedence than the brackets, the array type. The compiler will interpret the brackets first. The declaration in the previous example is an array. But what kind of objects are in the array? Then the pointer type, the asterisk, is interpreted. The objects in this array are pointers, an array of pointers. Then the data type is read: int. This is an array of pointers to int.

An element in this array of pointers is referenced using the same array subscript used to reference an element in any other kind of array. `numptrs[1]` is a pointer variable and the second element in the `numptrs` array. The elements of an array of pointers are variables themselves. You can use an element in this array just like any other pointer variable. You can assign addresses to it, or perform indirection on it. In the next example, the addresses of the integer variables are assigned to elements of the `numptrs` array, instead of to separately declared pointer variables. As shown in Figure 14-2, the elements of the `numptrs` array now have as their values the addresses of the three integers: `mynum`, `yournum`, and `ournum`.

```
numptrs[0] = mynum;
numptrs[1] = yournum;
numptrs[2] = ournum;
```

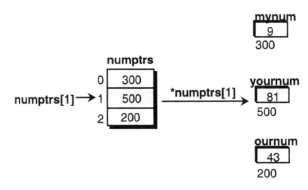

Figure 14-2: Array of pointers.

Once the elements of an array of pointers has been assigned the addresses of objects, you can then use those elements to reference the objects. To actually reference an object, you will need to perform an indirection operation on the element holding its address. In the case of the `numptrs` array, to reference an integer object you need to perform indirection on the pointer element holding that integer's address.

Referencing an object using an element of an array of pointers, will usually involve two operations. First you need to reference the pointer element you want in the array of pointers. You can do this with an array subscript index such as `[1]`. Then you need to perform the indirection operation on that pointer element using the indirection operator, *. In the next example, the second element of the `numptrs` array is used to reference an integer object. First the array subscript, `[1]`, references the second element, and then indirection is performed on that element, *.

```
*numptrs[1]
```

Remember that array subscript is just an indirection and offset operation. The actual indirections taking place in this case can be confusing. When array subscript is used with an added asterisk, there are really two indirections taking place. The array subscript itself is the first indirection. In the case of the first indirection, the type of the object pointed to is a pointer, one of the array elements. The first indirection references a pointer. The second indirection operates on that pointer to reference the object it points to. In this example, the second indirection operates on a pointer to an integer.

`numptrs[1]`   is equivalent to   `*(numptrs + 1)`

The asterisk on the array subscript is a second indirection.

`*numptrs[1]`   is equivalent to   `*( *(numptrs + 1))`

In the next example, both `printf` operations print out the `yournum` integer variable. In the second operation, an indirection on the second element of the `numptrs` array references the `yournum` integer variable.

```
printf("%d", yournum);
printf("%d", *numptrs[1]);
```

Each integer variable can now be referenced by the pointer elements of the `numptrs` array (see Fogire 14/3). In a sense, the array of pointers functions as an index with which to reference those integers. In the next example, each pointer element in `numptrs` is used to reference the integer variables and have them printed out in turn by `printf`. This is done simply by indexing through the `numptrs` array.

```
i = 0;
while (i < 3){
        printf("%d", *numptrs[i]);
        i++;
        }
```

Instead of referencing individual variables, arrays of pointers are usually used to reference elements of another array. An array of pointers becomes another way to reference elements of a given array. For an array of integers, you can define an array of pointers to integer that references each integer element. In the next example, an array of integers, `nums`, is defined along with an array of pointers, `numptrs`. Then address of each element in the `nums` array is assigned to a corresponding pointer element in the `numptrs` array. Now the `numptrs` array can be used to reference elements in the `nums` array.

```
int nums[3];
int *numptrs[3];

i = 0;
while (i < 3){
        numptrs[i] = &nums[i];
        i++;
        }
```

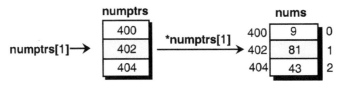

Figure 14-3 Array of pointers and array of objects.

The **printnum.c** program in LISTING 14-1, uses an array of pointers to integers to print out a set of integers. numptrs is the array of pointers to integers. Each pointer element in numptrs is assigned the address of an integer element in the nums array. Then, the numptrs pointer elements are used to print out the integers in the nums array. Notice how both an indirection and array subscript is used to reference the integer object in the printf function call.

LISTING 14-1:

printnum.c

```
#include <stdio.h>
#define MAX 3

int main(void)
        {
        int nums[MAX] = { 9, 81, 43 };
        int *numptrs[MAX];
        int i;

        for (i = 0; i < MAX; i++ )
                {
                numptrs[i] = &nums[i];
                }

        for (i = 0; i < MAX; i++ )
                {
                printf("%d %p\n", *numptrs[i], numptrs[i]);
                }

        return 0;
        }
```

Array of Pointers to Arrays

Instead of pointing to objects, you can define an array of pointers to point to other arrays. In this case, each element of the array of pointers holds the beginning address of an array. You can then use these pointer elements to reference the arrays. For example, you could have an array of pointer whose elements hold the beginning addresses of a set of strings, arrays of characters. You could then use the element of the array to reference those strings in string functions.

To better understand how arrays of pointers to arrays work, you need to take a closer look at how pointer variables works with arrays. A pointer variable can be used to hold the beginning address of an array, functioning much like the array name itself. In the following example, the first three declarations are arrays of characters. The arrays are used to hold character strings. Each array name is the address of the first element of the array. The pointer variable, `aptr`, can be set to the address of the first array by assigning to it the array name.

```
char author[10]={'D','i','c','k','e','n','s','\0'};
char writer[10] = { 'P', 'o', 'e', '\0'};
char poet[10] = { 'V','i','r','g','i','l','\0'};
char *aptr;

        aptr = author;

        puts(author);
        puts(aptr);
```

For the sake of this example, assume that the three arrays start at the addresses 800, 900 and 700, respectively. Because of the assignment of author to `aptr`, `aptr` holds the address represented by author . A function call to puts using either author or `aptr` references the same string, the string starting at address 800. In both function calls to puts, puts receives the same addresses, once from the array name, the other time from the pointer variable, `aptr`.

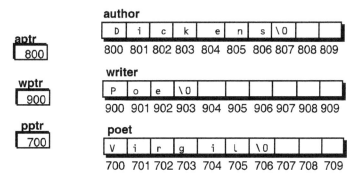

Figure 14-4: Pointers and arrays.

Other pointer variables can be declared and then assigned the beginning addresses of the other arrays. The assignments below result in the pointers and arrays illustrated in Figure 14-4.

```
char author[10]={'D','i','c','k','e','n','s','\0'};
char writer[10] = { 'P', 'o', 'e', '\0'};
char poet[10] = { 'V','i','r','g','i','l','\0'};

char *aptr;
char *wptr;
char *pptr;

        aptr = author;
        wptr = writer;
        pptr = poet;
```

You can replace the three pointer variables with an array of pointers to characters. Next is an example of such a declaration. nameptrs is an array whose elements are pointers variables, pointers to char.

```
        char *nameptrs[3];
```

You can use array subscripts to reference particular elements in the array. nameptrs[1] is the second element in the nameptrs array. In the next example, the character arrays are assigned to elements of the nameptrs array, instead of to separately declared pointer variables. As shown in Figure 14-5, the elements of the nameptrs array now have as their values the addresses of the three strings: author, writer, and poet. Since the elements of nameptrs now hold the beginning address of arrays, nameptrs can be said to be an array of pointers to arrays.

```
        nameptrs[0] = author;
        nameptrs[1] = writer;
        nameptrs[2] = poet;
```

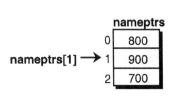
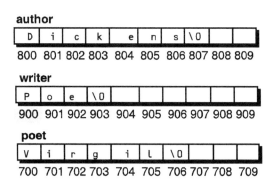

Figure 14-5: Array of pointers to arrays.

In the next example, the two calls to puts use the same address. One address is obtained from the array name and the other from an element of nameptrs. Both calls reference the same string. As shown in Figure 14-5, writer is an array name that is the address 900, and nameptrs[1] is a pointer element that holds the address 900. No indirection is required. Only the beginning address of the array is needed, and this the element already has.

```
puts(writer)
puts(nameptrs[1])
```

Each character array can now be referenced by the pointer elements of the nameptrs array. In a sense, the array of pointers functions as an index with which to reference those arrays. In the next example, each pointer element in nameptrs is used to reference the character arrays and have them printed out in turn by puts. This is done simply by indexing through the nameptrs array.

```
i = 0;
while (i < 3){
        puts( nameptrs[i] );
        i++;
        }
```

Usually when you have a set of data like the character arrays used in the previous example, it may be simpler to combined them into one two-dimensional array, an array of arrays. You can then assign the beginning address of each character array in the array of arrays to a pointer element in the array of pointers. In a sense, each pointer element would reference a row in the two-dimensional array.

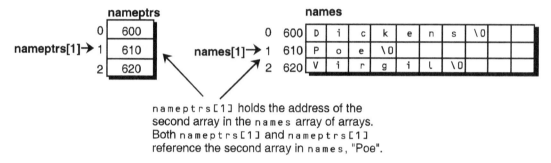

Figure 14-6: Array of pointers and Arrays of arrays.

In the **printnam.c** program in LISTING 14-2, the names array is a two-dimensional array of three rows initialized with the strings "Dickens", "Poe", and "Virgil" respectively. Each row functions as its own string having its own null terminator. The beginning address of each of these rows in the names array is assigned to a pointer element in the nameptrs array of pointers. The beginning address of each row is referenced using only the first dimension. As shown in Figure 14-6, names[1] references the second row starting at address 610. Having assigned the addresses, the nameptrs array is then used to pass the beginning address of each row to puts which uses the address to reference and print out the row as a string.

An array of pointers can also be a very convenient way to manage a collection of string constants. The array of pointers would hold the addresses of the string constants, and be used to reference them (see Figure 14-7). A string constant defines an array. It allocates and initializes a character array and has as its value the address of that array. In the next example, the string constants are defining and initializing character arrays. The addresses of those arrays are then assigned to elements in the nameptrs array. nameptrs is declared as an array of pointers to char. The address of each constant is assigned to one of those pointer elements. Initializations: array of pointers;

```
char *nameptrs[3];

nameptrs[0] = "Dickens";
nameptrs[1] = "Poe";
nameptrs[2] = "Virgil";
```

LISTING 14-2:

printnam.c

```
#include <stdio.h>

int main(void)
        {
        char names[3][10]={"Dickens","Poe","Virgil"};
        char *nameptrs[3];
        int i;

        for (i = 0; i < 3; i++)
                {
                nameptrs[i] = names[i];
                }

        for (i = 0; i < 3; i++)
                {
                puts(nameptrs[i]);
                }

        return 0;
        }
```

Just as you can initialize any array with a set of values, you can initialize an array of pointers with a set of addresses. Using the previous example, the addresses provided by the definitions of the string constants can be used to initialize the array of pointers. In effect the declaration of the array of pointers is combined with the assignment of string constants to those pointers. This is a common technique. The string constants are placed in the initialization block of the array of pointers, as shown in the following example.

In this declaration, three actions are taking place:

1. String constants are defined, returning as their value the beginning address of the string.
2. An array of three pointer objects to char is defined.
3. The addresses of the three string constants are assigned to the pointer elements in the array.

```
char *nameptrs[3] = {"Dickens",
                     "Poe",
                     "Virgil" };
```

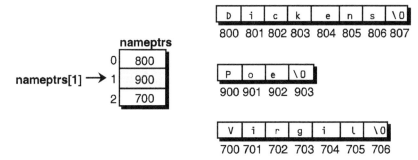

Figure 14-7: Array of pointers and string constants.

You can then reference a particular string using its index in the array of pointers. The call to puts below prints out the second string, "Poe".

```
puts(nameptrs[1]);
```

The **prtconst.c** program in LISTING 14-3 defines such an array of pointers to string constants. The string constants are then output using the array of pointers.

LISTING 14-3:

prtconst.c

```
#include <stdio.h>

int main(void)
        {
        char *nameptrs[3]={"Dickens","Poe","Virgil"};
        int i;

        for (i = 0; i < 3; i++)
                {
                puts(nameptrs[i]);
                }

        return 0;
        }
```

A Pointer to a Pointer

Recall that an array name is a pointer to the first object in the array. If that object is itself a pointer, then the array name is a pointer to a pointer. To understand how an array name for an array of pointers works, you need to first understand how a pointer to a pointer operates.

First take the example of a pointer variable that is a pointer to another pointer variable. In this case, a pointer to a pointer is a pointer variable that references another pointer variable. Pointer variables are variables themselves. You can assign the address of a pointer variable, in turn, to another pointer variable. A pointer variable that has the address of another pointer variable is referred to as a pointer to a pointer.

The declaration of a pointer to a pointer is specified with two asterisks. The first asterisk indicates that the variable is a pointer variable. The second asterisk specifies that the kind of object the pointer variable points to is also a pointer variable.

```
char **lptr;
```

In the next example, `letterptr` is declared as a pointer variable that points to a character, `lptr` is declared as a pointer variable that points to another pointer variable, and letter is a simple character variable. First letter is assigned the value 'H'. Then `letterptr` is assigned the address of the character variable letter. `lptr` is assigned the address of the pointer variable `letterptr`. An indirection on `letterptr` references letter in an assignment operation. The value of letter is changed to 'K'. Then a double indirection on `lptr` references letter through `letterptr`. The value of letter is changed to 'M'.

```
char  letter;
char *letterptr;
char **lptr;

letter = 'H';
letterptr = &letter;
lptr = &letterptr;

*letterptr = 'K';
**lptr = 'M';
```

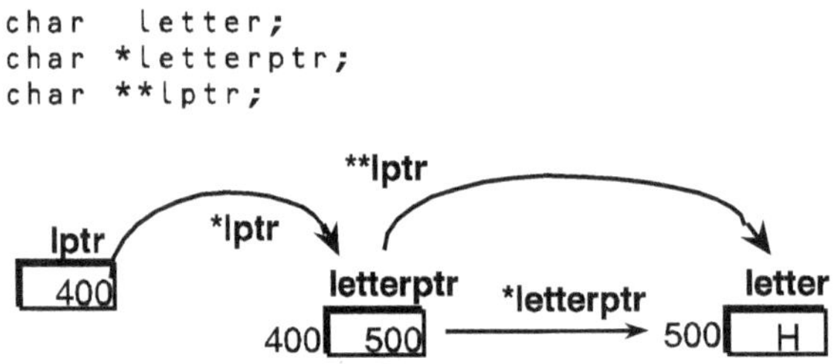

Figure 14-8: Pointer to a pointer, double indirection.

A pointer to a pointer uses double indirection to reference an object. The first indirection reference the pointer it points to, and the second indirection then operates on that pointer to reference the object that pointer points to. It is best to think of this double indirection as a set of nested indirection operations. The first indirection on `lptr` references a pointer variable at the address of `letterptr`. The second indirection uses the address in this referenced pointer variable to reference the character variable letter (see Figure 14-8.).

```
*lptr           references       letterptr
*(*lptr)        references       letter
```

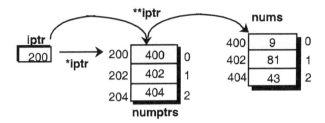

Figure 14-9: Pointer to a pointer as a working pointer for an array of pointers.

You will often need to use a pointer variable as a working pointer, referencing elements in an array. if the elements in the array are pointers themselves, then the working pointer must be a pointer to a pointer. It points to an array element that is a pointer.

The program **pnumptrs.c** in LISTING 14-4 is a rewritten version of the integer example described earlier in LISTING 14-1. Again an array of pointers to integers, numptrs, is defined and assigned the addresses of elements in an array of integers, nums. nums is then printed out using the array of pointers. Instead of using array subscripts to reference the pointer elements, a working pointer advances down the array of pointers, referencing each pointer element in turn. The working pointer, iptr, is defined as a pointer to a pointer. Notice the two pointer types, **, place before its name in its declaration. iptr is assigned the beginning address of the numptrs array, the array name (see Figure 14-9). Then, within the printf function call, two indirection operations are performed with iptr. The first indirection references the pointer element that iptr points to. Then the second indirection is performed on that referenced pointer element, and references the integer element it points to. The iptr working pointer then increments to the address of the next pointer element in the numptrs array.

LISTING 14-4:

pnumptrs.c
```
#include <stdio.h>
#define MAX 3
int main(void)
    {
    int nums[MAX] = { 9, 81, 43 };
    int *numptrs[MAX];
    int **iptr;
    int i;
    for (i = 0; i < MAX; i++ )
        {
        numptrs[i] = &nums[i];
        }
    iptr =  numptrs;
    while(iptr < (numptrs+3))
        {
        printf("%d\n", **iptr);
        iptr++;
        }

    return 0;
    }
```

You can just as easily use working pointers on arrays of pointer to arrays. The **pnameptr.c** program in LISTING 14-5 is a rewritten version of LISTING 14-1 using a working pointer to reference the array of pointers. The working pointer, `nptr`, is a pointer to a pointer. It is assigned the address of the first element in the `nameptrs` array, `nptr = nameptrs`. `nptr` is then used as a working pointer, incrementing through the array of pointers. An indirection on `nptr` references the currently pointed-to pointer element in the array as shown in Figure 14-10. That pointer element holds the address of a string constant. This is then passed to puts to print out the string constant.

LISTING 14-5:

pnameptr.c

```c
#include <stdio.h>

int main(void)
    {
        char *nameptrs[3]={"Dickens","Poe","Virgil"};
        char **nptr;

        nptr = nameptrs;
        while(nptr < (nameptrs+3))
            {
            puts(*nptr);
            nptr++;
            }

        return 0;
    }
```

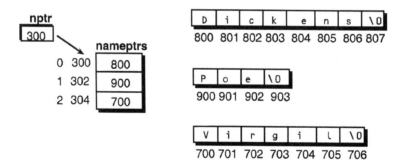

Figure 14-10: Pointer to element of array of pointers.

It would be an error to call puts with `nptr` alone as in `puts(nptr)`. `nptr` holds the address of a pointer, not the address of the first character in a character array. If passed the address in `nptr` instead of the address in `*nptr`, puts would try to print out the `nameptrs` array of pointers, thinking it was an array of characters.

As previously noted, the array name `nameptrs` is also a pointer to a pointer. `nameptrs` is the address of the first element in its array. The elements in its array are pointers themselves. The array name `nameptrs` can be used in an offset and indirection operation to reference a particular pointer variable in the array. The offset and indirection operations can, in turn, be represented by array subscripts. Both examples shown here reference the second pointer variable in the `nameptrs` array.

```
nameptrs[1];              *(nameptrs + 1)
```

You can, of course, perform an indirection on any pointer in order to reference the object it points to. For example, the second element in the `nameptrs` array holds the address of the first character in the "Poe" array. An indirection on the referenced second pointer element will, in turn, reference the first character variable in the array, 'P'. In the next example, the letter 'M' is assigned to the first character element in the array that `nameptrs[1]` references. `putchar` then prints out that character. (see Figure 14-11).

```
*nameptrs[1] = 'M';
putchar ( *nameptrs[1]);
```

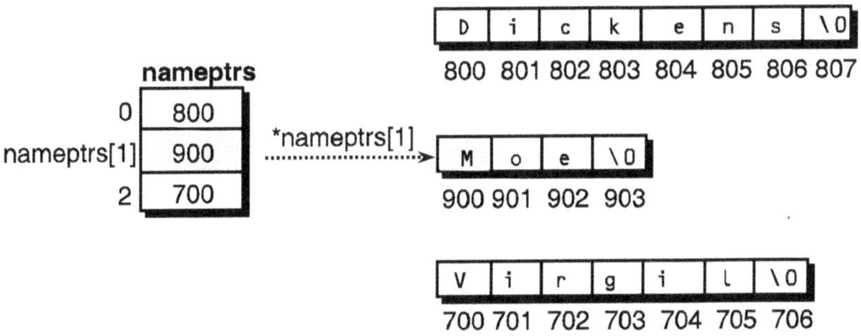

Figure 14-11: Pointer offset and indirection on element of array of pointers.

Notice how the indirection on the pointer element was performed. First the element was referenced using array subscripts, `nameptrs[1]`. Then the indirection operator was applied, `*`, giving us a combination of array subscript and indirection, `*nameptrs[1]`. When array subscript is used with an added asterisk, there are really two indirections taking place. The array subscript itself is the first indirection. In the case of the first indirection, the type of the object pointed to is a pointer. The first indirection operates on a pointer to a pointer. The second indirection operates on a pointer to a character.

```
nameptrs[1]    is equivalent to   *(nameptrs + 1)
```

The asterisk on the array subscript is a second indirection.

```
*nameptrs[1]   is equivalent to   *( *(nameptrs + 1))
```

To reference other character elements in the array referenced by a pointer element, the second indirection can be combined with an offset operation. Both examples shown here reference the fourth character in the array referenced by the second pointer element in the `nameptrs` array.

```
nameptrs[1][3];        *( *(nameptrs + 1) + 3)
```

This nested set of offset and indirection operations appears the same as that used for multidimensional arrays. In fact, the same array subscript used for multidimensional arrays can be used for arrays of pointers that reference other arrays. There is a crucial difference. The elements of a multidimensional array are arrays themselves, whereas the elements of an array of pointers are pointer variables.

For an array of pointers whose elements reference other arrays, you now have several ways of specifying references to objects in those arrays. The next example list several ways to specify how to reference the first character in the array referenced by the first pointer element in the `nameptrs` array. The array name `nameptrs` is the address of the first pointer element. A double indirection performed on `nameptrs`, references the first character variable in the array referenced by the first pointer element in the `nameptrs` array, `**nameptrs`. The same operation can be expressed using array subscript with an index of 0, `nameptrs[0][0]`. You can also use the combination of array subscript and an indirection operation, `*nameptrs[0]`, or you can specify the pointer offset operations with an offset of 0, `*((*(nameptrs+0))+0)`. The following examples are all equivalent:

```
nameptrs[0][0];        *( (*(nameptrs + 0)) + 0)
*nameptrs[0]           *(*(nameptrs + 0))
**nameptrs
```

Functions: A Pointer to Pointer and Pointer to Array

A parameter declaration for an array of pointers is very different than a parameter declaration for an array of arrays. The parameter for an array of pointers is a pointer to a pointer, whereas the parameter for an array of arrays is a pointer to an array.

Recall that a parameter for any array is a pointer to an element in that array. In the case of an array of pointers, an element of the array is a pointer. The corresponding parameter for an array of pointers is a pointer to a pointer. Remember also that parameters that are pointers can be declared using a set of empty brackets. This same notation can be applied to a parameter that is a pointer to a pointer. Instead of two pointer types, two asterisks, preceding the pointer name, you need only one asterisk, and then the empty brackets following the pointer name. Remember, that the empty brackets, when used in a parameter declaration, are just another way of declaring a pointer:

```
char *nptr[];
```

```
void pr_name(char**);

void main(void)
    {
    char *nameptr[3] = {"Dickens",
                        "Poe",
                        "Virgil"};
```

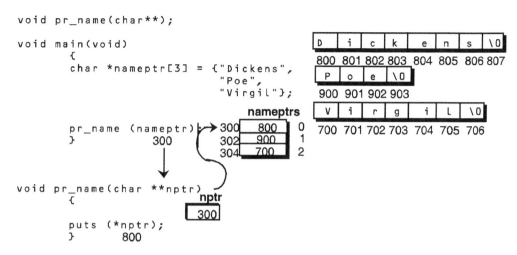

Figure 14-12: Pointer to a pointer as a parameter for array of pointers.

In Figure 14-12, the array name `nameptrs` is an argument in the function call of `pr_name`. The corresponding parameter variable, `nptr`, is declared as a pointer to a pointer. An indirection on `nptr` references the first element in `nameptrs`. This first element is a pointer to a char that holds the address 800. An indirection on `nptr` is used as an argument to puts. The indirection references the first element in `nameptrs`. puts will receive the value of this element, in this case the address 800.

LISTING 14-6A:

```
void pr_name(char *nptr[]);


int main(void)
    {
    char *nameptrs[3]={"Robert",
      "Mark","George"};

    pr_name (nameptrs);
    }


void pr_name(char *nptr[])
    {
    int i = 0;

    while (i < 3)
        {
        puts (nptr[i]);
        i++;
        }
    }
```

LISTING 14-6B:

```
void pr_name(char nptr[][20]);


int main(void)
    {
    char last[3][20] = {"Robert",
                  "Mark","George"};

    pr_name(last);
    }


void pr_name(char aptr [][20])
    {
    int i = 0;

    while (i < 3)
        {
        puts(aptr[i]);
        i++;
        }
    }
```

LISTING 14-7A:

```
void pr_name(char **nptr);


int main(void)
        {
        char *nameptrs[3] ={"Robert"
          ,"Mark","George"};

        pr_name (nameptrs);
        }


void pr_name(char **nptr)
        {
        char **cptr;


        cptr = nptr;
        while(cptr < (nptr+3))
              {
              puts (*cptr);
              cptr++;
              }
        }
```

LISTING 14-7B:

```
void pr_name(char(*lptr)[20]);


int main(void)
        {
        char last[3][20] ={"Robert",
                "Mark","George"};

        pr_name(last);
        }


void pr_name(char(*aptr)[20])
        {
        char (*tptr)[20];


        tptr = aptr;
        while(tptr < (aptr+3))
              {
              puts(*tptr);
              tptr++;
              }
        }
```

You need to be careful to distinguish between an array of pointers and an array of arrays. The corresponding parameters for each is different. In the case of an array of pointers, an element of the array is a pointer. The parameter must be a pointer to a pointer. In the case of an array of arrays, an element of an array of arrays is itself an array. The parameter must be a pointer to an array. The next example lists the different way of declaring each.

```
pointer to pointer      pointer to array
char **nptr;            char (*aptr)[4];
char *nptr[];           char aptr[][4];
```

LISTINGs 14.6 and 14.7 are examples of programs using an array of pointers and an array of arrays. LISTING 14-6 uses array subscripts. LISTING 14-7 uses pointer representation. The A part of each listing implements an array of pointers. The B part implements and array of arrays.

Because of their similarity it is easy to confuse the two types of declarations. One common error is try to declare a pointer to an array without the necessary parentheses. For example, the declaration show here is an invalid parameter declaration.

```
char *badptr[4]      invalid parameter declaration
```

This declaration declares badptr to be an array, an array of pointers. badptr becomes an array name. An array name evaluates to an address, not a variable, parameters must always be variables. You will receive a compiler error indicating that badptr is not a valid parameter.

argv and argc

Often, when you start up a program on your computer you will want to pass it arguments. Say you have a program to print files. When you start up the program, you would want to enter in the program name along with the names of the files to be printed. All C programs have the capability to handle such command line arguments. C programs automatically parse the command line words you entered in a program invocation and places them in string constants. For example, the command line invocation of the **a.out** program that follows, parses into two words: `myprint` and `termpaper.`, each of which are copied into their own string constant.

```
% myprint  termpaper
```

The special parameter variables `argv` and `argc` allow you to reference these string constants. `argv` and `argc` are defined as parameter variables in a program's main function. They reference the words used in a user's command line invocation of the program. `argc` is the count of the number of words the user provided in the command line. `argv` is a pointer to a pointer used to reference the words themselves. `argv` actually references an array of pointers. This array of pointers references the string constants that hold the command line words.

The following examples are two equivalent ways to declare `argv`. The first uses only pointer representation. The second uses a combination of pointer representation and array subscript.

```
int main (int argc, char **argv)
       {
       }

int main (int argc, char *argv[])
       {
       }
```

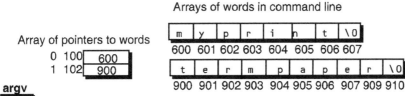

Figure 14-13: argv and argc.

In Figure 14-13, the value of `argc` is 2. The name of the program itself is included in the parse. `argv` is used to reference those words. Each words is placed in its own array. The addresses of those arrays are placed in an array of pointers. The address of the array of pointers is passed to `argv`. `argv` is a pointer to the first pointer element in that array of pointers.

You can reference a particular word through `argv` using array subscript. The first word is `argv[0]`. Figure 14-14 illustrates how array subscripts can be used to reference command line words. The following example prints out all the command line words, using array subscripts.

```
i = 0;
while(i < argc)
        {
        puts(argv[i]);
        i++;
        }
```

`argc` is used here to detect the end of the array. `argc` holds the number of words entered on the command line, including the program name. You can use this information in a variety of ways. One common use is to test for a valid number of program arguments. If you design a program that requires a specific number of arguments, you need some way to make sure that the user entered in those arguments. You could test the value of `argc` to see if it holds the value for the correct number of arguments. Remember that arguments start after the program name, so a program invoked with one argument will give `argc` a value of 2, one for the program name and one for the argument.

```
if (argc != 2)
        {
        fprintf(stderr,"Enter a filename \n");
        exit(1);
        }
```

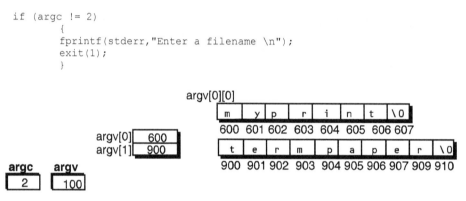

Figure 14-14: Using argv to reference command words.

Many program designs allow the user to enter in flags on the command line in order to set different options on the program. Such flags often exist as single letters. In the program itself you still need to reference these letters. In other words, you have to use a pointer to a pointer, `argv`, to reference an object in an array, the flag. In the next example, the first letter of a second word is treated as a letter flag. The array subscripts for two-dimensional arrays is used to reference a letter in its string constant. The first set of brackets references the second pointer element in the array of pointers which holds the address of the second command line string constant. The second set brackets references the first character in that second string constant.

```
switch(argv[1][0])
        {
        case 'f':
                printf("Greetings ");
                break;
        case 'c':
                printf("Hi ");
                break;
        }
```

The **greetarg.c** program in LISTING 14-8 uses `argc` and `argv` to manage command line arguments. The user is expected to add a name and a flag to the command line argument. `argc` is tested to check if the user entered in the correct number of arguments. The first character of the second argument is treated as a flag, printing out alternative greetings. If no flag is entered, then just the name is printed out. `argv[argc-1]` references the last argument no matter how many are entered. Arrays are indexed from 0, so `argc-1` indexes the last element.

LISTING 14-8:

greetarg.c
```c
#include <stdio.h>
#include <stdlib.h>

int main (int argc, char *argv[])
        {
        if ((argc < 2) || (argc > 3)) {
                printf("Invalid number of arguments\n");
                exit(1);
                }

        if (argc == 3)
                {
                switch(argv[1][0])
                        {
                        case 'f':
                                printf("Greetings ");
                                break;
                        case 'c':
                                printf("Hi ");
                                break;
                        }
                }
        printf("%s", argv[argc-1]);
        return 0;
        }
```

Run of LISTING 14-8

```
greetarg   f   justin
Greetings justin
greetarg   dylan
dylan
```

The array subscripts are really pointer offset expressions. You can always use the pointer offset expressions in place of the array subscript. The following examples listed here are all equivalent. The function call `puts(argv)` would be an error. The address of the command line string constant is in the array pointers, not in the pointer variable `argv`.

```c
*(argv + 0)
argv[0]
*argv

puts( *(argv + 0) );
puts(argv[0]);
puts(*argv);
```

You can apply any of the standard pointer operations to the array of pointers referenced by `argv`. You can have working pointers, declared as pointer to pointers, referencing this array of pointers. In the next example, wptr is assigned the same address as that held by argv. wptr is then used as a working pointer to increment through the array of pointers.

```
char **wptr;

wptr = argv;
while(wptr <  (argv + argc))
        {
        puts( *wptr);
        wptr++;
        }
```

argv is really a pointer variable. As a variable its value can be changed. You could also use argv as a working variable, incrementing down the array (see Figure 14-15).

```
i = 0;
while(i < argc) {
        puts( *argv);
        argv++;
        i++;
        }
```

You may run across programs in which there are clever uses of argv as a working pointer. Since argv is a pointer variable, the increment and indirection operations can be combined into the same expression, creating complex postfix and prefix operations. This often results in obscure code.

In the **greetinc.c** program in LISTING 14-9, the expression ***++argv* in the select statement is equivalent to argv[1][0]. The expression, ***++argv* first increments argv, ++argv, and then performs a double indirection, **argv. The increment places argv, which is already pointing to the first pointer, to point to the second pointer element in the array. The first indirection on argv references that second pointer element and the address of the second character array that it holds. The second indirection references the first character variable of the second character array. In this way the expression **argv accesses the first character in the third word.

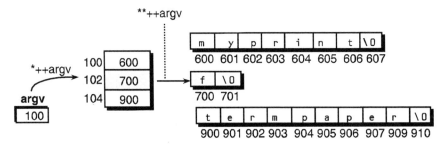

Figure 14-15: Incrementing argv.

If a user enters in only one argument, a name, the expression **++argv* in the printf function call is equivalent to argv[1]. The expression **++argv* increments argv, ++argv, and then performs indirection on argv, *argv. The increment sets argv to point to the second pointer in the array of pointers. Indirection on argv then references the second pointer, which holds the address of the second character array. If the user enters in an option with the name, then `*++argv` will be equivalent to `argv[2]`, argv having already been incremented to `argv[1]`, the option. `argv` will then reference the third pointer, which holds the address of the third character array, in this case, the name.

LISTING 14-9:

greetinc.c
```
#include <stdio.h>
#include <stdlib.h>

int main (int argc, char **argv)
        {
        if ((argc < 2) || (argc > 3)) {
                printf("Invalid number of arguments\n");
                exit(1);
                }

        if (argc == 3)
                {
                switch(**++argv)
                        {
                        case 'f':
                                printf("Greetings ");
                                break;
                        case 'c':
                                printf("Hi ");
                                break;
                        }
                }
        printf("%s",*++argv);
        return 0;
        }
```

Arrays of Pointers to Functions

You can define arrays of pointers to any type of object. You can define arrays of pointers to floats, array of pointers to structures, and even arrays of pointers to functions. With an array of pointers to functions, each element in the array can hold the address of a function. You can then use an element in that array to reference and call the function whose address it holds. This leads to the often confusing code in which you can use an array reference in a function call, in place of a function name.

In the next example, the array `stylefuncs` is declared as an array of pointers to functions. Its elements are initialized with a set of function names. Notice the parentheses placed around both the pointer and array data types (see Figure 14-16). The parentheses are needed because the pointer type, `*`, has a lower precedence that the function type, `()`. To have the array type, `[]`, apply to the pointer type, both have to be enclosed within parentheses, forcing precedence. The parentheses then placed around both the pointer and array data types declare this object as an array of pointers. The function data type, `()`, is then evaluated. This is an array of pointers to functions. The data type, in this case void, is the type of the function's return value. This is an array of pointers to functions with a return type of void.

```
void (*stylefuncs[3])(void) = { printformal,
                                printcommon,
                                printfriendly };
```

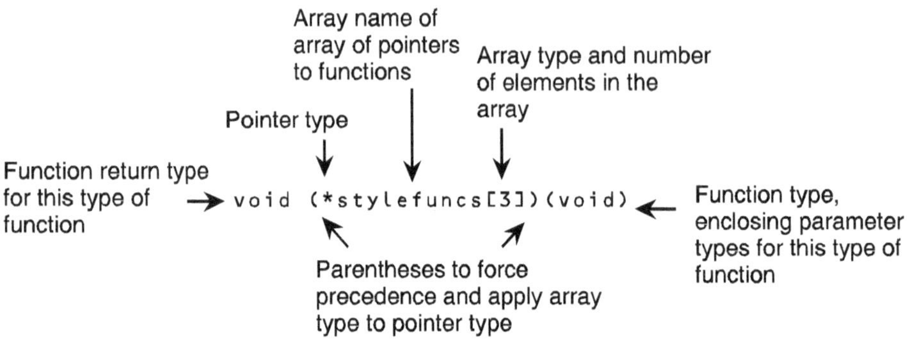

Figure 14-16: Declaration of an array of pointers to functions.

Recall that the function call operator, (), only requires the address of a function. This address can be obtained from a function name or an indirection on a pointer to a function that holds the address. The address of a function can also be obtained from an indirection on an element of an array of pointers to functions. These elements are themselves simply pointers to functions. You can use such an element in a function call, first referencing the pointer element in its array, and then performing an indirection on that pointer element to reference the function it points to. Once the function is referenced, the function call operation calls the function. The following example, the address of a function is obtained from the second element of the stylefuncs array. The array subscript [1] references that second element. The indirection operation references the function whose address the second element holds. The function call operation then calls that referenced function (see Figure 14-17).

```
(*stylefuncs[1])();
```

Notice the parenthesis placed around the indirection operator and the array brackets. As in the declaration, there is a precedence problem. The function call operator, (), has higher precedence that the indirection operator, *. Yet you need to perform the indirection on the array pointer element, not the function call. So parentheses are needed to force precedence, applying the indirection operation to the array element, and referencing the function address it holds, and only then performing the function call.

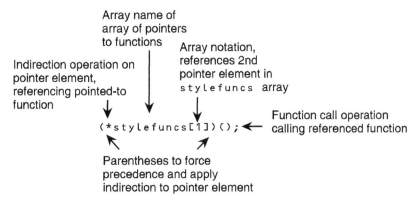

Figure 14-17: Function call using array of pointers to functions.

The program in Figure 14-18, illustrates how an array of pointers to functions works. The `stylefuncs` array is initialized with the addresses of three different functions. Then the user is asked to choose what function to call by entering in a number. The number, held in the variable choice, is used as an index to an element in the array of pointers to functions. If the user were to enter a 1, then the second element in the array of pointers would be referenced. In this case, the address of a function is obtained from the second element of the `stylefuncs` array. This element holds the address of the `printcommon` function, represented here as 700. An indirection on this element will reference that `printcommon` function. And a function call operation on this reference will, in turn, call the `printcommon` function.

There are, of course, several different ways you could write such a function call. For example, you could use the pointer offset and indirection operations in place of the array subscript, as shown here.

```
(* (*(stylefuncs + 1)) )();
```

Alternatively you could use array subscripts to write a function call using an element of an array of pointers to functions.

```
(*stylefuncs[1])();
```

Arrays of pointers to functions make it easier to design very flexible programs. You could use an array of pointers to functions as a collection of possible functions that a user could select from. The user could actually decide what function a program would execute. In the **styleptr.c** program in LISTING 14-10, the array `stylefuncs` is declared as an array of pointers to functions. Each pointer is initialized with an function name. When the user enters a choice, that choice becomes an index to the `stylefuncs` array of pointers to functions. To call a particular function, the address of the function is referenced by referencing the pointer element in the array (see Figure 14-18). In such a reference, you could use either array subscripts or pointer operations.

LISTING 14-10:

styleptr.c

```c
#include <stdio.h>
void printformal(void);
void printcommon(void);
void printfriendly(void);

void (*stylefuncs[3])(void) = { printformal,
                                               printcommon,
                                               printfriendly };

int main(void)
      {
      int choice;

      printf("Enter Greeting Code\n");
      scanf ("%d", &choice);

      if(choice < 3)
              (*stylefuncs[choice])();

      return 0;
      }

void printformal(void)
              {
              printf("greetings");
              }

void printcommon(void)
              {
              printf("hello");
              }

void printfriendly(void)
              {
              printf("hi");
              }
```

```
#include <stdio.h>

void printformal(void);
void printcommon(void);
void printfriendly(void);

void (*stylefunc[3])() = { printformal,
                           printcommon,
                           printfriendly };
```

stylefunc

```
int main(void)
    {
    int choice;
```

100	600
102	700
104	900

```
    printf("Enter Greeting Code\n");
    scanf ("%d", &choice);

    if(choice < 3)
        (*stylefunc[choice])();
    }

600 void printformal(void)
    {
    printf("greetings");
    }

700 void printcommon(void)
    {
    printf("hello");
    }

900 void printfriendly(void)
    {
    printf("hi");
    }
```

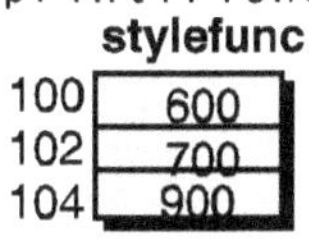

Figure 14-18: Array of pointers to functions.

Array of Pointers as an Index

Arrays of pointers are often used to construct indexes for sets of data. In many programs, you will have data that needs to be sorted. An array of pointers provides a very efficient, fast, and simple structure through which to sort that data. In effect, the array of pointers becomes an sorted index with which you can reference your data in sorted order.

There are several situations in which such an index is called for. One of these situations occurs if your data is so large that sorting it directly would be very inefficient. For example you may have a set of large strings that if sorted directly would entail a great deal of string copying. Another situation occurs when you have data consisting of records containing different fields. Suppose you need to perform several different sorts on the records, each sort using a different field. For example, if you have a set of employee records with name and id fields. You might need a sort of the records by the name field, and you might also need another sort of the records by id field.

In both cases the data is usually held in an array such as an array of strings or an array of structures. To create an index, you first define an array of pointer with the same number of elements. Then you assign the address of each data element to a corresponding pointer in the array of pointers. Each pointer in the array then hold an address of a record in the data array. Then, instead of physically sorting the data array, you sort the array of pointers instead. When sorting, you use the pointer element to reference the data you want to sort on. For example in the case of sorting strings, you need to use pointer elements to reference the strings you need to compare, test to see which is greater or less. Then, instead of switching strings in the data array, you only need to switch addresses in the array of pointers. Once you have finished the sort, you can then use the array of pointers to reference the data in a sorted manner.

LISTING 14-11:

strsort.c

```
#include <stdio.h>
#include <string.h>
#define MAX 3
void sortstrs(char**);

int main(void)
        {
        int i;
        char *strptrs[MAX];
        char mystrings[MAX][10]={"Virgil","Dickens","Poe"};

        for(i=0; i<MAX; i++)
                {
                strptrs[i] = *(mystrings + i);
                }
        sortstrs(strptrs);
        for(i=0; i<MAX; i++)
                {
                printf("%s\n", strptrs[i]);
                }

        return 0;
        }

void sortstrs(char **sptr)
        {
        int i, j;
        char *temptr;

        for(i = 0; i< (MAX - 1); i++)
                {
                for(j = i + 1; j < MAX; j++)
                        {
                        if( strcmp(sptr[i], sptr[j]) > 0)
                                {
                                temptr = sptr[i];
                                sptr[i] = sptr[j];
                                sptr[j] = temptr;
                                }
                        }
                }
        }
```

The **strsort.c** program in LISTING 14-11 uses an array of pointers to sort an array of strings. The mystrings two-dimensional array of characters holds the set of strings. The strings are not in alphabetical order. Each pointer element of the array of pointers strptrs, is then assigned an address of a string in `mystrings`. The `strptrs` array of pointers is then passed to the `sortstrs` function for sorting. Each string in `mystrings` is referenced through a pointer element in `strptrs`. To sort the strings, the pointers are sorted, not the strings themselves. To access the strings as an ordered set, the strings are referenced through the array of pointers (see Figure 14-19). `strptrs` is used to print out the `mystrings` strings in sorted alphabetical order.

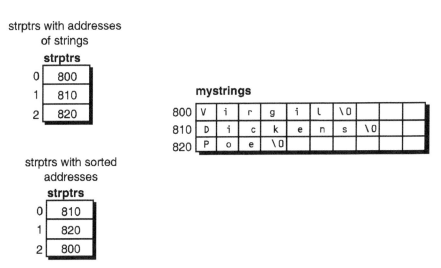

Figure 14-19: Array of pointers used for sorting strings.

To index records, you can use an array of pointers to sort a particular field in those records. Records are implemented in C as structures, and structure members function as record fields. To create an index on a particular structure member, you first define an array of pointer and then assign to each element the address of a structure element in the array of structures. Then you sort the pointers, by referencing the specified member in the structures. For example, suppose you have an array of employee structures as defined in the **strucptr.c** program in LISTING 14-12. And you need a sort based on the name member, sorting your structures by name. Having defined an array of pointers and assigning the address of each structure element to a corresponding pointer, you then need only sort the array of pointers. In performing the sort, you will need to use pointer elements to reference structure name members so that you can compare the different structures' names. Once you have completed the sort, you can then use the array of pointers to reference the array of structures sorted by name. Printing out the structures using this sorted array of pointers would then print out the structures sorted by name. You could do the same for the salary member using another array of pointers.

The **strucptr.c** program in LISTING 14-12 used an array of pointer to create such an index to an array of structures. The array is an array of structures, `emprecs`, is defined, along with an array of pointers, `ndxptrs`. The address of each structure element in the emprecs array is then assigned to a pointer element in the `ndxptrs` array. Using such an array of pointers to the structure elements, the structures can be sorted using one of the members as a key. Here, the id member is the key. These addresses held in the `ndxptrs` array are then sorted based on the id members of each structure element. Figure 14-19 shows the values of the `ndxptrs` array before and after sorting.

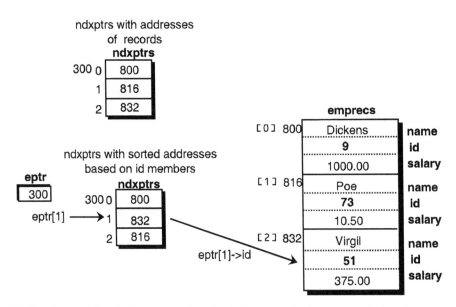

Figure 14-20: Array of pointers as index to data records in array of structures.

Using the ndxptrs array, the elements in the array of structures can then be printed out based on the sorted order of their id members. In this case, the first structure element will be printed out, followed by the third structure element, and finally the second structure element. This corresponds to a sorted order based on the values of their id members: 9, 51, 73.

Notice how an array offset and arrow operation on a pointer to an element in an array of pointers can reference the member of a structure in the array of structures. Figure 14-20 illustrates such an operation. For example, eptr[1]->id uses the second pointer element in the array of pointers to reference the id member of a structure element. First, an array offset on eptr references a pointer element of ndxptrs. eptr[1] references the second pointer element. This pointer element holds the address of a structure, 832. With this address, the structure can be referenced. The arrow operation on this address will perform an indirection to reference the structure and a member operation to reference a member in the structure. In this case, the id, member of the structure at address 832 is referenced, eptr[1]->id.

LISTING 14-12:

strucptr.c
```c
#include <stdio.h>
#define MAX 3
        typedef struct emp{
                char name[10];
                int id;
                float salary;
                } EMP;

 void sortids(EMP**);
 void printrec(EMP*);

 int main(void)
        {
        int i;
        EMP *ndxptrs[3];
        EMP emprecs[MAX]= { {"Dickens", 9, 1000},
                            {"Poe", 73, 10.50},
                            {"Virgil", 51, 375.00} };
        for(i = 0; i < 3; i++)
                {
                ndxptrs[i] = &emprecs[i];
                }

        sortids(ndxptrs);

        for(i = 0; i < 3; i++)
                {
                printrec(ndxptrs[i]);
                }
        return 0;
        }

void sortids(EMP **eptr)
        {
        int i, j;
        EMP *temptr;

        for(i = 0; i< (MAX - 1); i++)
                {
                for(j = i + 1; j < MAX; j++)
                        {
                        if(eptr[i]->id > eptr[j]->id)
                                {
                                temptr = eptr[i];
                                eptr[i] = eptr[j];
                                eptr[j] = temptr;
                                }
                        }
                }
        }

 void printrec(EMP *emptr)
        {
        printf("\nName is %s\n", emptr->name);
        printf("id is %d\n", emptr->id);
        printf("Salary %.2f\n",emptr->salary);
        }
```

Chapter Summary: Arrays of Pointers

Arrays of pointers have pointer variables as their elements. An array of pointers is often used to reference a set of data, such as a set of character arrays. Elements in an array of pointers can be referenced with either array subscripts or pointer operations. A working pointer can be declared to advance down the elements from one pointer to the next. Such a working pointer is declared as a pointer to a pointer. The type of object it points to is another pointer.

      The array name of an array of pointers is itself a pointer to a pointer. Indirection on the array name references the first pointer element in the array. A double indirection on the array name or working pointer references the object a pointer element points to.

      Pointers to pointers are used as parameters for functions that receive arrays of pointers as arguments. argv is a pointer to a pointer specifically designed as a parameter for the main function. argv holds the address of an array of pointers that references the command line arguments. All the words in a command line at the time the program is invoked are automatically parsed and stored in character arrays as strings. An array of pointers is generated to hold the addresses of these strings. argv holds the address of this array of pointers. As a parameter, argv is a variable. You can use it as a working pointer to advance down the array of pointers. The other main parameter, argc, holds the count of the number of words in the command line when the program is invoked. You can use it to determine the upper bound of the array of pointers referenced by argv.

      You can also use an array of pointers as an index for a set of data. The elements of an array of pointers can be set to the addresses of a set of data, such as character strings. Instead of physically sorting the character strings, you can sort the array of pointers instead. You can then use the array of pointers to reference the data in a sorted manner.

Exercises

1. Write a program with argv, taking as arguments your first name, your last name, and your age (approximate).

```
main(int argc, char *argv[])
        {
        printf("\n The first argument = %s\n",argv[1]);
        }
```

      Run of preceding program.

```
% a.out   baseball
The first argument = baseball
```

2. Rewrite your program using argc to test for the correct number of arguments.

3. Modify the program in LISTING 14-12 to index on the name member of the array of structures. Add a search function using only the array of pointers.

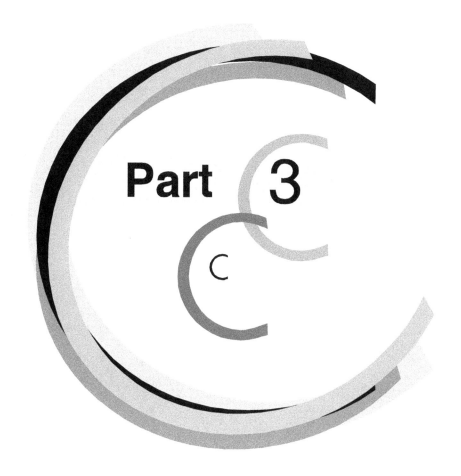

Part 3

Data Structures
and
File Management

Data Structures

and

Recursion

Part 3: Data Structures and File Managment

15. Data Structures and Recursion

Up till now, for most tasks, you only needed to define objects as variables or as elements of an array. Recall that you can also define objects dynamically. Such dynamic objects can be organized into very effective formats called data structures that you can then manage using recursion. Two common types of data structures are linked lists and trees. Linked list allow you to manage lists of data of varying length. Trees allow you to create and manage indexes that you can use to access records.

Data structures are characterized by their flexibility. For example, you can tailor a linked list to exactly the size of the list, lengthening it or shortening it as needed. Much of this flexibility is derived from the fact that a dynamic object is defined during the run of a program, not at compile time as with variables and arrays. As described in Chapter 5, you first allocate memory from unused free memory and assign its address to a pointer. You then use that pointer to reference that allocated memory as an object. Such a dynamic object only requires that you have a pointer with which to reference it. Should you need another object you only have to allocate the memory and assign its address to another pointer.

The type of a dynamic object depends solely on its pointer. A pointer to an integer will reference a dynamically allocated integer. A pointer to a structure will reference a dynamically allocated structure. In the case of data structures, you need to declare a structure type in which one of the members is itself a pointer. If you then dynamically allocated such a structure, then that structure would in turn contain a pointer. You could then allocate yet another object and assign its address to the pointer in the dynamically defined structure.

Using such a technique you can create a series of structure objects, each with a pointer used to reference another structure object. The pointer would be defined as a pointer to a structure of its own type. For example, in the type declaration of an EMP structure type, you could declare a pointer that points to a structure of the EMP structure type. In other words, the pointer would be pointer that points to another EMP structure, a structure of its own type. A structure with such a member is known as a self-referential structure. You can use self-referential structures to form data structures, such as linked lists or trees.

Linked lists and trees are often managed by recursive functions. Recursion is a non-intuitive process and can be very confusing when first examined. Though recursion can also be a way to perform mathematical calculations, in this text, recursion is presented as a method for managing data structures.

The topic of data structures is very extensive. There is a variety of different types of linked lists and trees. In this text, only the basic concepts are presented. This chapter will focus on simple forms of linked lists and binary search trees.

Linked Lists

A linked list is a list of several linked objects. Each object is a self-referential structure. A self-referential structure contains a pointer to another structure of the same type. Through its pointer, each structure is linked to other structures. Several of these linked structures form a linked list.

A linked list maintains a list of objects whose number may vary greatly from time to time. A list, that at one time may have only a few objects and at another time may have many objects, varies greatly in its storage requirements. To implement such a dynamic list with an array would require an array large enough to hold the maximum number of possible objects in the list. The maximum number would have to be somehow determined ahead of time, when the array is declared. A linked list suffers from no such constraints. A linked list only uses as much storage as the number of objects currently in the list. A linked list may expand to as many objects as are required at any given time (see Figure 15-1.). Each object is created as it is needed and destroyed when no longer required. Storage for each object is allocated dynamically at the time the object is needed. When the object is no longer needed, its memory is de-allocated, freed.

The memory used for a linked list is derived from the heap memory segment. There are four major data segments generated when a program is loaded into memory. The first is the program or text segment. This contains the instructions for the program. The second is the data segment, which contains memory for static and external variables. The fourth is the stack, which contains memory for automatic variables and function call information. The third, placed between the second and fourth segments, is the heap memory segment. This is all the remaining unused memory and is available for use during the run of the program. Linked-list objects are built from this memory, as shown in Figure 15-2. The memory is allocated for use by the program by memory allocation functions such as `malloc`.

You can use `malloc` to allocate memory for a linked-list object. Successive calls to `malloc` create other linked-list objects. When an object is no longer needed, a call of the free function will free up the object memory, making it available for use by later `malloc` function calls.

Figure 15-1: Linked list object.

The function `malloc` allocates memory for an object and returns the address of that memory. You then assign the address to a pointer accessible by the program. Without the pointer, the object cannot be referenced. A pointer variable is declared in the program, defining it in either the data or stack segment. The first call to `malloc` has the address of its allocated memory assigned to this variable. This establishes a connection between the program and the allocated object. Through the pointer, the program can reference the allocated object in the heap memory segment. This pointer is known as the head of the list. It holds the address of the first object in the list of objects.

It would be self-defeating to declare a pointer variable for each object in the list. To do so, you would again have to determine a maximum number of objects for the list and declare that many corresponding pointer variables. How then can successive objects in the list be referenced? To what pointer is the address of a new object assigned?

The type of object in a list is a structure, one of whose members is a pointer to a structure of its own type. A new object can have its address assigned to the member pointer of the last object in the list. When the first object is allocated, it contains a member that is a pointer variable itself. When the second object is allocated, its address is assigned to the pointer member of the first object. The address of the second object is now obtainable from the pointer member of the first object. The pointer member of the first object can, in turn, be referenced through the head pointer variable. The head pointer variable holds the address of the first object in the list. An indirection and member operation on the head pointer can access the pointer member in the first object. The pointer members are like steppingstones. Beginning with the first object, you can step from one object to the next. Each object will hold the address of the next object in the list. The pointer member of the last object will not hold an address. Its value will be the null value, 0.

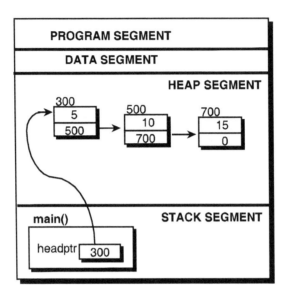

Figure 15-2: Linked list in memory.

The **linklist.c** program in LISTING 15-1 builds a simple linked list of three objects. Each object is a structure of two members, mynum and nextptr. mynum is a simple integer. Successive objects have their mynum member assigned multiples of 5;: 5 ,10, and 15. The nextptr member holds the address of the next object in the list. A new object is first allocated and its address assigned to a pointer variable called newptr. The newptr variable simply holds the address of the new object until it can be linked to the list.

Linking a new object to a list involves checking for a special case. Ordinarily you would simply attach the object to the last object already in the list, putting it at the end of the list. There is a special case that occurs when the very first object is allocated. At that point, the list is empty and the pointer variable used as head pointer for the list is null. In the case of the very first object, you need to assign its address to the head pointer. All the other objects that are allocated are simply attached to the last object in the list.

There are several ways to keep track of the last object in the list. A simple solution is to declare a pointer variable that will hold the address of the last object. In the following example, the pointer lastptr is used to keep track of the last object in the list. To attach a new object to the end of the list, the address of the new object is assigned to the nextptr member of the last object. The nextptr member of the last object is referenced through lastptr, lastptr->nextptr = newptr. The nextptr member of the new object is then set to 0 since it is now the last object in the list.

```
typedef struct numobj {
               int mynum;
               struct numobj *nextptr;
               } NUMOBJ;

int main(void)
      {
      NUMOBJ *headptr = 0;
      NUMOBJ *lastptr = 0;
      NUMOBJ *newptr;
      int i = 1;

      while(i <= 3)
            {
            newptr = (NUMOBJ*) malloc(sizeof(NUMOBJ));

            if(headptr == 0)
                  headptr = newptr;
            else
                  lastptr->nextptr = newptr;

            newptr->mynum = i * 5;
            newptr->nextptr = 0;
            lastptr = newptr;
            i++;
            }
      return 0;
      }
```

You now know how the beginning and end to the list are detected. The address of the first object in the list is held in the `headptr` variable. The last object in the list has a pointer member whose value is 0. The list is traversed starting with the address in the `headptr` variable and progressing from object to object using the address in each object's pointer member, in this example `nextptr`. The pointer member of each object holds the address of the next object. The object whose pointer member is 0 is the last object. A test for a zero value in an object's pointer member tests for the last object in the list.

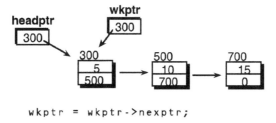

wkptr = wkptr->nexptr;

Figure 15-3: Linked list traversal with working pointer.

You need to use a working pointer to progress through the objects in a linked list, referencing each object in turn (see Figure 15-3). Just as a working pointer was used in Chapter 10 to reference each successive object in an array, a working pointer is also used to reference each successive object in a linked list. The working pointer obtains the address of the first object from the head of the list. It then obtains the address of each successive object from the pointer member of the current object. In the next example, the working pointer, wkptr, obtains the address of the first object from headptr. It then obtains the address of each successive object from the pointer member of the current object, nextptr.

```c
NUMOBJ *headptr;
NUMOBJ *wkptr;

wkptr = headptr;
while(wkptr != 0)
        {
        printf("%d", wkptr->mynum);
        wkptr = wkptr->nextptr;
        }
```

LISTING 15-1:

linklist.c

```c
/* Build a linked list of 3 objects and print them. */
#include <stdio.h>
#include <stdlib.h>

typedef struct numobj {
                int mynum;
                struct numobj *nextptr;
                } NUMOBJ;

int main(void)
        {
        NUMOBJ *headptr = 0;
        NUMOBJ *lastptr = 0;
        NUMOBJ *newptr;
        NUMOBJ *wkptr;
        int i = 1;

        while(i <= 3)
                {
                newptr = (NUMOBJ*) malloc(sizeof(NUMOBJ));
                if(headptr == 0)
                        {
                        headptr = newptr;
                        }
                else
                        lastptr->nextptr = newptr;
                newptr->mynum = i * 5;
                newptr->nextptr = 0;
                lastptr = newptr;
                i++;
                }

        wkptr = headptr;
        while(wkptr != 0)
                {
                printf("%d", wkptr->mynum);
                wkptr = wkptr->nextptr;
                }
        return 0;
        }
```

Deleting Linked List Objects

The last object in a linked list can be deleted simply by freeing the memory for that object and setting the pointer member of the previous object to 0. This can be a bit tricky since the address of the object before the last object needs to also be located. In the following example, `prevptr` keeps track of the objects before the current object is referenced by `wkptr`. When `wkptr` reaches the last object, `prevptr` will be pointed to the next to last object. If there is only one object in the list, it is deleted through `headptr`; otherwise, the end of the list is searched for using `wkptr`. The deleted object's memory is de-allocated with the free function. Figure 15-4 shows how `prevptr` and `wkptr` are used to delete the last object in a list.

```
NUMOBJ *headptr;
NUMOBJ *prevptr;
NUMOBJ *wkptr;

/* if there are objects in the list */
if(headptr != 0)
        {       /* if only one object in the list */
        if(headptr->nextptr == 0)
                {
                free(headptr);
                headptr = 0;
                }
        else
                {       /* find last and next-to-last object */
                wkptr=prevptr=headptr;
                while (wkptr->nextptr!=0)
                        {
                        prevptr = wkptr;
                        wkptr=wkptr->nextptr;
                        }
                free (wkptr);
                prevptr->nextptr = 0;
                }
        }
```

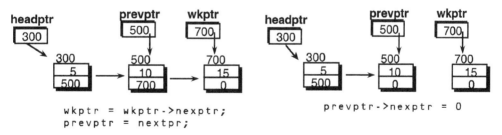

Figure 15-4: Deleting an object from a linked list.

In **numlist.c** program in LISTING 15-2, the user can alternately add objects to the list, print them out, as well as delete objects from the list. Instead of using `lastptr` to keep track of the last object in the list, the list is simply traversed to the end each time a new object is added.

LISTING 15-2:

numlist.c

```
#include <stdio.h>
#include <stdlib.h>

        typedef struct numobj {
                        int mynum;
                        struct numobj *nextptr;
                        } NUMOBJ;

void printlist(NUMOBJ*);
NUMOBJ *addobj(NUMOBJ*);
NUMOBJ *delobj(NUMOBJ*);

int main(void)
        {
        char choice[2];
        int more = 1;
        NUMOBJ * headptr = 0, *resptr;

        while (more != 0)
                {
                printf("Please enter choice\n");
                scanf("%s", choice);
                switch(choice[0])
                        {
                        case 'a':
                                resptr = addobj(headptr);
                                if (headptr == 0)
                                        headptr = resptr;
                                break;
                        case 'p':
                                printlist(headptr);
                                break;
                        case 'd':
                                resptr = delobj(headptr);
                                if(resptr == 0)
                                        headptr = 0;
                                break;
                        case 'q':
                                more = 0;
                        }
                }
        return 0;
        }

void printlist(NUMOBJ *headptr)
        {
        NUMOBJ *wkptr;

        wkptr = headptr;
        while(wkptr != 0)
                {
                printf("%d\n", wkptr->mynum);
                wkptr = wkptr->nextptr;
                }
        }
```

```
NUMOBJ *addobj(NUMOBJ *headptr)
        {
        NUMOBJ *newptr;
        NUMOBJ *wkptr;

                newptr = (NUMOBJ *) malloc(sizeof(NUMOBJ));
                newptr->nextptr = 0;
                printf("Please enter new number\n");
                scanf("%d", &newptr->mynum);

                if(headptr == 0)
                        {
                        return newptr;
                        }
                else
                        {
                        wkptr= headptr;
                        while (wkptr->nextptr != 0)
                                wkptr = wkptr->nextptr;
                        wkptr->nextptr = newptr;
                        return newptr;
                        }
        }

NUMOBJ *delobj(NUMOBJ *headptr)
        {
        NUMOBJ*prevptr;
        NUMOBJ*wkptr;

        if(headptr != 0)
                {
                if(headptr->nextptr == 0)
                        {
                        free(headptr);
                        return 0;
                        }
                        else
                        {
                        wkptr=prevptr= headptr;
                        while (wkptr->nextptr!=0)
                                {
                                prevptr = wkptr;
                                wkptr=wkptr->nextptr;
                                }
                        prevptr->nextptr = 0;
                        free (wkptr);
                        return prevptr;
                        }
                }
        }
```

Ordered Linked Lists

Ordered linked lists are created using a insert sort. Instead of simply placing a new object at the end of the list, the object is inserted into its ordered position in the list. The list is traversed as long as the data in the new object is greater than the data in the list object.

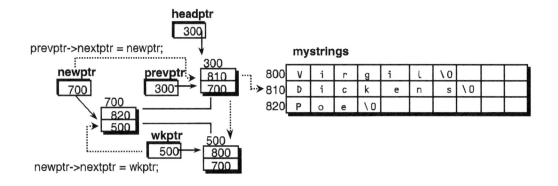

Figure 15-5: Ordered linked list of pointers to strings.

Two pointers are used to perform an ordered insert. One is a working pointer that traverses each object, and the other follows behind, keeping track of the previous object. When a list object is referenced whose data is greater than the new object's data, the point in the list for inserting the new object has been reached. The new object is inserted between the object referenced by the working pointer and the object referenced by the previous pointer. The address of the new object is assigned to the `nextptr` member of the previous object, the object referenced by the previous pointer. The address of the object referenced by the working pointer is assigned to the `nextptr` member of the new object. The previous object's `nextptr` member will now hold the address of the new object. The new object's `nextptr` member will hold the address of the currently referenced object.

Ordered insertions must check for one special circumstance. If the new object is to be inserted at the beginning of the list, then the head pointer must be changed to hold the address of that new object.

With an ordered insertion of the objects into a list, you can use a linked list in place of an array of pointers to index other data objects (see Figure 15-5). In Chapter 14, an array of pointers was used to index and sort an array of strings. Instead of an array of pointers, you can use an ordered linked list to index the strings. The data in each object will be a pointer to char and will hold the address of a string. Each object is inserted into the list by comparing the string it references to those referenced by other objects in the list.

Whereas an array of pointers places a limit on the number of objects that can be referenced, a linked list of pointers can vary the number of objects referenced to any degree. There is no limit. In the **ordlist.c** program in LISTING 15-3, an ordered linked list of pointers is used in place of an array of pointers to index and order a set of strings. The function insertobj places an object with the address of a string into the list. The function checks for a special condition. If the new object is to be inserted at the head of the list, the `headptr` variable must have its address changed to that of the new object.

LISTING 15-3: Ordered Linked List with Ordered Insert

ordlist.c

```c
#include <stdio.h>
#include <stdlib.h>
#include <string.h>

        typedef struct strobj {
                        char *strptr;
                        struct strobj *nextptr;
                        } STROBJ;

STROBJ *insertobj(STROBJ*, char*);
void printlist(STROBJ *);

int main(void)
        {
        STROBJ *headptr = 0, *resptr;
        int i;
        char mystrings[3][10] = { "Virgil","Dickens","Poe"};

        for(i=0; i<3; i++)
                {
                resptr = insertobj(headptr, mystrings[i]);
                if(resptr != 0)
                                headptr = resptr;
                }
        printlist(headptr);

        return 0;
        }

STROBJ *insertobj(STROBJ *headptr, char *str)
        {
        STROBJ *newptr;
        STROBJ *wkptr, *prevptr;

        newptr = (STROBJ *) malloc(sizeof(STROBJ));
        newptr->strptr = str;;

        prevptr = 0;
        wkptr = headptr;
        while((wkptr!=0) && (strcmp(str,wkptr->strptr)>0))
                {
                prevptr = wkptr;
                wkptr=wkptr->nextptr;
                }

        newptr->nextptr = wkptr;
        if(prevptr == 0)
                return newptr; /*insert at head of list*/
        else{
                prevptr->nextptr = newptr;
                return 0;
                }
        }
```

```
void printlist(STROBJ *headptr)
      {
      STROBJ *wkptr;

      wkptr = headptr;
      while(wkptr != 0)
            {
            printf("%s\n", wkptr->strptr);
            wkptr = wkptr->nextptr;
            }
      }
```

Recursion and Linked Lists

Up to now you have used loops to manage linked lists, moving from one object to the next with each iteration. You can also use recursion to manage linked-list objects. Though loops are clearer and easier to use on linked lists, recursion is far better for managing trees. The concept of recursion is difficult to understand. It is better to start out with simple recursive operations such as that used on linked lists, and the move to the more complex operations used on trees.

Linked lists use a simple type of recursion known as tail recursion. Tail recursion traverses a list, stopping at the tail, the end of the list. The discussion of recursion will begin by taking a closer look at how a linked list is traversed.

A linked list is traversed by a working pointer. The working pointer is assigned the address held by an object's `nextptr` member. This effectively changes the value held by the working pointer from the address of one object to that of the next. When the working pointer is given a 0 address, it has reached the end of the linked list.

In the previous programs, one pointer has been used to traverse the linked list. Though it may seem impractical, it is possible to declare a separate pointer for each object in the list and then reference each object through its own pointer. Each pointer could receive its value from the `nextptr` member of the previous object. In the following code, a list of two objects has already been created. The objects in the list are then traversed with three pointers: `headptr`, `secondptr`, and `endptr`. Each object in the list has its own pointer. A pointer obtains its own object's address from the `nextptr` member of the previous object. The last pointer, `endptr`, will have a value of 0.

```
NUMOBJ *headptr;
NUMOBJ *secondptr;
NUMOBJ *endptr;

/* This code traverses a list of 2 objects*/
printf("%d\n", headptr->mynum);
secondptr = headptr->nextptr;

printf("%d\n", secondptr->mynum);
endptr = secondptr->nextptr;

printf("%u\n", endptr);
```

This is, of course, not a very practical way to program a linked list. Notice, the overall format of this code. Each object has its own pointer. Each pointer receives its value from the `nextptr` member of the previous object. This member itself is referenced through a pointer. In this way, each pointer passes the address of the next object to the next pointer. The last object will pass a 0 value to the next pointer. In each case, the value of one pointer is being passed to another pointer.

Now recall that a function call can also pass the value of one pointer to another. In the code that follows, three function calls to three separate functions are used instead of assignments to pass addresses to pointers. Each function has its own `objptr` variable declared as a parameter. When one function calls another it passes the address of the next object to that function's `objptr`, effectively assigning to it the address of an object. Since the parameter variables declared in each function are scoped to that function, they may all have the same name.

Within each function is a call to another function. `printobj1` calls `printobj2` which in turn calls `printend`. When `printobj1` is called in main, it is passed the address of the first object, the address held by `headptr`. Then when `printobj1` calls `printobj2`, it passes the address of the second object to `printobj2`'s `objptr` variable. In `printobj1`, the address of the second object is held in the first object's member pointer `nextptr`. Finally when `printobj2` calls `printobjend`, it passes the contents of the second object's member pointer. Given that there are only two objects in this list, `printobjend` will be passed a 0 value. The second object's member pointer has a value of 0. Notice the test to check if `objptr` is 0. If it is 0, then no object's address has been passed and no print statement is executed.

```
int main(void)
      {
      NUMOBJ *headptr = 0;

      printobj1(headptr);
      }

void printobj1 (NUMOBJ *objptr)
      {
      if(objptr != 0)
            {
            printf("%d\n", objptr->mynum);
            printobj2(objptr->nextptr);
            }
      }

void printobj2 (NUMOBJ *objptr)
      {
      if(objptr != 0)
            {
            printf("%d\n", objptr->mynum);
            printobjend(objptr->nextptr);
            }
      }

void printobjend (NUMOBJ *objptr)
      {
      if(objptr != 0)
            {
            printf("%d\n", objptr->mynum);
            }
      }
```

Each of these functions is almost identical to each other. Only their names are different. Even the arguments in their function calls are identical. The same exact code is being executed over and over again. Instead of creating several different functions that do the same thing, you could just use the same function over and over again.

This is not a matter of simply calling the same function several times within a loop. The functions in the previous example do not simply repeat the same code. Within each function is a call to another function. This causes a kind of unfolding cascade effect. `printobj1` calls `printobj2` which in turn calls `printend`. When `printend` finishes its execution it returns to `printobj2`. When `printobj2` finishes its execution, it returns to `printobj1`. `printobj1` cannot finish execution of its code until all other functions have executed their code and returned.

Each function, except for the last, calls a function that has the same code. To replace them, a function is needed that calls a function with identical code. A function with identical code is the function itself. So you need to define a function that contains a function call to itself. Such a function is known as a recursive function.

The functions in the previous example can be replaced by one function that calls itself. This same code is rewritten in the next example using a single recursive function. You can think of each recursive call as generating a new copy of the function, complete with its own locally declared variables. The argument passed in each recursive call is the address of the next object. Given a list of two objects, the printobj function generates three versions of itself, one for each address passed. The first two copies reference objects in the list. Each copy has its own `objptr` variable that holds the address of an object. In this sense, there is a pointer variable for each object in the list. The last copy receives a null value. The null value is used to terminate the recursion.

The first copy of `printobj` is generated with the initial `printobj` function call. The argument for this first function call is the address held by `headptr`, the address of the first object in the list. The address in `headptr` is passed to the parameter variable `objptr`. A test is made to see if the value of `objptr` is 0. If not, then the object's `mynum` member is printed out. Then printobj is called again with the address held in the `objptr`'s pointer member `nextptr`, the address of the next object in the list. This time printobj is called from within the first call to printobj. The first copy of printobj is still in existence. The second call generates a new copy of printobj with its own `objptr` variable. This `objptr` receives the address of the second object in the list. From within this copy of printobj, printobj is called again. In this third copy of printobj, the `objptr` parameter will receive a value of 0. The test for the if expression will be false, preventing yet another printobj function call. The copies of printobj will then return. The recursive process unwinds back to the original function call that started it all.

It may help to look at how a recursive function call and its variables are managed on the stack. When a function is called, function call information and the function's variables are created on the stack. In a recursive process, each copy of a function will have its own set of variables and return value placed on the stack as it is called. The process stops when a recursive copy fails to issue a recursive function call. When this last recursive copy returns, a cascade effect takes place in which all the other copies return one by one. When a function returns, its variables are automatically destroyed, reducing the stack. The recursion unwinds back to the first copy of the recursive function.

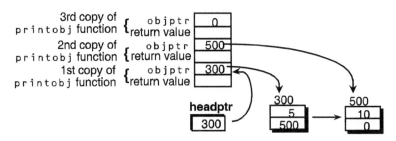

Figure 15-6: Recursive function and linked list.

In the recursive example that follows, three sets of variables and return values will be set up on the stack, one for each recursive function call. There will be three physically different `objptr` variables, each scoped to its own copy of the printobj function call. The value of the `objptr` variable in the last recursive copy will be 0. The value of the `objptr` variables in the first and second recursive copies will be the addresses of the first and second objects in the list. Figure 15-6 illustrates the `objptr` variables generated by recursive calls to printobj. Each `objptr` holds the address of an object in the linked list.

```
NUMOBJ *headptr = 0;

printobj1(headptr);

void printobj (NUMOBJ *objptr)
        {
        if(objptr != 0)
                {
                printf("%d\n", objptr->mynum);
                printobj(objptr->nextptr);
                }
        }
```

A recursive function always checks for a condition to stop the recursion. In the printobj function, this condition is a test of the `objptr` variable for a 0 value. The 0 value indicates the end of the list. If the function is passed a 0 value, no further function calls are performed. A recursive function should never be written without a condition that can stop the recursion. A recursive call without such a condition is like a loop with a test expression that is always true. A loop with a test condition that is always true is an infinite loop. A recursive call without a condition to stop the recursion leads to infinite recursion. The recursive calls never stop. The function keeps calling itself over and over again.

When a function finishes its execution, it returns to the function that called it. The same is true for recursive calls. Each recursive call generates its own copy of the function, complete with its own variables and return value. When the function returns, it returns a value to the copy of the function that called it. Just as the arguments of a recursive call are used to pass information from one copy of a function to the next, the return value can be used to pass information back to the previous copy.

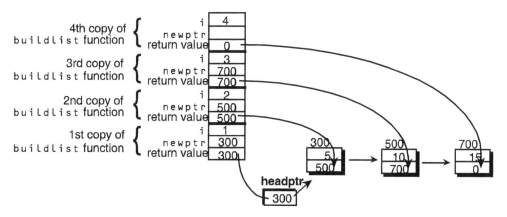

Figure 15-7: Recursion and return value.

In the **recurlst.c** program in LISTING 15-4, a linked list of three objects is generated recursively by the `buildlist` function. The `buildlist` function is designed to create a list of only three object, no more and no less. The test condition to end the recursion is a test to see if i is greater than 3. If i is greater than 3, no further recursive calls are performed and the function returns. If i is less than or equal to 3, then an object is created and its value assigned. The buildlist function is called again recursively, generating a new copy of the buildlist function with its own variables and return value. The buildlist function is passed an incremented value of i, i+1. The value of the i parameter variable in the new copy of the buildlist function will be 2.

LISTING 15-4 Recursive BuildinG of Linked List

recurlst.c

```
#include <stdio.h>
#include <stdlib.h>

        typedef struct numobj {
                        int mynum;
                        struct numobj *nextptr;
                        } NUMOBJ;

NUMOBJ *buildlist(int);
void printobj(NUMOBJ*);

 int main(void)
        {
        NUMOBJ *headptr = 0;
        int i = 1;

        headptr = buildlist(i);
        printobj(headptr);

        return 0;
        }

void printobj(NUMOBJ *objptr)
        {
        if(objptr != 0)
                {
                printf("%d\n", objptr->mynum);
                printobj(objptr->nextptr);
                }
        }

NUMOBJ *buildlist(int i)
        {
        NUMOBJ *newptr;

        if (i > 3)
                return 0;
        else
                {
                newptr = (NUMOBJ*) malloc(sizeof(NUMOBJ));
                newptr->mynum = i * 5;
                newptr->nextptr = buildlist(i + 1);
                return newptr;
                }
        }
```

Each recursive copy of buildlist returns the address of the new object it created. When the function returns to the copy of buildlist that called it, that address is assigned to the nextptr member of the previous object. As shown in Figure 15-7, each successive copy of `buildlist` references a successive object in the linked list. When a function returns, it returns to the function that references the previous object in the list. In a sense, objects are linked into the list backwards, starting from the last object. The very last `buildlist` function copy will return as its address the value 0. This will be assigned to the last object in the list. Then the address of the last object will be returned and assigned to the next-to-last object in the list. This continues until the first function call of `buildlist` is reached. In that case, the address of the first object in the list is returned and assigned to `headptr`.

Notice how the `buildlist` function is divided into two segments by the if-else statement. The test for the if-else statement is the test for the condition to end the recursive process. If this condition is met, actions are performed that do not include a recursive call. These are actions performed in the last recursive copy of the function. There are no further recursive calls. These actions are referred to as the basis case. If the condition is not met, actions, which include a recursive call, are performed. The recursion continues. This is the recursive case. In the recursive case, actions are performed for each copy of the function generated, except for the last copy.

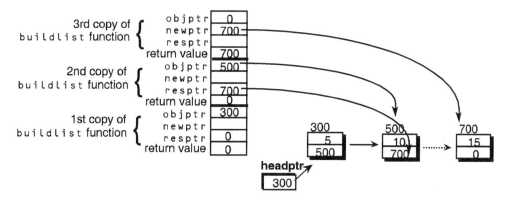

Figure 15-8: Adding an object in a linked list with the addobj recursive function.

In **numrecur.c** program in LISTING 15-5, the **numlist.c** program in LISTING 15-2 is rewritten with recursive functions. The `addobj` function recursively traverses the linked list from object to object. When the condition for ending the recursion is met, the end of the list has been reached. A new object is created and assigned values. The address of that new object is returned and assigned to the previous object in the list, as shown in Figure 15-8. All other copies of the `addobj` function will simply return 0. Only the last object in the list needs to have its `nextptr` member changed. It's `nextptr` member will be assigned the address of the new object.

Notice how the if-else statement in `addobj` and `delobj` divides the functions into a basis and a recursive case. In the basis case for the `addobj` function, a new object is created and its values assigned. In the recursive case, `addobj` is called recursively, and its return value is tested to see if a new address needs to be assigned to the pointer member.

The `addobj` function is first called with `headptr` as its argument. If the value of `headptr` is 0, then `addobj` will create the first object in the list and return its address. A special test is then made to see if the value of `headptr` is 0. If it is, then `headptr` is assigned the address returned by `addobj`. If there are already objects in the list, then the first call to `addobj` will return 0.

LISTING 15-5: Linked List with Recursive Functions

numrecur.c

LISTING 15-5: Linked List with Recursive Functions

numrecur.c

```c
#include <stdlib.h>
#include <stdio.h>

        typedef struct numobj {
                        int mynum;
                        struct numobj *nextptr;
                        } NUMOBJ;

void printobj(NUMOBJ*);
NUMOBJ* addobj(NUMOBJ*);
NUMOBJ* delobj(NUMOBJ*);

int main(void)
        {
        char choice[2];
        int more = 1;
        NUMOBJ * headptr = 0, *resptr;

        while (more != 0)
                {
                printf ("Please enter choice\n");
                scanf("%s", choice);
                switch(choice[0])
                        {
                        case 'a':
                                resptr = addobj(headptr);
                                if(headptr== 0)
                                        headptr = resptr;
                                break;
                        case 'p':
                                printobj(headptr);
                                break;
                        case 'd':
                                if(headptr != 0)
                                        {
                                        resptr = delobj(headptr);
                                        if(resptr == 0)
                                                headptr = 0;
                                        }
                                break;
                        case 'q':
                                more = 0;
                        }
                }
        return 0;
        }

void printobj(NUMOBJ *objptr)
        {
        if(objptr != 0)
                {
                printf ("%d\n", objptr->mynum);
                printobj(objptr->nextptr);
                }
        }
```

LISTING 15-5: Continued:

```
NUMOBJ *addobj(NUMOBJ *objptr)
        {
        NUMOBJ*newptr, *resptr;

        if(objptr == 0)
                {
                newptr = (NUMOBJ*) malloc(sizeof(NUMOBJ));
                newptr->nextptr = 0;
                printf("Please enter new number\n");
                scanf("%d", &newptr->mynum);
                return newptr;
                }
        else
                {
                resptr = addobj(objptr->nextptr);
                if(resptr != 0)
                        objptr->nextptr = resptr;
                return 0;
                }
        }

NUMOBJ *delobj(NUMOBJ *objptr)
        {
        NUMOBJ *resptr;

        if(objptr->nextptr == 0)
                {
                free (objptr);
                return 0;
                }
        else
                {
                resptr= delobj(objptr->nextptr);
                if(resptr == 0)
                        objptr->nextptr = 0;
                return objptr;
                }
        }
```

The delobj function performs the same kind of operations. The basis case removes the last object in the list and returns a 0 value to the next-to-last object. A 0 value is returned to the copy of the function that references the next to last object in the list. It's nextptr member is assigned the 0 value. All other copies will simply return the address of the object they reference. In the recursive case, if an address is returned from the recursive call, the nextptr member is left alone. If the first call to addobj returns a 0 value, then the list is empty, and the headptr must be assigned a 0 value.

Binary Search Trees and Indexes

A tree is designed to provide fast search capabilities. It is usually used to construct indexes. Objects in a tree will contain a key field. Searches are made for objects with specified keys. A tree can be searched much faster than a linked list. In a linked list, an item is searched for sequentially, from one object to the next. With a tree, objects can be arranged in such a way that only a very few may need to be searched in order to find a given key. There are a great many types of trees. In this chapter you will examine one of the most basic, the binary tree.

Binary Search Tree Structure: inorder, preorder, and postorder

A binary search tree is composed of nodes that branch out in two alternative directions (see Figure 15-9). Technically a tree node is simply a linked-list object with two member pointers instead of one. Both are structures created by memory allocation. In both cases, the object's pointer member will hold the address of another object, thereby linking the two. The only real physical difference is that a binary search tree object has two pointer members instead of one. Whereas an object in a linked-list is linked only to the next object, an object in a binary search tree can be linked to two other objects.

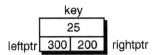

Figure 15-9: Binary search tree node.

A tree is conceptually imagined as a top-down structure. The first node in a tree is the root of the tree. The address of this first node is held in a variable usually called the root. Nodes linked to each other form branches. The last node in a branch is called a leaf. The first node, the root, is placed at the top. Each node has two pointer members. The two pointer members are often referred to as the right and left pointers. Through these pointers, the tree can branch to the right or to the left of the node. In traversing the nodes of a tree there are always two possible directions to take: the left side or the right side.

A new node is added at the end of a branch in the tree, much like an object in a linked list is added to the end of the list. A new key is created first. The tree is traversed in order to place the new key in a new node at the end of one of the branches. In a tree there are many possible branches to choose from. Each node branches off in two possible directions. As the tree is traversed, a decision must be made at each node to determine which direction to take, right or left. In a binary search tree, the decision is made by testing the value of the new key to the value of the key in the current node. If the new key is less than the key in the current node, then the left side is chosen. If the new key is greater than the key in the current node, the right side is chosen. Following this rule, you finally reach the end of a branch. The end of the branch is a node whose chosen pointer is 0. A new node is then created, and its key is assigned the value of the new key. The new node is attached to the end of the branch, becoming part of the tree.

In Figure 15-10, the new key 20 is added by first traversing the tree from the root. 20 is compared to the key of the root node, 25. 20 is less than 25 so the left branch is chosen. The next node to the left is then referenced. The new key is then compared to that node's key, 15. 20 is greater than 15, so the right branch is chosen. At this point, the right pointer of this node has a value of 0. The end of the branch has been reached. The new node is then created, and the new key, 20, is assigned to it. It is then attached to the right pointer member of the node whose key is 15.

Adding each node in this way establishes an ordered structure to the tree. A search for a particular item can be carried out in the same way a node is added. Starting at the root, a comparison is made between a given key and the root node's key. If the given key is greater than the node's key, the node to the right of the root is checked. If the given key is less than the node's key, the node to the left is checked. This process continues until the node with the same key is found. In each comparison, the search eliminates whole segments of the tree. The search quickly narrows down to the branch containing the searched-for-node. Figure 15-11 illustrates the search path for a node with a key of 20.

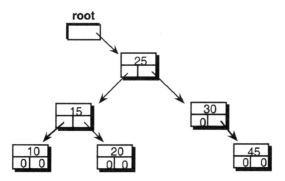

Figure 15-10: Binary search tree nodes.

A tree can be traversed, node by node, in three different ways: preorder, inorder, and postorder. To understand how this traversal takes place, it is helpful to think of the branches below each node's pointer as two subtrees. In inorder traversal, every node in the left subtree of a given node will be referenced first. Then the node's key will be referenced. And then every node in the right subtree will be referenced. This inorder traversal has the effect of traversing the keys in an ordered way. Printing the nodes of a tree in an inorder traversal prints out the keys a sorted order.

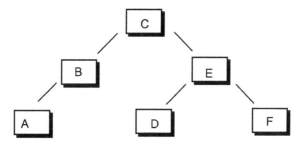

Figure 15-11: Binary search tree traversal operations.

```
Preorder: C, B, A, E, D, F
Visit the Root, Traverse the left subtree, then the right subtree.

Inorder: A, B, C, D, E, F
Traverse the left subtree. Visit the Root, then the right subtree.

Postorder: A, B, D, F, E, C
Traverse the left subtree, then the right subtree. Visit the Root
```

In Figure 15-13, the nodes 300, 500, and 600 form the left subtree of the root. 200 and 400 form the right subtree. The left subtree is traversed first. Node 500 forms the left subtree for node 300. This left subtree is first traversed. Node 500 does not have a left subtree. Its key, 10, is referenced. It does not have a right subtree either. Now all the nodes in 300's left subtree have been referenced. The key for 300, 15, can now be referenced. The right subtree for 300 is then traversed. This consists of the node 600, which has no subtrees. Its key, 20, is then referenced. Now all the nodes in the right subtree for 300 have been traversed, giving you the keys 10, 15, and 20. With 300, all the nodes in 100's left subtree have also been traversed. The key for 100, 25, can now be referenced. The same process continues for 100's right subtree, nodes 200 and 400. 200 has no left subtree, so its key, 30, is immediately referenced. 400 is the node is the right subtree of 200. It has no subtrees. Its key, 45, is the last to be referenced. If this inorder traversal is used to print out the tree, the key will be printed out as an ordered list with all the keys sorted: 10, 15, 20, 25, 30, 45.

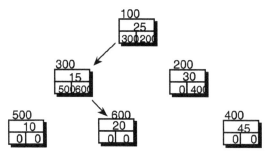

Figure 15-12: Search path for finding node with key of 20.

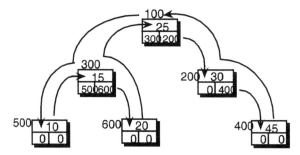

Figure 15-13: Direction of inorder traversal of nodes. The nodes are accessed as an ordered set.

Preorder traversal first references a node's key and then references every node in the left subtree, followed by every node is the right subtree. Postorder is the mirror image of inorder. Every node in the right subtree is referenced first, then the node's key, and then every node in the left subtree. Postorder provides you with a list of keys sorted in reverse.

Binary Search Trees and Recursion

Trees are usually managed with recursive functions. Very elegant recursive functions can be written to search, input, and print out binary search trees. As in the case of a recursive linked-list function, each node examined has its own copy of the recursive search function. Each recursive function call generates a copy of the function with its own automatic variable that is pointed to the node examined.

The **numtree.c** program in LISTING 15-6 maintains a binary search tree. Each node is a structure consisting of a key and two self-referential pointers, lptr and rptr. The key is an integer variable named mynum. The user is asked to add a node, print the nodes as an ordered set, or print the nodes as they are arranged in the tree.

The basis case of the addnode function is similar to the basis case of the addobj function in LISTING 15-5. A new node is created, and values are, assigned. This last recursive copy of the addnode function then returns the address of the new node to the recursive copy that called it.

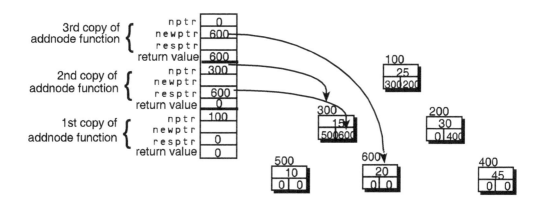

Figure 15-14: Adding a new node with a key of 20 to the binary search tree with the recursive addnode function.

In the recursive case of the addnode function, there is an if statement that chooses between two recursive function calls with two different arguments. The argument of one recursive function call is the left pointer of the node, lptr. The argument of the other recursive function call is the right pointer of the node, rptr. The test of the if statement compares the new key with the node's key. If the new key is less than the node's key, then the recursive call with the left pointer argument is called. The branch to the left of the node is traversed. If the new key is greater than the node's key, then the recursive call with the right pointer argument is called. The branch to the right is traversed. If the value of the pointer chosen is 0, then the next function call will have reached the end of a branch, and a new node can be added. The recursive process for adding a node is illustrated in Figure 15-14.

The printorder function is a recursive function to print out the nodes as an ordered list. In this function no decisions are made. Each node is to be referenced. This means that both branches of each node are to be traversed. The process begins with traversal down the left side of a node. When the end of the left-most branch has been reached, printing begins. As the left-side recursive call in each copy of the printorder function returns, the key is printed out. Then the branch to the right side of each node is traversed. When the recursive call for the right side returns, all the nodes below the current node have been traversed. That copy of the printorder function returns to the copy that called it.

LISTING 15-6: Binary search tree with Recursive Functions

numtree.c

```c
#include <stdio.h>
#include <stdlib.h>

        typedef struct node {
                        int mynum;
                        struct node *lptr;
                        struct node *rptr;
                        } NODE;

void printnodes(NODE*);
void printorder(NODE*);
NODE *addnode(NODE*, int);

 int main(void)
        {
        char choice[2];
        int more = 1, newnum;
        NODE *rootptr = 0, *resptr;

        while (more != 0)
                {
                printf("Please enter choice\n");
                scanf("%s", choice);
                switch(choice[0])
                        {
                        case 'a':
                                printf("Enter number\n");
                                scanf ("%d", &newnum);
                                resptr = addnode(rootptr,newnum);
                                if(rootptr == 0)
                                        rootptr = resptr;
                                break;
                        case 'p':
                                printorder(rootptr);
                                break;
                        case 'n':
                                printnodes(rootptr);
                                break;
                        case 'q':
                                more = 0;
                        }
                }
        return 0;
        }

void printorder(NODE *nodeptr)
        {
        if(nodeptr != 0)
                {
                printorder(nodeptr->lptr);
                printf("%d\n", nodeptr->mynum);
                printorder(nodeptr->rptr);
                }
        }
```

LISTING 15-6: Continued

```c
void printnodes(NODE *nodeptr)
    {
    if(nodeptr != 0)
        {
        printf("%d\n", nodeptr->mynum);
        printnodes(nodeptr->lptr);
        printnodes(nodeptr->rptr);
        }
    }

NODE *addnode(NODE *nptr, int num)
    {
    NODE *newptr = 0, *resptr;

    if(nptr == 0)
        {
        newptr = (NODE*) malloc(sizeof(NODE));
        newptr->mynum = num;
        newptr->rptr = 0;
        newptr->lptr = 0;
        return newptr;
        }
    else
        {
        if (num < nptr->mynum)
            {
            resptr = addnode(nptr->lptr, num);
            if(resptr != 0)
                nptr->lptr = resptr;
            }
        else
            if(num > nptr->mynum)
                {
                resptr = addnode(nptr->rptr, num);
                if(resptr != 0)
                    nptr->rptr = resptr;
                }
        return 0;
        }
    }
```

Binary Search Tree as Index

A binary search tree, as well as other types of trees, can be used as indexes for data records. Each node will contain another member that will hold a reference to the record. In LISTING 15-7, the binary search tree is used as an index for an array of structures. Each structure is a record of data. The key in the binary search tree is the name field of each record. Given a name, a record can be quickly retrieved by searching the binary search tree. The node has a new member, recno. recno is the number of the structure element in the array of structures. Once the node with the right key is found, the recno member of that node can be used to reference the record in the array of structures. The binary search tree index and the array of structures are illustrated in Figure 15-15.

The functions for maintaining the binary search tree and the array of structures are placed in two different source code files. The file **recs.c** contains a standard set of functions for adding and printing records in the array of structures. The **tree.c** file contains the set of functions used to manage the binary search tree. Notice that rootptr and the recursive functions are declared as external and static. This means that both these functions and `rootptr` are scoped to the **tree.c** file. They can be accessed only by functions defined within the **tree.c** file.

A set of access functions that simply call the recursive functions has been set up in the program. These access functions can be called in other files. In main, the access function `printrecords` is called. `printrecords` simply calls the recursive function `printorder` to print out an ordered list of the records from the binary search tree nodes. `addindex` is an access function called in the `addrec` function in **rec.c**. addindex calls the recursive function `addnode` to actually add a new node to the index.

This design has the benefit of hiding the recursive functions as well as `rootptr` from other parts of the program. Recursive functions initially called with the wrong values can result in infinite recursion. The function keeps calling itself until the system runs out of memory needed for each new copy of the function. Restricting access to the recursive functions provides a measure of control. The details managing both the binary search tree and the structure array are hidden within their respective source code files. Modification of the binary search tree would only require changing code in the **tree.c** file.

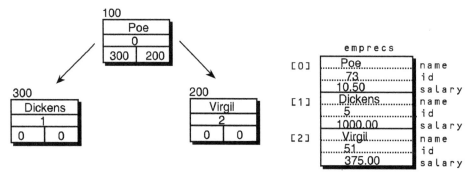

Figure 15-15: Binary search tree as index for records in an array of structures.

LISTING 15-7: Binary search tree as Index

types.h

```
        typedef  struct emp {
                    char name[100];
                    int  id;
                    float salary;
                    } EMP;
        typedef struct node {
                    int recno;
                    char name[30];
                    struct node *lptr;
                    struct node *rptr;
                    } NODE;
void addindex(char*, int);
void printrecords(EMP[]);
void printindex(void);
void outputrecs(EMP []);
void printrec(int, EMP[] );
void fillrec(EMP *);
void add_rec(EMP []);
void menu(void);
```

main.c

```c
#include  <stdio.h>
#include  "types.h"

 EMP emprecs[30];

 int main(void)
        {
        char choice[2];
        int more = 1;

        menu();
        while (more != 0)
                {
                printf("\nPlease enter choice: ");
                scanf("%s", choice);
                switch(choice[0])
                        {
                        case 'a':
                                add_rec(emprecs);
                                break;
                        case 'p':
                                printrecords(emprecs);
                                break;
                        case 'n':
                                printindex();
                                break;
                        case 'r':
                                outputrecs(emprecs);
                                break;
                        case 'm':
                                menu();
                                break;
                        case 'q':
                                more = 0;
                        }
                }
        return 0;
        }

void menu(void)
        {
        printf("\na = input a record\n");
        printf("p = print records ordered by name\n");
        printf("n = print the index nodes\n");
        printf("r = print the array of records\n");
        printf("m = print the menu\n");
        printf("q = quit program\n");
        }
```

recs.c

```
#include  <stdio.h>
#include  "types.h"

static int avail = 0;

void add_rec(EMP emps[])
        {

        fillrec(&emps[avail]);
        addindex(emps[avail].name, avail);
        avail++;
        }

void fillrec(EMP *emptr)
        {
        printf("\nEnter Name: ");
        scanf("%*[\n\t ]%[^\n]s", emptr->name);
        printf("\nEnter Id: ");
        scanf("%d", &emptr->id);
        printf("\nEnter Salary: ");
        scanf("%f", &emptr->salary);
        }

void outputrecs(EMP emps[])
        {
        int i;
        for (i = 0; i < avail; i++)
                {
                printrec(i, emps);
                }
        }

void printrec(int recno, EMP emps[])
        {
        printf("\n Employee Record %d ", recno);
        printf("\n\t NAME   :%s", emps[recno].name);
        printf("\n\t ID     :%d", emps[recno].id);
        printf("\n\t SALARY:%f\n", emps[recno].salary);
        }
```

tree.c
```
#include <stdio.h>
#include <stdlib.h>
#include <string.h>
#include "types.h"

 static NODE *rootptr;
 static void printorder(NODE*, EMP[]);
 static void printnodes(NODE*);
 static NODE *addnode(NODE*, char*,int);


 void printrecords (EMP emps[])
       {
       printorder(rootptr,emps);
       }
static void printorder(NODE *nodeptr, EMP emps[])
       {
       if(nodeptr != 0)
              {
              printorder(nodeptr->lptr,emps);
              printrec(nodeptr->recno, emps);
              printorder(nodeptr->rptr, emps);
              }
       }

 void printindex(void)
       {
       printnodes(rootptr);
       }

static void printnodes(NODE *nodeptr)
       {
       if(nodeptr != 0)
              {
              printf("\n%d", nodeptr->recno);
              printf("\n%s\n", nodeptr->name);
              printnodes(nodeptr->lptr);
              printnodes(nodeptr->rptr);
              }
       }

 void addindex(char *name, int recno)
       {
       NODE *resptr;

       resptr = addnode(rootptr, name, recno);
       if(rootptr == 0)
              rootptr = resptr;
       }

 static NODE *addnode(NODE *nptr, char *name, int recno)
       {
       NODE *newptr = 0, *resptr;

       if(nptr == 0)
              {
              newptr = (NODE*) malloc(sizeof(NODE));
              strcpy (newptr->name, name);
              newptr->recno = recno;
              newptr->rptr = 0;
```

```
            newptr->lptr = 0;
            return newptr;
            }
    else
            {
            if(strcmp(name, nptr->name) < 0)
                    {
                    resptr = addnode(nptr->lptr,name,recno);
                    if(resptr != 0)
                            nptr->lptr = resptr;
                    }
            else
                    if(strcmp(name, nptr->name) > 0)
                            {
                    resptr=addnode(nptr->rptr,name,recno);
                            if(resptr != 0)
                                    nptr->rptr = resptr;
                            }
            return 0;
            }
    }
```

Run of LISTING 15-7

```
a = input a record
p = print records ordered by name
n = print the index nodes
r = print the array of records
m = print the menu
q = quit program

Please enter choice: a

Enter Name: Justin

Enter Id: 44

Enter Salary: 2.39
Please enter choice: a

Enter Name: Valerie

Enter Id: 7

Enter Salary: 2508
Please enter choice
a

Enter Name: Christopher

Enter Id: 4

Enter Salary: 150043

Please enter choice: n
0
Justin

2
Christopher
```

```
1
Valerie

Please enter choice: p

 Employee Record 2
        NAME   :Christopher
        ID     :4
        SALARY:150043.00

Employee Record 0
        NAME   :Justin
        ID     :44
        SALARY:2.39

 Employee Record 1
        NAME   :Valerie
        ID     :7
        SALARY:2508.00

Please enter choice: r

 Employee Record 0
        NAME   :Justin
        ID     :44
        SALARY:2.39

 Employee Record 1
        NAME   :Valerie
        ID     :7
        SALARY:2508.00

 Employee Record 2
        NAME   :Christopher
        ID     :4
        SALARY:150043.00
Please enter choice: a

Enter Name: Marylou

Enter Id: 39

Enter Salary: 2508

Please enter choice: p

 Employee Record 2
        NAME   :Christopher
        ID     :4
        SALARY:150043.00

 Employee Record 0
        NAME   :Justin
        ID     :44
        SALARY:2.39

 Employee Record 3
        NAME   :Marylou
        ID     :39
        SALARY:2508.00
```

```
Employee Record 1
        NAME   :Valerie
        ID     :7
        SALARY:2508.00

Please enter choice: n
0
Justin

2
Christopher

1
Valerie

3
Marylou

Please enter choice: q
```

Chapter Summary: Data Structures and Recursion

A linked list is a list of dynamically allocated, self-referential structures. Each structure contains a member that holds the address of the next structure in the list. A pointer variable declared in the program holds the address of the first object in the list. This is the head of the list. A list is traversed with a working pointer that references each object in turn. It obtains the address of the next object from the pointer member of the object it currently references. The object whose pointer member is 0 is the last object in the list.

A linked list can be managed by recursive functions. A recursive function is a function that contains a function call to itself. Recursive functions must always have a test that will end the recursion. A recursive function is divided into two components: the basis case and the recursive case. The basis case consists of those actions performed when the test condition for ending the recursion is met. The recursive case consists of those actions performed when the function is called again.

A tree is used to implement indexes that can be quickly searched for given keys. The tree consists of structures that have several pointer members and a key. Each object in a tree is referred to as a node. The first node is called the root. From the root, the tree will continually branch in several directions.

A binary search tree has nodes that have two pointer members. The pointers branch to the left or to the right of the node. When a tree is searched, a decision is made to go in one direction or the other. The decision is determined by a comparison of a user-given key with the node's key. If the user-given key is less than the node's key, then the left branch is taken. If the user-given key is greater than the node's key, then the right branch is taken.

A binary search tree is easily managed with recursive functions. The recursive functions will contain two recursive calls, one for each branch. An inorder traversal of a binary search tree references the keys as an ordered sorted set. A preorder traversal references the keys as they have been placed in tree, and a postorder traversal references the keys in reverse sorted order.

A binary search tree, as well as other types of trees, can be used as indexes for data records. Each node will contain another member that will hold a reference to the record. In the case of an array of structures, each node holds the array offset of the record associated with the node's key.

Exercises

1. Add a search function to the linked list program in LISTING 15-2.

2. Add a recursive search function to the linked-list program in LISTING 15-5.

3. Add a search function to the binary search tree programs in LISTINGs 15.7.

4. Add a function to delete a node from a binary search tree.

Text Files

Character, Line, and Formatted

Stream I/O: Text and Binary

Opening and Closing Files: File Modes

Character Text Files: getc and putc

Line Text Files: fgets and fputs

Formatted Text Files: fscanf and fprintf

File Errors and End-of-File: ferror and feof

16. Text Files

Files are named storage areas on a storage medium such as a disk or tape. The storage consists of a series of bits arranged into bytes much like bytes in an array. The physical organization of the file on the disk is determined by the operating system. Each C compiler has a set of low-level system call functions that connect to and access files through the operating system. These system I/O functions all take a set of standard arguments and perform simple read and write operations on a file.

There is another set of C file functions that impose an abstract logical organization on files, regardless of their physical structure. They are known as the stream I/O file functions. These file functions establish a file interface that allows them to treat each file as a byte stream file. Such a file consists of a continuous stream of bytes. It can be read, written, and referenced, one byte at a time.

The stream I/O files can be further categorized into text stream and binary stream files. This chapter explains the stream I/O text files and their respective file functions. Character text, line text, and formatted text files are discussed in depth. The binary stream files are discussed in the chapter on record files, the next chapter. There is also a close association between the stream I/O text file functions and the input/output functions used for the keyboard input and screen output. This relationship will be discussed in the chapter on system calls, Chapter 18.

Stream I/O: Text and Binary

C was originally designed to work with UNIX. As such, its file interface reflects the file structure implemented for UNIX. At the time UNIX was developed, other operating systems physically implemented files in different ways. A decision was made with UNIX to implement physically all kinds of files as byte-stream files. One type of file is not physically different from another type of file. Instead, differences are shifted to the way a file is read and written. A file can be read as one kind of file or another kind of file. But physically it is the same as any other file, a byte stream.

Once bytes are read from a file, they can be organized or converted into different types of data. The stream I/O file functions, not only read a file as a series of bytes, but they interpret those bytes in different ways. In this sense, data is read from or written to a file differently depending on the file function used. A file can be characterized by the kind of file functions used to read and write to it. In this way, you can speak of different kinds of stream I/O files. The files are actually all the same, a stream of bytes, but those bytes are interpreted differently depending upon the file function that you use.

There are four major types of stream I/O files: character text, line text, formatted text, and record files. Each corresponds to a set of file functions used to read and write to them. The functions getc and putc read and write character text files, whereas the functions fgets and fputs read and write line text files. The file functions fscanf and fprintf are used to read and write formatted text files. The fread and fwrite functions will interpret a file as a record file.

You can access the stream of bytes in a file as either a text stream or a binary stream. In UNIX there is no distinction between text and binary streams. They are one and the same. In other systems, such as MS WINDOWS, there is a very real difference between a text and a binary stream (see Figure 16-1). When accessed as a text stream, most bytes in a MS WINDOWS file are treated as single characters. An exception is made for newlines. In MS WINDOWS, a newline is implemented with two characters: a carriage return, '\015', and a line feed, '\012'. As part of a text stream, these two characters will be interpreted and read as a single newline character, \n.

The characters in a text-stream file can be interpreted in different ways depending upon the file function used. The text stream can be read or written as a continuous stream of characters when the functions `getc` and `putc` are used. The text stream can be read or written as lines of text when the functions `fgets` and `fputs` are used. Using the functions `fscanf` and `fprintf`, a text stream can be formatted into separate fields whose characters can then be converted to specified values. This formatted I/O is the same as that used for `scanf` and `printf`.

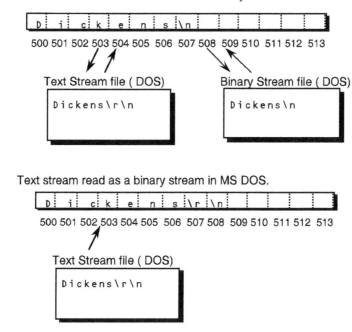

Figure 16-1: newline in text and binary streams in MS-WINDOWS.

When accessed as a binary stream, each byte is treated as a simple byte with its binary value. No decision is made as to how these bytes and their binary values are to be interpreted. A byte could be a character or part of an integer. The bytes are simply read into memory. The bytes in that memory may then be interpreted as an integer or character or structure, or any other kind of object. In MS WINDOWS, the newline is read and written as two separate bytes, the carriage return and line feed.

Record files are often implemented as binary files. A record is read and written to a file as a block of binary bytes. The file functions `fread` and `fwrite` are used to read and write records. `fread` and `fwrite` actually read and write a block of bytes, be it a record or an array.

Any file function can operate on either text or binary streams. It makes sense to reserve the character-based functions `getc`, `putc`, `fgets`, `fputs`, `fscanf`, and `fprintf` for text stream use, and the record functions `fread` and `fwrite` for binary stream use. There are exceptions. A dump of all the bytes and their numeric values would best be implemented with `getc` and `putc` operating on a binary stream. The binary stream would reference every byte in the file.

Opening and Closing Files: File Modes

For a program to access a file, your operating system needs to make a connection between the file and the program. The `fopen` function directs the operating system to establish such a connection. This is often referred to as opening a file. `fopen` takes as its arguments the file's name and the file mode with which the file will be opened. These arguments provide the operating system with the data file's name and the way that the file is to be accessed at this time. The `fclose` function directs the operating system to close off the connection, closing the file. The syntax for a `fopen` function call follows.

```
pointer-variable = fopen (filename, file-mode)
```

The `fopen` function returns a pointer to a structure of type `FILE`. A structure of type `FILE` holds variables that are used to manage a file. One of those variables is the file position indicator, which specifies the position in the file currently being referenced. The file position indicator is sometimes also referred to as a file pointer. Another variable is the file id, which is the operating system's identification of the file.

When you open a file, you need to assign the pointer to the `FILE` structure returned by `fopen` to a pointer variable in the program. This pointer variable is declared as a pointer to a structure of type `FILE`. File functions take as one of their arguments a pointer to a `FILE` structure. For a file function to operate on a particular file, you to pass it a pointer to the `FILE` structure for that file. For example, `fclose` takes as its argument the pointer to a file's `FILE` structure, and closes that file. In the next example, a file named myfile is opened, and the address of its `FILE` structure is assigned to the pointer variable `myfileptr`. The file is then closed with `fclose`. `myfileptr` is declared as a pointer to a structure of type `FILE`.

```
FILE *myfileptr;

myfileptr = fopen ("myfile", "r");

fclose(myfileptr);
```

There are three basic operations that you can perform on files: read, write, and update. You can read the data in a file, copying it into your program. You can write data in your program to a file, saving data in your computer memory onto a disk. You can also update data already in a file, overwriting data in a file with data in your program. The file mode specifies the type of operation that you want to perform on a file. You can open a file for just reading, or for writing only, or for update - reading and writing.

In C, there are several variations on these three basic operations. The file mode specified in the second argument of an `fopen` function call, determines which operations can be performed a file. The file mode itself consists of a string of one or more characters, each character predetermined to represent certain file operations such as read or write. For example, the r character specifies read operations, whereas the w character allows write operations.

In C, there are three basic file operations: reading, writing, and appending. Append is not the same as update. It merely allows you to add data on to the end of a file. The read, write, and append file modes are represented by the characters r, w, and a respectively. The first two of these three basic modes can be qualified to allow updating of a file, permitting you to read a write to the same file. The updating access is provided by the read write/qualifier is represented by the + character. The read/write qualifier allows you to both read and write to the same file. Any given mode may actually consist of several of these characters. For example, to open a file for update you will need both the r and + modes, "r+".

The basic file modes, r, w, and a, alone allow simple read, write, and append operations on character files. No update is allowed.

☐   r   Allows only reading from a file. The file must already exist. If the file does not exist, the `fopen` operation will fail. The file can only be read, not written.

☐   w   Allows only writing to a file. The file will be created. If the file already exists, it will be first destroyed, and then created as a new empty file.

☐   a   Allows only writing at the end of a file. As with the w mode, a file will be created if it does not exist. As with the `r` mode, if a file already exists, it will simply be opened, not first destroyed.

Shown here are examples of `fopen` functions using the different file modes. The file mode is the second argument for the `fopen` function. The file mode is a string, a character array. Often the string is specified as a string constant, the file mode encased in double quotes.

```
fopen("myfile", "r");     /* Read Only */
fopen("myfile", "w");     /* Write Only: Create */
fopen("myfile", "a");     /* Write Only: Append */
```

Updating Files: the + qualifier

Many file applications will require that you both read and write to the same file. To perform both read and write operations on a file, you need to add the read/write qualifier, +, to your `fopen` file mode argument. Any of the basic file modes can be qualified with the read/write qualifier, +. On an r mode, the + qualifier allow you to not only read a file, but also to write to it, "r+". Applied to the w mode, the + qualifier allows you to not only write to a file, but also to read from it, "w+". In effect, the combination of the either the r or w modes with the + qualifiers allow you to update a file. You can read data and overwrite that data with new data. There are subtle distinctions that you need to be aware of, as noted in the following explanations.

r+   As with the r mode, a file will be opened. The file can be both read from and written to. If the file does not already exist, the open operation will fail.

w+   As with the w mode, a file will be created. The file can be both written to and read from. If the file already exists, it will be first destroyed, and then created as a new empty file.

a+   As with the a mode, a file will be created if it does not exist. If a file does exist, it will simply be opened, not destroyed. The file can be both written to and read from. The file can only be written to at the end of the file. Data in the file that already exists cannot be over-written: it cannot be updated.

Shown here are examples of `fopen` functions using file mode arguments that open a file for update. Notice the + read/write qualifier in each file mode string.

```
fopen ("myfile", "r+");
fopen ("myfile", "w+");
```

True update capability is provided with the r+ and w+ modes. With both r+ and w+, any data can be overwritten. There are dangers in the way both r+ and w+ open files. Files that already exist can be destroyed if they are opened with the w+ mode. In this sense, w+ cannot update a file that already exists. On the other hand, r+ can update a file that already exists. If the file is new and does not already exist, r+ will not create it.

There is a common strategy used to avoid the destruction of an already existing file with w+ and, at the same time, overcome the inability of r+ to create a file. Two fopen statements are combined in nested if conditions. The first fopen statement has an r+ mode, and the second has a w+ mode. The one with the w+ mode would execute only if the one with the r+ mode fails. In other words, if the file already exists, simply open it. If the file does not exist, create it. If fopen fails to open a file, it returns a null value, NULL, as the file pointer. If both fopen function calls fail, then it may be advisable to stop the program. This is done with an exit command.

```
if((fileptr = fopen("myfile", "r+")) == NULL)
       {
       if((fileptr = fopen("myfile", "w+"))== NULL)
              {
              printf("File could not be opened\n");
              exit(1);
              }
       }
```

Keep in mind that the update mode consists of either both the r and + modes, or the w and + modes - r+ or w+. The + qualifier itself is not an update mode. It is literally the read/write qualifier. This distinction becomes critical when the + qualifier is applied to the append mode, a+. The a+ mode is not an update mode. In the a+ mode, any data written to the file is simply added to the end. Current data in the file cannot be written over. You cannot update a record in a file using this mode. Any attempt to update a record will simply write the new data as a new record to the end of the file. In this case, the + qualifier still allows both reading and writing, but the writing is restricted to adding new data to the end of the file.

```
fopen ("myfile", "a+");
```

Binary Files: the b qualifier

In many systems a further distinction is made between text and binary files. To open a binary file you need to further qualify your file mode a binary file mode. The binary file mode is represented by the character b. For example, in some systems, such as MS WINDOWS, record files are binary files. To open and read them you need the binary qualifier in your fopen file mode argument. MS WINDOWS also has a t qualifier that explicitly specifies a text file. In the next examples, the b qualifier is added to the file mode argument, indicating binary access.

```
fopen ("myfile", "rb");
fopen ("myfile", "wb");
fopen ("myfile", "ab");
```

To indicate binary record update, you need to add the + sign to the b qualifier.

```
fopen ("myfile", "r+b");
fopen ("myfile", "w+b");
fopen ("myfile", "a+b");
```

Character Text Files: getc and putc

A character text file consists of a stream of characters. The function `getc` and `putc` read and write one character at a time. When the file is opened, the file position indicator is set to the first byte in the file. When a character is read or written, the file position indicator advances to the next byte of the file. Successive calls to the `getc` function will eventually read all the bytes in the file.

     `getc` returns an integer value. The integer value will contain the one-byte character value read from the file, with one exception: When `getc` reaches the end of the file, it returns the end-of-file value, EOF. EOF is defined as an integer value, usually a -1. It is a value that cannot possibly be interpreted as a character.

     `putc` simply writes a character to a file. A file opened in the w mode will start as an empty file, and the file position indicator will reference the beginning of the file. When a character is written to the file, the file position indicator will advance past the byte just written, to the end of the file. Successive calls to `putc` write many characters to the file.

     In the **dispfile.c** program in LISTING 16-1, a file named myfile is opened and the address of its `FILE` structure is assigned to the pointer variable `myfileptr`. The file is then read and printed using `getc` and `putchar`. The pointer to the `FILE` structure, `myfileptr`, is passed to `getc`. `getc` then returns a character value read from the file. This return value is assigned to the variable inchar. When `getc` reaches the end of the file, it returns an end-of-file value, EOF. The test for EOF controls the loop. The file is then closed by passing the pointer to the `FILE` structure, `myfileptr`, to `fclose`.

LISTING 16-1:

dispfile.c

```
#include <stdio.h>

int main(void){
          FILE *myfileptr;
          int inchar;

          myfileptr = fopen("myfile", "r");
          while((inchar = getc(myfileptr)) != EOF)
                  {
                  putchar(inchar);
                  }
          fclose(myfileptr);
          return 0;
          }
```

     In the **copyfile.c** program in LISTING 16-2, `getc` and `putc` are used to copy one file to another, byte by byte. newfile is opened in the write mode, w.

     Though `getc` and `putc` usually operate on text files, they may also operate on binary files. Recall that opening a file with the b file mode qualifier will open the file as a binary stream. In UNIX, there is no difference between the text and binary streams. There is a difference in MS-WINDOWS. In MS WINDOWS, a file read as a text stream will convert a carriage return and line feed to a newline character, whereas a binary stream will not. In the **bindisp.c** program LISTING 16-3, **myfile** is opened and read as a binary stream. In MS WINDOWS, this means that carriage returns and line feeds will be read and printed out.

LISTING 16-2:

copyfile.c
```
#include <stdio.h>

int main(void){
          FILE *myfileptr;
          FILE *newfileptr;
          int inchar;

          myfileptr = fopen("myfile", "r");
          newfileptr = fopen("newfile", "w");
          while ((inchar = getc(myfileptr)) != EOF)
                {
                putc(inchar, newfileptr);
                }
          fclose(myfileptr);
          fclose(newfileptr);
          return 0;
          }
```

LISTING 16-3:

bindisp.c
```
#include <stdio.h>

int main(void)
          {
          FILE *myfileptr;
          int inchar;

          myfileptr = fopen("myfile", "rb");
          while((inchar = getc(myfileptr)) != EOF)
                {
                putchar(inchar);
                }
          fclose(myfileptr);
          return 0;
          }
```

Text Line Files: fgets and fputs

Character files are often used to hold lines of written text. A document or a letter is composed of lines of characters, each line terminated by a newline. Such files are often worked on by a text editor. In a text editor, working on a text file, a user types in a line and then hits the ENTER key to go to the next line. In this sense, lines can be seen as delimited by newline characters. The line text functions fgets and fputs access a file as a set of lines, each terminated by a newline character.

fgets reads a line from a file and places it in a character array. It then places a null character at the end, thereby making the line a string. The newline character is considered part of the line and is kept as part of the string. fgets takes three arguments: the address of a character array, the maximum number of characters to be read, and the file pointer. fputs, on the other hand, takes only two arguments: the character array and the file pointer. Shown here is the syntax, declaration, and an example of the fputs and fgets functions.

```
fgets (character array, maximum number, file pointer);      syntax
char *fgets(char *, int, FILE *);      declaration
fgets(buffer, 80, fileptr);

fputs (character array, file pointer);      syntax
int fputs(char *, FILE *);      declaration
fputs(buffer, fileptr);
```

LISTING 16-4:

getline.c
```
#include <stdio.h>
#define MAXLINE 80

int main(void)
      {
      char line[MAXLINE];
      FILE *fileptr;

      fileptr = fopen("myfile", "r");

      fgets(line, MAXLINE, fileptr);
      fclose(fileptr);
      return 0;
      }
```

It is impossible to predict how long a line in a text file is going to be. It could even be as long as the file itself. The line only ends when a newline character is reached, wherever in the file that might be. Arrays, on the other hand, have their size declared in the program. There is a danger that fgets would try to read in a line larger than the array, overwriting memory next to that array. For this very reason, fgets has a special argument whose purpose is to place a maximum limit on the number of bytes that can be read from a line. If the maximum is 80, fgets would read no more than 79 characters in a line of 100 characters. fgets always reads one less than the maximum specified, because it saves the last place for the null character, '\0'. The maximum should be determined by the size of the character array used. Often it is convenient to use a define symbol for the maximum, using the same symbol in the array declaration and the fgets function call, as shown in the program **getline.c** in LISTING 16-4.

LISTING 16-5:

putline.c
```c
#include <stdio.h>

#define MAXLINE 80

int main(void)
    {
    char line[MAXLINE] = "Dickens wrote before 1900\n";
    FILE *fileptr;

    fileptr = fopen("myfile", "w");

    fputs(line, fileptr);

    fclose(fileptr);
    return 0;
    }
```

fputs operates much in the same way as fgets, except that there is no need for a maximum (see **putline.c** in LISTING 16-5). Characters are simply being written to a file, and there is no limit on the amount of characters that can be written. fputs operates on a string, but does not write the null character at the end of the string.

The **copyline.c** program in LISTING 16-6, performs the same copy operation as that in LISTING 16-2. But instead of copying byte by byte, the file is copied a line at a time using fgets and fputs. Notice how the end of the file is tested for. fgets returns a NULL when it reaches the end of a file, not an EOF. You need to keep straight what value the different file functions return for an end of file detection. fgets and fread return a NULL, whereas getc and fscanf return an EOF.

LISTING 16-6:

copyline.c

```c
#include <stdio.h>

#define MAXLINE 80

int main(void)
    {
    char line[MAXLINE];
    FILE *myfileptr;
    FILE *newfileptr;

    myfileptr = fopen("myfile", "r");
    newfileptr = fopen("newfile", "w");

    while (fgets(line, MAXLINE, myfileptr) != NULL)
        {
            fputs(line, newfileptr);
        }

    fclose(myfileptr);
    fclose(newfileptr);
    return 0;
    }
```

Formatted Text Files: fscanf and fprintf

A formatted text file, though still a character file, is a very highly structured character file. In a formatted file, the user imposes a data organization on the file. The sequence of bytes in the file is still read as characters, but the characters are not used as characters. Instead, the characters are cut up into data fields. Each data field permits only a specified set of characters.

The idea behind a data field is very simple. In a program, there are variables of different types: integers, floats, characters, etc. How can the value of one of these variables be saved, using a character file? And how can it be saved in such a way that the value can be retrieved later? An integer variable with the value 237 exists as a two-byte integer in computer memory. In order to save this number as a character value, a conversion must take place. The integer 237 is converted to a sequence of three characters, '2', '3', and '7'. This sequence of three characters is then saved as character values in a text file. When retrieved, the sequence of three characters, '2' '3' '7', can then be converted back to a two byte integer value of 237.

The fscanf and fprintf file functions perform these conversions. fscanf and fprintf work in the same way as scanf and printf. They are very much the same functions, except that fscanf reads from a file, not a keyboard, and fprintf writes to a file, not the screen.

The fprintf arguments consist of a file pointer, a format string, and a list of values that are converted into their corresponding character representations. In the **putfield.c** program in LISTING 16-7, the %d symbol tells fprintf that the value in num is an integer. fprintf then performs an integer-to-character conversion, changing the integer value 237 into a set of three corresponding characters. The syntax, declaration, and an example of the fprintf function are listed here. The three dots, ..., making up the third argument in the fprintf declaration indicates that several different types of arguments may be listed. fprintf, like printf, is a function that take a varying number of arguments.

```
fprintf (file pointer, "format string", list of values);     syntax
int fprintf(FILE *, const char *, ...);          declaration
fprintf(fileptr, "%d %f", id, cost);
```

LISTING 16-7:

putfield.c

```
#include <stdio.h>

int main(void)
      {
      int num;
      FILE *fileptr;

      fileptr = fopen("myfile", "w");
      num = 237;

      fprintf(fileptr, "%d", num);

      fclose(fileptr);
      return 0;
      }
```

The fscanf arguments consist of a file pointer, a format string, and a list of addresses that reference objects that are to be assigned converted values read from the file. fscanf first reads in characters from a file and then converts them to a value that is then assigned to an object declared in the program. In the **getfield.c** program in LISTING 16-8, the %d tells `fscanf` to read the next sequence of numeric characters and convert them to an integer value. This integer value is then assigned to the variable num. The syntax, declaration, and an example of the `fscanf` function are shown here.

```
fscanf(file pointer, "format string", list of object
addresses);
    int fscanf(FILE *, const char *, ...);

    fscanf(fileptr, "%d %f", &id, &cost);
```

LISTING 16-8:

getfield.c

```
#include <stdio.h>

int main(void)
    {
    int num;
    FILE *fileptr;

    fileptr = fopen("myfile", "r");

    fscanf(fileptr, "%d", &num);

    fclose(fileptr);

    return 0;
    }
```

fscanf and Formatted Fields

Formatted text files are commonly used to implement character-based database files. A database can be seen as a table in which the columns are fields and the rows are records. An example of an employee database follows. The fields are name, id, and salary. The type of object needed to hold the data in each field is different. The name field requires a character array. The id field requires an integer variable. The salary field requires a float variable.

```
        name      id    salary
1       Dickens   34    8.56
2       Poe       23    50.70
3       Virgil    12    600.75
```

Since a formatted text file is basically a character file, you can us a simple text editor to create the file and enter in its data. There is one problem. When `fscanf` is reading from a file, how does it know that it has finished reading all the characters in a field? The answer to this can become complicated. The common solution is to use delimiters. `fscanf` is programmed to recognize a given set of characters as delimiters, marking the end of a field. These delimiters are the space, the tab, and the newline. They are commonly referred to as white spaces. These three delimiters are interchangeable. `fscanf` looks for all three. This allows a file to be set up in a very intuitive way. A record can be written on a line. Spaces can be used to delimit the fields in the record, except for the last field. Since a space and newline both serve equally well as a delimiter, a newline can be used as the delimiter for the last field. This allows each record to be written on its own line. Shown here is the file **mydata**, with the data written with white space delimiters.

mydata
```
Dickens  34  8.56
Poe      23  50.70
Virgil   12  600.75
```

In the **getrecs.c** program in LISTING 16-9, the file is read and printed out. fscanf is set up to read all three fields. Each time fscanf executes, it effectively reads a line of data, a record. Notice the test for the while statement. fscanf is a function and, as a function, has a return value. Like scanf, fscanf returns as its value the number of successful conversions. In this case, fscanf would return the value 3. If fscanf reads an end-of-file character, it will return an EOF value. Testing the return value of fscanf against an EOF value effectively tests for the end of the file.

LISTING 16-9:

getrecs.c

```
#include <stdio.h>

int main(void)
{
char name[10];
int id;
float salary;
FILE *fileptr;

fileptr = fopen("mydata", "r");

while(fscanf(fileptr,"%s%d%f",name,&id,&salary) != EOF)
        {
        printf("%s %d %f\n", name, id, salary);
        }

fclose(fileptr);
return 0;
}
```

The **calcsale.c** program in LISTING 16-10 presents a more complex application of fscanf. The program reads a data file with three fields: code, price, and name. The database is a set of records, each recording a transaction. The transactions may be retail, sale, or refund. For each record read, a calculation is performed to determine if this is a sale record and, if so, how much is lost in the sale's discount. The losses are totaled and printed out. A printout of the **costd** file follows. Notice the use of spaces as delimiters in the **costd** file.

costd
```
1 7.00   Keats
2 3.00   Dickens
1 230.00  Keats
3 7.00 Virgil
1 7000.00  Poe
```

LISTING16-10

calcsale.c
```c
#include <stdio.h>
#define RATE 0.10
#define SALE 1
#define RETAIL 2
#define REFUND 3
float discount(float);

int main(void)
     {
     int   code;      /* code from the file */
     char name[20];           /* consumer name */
     float  price, total = 0.00, loss;
     FILE *fileptr;

     fileptr = fopen("costd", "r"); /* open file */
     while((fscanf(fileptr,"%d%f%s\n",&code,&price,name))!=EOF)   {
            if (code == SALE){
                   printf( "%.2f %s\n",price ,name );
                   loss = discount(price) ;
                   total = total + loss;
                   }
            }
     fclose(fileptr);
     printf("Total loss is %.2f\n", total);
     return 0;
     }

float discount(float price)
     {
     float loss;
     loss = (price * RATE);
     return (loss);
     }
```

Output for LISTING 16-10:

```
7.00 Keats
230.00 Keats
7000.00 Poe
Total loss is 723.70
```

The [] Field Specifier

When dealing with strings, formatted files suffer from a frustrating limitation. Since the space delimits the end of a field, spaces cannot be allowed in a string. There is a way around this using a different string conversion specifier represented by braces, []. Braces literally specify a set of characters considered valid for a string field. Whereas %s reads in all characters except delimiters, you can use the braces to read in a specific range of characters for a string. %[a-m] specifies as valid input characters between a and m. %[A-Za-z] specifies all letters and the space as valid input. This would override the space as a delimiter, but then you could not use the space itself as a delimiter for this field. In this case, you could use a tab as the delimiter instead of a space.

If tabs are used as delimiters, the format string could be more easily written using another feature of braces, the circumflex symbol, ^. The circumflex symbol specifies invalid input. Characters are accepted until the invalid character is reached. The conversion specifier %[^\t] reads any character into a string until a tab is reached. In the next example, the string conversion specifier for the name field has been replaced by the braces conversion specifier with the circumflex and tab characters. The format string for the fscanf statement is "%[^\t]%d%f\n". For this to work, a tab character needs to be placed after each name field in the **mydata** file. The tab character itself will not show up. Instead you will see what appears to be several spaces between fields, which are in fact one tab character.

```
fscanf(fileptr,"%[^\t]%d%f\n",name,&id,&salary)
```

mydata
```
Charles Dickens       34   8.56
Edgar Allen Poe       23   50.70
Virgil                12   600.75
```

The format string has a newline constant at the end, \n. There is a problem with the %[^\t] conversion modifier. It will also read in any preceding spaces and newlines. In this case, it will include not only the name, but also the newline character from the preceding line. In the third record in the file, the newline before the name "Virgil" would be read in as part of the string, "\nVirgil". You can use several strategies to overcome this problem. The simplest, in this case, is to place a newline constant in the format string. Constants on the format string will match and skip corresponding characters in the file. At the end of the line, the newline constant matches and skips the newline in the file. The %[^\t] conversion modifier is then poised to read the name data on the next line. You can also implement a more flexible method using the field skipper modifier described later in this section.

The * Field Skipper and Invalid Data

Formatted files require a lot of care and coordination on the part of the programmer. The programmer must make sure that the fields in the file conform to the conversion specifiers and variables in the fscanf function call. The file itself must be correct. This can be a problem since a character file can be easily changed with a text editor. Since the file is processed sequentially, one corrupt field can throw off the reading of all other fields. In a sense, fscanf can lose its place. This happens because fscanf, as with scanf, does not skip fields with invalid input. It keeps trying to convert that same invalid data with the next conversion specifier. Everything can be thrown out of sync very easily.

mydata
```
Dickens   ti  8.56
Poe   23   50.70
Virgil   12   600.75
```

In the mydata file example above, the id field of the first record contains invalid data. When the program tries to read this id field, fscanf finds that the letter 't' is not valid input for an integer conversion. Integer conversions only accept numeric letters 0 through 9. The conversion for the id variable fails. If a conversion fails, fscanf stops and returns the number of successful conversions so far. The loop continues, calling fscanf again to read the next record. However, fscanf is still positioned at the failed input. "ti" is successfully read, but read as valid input for the string conversion for name. The 8 is then read as valid input for id. The period is invalid input for integers. .56 is then read as valid input for salary since the period indicates data for a floating point value. On the next record everything happens to be in sync again.

```
Output for corrupt data:        Dickens  0  0
                                ti  8  0.56
                                Poe  23  50.70
                                Virgil  12  600.75
```

The point to remember here is that fscanf does not stop only at delimiters. It also stops at invalid input. It knows what range of characters is valid for any given conversion specifier. Characters '0' through '9' are valid for numeric conversions. The dot, ., is a valid part of floating point conversions. Any character at all, except for a space, tab, and newline, is valid input for character strings.

You can detect a corrupted record by checking the return value of fscanf. The return value of fscanf is the number of successful conversions. If a conversion failed, the return value will be less than the number of conversion specifiers in the format string. In the next example, a new variable, valid, has been introduced which holds the return value of fscanf. If its value is less than the number of conversion specifiers in the format string, then a conversion has failed.

```
while((valid=fscanf(fileptr,"%s%d%f",
                                      name,&id,&salary))!= EOF){
        if (valid < 3)
                printf ("Invalid data in record \n");
        else
                printf("%s %d %f\n", name, id, salary);
        }
```

This solution is not yet complete. For the program to continue successfully it must skip over the bad data record. This can be done by using another feature of the format string, the asterisk, *. A conversion specifier, when used with an asterisk, skips over the data field for that conversion specifier. The asterisk can be thought of as a field skipper. In the next example, the asterisk with the second conversion specifier, %*d, forces the second data field, id, to be skipped. id is missing from the variable list in fscanf.

```
while((fscanf(fileptr,"%s%*d%f",name,&salary)) != EOF)
                printf("%s %.2f\n", name, salary);
```

The field-skipping feature can then be combined with the braces conversion specifier to skip over the rest of the bad data record. This technique takes advantage of the fact that the programmer has set up the newline as the end of the record. A newline placed within braces with a circumflex symbol, [^\n], will process everything until the newline is reached. Add an asterisk, "%*[^\n]", and fscanf simply skips over all the rest of the data in the line, until the newline.

```
while( (valid =fscanf(fileptr, "%s%d%f\n",
                                      name, &id, &salary)) != EOF){
        if (valid < 3){
                fscanf(fileptr,"%*[^\n]");
                printf("Invalid data in record \n");
                }
        else
                printf("%s %d %.2f\n", name, id, salary);
        }
```

fprintf and Formatted Fields

Instead of entering your data with a text editor, you may want to keep hands off the data file entirely. In that case, you can write a program to ask the user to input data, which is then written to the file using `fprintf`. In the **putrecs.c** program in LISTING 16-11, data is written to the file mydata by `fprintf`. There are spaces placed between the conversion specifiers in `fprintf`'s format string : "%s %d %f\n". Notice also that the newline character is in the format string. `fprintf` does not write in any delimiters to the file unless they are present in the format string. Placing the spaces and newline in the format string effectively writes the delimiters to the file. In fact, any character constants placed in the format string will be written to the file.

LISTING 16-11:

putrecs.c
```c
#include <stdio.h>

int main(void)
        {
        char name[10];
        int id;
        float salary;
        FILE *fileptr;
        char more[2];

        fileptr = fopen("mydata", "a");
        more[0] = 'y';
        while(more[0] == 'y')
                {
                printf ("Please enter all fields\n");
                scanf("%s%d%f", name, &id, &salary);

                fprintf(fileptr,"%s %d %f\n",name,id,salary);

                printf("Input another field?");
                scanf("%s", more);
                }
        fclose(fileptr);
        return 0;
        }
```

User-defined Delimiters and Formatted Fields

Anyone can create his or her own user-defined delimiters. User-defined delimiters are placed as constants in the format string of the `fscanf` or fprintf functions. The process can be dangerous. Any character constants in the format string must be found and matched in the data file. Care must be taken to make sure that the character constants also exist in the data file. In the next example, the comma is a user-defined delimiter. If a comma delimiter is missing in the file when `fscanf` attempts to read it, then a conversion failure will result. Only a comma in the data file is valid matching input for the comma constant in the format string. Any other input is rejected.

There is yet a further complication when using user-define delimiters. If a delimiter is valid input for a preceding field, it will be read as part of that field, not as a delimiter. For example, the comma delimiter does not work with strings, because the comma is simply recognized by the string conversion specifier as valid input for the string. The comma delimiter works for other conversion specifiers because the comma is invalid input for those fields (float and integer). `fscanf` then matches on the comma delimiter and goes onto the other field. For that reason the statement that follows would work, using a database of just id and salary fields.

```
fscanf(fileptr, "%d,%f", &id, &salary)
```

mydata
```
34,   8.56
23,   50.70
12,   600.75
```

When a string field is added, the comma delimiter fails. The `%s`, will read in the comma in the data file as part of the string. `fscanf` will then try to match the comma in the format string with a comma in the data file. However, the comma in the data file has already been read as part of the string. Not finding the comma, `fscanf` will fail.

```
fscanf(fileptr, "%s,%d,%f", name, &id, &salary)
```

mydata
```
Dickens,  34,  8.56
Poe,  23,  50.70
Virgil,  12,  600.75
```

There is a solution. Use the braces with the circumflex operator and the delimiter. This means that the delimiter cannot be part of a string.

```
fscanf(fileptr, "%[^,], %d, %f\n",name,&id,&salary)
```

The matching problem with user-defined delimiters raises another key point. Unless you are using user-defined delimiters, never place any character constants of any kind in the `fscanf` format string. In the next example, the format conversion symbols are bunched up next to each other. There are no character constants in the format string. If there are character constants in the format string, `fscanf` will try to match those constants with the data. If it does not find them, then conversion failures result.

```
fscanf(fileptr, "%s%d%f", name, &id, &salary)
```

Fixed Formatted Fields: Length Conversion Modifiers

You can also format fields as fixed length fields. In this case, delimiters are ignored. You place the number of characters for each field in the field's conversion specifier in `fscanf` and `fprintf`'s format string. In the next example, fixed lengths are specified for each field. The name field has 10 characters. The id field has 3 characters and the salary field has 8 characters.

```
fscanf(fptr,"%10s%3d%8f\n",name,&id,&salary)
```

In the **sdfrecs.c** program in LISTING 16-12, the data fields are fixed-length fields: `"%-10s%03d%08.2f"`. The fields are first input by the user and then written to the file in fixed format. The Left justification symbol, -, in the name field conversion specifier, places the name's characters in the file starting from the left. Both width modifiers for the decimal and floating point conversion specifiers are preceded with a 0. This will pad their numeric values with zeros when written to the file.

There are no spaces in either the fscanf or fprintf format strings. The newline character is explicitly placed in the format string in order to match and skip over newlines in the file. The data file is then closed and reopened. It is read with the fscanf function. The format string here also includes length specifiers.

The **mydata** file shows how the values are written to the file. Notice how the numeric fields are padded with zeros. In a fixed length numeric field, all the characters making up the field must be numeric, 0-9. Spaces would be read as invalid input.

LISTING 16-12:

sdfrecs.c
```c
#include <stdio.h>

int main(void)
        {
        char name[20];
        int id;
        float salary;
        FILE *fptr;
        char more[2];

        fptr = fopen("mydata", "w");
        more[0] = 'y';
        while (more[0] == 'y')
                {
                printf ("Please enter all fields\n");
                scanf("%s%d%f", name, &id, &salary);

                fprintf(fptr,"%-10s%03d%08.2f\n",name,id,salary);
                printf("Input another field?");
                scanf("%s", more);
                }
        fclose(fptr);
        fptr = fopen("mydata", "r");
while(fscanf(fptr,"%10s%3d%8f\n",name,&id,&salary)!=EOF)
                printf("%s %d %f\n", name, id, salary);
        fclose(fptr);

        return 0;
        }
```

mydata
```
Dickens        03400008.56
Poe            02300050.70
Virgil         01200600.75
```

File Errors and End-of-File: ferror and feof

A stream file function may return an EOF value for two possible reasons: the end of the file has been reached, or an error has occurred in accessing a file. The feof function will test a file's status to check and see if an error has actually occurred. The feof function returns a zero value if an error has occurred and a non-zero value if the end-of-file was detected. This function as well as the other error functions described here have to be called right after a file operation to be effective. In the **filechck.c** program in LISTING 16-13, the feof file function checks to see if the fscanf function returns an EOF value because it reached the end of the file or because an error occurred.

The `ferror` file function is used to check if a read or write error has occurred during a specific read or write operation. If an error should occur, then `ferror` will return a non-zero value . In LISTING 16-13, `ferror` is called after each `fscanf` to check if a read error has occurred.

The function `perror` prints out an system defined error message describing the error. When an error occurs, a code representing the error is placed in the system variable `errno`. The `perror` function uses the value of `errno` to reference a system defined message describing the error. `perror` takes a string as its argument, which it then concatenates to the beginning of the error message before printing it out.

Error messages are printed out to the `stderr` file stream. The `stderr` file stream is a special output stream separate from the standard I/O output streams used by `printf` and other output functions. Error messages can be explicitly written to this stream using `fprintf` and specifying `stderr` as the file pointer.

LISTING 16-13:

filechck.c
```c
#include <stdio.h>
int main(void)
        {
        char name[10];
        int id;
        float salary;
        FILE *fileptr;

        fileptr = fopen("mydata", "r");
        while(fscanf(fileptr,"%s%d%f",name,&id,&salary)        !=EOF)
                {
                if(ferror(fileptr) != 0)
                        {
                        fprintf(stderr,"%s read err\n",fileptr);
                        perror("mydata file");
                        }
                else
                        printf("%s %d %f\n", name, id, salary);
                }

        if(feof(fileptr) == 0)
                {
                fprintf(stderr,"%s EOF failed\n",fileptr);
                perror("mydata file");
                }

        fclose(fileptr);
        return 0;
        }
```

Chapter Summary: Text Files

Text files are files consisting of character data. Each byte can be read and interpreted as a character value. On some systems such files are referred to as ASCII files, on others simply as text files. In C, there are stream I/O file functions that implement three different types of text files: character, line, and formatted. Table 16-1 provides a complete list of all the text file functions.

A character text file is accessed with the file functions `getc` and `putc`. A file is referenced as a series of characters. `getc` returns an EOF value when the end of file is reached.

Table 16-1: Text File Functions

`FILE *fopen(`*char *fn, char *fm*`)`	Open a file with the name `fn` and mode `fm` and return a pointer to FILE
`int fclose(`*FILE *fp*`)`	Close the file referenced by `fp`
`int getc(`*FILE *fp*`)`	Retrieves and returns the next character in a file or EOF if the end of the file is reached.
`int putc(`*int ch, FILE *fp*`)`	Write character `ch` to a file `fp`.
`int fgetc(`*FILE *fp*`)`	Equivalent to `getc`
`int fputc(`*int ch, FILE *fp*`)`	Equivalent to `putc`
`char*fgets(`*char*s, int n, FILE*fp*`)`	Reads a line of characters into an array placing a null at the end. NULL is returned for end-of-file.
`int fputs(`*char *s, FILE *fp*`)`	Write string `s` to file `fp`
`int fprintf(`*FILE *fp, char *fmt, ...*`)`	Convert values to character data and write to a file.
`int fscanf(`*FILE *fp, char *fmt, ...*`)`	Read character data from a file, convert to specified values, and assign to listed objects. EOF is returned for end-of-file.
`void clearerr(`*FILE* fp*`)`	Clears end-of-file and error indicators.
`int feof(`*FILE *fp*`)`	Returns non-zero if end-of-file was reached and 0 if an error occurred
`int ferror(`*FILE *fp*`)`	Returns non-zero if error occurred for a file.
`void perror(`*char *s*`)`	Prints to `stderr` the string `s` and the system defined string for the error that has occurred.

A line text file is accessed with the file functions `fgets` and `fputs`. `fgets` views the file as a series of text lines, delimited by newlines. `fgets` reads a whole line into a character array and then adds a null character, making the character array a string. The line of text can then be manipulated as a string. `fgets` takes an argument that sets a maximum limit to the amount of characters it will read in. The limit is usually the same size as the character array into which a line is read. `fputs` simply writes a string to a file. Every character up to, but not including, the null character in a string is written to the file.

A formatted text file is accessed with the file functions `fscanf` and `fprintf`. `fscanf` takes three types of arguments: the file pointer, a format string, and a list of addresses of objects. Character data read from the text file is converted and assigned to the corresponding objects. `fprintf` also takes three arguments: the file pointer, a format string, and a series of values to be converted to character equivalents. `fscanf` and `fprintf` operate in the same way as `scanf` and `fprintf`, and use the same conversion specifiers and modifiers. Though record files are used more than formatted text files, formatted files have one advantage. In a formatted file, there is no limit on the length of the fields, whereas record files have fields of fixed length. In a formatted file, a data field could hold 3 characters or 3,000.

Exercises

Line text file exercises.

Write a program to read a text file line by line. Use `fputs`.

Write a program to receive input from the user line by line and write it to a file. Use `fputs`.

Combine both programs as functions in a program. One will be a `print_text` function to print out the contents of a file using `fgets`. The second will be a `write_text` function to write text to a file. Use menus and give the user an option to choose a function.

Modify exercise 11.3 to use a text file. Read a file line by line using `fgets()`. The user will provide a pattern that will then be searched for in each line of the file. Each line is searched for the presence of the pattern. If the pattern is found in a line, the line is printed out. Use the `argv` option for the name of the text file and the pattern. This means that the program will have two arguments: the file name and the pattern. Below, the program name is a.out, the file name is termpaper, and the pattern is time. You must create this file separately with your word processor.

Formatted text file exercises

Create a formatted text file of four fields: month, day, price, and store. Write a program to calculate the total cost for Mondays in the months of August and September (8 and 9). Print out the price and store for each matched record. At the end, print out the total cost. Cost is described below.

1. Set up a separate file of define commands for months and days. This file will be included into your main file. Below is a copy of part of the include file you will need.
```
#define   MONDAY   100
#define   TUESDAY  101
/*Do the MONTHS 1 - 12 */
#define   JANUARY  1
```

2. In the main function you need to open a file and read a file into the four variables. Use `fscanf`.

3. Create a separate function for calculating the cost. Cost is determined by
`price = price - (price * rate). The rate is 10 percent (0.10).`

4. To run your program, you must first create a separate file that has this data in it. Remember that the spaces are delimiters.

```
8  100        7.00   northside
1  101       20.00   westside
8  100        3.00   southside
8  103        6.00   northside
9  100       10.00   westside
9  105       13.00   northside
8  100       14.50   eastside
```

5. Below is a copy of the results you should get with this data.

```
7.00   northside
3.00   southside
10.00  westside
14.50  eastside
```
Total for Mondays in August and September is 34.50.

Record Files

Sequential and Random Access

Blocks of Bytes: **fread** and **fwrite**

Record Sequential Files and Blocks

Random Access Files: **fseek** and **ftell**

File Management Strategies

17. Record Files

The data in a file may be organized into a set of records. A record is an object that consists of a set of data fields. When a record is read into a C program, it is placed in a structure whose structure type corresponds to the record format. A structure variable is declared whose members are of the same type and size as that of the fields in the record. Reading a record into such a structure effectively reads a record from the file. Writing the structure to the record file effectively writes a record to the file. In terms of C programming, the record file can be thought of as an array of structures laid out in a file. Each record is like an element in an array, arranged sequentially one after the other, in the file.

A structure of a given structure type will have a fixed size. Writing structures of the same type to a file effectively organizes the file into fixed-sized blocks. Each block is the size of a structure.

The fixed size of the blocks in the file is important for later locating a specific record. For this reason, a record file is accessed as a binary file. A file accessed as a text stream may convert newlines to line feeds and carriage returns or add end-of-file characters. All this may change the size of the structure when written to the file. A file accessed as a binary stream, writes bytes exactly as they exist in the program. The data is still only a collection of bytes, but there are no conversions. Information is written into the file in exactly the same sequence of bit ones and bit zeros that exist in the program. In formatted text files, on the other hand, the two-byte integer value 237 is converted to a set of three characters. In binary files, the actual two bytes of the integer value are written directly into the file. In the file, those two bytes may not make any sense as characters.

The record file is still a byte-stream file, just as a text file is a byte stream file. The files are all physically the same. The user simply treats the information in them differently. Record files are different in that the information in them usually makes no sense as characters. If you use your word processor to look at a record file, a variety of strange characters will be displayed.

In UNIX, a record file is physically the same as text files. Both are byte-stream files. In other operating systems, particularly mainframe operating systems, a record file is physically different from text files. Furthermore, record files with different types of records are considered physically different. In C, the same file can be treated, at different places, as a record file, a text line file, or a text formatted file. The differences are in the functions used to access the file, not in the physical structure of the file itself.

A Block of Bytes: fread and fwrite

`fread` and `fwrite` are the block-handling file functions. `fread` and `fwrite` read and write whole blocks of data, unchanged, to and from a file. `fwrite` copies a block of data, a collection of bytes, from memory and writes them to a file. `fread` reads a block of bytes from a file into a block of bytes in memory. Unlike `fscanf` and `fprintf`, `fread` and `fwrite` do not perform any kind of conversions on the bytes in the block. If `fread` and `fwrite` operate on a binary stream, they effectively read and write whole blocks of data in their binary form, unchanged.

`fread` and `fwrite` take four arguments: the address of the block of bytes to be read or written, the number of bytes in the block, a repeat factor, and the file pointer. The repeat factor is usually 1 and will be explained later. A block can be any collection of bytes such as an array of characters. The syntax, prototypes, and examples for the `fwrite` and `fread` functions are listed here. `size_t` is usually an int.

```
fread(address of block, number of bytes to read, repeat, file pointer);
size_t fread(void *, size_t, size_t, FILE*);
```

```
fread(&employee, sizeof(EMP), 1, fileptr);
```

fwrite(*address of block*, *number of bytes to write*, *repeat*, *file pointer*);
```
size_t fwrite(void *, size_t, size_t, FILE*);
```

```
fread(&employee, sizeof(EMP), 1, fileptr);
```

A block may be the memory used for any data object, be it an array, a structure, or even a variable. The simplest kind of block is a character array. Because a character is the same size as a byte, it is easy to think of a character array as a block of bytes. Declaring a character array of 10 characters is the same as setting aside a block of 10 bytes. In the following example, the array `myblock` is treated as a block of bytes to be written to a file. A block, like an array, has a predetermined size. The second argument to `fwrite` is the number of bytes in the block, in this case the number of elements in the `myblock` array.

```
char myblock[3] = {'A','B','C'};

        fwrite(myblock, 3, 1, fileptr);
```

Any collection of bytes may be treated as a block. In the next example, an array of integers is written to the file. The integer values are written bit by bit, two bytes each. There is no conversion into characters, as performed with `fprintf`. In a binary file mode, the bit values of each byte are copied into the file exactly as they exist in memory. The number of elements in the integer array is not the same as the number of bytes in the array. To determine an accurate count of the number of bytes in the array, the number of elements is multiplied by the size of each element. The `sizeof` operator provides the size of each element in terms of bytes.

```
int numblock[3] = {'25','15','40'};

        fwrite(numblock, 3 * sizeof(int), 1,fileptr);
```

A block does not have to be an array. With the address and `sizeof` operators, any variable can be treated as a block. The `fwrite` and `fread` functions only require the address of the variable and the number of bytes it uses. In the next example, the double variable cost is treated as a block. The address operator obtains the address of the variable, and the `sizeof` operator provides the number of bytes it uses. cost's eight bytes of memory will be copied bit for bit to the file.

```
double cost = 9.56;

        fwrite(&cost, sizeof(double), 1,fileptr);
```

You can also use a structure variable as a block. A structure is a variable consisting of several different kinds of objects. Next is an example of the `employee` structure. The size of the structure variable is fixed. That size can be obtained with the `sizeof` operator. `sizeof(EMP)` provides the exact size of the `EMP` structure in terms of bytes. The size of the `EMP` structure is approximately 16 bytes (name = 10, id = 2, salary = 4).

```
typedef struct {
              char name[10];
              int id;
              float salary;
              } EMP;
EMP employee;
```

```
typedef struct emp{
 char name[10];
 int id;
 float salary;
 } EMP;


EMP employee = {"Dickens", 9, 1000};
float cost = 9.56;
char myblock[5] = {'A','B','C'};
FILE *fptr;

fptr = fopen("mydata", "w");

fwrite(myblock, 5,1, fptr);
fwrite(&cost, sizeof(float),1, fptr);
fwrite(&employee, sizeof(EMP),1, fptr);
```

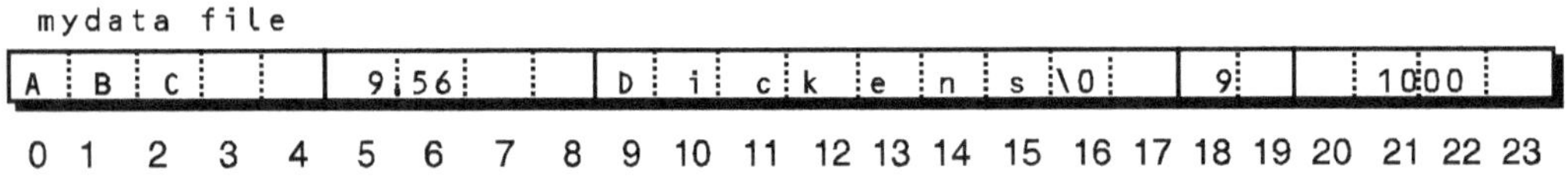

mydata file

A	B	C			9	56			D	i	c	k	e	n	s	\0		9			10	00	

0 1 2 3 4 5 6 7 8 9 10 11 12 13 14 15 16 17 18 19 20 21 22 23

Figure 17-1: fread and fwrite block format.

Given both the address and the size of a structure, fread and fwrite can treat the structure as a block (see Figure 17-1). The address operation applied to employee returns the address of the employee variable, &employee. The address of the employee structure variable can be treated as the address of the first byte in a block. The sizeof operation provides the size of the employee structure in bytes.

employee	a block, data treated as binary bits.
&employee	address of the first byte in the employee block.
sizeof(EMP)	number of bytes in employee.

Using these operations as arguments for fread and fwrite, records can be written directly from a structure variable to a file, and read directly from a file to a structure variable. The next example shows how you would use fread to read a record from a file into the employee structure.

```
fread( &employee, sizeof(EMP), 1, fileptr);
```

In the same way you can use fwrite to write the contents of an employee structure to a file.

```
fwrite( &employee, sizeof(EMP), 1, fileptr);
```

Record Sequential Files and Blocks: `fread` and `fwrite`

By themselves, `fread` and `fwrite` implement record sequential files. `fread` will progress sequentially through a file, record by record. `fwrite` will write sequentially one record after another to a file. Accessing a specific record would require that all previous records in the file be read first. Record-sequential files are useful for databases where most of the records on a regular basis are accessed in a batch mode. Figure 17-2 illustrates a record sequential file.

LISTING 17-1:

recwrite.c

```c
#include <stdio.h>

        typedef struct {
                    char name[100];
                    int id;
                    float salary;
                    }        EMP;

int main(void)
        {
        EMP emp;
        FILE *fileptr;
        char more[2];

        fileptr = fopen("mydata", "wb");
        more[0] = 'y';

        while (more[0] == 'y'){
                printf ("Please enter all three fields: ");
                scanf("%s%d%f",&emp.name,&emp.id,&emp.salary);

                fwrite(&emp, sizeof(EMP), 1, fileptr);

                printf("Input another field? ");
                scanf("%s", more);
                }
        fclose(fileptr);

        fileptr = fopen("mydata", "rb");
        while(fread(&emp,sizeof(EMP),1,fileptr) != 0)
                {
                printf("%s %d %.2f\n",emp.name,emp.id,
                                                    emp.salary);
                }
        fclose(fileptr);

        return 0;
        }
```

Run of **recwrite.c** program.

```
Please enter all three fields: Larisa 8 46
Input another field? y
Please enter all three fields: Aleina 9 52
Input another field? y
Please enter all three fields: Dylan 2 1000
Input another field? n

Larisa 8 46.000
Aleina 9 52.00
Dylan 2 1000.00
```

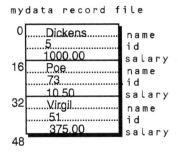

Figure 17-2: Record-sequential file.

In the **recwrite.c** program in LISTING 17-1, a file is opened first to write records. The emp structure variable is filled with new values within the loop. After each new set of values has been entered, the emp structure is written as a new record to the file. The writing of bytes to a file automatically advances down the file. The first record is written in the first 16 bytes. The second record entered is written in the next 16 bytes, and so on.

The file is then closed and reopened in the read file mode. In a loop, fread reads in each record one at a time. Within the loop, the record is printed out. The test for the end of the file is the NULL value. The while test expression both reads a record into a structure variable and tests the result of the fread function call for the end of the file, a NULL return value.

```
while(fread(&emp,sizeof(EMP),1,fileptr)!=NULL)
```

The third argument of the fread and fwrite functions is a repeat factor. It is used for conveniently reading and writing arrays. When using an array of structures, you may want to save the data in the array to a file for use later. You can use the repeat argument to read or write the array using only one fread or fwrite function call. In the **empafile.c** program in LISTING 17-2, the array of structures is read in from a file using the repeat argument. At the end of the program, the array is written back to the file, also using the repeat argument.

LISTING 17-2:

empafile.c

```c
#include <stdio.h>

#define MAX 3
        typedef struct emp{
                char name[100];
                int id;
                float salary;
                } EMP;

 int main(void)
        {
        EMP emprecs[MAX];
        int i;
        FILE *fileptr;

        fileptr = fopen("mydata", "rb");
        fread(emprecs,sizeof(EMP),3,fileptr);
        fclose(fileptr);

        i = 0;
        while (i < MAX)
                {
                printf("\n%s %d %.2f\n", emprecs[i].name,
                                emprecs[i].id, emprecs[i].salary);
                printf("Enter new values\n");
                scanf("%s%d%f", emprecs[i].name,
                                &emprecs[i].id, &emprecs[i].salary);
                i++;
                }

        fileptr = fopen("mydata", "wb");
        fwrite(emprecs,sizeof(EMP),3,fileptr);
        fclose(fileptr);

        return 0;
        }
```

Run of **emparfile.c** program.

```
Larisa 8 46.00
Enter new values
George 47 2.50

Aleina 9 52.00
Enter new values
Robert 41 8.75

Dylan 2 1000.00
Enter new values
Mark 36 122
```

Random Access Files: fseek and ftell

The `fseek` function is used to implement a random access file. `fseek` allows positioning of the file position indicator to any point in the file. A file can be thought of as an array of bytes. Each byte has its own offset. A file of 325 bytes can be thought of as an array of 325 bytes. Each byte, then, can be thought of as an element. With `fseek`, you can reference any particular byte in the file.

`fseek` references bytes through an offset. The offset is calculated from a point of origin. For a file there are three possible points of origin: the beginning of the file, the end of the file, and the current position in the file. These points of origin are represented by three symbolic constants defined in the stdio.h file: SEEK_SET, SEEK_END, and SEEK_CUR.

Offset from	**Point of Origin**	
The beginning of the file	first byte in the file	`SEEK_SET`
The current place in the file	current byte in the file	`SEEK_CUR`
The end of the file	last byte in the file	`SEEK_END`

The `fseek` function takes three arguments: a file pointer, an offset, and a point of origin for the offset. In a file consisting of 325 bytes, the `fseek` statement in the next example will position the file position indicator at the 245th byte. The offset is calculated from the beginning of the file as indicated by the SEEK_SET argument. Should you use the SEEK_END argument, then the offset is calculated from the end of the file. The function call `fseek(fileptr, 10L, SEEK_END)` will position the file pointer at 10 bytes from the end of the file, 325 - 10, the 315th byte. The syntax, prototype, and an example of the `fseek` function are shown here.

```
fseek(file pointer, byte offset (long), origin);
fseek(FILE*, long, int);
fseek(fileptr, 245L, SEEK_SET)
```

If the file position indicator is set to a given byte, it can then be offset from that position using `fseek` with the SEEK_CUR option.

```
fseek(fileptr,245L,SEEK_SET)   Position at 245th byte.
fseek(fileptr,20L,SEEK_CUR)    Position at 245 + 20, 265th byte.
```

`fseek`'s offset argument is a long integer. If an integer is used for this argument, it will automatically be converted to a long by the `fseek` function prototype. For the sake of consistency, any integer value used for offsets in these examples is cast to a long.

Combined with `fread` and `fwrite`, `fseek` allows reading and writing at any point in the file. In the **seekbyte.c** program LISTING 17-3, 10 bytes are read, starting with byte 245 in the file. Bytes 245 through 255 are copied into the buffer array.

This is of little use unless there is some organization to the file that allows one to calculate where information resides in the file. Record files impose such an organization. Record files usually contain only one kind of record. This record is always of the same size. For example, all records in a record file consisting of employee records have the same size, `sizeof(EMP)`. With this in mind, the file can be thought of as organized like an array of structure elements. In the employee example, the elements would be `EMP` structures. You can then think of `fseek` as offsetting on an array of `EMP` elements. However, record files are files, not arrays. The file offset is always calculated in terms of a number of bytes, not a number of records.

LISTING 17-3:

seekbyte.c

```
#include <stdio.h>

int main(void)
            {
            char buffer[10];
            FILE *fileptr;

            fileptr = fopen("myfile", "r+b");

            fseek (fileptr, 245L, SEEK_SET);
            fread(buffer, 10, 1, fileptr);

            fclose(fileptr);

            return 0;
            }
```

Recall that offsets on arrays involve a hidden multiplication of an element's place in an array by the size of an array element's type. This hidden multiplication provides the specific byte address of an element. In the same way, a multiplication of a structure's place in the file by the size of a structure type can provide a specific byte offset in the file for that particular structure. In this case, the multiplication by the size of the structure type must be provided explicitly. `fseek` will only offset by a number of bytes. In the case of the employee record file, in order to know which particular byte in the file to offset to, the place of the EMP structure in the file is explicitly multiplied by the size of EMP .

Given that the size of an EMP structure is 16 bytes, the first structure in the file will be located at the first byte, the second structure at the 16th byte, the third structure at the 32nd byte, and the fourth structure at the 48th byte. The place of a structure in a file can be thought of as the structure's record number. The record number of the first record is 0. The record number of the second structure is 1. The record number of the third structure is 2, and so on. To calculate the offset for the beginning byte of the third record, simply multiply its record number, 2, times the size of the EMP structure, 16. `2 * sizeof(EMP) = 2 * 16 = 32`. Given the record number and its multiplication by the size of its structure type, any record in the file can be randomly accessed (see Figure 17-3).

```
fseek(fileptr, 2L * sizeof(EMP), SEEK_SET);
fread(&employee, sizeof(EMP), 1, fileptr);
```

When a record is updated it is first read from the file, changed in the program, and then written back to the file. It is important to remember that the reading of the record will advance the file position indicator to the beginning of the next record. You need to use `fseek` again to reset the file position indicator back to the beginning of the just-read record before that record is written. In the next example, the salary field of record 2 is updated. The first `fseek` positions the file position indicator to the beginning of the third record in the file. After the `fread` operation, the file position indicator has been moved to the beginning of the fourth record. The second `fseek` resets the file position indicator back to the beginning of the third record.

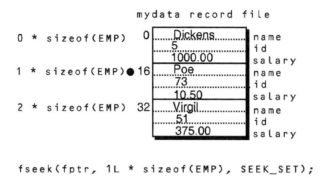

```
                              mydata  record  file

0 * sizeof(EMP)     0 ┌──────Dickens──────┐ name
                      │··········5··········│ id
                      ├───────1000.00──────┤ salary
1 * sizeof(EMP)● 16 │·······Poe···········│ name
                      │··········73·········│ id
                      ├───────10.50────────┤ salary
2 * sizeof(EMP)   32 │·······Virgil········│ name
                      │··········51·········│ id
                      └───────375.00───────┘ salary
```

```
fseek(fptr, 1L * sizeof(EMP), SEEK_SET);
```

Figure 17-3: Random access file and fseek.

```
fseek(fileptr, 2L * sizeof(EMP), SEEK_SET);
fread (&employee, sizeof(EMP), 1, fileptr);

employee.salary = 3000.00;

fseek(fileptr, 2L * sizeof(EMP), SEEK_SET);
fwrite (&employee, sizeof(EMP), 1 fileptr);
```

There is a clever way to reset the file position indicator in the second `fseek`. A negative offset combined with the SEEK_CUR option will offset backwards from the current byte. This can be dangerous. One has to make sure that the file position indicator is actually set to the next record. In the next example, the first `fseek` places the file position indicator at 32, 2 *16. The `fread` then advances the file position indicator by the size of the record to 48, 32 + 16. To update, the record needs to be written back to the same place, beginning at byte 32. The negative offset of 16 from the current position of 48 will place the file position indicator at 32, 48 - 16. This is, of course, assuming that the file position indicator is still at 48 when the `fseek` before the `fwrite` is called.

```
fseek(fileptr, 2L * sizeof(EMP), SEEK_SET);
fread (&employee, sizeof(EMP), 1, fileptr);

employee.salary = 3000.00;

fseek(fileptr, (long) -(sizeof(EMP)),SEEK_CUR);
fwrite (&employee, sizeof(EMP), 1 fileptr);
```

The **randrec.c** program in LISTING 17-4 is a program to update a file. There is one added `fseek` in this program, which at this point may seem redundant. In the `addrecord` function there is an `fseek` to place the file position indicator at the end of the file. This is done by an offset of zero bytes from the end of the file. This ensures that the file position indicator will be positioned at the end of the file. A new record can then be written to the end of the file. Similarly an offset of zero bytes from the beginning of the file will place the file position indicator at the beginning of the file.

The file position indicator can be reset to the beginning of the file with the rewind function. rewind is equivalent to an `fseek` with a zero offset from the beginning of the file.

```
fseek(fileptr, 0L, SEEK_END); /*End of File */
fseek (fileptr, 0L, SEEK_SET);        /* Top of file */
rewind(fileptr);
```

The number of records in a file can be determined by dividing the number of bytes in the file by the size of a record. To do so you need to first determine the size of the file. The position of the last byte in the file will also be the size of the file. An `fseek` with a 0L offset from the end of the file will place the file position indicator at the end of the file. The current position of the file position indicator can be obtained by the `ftell` function. Dividing this position by the size of a record gives the number of records in the file. In the following example, `fseek` positions the file position indicator to the end of the file, and `ftell` returns the position of the last byte. The result is then divided by the size of an `EMP` structure, giving the number of `EMP` records in the file.

```
long filesize, numrecs;

fseek(fileptr, 0L, SEEK_END);
filesize = ftell(fileptr);
numrecs = filesize / sizeof(EMP);
```

In the **randrec.c** program in LISTING 17-4, the function `printrev` prints the records out in reverse order. `ftell` is used to determine both the size of the file and the actual offset of each record. The `ftell` function takes a file pointer as its argument and returns a long value that is the current position of the file position indicator for that file. Notice how the variables used in the calculation of the offsets are all declared as long.

LISTING 17-4:

randrec.c

```c
#include <stdio.h>
#include <stdlib.h>

    typedef struct {
                char name[100];
                int id;
                float salary;
                }      EMP;

void addrecord(FILE*);
void updaterecord (FILE*);
void printrev(FILE*);

int main(void)
    {
    char choice[2];
    FILE *fileptr;
    int more = 1;

    if((fileptr = fopen("empfile1", "r+b")) == NULL)
            if((fileptr=fopen("empfile1","w+b"))==NULL)
                {
                printf("File could not be opened\n");
                exit(1);
                }
```

```
        while (more)
                {
                printf("Please enter choice: ");
                scanf("%s", choice);

                switch(choice[0])
                        {
                        case 'a':
                                addrecord(fileptr);
                                break;
                        case 'u':
                                updaterecord(fileptr);
                                break;
                        case 'p':
                                printrev(fileptr);
                                break;
                        case 'q':
                                more = 0;
                                break;
                        }
                }
        fclose(fileptr);
        return 0;
        }

void addrecord(FILE *fileptr)
        {
        EMP emp;

        printf ("Please enter all three fields: ");
        scanf("%s%d%f",emp.name,&emp.id,&emp.salary);
        fseek(fileptr, 0L, SEEK_END);
        fwrite(&emp, sizeof(EMP), 1, fileptr);
        }


void updaterecord (FILE  *fileptr)
        {
        EMP emp;
        long recordid;

        printf("Please enter record number: ");
        scanf("%ld", &recordid);
        fseek(fileptr, recordid*sizeof(EMP),SEEK_SET);
        fread(&emp, sizeof(EMP), 1, fileptr);

        printf("%s %d %.2f\n",emp.name,emp.id,emp.salary);
        printf ("Please enter all three fields: ");
        scanf("%s%d%f",emp.name,&emp.id,&emp.salary);

        fseek(fileptr, recordid*sizeof(EMP),SEEK_SET);
        fwrite(&emp, sizeof(EMP), 1, fileptr);
        }


void printrev(FILE *fileptr)
        {
        EMP emp;
        long recnums, filesize, i, curnum;
```

```
fseek(fileptr, 0L, SEEK_END);
filesize = ftell(fileptr);
recnums = filesize / sizeof(EMP);

for(i = (recnums-1); i >= 0; i--)
        {
        fseek(fileptr, i*sizeof(EMP),SEEK_SET);
        curnum = ftell(fileptr);
        fread(&emp, sizeof(EMP), 1, fileptr);
        printf("\nRecord Byte Offset = %ld",curnum);
        printf("\nRecord Number = %ld\n",i);
        printf("%s %d %.2f\n",emp.name,emp.id,emp.salary);
        }
}
```

Run of **randrec.c** program.

```
Please enter choice: a
Please enter all three fields: Cece 76 3000
Please enter choice: a
Please enter all three fields: Dylan 2 175
Please enter choice: p

Record Byte Offset = 16
Record Number = 1
Dylan 2 175.00

Record Byte Offset = 0
Record Number = 0
Cece 76 3000.00

Please enter choice: u
Please enter record number: 1
Dylan 2 175.00
Please enter all three fields: Chris 4 263

Please enter choice: p

Record Byte Offset = 16
Record Number = 1
Chris 4 263.00

Record Byte Offset = 0
Record Number = 0
Cece 76 3000.00

Please enter choice: q
```

File Management Strategies

There are many file management strategies that you can use to better access information in a file. Many of these such as indexes can have very complex implementations. There are a few that you can implement using only what you have learned so far. Two of these are referred to as management information and information hiding. In the case of management information you can reserve part of your file to hold information that you need to use to manage your file, information such as the number of records in a file. Information hiding is a strategy whereby you can protect certain critical data such as the value of a file pointer, restricting access to that data to one designated part of your program. Information hiding uses a method called encapsulation that, in C, scopes restricted data to a source code file. Both of these strategies are incorporated into the program in LISTING 17-6.

Management Information

With many record files, you will find that you may need to maintain certain information about the data in those files. For example, you may need to keep track of the number of records in a file, or the type of fields used in a record. To see how such Management information can be implemented and used, let us examine the problem of adding a new record to a file. Using the employee example, suppose that you have decided to make the employee id the same as the record number. This simplifies access letting you use the employee id to reference a record, since a record's id field is also its record number. But this raises another problem. When you add a new record, you will need to know that record's record number so that you can assign it to its id field. How is its record number determined? You will need to know how many records are in the file to begin with. You could simply use `ftell` to determine the size of the file and calculate the number of records in it. Another strategy is to just keep track of the number of records already entered into the file. You could keep this number saved in a section of the file that you have reserved for special Management information. That reserved section could be the bytes usually used for the first record in the file. The first record would then start at the second position, with a record number of 1. Instead of the first record number being 0, it would be 1.

To save this Management information, you could use the file function `fprintf`, instead of `fwrite`, treating the first bytes of the file like a formatted file. A file in C has only one physical form, the byte stream. It is the file functions which will treat a file as a specific type of file. Different file functions can be applied to the same file. A given file can be treated in one place as a record file by an `fread` or `fwrite` function. The same file can be treated in a different place as a formatted file by an `fscanf` or `fprintf` function.

At each session, the record number for the last record is retrieved from the information part of the file by using `fscanf`. At the end of the session, the last record number is saved to the information part of the file by using `fprintf`. There is an exception. In the first session, when the file is created, the record number of the last record is set to 0. Figure 17-4 shows how the space on the file for the first record is reserved for management information.

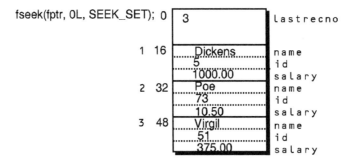

Figure 17-4: Management information in a file.

LISTING 17-5:

inforec.c

```c
#include <stdio.h>
#include <stdlib.h>

typedef struct {
                char name[100];
                long id;
                float salary;
                }       EMP;

long addrecord(FILE*, long);

int main(void)
    {
    FILE *fileptr;
    long lastrecno;
    int more = 1;
    char choice[2];
    EMP emp;

    if((fileptr = fopen("myfile", "r+b")) != NULL)
            fscanf(fileptr, "%ld", &lastrecno );
            else
            if((fileptr=fopen("myfile","w+b"))!=NULL)
                    {
                    lastrecno = 0;
                    fwrite(" ", 1, sizeof(EMP), fileptr);
                    }
                    else
                            exit(1);

    while (more)
            {
            printf("Please enter choice:");
            scanf("%1s", choice);

            switch(choice[0])
                    {
                    case 'a':
                            lastrecno=addrecord(fileptr,lastrecno);
                            break;
                    case 'q':
                            more = 0;
                            break;
                    }
        '   }

    fseek(fileptr, 0L, SEEK_SET);
    fprintf(fileptr, "%ld", lastrecno);
    fclose(fileptr);
    return 0;
    }
```

```
long addrecord(FILE *fileptr, long recno)
        {
        EMP employee;

        printf ("Please enter name and salary:");
        scanf("%s%f", employee.name, &employee.salary);

        recno++;
        employee.id = recno;

        fseek(fileptr, recno * sizeof(EMP), SEEK_SET);
        fwrite(&employee, sizeof(EMP), 1, fileptr);

        return(recno);
        }
```

The **inforec.c** program in LISTING 17-5 implements such a management information strategy. The variable `lastrecno` is passed to `addrecord`. `lastrecno` is initialized to 0 because it will be incremented to 1 before the new record is written. `addrecord` increments recno. It then returns the record number of the next record back to main to be placed in `lastrecno`. At the end of the program, before the file closes, the file position indicator is placed at the beginning of the file, `fseek(fileptr, 0L, SEEK_SET)`, and `lastrecno` is written to the file. You can add `updaterecord` and `menu` functions like those in LISTING 17-4.

Information Hiding and Encapsulation

A safe strategy in a large project is to hide the lower-level aspects of a set of operations from other parts of the program. In this case, the actual operations on a file can be hidden from other parts of the program by placing them within access functions. This technique is referred to as information hiding, hiding the implementation details of an operation. To read a file, a function call is made to a programmer-defined function for reading a file. Within that function, `fread` is called to actually read data in from the file. The `fread` function and the fileptr remain accessible only within this programmer-defined function. Other parts of the program do not call `fread` or in any way reference the file pointer. They simply issue a function call to the programmer-defined function for reading a file and pass it the address of a record variable to be filled.

Such a strategy protects the file from unplanned or unauthorized access and it reduces the potential for errors in actually reading the file. In LISTING 17-6, a set of file access functions are declared in the **file.c** file. The file pointer is declared as an external static variable. This means that it is known only to functions declared in the **file.c** file, the file access functions. Other functions in other parts of the program cannot reference the file pointer. They do not even know that the file pointer variable exists. The file pointer is effectively protected and hidden from other variables. No longer is a single file pointer value passed from function to function throughout the program. Instead, it is directly accessed by the file access functions in **file.c**, and only by those functions (see Figure 17-5).

The program in LISTING 17-6 is a revised version of LISTING 17-5 that incorporates file access using information hiding. A file is opened simply by calling the `openfile` function and passing the name of the file. A file is closed by a call to the closefile function. The file management information is now hidden within the `openfile` function. `lastrecno` is declared as a static external variable known only to the file access functions. It is incremented by a call to `setnextrecno`. Its value is obtained by a call to `getlastrecno`.

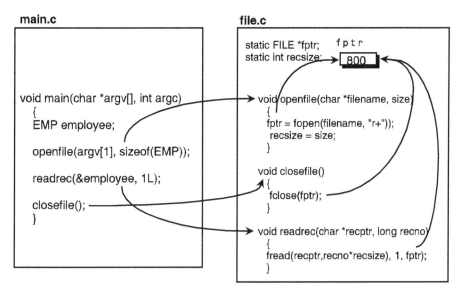

Figure 17-5: Information hiding and access functions.

Reading a specific record entails calling the readrec function with the address of the structure variable and the record number. A record is written by calling the `writerec` function with the same arguments as `readrec`.

The employee data is also hidden, but within the **emp.c** file. A series of employee access functions allow you to access this data. The EMP structure typedef is declared only within the **emp.c** file, not within any header files as in previous programs. This means that only functions within **emp.c** can access EMP structure data, and that EMP structures are only declared in functions defined in the **emp.c** file. Employee data remains entirely hidden within the **emp.c** file, accessible only through access functions such as print_recs and `add_rec`. These access functions are declared in the **emp.h** header file that is included in the **main.c** file. To add an employee record, the `add_rec` function is called within **main.c**. The `add_rec` function then adds an employee record using functions and structures defined in the **emp.c** file.

Functions are now divided into those that remain hidden within a source file, and those that are accessible outside the source file. Those that are publicly accessible are listed and declared in a header file, like the employee access functions defined in **emp.h**. Those that are only privately accessible by other functions defined within the source file, are declared as static within that source file, like the `output_rec` and `input_rec` functions in **emp.c**. The terms private and public appropriately describe the differences between such function. In fact, you will see that in C++, such private and public functions are explicitly defined.

Functions dealing with the same type of operations are grouped together in the same source code file. File access operations are in the **file.c** source file, whereas employee operations are in the **emp.c** source file. The source files serve to encapsulate the functions, hiding lower level functions and data, and allowing access through public functions. This kind of organization is referred to as encapsulation and is used extensively in C++ programming.

Notice also that there is also a kind of hierarchy built into the design that moves from specific operations to more general ones. At the top are the specialized functions to perform employee record operations such as add_rec. Such specialized functions are called in the main function. Then within the **emp.c** file, functions are defined to perform operations on employee data such as displaying records or inputting data. Finally, in **file.c**, very generalized file operations are performed such as writing data to a file are reading data from a file. Such a structure allows all file operations to be entire hidden from main functions. The main function only called employee functions that in turn call file functions. You can see this structure very clearly in the open file functions. In main, there is a call to the open_empfile function. In **emp.c**, the open_empfile function then calls the openfile function to actually open the file. In the process is adds information obtained from the EMP structure that is available only within the **emp.c** file. The close operation proceeds in much the same way. The close_empfile function calls the closefile function to actually close the file.

This design hides lower level operations from upper-level operations, dividing them by source code files. Should you need to change any lower level operations such as changing the way your file functions operate, the upper-level operation would not have to be touched. You would only modify those source code files that define the lower level functions. For example, if you decide to change the EMP structure you would only need to modify the **emp.c** source code file. No other source code file needs to be touched. So now you can modularize your code not just into separate functions, but also into separate source code files.

This particular design remains simple until you need to use several files at the same time. An array of file pointers could be declared, and an argument indicating the file pointer being referenced could be added to each access function. This could easily become very complicated. A simpler solution would be to set up a **file.c** file with its own set of file access functions for each file. This generates much more code and, of course, generates many new functions. Each file would have its own set of file access functions.

An even simpler solution is to use C++. C++ was designed for problems of this sort. In C++, structure type declarations are extended to include functions. A file object can be declared to include hidden data such as the file pointer as well as its own set of file functions. Chapters 19 discusses such applications.

LISTING 17-6

emp.h

```
void add_rec(void);
void print_recs(void);
void open_empfile(char*);
void close_empfile(void);
```

file.h

```
void openfile(char*, int);
void closefile(void);
long readrec(char*,long);
void writerec(char*, long);
long getlastrecno(void);
long setnextrecno(void);
```

main.c

```c
#include <stdio.h>
#include "emp.h"

 void menu(void);

int main(int argc, char *argv[])
            {
            int more = 0;
            char choice[2];

            open_empfile(argv[1]);

            menu();
            while (more == 0)
                    {
                    printf("\nPlease enter choice: ");
                    scanf("%1s", choice);

                    switch(choice[0])
                            {
                            case 'a':
                                    add_rec();
                                    break;
                            case 'p':
                                    print_recs();
                                    break;
                            case 'q':
                                    more = 1;
                            }
                    }

            close_empfile();
            return 0;
            }

void menu(void)
            {
            printf("\nEmployee Record Menu\n");
            printf("a = add a record\n");
            printf("p = print a record\n");
            printf("q = quit program\n");
            }
```

emp.c

```c
#include <stdio.h>
#include "emp.h"
#include "file.h"

#define NAMELEN 100

/* EMP structure */
        typedef  struct emp_type {
                char name[NAMELEN];
                long id;
                float salary;
                } EMP;

static EMP input_rec(void);
static void output_rec(EMP);

void open_empfile(char* filename)
        {
        openfile(filename, sizeof(EMP));
        }

void close_empfile(void)
        {
        closefile();
        }

void add_rec(void)
        {
        EMP emprec;

        emprec = input_rec();
        emprec.id = setnextrecno();
        writerec((char*)&emprec, emprec.id);
        }

static EMP input_rec(void)
                {
                EMP in_emp;

                printf("\nPlease enter last name: ");
                scanf("%*[\n\t ]%[^\n]s", in_emp.name);
                printf("Please enter salary: ");
                scanf("%f", &in_emp.salary);
                return(in_emp);
                }

void print_recs(void)
                {
                EMP emprec;
                long i, lastrec;

                lastrec = getlastrecno();
                for (i = 1; i <= lastrec ; i++){
                        readrec((char*)&emprec,i);
                        output_rec(emprec);
                        }
                }
```

```
static void output_rec(EMP out_emp)
            {
            printf("\n Employee Record \n");
            printf("\t NAME  : %s\n", out_emp.name);
            printf("\t ID    : %ld\n", out_emp.id);
            printf("\t SALARY: %.2f\n", out_emp.salary);
            }
```

file.c

```
#include <stdio.h>
#include <stdlib.h>
#include "file.h"

 static long lastrecno = 0;
 static FILE *fptr;
 static int recsize;

 void openfile(char *filename, int in_recsize)
      {
      recsize = in_recsize;

      if((fptr = fopen(filename, "r+b")) != NULL)
            {
            fseek(fptr, 0L, SEEK_SET);
            fscanf(fptr,"%ld", &lastrecno);
            }
      else
            if((fptr = fopen(filename, "w+b")) != NULL)
                  {
                  lastrecno = 0L;
                  fwrite(" ", 1, recsize, fptr);
                  }
            else {
                  printf("file open error\n");
                  exit(1);
                  }
      }

 void closefile(void)
      {
      fseek(fptr,0L, SEEK_SET);
      fprintf(fptr,"%ld", lastrecno);
      fclose (fptr);
      }

 void writerec(char *recptr,long recno)
      {
      fseek(fptr, recno * recsize , SEEK_SET);
      fwrite(recptr, recsize, 1, fptr);
      }

 long readrec(char *recptr, long recno)
      {
      long res;
      fseek(fptr, recno * recsize , SEEK_SET);
      res = fread (recptr, recsize, 1, fptr);
      return(res);
      }
```

```
long getlastrecno(void)
     {
     return (lastrecno);
     }

long setnextrecno(void){
     lastrecno++;
     return (lastrecno);
     }
```

Run of LISTING 17-6

```
Employee Record Menu
a = add a record
p = print a record
q = quit program

Please enter choice: a

Please enter last name: Justin
Please enter salary: 7.25

Please enter choice: a

Please enter last name: Chris
Please enter salary: 1045

Please enter choice: a

Please enter last name: Dylan
Please enter salary: 540

Please enter choice: p

 Employee Record
       NAME  : Justin
       ID    : 1
       SALARY: 7.25

 Employee Record
       NAME  : Chris
       ID    : 2
       SALARY: 1045.00

 Employee Record
       NAME  : Dylan
       ID    : 3
       SALARY: 540.00

Please enter choice: q
```

File Indexes: B-Trees

You have seen in chapter 15 how you can construct search tree to operate as indexes for data records, in that case, records that were elements in an array. You could also create a search tree that would reference records in a record file, using the record offset instead of a element number to access the record. Still, you would have to construct the search tree from scratch every time you started your program. For a large file, this could be very time consuming. Instead of a search tree that uses dynamic memory, you could construct a search tree using a record file. Each record would be the node in the search tree. In place of pointers you would use the offsets for next node records. Instead of using dynamic memory that disappears after use, you could use disk space that remains intact each time you use your program. In effect, you can create an index as a file.

Implementing a standard search tree as a record file has certain disadvantages. The node for a search tree is rather small, just a key, data number, and two pointers. One of the major costs to consider in any program is the time taken for disk access. Accessing your disk take a relatively large amount of time. With a search tree you will have a great many small records, each a node, that you will have to access. This could slow down your program significantly.

As an alternative, you could bunch several search nodes together in such a way that they could be retrieved as one record. Instead of one key and two node record numbers, you could have several keys and their respective node numbers arranged in an ordered list. This is the principle behind the b-tree. A b-tree provides a very efficient and fast way to implement an index in a file. A b-tree, in fact, is much faster than a search tree, able to reference records in extremely large files with great speed. It is the method of choice for accessing very large record files.

The b-tree combines two techniques, the search tree and ordered list. It uses the same node and pointer-like structure that you find in search trees. Each node has keys that you compare your search key to. Associated with each key is a record node number that operate like the pointers in a search tree. Unlike a search tree, the b-tree has several keys in the same node. These keys are organized like an ordered list. With such a node, you need to first find the key you want by searching through this ordered list of keys. Once you have found the key you want, then you can choose that key's node number. So instead of just comparing the search key to a single key as you would in a search tree, in a b-tree you need to search an ordered list of keys.

A b-tree node consists of a list of several ordered keys and associated node record numbers. You can think of the ordered keys as defining segments of a data. The first and last keys indicate all data less than or greater than a key. In the middle keys, the difference between one key and another defines a range of keys. For example, with a node consisting of the keys 45, 63, and 72, the keys 45 and 63 indicate the range of possible keys of 45 through 63. The first key indicates all possible keys from 1 to 45, and the last key indicates all possible keys greater than 72. Figure 17-6 shows this b-tree example both conceptually and its implementation in a record file.

Each key has a branch node number associated with it. This branch node number functions like a pointer in a search tree, referencing another node. In the case of middle keys, such a branch node will contain keys that fall within the range of the current key and its previous key. The keys in a branch node will be less than the current key and greater than the previous key. For example, suppose that key 63 has a branch node. The key prior to that is key 45. The branch node for key 63 can contain any keys between 45 and 63. This branch node could contain keys 53, 56, and 62, but not keys 31 or 75.

In the case of the first key, the branch node can contain any keys less than the first key. For example, the branch node for key 53 may contain any keys from 1 to 52, any less than 53. The last key has its own branch node that can hold keys greater than the previous key but less than the last key. The branch node for the last key 72 can hold keys greater than 63 but less than 72. There is also one extra branch node number in a b-tree node that is used for any keys greater than the last node. In a sense, the last key has two branch nodes associated with it, one less than its key and one for those greater than its key. This greater-than node can hold all keys greater-than the last key. For example, the greater-than node for the last key 72 can hold any keys from 73 on. Keep in mind that there is always one more node number than keys in a b-tree node. There is a node number for each key holding keys less than that key, and there is one last node number for keys that are greater than the last key.

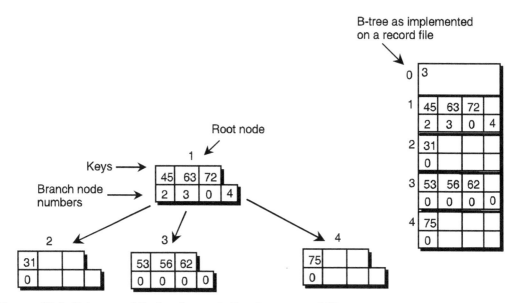

Figure 17-6: B-tree and its implementation in a record file.

Adding a new key involves first locating the node where it belongs, and then inserting the key in the ordered list of keys in that node. It is a recursive process, applying the same procedure to each node searched. The search for the right node begins with the root node and proceeds from one node to the next until the right one to add the new key to is found. Figure 17-7 illustrates the steps involved in adding a new key to a b-tree.

The key is first compared to the list of ordered keys in the node. The search will stop at the first key greater than the new key. This is the point in the list that the new key could be inserted. If there is room in the current node, then the key is simply inserted into that ordered list of keys. The keys greater than this key are simply moved over one, making room for the new key in the array of keys. If there is no room in the current node, then either a new node is created for it, or the search continues, recursively moving from one node to another.

If there is no space open, then the key where the search has stopped is checked to see if it has a branch node. If it has no branch node, then a new node is created that then becomes the branch node for that key. The new key is added as the first key in that branch node. If that key has a branch node, then that node needs to be searched. That node is recursively moved to and searched, just as the previous node was. The recursive procedure begins again. The ordered list of keys is searched, stopping at the first one greater than the new key. If there is room, the key is simply inserted at that point into the list of keys for that node. If there is no room, then the key where the search has stopped is checked to see if it has a branch node. If not a new one is created for the new key. If it does have a branch node, that branch node is recursively moved to and searched. The process continue this way until either a node is found with room for the new key, or the search stops at key that has no branch node, for which a new node can then be created and the new key placed there.

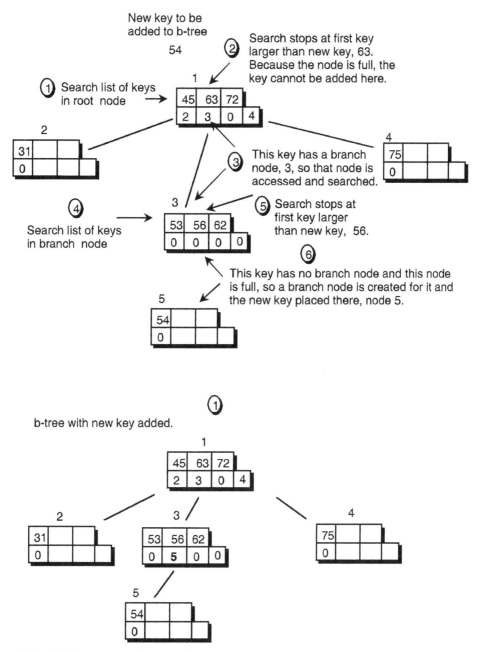

Figure 17-7: Adding a new key to a b-tree.

Figure 17-7 illustrates the process of adding a new key. The key 54 is added. First the root node is searched. 64 is the first key greater than 54 so the search of the root node's list of keys stops at 64. In this example, the nodes have only 3 keys, so the root node is full. Another key cannot be inserted. Key 64 also has a branch node, node 2. So the process moves to node 2. Node 2 holds keys between 45 and 64 which is what 54 is. The ordered list of keys for node 2 is searched, stopping at key 56. Key 56 is the first key greater than the new key, 54. Node 2 is full so the new key cannot be insert into it. However, there is no branch node for key 56. A new branch node is then created, node 3, and the new key, 54 is added there.

Using the b-tree to print out the ordered list involves the same type of inorder recursive function that was used for the search tree. There is one modification. Instead of recursively calling the inorder function with just a right and left node pointer, the inorder function is called separately for each key's branch node number. In a loop, the recursive function is called with each node number, except the last one. Following the function call and within the loop, any data associated with the key is printed out. Then, outside the loop, the inorder function is called with the last node number. The steps for an inorder recursive operation can be described as follows:

```
In a loop
        {
        recursive call to branch node for key;
        display the key;
        advance to next key
        }

recursive call to last branch node
```

An example of the recursive inorder function for a b-tree follows. The get_rec function is a function to retrieve and print the data referenced by a key.

```
void printorder(long nodeno)
        {
        NODEREC node;
        int i;

        readrec((char*)&node, nodeno, indexfid);

        for(i = 0; i < node.numkeys ; i++)
                {
                if(node.nodenums[i] != 0)
                        printorder(node.nodenums[i] );
                get_rec(node.keyrecs[i].recno);
                }

         if(node.nodenums[i] != 0)
                printorder(node.nodenums[i] );
        }
```

Figure 17-8 shows the inorder procedure for displaying keys in a b-tree. In the first node, the branch node of the first key is recursively called, node 2. It has only one key and no branches, so this key is then displayed, 31. The recursive call returns to node 1 where the first key is then displayed, key 45. Then the branch node for the next key is recursively called, node 3. The first key in node 3 has no branch node. It is just displayed, key 53. The next key does have a branch node, and this is then recursively called, node 5. Node 5 has only one key and no branch nodes. Its key is displayed, key 54. This recursive call then returns to node 3, and key 56 is then displayed. The next key has no branch node and is then displayed, key 62. The recursive call for node 3 then returns back to node 1. Its key, 63, is then displayed. The next key in node 1 has no branch node, so it is then displayed, key 72.

However, there is a last branch for node 1, node 4. This is then recursively called. Node 4 only has one key and no branch nodes, so this key is then displayed, key 75. The keys have then been accessed as an ordered list: 31, 45, 53, 54, 56, 62, 63, 72, 75.

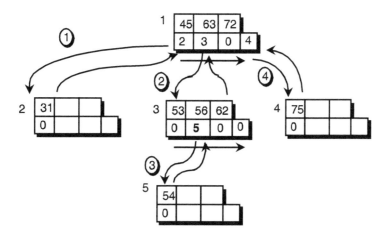

Figure 17-8: Searching a b-tree with inorder recursion.

When it comes to searching a file, you can see how effective and powerful a b-tree can be. The search process operates much like the recursive process for adding a key. You begin at the root and recursively search nodes until you find a match. First you search the ordered list of keys in the node. The search is for any key greater-than or equal to the search key. If no match is found, you will have stopped the search at the first key greater than the search key. You then recursively move to that key's branch node using its branch node number, searching the keys in that node. The process continues until a matched key is found. If the search has stopped at a greater-than key that has no branch node, then there is no such key in the b-tree. Figure 17-9 illustrates the search process on a b-tree.

In the search process, the more keys per node, the shallower and faster the search is. If you have nodes with 10 keys, you would only need two node accesses to search a b-tree of over a 100 possible keys. The first node searched would be the root node. The second node searched would be a branch node. In selecting a branch you may be eliminating over 90 other possible keys from the search. As you move from one branch node to another you eliminate vast portions of the b-tree from your search. If you have a b-tree three levels deep with evenly distributed nodes, then, with just three node accesses you could effectively search 1000 keys. With 4 levels it would be over a 10,000 keys, and 5 levels would be 100,000 keys. Such and effective operation depends on evenly distributed nodes, ones that are equally full, rather than having many nodes with just a few keys. This requires procedures to combine and split nodes as needed. Such a process is covered in more detail in texts on data structures. Only a simple version of a b-tree is presented here.

LISTING 17-7 is a data record management program that uses a b-tree to access records. The program is organized into separate source code files, one for each task. The **emp.c** file holds all functions for managing the employee records. The **file.c** file holds functions for lower level access of record files whether they be the employee data record file or the b-tree index file. The **btree.c** file holds the functions for managing the b-tree index. This contains all the recursive functions for adding a key or printing out the indexed file using the b-tree. In addition, the **btree.c** file has functions to display the b-tree so that you can see how the b-tree is constructed.

Searching the b-tree for key 54.

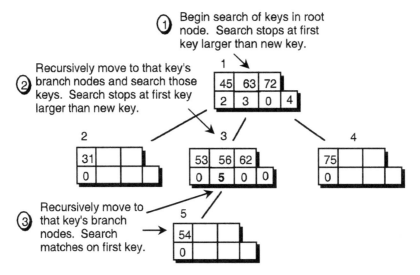

Figure 17-9: Searching a b-tree.

Notice how modularity is maintained. To access an employee record, functions in **main.c** will call an access function in **emp.c**. All employee operations are contained within functions in the **emp.c** file. Even the emp structure declaration are local to and hidden within the **emp.c** file. In turn, for a function in **emp.c** to access a data file, it will call an access function in the **file.c** file. That file will in turn manage data such as the FILE pointer that is hidden from the rest of the program. The b-tree functions are also modularized, with data such as the root record number hidden from the rest of the program.

In this program, the b-tree node is declared as a structure, NODEREC, containing two arrays, a keyrecs array and a nodenums array, and the integer numkeys. numkeys is the number of keys currently in the node. The keyrecs array is an array of KEYREC structures. Each KEYREC structure contains a key field that is an array of characters. In this program the employee name is used as the key and will be assigned here. The recno field of the KEYREC structure holds the record number of the employee record. This is the record number used to retrieve the employee record from the employee record file. Once you locate a key, you can then use the recno field in that KEYREC structure to retrieve the employee record that the key indexes. The nodenums array holds the record numbers used to retrieve other nodes in the b-tree record file. The b-tree record file is a file consisting solely of b-tree NODEREC records that can be read into a NODEREC structure. Figure 17-10 shows the NODEREC structure with its keyrecs and nodenums arrays.

```
typedef struct key_type {
        char key[KEYLEN];
        long recno;
        } KEYREC;

typedef struct noderec_type {
        int numkeys;
        struct key_type keyrecs[KEYNUM];
        long nodenums[NODENUMS];
        } NODEREC;
```

The `nodenums` array in the `NODEREC` structure contains a list of branch node numbers. Each element of the nodenums array corresponds to an element of the `keyrecs` array. `nodenums[4]` holds the branch node number for `keyrecs[4]`. There is one more `nodenums` element than `keyrecs` elements. This extra element is for the branch node number for keys greater than the last key.

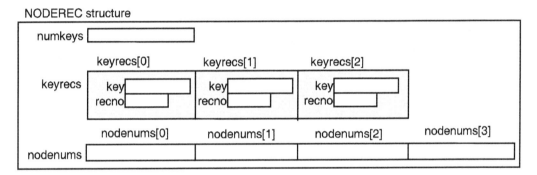

Figure 17-10: NODEREC structure with keyrec and nodenums arrays.

To add a record, the user enters 'a' at the menu prompt that then selects the `add_rec` function. `add_rec` creates the record and calls `writerec` to save it. It then calls `addindex` to add the new key to the b-tree index. `addindex` calls the recursive function `addnode` that locates the right node for the new key, and adds it there. First the function checks to see if it is passed a 0 node number. In this case it creates a new node and add the new key to it. The 0 passed to `addnode` indicates a situation in which the branch node of the first key greater than the new key, is 0, and a new node can then be added as the branch for that key.

If `addnode` receives a non-zero node number it then retrieves that node and searches its list of keys, stopping at the first key greater than the new key. If there is room in the node, then the new key just inserted at that point into the list of keys. If there is no room, then `addnode` is recursively called with that key's branch node number. This is the recursive case. If the first key greater than the new key has no branch, then its node number will be 0 and 0 is then passed on to the recursive call of `addnode`. If, on the other hand, it does have a branch, then that branch node will be retrieved and searched in that recursive call of `addnode`. The run of the program shown here after the listing of the program, adds several keys to the b-tree. Figure 17-11 shows the state of the b-tree after those keys have been added.

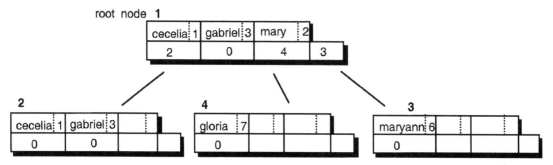

Figure 17-11: B-tree for program in LISTING 17.7-

LISTING 17-7- Program usinG b-tree index
index.h

```
void openindex(char *);
void closeindex(void);
 void print_rec_names (void);
 void printindex(void);
 void addindex(char *, int );
 void delindex(char *);
 void print_index_file(void);
```

emp.h

```
void menu(void);
void construct_emp(char *);
void destruct_emp(void);
void add_rec(void);
void print_emp_file(void);
void print_recs(void);
void del_rec(void);
void print_emp_idxfile(void);
void print_emp_index(void);
```

filedat.h

```
int openfile(char *, int );
void closefile(int );
long readrec(char *,long ,int );
void writerec(char *,long ,int );
long setnextrecno(int fid) ;
long getnextrecno(int fid);
void get_rec(long recno);

#define NAMELEN 100
```

main.c
```c
#include  <stdio.h>
#include "emp.h"

int main( int argc, char *argv[])
                {
                int more = 0;
                char choice[2];

                construct_emp(argv[1]);

                menu();
                while (more == 0)
                        {
                        printf("\n\tPlease enter choice:");
                        scanf("%1s", choice);

                        switch(choice[0])
                                {
                        case 'a':
                                add_rec();
                                break;
                        case 'p':
                                print_recs();
                                break;
                        case 'd':
                                del_rec();
                                break;
                        case 'r':
                                print_emp_file();
                                break;
                        case 'i':
                                print_emp_index();
                                break;
                        case 'x':
                                print_emp_idxfile();
                                break;
                        case 'm':
                                menu();
                                break;
                        case 'q':
                                more = 1;
                                }
                        }

                destruct_emp();
                return 0;
                }

void menu(void)
        {
        printf("\n\tEmployee Records with Index\n\n");
        printf("\ta = Add an employee record\n");
        printf("\tp = Print employee records by name\n");
        printf("\td = Delete employee record in index\n");
        printf("\ti = Print the index nodes only\n");
        printf("\tr = Print record file directly\n");
        printf("\tx = Print the index file directly\n");
        printf("\tq = quit program\n");
        }
```

emp.c

```c
#include <stdio.h>
#include "emp.h"
#include "filedat.h"
#include "index.h"

#define NAMELEN 30

        typedef  struct emp_type {
                char name[30];
                int  id;
                float salary;
                } EMP;

static int fid;

static EMP input_rec(void);
static void output_rec(EMP);


void construct_emp(char *filename)
        {
        fid = openfile(filename, sizeof(EMP));
        openindex(filename);

        }

void destruct_emp(void)
        {
        closefile( fid);
        closeindex();
        }

void add_rec(void)
        {
        EMP emprec;

        emprec = input_rec();
        emprec.id = setnextrecno(fid);
        writerec((char*)&emprec, emprec.id, fid);
        addindex(emprec.name, emprec.id);
        }

EMP input_rec(void)
                {
                EMP in_emp;
                printf("\n\tAdding a New Record\n");
                printf("\n\tPlease enter name: ");
                scanf("%*[\n\t ]%[^\n]s", in_emp.name);
                printf("\tPlease enter salary: ");
                scanf("%f", &in_emp.salary);
                return(in_emp);
                }

void print_recs(void)
                {
                printf("\n\tEmployee Records by Name\n");
                print_rec_names();
                }
```

```
void print_emp_index(void)
            {
            printf("\n\tThe Index by Nodes\n");
            printindex();
            }

void print_emp_idxfile(void)
            {
            printf("\n\tThe Index File\n");
            print_index_file();
            }

void del_rec(void)
        {
        char name[NAMELEN];

        printf("\n\tDeleting an Employee Record\n");
        printf("\n\tPlease enter name for record to be deleted: ");
        scanf("%*[\n\t ]%[^\n]s", name);
        delindex(name);
        }


void get_rec(long recno)
            {
            EMP emprec;

            readrec((char*)&emprec,recno, fid);
            output_rec(emprec);
            }


void output_rec(EMP out_emp)
            {
            printf("\n\t Employee Record \n");
            printf("\t NAME = %s, ID = %d, SALARY = %.2f\n", out_emp.name,
out_emp.id,out_emp.salary);
            /*
            printf("\t NAME   : %s \n", out_emp.name);
            printf("\t ID     : %d \n", out_emp.id);
            printf("\t SALARY : %.2f\n",out_emp.salary);
            */
            }


void print_emp_file(void)
            {
            EMP emprec;
            long i, lastrecno;

            lastrecno = getnextrecno(fid);

            printf("\n\tThe Employee Record File\n");
            for (i = 1; i <= lastrecno ; i++){
                    readrec((char*)&emprec,i, fid);
                    output_rec(emprec);
                    }
            }
```

btree.c
```c
#include <stdio.h>
#include <stdlib.h>
#include <string.h>
#include "filedat.h"
#include "index.h"

#define EXTLEN 4
#define KEYNUM 3
#define KEYLEN 100
#define NODENUMS (KEYNUM + 1)
#define NAMELEN 30


typedef struct key_type {
        char key[KEYLEN];
        long recno;
        } KEYREC;

typedef struct noderec_type {
        int numkeys;
        struct key_type keyrecs[KEYNUM];
        long nodenums[NODENUMS];
        } NODEREC;

 static int indexfid;
 static long root_rec = 0L;

 static void printorder(long);
 static void printnodes(long);
 static long addnode(long, char*, long);
 static long delnode( long nodeno, char *key);


 void openindex(char *filename)
        {
         char iname[NAMELEN + EXTLEN];
         NODEREC node;

        strcpy(iname, filename);
        strcat(iname, ".idx");

        indexfid =  openfile(iname, sizeof(NODEREC));

        if( getnextrecno(indexfid) == 0L)
                root_rec = 0L;
           else
                root_rec = 1L;
        }

 void closeindex(void)
        {
        closefile (indexfid);
        }

  void print_rec_names (void)
        {
        if(root_rec != 0)
                printorder(root_rec);
        }
```

```
static void printorder(long nodeno)
        {
        NODEREC node;
        int i;

        readrec((char*)&node, nodeno, indexfid);

        for(i = 0; i < node.numkeys ; i++)
                {
                if(node.nodenums[i] != 0)
                        printorder(node.nodenums[i] );
                get_rec(node.keyrecs[i].recno);
                }

         if(node.nodenums[i] != 0)
                printorder(node.nodenums[i] );
         }


 void printindex(void)
        {
        if(root_rec != 0)
                printnodes(root_rec);
        }


static void printnodes(long nodeno)
        {
        NODEREC node;
        int i, len;

        readrec((char*)&node,nodeno,indexfid);

        printf("\nNode %ld, Numkeys = %d\n", nodeno, node.numkeys);

        if(node.numkeys != 0)
                {
                printf("Keys & Recnos");

                for(i = 0; i < node.numkeys ; i++)
                        {
                        printf("   %s %-3ld", node.keyrecs[i].key,
node.keyrecs[i].recno);
                        }

                printf("\nNodenums      ");

                for(i = 0; i < node.numkeys ; i++)
                        {
        printf("   %-3ld%*s ", node.nodenums[i], (int) strlen(node.keyrecs[i].key), "
" );
                        }

                printf(" %-3ld\n", node.nodenums[i]);

                for(i = 0; i <= node.numkeys ; i++)
                        {
                        if(node.nodenums[i] != 0)
                                printnodes(node.nodenums[i] );
                        }
                }
```

```
        }

void addindex(char *key, int recno)
        {
        long resno;

        resno = addnode(root_rec, key, recno);
        if(resno == 1)
                root_rec = resno;
        }

static long addnode(long nodeno, char *key, long recno)
        {
        long resno, nextrecno;
        int k,i;
        NODEREC node;

        if(nodeno == 0)
                {
                 node.numkeys = 1;
                 node.nodenums[0] = 0;
                 node.nodenums[1] = 0;
                 node.keyrecs[0].recno = recno;
                 strcpy(node.keyrecs[0].key, key);

                nextrecno = setnextrecno(indexfid);
                writerec((char*)&node,nextrecno, indexfid);
                return nextrecno;
                }
      else
        {
        readrec((char*)&node,nodeno,indexfid);

        for(i = 0; i < node.numkeys && (strcmp( node.keyrecs[i].key, key) < 0) ; i++);


        if( node.numkeys < KEYNUM)  /* If room add into this recnode */
                {
                node.nodenums[node.numkeys + 1] = node.nodenums[node.numkeys];
                if (i < node.numkeys)
                        {
                        for(k = node.numkeys ; k >= i; k--)
                                {
                                node.keyrecs[k] = node.keyrecs[k - 1];
                                node.nodenums[k] = node.nodenums[k - 1];
                                }
                         }

                        node.numkeys++;
                        node.nodenums[i] = 0;
                        node.keyrecs[i].recno = recno;
                        strcpy(node.keyrecs[i].key, key);

                        writerec((char*)&node,nodeno,indexfid);
                         }
                else  /* if no room, go to next level until you find a node with room
*/
                        {
                         resno =  addnode(node.nodenums[i],key,recno);
                         if(resno != 0L)
                                {
```

```
                                node.nodenums[i] = resno;
                                        writerec((char*)&node,nodeno,indexfid);
                                        }
                        }
        return 0L;
         }
        }

  void delindex(char *key)
        {

        printf("Delindex and delete functions needed\n");

        }


void print_index_file(void)
        {
        NODEREC node;
        int i;
        long k, nextrecno;

        nextrecno = getnextrecno(indexfid);

                for (k = 1; k <= nextrecno ; k++)
                {
                readrec((char*)&node,k,indexfid);

                printf("\n\tNode %ld, Numkeys = %d\n", k, node.numkeys);
                printf("\tNodenums    Keys and Record Numbers\n");

                for(i = 0; i < node.numkeys ; i++)
                        {
                        printf("\t  %3ld         ", node.nodenums[i]);
                        printf("%-8s ", node.keyrecs[i].key);
                        printf(" %ld\n", node.keyrecs[i].recno);
                        }
                if(node.numkeys != 0)
                        printf("\t  %3ld\n", node.nodenums[i]);
                }
        }


file.c
#include <stdio.h>
#include <stdlib.h>
#include "filedat.h"
#define FILENUM 10

typedef struct filedat {
                        FILE *fptr;
                        int recsize;
                        long lastrecno;
                        char *fname;
                        int fileid;
                        } FILEDAT;

  static FILEDAT files[FILENUM];

  static int nextfile = 0;
```

```
long getnextrecno(int fid)
        {
        return (files[fid].lastrecno);
        }

long setnextrecno(int fid)
        {
        files[fid].lastrecno++;
        return (files[fid].lastrecno);
        }


int openfile(char *filename,int recsize)
        {
        int fid;

        fid = nextfile;

        if((files[fid].fptr = fopen(filename, "r+b")) != NULL)
                {
                fseek(files[fid].fptr, 0L, SEEK_SET);
                fscanf(files[fid].fptr,"%ld", &files[fid].lastrecno);
                }
        else
                if((files[fid].fptr = fopen(filename, "w+b")) != NULL)
                        {
                        files[fid].lastrecno = 0L;
                        fwrite(" ", 1, recsize, files[fid].fptr);
                        }
                else {
                        printf("file open error\n");
                        exit(1);
                        }

        files[fid].recsize = recsize;
        files[fid].fname = filename;
        nextfile++;

        return fid;
        }

void closefile(int fid)
        {
        fseek(files[fid].fptr,0L, SEEK_SET);
        fprintf(files[fid].fptr,"%ld", files[fid].lastrecno);
        fclose (files[fid].fptr);
        }

void writerec(char *recptr,long recno, int fid)
        {
        fseek(files[fid].fptr, recno * files[fid].recsize , SEEK_SET);
        fwrite(recptr, files[fid].recsize, 1, files[fid].fptr);
        }

long readrec(char *recptr,long recno,int fid)
        {
        long res;
        fseek(files[fid].fptr, recno * files[fid].recsize , SEEK_SET);
        res = fread (recptr, files[fid].recsize, 1, files[fid].fptr);
        return(res);
        }
```

In the run of the b-tree program in LISTING 17-7, the user first adds two records. The name fields of these records are used to create keys for them in the b-tree index. A new record is then added. The key for this new record, gabriel is inserted in the node 1 of the b-tree between cecelia and mary. The user then displays the list of records sorted by name. This operation uses the b-tree index to retrieve the records. The b-tree index itself is then displayed, showing the ordered list of keys in node 1. Then the record file is displayed directly, showing the order in which you entered the records. The record file is not sorted.

Two more records with their respective keys are then added, bonita and carolyn. The nodes in this example have only three keys. Since node 1 is now full, a new node is created. It branches off the first key of the first node, cecelia. cecelia now has a branch node, node 2. The bonita and carolyn keys are placed in node 2. Another record is then added, requiring yet another node. The maryann key comes after the mary key and so its node, node 3, is listed as the last branch node for node 1. Another record is then added whose key, gloria, requires yet another new node, node 4. It becomes the branch node for the mary key.

Run of **btree** program

```
Employee Records with Index

a = Add an employee record
p = Print employee records by name
d = Delete employee record in index
i = Print the index nodes only
r = Print record file directly
x = Print the index file directly
q = quit program

Please enter choice:a

Adding a New Record

Please enter name: cecelia
Please enter salary: 10.35

Please enter choice:a

Adding a New Record

Please enter name: mary
Please enter salary: 9.25

Please enter choice:i

The Index by Nodes

Node 1, Numkeys = 2
Keys & Recnos    cecelia 1      mary 2
Nodenums         0               0          0

Please enter choice:a

Adding a New Record
```

```
        Please enter name: gabriel
        Please enter salary: 183.02

        Please enter choice:p

        Employee Records by Name

         Employee Record
         NAME = cecelia, ID = 1, SALARY = 10.35

         Employee Record
         NAME = gabriel, ID = 3, SALARY = 183.02

         Employee Record
         NAME = mary, ID = 2, SALARY = 9.25

        Please enter choice:i

        The Index by Nodes

Node 1, Numkeys = 3
Keys & Recnos    cecelia 1      gabriel 3      mary 2
Nodenums         0              0              0          0

        Please enter choice:r

        The Employee Record File

         Employee Record
         NAME = cecelia, ID = 1, SALARY = 10.00

         Employee Record
         NAME = mary, ID = 2, SALARY = 9.25

         Employee Record
         NAME = gabriel, ID = 3, SALARY = 183.02

        Please enter choice:a

        Adding a New Record

        Please enter name: bonita
        Please enter salary: 8.17

        Please enter choice:a

        Adding a New Record

        Please enter name: carolyn
        Please enter salary: 7.95

        Please enter choice:i

        The Index by Nodes

Node 1, Numkeys = 3
Keys & Recnos    cecelia 1      gabriel 3      mary 2
Nodenums         2              0              0          0

Node 2, Numkeys = 2
Keys & Recnos    bonita 4       carolyn 5
```

```
Nodenums        0             0             0

        Please enter choice:a

        Adding a New Record

        Please enter name: maryann
        Please enter salary: 7.95

        Please enter choice:i

        The Index by Nodes

Node 1, Numkeys = 3
Keys & Recnos   cecelia 1      gabriel 3      mary 2
Nodenums        2             0             0         3

Node 2, Numkeys = 2
Keys & Recnos   bonita 4      carolyn 5
Nodenums        0             0             0

Node 3, Numkeys = 1
Keys & Recnos   maryann 6
Nodenums        0             0

        Please enter choice:a

        Adding a New Record

        Please enter name: gloria
        Please enter salary: 4.75

        Please enter choice:a

        Please enter choice:i

        The Index by Nodes

Node 1, Numkeys = 3
Keys & Recnos   cecelia 1      gabriel 3      mary 2
Nodenums        2             0             4         3

Node 2, Numkeys = 2
Keys & Recnos   bonita 4      carolyn 5
Nodenums        0             0             0

Node 4, Numkeys = 1
Keys & Recnos   gloria 7
Nodenums        0             0

Node 3, Numkeys = 1
Keys & Recnos   maryann 6
Nodenums        0             0

        Please enter choice:p

        Employee Records by Name

        Employee Record
        NAME = bonita, ID = 4, SALARY = 8.17
```

```
 Employee Record
 NAME = carolyn, ID = 5, SALARY = 7.95

 Employee Record
 NAME = cecelia, ID = 1, SALARY = 10.35

 Employee Record
 NAME = gabriel, ID = 3, SALARY = 183.02

 Employee Record
 NAME = gloria, ID = 7, SALARY = 4.75

 Employee Record
 NAME = mary, ID = 2, SALARY = 9.25

 Employee Record
 NAME = maryann, ID = 6, SALARY = 7.95

Please enter choice:r

The Employee Record File

 Employee Record
 NAME = cecelia, ID = 1, SALARY = 10.35

 Employee Record
 NAME = mary, ID = 2, SALARY = 9.25

 Employee Record
 NAME = gabriel, ID = 3, SALARY = 183.02

 Employee Record
 NAME = bonita, ID = 4, SALARY = 8.17

 Employee Record
 NAME = carolyn, ID = 5, SALARY = 7.95

 Employee Record
 NAME = maryann, ID = 6, SALARY = 7.95

 Employee Record
 NAME = gloria, ID = 7, SALARY = 4.75

Please enter choice:x

The Index File

Node 1, Numkeys = 3
Nodenums     Keys and Record Numbers
     2       cecelia   1
     0       gabriel   3
     4       mary      2
     3

Node 2, Numkeys = 2
Nodenums     Keys and Record Numbers
     0       bonita    4
     0       carolyn   5
     0
```

```
Node 3, Numkeys = 1
Nodenums      Keys and Record Numbers
    0           maryann    6
    0

Node 4, Numkeys = 1
Nodenums      Keys and Record Numbers
    0           gloria     7
    0

Please enter choice:q
```

Deleting Keys in a B-tree

Deleting an index key from an b-tree can follow the same strategy used to delete a node from a search tree. First you search for the key you want to delete, recursively moving from one node to another. Once you have located the key, you then need to check to see if it has a branch. If not, then all you need to do is delete the key. You can do this by simply overwriting the key with the next key, effectively moving the elements of the node's key array back by one. If you locate the key at the 2nd element, you just copy the contents of 3rd element to the 2nd element, overwriting and deleting it. You then copy the 4th element to the third element, and so on until you've moved the entire array back by one element starting from the element where you located the key.

If the key to be deleted has a branch, you will simply replace that key with one from its branch, instead of moving the node array back. The key you use to replace the located key is the one that is the last key in the branch node. You recursively move to the branch node, delete the last key, returning its contents back to your current node. You use the contents of the last key to overwrite and replace the deleted node.

This deletion operation is recursive. If the last key also has a branch node, then you have to recursively move to that branch node and delete its last key, copying it back to the last key in the previous node. You do this until you reach node with a last key that has no branch. You can then just delete that key from its node, and copy it back to the previous node. In other words, if a key has no branch node, then you can just delete it. But if a key has a branch node, you need replace the key with that branch node's last key. Since the last key is being moved up from the branch node to the current node, it needs to be deleted from the branch node. Again the deletion procedure kicks in. If the last key has no branch node you just delete it. If it has a branch node you need to copy the last key from that branch node back up to this one. And so on until you reach a last key that you can just delete, one with no branch nodes.

LISTING 17-8 contains the functions and declarations for deleting a key from the b-tree index. You just need to add them to the **btree.c** file. The `delnode` function is a recursive function that searches for the key to be deleted. First a node is read from the file into the node structure variable. Then its `keyrecs` array is searched for the key to be deleted. If the key is found, then the `delnode` basis case is executed. The basis case deletes the key from the node. If the key is not found, then the recursive case is executed. `delnode` is recursively called, moving to the first node whose key was greater than the deletion key. Recall that the search of the array is a search of an ordered list. The search will stop at the first key that is greater than the search key.

In the basis case, the key is deleted. There are two different ways in which the key is deleted, depending upon whether the key has a branch node. If the key has no branch node, it is just deleted. The node's `keyrecs` and `nodenums` arrays have their elements moved back by one starting from the key to be deleted. That key is overwritten and all other just move back one. The node then has one less key. `numkeys` is decremented by one, `node.numkeys--`.

If the key does have a branch node, then the key is simply replaced by the last key from that branch node. To do this, delnode calls another recursive function called getnode. The getnode function recursively locates the last key in a node. It then deletes that key and returns its contents to its calling function. getnode is recursive. Its basis case is if the last key has no branch node. In this case, the last key is simply deleted and its contents returned. The deletion is simply a matter of decrementing node.numkeys by one, node.numkeys--. The contents of the last key is copied to the krec structure of the lastrec structure. lastrec is then returned to the calling functions.

The recursive case is if the last key has a branch node. Then getnode is recursively called on that branch node. If the last key of that node also has a branch node then it, in turn, is recursively called by getnode. This continues until a node that meets the basis case is reached, a node whose last key does not have a branch node. With the basis case, the recursion begins to unwind. This is an example of a kind of tail recursion. The recursion moves down the b-tree from node to node until it reaches a leaf, a node with no branches. The basis case will return a copy of this leaf node's last key. This last key is returned to the previous recursive function call. This returned last key is assigned to a variable called newrec. The contents of this node's last key is then copied to the lastrec variable. The returned last key held by newrec is then copied to this node's keyrecs array, becoming the last key in this node. The former last key for this node, now held in lastrec, is then returned to its recursive function call. And so on, until the first function call of getnode in delnode is reached. Here the returned last key is used to overwrite the key to be deleted.

In the deletion process, empty nodes also need to be removed. Both delnode and getnode test for empty nodes. An empty node will have its branch entry deleted from the key that references it in the its parent node. delnode simply returns a -1 to indicate an empty node. getnode needs to return both the last key contents and a flag indicating whether the current node is empty or not. For this reason, getnode returns a LASTKEY structure that contains the integer nkeys and a KEYREC structure called krec. If, when returned, nkeys is 0, then a node knows that the branch node is empty and can delete the branch's node number entry from the nodenums arrays.

LISTING 17-8:

Delete functions and prototypes to be added to btree.c

```
typedef struct last_type {
    KEYREC krec;
    int nkeys;
    } LASTKEY;

static struct last_type getnode(long nodeno);
static long delnode(long nodeno, char *key);

void delindex(char *key)
    {
    long resno;

    resno = delnode(root_rec, key);
    if(resno == 1)
            printf("\tRecord deleted\n");
    else
            if(resno == 0L)
                {
                printf ("\tRecord not found \n");
                }
    }
```

```
static long delnode( long nodeno, char *key)
      {
      long resno;
      int k,i;
      NODEREC node;
      LASTKEY newrec;
      int empty = 0;

      if(nodeno == 0)
            {
            return 0L;
            }
      else
            {
            readrec((char*)&node,nodeno, indexfid);

      for(i = 0; i < node.numkeys && (strcmp( node.keyrecs[i].key, key) < 0) ; i++);

            if (strcmp(node.keyrecs[i].key, key) == 0)
                  {                         /* Basis Case */
                  if(node.nodenums[i] == 0)
                        {                   /* if no branch, just delete */
                        node.numkeys--;
                        for( ; i < (node.numkeys) ; i++)
                              {
                              node.keyrecs[i] = node.keyrecs[i + 1];
                              node.nodenums[i] = node.nodenums[i + 1];
                              }
                  node.nodenums[node.numkeys] = node.nodenums[node.numkeys + 1];
                        }
                  else        /* if branch node, replace */
                        {
                        newrec = getnode( node.nodenums[i]);
                        node.keyrecs[i] = newrec.krec;
                        if(newrec.nkeys == 0)
                            node.nodenums[i] = 0;
                        }

                  writerec((char*)&node,nodeno, indexfid);
                  if(node.numkeys == 0)
                        return -1L;
                    else
                        return 1L;
                  }
                  else  /* Recursive Case */
                        {                   /* if not found check next node */
                        resno =  delnode(node.nodenums[i],key);
                        if(resno == -1L)
                              {
                              node.nodenums[i] = 0;
                              writerec((char*)&node,nodeno, indexfid);
                              resno = 1L;
                              }
                        return resno;
                        }
            }
      }
```

```
static struct last_type getnode(long nodeno)
        {
        NODEREC node;
        LASTKEY lastrec;
        LASTKEY newrec;

        readrec((char*)&node,nodeno,indexfid);

        lastrec.krec = node.keyrecs[node.numkeys - 1];
        lastrec.nkeys = node.numkeys;

        if(node.nodenums[node.numkeys - 1] == 0)
                {
                node.numkeys--;
                node.nodenums[node.numkeys] = node.nodenums[node.numkeys + 1];
                writerec((char*)&node,nodeno,indexfid);
                lastrec.nkeys--;
                return(lastrec);
                }
        else
                {
                newrec = getnode(node.nodenums[node.numkeys - 1]);
                node.keyrecs[node.numkeys - 1] = newrec.krec;

                if(newrec.nkeys == 0)
                        node.nodenums[node.numkeys - 1] = 0;
                writerec((char*)&node,nodeno,indexfid);
                return(lastrec);
                }

        }
```

In the run of the btree program with the delete operation, the user first deletes bonita key. This involves a simple deletion operation. The bonita key has no branch node. It is simply deleted by moving the array for the node 2 back by one. Then the mary key is deleted. This involves a more complex deletion process. The mary key has a branch node, node 4. The last key for node 4 is ken. getnode will locate and copy this last key copied back up to node 1. Then the key augustine is deleted. augustine has as its branch, node 5. The last key in branch 5, antionette, is used to replace augustine. Finally, the gloria key is deleted. This is the last key in the 4th node. This fact is returned to node 1, for which the 4th node is a branch. The node 4 entry as the branch for the ken key is then removed, deleting 4 from node 1's list of nodenums.

Run of **btree** with delete operations

```
        Employee Records with Index

        a = Add an employee record
        p = Print employee records by name
        d = Delete employee record in index
        i = Print the index nodes only
        r = Print record file directly
        x = Print the index file directly
        q = quit program

        Please enter choice:i

        The Index by Nodes

Node 1, Numkeys = 3
Keys & Recnos    cecelia 1      gabriel 3     mary 2
Nodenums         2              0             4         3

Node 2, Numkeys = 3
Keys & Recnos    augustine 9     bonita 4      carolyn 5
Nodenums         5               0             0           0

Node 5, Numkeys = 1
Keys & Recnos    antoinette 10
Nodenums         0              0

Node 4, Numkeys = 2
Keys & Recnos    gloria 7     ken 8
Nodenums         0            0        0

Node 3, Numkeys = 1
Keys & Recnos    maryann 6
Nodenums         0              0

        Please enter choice:d

        Deleting an Employee Record

      Please enter name for record to be deleted: bonita
      Record deleted

        Please enter choice:i

        The Index by Nodes

Node 1, Numkeys = 3
Keys & Recnos    cecelia 1      gabriel 3     mary 2
Nodenums         2              0             4         3

Node 2, Numkeys = 2
Keys & Recnos    augustine 9     carolyn 5
Nodenums         5               0             0

Node 5, Numkeys = 1
Keys & Recnos    antoinette 10
Nodenums         0              0

Node 4, Numkeys = 2
Keys & Recnos    gloria 7     ken 8
```

```
Nodenums          0              0          0

Node 3, Numkeys = 1
Keys & Recnos    maryann 6
Nodenums          0              0
```

        Please enter choice:**d**

        Deleting an Employee Record

        Please enter name for record to be deleted: **mary**
        Record deleted

        Please enter choice:**i**

        The Index by Nodes

```
Node 1, Numkeys = 3
Keys & Recnos    cecelia 1      gabriel 3      ken 8
Nodenums          2              0              4          3

Node 2, Numkeys = 2
Keys & Recnos    augustine 9    carolyn 5
Nodenums          5              0              0

Node 5, Numkeys = 1
Keys & Recnos    antoinette 10
Nodenums          0              0

Node 4, Numkeys = 1
Keys & Recnos    gloria 7
Nodenums          0              0

Node 3, Numkeys = 1
Keys & Recnos    maryann 6
Nodenums          0              0
```

        Please enter choice:**d**

        Deleting an Employee Record

        Please enter name for record to be deleted: **augustine**
        Record deleted

        Please enter choice:**i**

        The Index by Nodes

```
Node 1, Numkeys = 3
Keys & Recnos    cecelia 1      gabriel 3      ken 8
Nodenums          2              0              4          3

Node 2, Numkeys = 2
Keys & Recnos    antoinette 10  carolyn 5
Nodenums          0              0              0

Node 4, Numkeys = 1
Keys & Recnos    gloria 7
Nodenums          0              0

Node 3, Numkeys = 1
```

```
Keys & Recnos    maryann 6
Nodenums            0              0

        Please enter choice:d

        Deleting an Employee Record

        Please enter name for record to be deleted: gloria
        Record deleted

        Please enter choice:i

        The Index by Nodes

Node 1, Numkeys = 3
Keys & Recnos    cecelia 1       gabriel 3       ken 8
Nodenums            2               0               0           3

Node 2, Numkeys = 2
Keys & Recnos    antoinette 10      carolyn 5
Nodenums            0               0               0

Node 3, Numkeys = 1
Keys & Recnos    maryann 6
Nodenums            0              0

        Please enter choice:q
```

Table 17-1: Record File Functions

```
size_t fread(void* p, size_t n, size_t r, FILE *fp)
```
Read data without conversion from a file into a block of bytes. n is the   number of bytes read and r is the repeat factor. p is a pointer that   references the block.

```
size_t fwrite(void* p, size_t, size_t, FILE *fp)
```
Write data without conversion from a block of bytes into a file. n is the   number of bytes written and r is the repeat factor. p is a pointer that   references the block.

```
int fseek(FILE *fp, long n, int origin)
```
Set the file position indicator to a specific byte offset in a file. The three points of origin are SEEK_SET, SEEK_END, SEEK_CUR. A non-zero value is returned if an error occurs.

```
long ftell(FILE *fp)
```
Returns the byte offset of the current file position or a -1L on an error.

```
void rewind(FILE *fp)
```
Reset file position indicator to the beginning of the file

```
int fgetpos(FILE *fp, fpos_t *p)
```
Records a file offset position in the fpos_t argument

```
int fsetpos(FILE *fp, const fpos_t *p)
```
Sets the file position to that recorded in the fpos_t argument.

Chapter Summary: Record Files

Records are implemented as structures in C. Structures are written and read to and from files using `fread` and `fwrite`. Both `fread` and `fwrite` are designed to work on binary files. `fwrite` writes a block of bytes to a file, bit by bit. `fread` reads a block of bytes from a file, bit by bit. `fread` and `fwrite` take as their arguments both the address of the block of bytes and the number of bytes in the block. Using the address operator and the `sizeof` operator allows a structure variable to be treated as a block. `fwrite` can write the bytes that make up a structure variable to a file, bit by bit.

`fread` and `fwrite` , by themselves, implement a record-sequential file structure. Together with `fseek`, they implement a random access file. With `fseek`, any byte offset in a file can be referenced. `fseek` can offset from the beginning of the file, the end of the file, or the current file position. Records in a record file are placed sequentially. The position of a record in a record file is referred to as the record number. The byte offset of a particular record in a file can be calculated by multiplying the record number by the size of the record. The file functions commonly used to implement record files are listed in Table 17-1.

A common file management strategy reserves a part of the file for database information. Another strategy places all the file functions within access functions that are defined within their own source code files. The file pointer is declared as a static external variable known only to these access functions. This hides the lower-level file operations from the rest of the program, as well as protects important data, such as the file pointer.

You can use a b-tree to index and access data in a record file. A b-tree is essentially search tree implemented in its own record file. You use recursive procedures to add, search, and a delete keys from your b-tree index. b-trees are powerful and efficient. In accessing just a few nodes you can effectively search large indexes. Managing b-trees is a complex process. Only a simplified version is presented here.

Exercises

1. Write a program to copy one record file to another record file. The record file uses a structure of the type described below. Open both files, one for reading and one for writing. In a loop, read a record from the original file and write the record to the copy file. Continue the loop until all the records in the original file have been read. Use `argv` arguments to get the file names from the user. `argv[1]` will be the name of the original file. `argv[2]` will be the name of the copy file.

```
1. name      20 characters.
2. id int
3. salary    double
```

2. Add both a find function and an update function to the program in LISTING 17-6.

3. Add functions to create a search tree index for the program in LISTING 17-6. The index will use the name field as a key. Instead of an array offset, the recno will be a file offset.

4. Add functions to search for a record in the program in LISTING 17-7. Also add a function to print out the records in the index file.

5. Modify the program in LISTING 17-7 to allow you to create several different indexes on the employee file using different keys: one for the name, another for the id, and one for the salary. How could you deal with duplicate keys?

System Calls
and
Stream I/O

System Calls

Stream I/O File Interface

File Functions and I/O

18. System Calls and Stream IO

The C programming language implements its own interface for accessing files. Whenever you compile a C program that uses files, your compiler will create a stream I/O file interface consisting of FILE structures, buffers, and system calls. The same stream I/O file interface is used for input/output functions such as `scanf` and `getchar`, as well as for user-designated files. This interface, in turn, makes calls to functions that interact directly with your operating system, actually reading, writing or opening files. Such functions are referred to as system calls. This chapter will closely examine system calls, the stream I/O file interface, and the implementation of the input/output functions.

System Calls

System calls are a small, restricted set of functions whose only purpose is to obtain data from a file. System calls are not standard to the C language. They may vary from one operating system to another. The original set of system calls discussed here was designed for the UNIX operating system. Many other systems have adopted the same names and syntax, with minor variations. The prototypes for system calls can usually be found in the header file **syscalls.h**.

There are six major system calls used to manage files: `open`, `close`, `creat`, `read`, `write`, and `lseek`. A file is opened with the `open` system call and closed with the `close` system call. `open` and `fopen` return two very different values. `open` returns the actual file descriptor assigned to the file by the operating system. The file descriptor is an integer that physically identifies the file. `fopen`, on the other hand, returns a pointer to a structure variable of type FILE. Within that structure are many variables used to manage access to the file, one of which is the file descriptor. In fact, `fopen` obtains the file descriptor from a call to `open`.

`open` takes three arguments: a filename, a file mode, and a permission. The permission is system dependent and is often 0. The `open` system call can open a file in a read, write, or update mode. The modes are represented by a symbolic constant that operates like a mask. The actual names for the symbolic constants may vary from system to system. The following are the UNIX symbolic constants for file modes:

`O_RDONLY`	read only
`O_WRONLY`	write only
`O_RDWR`	read and write

There are three system calls used to access a file: `read`, `write`, and `lseek`. Data is accessed in blocks. The `read` system call reads a block of bytes from a file, much like `fread`. `write` writes a block of bytes to a file, much like `fwrite`. `lseek` positions the file position indicator at a particular byte in the file. This is where the block will be either written or read by `write` or `read`. `lseek` operates very much like `fseek`.

`read` and `write` take three arguments: the file descriptor, the address of the block, and the number of bytes in the block to be read or written. Both the address of the block and the number of bytes are the same as the address and number arguments used for `fread` and `fwrite`. `lseek`, like `fseek`, takes three arguments: the file descriptor, the offset, and the point of origin. Both the offset and the point of origin arguments are the same as those in `fseek`. The syntax, prototype, and example for each are listed here.

```
read(file descriptor, address of block, number of bytes read);
int read(int, char*, int);
read(file id, &employee, sizeof(EMP));

write(file descriptor, address of block, number of bytes read);
int write(int, char*, int);
write(file id, &employee, sizeof(EMP));

lseek(file descriptor, byte offset, origin);
long lseek(int, long, int);
lseek(file id, (long) 1 * sizeof(EMP), 0);
```

In the next example, the myfile file is opened for writing. `lseek` moves the file position indicator to byte 245, and then `fwrite` writes the values of the mynums array as a block of 10 bytes. `close` then closes the file.

```
char mynums[5]={1,2,3,4,5};
int filed;

filed = open("myfile", O_WRONLY);

lseek(filed, 245L, SEEK_SET);
fwrite(filed, mynums, 5* sizeof(int));

close(filed);
```

The `open` system call will only open a file if it already exists. If the file does not exist, the system call fails. To create a new file, you need to use a different system call, `creat`. The `creat` function call takes as its arguments a file name and a permissions argument. The permissions argument is system-dependent. In UNIX, it is used to specify the permissions to be set up for the file. In other systems it may simply indicate an initial file mode. In the next example, the user creates a file, opening it with a write only permission.

```
creat("myfile", O_WRONLY);
```

Both `open` and `creat` return a -1 if they fail. You can use their return values to test to see if one or the other fails, allowing you to open a file if it already exists, or to create it if it does not yet exist. Should the file creation fail for some reason, you would then want to exit the program. The next example combines `open` and `creat` into a nested if statement in which the result of `open` is tested to see if the file exists. If not, then `creat` is called to create the file. Should that fail then the program exits with an error message. Notice how the result of `open` and `creat` are first assigned to filed, the integer file descriptor. Then the value of filed is tested to see if a -1 as returned.

```
if((filed = open("myfile", O_WRONLY)) == -1)
        {
        if((filed = creat("myfile", 0311)) == -1)
                printf("File could not be opened\n");
        }
```

There are times when you may find it preferable to use system calls instead of the stream I/O file functions. For example, you could use the system calls by themselves to implement a random access file. Since there is no buffer to manage, speed can be increased. Also, for stream I/O functions, file management problems can arise if the buffer is not written quickly enough. System calls operate directly on the file, immediately writing data.

In the **randsys.c** program in LISTING 18-1, the random access program from Chapter 17 (LISTING 17-6) has been rewritten using system calls instead of stream I/O file functions. With system calls there is not the easy interchange that stream I/O file functions enjoy. Whereas fscanf and fread can be used easily on the same file and can access that file in radically different ways, a file managed by system calls can only be read as block data using the read system call.

LISTING 18-1:

randsys.c

```c
#include <stdio.h>
#include <stdlib.h>
#include <fcntl.h>
#include <io.h>

typedef struct {
            char name[10];
            long id;
            float salary;
            }       EMP;

long addrecord(int ,long);
void printrecs(int);
void menu(void);

int main(void)
      {
      int filed;
      char buff[sizeof(EMP)];
      long lastrecord;
      int more = 1;
      char choice[2];

      if((filed = open("myfile", O_RDWR | O_BINARY)) > 0)
            {
            read(filed, buff, sizeof(EMP));
            sscanf(buff, "%ld", &lastrecord );
            }
            else
            if((filed = creat("myfile", 0311)) > 0)
                  {
                  lastrecord = 0;
                  write(filed, buff, sizeof(EMP));
                  }
                  else {
                        printf("File not be opened\n");
                        exit(1);
                        }
```

```
        while (more)
               {
               printf("Please enter choice:");
               scanf("%1s", choice);

               switch(choice[0])
                      {
               case 'a':
                      lastrecord=addrecord(filed,lastrecord);
                      break;
               case 'p':
                      printrecs(filed);
                      break;
               case 'q':
                      more = 0;
                      break;
                      }
               }
        lseek(filed, 0L, SEEK_SET);
        sprintf(buff, "%ld", lastrecord);
        write(filed,buff, sizeof(long) );
        close(filed);
        return 0;
        }

long addrecord(int filed,long nextrecord)
        {
        EMP employee;

        printf ("Please enter name and salary: ");
        scanf("%s%f", &employee.name,&employee.salary);
        nextrecord++;
        employee.id = nextrecord;
        lseek(filed, nextrecord * sizeof(EMP), SEEK_SET);
        write(filed, &employee, sizeof(EMP)) ;
        return(nextrecord);
        }

void printrecs (int filed)
        {
        EMP employee;

        lseek(filed,1L * sizeof(EMP), SEEK_SET);
        while(read(filed, &employee, sizeof(EMP)) > 0)
               {
               printf("Name is  : %s\n", employee.name);
               printf("Id is    : %ld\n", employee.id);
               printf("Salary is: %.2f\n", employee.salary);
               }
        }
```

In the version of the program in Chapter 17, the value of lastrecno was treated as formatted data and saved to the file using `fprintf` and `fscanf`. There is a great deal of difference between system calls and formatted file functions such as `fprintf`. In order to save formatted data to a file managed by system calls, the formatted data must first be transformed into block data. The function `sprintf` performs this task. `sprintf` operates in the same way as `fprintf`. It formats specified values into equivalent character values. Instead of writing these characters to a file, `sprintf` copies them into a character array. The character array can then be treated like a block and written to the file with the `write` system call. `sscanf` works like `fscanf`. `sscanf` reads data from a character array and formats it into the specified variable values. The characters in the character array itself can be read initially as a block from the file using `read`.

Stream I/O File Interface

When you open a file in a C program, a stream I/O file interface is set up to allow you to reference the file as stream of bytes. This stream I/O interface consists of a buffer and a structure of variables, the `FILE` structure, used to manage this buffer. When you read data from a file, the data is first read into this buffer from the file, and then the program copies the data from the buffer. In effect, your program never directly accesses a file. It only accesses the file buffer.

When `fopen` opens a file, it allocates a structure of type `FILE` containing variables with which to manage the file. One of those variables is a pointer to a character. It is used to reference a buffer. When the file is first accessed, a buffer is allocated that will hold bytes to be read or written to the file. Such file buffers are all managed by variables in structures of type `FILE`. Shown here is the structure type declaration for a FILE structure. It is located in the **stdio.h** file. The actual names of the variables in the structure may vary from system to system. In this example, _fid is the file descriptor provided by a call to `open`; _flag is the file mode the file was opened with; _buf is pointer that holds address of the character array used for the buffer; _ptr is a working pointer that advances down the array, character by character; _cnt is the count of characters not yet referenced (read) by _ptr.

```
typedef struct _iobuf{
        int _cnt;       /*count of characters left in _buf */
        char *_ptr;     /*pointer to next char to be read */
        char *_buf;     /*address of  buf*/
        int _flag;      /*read/write/update file permission*/
        int _fid;       /*O/S file id of the physical file */
        } FILE;
```

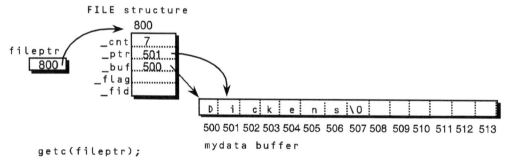

getc(fileptr);

Figure 18.1: FILE structure and file buffer-

The address of the allocated buffer for the file is assigned to the character pointer _buf in the FILE structure. The buffer is treated as an array of bytes, as shown in Figure 18-1. The pointer _ptr is moved along the array as bytes are accessed. _cnt is a count of the remaining unaccessed bytes in the array. When all the bytes have been accessed, a call goes out to a read system call to read in more bytes from the file into the array. Bytes are then accessed again from the beginning of the array.

This setup has several advantages. A file can be referenced byte by byte, without having to access the physical file for each byte. When a file is read sequentially, the only time it actually needs to be accessed is when the buffer needs refilling. The standard stream size of a buffer is 512 bytes. If a 1,000-byte file is read 10 bytes at a time, the file is only physically accessed 2 times, instead of 100.

In some systems the standard buffer size may be larger. You can even set the size yourself. With the function setvbuf you can make a file buffer larger or smaller. A larger buffer would reduce the number of actual file accesses. A buffer could also be tailored to the size of a record. setvbuf also allows you to use a different buffer instead of the one allocated for the file by the system.

There are also different ways in which you can have data read into your buffer. You can read data in a block at a time, as normally done, or you can read data in a line at a time. You can even specify no buffering at all, reading directly from the file. The way in which you read a buffer is referred to as the buffer mode. You set a buffer mode using the same setvbuf function that you use for setting the size of the buffer. There are three buffer modes: _IOFBF, _IONBF, and _IOLBF. The _IOFBF mode specifies the normal full buffering. The _IONBF mode specifies no buffering. Input and output access the file directly. The _IOLBF mode specifies line buffering. Input is read in one line at a time, and output is written one line at a time. This happens to be the default buffering for keyboard input. Buffers;

setvbuf takes four arguments: the file pointer, the address of a buffer, the buffer mode, and the size of the buffer. When changing only the buffer size, the buffer argument is NULL. The setvbuf function is called after the file is opened and before any other file functions operate on the file. The syntax, declaration, and example for setvbuf and setbuf are listed here.

```
setvbuf(file pointer, address of buffer, buffer mode, size of buffer);
int setvbuf(FILE*, char*, int, int);
setvbuf(fileptr, mybuff, _IOFBF, 1000);
```

In the next example, the buffer for fileptr is enlarged to 5,000 bytes. The buffer for myfptr is set to the mybuf array.

```
char mybuf[200]
FILE *fileptr, *myfptr;

fileptr = fopen("newfile", "r");
setvbuf(fileptr, NULL, _IOFBF, 5000);
myfptr = fopen("myfile", "r");
setvbuf(myfptr, mybuf, _IOFBF, 200);
```

User-defined File Functions

The stream I/O file functions do not directly access a file. Instead, they access a buffer. The buffer is, in turn, fed by lower-level system calls that directly access the file. For example, the code for fopen has a system call for open. The code for getc has a system call for read. You can write your own version of a stream I/O file function within which you can then place system calls. For example, you could write your own version of getc using the read system call. But you cannot write your own version of a system call. A system call such as read is really part of the operating system. It is not part of C.

The function `getc` is a typical example of such a file interface. `getc` reads a single character from a file. A stripped-down version of `getc` looks like this:

```
int getc(FILE *fileptr)
        {
        int nextchar;
        if (fileptr->_cnt < 0)
                {
                if(read(fileptr->_fid,fileptr->_buf,512))
                        return(EOF);
                fileptr->_cnt = 512;
                fileptr->_ptr = fileptr->_buf;
                }
        nextchar = *fileptr->_ptr;
        fileptr->_ptr++;
        fileptr->_cnt--;
        return(nextchar);
        }
```

`getc` is a basic operation that is often incorporated into other file functions. You could even design your own file functions that simply calls `getc` at some point. The following is a user-defined version of `fgets` that simply issues repeated calls to `getc`.

```
int fgets (char *buffer, int num, FILE *fileptr)
        {
        int i;

        for(i=0; (i < num) && (buffer[i] != '\n'); i++)
                        buffer[i] = getc(fileptr);
        i++;
        buffer[i] = '\0';
        }
```

If a file is opened for writing, the buffer is treated as a write buffer. Data to be written to a file is first assigned, byte by byte, to the buffer. The `FILE` structure variable `_cnt` keeps track of how many bytes have been filled. Only when the buffer is full is the data actually written to the file. Bytes are not actually placed into the file until the buffer is written. The basic function for writing to files is the `putc` function. A stripped-down version of `putc` follows.

```
int putc(FILE *fileptr, char newchar)
            {
            if (fileptr->_cnt > 512){
                    write(fileptr->_fid,fileptr->_buf,512);
                    fileptr->_cnt = 0;
                    fileptr->_ptr = fileptr->_buf;
                    }
            *fileptr->_ptr = newchar;
            fileptr->_ptr++;
            fileptr->_cnt++;
            return(newchar);
            }
```

Just as input file functions can be defined using `getc`, output file functions can be defined using `putc`. Below is a simplified example of `fputs`:

```
int fputs (char *buffer,FILE *fileptr)
            {
            int i;

            for (i = 0; buffer[i] != '\0'; i++)
                    putc(buffer[i], fileptr);
            }
```

Program design constraints may require that a file be actually written to without waiting for the write buffer to fill up. The writing of the buffer to the file is called "flushing the buffer." The function `fflush` is used to flush the buffer, forcing the data to be written to the file. Here is a simplified form of `fflush`.

```
int fflush(FILE *fptr)
            {
            write(fptr->_fid,fptr->_buf,fptr->_cnt);
            fptr->_cnt = 0;
            fptr->_ptr = fptr->_buf;
            }
```

With `fseek`, the situation becomes more complicated because the file is no longer being read sequentially. `fseek` will force a reset of the buffer each time it is executed. If a file is being read at the time of an `fseek`, its buffer will be cleared, leaving it empty for the next `read`. If the file is being written, its buffer will be flushed to the file.

When a file is opened for update, the situation becomes confusing. With update, the same buffer is being used for both reading and writing. A problem arises when an `fread` is called right after an `fwrite`, without flushing the buffer in between. When an `fread` follows an `fwrite`, data in the buffer that has not yet been written is lost. The buffer needs to be flushed to the file before an `fread` executes. The buffer can be flushed by either a call to the function `fflush` or by a call to `fseek`. When the file position indicator is re-positioned, the buffer is automatically flushed. The subsequent `read` or `write` function will then begin work with an empty buffer.

File Functions and Input/Output

For every file function there is a corresponding input/output function: `fscanf` and `scanf`, `fgets` and `gets`, `getc` and `getchar`, and so on. This is no coincidence. The input/output functions are really file functions. They have exactly the same kind of interface. The only difference is that they reference devices instead of files. The input functions take their input from the keyboard rather than a file. Output functions write their output to the screen, rather than to a file. But this is the only difference. In all other respects, input/output functions are file functions.

This may seem odd since the input/output functions are never explicitly opened by the programmer. Yet the files for input and output are set up with `FILE` structures and buffers. To understand how this can be done, you have to take a look at how the `FILE` structures for file functions are defined. An array of `FILE` structures is declared in **stdio.h**. In UNIX, the array is named _iob. This array is of a fixed size, usually 20 elements. This means that the user can have no more than 20 files open at the same time. By convention, the first two structure elements are reserved for the input/output functions. The first element, 0, is the `FILE` structure for all input functions. The second element, 1, is the `FILE` structure for all output functions. The third element, 2, is reserved for error output. The first file opened by `fopen` will then take the fourth element, 3, for its `FILE` structure. The next will take the fifth element, 4, and so on.

When `fopen` opens a file, it then returns the address of a `FILE` structure. The first file opened will be the fourth element, 3. The address returned will be the address of this structure, in this case `&_iob[3]`. Since it is already known that input functions will use the first element, `_iob[0]`, the address of the `FILE` structure for the input functions will always be the address of the first structure element, `&_iob[0]`. Stream file functions can then be used on this FILE structure.

```
fscanf(&_iob[0], "%d", &count);
getc(&_iob[0]);
```

In **stdio.h**, the addresses of the first three FILE structure elements are defined as the symbolic constants `stdin`, `stdout`, and `stderr`. Those symbolic constants can then be used in the file functions. The next example shows a common definition of these symbolic constants that you will find in your **stdio.h** file. See if you can locate this file on your system and examine its define operations.

```
#define stdin    (&_iob[0])
#define stdout   (&_iob[1])
#define stderr   (&_iob[2])
```

Next are some examples of how you could use these symbolic constants in some common file functions.

```
fscanf(stdin, "%d", &count);
getc(stdin);
putc(stdout, 'A');
```

As a further convenience, all file function operations dealing with input and output are defined as input and output macros. In this sense, there are few real input and output functions as such. There are input and output macros which expand to file functions that use `stdin` or `stdout`. Examples of the more common input and output define macros follow. All are listed in your **stdio.h** file.

```
#define getchar()    getc(stdin)
#define putchar()    putc(stdout)
#define scanf(x,y)   fscanf(stdin, x, y)
```

Buffered Input and Newlines

Now that you have seen the interface for input and output functions, you can come to better understand how they operate, particularly how they respond when input and output errors occur. Many of the difficulties that you may encounter with input or output functions are affected by the fact the file interface is buffered. Though, input and output operations may be buffered or unbuffered, for most systems buffered I/O is the default. Unbuffered input is take directly into the program. Buffered input is first placed in a buffer, and then the data is then read from that buffer.

Buffered input reads data in one line at a time. Both input and output operations are usually line buffered by default. When a user types characters on the keyboard, the characters are copied into the `stdin` buffer until the user presses the ENTER key inputting a newline. The newline character is also copied into the buffer. Input file functions then work on the characters in the buffer. Only when all the characters in the buffer are disposed of will new input be accessed from the keyboard.

LISTING 18-2:

getnames.c

```
#include <stdio.h>

int main(void)
              {
              char first[40];
              char last[40];

              printf("Please enter first name:");
              scanf("%s", first);
              printf("Please enter last name:");
              gets(last);
              return 0;
              }
```

Output of LISTING 18-2.

```
Please enter first name: Charles
Please enter last name:
```

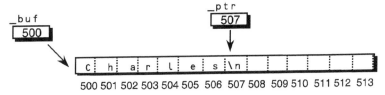

Figure 18.2: Input buffer and the position of the _ptr after the first scanf-

 Problems arise from the different ways in which file functions access this input. A classic problem is that of the dangling newline that results from mixing scanf and gets. In the **getnames.c** program in LISTING 18-2, the gets function obtains no input. When the program is run, the user is not even given the option to enter anything. The second prompt is just skipped. See the illustration of the input buffer after the first scanf in Figure 18-2, and the output of LISTING 18-2.

 Remember that, in the case of buffered I/O, the input functions do not access the keyboard directly. They only access the stdin FILE buffer. If there are any characters at all in the stdin file buffer, they will access those rather than read new characters from the keyboard. Recall also scanf always stops at a white space: a space, tab, or newline. In this case scanf stops at the newline. The buffer pointer does not retrieve the newline, leaving it in the input buffer.

 At this point, there is one more character left in the stdin buffer: the newline. gets then accesses stdin and finds a character already in the buffer, a newline. It takes the newline and has thus completed its job, since gets reads all characters until and including the newline. Finished, there is no need to get new characters from the keyboard. The user never has a chance to enter in the last name.

 If the subsequent input function was scanf instead of gets, there would be no problem. scanf retrieves and tosses away any initial white spaces. The newline would be tossed aside. scanf would then require new input, and stdin would have to go to the keyboard to get it, allowing the user to enter in the last name.

Flushing Buffered Input

Odd things can happen with your input, depending on what you type in. In the program in LISTING 18-3, the user typed in both the first and last name on the same line. Again, the second prompt will be skipped. But last will get the last name of Dickens, as shown in the **namescan.c** program in Figure 18-3.

The first scanf will stop at the white space at the end of "Charles." This is a space. The second scanf, seeing data already in the stdin buffer, will retrieve characters until it reaches a white space, reading in "Dickens." Since no characters were needed from the keyboard, the user has no chance to enter anything in at the last name prompt.

LISTING 18-3:

namescan.c

```c
#include <stdio.h>

int main(void)
        {
        char first[40];
        char last[40];

        printf("Please enter first name: ");
        scanf("%s", first);
        printf("Please enter last name: ");
        scanf("%s", last);
        return 0;
        }
```

Output of LISTING 18-3:

```
Please enter first name: Charles Dickens
Please enter last name:
```

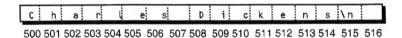

500 501 502 503 504 505 506 507 508 509 510 511 512 513 514 515 516

Figure 18.3: Input buffer and white spaces-

The problem here can be seen as one of flushing the stdin buffer. How do you get rid of extra input? One method is to use a loop to read any remaining characters from the input buffer, thus emptying it out. The while loop after each scanf in the **namflush.c** program in LISTING 18-4, will continue retrieving characters from the stdin buffer until and including the newline. Since the newline is always the end of the data, the buffer is flushed. Note that there is a null statement at end of the while loop's test expression:

```c
while (getchar() != '\n');
```

This flushing of the `stdin` buffer can also be accomplished with a `scanf`. The following statement first retrieves and skips over all characters until the newline using the brackets conversion specifier and the field skipper, `%*[^\n]`. Then it skips over the newline character with the character conversion specifier and again the field skipper, `%*c`.

```
scanf("%*[^\n]%*c");
```

LISTING 18-4:

namflush.c
```
#include <stdio.h>

int main(void)
        {
        char first[40];
        char last[40];

        printf("Please enter first name: ");
        scanf("%s", first);
        while (getchar() != '\n');
        printf("Please enter last name: ");
        scanf("%s", last);
        while (getchar() != '\n');
        return 0;
        }
```

Output of LISTING 18-4:

```
Please enter first name: Charles
Please enter last name: Dickens
```

Single Character Input

The problem of the dangling newline becomes a real aggravation when attempting simply to input a single character. The `%c` cannot be used in `scanf` to retrieve the input of a single character because white spaces are considered characters. The `%c` recognizes no delimiters. White spaces will not be skipped over. They will be retrieved just like any other character.

In the **getleter.c** program in LISTING 18-5, the user, in order to enter the single letter B, has actually entered two characters, B and the newline, \n. The first `scanf` retrieves the B for `firstletter`, but the second `scanf`, seeing remaining input, \n, in the `stdin` buffer takes the newline as its character.

Because it does not recognize delimiters, `%c` is a rare and dangerous format specifier. A safer technique treats the single character entry as if it were a string one character long. This way the string format symbol, %s, can be used. To guarantee that only one character is read in, a quantitative constraint can be placed on the string symbol, `%1s`, as shown in the **leterstr.c** program in LISTING 18-6. Instead of using a character variable for input, an array of two characters is used. One element is for the single character entry, the other is for the null character indicating the end of the string. By accessing the first element of the array, you can access the single character entry.

LISTING 18-5:

getleter.c

```
#include <stdio.h>

int main(void)
        {
        char firstletter, secondletter;

        printf("Please enter first letter: ");
        scanf("%c", &firstletter);
        printf("Please enter second letter: ");
        scanf("%c", &secondletter);
        return 0;
        }
```

Output of LISTING 18-5:

```
        Please enter first letter: B
        Please enter second letter:
```

LISTING 18-6:

leterstr.c

```
#include <stdio.h>

int main(void)
                {
                char firstletter, secondletter;
                char response[2];

                printf("Please enter first letter: ");
                scanf("%1s", response);
                while (getchar() != '\n');
                firstletter = response[0];

                printf("Please enter second letter: ");
                scanf("%1s", response);
                while (getchar() != '\n');
                secondletter = response[0];
                return 0;
                }
```

Run of LISTING 18-6:

```
        Please enter first letter: B
        Please enter second letter: D
```

There is an option to handling single-character input through the stdin buffer: It can be handled directly as unbuffered input. This entails reading directly from the operating system's interface with the keyboard. An operating system's interface with a file is given in the file's file descriptor, _fid.

The `stdin` also has a file descriptor. It can be directly referenced through the `stdin` structure, `stdin->_fid`. Having the file id, you can now use `read` to access the keyboard, directly..

```
char letter;
read( stdin->_fid, &letter, 1);
```

This statement reads one character from the keyboard and places it within the variable letter. It is now possible to write a function that takes unbuffered input. The `getch` function defined here performs such unbuffered input. Many compilers have already defined `getch` as part of their standard library. Check your own compiler documentation to see if `getch` is already provided.

```
int getch(void)
        {
        int letter;

        read( stdin->_fid, &letter, 1);
        return (letter);
        }
```

Accessing the I/O Buffer

Directly using variables in the `FILE` structure can help in some debugging problems. You can print out the `stdin` buffer to the screen using `_buf`, `_cnt`, and `_ptr`. The following example prints out the stdin buffer with the count of characters in it. `_cnt` is the count of remaining characters. (`_ptr` - `_buf`) is the count of characters already read. Together they are the count of all characters read into the buffer.

```
endbuf=stdin->_cnt + (stdin->_ptr - stdin->_buf);

for (i = 0; i < endbuf; i++)
        putchar(stdin->_buf[i]);
```

You can also use pointer indexing to print out just the unread portion of the buffer.

```
readcount = stdin->_ptr - stdin->_buf;

for (i = readcount; i < stdin->_cnt; i++)
        putchar(stdin->_buf[i]);
```

Chapter Summary: System Calls and Stream I/O

System calls provide lower-level access to files. System calls correspond to many of the stream I/O file functions. The major system calls are `open`, `close`, `creat`, `read`, `write`, and `lseek`. The actual names and arguments for these system calls are system-dependent. They may vary slightly from one operating system to another. System calls provide block access to a file. A file is read and written in blocks of bytes, much like `fread` and `fwrite`. They can even be used to implement random access files. The system calls are listed in Table 18-1.

Stream I/O file functions set up an interface with a file consisting of a structure of type `FILE` and a buffer. The `FILE` structure contains variables used to manage the file and the buffer. When a file is first read, a `read` system call reads data from the file into the buffer. Pointers within the `FILE` structure then access data in the buffer. The file functions use the system calls to actually access the file.

Table 18-1: System Calls

```
int open(char* n, int f, int p)
```
Open a file and return the file id. open takes three parameters: the file   name, the file mode, and the permissions.

```
int creat(char* n, int p)
```
Create a file and return its file id. The permission, p, is usually 0.

```
long lseek(int fid, long offset, int origin)
```
Position the file position indicator at the specified offset from the origin.

```
int read(int fid, char* buff, int n)
```
Read a number of bytes from the file into a block of memory. such as a buffer. The number of bytes read is returned.

```
int write(int fid, char* buff, int n)
```
Write a number of bytes to the file from a block of memory. such as a   buffer. The number of bytes written is returned.

This buffer interface allows a file to be easily accessed, byte by byte. The file is actually accessed very few times for every byte read. There are times when you may need to clear the file buffer. Both fseek and fflush will force a buffer to be written to the file.

The stream I/O file functions correspond to the input/output functions. In fact, the input/output functions are actually file functions. The FILE structures assigned to different files are obtained from an array of FILE structures. The first three are reserved for input/output operations. The first structure, _iob[0], is the FILE structure for input functions such as getchar and scanf. The second structure, _iob[1], is the FILE structure for output functions. The addresses of these FILE structures are defined as the symbolic constants stdin and stdout. Many input/output functions are simply macro definitions of file functions with either a stdin or stdout as the file pointer.

Examination of the FILE structure and buffer interface used for input functions provides a clearer understanding of some of the more mysterious errors that occur with input. Using different input functions on the same input can cause strange behavior, such as preventing the user from entering input.

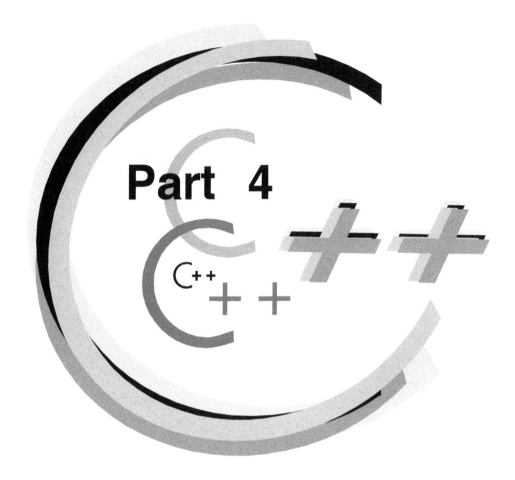

Part 4

Introduction to C++

Classes and Objects
Classes and Pointers
Inheritance
Derivation
Overloading

Classes and Objects

Structures, Classes, and Constructors

Structures

CLasses

Objects

Constructors

Destructors

Part 4: Introduction to C++

19. Classes and Objects

Though most programming languages can be classified as procedural, assembler, or function applicative languages, another category has recently emerged: Object oriented programming languages. Object oriented programming organizes a program into objects rather than procedures or individual instructions. An object consists of data and actions. The program is processed by sending messages to objects telling them to perform specific actions on its data. A common example of an object oriented program is a simple drawing program. A drawing program would consist of several drawing objects. There would be an object for drawing a circle, another for drawing a square, and still another for drawing a line. The circle object would contain instructions needed to draw a circle as well as any data such as the size and color of the circle. To have the program draw a circle, a message is sent to the circle object to draw a circle. The circle object then executes the instructions for drawing a circle. The main program would only consist of sending messages to objects. The objects themselves have the code for executing operations. The circle object contains all the code needed to draw a circle. This is a very different way of organizing program instructions. Instead of placing instructions within procedures, instruction are placed in objects. Instead of function calls, a program progresses by sending messages to objects. The objects then execute instructions. Instead of being procedure oriented or line oriented, the program is object oriented. In planning your program you can then think of the objects that would make up your program, rather than mapping out procedures.

C++ is a complete object oriented programming language that includes the features of the C Programming language. C++ has object oriented features such as classes, inheritance, and overloading. With C++ you can organize your program into objects. Each object will have its own set of functions that you can instruct the object to execute. You can create complex objects making use of inheritance rules. And you can use overloading to extend the functionality of operators.

You can have many different types of objects in C++. In fact, object types are user-defined. In this respect, objects are very much like structures. Just as you can define the type of a structure, so also you can define the type of an object. Such object type declarations are called class declarations. A class in C++ is similar to a structure type in C. A class specifies the type of an object. When you declare an object in C++ you use as its type its class name.

Just as you can have many different structure types, you can have many different classes - many different object types. You can create whatever types of objects you want. For example, you can have circle drawing objects or square drawing objects. For circle drawing objects you would have a circle class. This circle drawing class would be the type for all circle drawing objects.

What is different about class definitions is that they include the functions for objects of that class. You will find that you will be writing most of the code for you program in the class definition, not in the actual program. This is typical of many object oriented programs. The program itself is very brief. Most of the code is placed in class definitions. The code itself becomes part of the type specifications for an object. You can think in terms of a type of code. Objects in the same class will have the same type of code. The circle drawing objects will all have the same type of code for drawing circles.

C++ Structures

To understand how C++ classes and objects work it is helpful to first examine how C++ structures function. A C++ structure is similar to C structures and yet incorporates many of the features found in C++ classes. You can declare a function as a member of a C++ structure, just as you can in C++ classes. C++ structure types are declared by the user in structure type declarations, just as C structure types are. In fact, you can think of C++ classes as enhanced versions of the structure type declarations.

C++ Structure Declarations

The syntax for a C++ structure type declaration consists of the keyword `struct` and a type name followed by the list of structure member declarations enclosed in braces. A structure variable is declared using only the type name. C++ structures do not have tags, like C structures do. Instead they have type names that identify the structure type. In the next example a structure type is declared with the type name calc and a list of members. The structure variable `mycalc` is then declared using the type name calc.

```
struct calc {
            double price;
            double cost;
            };

calc mycalc;
```

In C++ you no longer need to use a `typedef` name for a structure, nor will you need to use the `struct` keyword in a structure variable declaration. In effect, C++ now treats structure types much in the same way as a standard type. In the structure type declaration you are defining a type whose name you can use just as you would any other type. In the previous example, the user defines a structure type called calc, and the calc type can then be used as the type in a variable declaration.

The syntax for a C++ structure does appear the same as that of a C structure. The similarity of C and C++ structure type declarations can be misleading. In the C++ structure, a type name follows the `struct` keyword, whereas in a C structure a tag name follows the `struct` keyword. When declaring a C++ structure variable you need only use the type name, whereas a C structure variable will require the keyword struct and the tag name. However, in C you can simulate a type name by using a `typedef` to give a type name to the structure.

Member Function Declarations

You define a structure to hold data that you then use in your program. You will often find that you need to define certain functions to perform operations on that data. In this sense, you may have a set of functions specifically associated with the data in the structure. In such cases the data and functions are designed to work together. In this way, functions can be considered part of the structure. Data and the functions that work on data form abstract data types. You can think of a structure type as including not only data but the functions that operate on that data. In the next example, the data in the `mycalc` structure is operated on by the input and price functions. You can think of these functions and the `mycalc` structure forming one abstract data type. You shall see that C++ structures are specifically designed to incorporate such abstract data types.

```
struct calc {
            double price;
            double cost;
            };

void user_input(calc* cptr)
      {
      printf("\nPlease enter cost: ");
      scanf ("%lf", &cptr->cost);
      }

void calc_price (calc* cptr)
      {
      cptr->price = cptr->cost + (cptr->cost * MARGIN);
      printf("Price is %.2f\n", cptr->price);
      }

int main()
      {
      calc mycalc;

      user_input(&mycalc);
      calc_price(&mycalc);
      }
```

A structure in C++ operates much like a structure in C with one crucial difference. C++ structures may have as their members functions. This is a significant departure from C structures. A normal C structure has as its members data objects such as variables or arrays. The structure type declaration will contain the variable or array declarations of each member. A C++ structure can also have data objects as members. They are declared in the same way as data objects in a C structure. However, the C++ structure type declaration can also include functions. You can declare a function as a member of a structure.

This requires a new way of thinking about functions. Remember the difference between a declaration and a definition. A declaration only specifies type and name information, whereas a definition actually creates an object. In a structure type declaration, members are declared, not defined. The same is true for function members in a C++ structure. When specifying a function as a member of a C++ structure, you need to declare it, not define it.

You have already seen the difference between a function declaration and a function definition in Chapter 6. A function definition is the actual function code, whereas the function declaration specifies only the name and type information about the function. The function declaration includes the return type and, in C++, the parameter types. In this sense, you declare a function as a member of a structure by placing its function declaration in the structure type declaration. A structure type declaration may then include declarations of data objects such as variables, and declarations of functions.

Whereas a variable declaration will provide all the information needed to create a variable, a function declaration does not. A function declaration only provides the name of the function and its return and parameter types. It says nothing about the programming code that makes up the function. In your program, the function declaration is only used to convey name and type information about one function to another. A function declaration in a structure needs to not only specify name and type information, but also the actual code that makes up the function.

Again, this is a new way of thinking about function. Usually the function definition is the place where you write out the function code, the statements and variable declarations that make up the function. In the case of structures, the function code is placed in a function declaration. The function is not physically defined as in a normal function declaration. It is, instead declared. The actual code that makes up a function is placed in a declaration and treated as type information. In this sense, a function declaration is expanded to include not only the name and type information, but also the actual function code. Creating a structure object will then not only define corresponding member objects such as variables, but also define functions declared as members. In this sense, each structure object will have its own member functions, just as it has its own member variables or member arrays. A function and its code is created as part of the structure object. Until then, the function is not defined, it does not exist. It is only type information, part of the type information specified in the structure type declaration.

A member function declaration is placed outside of the structure type declaration much like a regular function definition. This means that you write the code for a member function outside of the structure type declaration. A declaration of the member function is then placed within the structure type declaration.

A member function is written much like other function definitions except that the structure name and the function scoping operator is placed before the function name. The function scoping operator is a double colon, `::`. A function declaration is then placed within the structure to identify the function as a member. In the next example, the functions `user_input` and `calc_price` have been declared as member functions of the calc structure. Notice how the member function declarations are placed in the list of structure members. The code for each function is then written out and scoped as part of the calc structure declaration. Each function name is preceded by the calc keyword and two colons. The `user_input` name is preceded by calc:: - `calc::user_input`. The following code does not actually define the function. It specifies the data objects and statements that will make up the function if a calc variable of type calc is defined. At this point the code does not constitute a function definition, it is rather a function declaration that is part of a larger structure type declaration. This function declaration is only type information. There is no actual defined function at this point.

```
struct calc {
            double price;
            double cost;
            void user_input(double*);
            void calc_price(double*, double);
            };

void calc::user_input(double *costptr)
        {
        printf("\nPlease enter cost: ");
        scanf ("%lf", costptr);
        }

void calc::calc_price (double *priceptr, double cost)
        {
        *priceptr = cost + (cost * MARGIN);
        printf("Price is %.2f\n", *priceptr);
        }

int main()
        {
        calc mycalc;

        mycalc.user_input(&mycalc.cost);
        mycalc.calc_price(&mycalc.price, mycalc.cost);
        }
```

When the `mycalc` structure variable is declared, it defines as its members the members declared in the calc structure type declaration. `mycalc` will have a cost and price member. It will also have two function members, `user_input` and `calc_price`. They will then be actual defined functions that can be called as part of the `mycalc` structure variable (see Figure 19-1).

When calling a member function, you need to reference the member function using the member operator, the period. The name of the structure variable is placed before the member operator and the function name followed by parenthesis and arguments is placed after the member operator. In the next example, the `user_input` function is called as a member of the `mycalc` structure. `user_input` must first be referenced with the member operator and the structure variable name - `mycalc.user_input()`. Once referenced, you can call the function with the function call operator, `()`.

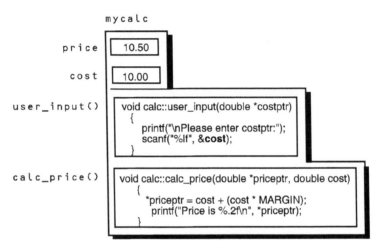

mycalc structure

Figure 19-1: The mycalc structure with member functions-

Scoped members

Variables and arrays declared as members of structures are scoped to that structure's member functions. A member variable can be thought of as an external variable scoped to the member functions. This means that a member variable's name can be used in any of the member functions as if it were an external variable. The member variable is external only to the member functions. To reference a member variable in your program you need to use the structure name and the member operator.

This scoping feature allows you to write code in such a way that both the data and the functions that operate on that data are both encased within a data object, in this case a structure. You can now think of a structure as an abstract data object, consisting of functions operating on data.

In the **calcobj.cpp** program in LISTING 19-1, The calc structure is declared with the member variables price and cost, as well as the member functions `user_input` and `calc_price`. The member variable cost is directly referenced within the `user_input` function. Since `user_input` is declared as a member of the calc structure, its reference of cost references the cost member of the calc structure.

The same is true of the reference of cost and price in the `calc_price` function. Both are members of the same structure that `calc_price` belongs to.

This scoping of members allows data to be operated on within the confines of the structure. Unlike the previous example, cost and price need never be referenced in the main program (though they could be). Instead, the function call to the `user_input` function will operate on the cost member to input a value to it. The function call to the `calc_price` will use cost and price to determine a new price. In a sense, the function call to these member function sends a message to the structure to perform some action on data. The main program does not need to reference the data nor know how the functions operate on it. The main program simply issues a function call that, in effect, sends a message to the structure to perform some task, in this case to calculate a price(see Figure 19-2).

LISTING 19-1: Calc structure and member functions scoped data

calcobj.cpp

```
#include <stdio.h>

#define MARGIN 0.05

struct calc {
            double price;
            double cost;
            void user_input();
            void calc_price();
            };

void calc::user_input()
      {
      printf("\nPlease enter cost: ");
      scanf ("%lf", &cost);
      }

void calc::calc_price ()
      {
      price = cost + (cost * MARGIN);
      printf("Price is %.2f\n", price);
      }

int main()
      {
      char response[2];
      calc mycalc;

      response[0] = 'y';
      while (response[0] != 'n'){
            mycalc.user_input();
            mycalc.calc_price();
            printf("Enter another? (y/n):");
            scanf("%s", response);
            }

      return 0;
      }
```

It is important to remember that the member functions are specified in the structure type declaration. The function code is part of the structure type declaration. The function code of a member function does not define a function as it does with regular non-member functions. In LISTING 19-1 only one function is explicitly defined, the main function. `calc_price` and `user_input` as written here are type information, part of the structure type declaration. They specify a type of possible function, not an actual function such as main.

When a structure variable is declared, only then are the member functions defined. They are defined as members of the that specific structure variable, in this case the `mycalc` structure variable. There is then a `mycalc user_input` function and a `mycalc calc_price` function. If another structure variable of type calc is declared, it would define its own `user_input` and `calc_price` member functions.

LISTING 19-2: Calc structure in calc-h file

calc.h

```
#define MARGIN 0.05

struct calc {
            double price;
            double cost;
            void user_input();
            void calc_price();
            };

void calc::user_input()
        {
        printf("\nPlease enter cost: ");
        scanf ("%lf", &cost);
        }

void calc::calc_price ()
        {
        price = cost + (cost * MARGIN);
        printf("Price is %.2f\n", price);
        }
```

main.cpp
```
#include <stdio.h>
#include "calc.h"

int main()
        {
        char response[2];
        calc mycalc;

        response[0] = 'y';
        while (response[0] != 'n'){
                mycalc.user_input();
                mycalc.calc_price();
                printf("Enter another? (y/n):");
                scanf("%s", response);
                }

        return 0;
        }
```

To emphasis the fact that the function member declarations are only type information and part of the structure type declaration, it may be helpful to place them in a separate header file. A header file is used to hold structure type declarations. A C++ structure type declaration would include the member function declarations. They should be placed together in the same header file. In LISTING 19-2 the structure type declaration and member functions for the calc structure are placed in the **calc.h** file. The **calc.h** file is then included into the **main.cpp** file. The only actual function definition in this program is definition of the main function (see Figure 19-2).

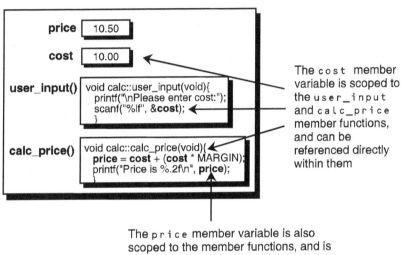

mycalc structure

The `cost` member variable is scoped to the `user_input` and `calc_price` member functions, and can be referenced directly within them

The `price` member variable is also scoped to the member functions, and is here directly refrenced within `calc_price`.

Figure 19-2: The `mycalc` structure, using scoped member references- Member variables in a structure are scoped to member functions and can be directly referenced within them as shown here.

Inline functions and the const qualifier

C++ makes use of inline functions and the const qualifier to replace the use of preprocessor constant and macro directives. Instead of using a define directive to create symbolic constant you can declare variable with the const qualifier and initialize it with a value. Such a variable if the equivalent of a symbolic constant. Its value can never be changed. The const qualifier is also used in C for the same purpose, but its use in C++ is much more widespread (see chapter 2 for a discussion of the const qualifier)

```
const rate = 0.5;
```

Inline functions are a C++ feature that eliminates much of the need for define macros. You define an inline function by placing the keyword inline before the function definition. The function definition is written as you would any standard function definition, including parameters variables and return statements. In fact, inline functions operate much like standard functions, receiving arguments and returning values. However, like define macros, inline functions become inline statements in your program, not separate function calls. You can have more than one statement in your inline function, in which case, more than one statement is generated in the program. With inline functions you have all the advantages of both functions and macros, particularly the argument handling of a function and the efficiency of a macro. The next example is an inline function for the `mymax` macro.

```
inline int mymax (int num1, int num2)
      {
      if ( num1 > num2)
             return num1;
      else
             return num2;
      }
```

You can define inline functions for structures and classes by simply defining the function within the structure or class declaration. Any function defined within a structure or class declaration is taken to be an inline function. The keyword inline is not required in this case. The inline function becomes a member function scoped to the class or structure just as any member function is. It is accessed in the same way as other member functions and, in the case of classes, can be either private or public. In the next example, `calc_price` is defined an incline function for the calc class, whereas a `user_input` is a standard member function for calc.

```
class calc {
             private:
                    double price;
                    double cost;
             public:
                    void user_input();
                    inline void calc_price ()
                           {
                           price = cost + (cost * MARGIN);
                           }
             };

void calc::user_input()
      {
      printf("\nPlease enter cost: ");
      scanf ("%lf", &cost);
      }
```

Classes

You can think of a class as a structure with added features. In a sense, a class is an extension of a structure. A class declares a type of object made up of members that you specify. Just like a structure, a class is made up of members of which some may be functions. Functions take on a special significance in a class. They become the way in which member data is accessed. In this sense, member functions are often referred to as access methods. They are methods for accessing class data.

Members of a class can be qualified as private, public, or protected. Private members can only be referenced by member functions. Public members can be referenced in your program by simple use of a member operator. In other words, public members can be reference by the programmer in the program, just like structure members. As with a structure member, you reference a public member by using the member operator preceded by the class variable's name. In fact a class with only public members is identical to a structure.

LISTING 8-14: Chapter 8 style program:

greet.c
```c
#include <stdio.h>
        static int style = 1;

 void setstyle()
                {
                printf ("Please enter style:");
                scanf("%d", &style);
                }
void printintro()
                {
                switch (style)
                        {
                        case 1:
                        printf("greetings");
                                break;
                        case 2:
                        printf("hello");
                                break;
                        }
                }
void printexit()
                {
                switch (style)
                        {
                        case 1:
                        printf("farewell");
                                break;
                        case 2:
                        printf("goodbye");
                                break;
                        }
                }
```

main.c
```c
#include <stdio.h>
 void setstyle();
 void printintro();
 void printexit();
int main()
                {
                int i;
                setstyle();
                for (i = 0; i < 3; i++)
                        {
                        if (i == 0)
                        printintro();
                        printf ("Number %d\n", i);
                        if (i == 2)
                        printexit();
                        }

                return 0;
                }
```

LISTING 19-3:

style.h
```
#include <stdio.h>

        class styles {
                private:
                        int style;
                public:
                        void setstyle();
                        void printintro();
                        void printexit();
                        };
 void styles::setstyle()
                {
                printf ("Please enter style:");
                scanf("%d", &style);
                }
 void styles::printintro()
                {
                switch (style)
                        {
                        case 1:
                        printf("greetings");
                                break;
                        case 2:
                        printf("hello");
                                break;
                        }
                }
void styles::printexit()
                {
                switch (style)
                        {
                        case 1:
                        printf("farewell");
                                break;
                        case 2:
                        printf("goodbye");
                                break;
                        }
                }
```

main.cpp
```
#include <stdio.h>
#include "style.h"
 int main()
                {
                styles mystyle;
                int i;
                mystyle.setstyle();
                for (i = 0; i < 3; i++)
                        {
                        if (i == 0)
                        mystyle.printintro();
                        printf ("\nNumber %d\n", i);
                        if (i == 2)
                        mystyle.printexit();
                        }
                return 0;
                }
```

Private members cannot be referenced in this way. Private members are private to the class. A private member can be referenced within a member function, but it cannot be referenced publicly through a member operation. In this sense, the private members are hidden from the rest of the program. Only the member functions even know that they exist. This is the concept of data hiding and it prevents data that needs to be protected from accidental change in the program. You can only change a private member by calling a public member function that can then change it (see Figure 19-3).

This private/public organization in classes achieves what is done using external static variables scoped to source files. In LISTING 8-14, a static external variable called style in the **greet.c** source code file was used to hide the variable from the rest of the program. Then functions were called to change and access that hidden variable. The private/public organization of class members allows you to do the same thing, but without resorting to source code files and external static variables.

In the **style.h** file in LISTING 19-3 the greet class declares the style variable as a private member and the `setstyle`, `printintro`, and `printexit` functions as member functions used to access the style private member. style remains hidden within the class and cannot be referenced in the program. The member functions are public and can be called in the program. Only through them can the style member be accessed or changed. The compiler will not allow you to publicly reference the private style member. The reference `mystyle.style` would be illegal (see Figure 19-3).

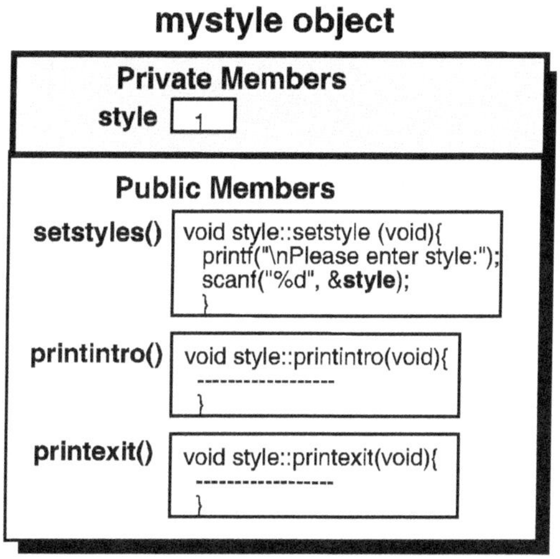

mystyle object

Figure 19-3: The mystyle object using private members as hidden data.

Class Declarations

Designing a class involves determining private data and the functions that access that data. The data and actions constitute the object. Function calls throughout the program are messages sent to the object to perform certain actions. Before declaring a class you should decide on what data and functions you will need in this class and which of these should be private or public.

The declaration of a class is very much the same as that of a C++ structure declarations, except that the class declaration qualify members as public, private, or protected. The class declaration consists of a list of members that may include functions. The syntax for a Class type declaration consist of the keyword class and a class name followed by the list of class member declarations enclosed in braces. The list of class members is divided into private, public, and protected sections, each preceded by the tag private, public, and protected respectively. Each tag is entered in on a line of its own with a colon with a colon after it.

All three are not required in a class declaration. Should your class only have public and private members you only need to include those tags. You could leave out the protected tag. If your class only has public members you could also leave out the private tag. In the next example a class is declared with the name calc and a list of private and public members. The public and private tags are entered in a line of their own at the head of their respective lists.

```
class calc {
        private:
                double price;
                double cost;
        public:
                void user_input();
                void calc_price();
        };

void calc::user_input()
        {
        printf("\nPlease enter cost: ");
        scanf ("%lf", &cost);
        }

void calc::calc_price ()
        {
        price = cost + (cost * MARGIN);
        printf("Price is %.2f\n", price);
        }
```

Member function declarations are placed outside of the class declaration much like a regular function definitions. This means that you write the code for a member function outside of the class declaration, just as you would with a structure type declaration. The function scoping operator, ::, is placed before the function name. A declaration for the function is then placed within the class declaration to identify the function as a member. In the previous example, the functions user_input and calc_price have been declared as member functions of the calc class. The code for each function is then written out and scoped as part of the calc class declaration. Each function name is preceded by the calc keyword and two colons.

Members of a class (private, public, and protected) are scoped to that class's member functions. As in the case of structures, a member variable can be thought of as an external variable scoped to the member functions. You can reference member variables, including private ones, in any of the member functions. In fact this is the only way to reference private members. Public members, on the other hand, can also be referenced in your program using the class member operator. In the previous example, the private member cost is referenced within the member function user_input.

The class declaration is only a type declaration, it is only type information. In fact, the term class declaration can be somewhat misleading. The class declaration does not define any actual objects. Like the structure type declaration, it is only type information. This is particularly true of the function declarations for class function members. Such a function declaration does not actually define the function. The function declaration is only type information. It specifies the data objects and statements that will make up the function if an object of that class is defined. There is no actual defined function at this point.

Defining Class Objects

You define a class object much as you do a structure. You enter in the class name followed by the name of object. This defines an object whose type is that class. In defining the object, all the members, including functions are then defined. You can then access the data members of the object, or call its function members. The next example defines a object called `mycalc` whose type is the calc class.

```
calc mycalc;
```

LISTING 19-4: Calc functions and classes

calcpriv.cpp

```cpp
#include <stdio.h>

#define MARGIN 0.05

class calc {
        private:
                double price;
                double cost;
        public:
                void user_input();
                void calc_price();
                };

void calc::user_input()
    {
    printf("\nPlease enter cost: ");
    scanf ("%lf", &cost);
    }

void calc::calc_price ()
    {
    price = cost + (cost * MARGIN);
    printf("Price is %.2f\n", price);
    }

int main()
    {
    char response[2];
    calc mycalc;                    /* defining class object */

    response[0] = 'y';
    while (response[0] != 'n'){
            mycalc.user_input();   /* member function */
            mycalc.calc_price();   /* member function */
            printf("Enter another? (y/n):");
            scanf("%s", response);
            }
    return 0;
    }
```

In the program, you can use the class member operator to access public members of a class object. The class member operator is the same as the structure member operator, the period. The class object name is placed before the period and the public member is placed after the period. In the main function, the class member operator is used with the `mycalc` object name to reference the `user_input` member, a public member (see Figure 19-4)

```
mycalc.user_input()
```

In this sense, you have yet another way to reference a function. You have seen that a function can be referenced using the function name or an indirection on a pointer to a function. Now you see that a function can be referenced using the class member operator (see Figure 19-4).

In the **calcpriv.cpp** program in LISTING 19-4 the calc program has been redesigned using a class. The calc class has two private members, the variables price and cost. There are two functions that operate on these private variables, `user_input` and `calc_price`. In the main function, an object is defined of type calc, `mycalc`. The definition of the `mycalc` object will define its private and public members, the private members price and cost as well as the public members `user_input` and `calc_price`. The `user_input calc_price` functions are referenced with the class member operator and then used in function calls as designated by the function call operator, ().

mycalc object

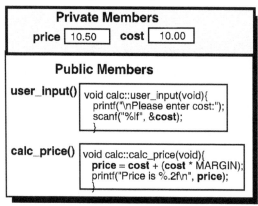

Figure 19-4: The mycalc object. The class type of this object is calc. price and cost are private members. user_input and calc_price are public members.

You can define more than one object of the same class. Each object will have its own private and public members. In LISTING 19-5 two objects of type calc are declared, `mycalc` and `yourcalc`. Each has its own private cost and price members and public `user_input` and `calc_price` members.

It is important to keep in mind that class declarations are type declarations, consisting of only type information. To emphasize this difference, the class declaration is often placed in a header file, just as structure type declarations are. In fact it may be more accurate to refer to class declarations as class type declarations. They declare a certain type of class, just as structure type declaration declare a certain type of structure. In LISTING 19-5 The class type declaration for calc is placed in its own **calc.h** header file and included into the **main.cpp** source code file.

LISTING 19-5:

calc.h - header file for calc class type declaration

```
#define MARGIN 0.05

class calc {
                private:
                        double price;
                        double cost;
                public:
                        void user_input();
                        void calc_price();
                        };

void calc::user_input()
        {
        printf("\nPlease enter cost: ");
        scanf ("%lf", &cost);
        }

void calc::calc_price ()
        {
        price = cost + (cost * MARGIN);
        printf("Price is %.2f\n", price);
        }
```

main.cpp

```
#include <stdio.h>

#include "calc.h"

int main()
        {
        calc mycalc;
        calc yourcalc;

                mycalc.user_input();
                mycalc.calc_price();

                yourcalc.user_input();
                yourcalc.calc_price();
        return 0;
        }
```

Using Classes and Objects

You can, of course, declare many different types of classes. In the **bookobj.cpp** program in LISTING 19-6, the **book.c** program from Chapter 7 is rewritten in C++ using a bookrec class type declaration. The book structure is now declared as a private member of the bookrec class. The functions that operate on the structure are now member functions of the bookrec class (see Figure 19-5). The actual program consists only of declaring a bookrec object, in this case book, and calling different bookrec member functions (see Figure 19-5).

LISTING 19-6:

bookobj.cpp

```
#include <stdio.h>

#define  YEAR  1980

 struct bookdat {        /* Book structure */
                        int year;
                        float price;
                        };

class bookrec {
        private:
                bookdat book;
        public:
                void input_rec();
                void calc_price();
                void output_rec();
                };

 void bookrec::input_rec()
        {
        printf("\nPlease enter year published: ");
        scanf("%d", &book.year);
        printf("\nPlease enter book price: ");
        scanf("%f", &book.price);
        }

 void bookrec::calc_price()
        {
        if (book.year < YEAR)
                book.price *= 0.5;
        }

 void bookrec::output_rec()
        {
        printf("\n\n Book Record \n");
        printf("\t YEAR  : %d \n", book.year);
        printf("\t PRICE : %.2f \n\n", book.price);
        }


 int main()
        {
        bookrec mybook;

        mybook.input_rec();
        mybook.calc_price();
        mybook.output_rec();

        return 0;
        }
```

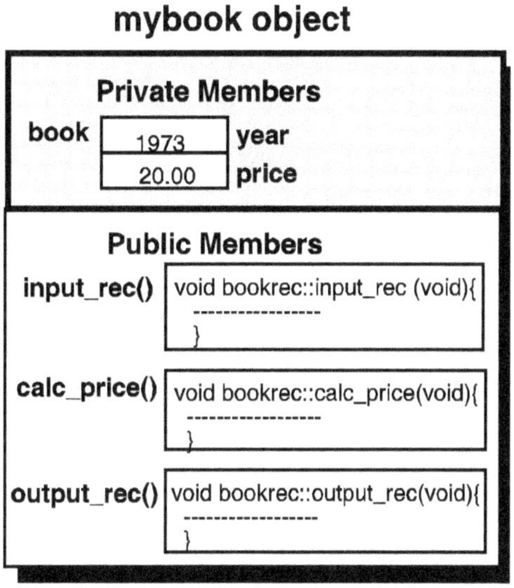

mybook object

Figure 19-5: The mybook object using the structure book as a private member.

As a further comparison, the **calcprof.cpp** program in LISTING 19-7 implements the program from Chapter 6, LISTING 6-28 as a C++ program. The calc class includes all the data and functions for calculating the price. The variables price, cost, profit, and `wholesale_price` are now private members of the calc class. The functions `user_input`, `calc_price`, `calc_profit` are now public members of the calc class. An object of that type of class is then declared, defining these member functions and variables. Member operations on this `mycalc` object reference member functions, which are then called to perform certain operations for calculating the price.

The `print_price` function has been added. This is because the price variable is now a private member of the `mycalc` object and cannot be directly accessed from the program. Instead a member function is declared that, when called, will access the price member and, in this case, print it out. In this sense, member functions can be thought of as access methods. They are methods by which the private data in a class can be operated on (see Figure 19-6).

You can think of a class as a kind of task. If you have a task that requires several actions and depends on the integrity of specific variables, you may have a candidate for a class. In the program in LISTING 19-8 as with many programs, one task that needs to be performed is that of managing a user response. The `user_response` is used to control a loop that drives the program. In the program this task has been organized into a class, the response class. The method for getting a user response is place entirely within this class. The response variable that holds the user response is now a private member of this class. In the main function, you only call member functions of the response object. In a sense, you send a message to the response object to get a response from the user. The response object then does the rest.

LISTING 19-7:

calcprof.cpp
```cpp
#include <stdio.h>
#include <stdlib.h>
#include <string.h>
#define MARGIN 0.05

class calc {
        private:
                double price;
                double cost;
                double profit, wholesale_price;
        public:
                void user_input();
                void calc_price();
                void calc_profit();
                void calc_print();
                };

void calc::user_input()
        {
        printf("\nPlease enter cost: ");
        scanf ("%lf", &cost);
        printf("\nPlease enter wholesale price: ");
        scanf ("%lf", &wholesale_price);
        while (getchar() !='\n');
        }

void calc::calc_price ()
        {
        price = wholesale_price + (wholesale_price * MARGIN);
        }

void calc::calc_profit()
        {
        profit = (price - cost);
        }

void calc::calc_print()
        {
        printf("Profit = %.2f\n", profit);
        }

int main()
        {
        char response[2];
        calc mycalc;

        response[0] = 'y';
        while (response[0] != 'n'){
                mycalc.user_input();
                mycalc.calc_price();
                mycalc.calc_profit();
                mycalc.calc_print();
                printf("Enter another? (y/n):");
                scanf("%s", response);
                }
        return 0;
        }
```

Notice how the class type declarations for calc and response were placed in their own header files, **calc.h** and **response.h**. You can now see how many of your C++ programs will consist mostly of several .h header files. These header files will declare class types. Most of the code for your program will be in these header files in the form of member function declarations. This underscores the fact that much of C++ programming consists of type information, specifying the types of different objects, including the actions those objects can take - the statements they can execute and the variables they can define.

LISTING 19-8: Calcfuncs with Response Class

calc.h

```cpp
#define MARGIN 0.05

class calc {
        private:
                double price;
                double cost;
                double profit, wholesale_price;
        public:
                void user_input();
                void calc_price();
                void calc_profit();
                void calc_print();
                };

void calc::user_input()
        {
        printf("\nPlease enter cost: ");
        scanf ("%lf", &cost);
        printf("\nPlease enter wholesale price: ");
        scanf ("%lf", &wholesale_price);
        while (getchar() !='\n');
        }

void calc::calc_price ()
        {
        price = wholesale_price + (wholesale_price * MARGIN);
        }

void calc::calc_profit()
        {
        profit = (price - cost);
        }

void calc::calc_print()
        {
        printf("Profit = %.2f\n", profit);
        }
```

response.h

```
class response {
        char res[2];
        public:
        void initresponse();
        void getresponse();
        int testresponse();
        };

        void response::initresponse()
                {
                res[0] = 'y';
                }

        void response::getresponse()
                {
                printf("Enter another? (y/n):");
                scanf("%s", res);
                }

        int response::testresponse()
                {
                if(res[0] == 'n')
                        return 0;
                        else
                        return 1;
                }
```

main.cpp

```
#include <stdio.h>

#include "calc.h"
#include "response.h"

int main()
        {
        response res;
        calc mycalc;

        res.initresponse();
        while (res.testresponse() == 1){
                mycalc.user_input();
                mycalc.calc_price();
                mycalc.calc_profit();
                mycalc.calc_print();
                res.getresponse();
                }

        return 0;
        }
```

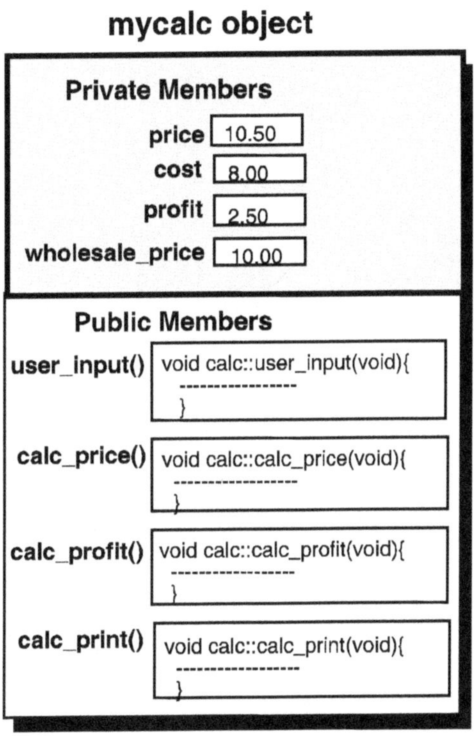

mycalc object

Figure 19-6: The mycalc object.

Friend Functions

The restrictions on private data are designed to protect certain data from inadvertent changes. Normally, the private data of a class can only be accessed through its own member functions. However, it is possible for a class to allow other ordinary program functions to have access to its private members. Such functions are known as friend functions. They are friends of the class with the same access to private members that member functions have. When you define such a friend function you can include references directly to the private members, using private variables in expressions or statements. You can think of a friend function as a way of allowing controlled access to private members. Only the functions designated by a class as friends can access its private members.

You designate a function as a friend of a class by including that function's declaration, preceded by the keyword friend, within the class declaration. You simply list it along with other member function declarations. The class will then treat the friend function as one of its own, allowing full access to all its members. To be a friend, the function has to be listed in the class declaration with the keyword friend. There is no way to make such a connection other than through the class declaration. In the next example, the function discount is a friend function. It has access to the cost and price private members of the calc class. Notice the preceding keyword friend in its declaration.

LISTING 19-9:

calcfrnd.cpp

```
#include <stdio.h>

#define MARGIN 0.05

class calc {
                private:
                        double price;
                        double cost;
                public:
                        void user_input();
                        void calc_price();
                        friend float discount();
                        };

void calc::user_input()
        {
        printf("\nPlease enter cost: ");
        scanf ("%lf", &cost);
        }

void calc::calc_price ()
        {
        price = cost + (cost * MARGIN);
        printf("Price is %.2f\n", price);
        }

float discount();

 calc mycalc;

int main()
        {
        char response[2];
        float disprice;

        response[0] = 'y';
        while (response[0] != 'n'){
                mycalc.user_input();
                mycalc.calc_price();
                disprice = discount();
                printf("Enter another? (y/n):");
                scanf("%s", response);
                }
        return 0;
        }

float discount()
        {
        return(mycalc.price * .75);
        }
```

```
class calc {
        private:
                double price;
                double cost;
        public:
                void user_input();
                void calc_price();
                friend float discount();
        };
```

The friend function is not restricted to just working with the members of that class. It is a regular program function that can access objects in your program. In this way you can define a function that can work both with variables you declare in your program and with private members in objects. In the **calcfrnd.cpp** program in LISTING 19-9, the discount function is listed within the calc class declaration as a friend function. It useses the price private member to calculate a special discount of 25 percent. **discount** has its own function declaration before the main function. It is defined as a separate function after main, just as regular functions are defined. Its function call in main consists only of the its function name, unlike the preceding two calls to function members of `mycalc`, `user_input` and `calc_price`. The value that is returns is assigned to a locally declared variable in main called discprice.

Classes and Constructors: Initialization

Suppose you need to initialize private members in an object. You cannot access the members directly. Nor can you perform any kind of initialization when you declare the class type of an object. A class type, like a structure type, is only type information. To initialize private members you will need to use either an access function that you call in your program, or a special built-in constructor function that automatically executes when you define the object.

Class type declarations can appear misleading. When you write out a class type declaration, you may need to declare variables such as integer or floating point variables. These declarations appear to be the same as those you write when defining internal variables within your functions. However, internal variable declaration within a function both declare and define a variable, creating an object of that type such as an integer or floating point object. Whereas, within a class type declaration, any variable declarations you make are only declarations, not definitions. They provide only type information, name and type. There is no actual definition of an object. For this reason you cannot have any initializations within a class type declaration, because there are no objects yet to assign values to. (The same holds true for structure type declarations as discussed in Chapter 7).

Initialization using access functions

A simple way to initialize private members is to define an access function in which you specify assignment operations for those members. You then call that function in your program before any members are used. You, as the programmer, need to carefully manage all this yourself. You have to be sure to explicitly call the initialization function before the object is accessed.

In the **calcinit.cpp** program in LISTING 19-10, the user defines an initialization function called `initcalc`. This function initializes the count variable to 0. `initcalc` is called right after `mycalc` is defined.

LISTING 19-10:

calcinit.cpp

```
#include <stdio.h>
#define MARGIN 0.05

class calc {
            private:
                    int count;
                    double prices[50];
                    double cost;
            public:
                    void user_input();
                    void calc_price();
                    void initcalc();
                    };

void calc::initcalc()
        {
        count = 0;
        }

void calc::user_input()
        {
        printf("\nPlease enter cost: ");
        scanf ("%lf", &cost);
        }

void calc::calc_price ()
        {
        prices[count] = cost + (cost * MARGIN);
        count++;
        }

int main()
        {
        char response[2];
        calc mycalc;

        mycalc.initcalc();

        response[0] = 'y';
        while (response[0] != 'n'){
                mycalc.user_input();
                mycalc.calc_price();
                printf("Enter another? (y/n):");
                scanf("%s", response);
                }
        return 0;
        }
```

Constructor Functions

C++ provides a way to perform initializations without having to explicitly call an access function. In C++, you can define what is called a constructor function. A constructor function is automatically executed when an object of that type is created. When your program, in executing its statements, comes to a declaration of a class type object, it will not only define that object, creating it, but also execute that object's constructor function. If a class has a constructor function, then an object declaration of that class type will not only define the object but also execute a function, the constructor function. With constructor functions you now need to look at object declarations as not only creating objects, but also executing code.

A constructor function has the same name as that of the class. Whatever statements you place in a constructor function will be executed whenever an object of that class is created. Unlike other functions, the constructor function has no return type. You do not specify a return type in its declaration. An example of the constructor function for the calc object type follows.

```
calc::calc()
       {
       count = 0;
       }
```

You need to enter the declaration of the constructor function into your class declaration, along with your other member function declarations. However, the constructor declaration will not have a return type. You need to place the constructor declaration in the list of public members, so that it can automatically be accessed and executed by your program.

```
calc();
```

In LISTING 19-11, the constructor for calc is listed as a public member function with no return type. Its declaration also has not return type. When the `mycalc` object is defined, its constructor function is automatically executed, initializing count to 0.

Suppose that initialization values may differ from one object to the next. In the previous example, members of any object declared for that class type will all be initialized with the same value. The count member will always be initialized with 0 whenever you define a calc object. Suppose that there are members of a class that you would want to initialize differently whenever you create an object. Instead of initializing with zero, perhaps you would want to initialize count in one object with 5 and in another 3. Of course it doesn't make much sense to do this with count. But there are situations where you would want such flexibility. For example, if your object dynamically allocates an array, you may want to specify different sizes for the array size.

The difference here is between initializing members in the class type declaration, and initializing members when you define an object of the class type. If you initialize members in a class type declaration, then any object of that class will always have its members initialized with those values. All calc objects will have their count member always initialized to 0. If you initialize member when their objects are defined, you could specify different initial values for members in each object. Each calc object could have their count member initialized with a different value.

A simple way to initialize member at object definition is to define an access function that takes arguments. You could then execute the access function explicitly, providing as arguments the initialization values for different members. This is the same method describe previously, but with arguments added.

Though this approach works, a more common method is to use the constructor function. You can define the constructor function to include parameters. The constructor function can take arguments into its parameters and use them to initialize members. In the next example, the calc constructor now takes an argument. The argument is passed to the num parameter variable that is then used to initialize the count member.

LISTING 19-11:

calc.h

```
#define MARGIN 0.05
#define MAXPRICES 10

class calc {
            private:
                    int count;
                    double prices[MAXPRICES];
                    double cost;
            public:
                    calc();
                    void user_input();
                    void calc_price();
                    };

  calc::calc()
        {
        count = 0;
        }

void calc::user_input()
        {
        printf("\nPlease enter cost: ");
        scanf ("%lf", &cost);
        }

void calc::calc_price ()
        {
        if(count < MAXPRICES)
                {
                prices[count] = cost + (cost * MARGIN);
                count++;
                }
          else
                printf("Array if Full\n");
        }
```

main.cpp
```
#include <stdio.h>
#include "calc.h"
int main()
        {
        char response[2];
        calc mycalc;

        response[0] = 'y';
        while (response[0] != 'n'){
                mycalc.user_input();
                mycalc.calc_price();
                printf("Enter another? (y/n):");
                scanf("%s", response);
                }
        return 0;
        }
```

```
calc::calc(int num)
      {
      count = num;
      }
```

How then do you specify arguments for a constructor function, especially since you usually do not explicitly call a constructor function? When a constructor function has arguments, you can explicitly call it in the object's declaration. You can then specify the arguments in the argument list of the constructor function call. After entering the object declaration, you enter an equal sign followed by the constructor function name and its argument list. The constructor function name is always the same as the class type of the object. In the next example, the constructor function for the mycalc object is called with the argument 5. The value 5 will be passed to the num parameter that is then used to initialize mycalc's count member. The function call is made as part of the declaration of the mycalc object.

```
calc mycalc = calc(5);
```

There is an alternative way for you to specify constructor arguments. C++ allows you to simply list constructor arguments next to an object's declaration. The argument list is a list of values enclosed in parentheses. You simply place that next to the object name in the object's declaration. Any arguments placed in an object declaration are assumed to be arguments for the object's constructor function. Recall that an object declaration not only creates an object, but automatically executes its constructor function. It makes sense then to specify arguments for the constructor function in the object's declaration. In the next example, the declaration of mycalc both defines the object and passes as an argument to its constructor function, the integer value 5.

```
calc mycalc(5);
```

Different calc objects could then have different initialization values for their count member. In the next example, the count member of the yourcalc object will be set to 12, whereas the count member of the ourcalc object will be set to 3.

```
calc yourcalc = calc(12);
calc ourcalc = calc(3);
```

Suppose you define an object that has a constructor expecting arguments, but you specify no arguments. In that case the values of the constructor parameters would be undefined. You can avoid this problem by specifying default values for your constructor arguments. If you should not specify any arguments when you define an object, then the default values will be used as the arguments. You specify the default values in the parameter list of the constructor function. Following each parameter declaration you enter an equal sign and the default value. Next is an example of the calc constructor with a default value. If no argument is specified for a calc object, then num will be initialized with the default value 3.

```
calc::calc(int num = 3)
      {
      count = num;
      }
```

As a more practical example, suppose that you have an object that dynamically allocates an array based on an initial size. By using an argument in your constructor function you could have an array of different size for each object. Should you need an object with a small array you just need to use a small number for the argument. In the next example, two different objects of the same type, the calc class, have two different initialization values. The yourcalc object passes the value 12 to its constructor, whereas `ourcalc` passes 3 to its constructor.

```
calc yourcalc(12);
calc ourcalc(3);
```

Destructors

Variables that you define in your functions exist only during the execution those functions. Each time a function is called it creates anew its declared variables. When it finishes execution and returns to the function that called it, those variables are destroyed. The same is true for class objects. When you declare an object within a function, it will be created anew whenever that function is called, and be destroyed when it finishes execution and returns to the calling function.

Bearing this in mind, in certain cases there may be operations you would want performed on an object before it is destroyed. You could define an access function to do this, but then you would always have to remember to call it in every function that you define such an object. Instead you can define what is called a destructor function to automatically perform such operations for you whenever an object is destroyed.

A destructor function consist of the same name as the class type, but preceded by a tilde. Whenever an object of that class type is destroyed, its destructor function is executed. Like the constructor function, the declaration of a desctructor function has no return type. You also need to enter the declaration for the destructor function in the list of public members.

```
file::~file()
        {
        fclose (fptr);
        }
```

As an example, let us take the task of managing files. Whenever you use a file, you not only need to open it, but you also need to close it. Failure to close a file could result a serious loss of data. Suppose that there are files that you only want opened and closed once within a function. You could create an object with a constructor function to open the file and a destructor function to close the file.

In LISTING 19-12, the file class uses a constructor function to open a file and a destructor function to close the file. The destructor function is named with a preceding tilde and the name of the class, in this case, ~file. In the main function, the declaration of `myfile` passes the arguments for the name of the file and the file mode to the object's constructor functions. The constructor function then opens a file using that name and file mode. The access function `readbuf` is then used to read the file line by line using `fgets`. `printf` then displays each line. The main function then ends, but as it ends, it destroys the `myfile` object, activating its destructor function. The destructor function then closes the file, just before `myfile` object is destroyed.

LISTING 19-12:

file.h
```
#include <stdio.h>
#define BUFSIZE 1000
        class file
          {
                private:
                        FILE *fptr;
                public:
                         file(char*, char*);
                         ~file();
                        void writeline(char*);
                        char* readline(char*);
                };

        file::file(char *filename, char *mode)
                        {
                        if((fptr = fopen(filename, mode)) == NULL)
                                {
                                printf("file open error\n");
                                exit(1);
                                }
                        }
        file::~file()
                        {
                        fclose (fptr);
                        }

        void file::writeline(char *buf)
                        {
                        fputs(buf, fptr);
                        }

        char* file::readline(char *buf)
                        {
                        char *res;

                        res = fgets(buf, BUFSIZE, fptr) ;
                        return res;
                        }
```
main.cpp
```
#include <stdlib.h>
#include  "file.h"
#define BUFSIZE 1000

        int main()
                {
                char buf[BUFSIZE];
                file myfile("mytext", "r");

                while (myfile.readline(buf) != 0)
                        {
                        printf("%s", buf);
                        }
                return 0;
                }
```

Using Constructors and Destructors with Dynamic objects

Constructors and destructor functions are commonly used to first dynamically create objects, allocating memory for their use, and then later destroying those objects, freeing up their memory when it is no longer needed. Suppose that you have an object that you want to create dynamically, making use of allocated memory. You will need to make sure that the object is first created, allocating memory for it, and then, when no longer needed, the object is destroyed, freeing that memory for other uses. You could do this explicitly by declaring access functions to create objects and then destroy them. However, constructor and destructor functions could do this for you automatically. By dynamically creating objects in a constructor you ensure that the needed memory is allocated whenever an object of that type is defined. By destroying objects in a destructor function, you ensure that the allocated memory is freed for use, now that it is no longer needed.

In C++, you use the new operation to dynamically create new objects, and the delete operation to destroy them. Though you can still use `calloc` and `malloc`, the C++ new operation provides a clearer and more effective way of allocating memory. new is often used to dynamically create data structure components and arrays. The creation of data structures is discussed in more detail in the next chapter.

To use the new operation to create elements for an array, you simply enter the keyword new followed by the type of objects in the array with the number of elements enclosed in brackets. new will return the beginning address of the newly created elements. You can then assign that address to a pointer. In the next example, the user creates elements for an array of 20 characters, and assigns the beginning address of that memory to the pointer **str**.

```
str = new char[20];
```

Once you have finished using the created elements, you can delete them up using the delete operation. delete will destroy the elements, de-allocating the memory they used. If you do not delete the created elements, they will continue to take up memory. To delete created elements you use the delete operation followed by the pointer that holds the beginning address of that memory. In the next example, the user deletes the elements whose address **str** holds.

```
delete str;
```

In the **calconst.cpp** program in LISTING 19-13, is an example of the use of dynamically created elements using constructor and destructor functions. The size of an array is dynamically determined by a value passed to the calc object's constructor function in its definition. As shown in the next example, the value 15 is passed to the `mycalc` constructor when it is defined. The `mycalc` constructor will then use this value to create a prices array of 15 elements.

```
calc mycalc(15);
```

prices is actually a pointer to a double. The program will dynamically create the element, allocating memory and assigning its beginning address to prices. Pointer operations on the prices pointer will then reference these elements as members of an array. Dynamically allocated array were discussed in Chapter 10, using calloc to allocate the memory. In this example, calloc is not used. Instead the C++ operation new is used to dynamically create the elements for the array. In the **calconst.cpp** program, the user creates elements for an array of doubles, the number of which is determined by value passed to `maxp`.

```
prices = new double[maxp];
```

The destructor function will use the delete operation to delete the dynamically created elements, freeing up the allocated memory used for them. An object's destructor function will execute automatically when it is destroyed. In this case, the `mycalc` object will be destroyed when the program ends, first executing its destructor function to delete the elements that its constructor function allocated.

```
delete prices;
```

LISTING 19-13:

calconst.cpp
```cpp
#include <stdio.h>
#define MARGIN 0.05

class calc {
            private:
                    int count;
                    int maxprices;
                    double *prices;
                    double cost;
            public:
                    void user_input();
                    void calc_price();
                    void print_prices();
                     calc(int);
                    ~calc();
                    };

  calc::calc(int maxp = 10)
       {
       count = 0;
       maxprices = maxp;
       prices = new double[maxp];
       }

  calc::~calc()
       {
       delete prices;
       }

 void calc::user_input()
       {
       printf("\nPlease enter cost: ");
       scanf ("%lf", &cost);
       }
```

```
void calc::calc_price ()
        {
        if(count < maxprices)
                {
                prices[count] = cost + (cost * MARGIN);
                printf("Price is %.2f\n", prices[count]);
                count++;
                }
          else
                printf("Array if Full\n");
        }



void calc::print_prices()
        {
        int i;

        printf("\nList of Prices\n");
        for(i=0;i<count;i++)
                printf("%.2f\n", prices[i]);
        }

int main()
        {
        char response[2];
        calc mycalc(15);

        response[0] = 'y';
        while (response[0] != 'n'){
                mycalc.user_input();
                mycalc.calc_price();
                printf("Enter another? (y/n):");
                scanf("%s", response);
                }
        mycalc.print_prices();

        return 0;
        }
```

Nested Objects

You can next class objects inside of each other. That is, a class type may have as one of its members an object of another class. As with nested structures, the nesting must be hierarchical. A class cannot contain a class object that in turn contains a class object of the first outer class.

LISTING 19-14 is an example of a nested object. The emp class contains a declaration of a recfile class. This program incorporates all what you have discussed so far. Notice the constructor and destructor functions for recfile. The program performs simple sequential record file operations on an employee database file.

LISTING 19-14: Record File Program using Nested Objects

recfile.h

```
#include <stdlib.h>
        class recfile {
                        FILE *fptr;
                        long recsize;
                public:
                        recfile(long);
                        void openfile(char*);
                        void closefile();
                        void writerec(void*);
                        int readrec(void*);
                        void reset();
                };

  recfile::recfile (long size)
                {
                recsize = size;
                }

void recfile::openfile (char *filename)
                {
                if((fptr = fopen(filename, "r+b")) == NULL)
                        {
                        if((fptr = fopen(filename, "w+b")) == NULL)
                                {
                                printf("file open error\n");
                                exit(1);
                                }
                        }
                }
void recfile::closefile()
                {
                fclose (fptr);
                }
void recfile::writerec(void *recptr)
                {
                fwrite(recptr, recsize, 1, fptr);
                }
int recfile::readrec(void *recptr)
                {
                int res;

                res = fread (recptr, recsize, 1, fptr) ;
                return(res);
                }

void recfile::reset()
                {
                fseek (fptr, 0L, 0);
                }
```

emp.h

```
#include <stdio.h>

#include "recfile.h"

        struct EMP {
                char name[100];
                long id;
                double salary;
                };
        class emp {
                private:
                        EMP emprec;
                        recfile empfile;
                        void input_rec();
                        void output_rec();
                public:
                         emp(char*);
                        ~emp();
                        void add_rec();
                        void print_rec();
                        void find_rec( void);
                };

    emp::emp(char *filename):empfile(sizeof(EMP))
            {
            empfile.openfile(filename);
            }

    emp::~emp()
            {
            empfile.closefile();
            }

    void emp::add_rec()
            {
            input_rec();
            empfile.writerec( &emprec);
            }

    void emp::input_rec()
            {
            printf("\nPlease enter last name: ");
            scanf("%*[\n\t ]%[^\n]s", emprec.name);
            printf("\nplease enter employee id: ");
            scanf("%ld", &emprec.id);
            printf("\nplease enter employee salary: ");
            scanf("%lf", &emprec.salary);
            }
    void emp::print_rec()
            {
            empfile.reset();
            while( empfile.readrec(&emprec) != 0)
                    {
                    output_rec();
                    }
            }
```

```
void emp::output_rec()
        {
        printf("\n\n Employee Record \n");
        printf("\n\t NAME  : %s \n", emprec.name);
        printf("\n\t ID    : %ld \n", emprec.id);
        printf("\n\t SALARY: %f \n\n", emprec.salary);
        }

void emp::find_rec( void)
        {
        long id;

        printf("Please enter record id: ");
        scanf("%ld", &id);
        empfile.reset();
        while  ( (empfile.readrec(&emprec) != 0)
                                        && (id != emprec.id));

        if (id == emprec.id )
                output_rec();
         else
                printf("Record not found\n");
        }
```

choice.h

```
class choice {
        private:
                char res[2];
                int more;
        public:
                choice();
                int getchoice();
                int testchoice();
        };

choice::choice()
        {
        more = 1;
        }

int choice::getchoice()
        {
        printf("Please enter choice\n");
        scanf("%s", res);
        if(res[0] == 'q')
                more = 0;
        return(res[0]);
        }

int choice::testchoice()
        {
        return(more);
        }
```

main.cpp

```cpp
#include <stdio.h>
#include "emp.h"
#include "choice.h"

        void menu();

        int main()
                {
                emp employee("myemps");
                choice sel;

                menu();
                while (sel.testchoice())
                        {
                        switch(sel.getchoice())
                                {
                                case  'i':
                                        employee.add_rec();
                                        break;
                                case  'f':
                                        employee.find_rec();
                                        break;
                                case  'p':
                                        employee.print_rec();
                                        break;
                                default:
                                        printf("invalid input\n");
                                }
                        }
                return 0;
                }

        void menu()
                {
                printf("\ni = input a record\n");
                printf("f. = find a record\n");
                printf("p = print a record\n");
                printf("q = quit program\n\n");
                }
```

Program examples

The following programs incorporate many of the C++ features that have been discussed so far. The program in LISTING 19-15 is a rewritten version of the **book.c** program from LISTING 7-15. In this version, the booklib class type manages an array of bookrec structures. The bookrec structure is a record containing the title, year, and price of a book. The booklib class type has several private members: nextbook, maxbooks, books, and calc_price. nextbook keeps track of the number of structures used in the array. maxbooks is the number of structures in the array. books is used as a pointer to an array of structures. calc_price is a function called only by another booklib function, add_book.

The declaration of the lib object includes arguments for its constructor function. The booklib constructor function takes two arguments, the size of the bookrec array and a year date. The size is used to dynamically allocate the array and set the value of maxbooks which is used in functions to detect the maximum number of elements in the array. The year is used in `calc_price` to calculate a discount price for books published before the specified year. Default values have been specified for both arguments. If the programmer declares a collection object without specifying any arguments, then the default values will be used, in this case 10 for max and 0 for yr.

There are three public members. The three public members are functions for adding a book record - `add_book`, printing out the book records already entered - `output_books`, and a menu to display choices. Each is called through a class member operation on the lib object name.

LISTING 19-15: Book library

choice.h

```
class choice {
        private:
                char res[2];
                int more;
        public:
                choice();
                int getchoice();
                int testchoice();
        };
choice::choice()
        {
        more = 1;
        }
int choice::getchoice()
        {
        printf("Please enter choice\n");
        scanf("%s", res);
        if(res[0] == 'q')
                more = 0;
        return(res[0]);
        }
int choice::testchoice()
        {
        return(more);
        }
```

books.h

```
struct bookrec {        /* Book structure */
                char title[100];
                int  year;
                float price;
                } ;
class booklib {
        private:
                int nextbook;
                int maxbooks;
                int Year;
                bookrec *books;
                void calc_price();
        public:
                booklib (int, int);
                ~booklib();
                void add_book();
                void output_books();
                void menu();
        };
```

```
booklib::booklib(int max=10, int yr= 0)
      {
      nextbook = 0;
      maxbooks = max;
      Year = yr;
      books = new bookrec[maxbooks];
      }

 booklib::~booklib()
      {
      delete books;
      }

void booklib::add_book()
      {
      if(nextbook < maxbooks)
            {
            printf("\nPlease enter title: ");
            scanf("%*[\n\t ]%[^\n]s", books[nextbook].title);
            printf("Please enter year published: ");
            scanf("%d", &books[nextbook].year);
            printf("Please enter book price: ");
            scanf("%f", &books[nextbook].price);
            calc_price();
            nextbook++;
            }
        else
            printf("Library is full\n");
      }

void booklib::calc_price()
      {
      if (books[nextbook].year < Year)
            books[nextbook].price *= 0.5;
      }

void booklib::output_books()
      {
      int i;

      for(i=0; i < nextbook; i++)
            {
            printf("\n\n Book Record \n");
            printf("\t TITLE: %s \n", books[i].title);
            printf("\t YEAR : %d \n", books[i].year);
            printf("\t PRICE: %.2f \n\n", books[i].price);
            }
      }

void booklib::menu()
            {
            printf("a. add books to library\n");
            printf("p. print books in library\n");
            printf("q. quit library\n");
            }
```

main.cpp

```
#include <stdio.h>
#include "books.h"
#include "choice.h"

 int main()
        {
        booklib lib(10, 1980);
        choice sel;

        lib.menu();
        while (sel.testchoice())
              {
              switch(sel.getchoice())
                    {
                    case 'a':
                          lib.add_book();
                          break;
                    case 'p':
                          lib.output_books();
                          break;
                    case 'm':
                          lib.menu();
                          break;
                    }
              }
        return 0;
        }
```

The program in LISTING 19-16 takes the implementation of class objects to the extreme. The entire program consists of only one declaration and one function call, a declaration of a collection object named `mycolls`, and a call to that object's `select_coll` member function, `mycolls.select_coll()`. The rest of the program consists entirely of type information held in header files, specifically class type declarations for the collection, `bookcoll`, and `booklib` class types. Within the collection class declaration, there are declarations of `bookcoll` objects, and within the `bookcoll` class declaration there is a declaration of a `booklib` object. These nested objects are not created until the collection object `mycolls` is created by its declaration in the main function. Until then they remain only type information as do any declarations within a class type.

The program is designed to manage three book collections. These collections are declared within the collection class: mystery, romance, and sci-fi. These declarations include arguments for their constructor functions. The `bookcoll` constructor function takes two arguments, the size of the `bookrec` array and a year date. These are passed on to the `booklib` constructor function which will actually use them to manage the book records.

The collection class consists essentially of a menu from which to make a selection of what collection you want to work on. Upon making a choice, a call is make to the manage_coll function of that object. If you choose mystery, then `mystery.manage_coll` is called. The book collections are objects of the `bookcoll` class type. The `bookcoll` class consists also of just a menu from which to make a choice. But in this case the choices are for operations you want to perform on the collection such as adding records or printing them out. `bookcoll` contains a `booklib` object, `libcol`, whose functions are used to perform the operations. The `booklib` class is the same class as used in the previous listing, LISTING 19-15 and is not repeated here. **books.h** for this program is the **books.h** described in LISTING 19-15.

The program begins with a call to the mycolls select_col function. This generates a menu of collection choices. Upon selecting a collection, that collection object's manage_coll function is called that in turn generates a menu of choices of actions you can take on the collection, such as adding records or printing out records. Upon selecting an action to take, the corresponding libcol object's function is called to perform the action. The libcol is an object of type booklib which performs all actual operations on the book array.

The booklib object is a private member of the bookcoll class. This make the functions used to manage the book arrays essentially private members, hidden from the program. This can provide another level of control, making not only data private such as nextbook and maxbooks, but also the methods of accessing that data such as add_book and output_coll. Not only data is hidden and protected, but also the way you access that data.

LISTING 19-16: Program of nested class objectsbookcoll.h

```cpp
class bookcol{
            private:
                booklib libcol;
            public:
                 bookcol(int, int);
                void menu_coll();
                void manage_coll();
                };

  bookcol::bookcol(int max=10, int yr= 0):libcol(max, yr)
        {
        }

void bookcol::manage_coll()
        {
        choice sel;

        libcol.menu();
        while (sel.testchoice())
                {
                switch(sel.getchoice())
                        {
                        case 'a':
                                libcol.add_book();
                                break;
                        case 'p':
                                libcol.output_books();
                                break;
                        case 'm':
                                libcol.menu();
                                break;
                        }
                }
        }
```

colls.h

```
class collection{
            private:
                    bookcol mystery;
                    bookcol romance;
                    bookcol scifi;
            public:
                    collection();
                    void menu_coll();
                    void select_coll();
                    };


    collection::collection():mystery(10,1980),romance(30,1960),scifi(15,1975)
        {
        }

void collection::menu_coll()
                {
                printf("m. mystery\n");
                printf("r. romance\n");
                printf("s. scifi\n");
                printf("q. quit\n");
                }

void collection::select_coll()
        {
        choice sel;

        while (sel.testchoice())
                {
                menu_coll();
                switch(sel.getchoice())
                        {
                        case 'm':
                                mystery.manage_coll();
                                break;
                        case 'r':
                                romance.manage_coll();
                                break;
                        case 's':
                                scifi.manage_coll();
                                break;
                        case 'q':
                                break;
                        default:
                                printf("Invalid Choice\n");
                        }
                }
        }
```

main.cpp

```
#include <stdio.h>
#include <stdlib.h>
#include <string.h>
#include "choice.h"
#include "books.h"
#include "bookcoll.h"
#include "colls.h"

 void menu();

        int main()
                {
                collection mycolls;

                mycolls.select_coll();

                return 0;
                }
```

When you specify arguments for a nested object, you do not do so in its declaration. Instead you need to specify those arguments in the declaration of the outer object's constructor function. You first have the declaration of the constructor function name and argument list. After the argument list you enter a colon followed by the nested object's constructor name and its argument list. You can use parameters of the outer constructor, as arguments to the nested constructor, effectively passing values from the outer constructor to the inner constructor.

The `bookcoll` object needs to pass the max and year information given to its constructor, onto the constructor function for its nested `booklib` object, `libcol`. This becomes complicated because the constructor functions for nested objects are always executed before the constructor functions for the outer object, the object it is declared in. So the `booklib` constructor function is executed before the `bookcoll` constructor function. However, it is to the `bookcoll` constructor function that the max and year values are passed, `svalues` that the `booklib` constructor needs for its arguments.

You can easily pass the arguments of an outer constructor to that of a nested object's constructor. For, though the nested object's constructor is executed first, it is the outer object's constructor that is called first, passing arguments to its parameter variables. Next is the `bookcoll` constructor function. The `bookcoll` constructor is called first and arguments are passed to its parameters max and year, which are then used as arguments for the call to the `booklib` constructor. This effectively passes the argument specified for `bookcoll` down to the `booklib` constructor. The `booklib` constructor is then executed in full, and, after, its execution, the rest of the `bookcoll` constructor is executed. In the `bookcol` constructor, the name of the declared object is used, libcol, not the object type, `booklib`. Just as values are passed to a contractor in an object declaration, so also, in the case of nested objects, values are passed to a constructor using the object's name and the list of values. Though the object's name and values are placed in the current classes constructor, not in the classes list of declarations where the object is declared. The declaration of `libcol` in the `bookcoll` class cannot have an argument list for its constructor. Within `bookcoll` 's constructor, you can specify `libcol` with an argument list for its own constructor. Again, recall that you are only dealing with type information at this point and you cannot assign a value to a type, only to an object that has been defined. The declaration of `libcol` is only type information for the `bookcoll` class. Constructors, on the other hand, are executed only when an object is defined. A constructor can then assign values to members of the already defined object.

```
void bookcol::bookcol(int max=10, int yr= 0):libcol(max, yr)
      {
      }
```

Chapter Summary: Classes and Objects

C++ extends the C programming language providing object oriented programming capabilities. The standard features of ANSI C are included in C++. However, C++ enhances certain features and adds new ones. With C++ you can organizes your program as an object oriented process. Instead of seeing a program as a series of function calls, you can think of your program as a set of objects that can perform different tasks. To have an object perform an certain task you sent it a message to do so. Function calls operate like messages sent to objects. Objects will contain both the data and the functions with which to perform its tasks. You can now compartmentalize your program, breaking it down into different class objects, each performing different tasks.

Structures in C++ can have functions as members. These member functions are declared as part of the structure type, and remain undefined until a structure variable is defined. Data members of a structure such as variables or arrays are scoped to its members functions and can be directly referenced within them. Member function declarations for a structure are part of that structure's type declaration. They remain type information, just as the structure type declaration is only type information.

Classes have all the same capabilities of C++ structures. You can declare member functions and data members are scoped to those functions. In addition, you can control the accessibility of members by classifying them as either private, protected, or public. Public members are open to use anywhere in your program. Private members can only be referenced by member functions for that class. Protected members provide partial access (they are discussed in Chapter 21). Like C++ structures, class declarations are only type information. The declarations of class data and function members can be thought of as a class type declaration. For this reason, class declarations, including their member function declarations could be placed in a **.h** header file, just as you would structure type declarations.

You cannot initialize members in class declarations. A class declaration is only type information. Its members are not defined until an object of that class is declared, much as you would declare a structure variable. To initialize members of a class you can use a constructor function. A constructor function is a special class function that is executed automatically whenever and object of that type of class is defined. You can use this constructor function to assign values to members. When an object is defined, its constructor function will be called and those values assigned to its members. You can even pass initial values to an object's constructor function and have these values assigned to the object's members. Destructor functions are special class functions that are automatically executed when an object is undefined. For example and object that is an automatic variable will become undefined when the function it is defined in finishes execution and returns. At that point, the object's destructor function will be executed just before the object is destroyed.

Exercises

1. Rewrite the **calcsale.c** program in LISTING 16-10 using C++. Use class objects for managing your file and the calculations on the data.

2. Rewrite the following program using C++. Create a class object to manage the employee data.

```
typedef  struct emp { /* EMP structure */
             int  id;
             float salary;
             } EMP;

int main()
      {
      EMP employee;
      int years;

      printf("\nplease enter employee id: ");
      scanf("%d", &employee.id);
      printf("\nplease enter years experience: ");
      scanf("%d", &years);
      employee.salary = years * 10000.00;
      printf("\n\n Employee Record \n");
      printf("\n\t ID: %d \n", employee.id);
      printf("\n\t SALARY:%f\n\n", employee.salary);
      }
```

3. Modify the program in LISTING 19-14 so that the program consists one function call, just as 19.16 does.

Pointers and Classes

Pointers, References, and Friends

20. Objects and Pointers

In C++, pointers to objects work much as they do with structures, with some key exceptions. You can define pointers to objects and use class pointer operations to reference it public members. However, pointers to object are restricted from accessing private members, unless that pointer is declared within a friend function. You can define arrays of objects and use pointer operations to reference objects in the array.

You can also define pointers to members of a class. However, pointers to class members operate very differently than pointers to structure members. In C++, a pointer to a class member does not hold the address of a particular object's member. Instead it is set to reference a member of a particular name within a class. Then when you reference an object you can use the pointer to reference that object's member. You can never use the pointer to directly reference the member. You always first have to reference a particular object either with that object's name or with a pointer to that object.

You can use class objects to implement data structures such as linked lists. These applications involve other features of C++ such as friend classes and static members. A class that is a friend of another provides it with access to its private members. The new operation is used to dynamically create new objects that can then be linked using pointers to objects. Arrays often make use of static members that are single global members of a class that you can use to manage an array.

In addition to pointers, C++ also supports references. A reference operates as another name for an object. With a reference you can implement call-by-reference operations without resorting to pointers and pointer operations such as indirection. In most cases where you would need a pointer to an object or variable, you could, instead, use a reference, providing a much more elegant way to reference the object.

This chapter will first deal with pointers and references and their use with functions. Then arrays of objects and static members will be discussed, followed by an examination Friend classes and the new operation. Finally the use of classes to implement a linked list data structure will be presented, incorporating both the use of friend classes and the new operation.

Pointers to Objects

Just as you can declare pointers to structures, you can also declare pointers to objects. You declare a pointer to an object by entering the class type followed by the pointer type and the name of the pointer variable. In the next example, `cptr` is declared as a pointer to a class object of type calc.

```
calc *cptr;
```

Just as with a structure, you can use the address operator to obtain the address of an object. This address could then be assigned to a pointer to that type of object. In the next example, the address operation on the `mycalc` object obtains the address of `mycalc` that is then assigned to the `cptr` variable.

```
cptr = &mycalc;
```

Once a pointer has the address of an object, you can use it to reference the object's public members. A pointer to an object uses a class pointer operator to reference members. The class pointer operation uses the same symbol as the structure pointer operator. Both consist of an arrow made with a dash followed by a greater than sign, ->. In the next example, the class pointer operation using `cptr` references the `calc_price` function, executing a function call.

```
cptr->calc_price();
```

You cannot, however, use a pointer to reference any of the private members. Private member remain hidden whether you use the class member operator, . , or the class pointer operator, ->. The next example brings all these elements together, declaring a pointer, assigning an address of an object, and then using the pointer to reference a member of that object.

```
calc mycalc;
calc *cptr;

cptr = &mycalc;

cptr->calc_price();
```

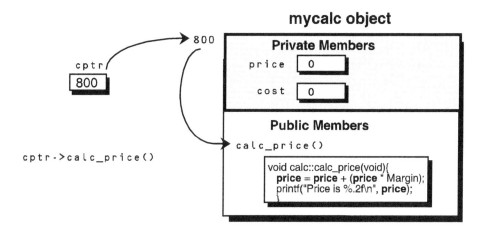

Figure 20-1: Pointer to class object referencing an object member.

Pointers to Class Members

C++ does not allow you to declare an ordinary pointer as a pointer to a member of class. Unlike structures in C, where you can declare pointers that directly reference structure members, you cannot have a pointer directly referencing a class member. Using the calctot class in the following example, you could not assign the address of the total member to the totptr pointer declared in the program, even though total is a public member of calc and can be accessed otherwise. An attempt to assign the address of the mycalc's total member to totptr or any other pointer is illegal and will result in a compiler error.

```
class calctot {
            private:
                    double price;
            public:
                    double total;
                    void calc_price(void);
            };

calc mycalc;
double *totptr;

totptr = &mycalc.total          Illegal Operation
```

C++, does have a special kind of pointer that, when used with an object reference, allows that pointer to directly reference a class member. These are known as pointers to class members. A pointer to a class member not only requires the type of the member, but also the type of its class. The type of a class member actually consists of two components, the standard data type, and the class type. In the `calctot` class used in preceding example, the type of the total member is `double calctot::`. double is its data type and `calctot::` is its class type. The class type for a member is denoted by the class name followed by two colons.

When you declare a pointer to a class member you need to include both the standard data type and the class type in the pointer declaration. In the next example, the pointer `tptr` is declared as a pointer to member of the `calctot` class that is a double.

```
double calctot:: *tptr;
```

A pointer to a class member is literally just that. It a pointer that points to a member of a class, not a member of a particular object. A pointer to a class member uses class type information to later reference a particular member. In this respect, you do not assign to it the specific address of a defined object's member. Instead you assign the relative address of a member as provided by a class declaration. Then when you reference an object, you can then use the pointer to reference one of its members. You can think of the relative address as an offset, how many bytes from the beginning of an object where you would find the member. No particular address is involved. This kind of information can be provided by the class directly, rather than by a particular object.

To use such a pointer you need to first reference an object of that class, and then that object's member can be accessed. You are actually declaring a pointer that is scoped to that class. It can only be used to reference members of objects for that class, and then, only with members of the same data type.

In the next example, mycalct is declared as an object of class type `calctot`. `tptr` is declared as a pointer to a member of the `calctot` class that is a double. The relative address of the total member of the mycalct class is then assigned to `tptr`. The `calctot` class type is used in the address calculation, not a defined object. In effect, `&calctot::total` is providing type information to `totptr` on where to locate the total member when an actual `calctot` object is referenced.

```
double calctot::*tptr;

totptr = &calctot::total;
```

To use a pointer to a member, you first reference an object of its class and then use indirection to reference the member. In the next example, `tptr` is used to reference the total member of the mycalt object. Notice the combination of the class member operator, ., and the indirection operator, *. The class member operator first references the `mycalc` object, and then the indirection on `tptr`

```
mycalc.*tptr = 34.00;
```

Pointers to members have the same scoping restrictions as pointers to objects. Unless a pointer to a member is defined within a friend function, it cannot reference a private member. For example, any attempt to assign the address of the private member price to `tptr` will result in a compiler error. Only public members can be accessed by pointers to members (with the exception of friend functions).

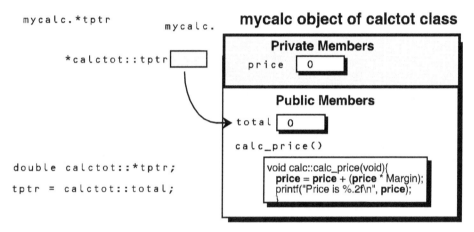

Figure 20-2: Pointer to member.

Pointers to members are often used to reference member functions. In this case you would need to declare a pointer to a class member that is a function. Such a pointer is not a simple pointer to a function. The pointer references the functions as member of a class. Such a declaration can appear complex. You need to enclose both the class type and the pointer type within parenthesis. The pointer type, the asterisk - *, has less precedence that the function type, the parentheses - (). To ensure the precedence of the pointer type it is enclosed within parentheses. In the next example, the user declares a pointer to a member function called `calptr`. `calptr` points to a member function of the calc class that has no return type or parameters (void).

```
void (calc:: *calptr)(void);
```

As with data members, you use class information to assign a relative address to the pointer. In the next example, the `calctot` class is used to provide `calptr` with information on where to locate the `calcprice` member function. You can then use `calptr` to reference the `calcprice` members of `calctot` class objects.

```
calptr = &calctot::calcprice;
```

In the next example, the `mycalc` object is first referenced, and then an indirection on `calptr` references `mycalc`'s `calcprice` function. `mycalc` and `calptr` are enclosed in parenthesis because the function call operator, `()`, has a higher precedence than the class member or indirection operators, `.` and `*`.

LISTING 20-1:

calcptr.cpp
```cpp
#include <stdio.h>
const double Margin = 0.05;

class calc {
        private:
                double price;
                double cost;
        public:
                double total;
                void user_input(void);
                void calc_price(void);
        };

void calc::user_input()
    {
    printf("\nPlease enter cost: ");
    scanf ("%lf", &cost);
    }

void calc::calc_price (void)
    {
    price = cost + (cost * Margin);
    printf("Price is %.2f\n", price);
    }

int main(void)
    {
    calc mycalc;
    calc *cptr;                 /* pointer to calc class object */
    double calc:: *tptr;        /* pointer to public member */
    void (calc:: *calptr)(void);   /* pointer to public member
                                        function */

    cptr = &mycalc;
    cptr->user_input();
    calptr = &calc::calc_price;   /* calptr set to reference the
                                     calc_price functiosn in any calc
                                        object */
    (mycalc.*calptr)();           /* calptr first locates calc_price
                                     in mycalc and then references it */

    tptr = &calc::total;      /* set to reference a total member in
                                  any calc object */
    mycalc.*tptr = 45.00;
    printf("The total is %.2f", mycalc.*tptr );

    return 0;

    }
```

```
(mycalc.*calptr)();
```

The **calcptr.cpp** program in LISTING 20-1 shows examples of the use of pointers to data members and pointers to member functions. There are three pointers in this program, cptr, tptr, and calptr. cptr is a pointer to a calc object. It is assigned the address of the mycalc object and then references and calls the user_input member function of mycalc. The tptr pointer is a pointer to a double member of the calc class. It is assigned the relative address of the calc class's total member. A reference of mycalc and an indirection on tptr is then used to reference the mycalc total member and assign the value 45.00 to it. calptr is a pointer to a calc member function that has not return value or parameter list. calptr is assigned the relative address of calc_price. calptr is then used in a function call operation to reference and call the calc_price member function of the mycalc object.

References to Objects

In C++ there are two ways in which you can use an object's address to reference members of that object, pointers and references. Pointers to objects operate much like pointers to structures, using indirection and member operations. References operate more as another name for an object, allowing you to dispense with the operators you would normally use with pointers. A reference can access an object with the same syntax as an object name. References are often used in functions to implement call-by-reference operations.

The use of a reference appears exactly like the use of an object's name. You would use the name of reference, just as you would use the name of an object, whereas a pointer would require special operators such as the indirection and class pointer operators.

A reference is a constant that must be initialized when it is declared. You cannot declare a reference without initializing it. To initialize a reference you assign it the name of an object. A reference can only reference one particular object. You cannot change it to reference another object. In this respect a reference is always a reference of one specific object, not of a type of object as with pointers.

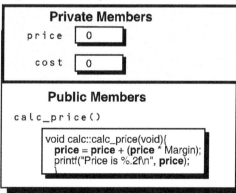

Figure 20-3: Reference as another name for an object.

You define a reference using a class type followed by an ampersand preceding the reference name. After the reference name comes the initialization to the object that the reference will refer to. This consists of only the equal sign, followed by just the object name. No address operator is needed, as is the case with pointers. You only need the name of the object. In the next example, `newprice` is a reference that can be used to reference the `mycalc` object.

```
calc &newprice = mycalc;
```

LISTING 20-2:

calcref.cpp

```
#include <stdio.h>

const double Margin = 0.10;

class calc {
            private:
                    double price;
                    double cost;
            public:
                    void user_input(void);
                    void calc_price(void);
            };

void calc::user_input()
        {
        printf("\nPlease enter cost: ");
        scanf ("%lf", &cost);
        }

void calc::calc_price (void)
        {
        price = cost + (cost * Margin);
        printf("Price is %.2f\n", price);
        }

int main(void)
        {
        calc mycalc;
        calc *cptr;
        calc &newprice = mycalc;

        cptr = &mycalc;

        mycalc.user_input();

        cptr->calc_price();
        newprice.calc_price();
        mycalc.calc_price();

        return 0;
        }
```

Note that the reference data type is yet another use of the ampersand. In a reference declaration you place the ampersand just before the reference name, in the same place where you would put the pointer type, the asterisk, in a pointer variable declaration. In the next example, `mycalc` is defined as an object of type calc, and `newprice` is a reference that accesses that `mycalc` object. You can now use `newprice` as you would use the `mycalc` object name. A member operation on `newprice` is used to call the `calc_price` function.

```
calc mycalc;
calc &newprice = mycalc;;

newprice.calc_price();
```

In the **calcref.cpp** program in LISTING 20-2, shows both the use of pointers and references to objects. `cptr` is declared as a pointer to a class object of type calc, and `newprice` is declared as a reference to the `mycalc` object. In the first statement, the address operation on the `mycalc` object obtains the address of `mycalc` which is then assigned to the `cptr` pointer variable. The `newprice` reference already references `mycalc` as specified in its initialization. Three references of the `calc_price` function then follow. The first uses the pointer variable `cptr` with the class pointer operation to reference the `calc_price` member. The second uses the `newprice` reference with the class member operation. And the third uses the object name `mycalc` with a class member operation. Both the reference and the object name use the class member operator, ., whereas the pointer variable needs to use the class pointer operator, ->.

Objects and Functions

You can use objects as arguments and parameters in function calls just as you would use structures. You can perform call-by-value operations in which you pass the values of one object into a corresponding locally declared parameter object. And you can perform call-by-reference operations in which you pass only the address of an object, using it to directly reference the object from within the called function. You can also implement call-by-reference operations using references. In this case the reference is a parameter that will refer to the object listed as its corresponding argument. Using the reference name in the called function will directly reference that object in the calling function, without resorting to pointers.

call-by-value and objects

In a call-by-value operation, you pass an object to a function by listing that object as an argument in a function call. The corresponding parameter to that argument is an object of the same type. The values of the argument object are copied into the members of the parameter object. In the **numval.cpp** program in LISTING 20-3, the `mynum` object is passed to the `newnum` parameter object in the `enternum` function.

In call-by-value operations such as these, you need to keep in mind that the parameter object is the object being operated on within the function, not the argument object in the calling function. The use of access functions can be misleading in this respect. The function call to `get_num` and `print_num` in the `enternum` function affects the num member of the `newnum` object, not the `mynum` object.

In a call-by-value operation, also be aware that you may be passing a great deal of data. When you pass the value of an object to its parameter, you are copying all the data in that object the corresponding parameter object.

LISTING 20-3:

num.h

```
class num {
            private:
                    int number;
            public:
                    void get_num(void);
                    void print_num(void);
            };

void num::get_num (void)
        {
        printf("Enter Num\n");
        scanf("%d", &number);
        }

void num::print_num (void)
        {
        printf("Num is %d\n", number);
        }
```

numval.cpp

```
#include <stdio.h>
#include "num.h"

    void enternum(num);

    int main(void)
            {
            num mynum;

            mynum.get_num();
            enternum(mynum);
            mynum.print_num();
            return 0;
            }

    void enternum(num newnum)
            {
            newnum.print_num();
            newnum.get_num();
            newnum.print_num();
            }
```

call-by-reference with pointers

In a call-by-reference operation, you pass the address of an object to a pointer variable that points to that type of object. You can obtain the address of the object using an address operator on the object name. Within the called function, the pointer parameter will hold the address of this object. You can then use the class pointer operator to reference members of that object. In the **numptr.cpp** program in LISTING 20-4, the address of the `mycalc` object is passed to the `nptr` pointer parameter in the `enternum` function. The nptr pointer is then used to reference `print_num` and `get_num` members of `mycalc`. Note that these are the member function of the `mycalc` object defined in the main functions. The calls to these functions will change the number member of `mycalc`.

LISTING 20-4:

numptr.cpp

```
#include <stdio.h>
#include "num.h"

        void enternum(num *);

        int main(void)
                {
                num mynum;

                mynum.get_num();
                enternum(&mynum);
                mynum.print_num();
                return 0;
                }


        void enternum (num *nptr)
                {
                nptr->print_num();
                nptr->get_num();
                nptr->print_num();
                }
```

LISTING 20-5:

numref.cpp

```
#include <stdio.h>
#include "num.h"

        void enternum(num&);

        int main(void)
                {
                num mynum;

                mynum.get_num();
                enternum(mynum);
                mynum.print_num();
                return 0;
                }

        void enternum(num &fnum)
                {
                fnum.print_num();
                fnum.get_num();
                fnum.print_num();
                }
```

call-by-reference with references

Instead of a pointer, you could use a reference as your parameter in a call-by-reference operation. The reference parameter can directly reference its corresponding object listed in the argument list. It is literally another name for that object, an alias for that object. Recall that a reference uses the same standard member operations as that used with an object name. It does not use pointer operators such as the indirection operator. Also, you declare a reference using the reference type, the ampersand, instead of the pointer type, the asterisk.

In the **numref.cpp** program in LISTING 20-5, the `fnum` parameter reference is made a reference to its corresponding object in the argument list, the `mynum` object. Then member operations on `fnum` references the `print_num` and `get_num` members of `mynum`. As with the pointer operations, the `mycalc` function members are being referenced, changing the number member of the `mycalc` object defined in the main function. The prototype for `enternum` how lists a reference to a num class object. The ampersand is place after the class name, `void enternum(num&)`.

Pointers and Friend Functions

Ordinarily, pointers to objects cannot access the private members of objects. However, friend functions provide an exception to this restriction. A pointer to an object defined within a friend function can access the private members of objects of that class. You can also define a pointer to a private member. In the next example, the function `setprice` is defined in the calc class as a friend function. Any pointers defined in `setprice` can then access private members of calc class objects. `cptr` is declared a pointer to a calc class object. It is then assigned the address of the `mycalc` object. Since setprice is a friend function of calc objects, `cptr` can reference the cost private member of the `mycalc` object, `cptr->cost`. Using the class pointer operation on `cptr`, the price member of `mycalc` is assigned the value 53.00.

```
class calc {
            private:
                    double price;
                    double cost;
            public:
                    double total;
                    void calc_price(void);
                    friend float setprice(void);
            };

float setprice(void)
        {
        calc mycalc;
        calc *cptr;
        double calc::*priceptr;

        cptr = &mycalc;
        cptr->cost = 53.00;

        priceptr = &calc::price;
        mycalc.*priceptr = 45.00;
        }
```

Within a friend function you can also assign the address of a private member to a pointer to a member. In the previous example, `priceptr` is declared as pointer to a member of the calc class that is a double. Normally, it would be restricted only to doubles that are public members. Within the friend function it can be assigned addresses of doubles that are private members. In the example, `priceptr` is assigned the address of the `mycalc` object's private member price. An indirection on `priceptr` then references the price member. Here the indirection on `priceptr` is used to set the value of the price member of `mycalc` to 45.00

A friend function is particularly effective for implementing a kind of call-by-reference operation on an object that can reference all members of that object, both public and private. In the **setprice.cpp** program in LISTING 20-6, `setprice` is modified to receive the address of an object in is `cptr` parameter. `cptr` is a pointer to an object of class calc. Since `setprice` is a friend function, `cptr` can reference both public and private members, including cost and price. Notice also the way the `priceptr` pointer to a member is reference with `cptr`, `cptr->*priceptr`. `cptr->` references the object, and then `*priceptr` refrences the pointed to member, in this case, price.

LISTING 20-6:

setprice.cpp
```
#include <stdio.h>

        const double Margin = 0.05;

        class calc {
                        private:
                                double price;
                                double cost;
                        public:
                                double total;
                                void calc_price(void);
                                friend void setprice(calc*);
                        };

        void calc::calc_price (void)
                {
                price = price + (price * Margin);
                printf("Price is %.2f\n", price);
                }

 void setprice(calc*);

        int main(void)
                {
                calc mycalc;

                setprice(&mycalc);
                return 0;
                }

        void setprice(calc *cptr)
                {
                double calc:: *priceptr;

                cptr->cost = 53.00;

                priceptr = &calc::price;
                cptr->*priceptr = 45.00;
                }
```

Arrays of Objects

Just as you can define an array of structures, you can also define an array of class objects. In this case, the type of each object in the array is of a class. You can then reference each object as an element in the array, using array subscripts or the pointer offset, increment, or index operations. The next example defines an array called `ournums` that consists of 30 num objects. There is then a reference to the fifth object using an array subscript.

```
num ournums[30;

ournums[5]
```

To call a particular object element's function, you would need the array name, the array subscript with the element number, and a class member operation to reference the function. The next example calls the `print_num()` function of the fifth object element in the `ournums` array.

```
ournums[5].print_num();
```

Instead of array subscripts, you can use pointer operations to reference object elements. The next example uses pointer offset operations to reference the fifth object element and its `print_num` function. Note that the indirection and offset operation, `*(ournums + 5)`, references the fifth element, and then the class member operation references the fifth element object's `print_num` function.

```
(*(ournums + 5)).print_num();
```

Working pointers operate in the same way on class object arrays as then do on other arrays. The next example defines a pointer to a num class, `numptr`, and then assigns the address of the first object in the `ournums` array to it. `ournums` is an array name and as such is the address of the first element of the array, in this case, the address of the first num object. `numptr` is then uses increment operations within a loop to advance from one object element to another. A class pointer operation is used to reference the `print_num` function of the object element currently pointed to.

```
num ournums[10];
num *numptr;

numptr = ournums;
while (numptr < (ournums + 10))
        {
        numptr->print_num();
        numptr++;
        }
```

The **numarr.cpp** program in LISTING 20-7 shows the use of array subscript and pointer operations on class object arrays. `ournums` is defined as an array of num objects. `count` keeps track of how many objects in the array are used. In the first loop, the `get_num` function of the next available object is referenced using array subscripts. In the second loop, `numptr` is used as a working pointer to advance down the array from object to object, referencing each object's `print_num` function to display its number.

LISTING 20-7:

numarr.cpp

```
#include <stdio.h>

        class num {
                        private:
                                int number;
                        public:
                                void get_num(void);
                                void print_num(void);
                        };

        void num::get_num (void)
                {
                printf("Enter Num\n");
                scanf("%d", &number);
                }

        void num::print_num (void)
                {
                printf("%d\n", number);
                }

        const int Max = 30;

        int main(void)
                {
                num ournums[Max];
                num *numptr;
                int count = 0;

                char answ[2] = "y";

                while(answ[0] == 'y')
                        {
                        ournums[count].get_num();
                        count++;
                        printf("Again (y/n): ");
                        scanf("%1s", answ);
                        }

for(numptr=ournums; numptr < (ournums+count); numptr++)
                        {
                        numptr->print_num();
                        }

        return 0;
        }
```

Static members

Suppose that you have an array, and you want to keep track of how many elements are being used. You could define a structure with a member that is the array and another an integer to keep count of the elements used. Or you could use a static member. A static member is a member of a class that is global to all objects defined for that glass. It is a kind of scoped global variable. Recall that an static external variable in C are scoped to the functions defined in its source code file. Static class members are also scoped, but scoped to all the objects of their class. As a global variable, there can be only one instance of a static member. In this respect, a static member is associated more with the class than with any particular object. Whereas each object has its own class members, there is only one instance of static member. Each object can access this one static member.

A static member works more with the class as a whole, rather than as part of one individual object in that class. As such, a static member is defined when it initialized with a value. You do not have to first define an object. You initialize a static member outside of the class declaration, just as you would initialize an external variable. The initialization does requires the class type and scoping operator. The next example shows a class declaration called numc that defines a static member called count. count is initialized to zero outside the class declaration much like an external variable. The initialization includes the class type and scoping operator, numc::. At this point, though there are no numc objects defined, there is the static variable count that will operate as a scoped external member for all future numc objects. There will be only one count variable though there may be many numc objects.

```
class numc{
      public:
            static int count;
            int num;
      }

int numc::count = 0;
```

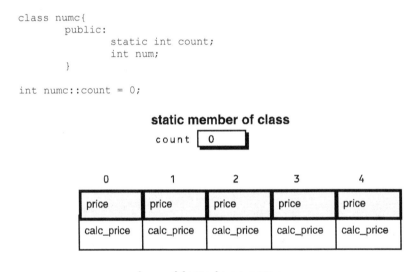

static member of class

count   0

class objects in an array

Figure 20-4: Static members accessible to all objects of a class.

You can access a static member using either the class name and the class scope operator, ::, or you can use any of the class objects' name and the member operator. In the next example, both statements access the same static member, count.

```
numc::count++;

mynum.count++;
```

Though you could use different object names to access a static member, they all would access that one single static member, in this case, count. In the next example, both references of count using mynum and yournum access the one same static member.

```
numc mynum;
numc yournum;

mynum.count++;
yournum.count++;
```

LISTING 20-8:

numc.cpp

```c
#include <stdio.h>

class numc {
            private:
                    int number;
            public:
                    static int count;
                    void get_num(void);
                    void print_num(void);
            };

void numc::get_num (void)
        {
        printf("Enter Num\n");
        scanf("%d", &number);
        }

void numc::print_num (void)
        {
        printf("%d\n", number);
        }

int numc::count = 0;

const int Max = 30;

int main(void)
        {
        numc mynum[Max];
        char answ[2] = "y";
        int i;

        while(answ[0] == 'y')
                {
                mynum[numc::count].get_num();
                numc::count++;

                printf("Again (y/n): ");
                scanf("%1s", answ);
                }
printf("The number entered is %d\n", numc::count);
        for(i = 0; i < numc::count; i++)
                {
                mynum[i].print_num();
                }
return 0;
}
```

Static members are often used with arrays of objects. With an array of objects, there is usually certain information that you may need to manage the array, such as the number of objects used in the array. Also, each object may have to access certain common information. All such information could effectively be held in static members, members global to and yet scoped to those array objects. Instead of placing the information in regular external variables, you can just define static members for it. In the **numc.cpp** program in LISTING 20-8, an array of numc objects is defined. The numc class has a static member called count that keeps track of the number of object used in the array. It is initialized outside the class declaration to 0. In a loop, the user is prompted to enter in a number for an object. The static member, count, keeps track of how many objects are used. count is referenced using the class name and scope operator, numc::count. In the next loop, the number members of each object in the array is printed out. The static member count indicates the last object used.

Keep in mind that static members are global to all objects of a class. This presents a slightly restricted way of thinking about a class. Instead of a more general class, a class with static members tends to be tailored to a specific task. So instead of a general numc class, you would have a class for a particular list of numbers, say a numitems class for a list of the number of items sold in a particular store. The **mystbook.cpp** program in LISTING 20-9, manages a list of mystery books using an array of mystbook class objects. The mystbook class uses the bookcount static member to keep track of how many mystery books there are. A class reference to the static member bookcount is used in the main function to determine how many books objects to output, mystbook::bookcount. mystbook also has a static function, menu. Just as data members can be static, so also member functions can be static. In this case, the mystbook objects only need the one single copy of the menu function. For each object, the menu will be the same. So only one instance of the menu function is needed. It is also referenced in main using the class scope operation, mystbook::menu().

LISTING 20-9:

mystbook.cpp
```cpp
#include <stdio.h>
        const int Max = 30;
        class mystbook {
                private:
                        char title[100];
                        int  year;
                public:
                        static int bookcount;
                        static void menu(void);
                        void input_book(void);
                        void output_book(void);
                };

 void mystbook::input_book()
     {
     if(bookcount < Max)
            {
            printf("\nPlease enter title: ");
            scanf("%*[\n\t ]%[^\n]s", title);
            printf("Please enter year published: ");
            scanf("%d", &year);
            bookcount++;
            }
        else
            printf("Library is full\n");
     }
```

```
void mystbook::output_book()
        {
                printf("\n\n Book Record \n");
                printf("\t TITLE: %s \n", title);
                printf("\t YEAR : %d \n\n", year);
        }

void mystbook::menu(void)
                {
                printf("a. add books to library\n");
                printf("p. print books in library\n");
                printf("q. quit library\n");
                }

int mystbook::bookcount = 0;

int main(void)
        {
        mystbook books[Max];
        int i;
        int more = 1;
        char choice[2];

        mystbook::menu();
        while (more == 1)
                {
                printf("Enter choice: ");
                scanf("%1s", choice);

                switch(choice[0])
                        {
                        case 'a':
                                books[mystbook::bookcount].input_book();
                                break;
                        case 'p':
                                for(i= 0; i< mystbook::bookcount; i++)
                                        {
                                        books[i].output_book();
                                        }
                                break;
                        case 'm':
                                mystbook::menu();
                                break;
                        case 'q':
                                more = 0;
                                break;
                        }
                }
        return 0;
        }
```

Pointers to Allocated Objects: new

Data structures such as linked lists are created using allocated objects. In Chapter 15 you saw how allocation functions such as `malloc` and `calloc` created such objects, returning to the program their addresses. Through pointers you could then reference these objects. C++ uses much the same process. The allocation of an object has been streamlined to just one operation invoked by the new command. You no longer need to use allocation functions like `malloc` . You only need to use new.

The new operation takes as its argument a specified type. It then creates an object of that type and returns its address. You can then assign that address to a pointer that you can then use to reference the object. In the next example, the user creates an integer object using the new operation and assigns the resulting address to the pointer `costptr`.

```
int *costptr;

costptr = new int;
```

You can also use the new operation to dynamically allocate objects for use as arrays. In this case the type would include the array type, [], and the number of elements in the array, as well as the type of objects. In the next example, the user creates an array of 10 characters. The type for an array of 10 character is char[10].

```
char *str;

str = new char[10];
```

To dynamically allocate an object for a structure, you need only to specify the structure type. In the next example, the user allocate memory for a node structure and assigns its address to the `nodeptr` pointer.

```
struct node {
            char key[10];
            node *rptr;
            node *lptr;
            };

node *nodeptr;

nodeptr = new node;
```

You can also use new to create a class object. In the next example, the new operation creates a `newobj` object. The address is assigned to `objptr` which can then can then use indirection to reference that `newobj` object.

```
class numobj {
            int mynum;
            numobj *nextptr;
            };

numobj *numptr;

numptr = new newobj;
```

Once you no longer need to use an object, you can destroy the object the delete operation, effectively de-allocating its memory. delete returns the memory to the pool of unused free memory available to your program for allocation by new. If you do not delete a dynamically allocated object that you no longer need to use, its memory remains marked as in use and unavailable.

For example, say you have implemented a linked list using dynamically allocated objects. Should you remove an object from a linked list, you would then need to delete that object. The delete operation takes as its argument the pointer that holds the address of the object to be de-allocated. The next example shows the operation for deleting a `newobj` object whose address is held by `numptr`.

```
delete numptr;
```

You can also apply the delete operation to dynamically allocated arrays. In this case the argument is the pointer that holds the address of the first element in the array. delete will remove the entire array. The next example shows the delete operation de-allocating the memory for the `str` array.

```
delete str;
```

Applying delete to an array of objects requires that you include the array type, the set of empty brackets - [], before the pointer that holds the array address. The next example shows both the allocation of an array of `mystbook` objects and its de-allocation with the delete operation.

```
mystbook *booksptr;

booksptr = new mystbook[10];

delete [] booksptr;
```

Friends Class: scoping between classes

You have seen how classes hide and protect their private members from the rest of the program, even other classes. An object completely hides its private data from any other object. No other object can access it. There are situations when one object may have to access the private data held by another object. In other words, an object may need to share its private data with another object. Such is the case in Data Structures. For example, a linked list composed of objects needs to allow the head pointer to access the first object.

One solution is to make such private data, public. But this would open up the data to any other object, or even to any function, allowing a change anywhere in your program. Instead, you only want to allow access to an object only by another specified type of object. The friend class specification allows you to do this.

The friend class provides a way for one object to access the private data in another. In this sense, an object can be said to have friends. Any object of a friend class can access the private data of that object. Accessibility is limited only to its friends. To other objects and to the rest of the program, that object's private data remains hidden and inaccessible. At the same time, keep in mind that the friend class relationship works by class, not individual objects. All the objects of a certain class are open to all the objects of its friend class.

You specify a friend class in a class type declaration by entering the keyword friend, followed by the keyword class, and then the name of the friend class. This entry in placed in the class declaration as you would enter a member. The next example shows the entry you would make in class declaration to make the class list a friend of that class.

```
friend class list;
```

In the next example, the list class is made a friend of the `numobj` class. An object of the list class can now access the private data of any `numobj` object, referencing their `mynum` or `numobj` members.

```
class numobj {
            friend class list;
            int mynum;
            numobj *nextptr;
            };
```

The friendship relationship here is one-sided. list has access to `numobj` objects, but `numobj` objects do not have access to the private members of list objects. You can make classes friends of each other. In each class declaration you would enter the friend class specification. In such a case the objects of the two classes could access each other's private members.

In the following example, the calc and item classes are specified as friends of each other. Each also has a pointer to the other class. The iptr member of the calc class can be assigned the address of an item object, and then, through that pointer, a calc object can reference the private members of the item object. The same is true for an item object. The `cptr` member of the item object can be assigned the address of a calc object and, through it, the item object can access the private members of the calc object.

```
class item;            /* forward declaration */
class calc {
            private:
                    friend class item;
                    double price;
                    item *iptr;
            public:
                    void calc_price(void);
            };

class item {
            private:
                    friend class calc;
                    double cost;
                    calc *cptr;
            public:
                    void discount(void);
            };
```

Notice also the forward declaration of item. Since the term item is used in the calc declaration before the item class is actually declared, you need to provide a forward declaration, informing the compiler that, at that point, that the term item refers to a class.

You can also narrow the friend declaration to just a member of another class. Suppose that you have a member function in one class that needs to access the private members of another class. You could then enter just that member function as a friend, instead of the entire class. In the friend entry you will need to include the class scope operation and the class name. You would enter the keyword friend, followed by the member function declaration whose function name would be preceded by the class name and class scope operator. The next example shows what the entry for making the `calcprice` member function of calc a friend.

```
friend void calc::calcprice(void);
```

The next example shows how a member function can be declared a friend of another class. The `calc_price` member of the calc class is declared as a friend of the sum class. `calc_price` can then access the private members of any sum objects, such as a sum object's price member.

```
class calc {
                private:
                        double price;
                public:
                        void calc_price(void);
                };
class sum {
                private:
                        double price;
                public:
                        friend void calc::calc_price(void);
                };
```

Linked List Data Structures: friend classes

As described in Chapter 15, you can create data structures such as linked lists using structures that point to other structures. In C++ you can use class objects in the place of structures as components of a data structure. A linked list can consist of a list of objects. Each object would contain a pointer to another object of the same class type. These objects would then be managed by another object that would contain functions for managing the linked list such as functions to add and delete objects or to print the list of objects out. This list management object would also contain the pointer to the first object, the head pointer. The list management object would hide the management routines and head pointer as private data from the rest of the program. To perform an operation on a list such as adding a new object, you would call an access function that in turn would call a private list management function to add an object to the list.

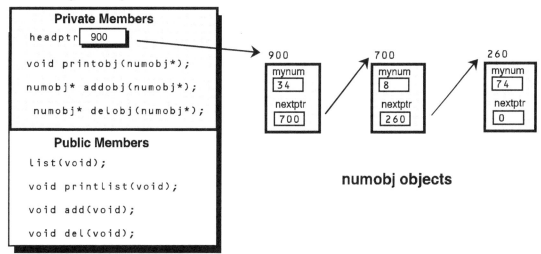

Figure 20-5: Linked list implemented with friend classes.

This means that a linked list in C++ requires two different types of classes. One is for the objects themselves and would contain the list object data and the pointer to the next object in list. The other class would contain the head pointer and the list management functions, as well as a public access methods for list operations. There are now then two classes, one of which has to access private data in another. The list management class has to be able to access and change the pointers in the list element class as well as add information to its private data members.

In the **list.cpp** program in LISTING 20-10, two classes are declared, the numobj and the list class. The numobj class is the class used for list objects. Each object is created by the new operation as a numobj object. The list class is the class used for the list management object. This class declares the list management functions that perform operations on the list objects, as well as the access methods by which the program can operate on the list. This class also declares the head pointer that holds the address of the first object in the list.

A list class object will need to access the private data of the numobj class objects in its linked list. To allow such access, the class type declaration of the numobj class specifies that the list class as its friend, friend class list;. Any list object will have access to any private data in a numobj object. At the same time, only a list object has such access. To all other objects and program functions, the numobj data remains inaccessible and hidden.

LISTING 20-10: Linked List C++ version

list.h

```
class numobj {
                friend class list;
                int mynum;
                numobj *nextptr;
                };


class list {
        private:
                numobj *headptr;
                void printobj(numobj*);
                numobj* addobj(numobj*);
                numobj* delobj(numobj*);
        public:
                 list(void);
                void printlist(void);
                void add(void);
                void del(void);
                };
    list::list(void)
        {
        headptr = 0;
        }
void list::printlist(void)
        {
        printobj(headptr);
        }
```

list.h (continued)

```
void list::printobj(numobj *objptr)
        {
        if(objptr != 0)
                {
                printf ("%d\n", objptr->mynum);
                printobj(objptr->nextptr);
                }
        }

void list::add(void)
        {
        numobj *resptr;
        resptr = addobj(headptr);
                if(headptr== 0)
                                headptr = resptr;
        }

numobj* list::addobj(numobj *objptr)
        {
        numobj *newptr, *resptr;

        if(objptr == 0)
                {
                newptr = new numobj;
                newptr->nextptr = 0;
                printf("Please enter new number\n");
                scanf("%d", &newptr->mynum);
                return newptr;
                }
        else
                {
                resptr = addobj(objptr->nextptr);
                if(resptr != 0)
                        objptr->nextptr = resptr;
                return 0;
                }
        }

void list::del(void)
        {
        numobj *resptr;
        if(headptr != 0)
                {
                resptr = delobj(headptr);
                if(resptr == 0)
                        headptr = 0;
                }
        }
```

list.h (continued)

```
numobj* list::delobj(numobj *objptr)
        {
        numobj *resptr;

        if(objptr->nextptr == 0)
                {
                delete objptr;
                return 0;
                }
        else
                {
                resptr= delobj(objptr->nextptr);
                if(resptr == 0)
                        objptr->nextptr = 0;
                return objptr;
                }

        }
```

list.cpp

```
#include <stdio.h>
#include "list.h"

 int main(void)
        {
        char choice[2];
        int more = 1;
        list mylist;


        while (more != 0)
                {
                printf ("Please enter choice\n");
                scanf("%s", choice);
                switch(choice[0])
                        {
                        case 'a':
                                        mylist.add();
                                        break;
                        case 'p':
                                        mylist.printlist();
                                        break;
                        case 'd':
                                        mylist.del();
                                        break;
                        case 'q':
                                        more = 0;
                        }
                }
        return 0;
        }
```

Chapter Summary: Classes and Pointers

You can define pointers to objects that can reference an object's public members. However, you cannot declare a pointer that points directly to a specific member of an object. For this you need to use a special kind of pointer called a class member pointer. A class member pointer is scoped to that class and is assigned the class member reference using the class type and the member name. To reference the member in a particular object, you need to first reference the object with the object name and class member operation. Then the class member pointer will reference the object's member.

C++ introduces an new feature called references that operate much like pointers. A reference is a pointer that has special features not found in ordinary pointers. When you use a reference, it automatically performs indirection, immediately referencing the object it points to. A reference can use a class member operator to reference class members, instead of the class pointer operator. In fact, the use of a reference appears exactly like the use of an object's name. You would use the name of reference, just as you would use the name of an object, whereas a pointer would require special operators such as the indirection and class pointer operators.

Static members are scoped external members of a class that can be referenced by any object defined for that class. There is only one instance of a static member in a class, and each object can reference that single member. Static members are often used to manage arrays of objects, holding such information such as the number of object used in an array.

In certain cases, an object of one class will need access to the private members of another. For this you need to declare one class as the friend of another. A friend class has complete access to the private members of a given class's objects. In the case of linked lists, the list management class needs access to the private members of the list node class. The list management class is made a friend of the node class, permitting such access.

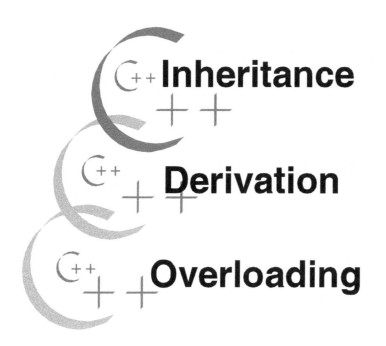

Inheritance

Derivation

Overloading

Function Overloading

Operator Overloading

Derived Classes

Protected Members

Virtual Functions

Inheritance Hierarchies

Multiple Inheritance

21. Inheritance, Derivation, and Overloading

Inheritance, derived classes, and overloading are perhaps the most effective and advanced features of C++. With inheritance you can combine different classes to make a single coherent class called a derived class. You can organize your classes into a hierarchy of classes beginning at the top with very general classes that can be part of many different classes, and ending at the bottom with classes that perform very specific tasks. If you have a complex task that you want a class to perform, then, instead of composing a large class from scratch, you can just combine classes in your hierarchy to create the derived class that you need. Using inheritance you can easily create powerful and complex classes.

Overloading is used primarily for operators and classes. The standard C++ operators can be used on classes provided you define the actions the operator must take. Classes are user-defined and the compiler has no prior knowledge of them, as it does with the standard types. If you want to use an operator on a class, you need to provide the operations that the operator should perform on the class. For example, to use the + operator with two classes you need to define special function for the + operator that adds the specific class members that you want added. You could then use two objects of that class with the + operator. Overloading allows you to use objects of the classes you defined with the standard operators, instead of always having to call functions to perform tasks on an object. This can make for a much clearer and easier programming.

Overloading

Overloading allows you to define different operations for the same function name or operator. It is most often implemented for operators used with classes. For example, you could define your own function for handing the assignment operation between two class objects. This is referred to as operator overloading because is add more operations to the ones that an operator already performs. The + operator is already used to add the values of two standard types such as integers or floats. However, you could create and add your own + operation for two classes that the + operator would then also execute.

Function Overloading

Normally in C you can only use one name per functions. Remember that a function is identified not only by its name but also its type, the type of its return value and the type of is parameters. The return and argument types of a function make up its signature, uniquely identifying it. Recall that in C that you declare a function by specifying the function's name with its return and parameter types. If you gave the wrong type, then the compiler would think there were two different functions with the same name. The return and parameter types identify a function just as much as a function name does.

In C++ you can define functions that have the same name, but with different parameter types. The return type always has to remain the same. The different parameters types are used by your compiler to determine what function you are referring to at any given time. Defining different functions with the same name is called function overloading. Each of these functions needs to have differing parameter types. The compiler uses these different signatures (parameter types) to distinguish functions with the same name. In the next example, two functions of with the same name and return type, but with different parameter lists are declared. Both have the function name `mult` and both return an integer. However one multiplies integers and the other multiplies doubles. The first function has as its arguments two integers. It will call the `mult` function whose parameters list consists of a (int, int).

The second function call has two doubles as its arguments. So it will call the function with the parameter list (double, double), the second function declared.

```
int mult(int, int);
int mult(double, double);

mult(4, 8);

mult(7.25, 2.39);
```

Both return an integer value. Bear in mind that you cannot change the return type. I you were to declare function named `mult` that returned a double, the compile what consider an attempt to re-declare `mult` and give you a compiler error. A declaration like `double mult(double, double)` would be invalid.

Each overloaded function is considered separate functions. You need to define each one in your program. Each will have the same name and return type, but different parameters. Your compiler will be able to tell the functions apart by their parameter types. Since the function's names and return types are the same, their parameter types are used to identify them. In the next example, two versions of `printrec` use different structures as the parameters. The first is designed to print employee records and the second is designed to print contractor records.

```
void printrec(EMP);
void printrec(MANG);
main()
        {
        EMP emp;
        CONTR acme;

        printrec(emp)

        printrec(acme);
        }

void printrec(EMP employee)
                {
                printf("%s", employee.name);
                printf("%d", employee.salary);
                }

void printrec(CONTR contractor)
                {
                printf("%s", contractor.name);
                printf("%d", contractor.bid);
                }
```

Your compiler will be able to tell the function you want to use by the differing type and number of arguments you use when you call it (its signature). In the previous example, the first call to `printrec` will call the `printrec` function with the `EMP employee` parameter and print out an employee record. The second call to `printrec` will call the `printrec` function with the `CONTR contractor` parameter and print out the contractor record.

A differing number of arguments will also distinguish two overload functions. Say, for example, you wanted to have two `printrec` functions for EMP, one for displaying the base record and one for displaying the record and a bonus. The bonus would be provided by a separate argument to

printrec. In the next example, there is yet another version of printrec, this time one that has the
EMP parameter and a double parameter.

```
void printrec(EMP);
void printrec(EMP, double);
void printrec(MANG);

The new function would be defined as such:

void printrec(EMP employee, bonus double)
            {
            printf("%s", employee.name);
            printf("%d", employee.salary);
            printf("%d", employee.salary + bonus);
            }
```

The following function call would call that version of printrec.

```
        printrec(emp)
```
Though you can define an overloaded function to execute any statements you want, it makes
sense to have it perform operations similar to those with the same name. A programmer should have
some idea of what the different versions of a function do. Functions that share the same name and have
the same return type, should perform similar tasks. Otherwise, a programmer could execute a function
call and have radically different results depending up the arguments used. In this respect it may be
more appropriate for there the printrec function for EMP and the one for CONTR to have different
names, say printemp and printcontr. These in turn could be overloaded for variations on printing
out the respective records.

```
void printemp(EMP);
void printemp(EMP, double);
void printcontr(MANG);
void printcontr(MANG, double);
void printemp(EMP employee)
            {
            printf("%s", employee.name);
            printf("%d", employee.salary);
            }

void printemp(EMP employee, bonus double)
            {
            printf("%s", employee.name);
            printf("%d", employee.salary);
            printf("%d", employee.salary + bonus);
            }

void printcontr(CONTR contractor)
            {
            printf("%s", contractor.name);
            printf("%d", contractor.bid);
            }

void printcontr(CONTR contractor, double penalty)
            {
            printf("%s", contractor.name);
            printf("%d", contractor.bid + penalty);
            }
```

When the arguments in a function call of an overloaded function do not exactly match the argument list in any of those functions, then the compiler tries to find the best match. Standard conversion will be tried first, the same conversion used by C for arguments in function calls. If that should fail, the compiler will try to user-defined conversion such as those specially defined for classes. The compiler follows these steps.

1. Look for exact matches.
2. Use standard conversions to generate exact matches.
3. Use user-defined conversions to generate matches.

It is easy to define ambiguous overloaded functions where, in certain circumstances, the compiler is unable to determine what function to call. For this reason it is best use function overloading sparingly. When call overloaded functions be careful to use arguments of the exact match to the parameter list of the particular function you want. Relying on conversions to do it for you can result in calling the wrong function or a compiler error for an ambiguous function call. If necessary, you can use casts in your argument list to insure that the types correctly match the functions parameters.

Even when arguments appear to match exactly, ambiguities can result. For example, in C++ the value 0 can match either an integer or a pointer. Using it to call either version of disp in the next example will result in a function call ambiguity error.

```
void disp(int num);
void disp(int *nptr);
disp(0);                              /* ambiguity error */
```

Operator Overloading

C++, like C, has a designated set of operators consisting of specified symbols such as + and *. These symbols can be used as operators in expressions to perform operations on operands. For example, the + operator will add two operands, two values. 5 + 7 add 5 and 7, resulting in 12. Using operator symbols like + and * in expressions, can be misleading. You may think that operator symbols are somehow different from functions. In fact, they are not. When you use an operator, you are in fact calling a pre-defined function that actually performs the operation. The operands are actually the arguments for that function, and the result of the operation is the return value of that function. Each operator is associated with a pre-defined function that actually performs the work.

When an operator is used, its associated function is called and its operands are passed as arguments to that function. Upon being called, the associated function performs the work and returns the result as its return value. For example, when you use the + operator, an associated addition function is called to actually add the two operands. Those operands are passed as arguments to that addition function. The result of the addition becomes the return value of the addition function.

To understand operator overloading you need to see operations as function calls. The expression `4 + 5` is equivalent to `add(4,5)`, where add is a function to add two integers. Notice that operands of one type require different actions than operands of a different type. In other words, the operation to add two integers is very different from the operation to add two floats. The addition of floating point values requires much more work than the addition of integers. So the addition operator actually has several pre-defined functions associated with it, one for each data type. If you use float as operands for an addition operation, then the function for adding floats is called. If you use integers as operands for an addition operation, then the function for adding integers are called. The same operator, +, has several associated functions each using different operand types. You can begin to see that this looks a lot like function overloading. And indeed it is. An operator is like a series of functions with the same name and differing parameter types. Depending upon the type of arguments you use, one of the functions is selected. You can see then that the type of operands you use with an operator will select and execute one of several associated functions.

For the basic data types such as char, int, and float, operators already have a set of pre-defined associated functions. They cannot be changed. There are no pre-defined functions for any class or structure types that you may declare. You need to define associated operator functions for any class types. For example, suppose you have a class type that can be added. You could define a function to add the two objects of that type, but you can also define an associated operator function that will allow you to then use the addition operator with the two objects. The associated operator function becomes one more associated function for that operator. When you use two class type operands with that operator, the compiler knows to use the associated function that you defined for it.

In effect, you are overloading the operator just as you are overloading a function. Different operations can use the same operator symbol with differing operands, just as different functions can use the same name with differing parameter types. Defining new associated functions for operators is referred to as operator overloading.

You can overload most of the operators already defined for C++, with a few exceptions. However you cannot create any new operators of your own. You can only overload those that already exist. Nor can you change the associativity or precedence of these operators. For example, any operation using *, overloaded or not, takes precedence over operations using +. In general you can easily overload any of the arithmetic, relational, equality, and assignment operators. However, there are four operators that require special treatment, the assignment operator =, the subscript operator [], the function call (), and the class or structure pointer operators ->. The operators can only be overloaded as members of a class. Certain operators such as the conditional operator ?:, the class scope operator ::, and structure or class member operators ., cannot be overloaded at all. Table 21-1 list the different operators that you can overload.

At least one operand in an overloaded operator function must be a user-defined type. That is, it must be either a struct or a class. An attempt to create an overload function using any of the defined standard data types like int or float would conflict with the functions for that operator that already use those data types. For the + operator, there is already a function that uses float data types. You cannot create one of your own. However, there are no predefined operator functions for any of the type you create, such as `struct` or `class` types.

Defining overloaded operators

You define an operator overload function using the operator operation with the operator attached to it that you want to overload. For example, `operator+` will overload the + operator, and `operator=` will overload the assignment operator. Following the keyword operator with its attached operator, is a parameter list specifying the types for the operator's operands. The number of parameter depends upon the number of parameter already defined for the operator. Some, like the – operator can be either the unary - operator taking only one operand, or the arithmetic subtraction operator taking two operands. If an operator takes two operands then the first parameter corresponds to the left operand and the second parameter corresponds to the right. The return type precedes the operator keyword. The next examples show the syntax for both a unary and binary operations.

```
return type operatorop ( operand type )
return type operatorop ( left operand type , right operand type )
```

Keep in mind that at least one of the operands must be a user defined type such as a `class` or `struct`. However, though one must be user-defined, the other can be a standard type. You could have one operand be a structure and the other be a regular integer, or even a pointer to an integer. In the next example, the + operator is overloaded to perform a special operation on an `emprec` structure and a double value. It adds the double value to the salary field of the `emprec` structure, returning the resulting value.

```
struct emprec {
        char name[30];
        double salary;
        }

main()
        {
        emprec dylan;
        double newsalary;

        newsalary = dylan + 8.50;
        }

double operator+(emprec myemp, double raise)
        {
        double res;

        res = myemp.salary = raise;
        return raise;
        }
```

Operator overloading is often used for relational operators. The next example, create an overloaded > operation using operands of type `emprec`.

```
main()
        {
        emprec dylan, chris;

        if(dylan > chris)
                printrec(chris);
        }

int operator>(emprec empleft, emprec empright)
        {
        if(strcmp(empleft.name, empright.name) > 0)
                return 1;
        else
                return 0;
        }
```

Part of the difficulty of working with operation overloading is its power. You can, in effect, change the very meaning of an operator for your user-defined types. You could have an addition operator performing subtraction, or a logical operator printing data. It is up to you to write the overload function, and you can put in any statement that you want.

It is important, though, that you implement operator overloading in an intelligible way. Overloaded operators should perform tasks similar to their original used with standard data types. That way a programmer has some idea of what is being accomplished when the overloaded operator is used. For example, an overloaded assignment operator should perform some kind of assignment operation assigning values in the left operand to those in the right. An overloaded < operation should perform some kind of less-then comparison.

Table 21-1: Operators for Overloading

Arith	Relational	Logical	Assignment	Special	Bitwise
+	>	&&	=	[ ]	&
−	<	||	+=	( )	|
*	>=	−=	−>		^
/	<=	!	*=	−>*	~
%	==		/=	,	&=
	!=		%=		|=
			++		^=
			−−		>>
					<<

Operators whose overload function must be class member function

```
    =
    [ ]
    ( )
    −>
```

Overloaded Operations for Classes: member operator overload functions

If the left hand operand of an overload operation is a class, then the operator function has to be member of that class. This also means that unary operator overloads that have a class as their operand, must be implemented as member functions of the operand's class. Also, overload operator functions for the operators =, [], (), and −> can only be defined as class member functions. You cannot define an independent overload function for the =, [], (), or −> operators. In effect, in most cases where your overload operation used operands that are classes, you will need to define the operator function as member of one of those classes.

When defining an operator function as a member of a class, you do not declare the left operand in the operator function's parameter list. As a member function, the operator function already has direct access to class members. In effect, the declaration of that class as the left operand is implied. Only the right operand needs to be declared in the parameter list, and in the case of unary operations, no explicit parameter declarations are required at all. You can think of the operands used with a member operator function as translating into a function call the left hand object's member operator function using the right hand object as its argument. The following show the translation for a member operator > function.

leftobject > rightobject   is equivalent to   *leftobject . operator> (rightobject)*

To define an operator function as a class member, you first enter the return type followed by the class name and scope operator with the keyword operator with the operator symbol attached. The next example defines the overload of the > operator as a member of the emp class. Its operands are emp class objects. The left operand is implied and is not listed in the operator > function's parameter list.

Only the parameter for the second operand is listed. The function compares the name fields of the emp class's erec structure. erec is a structure of type emprec containing a name and salary field.

```
int emp::operator>( emp rightemp)
      {
      if(strcmp(erec.name, rightemp.erec.name) > 0)
             return 1;
      else
             return 0;
      }
```

You then declare the function in the body of the class using the operator keyword with the attached operator and the list of parameters as well as the return value. The declaration of the operator function defined in the previous example follows.

```
int operator>( emp);
```

In your program, you can then use the > operator to compare two emp objects. The > operator will call the left hand object's operator > function, comparing the name fields of each object's erec structure.

```
emp myemp;
emp newemp;

if(myemp > newemp)
      myemp.output_rec();
```

A listing of the body of the emp class with the operator> member function follows.

```
struct emprec {
      char name[10];
      double salary;
      };

class emp {
      private:
             emprec erec;
             recfile empfile;
      public:
             int operator> (emp);
             void input_rec(void);
             void output_rec(void);
      }

int emp::operator> (emp rightemp)
      {
      if(strcmp(erec.name, rightemp.erec.name) > 0)
             return 1;
      else
             return 0;
      }
```

The implementations of the =, [], and () operator overloads as class member functions are special cases, yet very common. They will each be examined in turn.

Member Overloaded Functions for = Operator: assignment operations

Operator overloading is used most often for the assignment operators, = . Often you will need to assign the value of one class object to another. The = operator has a default copy operation that it will perform on the assignment of two objects. This copy operation is a member-wise copy of the value of each member to the corresponding members of another object, bit by bit. To perform such basic assignment operations you do not need to overload the assignment operator.

In many cases, generating a copy of an object requires special handling of some of its members. In such cases you would have to overload the = operator for this class. For example, if a members of an object you are copying references allocated memory, you would have to take care to also allocate memory for the pointer members in the corresponding object. To do this, you would have to overload the = operator to perform the needed memory allocation.

To overload an assignment operator for a class, you have to define a member overload operator function for the assignment operator. By defining a member function for the = operator, you can use the = operator to write assignment operations. In the next example, the value of one bookrec object is assigned to another using the = operator. The = operator actually calls the bookrec = operator function, with the two operands, the two bookrec objects, as the argument for the = operator function. The **books.cpp** program in LISTING 21-1 shows the definition of the bookrec member overload = operator function.

```
bookrec newbk;
bookrec tempbk;

tempbk = newbk;
```

The return type for an operator = function is the type of the class. Recall that the result of an assignment operation is the value assigned. In this case the value assigned is the value of a class. To cut down on the memory required to contain such a copy of a class, operator = functions are often defined to return a reference instead, as is the case in this example. You define a member overload operator function for = by first entering its return type followed by the class name and class scope operator, and then the keyword operator with the = symbol attached to it. The argument list follows. It will contain a parameter declaration for the second operand. For member overload operator functions, the first operand is implicit and always assumed to be an object of the class for which it is a member. As such, the member operator function can directly reference its object's members, the member of the first operand. The second operand is then declared as the first parameter of the operator = function. The second operand of an assignment operation is the value assigned. In this case the value assigned is the value of another bookrec object. Again to save on space, this operand is often passed as a reference instead of an object's value. The following example shows the definition of the member overload = operator function for the bookrec class.

```
bookrec &bookrec::operator=(bookrec &rbrec)
        {
        book.year = rbrec.book.year;
        book.price = rbrec.book.price;
        strcpy(book.titleptr = rbrec.book.titleptr);
        return rbrec;
        }
```

LISTING 21-1:

books.cpp
```cpp
#include <stdio.h>
#include <string.h>

 struct bookdat {        /* Book structure */
                        int year;
                        float price;
                char* titleptr;
                        };
class bookrec {
        private:
                bookdat book;
        public:
                 bookrec();
                void input_rec(void);
                void output_rec(void);
                bookrec &bookrec::operator=(bookrec&);
                };
 bookrec::bookrec()
                {
                book.titleptr = new char[100];
                }
 bookrec &bookrec::operator=(bookrec &rbrec)
                {
                book.year = rbrec.book.year;
                book.price = rbrec.book.price;
                strcpy(book.titleptr, rbrec.book.titleptr);
                return rbrec;
                }

void bookrec::input_rec(void)
        {
        printf("\nPlease enter title: ");
        scanf("%*[\n\t ]%[^\n]s", book.titleptr);
        printf("\nPlease enter year published: ");
        scanf("%d", &book.year);
        printf("\nPlease enter book price: ");
        scanf("%f", &book.price);
        }

void bookrec::output_rec(void)
        {
        printf("\n\t TITLE : %s \n", book.titleptr);
        printf("\t YEAR  : %d \n", book.year);
        printf("\t PRICE : %.2f \n\n", book.price);
        }

int main(void)
        {
        bookrec mybook;
        bookrec tempbk;

        mybook.input_rec();
        tempbk = mybook;
        tempbk.output_rec();

        return 0;
        }
```

An assignment of one `bookrec` object to another consist mainly of assigning the different members of their respective book `bookdat` structure to each other. `rbook` is a reference to the right hand operand, the second operand, in the assignment operation. The object of which this assignment function is a member, is the left hand operand, the first operand. Its assignment function can directly reference its own members. So the book member of the first operand is referenced directly as book, whereas the book member of the right hand operand is referenced through the assignment function's parameter, rbrec.book.

Though the assignment operation for a class is written with a right and left object around a = operator, you can think of it as translating into a function call of the left hand object's assignment function with the right hand object as its argument. `tempbk = newbk` becomes `tempbk.operator=(newbk);`

```
tempbk = newbk    is equivalent to  tempbk.operator=(newbk)
```

The `titleptr` member of the book structure in each object requires special handling. `titleptr` is a pointer to allocated memory, and array of characters created in the `bookrec` constructor whose address is assigned to the `book.titleptr` pointer. `strcpy` is used to copy the contents of the allocated array used for assigned object to the allocated array used by the object being copied to. A = overload function has to be used to provide the `strcpy` operation, because the allocated arrays are not part of the objects. Only the book.titleptr pointers are part of the objects. If you were to use the default memberwise copy operation instead of defining a = overload function, then the address in the `book.titleptr` pointer in the assigned object would be copied to the `book.titepltr` pointer in the copied-to object. The contents of the corresponding array would not be copied. Instead the `book.titleptr` members of each object would point to the same allocated array, and the `book.titleptr` member of the object being copied to would lose the address of its originally allocated array.

Member Overloaded Functions for [] Operator: array reference

The member overload functions for the `[]` and `()` operators are normally used to operate on class member arrays, `[]` more so than `()`. The `[]` operator is used to reference elements of an array that is a member of a class, and the `()` operator is often used to provide an increment of an integer or pointer that is being used to reference elements of such an array. As previously noted both `[]` and `()` operator functions can only be member functions of a class. This means that their left hand operands must be a class. They are then used to operate on an array that is a member of that class.

Recall how in LISTING 19-11 the calc class was used to manage an array of prices. Manipulation of array had to be carried out by calling access functions for that class. What if, instead, you wanted to directly reference the elements of that array, while, at the same time, maintaining some control over it such as checking for array bounds or keep track of how many elements have been used. You would still need a class, but one that provides direct access to the elements of the class's member array. At the same time you would want to use the same array notation to reference array elements that you would with any other array, `[]`. Defining a member overload function of the `[]` operator for the class will allow you to do just that.

The operator `[]` takes two operands, the name of a class object which is place before the `[]` operator, and an integer value placed with the enclosing `[]` operator. In the next example, `mycalc` object of the `calc` class is the first operand for `[]` and 2 is the second operand. The integer value used as the second operand is used to index the array.

```
mycalc[2]
```

The `[]` operator member function will not include the first operand in its parameter list since this is already implied. Since operator member functions always have as their first operand their class, this first operand is implicit. Furthermore, as a member function, operator function can directly reference members of that class. The next example shows the definition of the operator `[]` function for the calc class.

```
double &calc::operator[](int index)
        {
        return prices[index];
        }
```

The function is then declared in the body of the `bookrec` class as follows. A complete declaration of the `calc` class follows. Notice the declaration of the `prices` array as an array of 10 double elements. The `calc` class is designed to manage this array, yet provide direct access to it through the `[]` operator function.

```
const int Max = 10;

class calc {
            private:
                    double prices[Max];
            public:
                    int count;
                    calc(void);
                    double &operator[](int);
            };

  calc::calc(void)
        {
        count = 0;
        }

  double &calc::operator[](int index)
        {
        return prices[index];
        }
```

You can then reference elements of the prices array in the calc class with the same array notation you would use for any other array, though, in this case, you would be calling the `operator[]` member function of the calc class.

```
        printf("%f", mycalc[2]);
```

The calc `operator[]` function returns a reference to a double element, not the value of that element. This means that you could use an `operator[]` reference of calc's prices array in the right hand side of an assignment operation.

```
        mycalc[2] = 3.50;
```

LISTING 21-2:

calcover.cpp

```cpp
#include <stdio.h>
#include <stdlib.h>

const int Max = 10;

class calc {
            private:
                    double prices[Max];
            public:
                    int count;
                    calc(void);
                    double &operator[](int);
                    };

  calc::calc(void)
        {
        count = 0;
        }

  double &calc::operator[](int index)
                {
                if(index < 0 || index >= Max)
                        {
                        printf("Array out of bounds\n");
                        exit(1);
                        }
                else
                        return prices[index];
                }

int main(void)
        {
        char response[2];
        calc mycalc;
        int i;

        response[0] = 'y';
        while (response[0] != 'n'){
                printf("Please enter price: ");
                scanf("%lf", &mycalc[mycalc.count]);
                mycalc.count++;
                printf("Enter another? (y/n):");
                scanf("%s", response);
                }

        for(i = 0; i < mycalc.count; i++)
                {
                printf("%f\n", mycalc[i]);
                }

        return 0;
        }
```

One of the advantages of using an overload operator function is that you can modify it to better perform its task. One command change is to include within the operator[] member function a check for array bounds. Even standard array notation does not perform such a check. In the following version of the calc `operator[]` function a check for array bounds has been added. Any attempt to index off the end of the array will result in an error message, instead of just progressing to the next chunk of memory as standard arrays do.

```
double &calc::operator[](int index)
        {
        if(index < 0 || index >= Max)
                {
                printf("Array out of bounds\n");
                exit(1);
                }
        else
                return prices[index];
        }
```

The **calcover.cpp** program in LISTING 21-2 shows the modified version of calc that include the `[]` operator overload member function. First elements of the array are filled. Then the `calc []` operator function is used to reference and display those elements.

Member Overloaded Functions for () Operator: array iteration

Notice how in LISTING 21-3, the increment from one element to another was explicitly managed with a for loop and an integer variable. Instead of such an explicit operation, you an use an overload of the `()` operator to manage the incrementation from one element to the next. An overload of the `()` operator as a member function is often used for array iteration as an increment operation returning successive elements of a member array. The first call of the `()` operator function will return the value of the first element in the array, the second call returns the second element, and so on. A definition of the `()` operator function for the prices array follows. The function used an integer member called `i` to keep track of the last element referenced. It checks for the number of elements used held in the count member. When `i` reaches that count, the operator `()` function returns a 0 indicating the end of the used elements in the array.

```
double calc::operator()()
        {
        if(i < count)
                {
                return prices[i++];
                }
        else
                return 0;
        }
```

The call of this operator `()` function consists of the class name, `calc`, followed by the `()` operator. This appears just like a function call, but calc is not a function name. It is a class name. Used with `()`, it calls the `calc` class's operator `()` member function which returns as its value the next element in the prices array. In the next example, the value of the next element of the prices array in `mycalc` is returned by its `()` function and is then assigned to `pricetemp`.

```
calc mycalc;
double pricetemp;

        pricetemp = mycalc()
```

The loop in the main function to print out the array can now be written with no management variables to initialize or increment.

```
while ( (pricetemp = mycalc()) != 0)
            {
            printf("%f", pricetemp);
            }
```

The **opmem.cpp** program in LISTING 21-3 shows the implementation of the operator () member function in the calc class.

LISTING 21-3:

opmem.cpp

```
#include <stdio.h>
#include <stdlib.h>

const int Max = 10;

class calc {
            private:
                    double prices[Max];
            public:
                    int count;
                    int i;
                    calc(void);
                    double &operator[](int);
                    double operator()();
                    };

  calc::calc(void)
      {
      count = 0;
      i = 0;
      }

  double &calc::operator[](int index)
            {
            if(index < 0 || index >= Max)
                    {
                    printf("Array out of bounds\n");
                    exit(1);
                    }
            else
                    return prices[index];
            }
```

```
        double calc::operator()()
                {
                if(i < count)
                        {
                        return prices[i++];
                        }
                else
                        return 0;
                }

int main(void)
        {
        char response[2];
        calc mycalc;
        double pricetemp;

        response[0] = 'y';
        while (response[0] != 'n'){
                printf("Please enter price: ");
                scanf("%lf", &mycalc[mycalc.count]);
                mycalc.count++;
                printf("Enter another? (y/n):");
                scanf("%s", response);
                }

        while ( (pricetemp = mycalc()) != 0.0)
                        {
                        printf("%.2f\n", pricetemp);
                        }

        return 0;
        }
```

This implementation still has several limitations. You will need a special function to initialize i if you want to perform another iteration using the operator () function. An alternative design would be to create a separate and more general class that iterates through doubles. This class would be a friend of the calc class and could reference its prices member array.

Constructor Overloading

Just as you can overload functions, you can also overload constructor functions. You could have several constructor functions for a class, and select different ones when you declare different objects of that class. The parameter types for each constructor function need to differ. It is by matching the type and number of arguments you use in an object declaration, that a particular constructor function is chosen.

In **bookcon.cpp** program in LISTING 21-4, there are four constructor functions, one that is executed if there are no arguments listed with an object definition, and another that is executed if an integer value is listed, still another if a double value is listed, and finally one if both an integer and a double are listed with an object definition. The first sets the year member of the bookrec class to 1980, and the discount to 0.50. These serves as default values. The second sets the year to the value the user lists with the object definition. That value is passed to the newyear parameter whose value is then assigned to the year member. The third sets the value of the discount member, receiving a double value. The fourth sets both the year and discount members using an integer and a double value listed with the object definition.

The compiler determines which one to execute by comparing the types of the arguments supplied with the object definition with those of the different constructor functions. It searches for an exact match, and, if found, executes that function. If there is no exact match, then the compiler will performs conversion to try to generate an exact match.

```
bookrec::bookrec(void)
       {
       year = 1980;
       discount = 0.50;
       }

bookrec::bookrec(int newyear)
       {
       year = newyear;
       discount = 0.50;
       }

bookrec::bookrec(double ndiscount)
       {
       year = 1980;
       discount = ndiscount;
       }

bookrec::bookrec(int newyear, double ndiscount)
       {
       year = newyear;
       discount = ndiscount;
       }
```

Each constructor function also needs to be declared within the body of the class. The following are declarations of the previous constructor functions.

```
                  bookrec(void);
                  bookrec(int);
                  bookrec(double);
                  bookrec(int,double);
```

Be careful to make sure that overloaded constructor functions can be easily distinguished from one another. Otherwise ambiguous constructor function calls could result where the compiler or even the programmer is not sure what constructor should be called.

LISTING 21-4:

bookcon.cpp

```
#include <stdio.h>

 struct bookdat {       /* Book structure */
                        int year;
                        float price;
                        };
```

```
class bookrec {
      private:
              bookdat book;
              int year;
              double discount;
      public:
              bookrec(void);
              bookrec(int);
              bookrec(double);
              bookrec(int,double);
              void input_rec(void);
              void calc_price(void);
              void output_rec(void);
              };

      bookrec::bookrec(void)
              {
              year = 1980;
              discount = 0.50;
              }

      bookrec::bookrec(int newyear)
              {
              year = newyear;
              discount = 0.50;
              }

      bookrec::bookrec(double ndiscount)
              {
              year = 1980;
              discount = ndiscount;
              }

      bookrec::bookrec(int newyear, double ndiscount)
              {
              year = newyear;
              discount = ndiscount;
              }

void bookrec::input_rec(void)
      {
      printf("\nPlease enter year published: ");
      scanf("%d", &book.year);
      printf("\nPlease enter book price: ");
      scanf("%f", &book.price);
      }

void bookrec::calc_price(void)
      {
      if (book.year < year)
              book.price *= discount;
      }

void bookrec::output_rec(void)
      {
      printf("\t YEAR  : %d \n", book.year);
      printf("\t PRICE : %.2f \n\n", book.price);
      }
```

```
int main(void)
      {
      bookrec mybook;
      bookrec newbook(1995);
      bookrec cheapbk(2.35);
      bookrec salebk(1972, 4.95);

      salebk.input_rec();
      salebk.calc_price();
      salebk.output_rec();

      return 0;
      }
```

Inheritance and derived classes

Some classes that you define may perform very specialized tasks, while others may perform very general tasks. For example you may have a class for just managing file operations on a file, whereas you may have another class for managing a certain type of record on a file, such as an employee record. In many cases the specialized class will need to include the same code as that for the generalized class. A class for an employee record file would not only need the code for managing employee records, but also the code for file operations on the employee record file. These file operation may be the same as those used in a more generalized record file class. Dereference (see Indirection) "

Instead of repeating generalized code within specialized classes, C++ provides a way in which you can automatically incorporate the code of generalized classes within those of specialized classes. You can create two separate classes, one for generalized code, and another for the specialized code. The class for specialized code can then inherit the code from the generalized class forming a new class that combines the two. A class that inherits from another class is called a derived class. The class from which it inherits is called the base class. The generalized class would be a base class, and the specialized class would be the derived class. For example, the specialized employee record class could just inherit the generalized code for operations on a record file from the record file class. In this case, all the code for the record file class becomes joined with that of the employee record class, making one large employee record class that contains all the generalized code for file operations from the record file class. The employee record class would then be a derived class, deriving much of its code by inheriting it from the record file class, its base class.

When one class inherits from another, in effect, a complex class is created that consists of two classes. The derived class has been extended to include the base class. The base class still exists with all its private and public members. In fact, the derived class cannot access the private members of that base class. The derived class has to rely on the same base class's access functions to access base class members. When a class inherits from another, you are actually joining the two classes into one complex class, the derived class. This is similar to the process of nested objects, where one object is declared within another. The difference with inherited classes is that they create only one object consisting of several joined classes. These joined classes make up the derived class for the object.

At the same time, there are ways you can have the different classes of a derived class share their members. A special category of members called protected members can be shared by classes in a derived class, and yet still be private to the object. You can specify that the derived class have direct access to public members of the base class, treating those members as if they were its own. Classes with different versions of the same function can share those versions. Such member functions are called virtual functions. With protected members, a public specification, and virtual functions, an object that has derived class incorporating a base class, can operate much like an object with one class.

Bear in mind that inheritance, when taken to extremes, can become unwieldy. With very deeply nested inheritance it can be difficult to keep track of what is actually being declared in a class object, since many members may be inherited rather than explicitly declared.

Base and Derived Classes

You can think of derived classes as a way of automatically building a specialized structure, retrieving common information held in a more generalized structure. Take the example of employee records at a college. Employees could be administration, staff, or teachers. For each group the employee record would be slightly different. The teacher record may contain grant information, while the staff record may have pay scales. All would have basic information such as name and salary, duplicating the fields for such basic information in each specialized structure. Maintaining such a scheme would be difficult if you ever needed to change the fields for the basic information. Suppose you need to add a middle initial field. You have to add it to every specialized structure. Any modification of these common fields means tracking down and changing every specialized structure.

Instead of a series of complete specialized structures, you could use a derived class and its base class. The fields for the basic information could be placed into one base class, instead of being duplicated in different structures. In this case the base class could be called `employee`, and would contain such fields as `name` and `salary`. `employee` would then function as a base class for two specialized derived classes, one for teachers and one for staff. The derived classes would contain fields for specialized information. A `teacher` class would be a derived class whose base class is `employee`. As a derived class, `teacher` would include the `employee` base class, incorporating all its fields. There is now only one class for basic information, the `employee` class. Should those fields ever need to be changed, only that once class needs to be modified.

When declaring a derived class you need to designate its base class. After the class name and before the opening brace, you enter a colon followed by the name of the base class. In most cases you will precede the bass class name with the keyword `public`. In the next example teacher will inherit the `employee` class, together forming one derived class.

```
employee class {
        char name[30];
        float salary;
    public:
        void dispsal(void) {printf("%f",salary);}
        };

teacher class : public employee {
        float grant1;
        int tenure;
    public:
        void dispgrant(void) {printf("%f",grant1);}
        }
```

Public Member Inheritance

A derived class is formed by including a base class. However, this inclusion maintains a separateness for the base class. The base class retains its own private members, and the derived class cannot access them. A base class's public members can be either private to the derived class or become public members. To designate them as public, you need to enter in the keyword public before the name of the base class in the derived class declaration. In the previous example, the keyword public precedes the base class employee in the declaration of the teacher class.

Should you leave out the keyword `public`, then, by default, the base class will be made entirely private to the derived class. Public access of base class public members will be denied. You can explicitly designate a base class as private by using the keyword private in place of public in the derived class declaration. In either case, it is always best to include either public or private in the derived class declaration so that it is clear whether the base class public members are publicly accessible or not.

As public members, base class member can be directly access through the derived class. All the public members of the base class will become public members of the derived class. In the previous example, the `teacher` class not only inherits the `employee` class, but also has direct access to the public member of the `employee` class such as `employee` public member function `dispsal`. In the next example the call to `dispsal` is valid, since `dispsal` is now a public member of the employee derived class.

```
employee dylan;

    dylan.dispsal();
```

If, however, the public keyword had been left out of the declaration of the teacher class, then `dispsal` would be private and the function call of `dispsal` in the previous example would be invalid.

Inheritance Hierarchies

You can apply inheritance to several classes, not just two. Instead of having just one base class and one derived class, you can have a derived class that is, in turn, a base class for yet another derived class. One class inherits another, which, in turn, inherits another, and so on until a top level base class is reached that does not inheriting. These inheriting classes form a hierarchy, beginning with the most general class at the top and moving to more specialized classes at the bottom.

The final derived class consists of all the classes in the hierarchy. All combine to form one derived class. The name of the class is the name of the first derived class, the last class at the bottom of the hierarchy. In the next example, there are three classes, two of which are declared as derived classes. `sale` is the derived class at the bottom of the hierarchy. It will inherit the `price` class that will in turn inherit the `inventory` class. The `price` class is a derived class that operates as the base class for `sale`. This is an example of a class that is operates as a base class to one class and as a derived class for another classes. `retail` is a base class for `sale`, but a derived `class` for inventory. All such middle classes in a class hierarchy have this double role, both as inheritor and as a base. Finally, `inventory` is the base class for `retail`. It is not a derived class, and, at this point, the inheritance hierarchy tops out.

```
inventory class {
            char name[30];
            int item_num;
      public:
            void itemdisp(void) {printf("%d",item_num);}
            };

retail class : public inventory {
            float price;
      public:
            void pricedisp(void) {printf("%f",price);}
            float getprice(void) {return price);}
            }

sale class : public retail {
            float calcsale(void){ return (getprice() * .80)};
      public:
            void saledisp(void) {printf("%f",calcsale());}
            }
```

In the following example, the sale price of a radio is displayed along with its item number. The inventory's itemdisp function is a public function for the sale derived class. Its public members where inherited by retail as public, which in turn was inherited by sale as public. The public members of all the inherited classes are public members of the derived class they make up.

```
sale radio;

      radio.itemdisp();
      radio.saledisp();
```

You can define an object using a derived class at any point in the inheritance hierarchy. You could define an object of the retail class, that would include just the inventory class. Of course, the sale class would not be part of this derived class. In the next example, the user defines three objects; newitem, oldprice, and lamp. newitem consists of only the inventory class. oldprice is an object of a derived class holding the retail class with its inventory base class. lamp is an object with a derived class consisting of the sale, retail, and inventory classes.

```
inventory newitem;
retail oldprice;
sale lamp;

      newitem.itemdisp()

      oldprice.itemdisp();
      oldprice.pricedisp();

      lamp.itemdisp();
      lamp.pricedisp();
      lamp.saledisp();
```

Derived Classes and Nested Classes

Designing inheritance hierarchies can become very involved. You have to be very aware of what members different classes in the hierarchy contain and how they are being inherited. Sometimes it is more appropriate to use a nested class instead of a derived class. A nested class is a class whose object is declared within another class. The programs in Chapter 19 had numerous examples of nested class objects. A simple rule of thumb to use when deciding whether to use a nested or derived class is the IS-A and HAS-A test. Is the new feature provided by a class something that a class has or is it something it is a part of. If it is something that it has, then a nested class is called for. If, instead, it is something that it is part of, then a derived class is needed. For example, a retail item is part of inventory, but it has a price. Price is an attribute of the retail item, but inventory is what the item is.

Protected Members

When classes are inherited to form a derived class, the different classes making up this derived class retain their private members. Private members remain private to those classes and can only be accessed by their own member functions. In the previous declaration of the `sale` derived class, the private member of `inventory`, `item`, is inaccessible to either `retail` or `sale` member functions. Neither of those classes can access that private member. They could only call inventory's `itemdisp` function to display it for them. Similarly, the `retail`'s class private member price was inaccessible to the `sale` class. To obtain the value of price, the sale class has to call one of `retail`'s public access function, `getprice`, that obtained the price for the sale class.

Should you want the private members of one class to be accessed by the member functions of another class, you could make the private members public. But making the private members of any class public makes them accessible to the program at large. The members are no longer hidden within the object, defeating much of the purpose for having of class objects.

There is a way to make a member accessible to other classes in your derived class, and yet have them retain their private status in regards to the object as a whole. For this purpose you can use yet another category of class members, the protected category. A protected member is used for derived classes. A protected member is accessible to any of the classes making up a derived class, and, at the same time, the protected member is private to the entire derived class. The object will treat a protected member as private in regards to the rest of the program. Only members within the derived class can access the protected member. At the same time, all the member functions of all the different classes making up the derived class will be able to access the protected member.

To declare a protected member, you first need to enter the protected keyword into your class type declaration. You enter the keyword protected followed by a colon. In the following lines you enter in the declarations of any members you want protected. These members can then be accessed by any of the member functions in any of the other classes making up the derived class.

In the following inheritance hierarchy, the `sale`, `retail`, and `inventory` class have been modified to incorporate protected members. `item_num` is now a protected member of `inventory`, and, as such, is accessible to all other classes making up the derived class. Both `retail` and `sale` member functions can now directly reference `item_num`. The same is true for `price` in the `retail` class. `price` is a protected member of retail and as such is accessible to `sale` and its member functions. The `sale` member function `calcsale` can now directly access `price`. As protected, `item_num` and price are accessible to other classes further down in the inheritance hierarchy. `item_num` is accessible to both `retail` and `sale`, and `price` is accessible to `sale`. However, both remain private to the entire derived class. This means that neither price nor `item_num` can be accessed by your program.

```
inventory class {
      protected:
              char name[30];
              int item_num;
      public:
              void itemdisp(void) {printf("%d",item_num);}
              };

retail class : public inventory {
      protected:
              float price;
      public:
              void pricedisp(void) {printf("%d %f", item_num, price);}
              }

sale class : public retail {
      private:
              float calcsale(void){ return price * .80)};
      public:
      void saledisp(void) {printf(" %d %f", item_num, calcsale());}
              }
```

Scoping of Derived Class Members

Scoping rules for classes making up a derived class follow much the same rules as those for external and internal variables. Class members that have unique names are easily identified. However, if members of different classes have the same name, their use in other classes become ambiguous. In such a case, you can identify the member you want by preceding its name with its class name and the class scope operator, : :. If no scope is specified then, by default, the member of the member function's class is used.

```
cost class {
      protected:
              float price;
      public:
              void pricedisp(void) {printf("%f",price);}
              }

discount class : public cost {
      protected:
              float price;
              void calcdis(void);
      public:
              void specialdisp(void);
      }

void discount::calcdis(void)
      {
      discount::price = cost::price * .80)
      };

void discount::specialdisp(void)
      {
      calcdis();
      printf("%f", price);
      }
```

In the previous example, a member of cost and a member of discount both have the same name, price. In this example, the price member of the base class is protected and so directly accessible to the discount class. To distinguish the references to the cost price member, they are preceded by the cost class name and class scope operator, cost::price.

The reference to price without any class scope, will automatically default to the price member of discount, not cost. The class name and scope operator can be used if wished, to more clearly distinguish the two, as done in the calcdisp member function. The simple reference to price in the specialdisp function will automatically reference the price member of discount.

Virtual Functions

There are situations in which the member functions of a base class will need to call member functions of the derived class. For example, a base class that draws figures such as circles and squares may be combined with a derived class that has functions to draw circles and squares of a certain shade and color. The base class, in this case, should use the circle drawing function in the derived class to draw a circle, not its own circle drawing function.

When you declare the base class, it has no knowledge of its derived class. The base class does not know what functions or data members the derived class will contain. So, in effect, it cannot call a derived class's function. There is way for the base class to dynamically identify a derived class's function. Special member functions called virtual functions will allow a base function to dynamically identify and reference derived class functions when the derived class is constructed. In effect, a virtual function declared within a base class sets aside an empty slot to be filled by the derived class. A virtual function is actually a pointer to a function. The address of a derived class function is then assigned to this pointer when the derived class is created. When the base class then calls this virtual function, it is actually referencing and calling the derived class function. This process is known as dynamic binding. The virtual function is dynamically bound to a derived function when an object is defined, not when the class is declared.

A virtual function is declared in the base class with the same type as that of the derived class function it is going to reference. This includes the same return type and parameter list, as well as the same function name. The keyword virtual is placed before the function declaration.

```
virtual void printrec(int);
```

The function in the derived class that the base class virtual function refers to, also has its declaration preceded by the keyword virtual. The derived class function is also declared in its entirety within the derived class. Then, within the base class, any function call of the virtual function will actually call that derived class function.

In the next example, the employee and teacher classes are modified to manage a virtual function. The employee class is a base class that needs to display the income of an employee. However, that income, in the case of teachers, is calculated using information in the teacher class, namely grants. A teacher's income is consists of both grants and salary. This can only be calculated by a function in the teacher class. So a virtual function is declared in the employee base class called print_income, and a corresponding function is declared in the teacher class. When an object of the teacher class is defined, the address of its print_income function will be assigned to its employee's base class print_income virtual function. When print_income is called in the program, the employee class print_income virtual function will reference the teacher class print_income function.

```
employee class {
            char name[30];
        protected:
            float salary;
        public:
            virtual void print_income(void);
            };

teacher class : public employee {
            float grant1;
            int tenure;
        public:
            virtual void print_income(void);
            }

void teacher::print_income(void)
        {
        print("%f", salary + grant1);
        }
```

In the previous example, the base class by itself has no defined function for `print_income`. There is only the virtual function declaration that is really a pointer to a function. A virtual function declaration that within its class has no corresponding function definition is called a pure virtual function. A class that contains a pure virtual function cannot alone be use for an object definition. In its current version, you could not define an object of class employee. `employee` contains a pure virtual function, `print_income`, that is really just a pointer. It needs a derived class that has defined `print_income` function that it can reference.

```
employee class {
            char name[30];
        protected:
            float salary;
        public:
            virtual void print_income(void);
            };

void employee::print_income(void)
        {
        print("%f", salary);
        }


teacher class : public employee {
            float grant1;
            int tenure;
        public:
            virtual void print_income(void);
            }

void teacher::print_income(void)
        {
        print("%f", salary + grant1);
        }
```

In most cases, the base class will also have its own function definition for a virtual function. You can think of such a definition as operating like a default. If the derived class has no function for the base classes virtual function, then the base class can use its own function definition. Such a base class can then be used to define its own objects. The object will just use the base classes definition of the virtual function.

Even if the base class does define its own function for its virtual function, its virtual function will still reference the derived classes function. The base class's function definition remains unused. In the next example, even though employee has defined its own print_income function, its virtual function will still reference teacher's print_income function. The income will be calculate using both grant1 and salary, not just salary as in the employee version of print_income.

This becomes clearer if you keep in mind that the virtual function declaration is the base class is really a pointer to a function. The virtual function is still assigned the address of the teacher class's print_income function, even thought employee has its own print_income function. If employee is used alone to define an object without the teacher class, the address of empolyee's print_income function is assigned to its virtual function. In this case its virtual function will reference the employee definition of print_income. The same thing happens if employee is included in a derived class that does not have a print_income function. In this respect, you can think of employee's definition of print_income as a default that is used if there is no derived class that has a print_income function.

In the next example, emprec is defined solely as an employee object. The function call to print_income will use employee's print_income function, displaying only the salary. teachrec is defined as an object of the teacher derived class. The function call to print_income will use teacher's print_income function. Both call the same virtual function in their respective employee classes. But recall that the virtual function is a pointer. In the case of emprec, that pointer holds the address of employee's print_income function and so reference it. In the case of teachrec, a derived class, that pointer holds the address of teacher's print_income function and so references it.

```
employee emprec;
teacher teachrec;

emprec.print_income();        /* employee version */

teachrec.print_indome();      /* teacher version */
```

The program in LISTING 21-5 makes crucial use of virtual functions. In this program, a linked list is used to manage a list of book records. Each node in the linked list contains a pointer to the data record. The linked list is designed so that its class can be used in different programs with any data record. In this case, it is used with book records. The linked list class manages all actions on the list including printing the records in the list. However, printing records in the list requires a print function that knows what the record is. The list class is purposely designed not to know what the record is so that it can be used with many different types of records. Only the book class knows what the book record is. This is a situation where the base class, the list class, needs to call a function in its derived class, the book class. The book class has a printrec function that prints out its book record held in a structure called bookrec. The list class uses a virtual printrec function to connect to the book class's printrec function. When the book derived class is created, then the printrec function of its list base class will be assigned the address of bookrec's printrec function. The function call of printrec in the list class's printobj function will actually call book's printrec function, printing out the bookrec structure. Though list has defined its own printrec function, it is ignored when list is included as part of a derived class.

A virtual function is also used for deleterec. deleterec deletes a bookrec structure. Again, the list class does not know what type of structure it is deleting. This is left up to the book class to determine. list's deleterec virtual function will reference book's deleterec function.

The program in LISTING 21-5 has an inheritance hierarchy consisting of three classes; list, book, and collection. The collection class is a derived class whose base class book. book is, in turn, a derived class whose base class is list. The list class manages the list that holds the book records. The book class manages the book records themselves. And the collection class manages a particular collection of books.

LISTING 21-5: book linked list: C++

list.h

```
        struct OBJ {
                        void *recptr;
                        OBJ *nextptr;
                        };

        class list {
                private:
                        OBJ *headptr;
                        void printobj(OBJ*);
                        OBJ* addobj(OBJ*, OBJ*);
                        OBJ* delobj(OBJ*);
                protected:
                        void printlist(void);
                        void addlist(void*);
                        void dellist(void);
                public:
                        list(void);
                        virtual void printrec(void*);
                        virtual void deleterec(void*);
                };

        list::list(void)
        {
        headptr = 0;
        }

void list::printrec(void * rptr)
        {
        printf("record");
        }

void list::deleterec(void * rptr)
        {
        delete rptr;
        }

void list::printlist(void)
        {
        printobj(headptr);
        }

void list::printobj(OBJ *objptr)
        {
        if(objptr != 0)
                {
                printrec(objptr->recptr);
                printobj(objptr->nextptr);
                }
        }
```

```
void list::addlist( void *recptr)
        {
        OBJ *resptr;
        OBJ *newptr;

        newptr = new OBJ;
        newptr->recptr = recptr;
        resptr = addobj(headptr, newptr);
                if(headptr== 0)
                                headptr = resptr;
        }

OBJ * list::addobj(OBJ *objptr, OBJ *newptr)
        {
        OBJ *resptr;

        if(objptr == 0)
                {
                newptr->nextptr = 0;
                return newptr;
                }
        else
                {
                resptr = addobj(objptr->nextptr, newptr);
                if(resptr != 0)
                        objptr->nextptr = resptr;
                return 0;
                }
        }

void list::dellist()
        {
        OBJ *resptr;
        if(headptr != 0)
                {
                resptr = delobj(headptr);
                if(resptr == 0)
                        headptr = 0;
                }
        }

OBJ* list::delobj(OBJ *objptr)
        {
        OBJ *resptr;

        if(objptr->nextptr == 0)
                {
                deleterec(objptr->recptr);
                delete objptr;
                return 0;
                }
        else
                {
                resptr= delobj(objptr->nextptr);
                if(resptr == 0)
                        objptr->nextptr = 0;
                return objptr;
                }
        }
```

book.h

```
        struct BOOKREC {        /* Book structure */
                    char title[100];
                    int  year;
                    float price;
                    };

class book: public list{
                    void calc_price(BOOKREC*);
                protected:
                    int year;
                    void input_rec(BOOKREC*);
                    void deleterec(void*);
                    void add_book(void);
                public:
                    void printrec(void*);
                };

void book::add_book()
    {
    BOOKREC *bookptr;

    bookptr = new BOOKREC;
    input_rec(bookptr);
    addlist((void*) bookptr);
    }

void book::input_rec(BOOKREC *bookptr)
    {
    printf("\nPlease enter title: ");
    scanf("%*[\n\t ]%[^\n]s", bookptr->title);
    printf("Please enter year published: ");
    scanf("%d", &bookptr->year);
    printf("Please enter book price: ");
    scanf("%f", &bookptr->price);
    calc_price(bookptr);
    }

void book::calc_price(BOOKREC *bookptr)
    {
    if (bookptr->year < year)
            bookptr->price *= 0.5;
    }

void book::printrec(void *ptr)
    {
    BOOKREC *bookptr = (BOOKREC*) ptr;
    printf("\n\n Book Record \n");
    printf("\t TITLE: %s \n", bookptr->title);
    printf("\t YEAR : %d \n", bookptr->year);
    printf("\t PRICE : %.2f \n\n", bookptr->price);
    }

void book::deleterec(void *ptr)
    {
    BOOKREC *bookptr = (BOOKREC*) ptr;
    delete bookptr;
    }
```

coll.h

```
class collection: public book {
      void menu_coll(void);
      public:
      void manage_coll(void);
      collection(void);
      };

      collection::collection()
      {
      year = 1980;
      }

void collection::menu_coll(void)
      {
      printf("a. add books to collection\n");
      printf("d. delete a book in collection\n");
      printf("p. print books in collection\n");
      printf("q. quit collection\n");
      }

void collection::manage_coll(void)
      {
      char choice[2];
      int more = 1;

      menu_coll();
      while (more != 0)
            {
            printf("Please enter choice\n");
            scanf("%s", choice);
            switch(choice[0])
                  {
                  case 'a':
                        add_book();
                        break;
                  case 'p':
                        printlist();
                        break;
                  case 'd':
                        dellist();
                        break;
                  case 'm':
                        menu_coll();
                        break;
                  case 'q':
                        more = 0;
                  }
            }
      }
```

main.cpp

```cpp
#include <stdio.h>
#include <string.h>
#include "list.h"
#include "book.h"
#include "coll.h"

void menu(void);

int main(void)
        {
        collection mystery;
        collection romance;
        collection scifi;
        char choice[2];
        int more = 1;

        while (more != 0)
                {
                menu();
                printf("Please choose book collection\n");
                scanf("%1s", choice);
                switch(choice[0])
                        {
                        case 'm':
                                mystery.manage_coll();
                                break;
                        case 'r':
                                romance.manage_coll();
                                break;
                        case 's':
                                scifi.manage_coll();
                                break;
                        case 'q':
                                more = 0;
                                break;
                        default:
                                printf("Invalid Choice\n");
                        }

                }
        return 0;
        }

void menu(void)
                {
                printf("m. mystery\n");
                printf("r. romance\n");
                printf("s. scifi\n");
                printf("q. quit\n");
                }
```

Multiple Inheritance

A derived class can have several base classes instead of just one. In such a case, the derived class inherits multiple classes. It will contain several base classes instead of just one. The derived class can make use of all the members of its base class. Multiple inheritance is often used when a class needs to inherit from different types of classes. For example, information about a teacher may not only be contained in standard employee information, but also in information about research projects that the teacher may be a part of. A full record about a teacher would need to draw on both sources of information.

The base classes are listed after the class name and the colon in the class declaration. Each base class is separated by a comma and has its own public and private designation. In the next example the `teacher` class is a derived class with two base classes, `research` and `employee`. `teacher` will have access to all the members in both classes.

```
research class {
        protected:
                char projname[30];
                float funding;
        public:
                void dispfund(void) {printf("%f",funding);}
                };

employee class {
        protected:
                char name[30];
                float salary;
        public:
                void dispsal(void)  {printf("%f",salary);}
                };

teacher class : public employee, public research {
                float grant1;
                int tenure;
        public:
                void dispgrant(void) {printf("%f",grant1);}
                }
```

In the next example, the `chris` teacher class calls the `dispfund` function in its research base class and then the `dispsal` function in its employee base class. Finally it calls the `dispgrant` function in its `teacher` class.

```
teacher chris;

chris.dispfund();
chris.dispsal();
chris.dispgrant();
```

The program in LISTING 21-6 uses multiple inheritance for its derived class. The `emp` class is a derived class whose base class are tree and `recfile`. From both the tree and `recfile` base classes, `emp` inherits all the functions for managing a record file and a search tree. The tree class makes use of a virtual function, `printrec`. When an object of the `empfile` class is created, the `printrec` virtual function (really a pointer to a function) in its tree class, will be assigned the address of `printrec` function in its `empfile` class. The call of `printrec` in the tree class's `printnode` function will call the `empfile` class's `printrec` function. The tree class version of the `printrec` function is ignored.

A virtual function is not used for `build_index`. The `build_index` function is called if the employee file already exits when the `empfile` object is created. It used the employee file to build a current version of the index. A logical place to call `build_index` would be in the constructor for the file class of the `empfile` derived class. The `filerec` class constructor will check to see if the file already exists. However, you cannot call virtual functions within class constructors. A call to build_index would only call a file class version of build_index, not the empfile class version.

The empfile class constructor checks to see if the next record number is 0. This way it knows whether to call build_index or not. If the number is greater than 0, then the file must already exist and build_index needs to be called. The index is built within the constructor before any action can be take on the file by the program.

Notice also how the constructor of the filerec base class is initialized by the empfile derived class. This is similar to the initialization of nested classes, except that class names are used instead of object names. The filerec base class constructor needs to receive the file name and the number of bytes in a record. This information is passed onto it by the empfile constructor. The empfile class already knows the size of a record, but receives the name from its object declaration. The initialization values for the filerec class are listed after the parameter list of the empfile class's constructor and preceded by a colon and the class name, as shown here.

```
empfile::empfile(char *fname): filerec((long)sizeof(EMP), fname)
```

Notice how the fname parameter for the empfile constructor is used as an argument for the filerec constructor. The empfile constructor's parameters will first receive their argument values, and then they can be used as arguments for other class constructors, in this case, filerec. When the programmer declares an object of class empfile with the initialization value "myfile", empfile("myfile"), the string "myfile" is passed to the fname parameter of the empfile class constructor. Then from fname, "myfile" is passed to the filerec class constructor into its filename parameter and then uses that to open the file.

LISTING 21-6: Tree Index C++ example with inheritance, protected members, and virtual functionstree.h

```
struct NODE{
            long recno;
            char key[100];
            NODE *lptr;
            NODE *rptr;
            } ;

class tree {
  private:
        NODE *rootptr;
        void printorder(NODE*);
        void printnodes(NODE*);
        long findnode(NODE *, char*);
        NODE *addnode(NODE*, char*, long);
  protected:
        tree(void);
        void addindex(char*, long);
        virtual void printrec(long);
  public:
        long findrec(char*);
        void printrecords(void);
        void printindex(void);
        };
```

```
        tree::tree(void)
        {
        rootptr = 0;
        }

void tree::printrec(long recno)
        {
        printf("%ld\n", recno);
        }

 void tree::printrecords (void)
        {
        printorder(rootptr);
        }

 void tree::printorder(NODE *nodeptr)
        {
        if(nodeptr != 0)
                {
                printorder(nodeptr->lptr);
                printrec(nodeptr->recno);
                printorder(nodeptr->rptr);
                }
        }

 void tree::printindex(void)
        {
        printnodes(rootptr);
        }

 void tree::printnodes(NODE *nodeptr)
        {
        if(nodeptr != 0)
                {
                printf("%d\n", nodeptr->recno);
                printf("%s\n\n", nodeptr->key);
                printnodes(nodeptr->lptr);
                printnodes(nodeptr->rptr);
                }
        }

 void tree::addindex(char *key, long recno)
        {
        NODE *resptr;

        resptr = addnode(rootptr, key, recno);
        if(rootptr == 0)
                rootptr = resptr;
        }

 NODE *tree::addnode(NODE *nptr, char *newkey, long recno)
        {
        NODE *newptr = 0, *resptr;

        if(nptr == 0)
                {
                newptr = (NODE*) malloc(sizeof(NODE));
                strcpy (newptr->key, newkey);
                newptr->recno = recno;
                newptr->rptr = 0;
```

```
                newptr->lptr = 0;
                return newptr;
                }
        else

                {
                if(strcmp(newkey, nptr->key) < 0)
                        {
                        resptr = addnode(nptr->lptr,newkey,recno);
                        if(resptr != 0)
                                nptr->lptr = resptr;
                        }
                else
                        if(strcmp(newkey, nptr->key) > 0)
                                {
                        resptr=addnode(nptr->rptr,newkey,recno);
                                if(resptr != 0)
                                        nptr->rptr = resptr;
                                }
                return 0;
                }
        }

long tree::findrec(char *key)
        {
        long recno;

        recno = findnode(rootptr, key);
        return recno;
        }

long tree::findnode(NODE *nptr, char *key)
        {
        long recno;

        if(nptr == 0)
                {
                return 0;
                }
          else
                {
                if(strcmp(key, nptr->key) == 0)
                        return nptr->recno;
                else
                        if(strcmp(key, nptr->key) < 0)
                                recno = findnode(nptr->lptr,key);
                        else
                                if(strcmp(key, nptr->key) > 0)
                                        recno = findnode(nptr->rptr,key);
                return recno;
                }
        }
```

file.h

```
class filerec {
        private:
                FILE  *fptr;
                long recsize;
                long lastrecno;
        protected:
                filerec(long, char *);
                ~filerec(void);
                long readrec(void *, long);
                void writerec(void *, long);
                void reset(void);
                long setnextrecno(void);
                long getlastrecno(void);
                };

  filerec::filerec(long size, char *filename)
                {
                recsize = size;

                if ( (fptr = fopen(filename, "r+b")) != NULL){
                        fseek(fptr, 0L, 0);
                        fscanf(fptr, "%ld", &lastrecno);
                        }
                    else
                        if ( (fptr = fopen(filename, "w+b")) != NULL){
                                lastrecno = 0L;
                                }
                            else {
                                printf("file open error\n");
                                exit(1);
                                }
                }

  filerec::~filerec(void)
                {
                fseek(fptr,0L, 0);
                fprintf(fptr,"%ld", lastrecno);
                fclose (fptr);
                }

void filerec::writerec(void *buf, long recno)
                {
                fseek(fptr, (recno * recsize), 0);
                fwrite(buf, recsize, 1, fptr);
                }

long filerec::readrec(void *buf, long recno)
                {
                long res;

                fseek(fptr, (recno * recsize) , 0);
                res = fread (buf, recsize, 1, fptr);
                return(res);
                }

long filerec::getlastrecno(void)
                {
                return (lastrecno);
                }
```

```
long filerec::setnextrecno(void)
                {
                lastrecno++;
                return (lastrecno);
                }
void filerec::reset(void)
                {
                fseek (fptr, 0L, 0);
                }
```

emp.h

```
    struct EMP {
                char name[100];
                long id;
                float salary;
                } ;

class  empfile : public filerec, public tree {
                void output_rec(EMP);
                void input_rec(EMP*);
        protected:
                void build_index(void);
                virtual void printrec(long);
         public:
                empfile(char *);
                void find_emp(void);
                void add_rec(void);
                void print_file(void);
                void menu(void);
        };

 empfile::empfile(char *fname): filerec((long)sizeof(EMP), fname)
                {
                if(getlastrecno() > 0)
                  build_index();
                }

 void empfile::build_index(void)
                {
                long i, lastrec;
                EMP emprec;
                lastrec = getlastrecno();
                for (i = 1; i <= lastrec ; i++)
                        {
                        readrec((char*) &emprec, i);
                        addindex(emprec.name, emprec.id);
                        }
                }

    void empfile::add_rec(void)
                {
                EMP emprec;

                input_rec(&emprec);
                emprec.id = setnextrecno();
                writerec(&emprec,emprec.id);
                addindex(emprec.name, emprec.id);
                }
```

```
void empfile::input_rec(EMP *emptr)
      {
      printf("\nPlease enter last name: ");
      scanf("%*[\n\t ]%[^\n]s", emptr->name);
      printf("\nplease enter employee salary: ");
      scanf("%f", &emptr->salary);
      }

void empfile::print_file(void)
      {
      long i, lastrec;

      lastrec = getlastrecno();
      for (i = 1; i <= lastrec ; i++){
            printrec(i);
            }
      }

void empfile::printrec(long recno)
      {
      EMP out_emp;

      readrec((char*) &out_emp, recno);
      printf("\n\n Employee Record \n");
      printf("\n\t NAME  : %s \n", out_emp.name);
      printf("\n\t ID    : %ld \n", out_emp.id);
      printf("\n\t SALARY: %f \n\n", out_emp.salary);
      }

void empfile::find_emp(void)
      {
      char empname[100];
      long recno;

      printf("Please enter employee name: ");
      scanf("%*[\n\t ]%[^\n]s", &empname);

      recno = findrec(empname);

      if (recno != 0)
            printrec(recno);
      else
            printf("Record not found\n");
      }

void empfile::menu(void)
      {
      printf("\nEmployee Records Menu\n");
      printf("\na = add a record\n");
      printf("f = find a record\n");
      printf("p = prints a records\n");
      printf("i = print index\n");
      printf("r = print record file\n");
      printf("m = display menu\n");
      printf("q = quit program\n\n");
      }
```

main.cpp

```cpp
#include <stdio.h>
#include <stdlib.h>
#include <string.h>
#include "tree.h"
#include "file.h"
#include "emp.h"

        int main(void)
                {
                empfile myemps("myfile");
                int more = 0;
                char response[2];

                myemps.menu();

                while (more == 0){
                        printf("Please enter choice :");
                        scanf("%s", response);
                        switch(response[0])
                                {
                                case  'a':
                                        myemps.add_rec();
                                        break;
                                case  'f':
                                        myemps.find_emp();
                                        break;
                                case  'p':
                                        myemps.printrecords();
                                        break;
                                case 'i':
                                        myemps.printindex();
                                        break;
                                case 'r':
                                        myemps.print_file();
                                        break;
                                case 'm':
                                        myemps.menu();
                                        break;
                                case  'q':
                                        more = 1;
                                        break;
                                default:
                                        printf("invalid input\n");
                                }
                        }
                return 0;
                }
```

Chapter Summary: Inheritance, Derivation, and Overloading

Classes can be combined together by inheritance to form a derived class. A derived call inherits a base class, that can, in turn, inherit yet another base class. The inheritance relationship of such classes forms an inheritance hierarchy. Such a hierarchy begins with the more general class and becomes specific the further down the hierarchy. At the bottom of the hierarchy are derived classes the perform specific tasks. Inheritance can be single or multiple. A derived class can have two base classes that it inherits. The base classes are listed in the derived class declaration after the class name.

A base class retains its own private member, which cannot be accessed by the derived class. However members can be classified as protected, making them accessible to the other classes the make up the derived class, but private the entire derived class. You can also declare virtual functions in which a base class can call a function defined in a derived class. A virtual function is really a pointer to function that is assigned the address of its corresponding derived class function when an object of that class is defined.

You can also overload the standard C++ operators and use them with the classes that you declare. To overload an operator you declare your own operator function that has user-defined classes as its parameters. The parameter are operands for the operator. If the left hand operand is a class, you need to define the operator function as a member of that class. The =, (), [], and -> operators also require that any operator functions be defined as members of a class. Operator overloading allows you to use operators on class objects, rather than always having to resort to function calls.

Exercises

Modify the program in LISTING 21-6 to use a btree instead of a search tree.

Rewrite the program in LISTING 21-5 to use three different derived classes specialized for mystery, romance, and sci-fi. Each would inherit the base classes such as `coll`, `bookrec`, and `list`.

Design a string class and define overloaded operator functions for the =, >, and < operators that you can use to compare to other string classes.

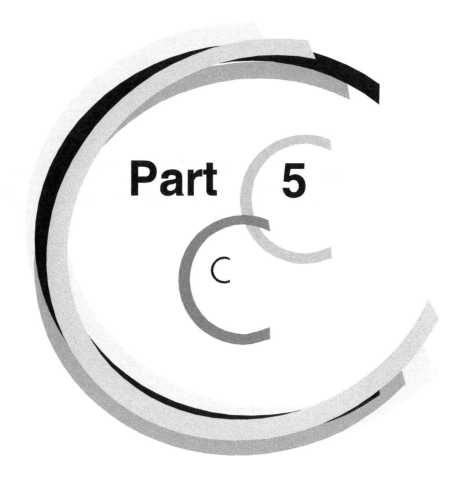

Part **5**

The Preprocessor

Bitwise Operations

Make

Formatted IO

Conversions

C Topics

The Preprocessor

Macros, Headers, and Inclusions

Symbolic Constants

Macros

Header Files

Conditional Inclusions

Part 5: C Topics

22: The Preprocessor

The preprocessor provides a great deal of flexibility in managing C programs. The #define directive is used to create macros and symbolic constants. The include directive allows replicated code, such as function declarations, to be placed in one file and included in different source code files. The conditional directives allow a programmer to specify whether or not a segment of code should be compiled.

There is a newline after the preprocessor directive and its arguments, and a pound sign, #, before the directive term such as #define. The pound sign is sometimes referred to as the cross-hatch or the sharp sign. The pound sign and the newline form the boundaries, the beginning and end, of any preprocessor directive. The preprocessor looks for the pound sign, and when it finds it, it knows that it has been issued a directive. Though the pound sign is usually placed in the first column of the source code file, C allows the preprocessor directive to be indented. The following is an example of a `#define` preprocessor directive.

```
#define RATE    0.50
```

You have to enter a preprocessor directive all on one line. However, for the sake of clarity, you can enter a directive on several lines if you escape the newline character for each line except the last one. You escape a newline by entering a backslash, \, just before you press ENTER. The preprocess will automatically remove escaped newline characters, effectively joining such lines into one line. The following two lines:

```
#define RATE  \
0.50

will be read as one line

#define RATE    0.50
```

define and Symbolic Constants

The `#define` directive is a preprocessor directive that you can use to simulate a symbolic constant. The `#define` directive consists of the `#define` keyword, a `#define` symbol, and a replacement text. By convention, the `#define` symbol is usually written in upper case.

The `#define` directive can be thought of as a global substitution directive. It replaces a symbol with a replacement text throughout the source code file. In the next example, the symbol RATE is defined as the text 0.50.

```
#define RATE    0.50
```

In LISTING 22-1, the `#define` directive performs a global substitution. The collection of characters making up the symbol RATE, wherever it exists in the file, will be replaced with the text of characters 0.50.

LISTING 22-1:

```
#include <stdio.h>

#define  RATE  0.50

int main(void)
      {
      int count;

      count = RATE * 5;
      printf("count = %d, rate = %.2f\n",count, RATE);

      return 0;
      }
```

The preprocessor takes this code and generates its own code with the text substituted in. This is the version of the code that the compiler actually sees:

```
int main(void){
      int count;

      count = 0.50 * 5;
      printf("count = %d, rate = %f\n",count, 0.50);

      return 0;
      }
```

The preprocessor is not part of the compiler. It is the programmer's responsibility to make sure that the substituted text makes sense to the compiler. If the #define directive in LISTING 22-1 were written as:

```
      #define  RATE  0M5g
```

The program as it is sent to the compiler would look like this:

```
int main(void)
      {
      int count;
      count = 0M5g * 5;
      printf("count = %d, rate = %f\n",count, 0M5g);

      return 0;
      }
```

If there is a change in the replacement text, it only needs to be made in one place: the #define directive. In the previous example, if the rate changes to 0.75, only the #define directive needs to be changed. This is helpful in large programs where symbols like RATE are used many times.

```
#define  RATE  0.75
```

Macros: define with Arguments

A #define symbol can be used to represent not only constants, but also expressions and even whole statements. The #define directive does not recognize statements or expressions. It only performs a substitution on text, whatever it may be. In LISTING 22-2, the #define symbol MULT is replaced by an arithmetic expression. The #define symbol GREETING is replaced by a function call.

LISTING 22-2:

```
#include <stdio.h>

#define   RATE   0.10
#define   GREETING   printf("Hello\n")
#define   MULT   (4 * 5)

int main(void)
       {
       int res;

       GREETING;
       res = MULT;
       printf("Rate is %.2f, Res = %d\n", RATE, res);

       return 0;
       }
```

The preprocessor will generate the following code based on the program in LISTING 22-2. This is what the compiler will actually receive:

```
int main(void)
           {
           int res;

           printf("Hello\n");
           res = (4 * 5);
           printf("Rate is %.2f, Res = %d\n", 0.10,res);

           return 0;
           }
```

It makes sense to give the MULT symbol arguments so that it could generate the symbols for multiplication operands other than 4 and 5. The #define directive has this capability. The term "arguments" is misleading. A #define symbol with arguments looks similar to the code for a function definition. It is not. It is really a text substitution operation. The #define symbol will expand to replacement text specified in its #define directive. In this sense, a #define symbol with arguments can best be described as a macro.

A #define symbol with arguments is usually written in lower case. It is important that there be no spaces between the symbol name and the arguments. The name must be right next to the opening parenthesis for the arguments. Figure 22-1 displays a #define directive with arguments.

```
#define   mult(x,y)   (x) * (y)
```

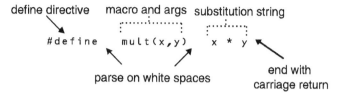

Figure 22-1: define macro with arguments.

The #define symbol `mult` has arguments that appear to form a parameter list. The `x` and `y` in the parameter positions `(x,  y)` are not parameter variables. They can be thought of more as substitution markers. This is strictly a word processing-like operation. Whatever text is in the `x` position will be substituted for all the x positions in the replacement text.

The arguments are only text substitution directives. Whatever text is found in the argument position is mapped into the replacement text. In the next example, the macro arguments for `mult` are x and y. The macro `mult` replaces the x and y positions in the replacement text with the text found in the respective x and y argument positions (5, 4). The text found in the x's position will be placed wherever the x occurs in the replacement text. The final constructed text is then sent to the compiler. The text does not necessarily have to make sense.

```
mult(5,4)          is replaced by    5 * 4
mult(john,53)      is replaced by    john * 53
mult(7&0%,yl!)     is replaced by    7&0% * yl!
```

In LISTING 22-3, the #define macro `mult` will take the symbols in its argument positions, 4 and 5, and replace them for every x and y in the replacement text. It is a simple text substitution.

LISTING 22-3:

```
#define  mult(x,y)  (x) * (y)

int main(void)
        {
        int res;
        res = mult(4,5);

        return 0;
        }
```

After the preprocessor has executed, this is what the compiler will receive.

```
int main(void)
        {
        int res;
        res = (4) * (5);

        return 0;
        }
```

The use of the mult #define symbol with arguments looks exactly like a function call. It is not, and should never be thought of as one. A macro should be thought of as another way of writing an expression, not a function. Just as the #define directive is used to #define constants, a macro can be thought of as defining an expression. The mult macro expands to inline code, in this case an arithmetic expression.

Once you start thinking of a macro as an expression, you realize that the same kinds of problems found in expressions are also found in macros. Like expressions, macros must deal with problems of associativity, precedence, and side effects. Precedence and associativity problems can occur when a macro is combined with other expressions and when a macro's arguments are expressions themselves.

When a macro is combined with other expressions, precedence and associativity rules can cause unintended results. These occur if you do not place the operands in a `#define` macro within parenthesis. Take the example of the `mult` macro written without parenthesis around its operands.

```
mult(x,y)   x * y
```

In the next example, the division and multiplication operators associate from left to right. The division is performed first, instead of multiplication.

```
21 / mult(4,5)       is      21 / 4* 5
                             (21/4)  *  5
```

Precedence and associativity can always be overcome by using parentheses. That is the solution here. A #define macro should always have a set of parentheses placed at the beginning and the end of its replacement text.

```
#define mult(x,y) (x * y)
```

```
21 / mult(4,5)       is      21 / (4 * 5)
```

When the replacement text in a macro's argument is an expression, precedence and associativity problems can arise within the macro's expression. In the next example, precedence first multiplies 2 with 5 then adds the result to 4, though this is clearly not the intention of the user.

```
mult(4+2,5)          is      4 +  2 * 5
                             4 + (2 * 5)
```

Again the solution is parentheses, but this time the parentheses are placed around the argument symbols in the replacement text.

```
#define mult(x,y)  ( (x) * (y))
```

```
mult(4+2,5)              is      ((4 +  2) * 5)
```

Multiple increment operations on the same variable are to be avoided in #define macros just as in expressions. A macro whose argument is an increment may generate an expression with multiple increments. In the following example, if the square macro is thought of as a function call, the square macro looks as if it is incrementing i only once. In fact, it generates an expression in which i is incremented twice.

```
square(i++)          is      i++ * i++
```

A macro has a performance advantage over a function in the same way that an expression has a performance advantage over a function. There are functions that can be easily written as expressions. Functions that can be written as single expressions could be replaced by a macro that will expand to an expression. In the next example, a greater-than comparison is defined with a macro.

```
#define  max(x,y)   ((x > y) ? x : y)
```

As with constants, a macro has the advantage of defining an expression only once and then using it many times throughout the program. If the expression ever needs to be changed, you only need to modify the #define macro.

include: Header Files

Often extern declarations are used in many different files throughout the program. Instead of being retyped in each file, they can be placed in a header file and included simply with the include directive. This makes maintenance of extern declarations very manageable. By convention, the extension of a header file is .h. In LISTING 22-4, the function declarations and extern declaration are placed in the header file **funcs.h**. The include directive is placed in each file. The preprocessor will include the **funcs.h** file in each of the .c files when each is compiled.

LISTING 22-4:

funcs.h
```
 float calc(int, int);
 float add(int, int);
 extern float calcres;
```

```
main.c
#include "funcs.h"

int main(void)
                {
                float res;

                res = calc(4,5);

                return 0;
                }
```

calc.c

```
 float calcres;

float calc(int x, int y)
                {
                calcres = (x * y) * 0.05;
                return (calcres);
                }

float add(int x, int y)
                {
                calcres = x + y;
                return (calcres);
                }
```

The header file is also used for structure type declarations. A structure's type is user-defined. The compiler must be told what it is. Since each file is compiled separately, the structure type declaration must be provided in each source code file where structures of that type are used. A simple way to deal with this problem is to place the structure definition in a header file and place an include directive for this file in each source code file. The structure type definition is placed in a .h file. Then the .h file is included.

Conditional Directives

Conditional preprocessor directives perform operations based on a specified condition. They are often used to include code into a program. If the condition is met, the designated code is included into the program and sent to the compiler. If the condition is not met, the designated code is not included, and the program is sent to the compiler without that code. There are two ways to test conditions: conditional definitions and conditional decisions. Conditional definitions are true if a symbol has been defined or undefined. It does not matter what the symbol represents. It only matters that it has been defined. The conditional definition directives are `#ifdef` and `#endif`.

Conditional decisions perform much like an `if` statement. A defined symbol is compared to a possible integer value that it may represent. The conditional decision directives are `if` and `elif`. An operation called defined can be used with the conditional decision directives to effect a conditional definition process. The defined operation takes a preprocessor symbol as its argument. If the symbol is defined, the defined operation results in a true value. If used as the test in an if directive, the test would be true if the symbol were defined.

Conditional definitions: ifdef and endif

The `#ifdef` directive conditionally includes program code. The conditional test is a `#define` symbol. If the symbol is defined, the test is true. If the symbol is not defined, the test is false. The `#define` symbol can be defined to represent anything at all. It does not matter what it represents, only that it is defined. It may even be defined to represent nothing at all.

Conditional definitions are often used as a way to insert debugging code. During the development process, the debugging code is included into the program. Debugging code usually consists of a series of `printf` statements used to check the changing values of variables. These `printf` statements are placed within `#ifdef` and `#endif` directives throughout the program. The test condition is a `#define` symbol. This symbol is then defined in a #define directive, making the `#ifdef` test true. When the program is finished, it can be compiled without the debugging statements by simply removing the #define directive for that symbol.

In LISTING 22-5 debugging statements are placed in the program to print out the addresses held in working pointers. The symbol used for the `#ifdef` test is MYDEBUG. MYDEBUG is then defined in its own `#define` directive. It is not defined to represent anything. `#ifdef` only requires that the symbol be defined, not that it represent anything. To remove the debugging statements, you simply eliminate the `#define` directive for MYDEBUG from the source code file by either deleting it with your editor or turning it into a comment with the comment symbols, `/* */`.

The #else directive can be combined with the `#ifdef` directive to provide a choice between two alternatives depending upon whether a given symbol has been defined. In LISTING 22-6 MYDEBUG is defined, then the debugging format of `*nptr` is printed out. Otherwise, only the value of `*nptr` is printed. `#ifdef`, `#else`, and `#endif` enclose a series of statements. Between `#ifdef` and

#else you can enter several statements. The same is true for #else and #endif or #ifdef and #endif.

LISTING 22-5:

```
#include <stdio.h>
#define MYDEBUG

int main(void)
        {
        char name[10] = "Dickens";
        char *nptr;

        nptr = name;
#ifdef MYDEBUG
        printf("nptr = %p, name = %s\n", nptr, name);
#endif

        while (*nptr != '\0')
                {
#ifdef MYDEBUG
                printf("nptr= %p,*nptr=%c\n",nptr,*nptr);
#endif
                nptr++;
                }
        return 0;
        }
```

LISTING 22-6:

```
#include <stdio.h>
#define MYDEBUG

int main(void)
        {
        char name[10] = "Dickens";
        char *nptr;

        nptr = name;
#ifdef MYDEBUG
printf("nptr = %p, name = %s\n", nptr, name);
#endif

        while (*nptr != '\0')
                {
#ifdef MYDEBUG
                printf("nptr = %p\n", nptr);
                printf("*nptr = %c\n", *nptr);
#else
                putchar(*nptr);
#endif
                nptr++;
                }
        return 0;
        }
```

Sometimes a program will include header files that have been designed for other applications. In that case, a header file may define a symbol differently from the way it is used in the current program. The preprocessor does not allow a symbol to be re-defined unless it is first undefined. The `#undef` directive undefines a symbol. It can then be re-defined. In LISTING 22-7 MAXCHARS is defined in the header file **maxs.h**. It is then undefined in the program and re-defined with a new value.

It may also be the case that the programmer may not know if a header file actually defines a symbol needed in the program. The `#ifndef` directive tests to see if a symbol has already been defined. The `#ifndef` directive is the same as the `#ifdef` directive, except that its test is true if the symbol has not been defined. In LISTING 22-7 an `#ifndef` tests whether the symbol MAXLINES has been defined. If not, it then defines MAXLINES.

LISTING 22-7:

maxs.h

```
#define MAXCHARS 30


getlines.c

#include <stdio.h>
#include "maxs.h"

#ifndef MAXLINES
#define MAXLINES 5
#endif

#undef MAXCHARS
#define MAXCHARS 160


int main(void)
        {
        char lines[MAXLINES][MAXCHARS];
        int i, j;

        for(i=0; i < MAXLINES; i++)
                {
                fgets(lines[i] , MAXCHARS, stdin);
                }
        return 0;
        }
```

Conditional decisions: if, elif, and defined()

A conditional decision tests the value of a defined symbol, not simply whether or not a symbol has been defined. The `#if` and `#elif` directives are conditional decision-making directives. The test used in an `#if` directive is an integer constant expression. This constant expression will evaluate to either zero or non-zero. A non-zero value is true, and a zero value is false.

The test expression must be a constant integer expression. Expressions other than constant integer expressions are not allowed. A constant integer expression is any expression whose operands are constant integers. A relational expression with constant integer operands is a constant integer expression. An equality expression with constant operands is also a constant integer expression. Usually, one operand is a `#define` symbol and the other is a constant to which the symbol is compared.

In LISTING 22-8, a conditional decision structure is used instead of a conditional definition. In this case, the value defined for MYDEBUG is important. The conditional decisions permit a more sophisticated structure. Several levels of debugging can now be specified. MYDEBUG is then set to one of those levels.

LISTING 22-8:

```
#include <stdio.h>
#define MYDEBUG 2

int main(void)
        {
        char name[10] = "Dickens";
        char *nptr;

        nptr = name;
#if MYDEBUG > 0
printf("nptr = %p, name = %s\n", nptr, name);
#endif

        while (*nptr != '\0')
                {
#if MYDEBUG == 0
                putchar(*nptr);
#elif MYDEBUG == 1
                printf("nptr = %p\n", nptr);
#elif MYDEBUG == 2
                printf("nptr = %p\n", nptr);
                printf("*nptr = %c\n", *nptr);
#endif
                nptr++;
                }

        return 0;
        }
```

#if and #elif are often used to choose among several possible system configurations. A program may be compiled for several different operating systems, using that system's C compiler. Though many of the input/output operations have been standardized in the standard library functions, there are still many system-dependent operations. For example, a C compiler may have a special set of system-specific functions to access and manage file directories. UNIX, MS WINDOWS, and Macintosh file directories are all accessed in very different ways. The prototypes and #define symbols for each may be placed in different header files and then included when appropriate. In LISTING 22-9, the symbol SYSTEM is used to determine which system-specific header file to include.

LISTING 22-9:

```
#include <stdio.h>
#define SYSTEM 2

#if SYSTEM == 1
        #include "unix.h"
#elif SYSTEM == 2
        #include "MS Windows.h"
#elif SYSTEM == 3
        #include "mac.h"
#else
        #include "mysys.h"
#endif

int main(void)
        {

        return 0;
        }
```

You can combine a conditional decision with a defined preprocessor operation to implement a conditional definition structure. The defined operation takes a symbol as its argument. If the symbol has been defined, the defined operation results in a 1. If the symbol is undefined, the defined operation results in a 0. In LISTING 22-10 a choice is made between several possible definitions. Only the symbol MS WINDOWS is defined. It will be chosen. It does not matter that it has been defined with no value. It is still defined.

LISTING 22-10:

```
#include <stdio.h>
#define MS WINDOWS

#if defined(UNIX)
        #include "unix.h"
#elif defined(MS WINDOWS)
        #include "MS Windows.h"
#elif defined(MAC)
        #include "mac.h"
#endif

int main(void)
        {

        return 0;
        }
```

Bitwise Operations

Masks, Shifts, and Fields

Logical Operations

Masks

Shift Operations

Bit Fields

23. Bitwise Operations

The bitwise operations allow a programmer to manipulate specific bits in an integral object. The operations perform bit level logical operations on each bit in an integer. The bitwise operations can be combined with masks to turn specific bits on and off.

Bits can also be organized into bit fields, several bits to a field. Bit fields are declared as members of a structure. A variable can then be declared as a structure of bit fields. Each field is referenced with the member operator, just as members of a structure are referenced.

Bitwise Logical Operations: &, |, ^, ~

Bitwise operations take integral objects as their operands. The integral objects may be of any integral type, whether it be long, character, or simply integer. The integral objects are operated on bit by bit, not as a whole. For example, the logical bitwise operators & and | will compare bit by bit the bits in two integral objects.

The bitwise operations are expressions. They result in a value that is a modified form of the integral objects operated on. The integral objects themselves are not changed. In a sense, the resulting value of a bitwise operation is constructed bit by bit from operations on the bits of the integral operands. A bitwise operation can almost be thought of as an operation on an arrays of bits, each bit constituting an element of an array that is the integral object. The integral objects are, of course, not arrays. But their bits are referenced in bitwise operations as if they were individual elements.

Bitwise AND: &

The bitwise AND operation, &, compares the bits in two integral operands. It builds a resulting value bit by bit based on these comparisons. If two corresponding bits in the two operands have a binary 1 value, then the corresponding binary bit in the resulting value will have a binary 1 value. If either, or both, of the corresponding bits in the two operands has a binary 0 value, then the corresponding bit in the resulting value will be given a binary 0 value. s

There is a kind of analogy here to the logical AND operation, &&. A logical AND expression is true if both operands are true. If either operand, or both, is false, then the expression is false. In a bitwise AND operation, &, if both bits are a binary 1, then the result is a binary 1. If one or the other, or both, is a binary 0, then the result is a binary 0. In Figure 23-1, two character values are operated on by a bitwise AND operator. They are presented in their binary form to show better how comparisons are made.

$$
\begin{array}{r}
\& \ \ 0\ 1\ 0\ 0\ 1\ 0\ 0\ 1 \\
\underline{0\ 1\ 1\ 0\ 1\ 0\ 0\ 0} \\
0\ 1\ 0\ 0\ 1\ 0\ 0\ 0
\end{array}
$$

Figure 23-1: Bitwise AND operation.

Bitwise OR: |

The bitwise OR operation, |, also compares the bits in two integral operands. A resulting value is generated bit by bit based on each comparison. If either of two corresponding bits in the integral operands has a binary value of 1, or if they both have a binary 1 value, then the corresponding bit in the resulting value will be given a binary 1 value. Only if both corresponding bits in the integral operands have a binary 0 value will the corresponding bit in the resulting value be given a binary 0 value.

This is analogous to the logical OR operation, | |, in which a logical expression is true if either operand is true. A logical OR expression is false only if both operands are false. In a bitwise OR operation, |, if both of the corresponding bits in the integral operands have a binary 0 value, the corresponding bit in the resulting value will be given a binary 0 value. Otherwise, the corresponding bit in the resulting value will be given a binary 1 value. In Figure 23-2, a bitwise OR operation is performed on two character values.

```
    0 1 0 0 1 0 0 1
|   0 1 1 0 1 0 0 0
    ───────────────
    0 1 1 0 1 0 0 1
```

Figure 23-2: Bitwise OR operation.

Bitwise One's Complement: ~

The one's complement operator, ~, is a unary operator. It takes one integral operand. In the one's complement operation, the corresponding bit in the resulting value is set to the opposite of that of the operand's bit. If an operand's bit is a binary 1, then the corresponding bit of the resulting value will be a binary 0, and vice versa. The one's complement operation results in a value that is the bitwise mirror image of the operand. All bits set to 1 in the operand are set to 0 in the resulting value. All bits set to 0 in the operand are set to 1 in the resulting value, as shown in Figure 23-3.

```
      0 1 0 0 1 0 0 1
~     ───────────────
      1 0 1 1 0 1 1 0
```

Figure 23-3 Bitwise One's Compliment operation.

Bitwise Exclusive OR: ^

An exclusive bitwise OR operation is similar to the bitwise OR. In an exclusive bitwise OR operation, if one of the corresponding bits in the two operands is a binary 1 and the other is a binary 0, then the corresponding bit in the result is given a binary 1. If both corresponding bits have a binary 1 value or both have a binary 0 value, then the corresponding bit of the resulting value is a binary 0. Figure 23-4 shows two corresponding bits result in a 1 only if they are different, not if they are the same.

```
      0 1 0 0 1 0 0 1
^     0 1 1 0 1 0 0 0
      ───────────────
      0 0 1 0 0 0 0 1
```

Figure 23-4: Bitwise Exclusive OR operation.

Masks

Bitwise logical operations are used to manage the values of particular bits in an integral object. The integral object is treated like an array of bits. Individual bits are referenced in bitwise logical operations in which one operand is the integral object and the other is a constant. The constant is a predetermined value whose bits will interact with those of the integral object in such a way as to affect a specific bit. Such a constant is often referred to as a mask. A combination of bitwise operations and assignment operations can actually change the values of individual bits to either a binary 1 or a binary 0.

It is easy to construct a mask using octal values. A octal value easily maps to a binary representation. Figure 23-5 is a table of octal values and their binary equivalent. An integer can be thought of as being divided into sets of three bits. Each number in an octal value will correspond to the binary value of each of these sets of three bits. The octal value 021 is equivalent to the binary value of 000 010 001. The binary equivalent of an octal 75 is 000 111 010. The octal 0 maps to a binary 000; the octal 2 maps to a binary 010; and the octal 1 maps to a binary 001.

Using octal values allows a mask to be easily constructed where one bit is set to 1 and the others are set to 0. Such a mask is used to reference the corresponding bit in the integral object. To reference the third bit in an 8-bit character variable, a mask consisting of the octal value 004 is used. The binary equivalent of an octal 004 is 000 000 100.

Octal Binary Values

Binary value	Octal number
000	0
001	1
010	2
011	3
100	4
010	5
110	6
111	7

Figure 23-5: Table of Octal Binary Values

Setting Bits On: |=

A bit in a given integral object can be set to 1 by combining the bitwise OR operation with an assignment operation. First, a bitwise OR operation is performed on both the integral object and a mask whose value references that specific bit. The resulting value of the bitwise OR operation will include all the bits already set to 1 in the integral object as well as the bit set to 1 in the mask. This resulting value is then assigned to the integral object, becoming the object's new value. In this new value, the bit referenced by the mask is set to 1. =

In Figure 23-6, the third bit in the character variable flags is set to 1 using bitwise OR and assignment operations. Both the assignment and bitwise operations can be performed by a bitwise assignment operation. The bitwise OR assignment operation, |=, performs the bitwise OR operation on the operands and then assigns the result to the left operand. Bitwise assignment operations are structured in the same way as arithmetic assignment operations.

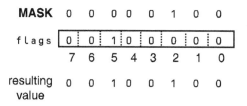

Figure 23-6: Bitwise OR assignment operation.

Setting Bits Off: &=, ~

Setting a bit to 0 is more involved than setting it to 1. All the bits in the integral object must retain their values, except for the one bit referenced. In a bitwise AND operation, if one bit is 0 and the other is 1, then the result will be 0. In this sense, a bitwise AND operation can be used to set a bit that is 1 to 0. However, the AND operation must be done is such a way that the value of any of the other bits is not changed.

To set a bit that is 1 to 0 without affecting the other bits requires a combination of the one's complement operation and the bitwise AND operation. The one's compliment operator, ~, is first applied to the mask that references the specific bit. The one's complement operation will result in a value in which the specified bit is set to 0 and all the other bits are set to 1. The AND operation then uses this inverted value as a mask for the integral object. Since the specified bit in the mask is 0, the corresponding bit in the resulting value will be 0. Since all other bits in the inverted value are 1, any bits set to 1 in the integral object will be carried over into the resulting value. The resulting value is then assigned to the integral object.

In Figure 23-7, the character object flags has its third bit set back to 0 using a combination of a one's complement on the bit's mask and the bitwise AND operation. Like the bitwise OR assignment operator, there is also a bitwise AND assignment operator, &=, ~..

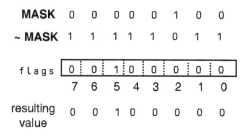

Figure 23-7: Bitwise AND assignment operation.

Toggling Bits : ^=

The exclusive OR is used to toggle a bit. If a bit is set to 1, the exclusive OR will set it to 0. If a bit is set to 0, the exclusive OR will set it to 1. The bit is turned on if it is off, and turned off if it is on.

In an exclusive OR, bit values that are the same result in a 0 value. Bit values that are different result in a 1. In the mask, the specified bit is always 1. If its corresponding bit in the integral object is also to 1, then both bits will be the same, and the result will be a 0 value. If the corresponding bit in the integral object is a 0, then the bits will be different, and a 1 value will result. In other words, if the integral object's bit is 0, the corresponding bit in the resulting value will be 1. If the integral object's bit is 1, then the corresponding bit in the resulting value will be 0. The resulting value is then assigned to the integral object.

In the mask, only one specified bit is set to 1. All others are set to 0. In the integral object, any other bits set to 1 will be different from the corresponding bit in the mask, which will be 0. The 1 setting for such bits will be carried over into the resulting value. In Figure 23-8, the third bit of the flags variable is toggled on and off. The exclusive OR also has a bitwise exclusive OR assignment operator, ^=.

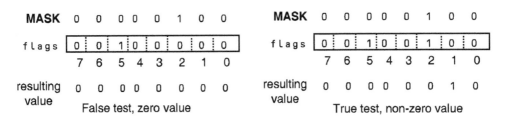

Figure 23-8: Bitwise Exclusive OR assignment operations.

Testing a Bit : &

Bitwise operations are expressions that can be used as test expressions for control statements, such as while and if. Their resulting value can be a zero or non-zero value. A zero value will be false, and a non-zero value will be true. A zero value is literally a value in which all the bits are set to 0. A bitwise operation that results in a value in which all the bits are set to 0 can be thought of as being false. If any of the bits in the result is set to 1, the bitwise operation can be thought of as being true.

```
MASK   0  0  0 0  0  1  0  0           MASK   0  0  0 0  0  1  0  0

flags [ 0 : 0 : 1:0 : 0 : 0 : 0 : 0 ]  flags [ 0 : 0 : 1:0 : 0 : 1 : 0 : 0 ]
        7  6  5  4  3  2  1  0                  7  6  5  4  3  2  1  0

resulting  0  0  0 0  0  0  0  0        resulting  0  0  0 0  0  0  1  0
value      False test, zero value      value      True test, non-zero value
```

Figure 23-9: Bitwise AND operation as a test expression.

To test for the value of a specific bit, a bitwise AND operation is used as a test expression. Its operands are the integral object and the mask for that specified bit. Since all but one of the bits in the mask are 0, all but the specified bit in the result will necessarily be 0. If the specified bit in the integral object is also 0, then all the bits in the result will be 0. In that case the result of the bitwise AND operation will then be zero, and the test will be false. If the specified bit in the integral object is set to 1, then the corresponding bit in the result will be 1. The result of the AND bitwise operation will then be a non-zero value, and the test will be true. In Figure 23-9, the third bit of the flags variable is tested in both an if and a while statement.

In LISTING 23-1, the program in LISTING 4-21 has been rewritten using bitwise operations and masks. The three greeting options are defined as octal values. FORMAL is defined as an octal 01 and references the first bit in the integer greeting, 001. COMMON is defined as an octal 02 and references the second bit in the integer, 010. FRIENDLY is defined as an octal 04 and references the third bit in the integer, 100. The second bit of the greeting integer is then set to 1 with the bitwise OR assignment operation, greeting |= COMMON. In the test expression of each if statement, the bitwise AND operations test to see if a given bit is on. The expression greeting & FORMAL tests the first bit. The first bit is 0 so the expression results in a 0 and the test is false. The expression greeting & COMMON tests the second bit. The second bit is 1 so the expression results in a non-zero value (2 in this case). The non-zero result makes the test true.

LISTING 23-1:

```c
#include <stdio.h>

#define FORMAL 01
#define COMMON 02
#define FRIENDLY 04

int main(void)
    {
    int greeting = 0;

    greeting |= COMMON;

    if ((greeting & FORMAL) != 0)
        printf("greetings");
    else
        if ((greeting & COMMON) != 0)
            printf("hello");
        else
            if ((greeting & FRIENDLY) != 0)
                printf("hi");
            else
                printf("Invalid Greeting");
    return 0;
    }
```

Bitwise Shift Operations: <<, >>

The bitwise shift operators produce a result in which the binary values of an operand are shifted. The shift operators take two operands. The first is an integral object whose binary values are used to generate the shifted resulting value. The second is an integer specifying how many places the binary values are to be shifted.

The left shift operator, <<, shifts binary values to the left. Values shifted off the end of the object are lost, and bits at the beginning of the object whose values have been shifted over have their values replaced with 0.

The right shift operator, >>, operates in the same way as the left shift operator, except that it shifts values to the right. Both the left and right shift operators have corresponding bitwise shift assignment operators. A bitwise shift operator first generates a result in which the bit values of an operand have been shifted and then assigns that result to the operand.

The shift operators effect bit-level multiplication and division by powers of 2. The power is the number of places shifted. Shifting a value one bit to the left effectively multiplies it by 2. Shifting the value two bits to the left multiplies it by 4. Shifting the value two bits to the right divides it by 4. In the following example, the value of num is continually divided by 2 with a right shift operation.

```
int num = 100;
while(num > 0)
        {
        printf("The value of num is %d\n", num);
        num >>= 1;
        }
```

LISTING 23-2:

```
#include <stdio.h>
#define BYTEBITS 8

int main(void)
        {
        int num;
        int i = 0;

        printf("Enter number to be printed out in binary ");
        scanf("%d", &num);

        while(i < (sizeof(int) * BYTEBITS))
                {
                if(num & 01)
                        putchar('1');
                else
                        putchar('0');
                num >>= 1;
                i++;
                }
        return 0;
        }
```

The bitwise shift operations are often combined with masks to print out the binary equivalent of an integer. In the LISTING 23-2, the integer num is shifted to the right each time through the loop. A mask consisting of an octal 1, 01, is tested with the integer num. An octal 1 will test the value of the first bit only. If the bit is 1, the test will be true. In that case a '1' will be printed out. If the bit is 0 then the test will be false. A 0 will then be printed out. The `sizeof` operator is used to determine the size of an integer. In the case of a 2 byte integer fifteen bits will be printed - 0 to 15.

```
while(i < 16)
        {
        if(num & 0100000)
                putchar('1');
        else
                putchar('0');
        num <<= 1;
        i++;
        }
```

Integers are often represented with the most significant bit printed first, 15 to 0. In this case, the bits are shifted to the left. In this example a 2 byte 15 bit integer is assumed. The mask is an octal 0100000. The first five zeros reference the first fifteen bits. Each octal number represents three binary bits. The 1 references the 16th bit.

LISTING 23-3:

```
#include <stdio.h>
#define BYTEBITS 8

int main(void)
        {
        int num, bits, mask = 01;
        int i = 0;
        printf("Enter number to be printed out in binary ");
        scanf("%d", &num);
        bits = sizeof(int) * BYTEBITS;
        mask <<=  (bits - 1);
        while(i < bits)
                {
                if(num & mask)
                        putchar('1');
                else
                        putchar('0');
                num <<= 1;
                i++;
                }
        return 0;
        }
```

The actual size in bytes of an integer may vary from one computer to another. On one system an integer may be two bytes, 16 bits. On another system an integer may be four bytes, 32 bits. The program in LISTING 23-3 calculates the number of bits in an integer using the `sizeof` operator. The mask used in an integer variable initialized to an octal 1. The left-shift operator is then used to move the 1 to the left-most bit.

Bit Fields

Bit fields are members of a bit field structure. A bit field structure consists of integers whose bits are allocated to the bit field members of the structure. A bit field itself is declared with a name followed by a colon and the number of bits to be allocated for this field. A bit field may consist of only one bit or several bits.

In the next example, `myfields` is a structure variable whose members are bit fields. `myflag` and total share the same unsigned integer. `myflag` references the first bit in the integer, and total references the next four bits. Each field can be assigned values up to the maximum possible for the size of the field. `myflag` can only hold values 0 and 1. total can hold values from 0 to 15 (24)

```
struct {
        unsigned myflag: 1;
        unsigned total: 4;
        } myfields;

myfields.myflag = 1;
myfields.total = 9;
```

Unnamed bit fields can be added for padding. In the following declaration, a padded field is placed between myflag and total. total now references bits 4 to 8 in the integer.

```
struct {
        unsigned myflag: 1;
        unsigned           : 2;
        unsigned total: 4;
        } myfields;
```

If the sizes of all the fields sum to a size greater than an integer, then two integers are allocated for the structure. The bit fields in the second integer will be aligned. A bit field may not overlap two integers.

Bit fields operate at a very low level and as such tend to be implementation dependent. Check your compiler for specific on how Bit fields actually operate on memory.

24

Make

Suffix Rules and Libraries

Implied Dependencies

Pre-defines Variables

Suffix Rules

Library Dependencies

24. Make

You will often be working with a program that has many source code files. As you develop the program, making modifications, you will need to compile the program over and over again. However you need only compile those source code files in which you made changes. The linker then links the newly generated object code files with previously compiled object code files creating a new executable file. The fact that only a few of your source files have to actually be compiled, drastically cuts down on the work of the compiler. Each time you need a new executable program you do not need to recompile each source code file.

It can be very difficult in large programs with many source code files to keep track of which files have been changed and need to be compiled, and which files need only to be linked. A utility called the Make utility will do this for you. Make was designed for a development environment in which different source code files in a program are constantly being modified. Make keeps track of which source files have been changed and which have not. It then recompiles only those that have been changed, linking them with the rest of the object code files to create a new executable file. Different features and options of the Make utility are described in Table 24-5.

Most C compilers will include a Make utility with which you can manage your programs. Though the actual implementation of Make may differ depending upon the compiler you use or the operating system you are working on, all use the same basic structure originally designed for the UNIX Make utility. Make was originally a UNIX utility that was later transported to other systems. The following examples of Make are based on the UNIX Make utility since the UNIX version remains a simple and easy to understand implementation of Make. In the next example, the user enters the command make on the command line to invoke the Make utility. Make then compiles those files that have recently been modified and creates a new executable file. Make displays each Unix command it executes, in this case, compiler commands to compile a program.

```
$ make
cc -c main.c
cc -c io.c
cc main.o io.o
$
```

If all the files in your program are up to date, then the Make utility only returns a messages telling you so.

```
$ make
'a.out' is up to date.
$
```

To understand how the Make utility works, you need to realize that it uses a source code file's time stamp to determine whether or not it should be compiled. Whenever a file is created, re-created, or modified in any way, a new time stamp is placed on it by the Unix operating system. If you create a file at 1:00 that file is stamped with the time 1:00. If you then change the file at 6:00, the file is re-stamped with the time 6:00. When compiling a program, only those source code files that have been changed need to be recompiled. Since the change of any file changes the time stamp, the time stamp can be used to determine which files need to be compiled. In this way, Make knows which files need to be compiled and actually selects the files to be compiled for the programmer.

In the next example, the user manages a program consisting of two source code files: **main.c** and **io.c**. Both files have corresponding object code files: **main.o** and **io.o**. These are used to create an executable file called **a.out**. If either **main.c** or **io.c** have been modified since **a.out** was last created, then make will again compile the modified source code file, generating a new object code file and then create a new executable file. Below, is a Unix listing of all files that specifies the time the file was last modified just before the name of the file at the end of the line. All files, except for **main.c**, have times earlier than the executable file **a.out**.

```
$ ls -l
total 56
-rwxr-xr-x  1 chris     48728 Nov   3 04:31 a.out
-rw-r--r--  1 chris       256 Nov   3 04:30 io.c
-rw-r--r--  1 chris      2080 Nov   3 04:30 io.o
-rw-r--r--  1 chris       136 Nov   3 05:05 main.c
-rw-r--r--  1 chris       604 Nov   3 04:30 main.o
-rw-r--r--  1 chris        66 Nov   3 03:00 types.h
```

The user then executes the make command. Make finds that **main.c** was changed more recently than **a.out**, so **main.c** is compiled creating a new **main.o** file. Both the new **main.o** and the old **io.o** file are then used to create a new **a.out** file. The following file listing shows that the times for **main.o** and **a.out** are now more recent than **main.c**.

```
$ make
cc -c main.c
cc main.o io.o
$ ls -l
total 56
-rwxr-xr-x  1 chris     48728 Nov   3 05:06 a.out
-rw-r--r--  1 chris       256 Nov   3 04:30 io.c
-rw-r--r--  1 chris      2080 Nov   3 04:30 io.o
-rw-r--r--  1 chris       136 Nov   3 05:00 main.c
-rw-r--r--  1 chris       604 Nov   3 05:05 main.o
-rw-r--r--  1 chris        66 Nov   3 03:00 types.h
$
```

Make does not automatically compile any source code file that has been changed. You need to first provide the Make utility with a coded set of instructions that tell Make how to determine what files are to be compiled. These instructions are often referred to as dependency lines and are placed in a file called **makefile**. Make will automatically read and execute the dependency lines that it finds in the **makefile**.

By default, Make will look for a file called **makefile** in your current working directory in your operating system. Each directory can have its own file called **makefile**. Suppose that you needed to have more than one **makefile** in your current directory. Using the -f option, Make can read a file that contains dependency lines, but has a name other than "**makefile**". In the next example, the user reads dependency lines from a file called **prog.mak**. By convention, such files often have the extension **.mak**. However, this extension is not required. Other Unix Make options are listed in Table 24-5, and are commonly found in Make utilities used on other systems.

```
$ make -f prog.mak
```

```
cc -c io.c
cc main.o io.o
$
```

Another Make option that you may find helpful as you learn Make, is the -n option. With this options, Make does not execute any actual commands. Instead it only displays those commands that would be executed by Make. In this way you can see how your Make instructions are operating, and if they are performing as you want them to. In the next example, the make command does not actually compile the program. It only displays the cc commands that Make would execute.

```
$ make -n
cc -c io.c
cc main.o io.o
```

The makefile: dependency Lines

The Make utility works on a file called **makefile** which consists of Make commands. Such Make commands are made up of dependency lines followed by operations to be executed. Let us first take a look at the concept of dependency as it is used in Make.

A dependency specifies a dependency relationship between files. Make operates in terms of dependencies. A source code file is used to create an object code file which in turn is used to create a runnable program. The program can be said to be dependent on the object code file which in turn is dependent on the source code file. You need to specify the dependency relationship between a source code file and an object code file in a dependency line. In another dependency line you need to specify the dependency relationship between an executable file and all its object code files.

A dependency line can be thought of as a kind of conditional statement. The dependency relationship is its test condition. If an object code file depends on a source code file and the source code file has been recently modified, then the test condition is true and the file is then recompiled. However, the syntax for a dependency line is a bit more complex than a standard conditional statement. A dependency line consists of three components: a target file, a list of dependency files, and a command. If any of the dependency files has been modified more recently than the target file, then the command is executed. The target file and the dependent files are written on the same line, separated by a colon. You can either place the command on the same line, separated from the dependent files by a semicolon, or you can place the command on the next line preceded by a tab. You can list more than one command if you wish. When entered on the same line you separate Unix commands with semicolons. On separate lines, each command has to be preceded by a tab. The dependency line ends with a following empty line. In these examples the command is an invocation of the cc compiler, compiling a source code file or linking object code files. The syntax for a dependency line is as follows:

```
target file : dependent files ; command
empty line

target file : dependent files
tab    command
empty line
```

In the following **makefile** you construct the dependency lines for a C program consisting of two source code files: **main.c** and **io.c**. In such a two-file program there are really five files to manage. For each .c file there is a corresponding .o file. There is the executable file, **a.out**. You need to set up your **makefile** with dependency lines to manage all of these files, specifying dependencies for each. An object code file (.o) is dependent on a source code (.c) file. An executable file, **a.out**, is dependent on several object code files (.o) . In this example, **a.out** is dependent on (made up of) the two object code files **main.o** and **io.o**. Each object code file is, in turn, dependent on their respective source code files; **main.o** on **main.c** , and **io.o** on **io.c** (see Figure 24-1).

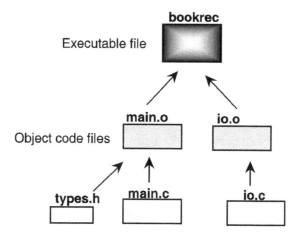

Figure 24-1: Dependency diagram. bookrec depends on both main.o and io.o. main.o depends on both main.c and types.h. io.o depends only on io.c.

In the **makefile**, three dependency lines are needed for the **a.out**, **main.o**, and **io.o** files respectively. The linking and compilation of the program are split up among the different dependency lines. The Unix command for the **a.out** target only links the two object code files, creating a new executable file. It invokes cc with only object code files (.o), causing only the linker to be invoked. The Unix commands for the **main.o** and **io.o** targets only compile, creating .o object files. The -c option used with cc means that no linking is done, only compilation, generating the object code file for this source code file.

makefile

```
a.out : main.o io.o
        cc main.o io.o

main.o : main.c
        cc -c main.c

io.o : io.c
        cc -c io.c
```

The flow of control for a dependency line operates somewhat like a series of function or procedure calls. Control is transferred from one dependency line to another, each time checking the time stamps of files in the list of dependent files. The flow of control operates according to three basic rules applied to each dependency line.

1. Start checking the list of dependent files. Take the first dependent file and check to see if it is itself a target file in another dependency line. If it is, then suspend operation on the current dependency line and transfer control to that other dependency line. This operation is similar to a function call, where control is transferred from one part of the program to another. The target files form a left hand column on the left edge of the file.

2. When control has returned to the dependency line after another dependency line has finished, or if the dependent file is not itself a target file , then continue on to the next dependent file in the list of dependent files. Check, in turn, to see if this next dependent file is itself a target file in another dependency line. If so transfer control.

3. After all the dependent files have been processed, Make then checks if any of the time stamps for the dependent files is more recent than that of the target file. If so, the dependency line executes the Unix command. If not, the Unix command is not executed.

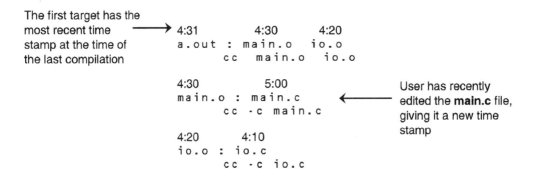

Figure 24-2: dependency lines with time stamps illustrated before executing the make utility and after changing the main.c file.

Figure 24-2 is an example of a **makefile** dependency lines with time stamps added in. Suppose you modify **main.c**, saving it at 5:00. When you do so, Unix gives **main.c** a new time stamp of 5:00. Then you execute the make command to update your program, incorporating the changes you just made. The Make utility reads the dependency lines in your makefile. Make then starts at the first dependency line which happens to have target file **a.out**. It then starts on the first dependent file in that line: **main.o**. Is **main.o** itself a target file in another dependency line? It is. Control is transferred to that line. Make then examines the first dependent file in the **main.o** dependency line. It is **main.c**. Is **main.c** itself a target file? It is not. This is the only dependent file for **main.o**. The next step is to check if the timestamp of any of the dependent files is more recent than the target file, **main.o**. There is only one dependent file, **main.c**, and its time stamp is more recent than that of **main.o**. The time stamp for **main.c** is 5:00 than the time stamp for **main.o** is 4:30. The Unix command for the **main.o** dependency line, is then executed. The Unix command is a cc command to recompile **main.c**. The recompilation of **main.c** creates a new **main.o** file with a new time stamp. The time stamp of **main.o** is now 5:05. The dependency line ends and returns control to the dependency line it came from, **a.out**. Figure 24-3 points out the different time changes to files in the **main.o** and **a.out** dependency lines.

Once back at the **a.out** dependency line, Make continues down the list of dependent files. It finds **io.o**. It then asks if **io.o** is itself a target in another dependency line. It is. Control is transferred to that dependency line. In the **io.o** dependency line, Make examines files in the dependency list. The only dependent file is **io.c** which is not itself a target file. Nor is its timestamp more recent than the target file, **io.o**. So the Unix command for the **io.o** dependency line is not executed, and control returns to the dependency line it came from, **a.out**.

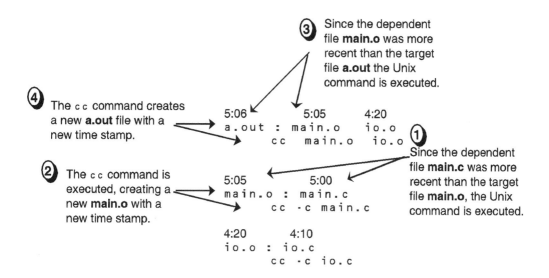

Figure 24-3: Make utility executing dependency lines and changing time stamps

Again back at the **a.out** dependency line, Make has now finished processing a.out's list of dependent files. It then checks if there any dependent files whose timestamp is more recent than the timestamps of the target file. There is one. The time stamp for **main.o**, 5:05 is now more recent than the time stamp for **a.out**, 4:31. So the Unix command for the **a.out** dependency line is executed. The Unix command is a cc command that links the .o files into a new **a.out** file. This operation will create a new **a.out** file with a new time stamp, in this case 5:06. Notice that 5:06 is more recent than all the other files in the dependency lines. Figure 24-4 illustrates the flow of control from one dependency line to another and back again.

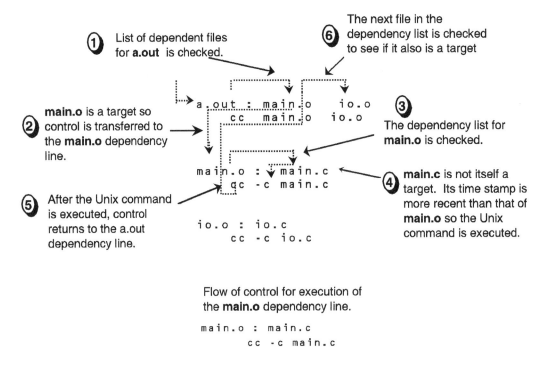

Figure 24-4: Makefile flow of control for lib.o dependency lines.

Header Files

Dependency relationships can be set up between files of any type, not just source code and object code files. For example, you can set up a dependency relationship between an object code file and what is known in C programs as a header file. A header file is a text file that contains segments of source code that are inserted into your main source code files by your compiler. They become an actual part of the program. In this respect, an object code file may not only be dependent on a source code file, but also a particular header file.

To use a particular header file, you need to explicitly instruct the compiler to include that header file with the source code file. You do so by entering a special include instruction in your source code file. In the **io.c** file, the include instruction `#include<stdio.h>` instructs the compiler to include source code contained in the **stdio.h** header file. By convention, header files all have the **extension .h** attached to their names. In the next example, the header file called **types.h** is created for the **bookrecs** program. **types.h** contains the prototype declarations that were previously in the **main.c** file. An include instruction in **main.c** instructs the compiler to include the prototype declaration in **types.h** as part of the **main.c** source code. Both **main.c** and **types.h** are now used to create the **main.o** file.

types.h

```
void bookinput(char[], float*);
void printbook(char[], float);
```

main.c

```
#include "types.h"

int main(void)
            {
            char title[20];
            float price;

            bookinput(title, &price);
            printbook(title, price);

            return 0;
            }
```

io.c

```
#include <stdio.h>

void bookinput(char title[], float *price)
            {
            printf("Please enter book record : ");
            scanf("%s%f", title, price);
            }

void printbook(char title[], float price)
        {
        printf("The book record is: %s %.2f\n",title,price);
        }
```

You can now see how the **main.o** file depends on the both the **main.c** source code file and the **types.h** header file. Should you make changes to the **types.h** file, you would want to have Make generate a new **main.o** file. To do this, you need to place **types.h** as a dependent file in the **main.o** depdency line. If there are any changes to either **main.c** or to **types.h** header file, then **main.c** will be recompiled.

makefile

```
a.out : main.o io.o
        cc main.o io.o

main.o : main.c types.h
        cc -c main.c

io.o : io.c
        cc -c io.c
```

Implied Make Dependencies

The Make utility has a set of implied dependency relationships that it automatically applies to source code and object code files. Though these implied dependencies were originally defined for use in Unix, many have been carried over to other operating systems. In Unix, the source code file for any given programming language must contain a specific suffix. C source code files **require .c** suffixes. Fortran files require a .f suffix. .s is used for assembler source code files. Make will examine the source code file suffix of a corresponding object code file in a dependency list, and automatically invoke the appropriate compiler for that source code file. This means that, using implied dependencies, you can dispense with the dependency lines for compiling source code files. You can then reduce your **makefile** to one Unix command, the command to link files. The source code file extensions and their corresponding programming language compilers are listed in Table 24-4.

Exactly how Make implements implied dependencies is discussed later during the examination of suffix rules. Using such rules you will learn how to create your own implied dependencies. For now it is enough to know that you can drastically reduce the number of dependency lines in your **makefile** if you wish to do so.

In the next example, by relying on implied dependencies, the **makefile** for the **bookrecs** program only needs two dependency lines. When examining the dependency list for the **bookrecs** dependency line, Make will look for corresponding source code files in the current directory. It will find **main.c** and **io.c**. Since these files have a .c extension, the dependency line would recognize these as C source codes and would invoke the cc compiler if necessary. Suppose the user recently modified **io.c**. Then Make would know to compile **io.c** with the C compiler, cc -c.

makefile

```
bookrecs : main.o io.o
        cc main.o io.o -o bookrecs
```

Run of make command.

```
$ ls *.c
main.c io.c
$ make
cc -c io.c
cc main.o io.o -o bookrecs
```

To denote the dependency of header files on an object code file, you need to add a dependency line but without a following Unix command. Make will locate the source code file and compile it to create the object code file. In the next **makefile** example, another dependency line is added for the **main.o** and **types.h** dependency.

makefile

```
bookrecs : main.o io.o
        cc main.o io.o -o bookrecs

main.o: types.h
```

Specifying Dependency Lines using Target Arguments

Suppose that you want to use Make to execute a specific Unix command for you. For example, suppose you would like to use Make to execute the Unix command to print out all your source code files. Instead of entering in all your source code files on the command line each time you want to print them out, you can have Make do it for you. Remember that the Unix command in a dependency line can be any Unix command, not just a cc compiler command. You can enter a dependency line whose Unix command is an lp command to print files.

You would then be using your **makefile** for two very different purposes: to compile a program, and to print files. You will have dependency lines that compile your program, as well as another dependency line to print your files. Whereas the dependency lines for compiling are all inter-dependent, the one for printing would be independent of any other dependency lines. You do not want to print each time you compile and visa verse. You could have a dependency line, whose target , is not listed as a dependent file in any other dependency line. Such a dependency line would be disconnected from all others. The target itself does not have to be an actual file. It can be what is known as a zero length file, one that Make creates for its own purposes. In the next example, the user creates such a dependency line whose target is the word print. **print** is a zero length file created by Make. It is not one that you have created.

makefile

```
bookrecs: main.o io.o
        cc main.o io.o -o bookrecs

main.o : main.c
        cc -c main.c

io.o : io.c
        cc -c io.c

print :
        lp main.c io.c &
```

Since the target in such a dependency line is not in any way related to any other dependency line, how then could it ever be executed? By default, Make begins processing with the first dependency line in the **makefile**. However, you can direct Make to begin processing with a specific dependency line by using its target as an argument on the command line. If you list the target of a dependency line, then Make will execute that dependency line, ignoring the others. In the previous **makefile**, the last dependency line only prints files. Its target is the word print. There is no dependency list so that if this dependency line is ever processed, it will always execute its Unix command. This dependency line is actually a way to use Make to print out all the source code files in the background, &.

```
$ make print
lp main.c io.c
$
```

You can actually specify any target on the command line. For example, you could explicitly specify **main.o** as a target on the command line. Then Make would only execute the **main.o** dependency line, checking to see if the **main.c** file should be compiled. For this **makefile**, the make command by itself and make with the **bookrecs** argument have the same effect. **bookrecs** is the target of the first dependency line in the file and thus also the default. The next two commands are equivalent.

```
$ make
$ make bookrecs
$
```

Updating a file's time stamp: touch and -t

Using the previous **makefile** as an example, suppose you have added some new options to your cc command and want to recompile your program to include those new options such as the -O optimizing option. Since you have not actually modified any of your source code or header files, Make will consider the program to be up to date and not recompile. You need to be able to change the time stamp of the source code files for the program. You could edit each one making minor changes. You could also use the touch command to directly change the time stamp of your files. The touch command is designed to go hand in hand with Make. It allows you to force execution of dependency lines, even though you may not have actually changed any files. Make looks only at the time stamp of files, not whether they have actually been modified or not. In the next example, the touch command updates the time stamps of the **main.c** and **io.c** files. Then, when the user executes the make command, the program is recompiled.

```
$ touch main.c io.c
$ make
cc -c -O main.c
cc -c -O io.c
cc main.o io.o -o bookrecs
$
```

Should you not want a target file recompiled, even though you may have changed one of its dependent files, you can update the target file using Make's -t option. Enter the option -t and the target as an argument on the command line. In the next example, the user updates **io.o** using the -t option. Even if the user has previously changed **io.c**, the **io.o** target will now be up to date and not be recompiled. However, when the make command is executed, the **io.o** is now more recent than the **bookrecs** target in the **bookrecs** dependency line, so the program is again linked. Notice that **main.c** is not compiled.

```
$ touch io.c
$ make -t io.o
touch(io.o)
$ make
cc main.o io.o -o bookrecs
$
```

Make Variables

You may often need to use a list of filenames in more than one place in a **makefile**. Instead of retyping the list in each dependency line that you use it, you could assign the list to a variable and use the variable in its place. In your **makefile** you can define variables and assign values to them. You can then evaluate the variables in different dependency lines throughout the **makefile**. To evaluate a make variable you first encase the variable name within parentheses, and then precede the parentheses with a dollar sign, $. For example, if you assign a variable a list of filename, then, when you evaluate the variable, the list of filenames that it holds will be substituted for the variable name.

In the next makefile example, a list of object code files is assigned to a variable called OBJECTS. In previous **makefile** examples, the **bookrecs** dependency line required that you enter in the list of object code files both in the list of dependent files and also in the cc command to link those files. In this **makefile**, you simply enter in an evaluation of the OBJECTS variable in both places., $(OBJECTS). Also in the **makefile**, CFILES variable is defined and assigned the list of all C source code files. This variable is then used in the print dependency line to provide the lp command with a list of all C source code files. Make variables operates somewhat like shell variables. You use the assignment operator to assign a string to a variable. Then the dollar sign is used to evaluate the variable. However, unlike shell variables, when evaluating a variable you must place the variable name within parentheses.

makefile

```
CFILES = main.c io.c
OBJECTS = main.o io.o

bookrecs : $(OBJECTS)
        cc $(OBJECTS) -o bookrecs

main.o : main.c
        cc -c main.c

io.o : io.c
        cc -c io.c

print :
        lp $(CFILES) &
```

A Make variable has as its value a string. The string can be any set of characters. For example, in the next **makefile** example, the string "Printing out the source code files" is assigned to the variable PRINTNOTICE. This variable is then evaluated in the print dependency line as the argument to an echo command. The string is displayed on the screen, notifying the user that the source code files are being printed. The echo command itself is precede by an @ operator that suppresses display of the actual echo command. Make will display each command that is executes, unless instructed not to with the @ operator.

The list of filenames assigned to a variable is really just a string. Just as you can assign filenames to a variable, you can also assign compiler options. The options are really just strings as far as the variable is concerned. Options are represented with a dash followed by a letter code and sometimes an argument. In the next make example the variable LINKFLAGS holds the linker option -o followed by a filename. This option allows the user to specify another name for the executable file, in this case **bookrecs**.

makefile

```
CFILES = main.c io.c
OBJECTS = main.o io.o
LINKFLAGS = -g -o bookrecs
PRINTNOTICE = Printing out the source code files

bookrecs : $(OBJECTS)
        cc $(LINKFLAGS) $(OBJECTS)

main.o : main.c
        cc -c main.c

io.o : io.c
        cc -c io.c

print :
        @echo $(PRINTNOTICE)
        lp $(CFILES) &
```

Run of `make` command.

```
$ make print
Printing out the source code files
lp main.c io.c &
```

Make Pre-defined Variables

When execute the make command, Make defines all exported variables from the shell, as well as defining several standard variables for Make's own use. The pre-defined variables hold compiler command names and compiler options. For example, CC holds the command name of the system's C compiler, usually cc. FC holds the command name of the system's Fortran compiler. Compiler options are held in variables whose names end with "FLAGS". For example, CFLAGS holds the standard C compiler options such as -o that invokes the optimizer. FFLAGS holds the Fortran compiler's standard options. The Pre-defined Make variables are listed in Table 24-1.

The predefined variables are useful if you have several different compilers for the same computer language, or if the system compiler should change frequently. Suppose that you have several different C compilers on your system to choose from. One of them will be considered the default and have its name assigned to the CC variable. However, in your **makefile**, you can change the value of any of the predefined variables. To use one C compiler or the other, just assign that compiler's command name to the CC variable. The same is true for the option variables. To add the -g option to the CFLAGS variable, just assign -g -o to it in your **makefile**. In the next **makefile** example, the user decides to use the ccp compiler instead of the standard cc compiler. In the dependency lines, instead of using the cc command, the user evaluates the CC variable to obtain the C compiler command name needed. The user changes the CFLAGS variable as well. Both CFLAGS and LINKFLAGS now include the -g option which prepares the compiled code for use in a symbolic debugger.

makefile

```
CC = ccp
CFLAGS = -g -O
CFILES = main.c io.c
OBJECTS = main.o io.o
LINKFLAGS = -g -o bookrecs
PRINTNOTICE = Printing out the source code files

bookrecs : $(OBJECTS)
        $(CC) $(LINKFLAGS) $(OBJECTS)

main.o : main.c
        $(CC) $(CFLAGS) -c main.c

io.o : io.c
        $(CC) $(CFLAGS) -c io.c

print :
        @echo $(PRINTNOTICE)
        lp $(CFILES) &
```

Run of `make` command.

```
$ make
ccp -g -O -c main.c
ccp -g -o bookrecs main.o io.o
```

The advantage of using the predefined variable is that the command names held in them are also used in implied Make operations, ones that you do not explicitly enter in a dependency line.

Table 24-1: Pre-defined Variables

Variable	Default Value	Description
CC	cc	C Compiler.
CFLAGS	-O	Options for the C Compiler.
AS	as	Assembler
ASFLAGS		Options for Assembler
FC	f77	Fortran Compiler.
FFLAGS		Options for Fortran Compiler
ld	ld	Loader to link object code files.
LDFLAGS		Options for loader.
LEX	lex	Lexical Analyzer: creates .c files from .l files.
LFLAGS		Lexical options
MAKE	make	The Make utility.
MAKEFLAGS	b	Options for Make

Make special variables

Make has a set of specially defined variables that hold information about the current dependency line. Their values change from one dependency line to another. There are three special variables that you can use in any ordinary dependency line: $@, $$@, and $?. The $@ and $$@ variable hold the name of the current target. The $? variable holds a list of those dependent files whose time stamps are more recent than those of the target file. Some of the special variables apply only to special kinds of dependency lines. For example, the $* and $< are used only with suffix rules and the $% is used only with library dependency lines. They are discussed in later sections. The Make special variables are listed in Table 24-2.

In the previous **makefile** example, the print dependency line printed out all your source code files. Suppose you want to print only those files in the dependency list that you most recently changed. The $? variable will hold the names of the most recently changed source code files in the dependency list. You can use that variable with the lp command to print out only the recently changed files. In the next example, only the **main.c** file has been changed since the print dependency line was last executed.

makefile

```
bookrecs : main.o io.o
        cc main.o io.o -o $@

main.o : main.c
        cc -c main.c

io.o : io.c
        cc -c io.c

print : main.c io.c
        lp $?
        @touch print
```

Run of make command.

```
$ make print
lp main.c
$
```

There is a touch command after the lp command in the print dependency line. The touch command updates the time stamp for print. The @ before touch is a special Make instruction to suppress display of the command.

The $@ variable holds the name of the target. It becomes helpful when you need to reference the target name in a dependency line's Unix command. In the previous **makefile** example, instead of repeating the term **bookrecs** in the cc command, the $@ variable is used. This would ensure that if you ever change name of the target, the same name would be used in the cc command as the name of the executable file.

```
$ make
cc main.o io.o -o bookrecs
$
```

Table 24-2: Dependency Line Special Variables

	`$@`	The name of the target file in a dependency line
files.	`$$@`	The name of the target file. This variable can only be used in the list of dependent
	`$?`	The dependent files that are more recent than the target. This variable can only be used in the Unix command of a dependency line.
	`$%`	Member files of a library file that are more recent than the library file. If iolib.a is composed of input.o and input.o is more recent than iolib.a, then `$%` evalueates to input.o.
	`$<`	In suffix rules, this variable evaluates to the dependent files that are more recent than the target. (like `$?`)
	`$*`	In suffix rules, this variable evaluates to the name of the target file without its suffix (like `$@`)

Make Special Targets

In addition to the special variables, Make has a set of special targets used to provide different features. A special target is preceded by a period and entered in uppercase. For example, the special target `.SILENT` will suppress the usual display of Unix commands as they are executed in depedency lines. The special target `.IGNORE` will allow your **makefile** to continue execution even if a Unix command fails. By default, Make will stop if it executes a Unix command the returns an error code. The `.IGNORE` special target ignores all error codes.

The `.PRECIOUS` special target specifies those targets you do not want removed should Make be interrupted. In some cases you need to retain the target file in order to perserve its time stamp. For example, the time stamp of the print target file is used print out those files that have recently been changed. If, for some reason, the lp command in the print depedency line, is interrupted during its execution, then Make will, by default, remove the target, the print file. However, you can overide this default action by listing print with the `.PRECIOUS` special target. The print file will not be removed.

The `.DEFAULT` special target is executed if there is no dependency line or builtin rule to handle a target. For example, if the user enters as an argument to make, a target that does not exist, then the `.DEFAULT` target is executed. (Note that a target does not have to be explicit, it could be builtin).

In the next **makefile** example, the user suppresses the display of commands with the `.SILENT` target, ignores command errors with the `.IGNORE` target, perserves the print target in case of interruptions, and outputs an error message if there is not dependency line, explicit or implied, for the target.

makefile

```
.SILENT:

.IGNORE:

.PRECIOUS: print

bookrecs : main.o io.o
        cc main.o io.o -o $@

main.o : main.c
        cc -c main.c

io.o : io.c
        cc -c io.c

print : main.c io.c
        lp $?
        touch print

.DEFAULT:
        echo The target $@ does not exist.
```

Run of `make` command.

```
$ make myindex
The target myindex does not exist
$
```

There are other special targets such as `.SUFFIXES:` that are described later. The Make special targets are listed in Table 24-3.

Table 24-3: Special Targets

`.DEFAULT:` Unix Commands	This target is executed if there is no dependency line for a specified target.
`.IGNORE:`	Ignore error values returned by Unix commands. Continue on with makefile execution
`.PRECIOUS:` targets	Should make be interrupted, the targets listed with .PRECIOUS are not removed.
`.SILENT:`	Commands are not displayed when executed.
`.SUFFIXES:` suffixes	Add suffixes to the list of valid suffixes referenced by suffix rules. If not suffixes are listed, the list of valid suffixes is erased.

Suffix Rules

A suffix rule is a special dependency that specifies how files with different suffixes depend on each other. For example, the **main.c** file and the **main.o** file have same name but different suffixes: .c and .o. A suffix rule for files ending in .c and .o would show how a **main.o** file depends on a **main.c** file. In other words, how you would use a **main.c** file to create a **main.o** file.

Suffix rules provide generality to the dependency line. Instead of applying to one specific set of files, a suffix rule applies to whole categories of files. The categories are determines by the suffixes. For example, you can write a suffix rule that applies to all files ending in .o and those ending in .c. Because of this generality, suffix rules can drastically reduce the number of dependency lines you may need in your makefile. This is particularly true of dependency lines are perform the same actions and differ only according to the name of the files specified. In previous **makefile** examples, the **main.o** and **io.o** dependency lines are identical in every respect except for the names of their files. Both perform the same action, specifying how a .o file depends on a .c file and how the cc command create the .o file. You can replace both of these dependency lines with one suffix rule the specifies the dependency of .o and .c files. Moreover, this suffix rule would apply to all files you may later add that end in .c and .o. You would not have to add any new dependency lines for them.

The target of a suffix rule consists of a sequence of two suffixes, each beginning with a period. The second suffix depends on the first suffix. The target for a suffix rule for `.c` and `.o` files, would consist of the suffix .c followed by `.o`: `.c.o`. A `.o` file depends on a `.c` file. The syntax for a suffix rule follows.

```
.suf1.suf2:
        Unix command
```

The suffix rule has no list of dependent files following the colon. In a sense, the dependent files are those specified by the first suffix in the target and the target file is the one specified by the second suffix. In the case of a .c and .o dependency, if you change a .c file and then execute Make, the .c.o suffix rule would be activated and its Unix command executed. The .c.o suffix rule will be activated for each .c file that has been recently changed. However, each time you activate the rule, in the Unix command you need to be able to reference the particular .c file you are dealing with at the time. When the .c.o suffix rule is invoked for say the **main.c** file, you need to be able to reference the **main.c** file in the Unix command. The $< special variable evaluates to the name of the current dependent file that is causing the suffix rule to activate. For example, if you change your **main.c** file, then, in the .c.o suffix rule, $< will be set to **main.c**. If you change several .c files, then $< will be set in turn to each one as the suffix rule is invoked for them.

You can now construct a suffice rule for the source code files and their object code files. The target consists of the suffixes **.c.o** and the Unix command consists of the cc -c command with the $< special variable.

```
.c.o:
        cc -c $<
```

In the next **makefile** example, the dependency lines for the **main.o** and **io.o** files are now replaced by the `.c.o` suffix rule. Should you have a program consisting of many source code files, you now only need one suffix rule to cover them all, instead of a dependency line for each one.

makefile

```
bookrecs : main.o io.o
        cc main.o io.o -o bookrecs

.c.o:
        cc -c $<

print : main.c io.c
        lp $?
        @touch print
```

Run of make command.

```
$ make
cc -c main.c
cc -c io.c
cc main.o io.o -o bookrecs
```

Another special variable used in suffix rules is $*. This variable holds the name of the current target without its suffix. If the current target was **main.o** then the value of $* would be just main. The variable is helpful when you need to specify the name of the target in the Unix command, without its extension. For example, if you want to make a backup copy of the object file, but give it the extension .bak you could specify the target with $*.o and the backup name with $*.bak. The $@ variable holds the full name of the target, whereas the $* variable only holds the target name without its suffix. In the next example, the backup command is added to the suffix rule.

```
.c.o:
        cc -c $<
        cp  $*.o  $*.bak
```

Using the above suffix rule in your **makefile**, an object code file is copied after the source code file is compiled.

```
$ make
cc -c main.c
cp main.o main.bak
cc -c io.c
cp io.o io.bak
cc main.o io.o -o bookrecs
```

Implied Make Dependencies and the Standard Suffix Rules

The Make utility has a standard set of suffix rules that automatically provide make with built-in dependencies. The standard suffix rules are found in a file called . Make automatically applies these rules to any files for which there are not explicit dependency lines. Using just the suffixes of files and the appropriate suffix rule, Make can execute the appropriate Unix command. For example, if you do not specify a dependency line for the **main.o** file, then Make will use the standard suffix rule for .c and .o files to determine that **main.o** depends on **main.c** and, if more recent, should recompile **main.c**. Below is an example of the standard .c.o suffix rule.

```
.c.o:
        $(CC) $(CFLAGS) $<
```

The standard suffix rules allow you to assume an implied dependency between source code and object code files. In Unix, the source code file for any given programming language must contain a specific suffix. C source code files require a .c suffix. Fortran files require a .f suffix. .s is used for assembler source code files. There is a standard suffix rule for each type of source code file that invokes the appropriate compiler. The suffix rule for .f.o invokes the Fortran compiler for Fortran source code files.

Make will examine the source code file suffix of a corresponding object code file in a dependency list, and automatically invoke the appropriate compiler for that source code file. This means that, using implied dependencies provided by the standard suffix rules, you can dispense with the dependency lines for compiling source code files. You can then reduce your **makefile** to one Unix command, the command to link files. The source code file suffixes and their corresponding programming language compilers are listed in Table 24-4.

In the next **makefile** example, by relying on implied dependencies provided by the standard suffix rules, the **bookrecs** program only needs one dependency line When examining the dependency list for the **bookrecs** dependency line, Make will look for corresponding source code files in the current directory. It will find **main.c** and **io.c**. Since these files have a .c extension, Make will activate the standard suffix rule for .c and .o files. If the user recently modified **io.c**, then Make would use the standard .c.o suffix rule to compile **io.c** with the C compiler, cc -c.

makefile

```
bookrecs : main.o io.o
        cc main.o io.o -o bookrecs
```

Run of make command.

```
$ ls *.c
main.c io.c
$ make
cc -O -c main.c
cc -O -c io.c
cc main.o io.o -o bookrecs
$
```

If you specify a dependency line without any Unix command, then Make will apply the appropriate standard suffix rule to the target. This means that you can activate the suffix rules based on dependencies that you specify. For example, the **main.o** file depends not only on the **main.c** file but also on the **types.h** file. You can create a dependency line consisting just of the **main.o** target and the **types.h** dependent file, with no following Unix command. If, during the execution of the **makefile**, **types.h** is more recent than **main.o**, then, because there is no Unix command, Make will use the suffix rule for updating .o files to determine what Unix command to execute for this dependency line.

In effect, though implied dependencies work fine for source code files, you need to explicitly specify the dependencies for header files in their own dependency lines. Using the **bookrecs** example, this means that though you do not need a dependency line for the **main.o** and **main.c** dependency, you do need one for the **main.o** and **types.h** dependency. In the next **makefile** example, there is a dependency line for **main.o** with **types.h** as its dependent file.

makefile

```
bookrecs : main.o io.o
        cc main.o io.o -o bookrecs

main.o: types.h
```

Run of `make` command.

```
$ make
cc -O -c main.c
cc main.o io.o -o bookrecs
$
```

Table 24-4: Standard Suffixes

filename.`c`	C source code file
filename.`p`	Pascal source code file
filename.`f`	Fortran source code file
filename.`s`	Assembler source code file
filename.`r`	Ratfor source code file
filename.`l`	Lex source code file
filename.`y`	Yacc source code file

Creating Suffix Rules for your own Suffixes

Suppose that you want Make to manage files that have a suffix that you made up. The suffix for a file can be any set of characters. For example, say you want to automatically backup your updated C source code files. Your C files have the suffix .c, but you want to give the copies a suffix that you have made up yourself, .bk for backup. You now want to create a suffix rule that will automatically copy updated C files giving the copies the suffix `.bk`. You can easily create such a suffix rule using the target `.c.bk`. Before you can use the new suffix rules, you need to inform Make that the new suffix is a valid suffix that can be applied to suffix rules. Make maintains a list of valid suffixes, including the standard suffixes such as `.c` and `.o`. You can add to this list as many suffixes of your own as you want. You add a suffix using a dependency line whose target is the special target `.SUFFIXES`. You then list your new suffixes after the colon. Before you create a suffix rule for the .c and .bk suffixes, you need to add `.bk` to the suffix list using the `.SUFFIXES` target.

```
.SUFFIXES: .bk
```

You can now create a suffix rule for `.bk` files using the target `.c.bk`. Notice the use of the special variables `$<` and `$@` to specify the dependent file and the target file. `$<` holds the filename with the .c extension, `$*` will hold the filename the **.bk** extension.

```
.c.bk:
        cp $< $@
```

In the next **makefile** example, the user adds .bk suffix to the list of valid suffixes and then add the suffix rule for .c.bk files. The actual backup file, in this case main.bk, placed in the list of dependent file in the **bookrecs** dependency line.

makefile

```
.SUFFIXES: .bk

bookrecs : main.o io.o main.bk
        cc main.o io.o -o bookrecs

.c.o:
        cc -c $<

.c.bk:
        cp $< $@
```

Run of touch command.

```
$ touch main.c
$ make
cc -c main.c
cp main.c main.bk
cc main.o io.o -o bookrecs
$
```

Library Dependencies: Suffix Rules

There is also a special implied dependency for libraries and their member files. Make is able to compile and replace a member file in an archive automatically for you. You only need to specify the member with its library name on the dependency line. Specifying a library member takes the form library(member). The member file is enclosed in parenthesis and preceded by the library name. To specify the **input.o** member of the **iolib.a** library you enter **iolib.a(input.o)**. Make will then use a special library suffix rule to determine if the library member needs updating. If so, Make will recompile the source code file for the library member and then, using the ar command with the r option, will write the resulting object code file to the library file. For example, the **iolib.a** library consists of the **input.o** and **print.o** files. In the next **makefile** example, the user specifies both files as member of the **iolib.a** library on the **bookrecs** dependency line: **iolib.a(iput.o) iolib.a(print.o)**. If you should change **input.c**, then, when you execute make, **input.c** will be recompiled and the resulting **input.o** file will be written to the **iolib.a** library.

makefile

```
bookrecs : main.o iolib.a(input.o) iolib.a(print.o)
        ranlib iolib.a
        cc main.o iolib.a -o bookrecs
```

Run of `touch` command.

```
$ touch input.c
$ make
cc -c -O input.c
ar rv iolib.a input.o
a - input.o
rm -f input.o
ranlib iolib.a
cc main.o iolib.a -o bookrecs
$
```

The standard library suffix rule will also remove the object code file after it has been copied to the library file. At this point, the object code file is no longer needed since it has already been added to the library.

Library Suffix Rule

The standard library suffix rule uses the special suffix .a to denote library files. A library file does not actually have to have a .a extension. The .a extension used in the target of the library suffix rule applies to all library files, no matter what their extension or lack of one. In the library suffix target, the .a is preceded by a .c indicating that the library file depends on C source code files, files with a .c extension. An example of a standard library suffix rule follows.

```
.c.a:
        cc -c $<
        ar rv $@ $%
        rm -f $%
```

The library suffix rule has three Unix commands. The first compiles the source code file, creating an object code file. In the cc command, the $< variable references the current .c file that needs to be updated. For example, if the **print.c** file had been changed, then the value of $< would be **print.c**. The second command is an archive command that adds the object code file to the library file. In the ar command, the $@ variable holds the name of the target file, in this case the library file. If the target library is **iolib.a**, then the value of $@ would be **iolib.a**. The $% variable holds name of the library member that is being updated. If the **print.o** member file needed to be updated, then $% would hold that member name, **print.o**. In the last command, the rm command removes the object code file. Again the $% variable holds the name of the member file.

makefile

```
bookrecs : main.o iolib.a(input.o) iolib.a(print.o)
        ranlib iolib.a
        cc main.o iolib.a -o bookrecs

.c.o:
        cc -c $<

.c.a:
        @cc -c $<
        @ar r $@ $%
        @echo Member $% updated in library $@
```

Run of `make` command.

```
$ touch main.c print.c input.c
$ make
cc -c  main.c
Member input.o updated in library iolib.a
Member print.o updated in library iolib.a
ranlib iolib.a
cc main.o iolib.a -o bookrecs
$
```

The `$%` variable is a special variable used only with library dependencies. You can use it in either dependency lines that have library members, or in the library suffix rule.

You can, if you wish, create your own library suffix rule using the `.c.a` target. Suppose for example you do not want the object code file deleted after it is added to the library. In the next **makefile** example, the user creates a library suffix rule that does not delete the object code file. It also suppress the messages each of the Unix commands would output by preceding them with an `@` operator. Instead of the command outputs, the suffix rule prints a message saying what member file is being updated to what library.

Libraries and directories

A you develop larger programs, you may end up using several libraries, each with their own set of source code files. One way of keeping your libraries organized is to place them in their own directories. You could then create a separate **makefile** for each directory that updates that library. The source code files and **makefile** for your main program would reside in their own directory. Though you could explicitly run each **makefile** in the library directories, you can also instruct your main **makefile** to change to those directories and execute the makefiles in them.

For the next example, the user has created a directory called **iodir** in which is placed the files for the **iolib.a** library: **input.c** and **print.c** as well as the **iolib.a** file. Within the **iodir** directory, the user create a **makefile** consisting of one dependency line that is used to update members of the **iolob.a** library. In **iodir**'s parent directory resides the program source code files such as **main.c** as well as the executable file **bookrecs**. The **makefile** in the parent directory as shown below, specifies two Unix commands for special target that the user named **ilib**. The **ilib** target will always be out of date. Its dependency line holds the cd command that changes to the **iodir** directory, and a make command to execute the **makefile** in the **iodir** directory. Since **ilib** is always out of date, the library will always have its **makefile** run to check for any out of date members.

makefile

```
bookrecs : main.o ilib
        cc main.o iodir/iolib.a -o bookrecs

ilib:
        cd iodir ; make
```

makefile in iodir library directory

```
iolib.a:iolib.a(input.o) iolib.a(print.o)
        ranlib iolib.a
```

Run of `touch` command.

```
$ touch iodir/input.c
$ make
cd iodir; make
cc -c -O input.c
ar rv iolib.a input.o
r - input.o
rm -f input.o
ranlib iolib.a
cc main.o iodir/iolib.a -o bookrecs
$
```

Sometimes targets for programs and libraries in a **makefile** are separated so that you could independently update a library. In this case you would use a zero-length target consisting of a name you made up for use in the **makefile**. In the next **makefile** example, the target **ilib** is a name made up by the user to serve as a target for the dependency line that manages the **iolib.a** library. The user can now either update the library or compile the program by invoking make with either an **ilib** or **bookrecs** argument. Notice that the **bookrecs** dependency line is no longer connected to the **ilib** dependency line. If you change a library member file such as **print.c** and then invoke make with the **bookrecs** target to compile the program, the library is not going to update the changed member. To restore the connection, you need to create a new dependency line using **ilib** and **bookrecs** as dependent files. The target can be any name you make up such as the term all. In the **makefile** example, the all dependency line is the first one listed. When you enter make with no arguments, this will be the default. Make will first update the library using the **ilib** dependency line, and then update the program using the **bookrecs** dependency line. **ilib**, in turn, will change to the **iodir** directory and execute the **makefile** that updates the **iolib.a** library file.

makefile

```
all: ilib bookrecs

bookrecs : main.o iodir/iolib.a
        cc main.o iodir/iolib.a -o bookrecs

ilib:
        cd iodir ; make iolib.a


makefile in iodir library directory

iolib.a:iolib.a(input.o) iolib.a(print.o)
            ranlib iolib.a
```

Run of `make` command.

```
$ touch iodir/input.c
$ make ilib
cd iodir; make
cc -c -O input.c
ar rv iolib.a input.o
r - input.o
rm -f input.o
ranlib iolib.a
$
$ touch main.c iodir/print.c
$ make all
cd iodir; make
cc -c -O input.c
ar rv iolib.a input.o
r - input.o
rm -f input.o
ranlib iolib.a
cc -O -c main.c
cc main.o iodir/iolib.a -o bookrecs
$
```

A makefile Example

Bringing together all these features, you can now create a powerful **makefile**. In the next **makefile** example, the user first defines variables to hold different lists of filenames and compiler options. The different variables are then used throughout the dependency lines. The .`PRECIOUS`: special target prevents removal of print.

Two suffix rules follow, one for creating object code files from C source code files, and the other for updating libraries. The target for the object code files is .`c.o`. The $< variable holds the name of the C source code file that needs to be compiled. The target for the suffix rule for making libraries is .`c.a`. The out of date member's C source code file is compiled, creating a new object code file. The $< holds the name of the member's C source code file, such as **print.c**. This object code file is then written to the library using the ar command. The $@ variable holds the name of the library, in this case, **iolib.a**. The $% variable holds the name of the member to be written to the library, such as **print.o**. The @ operator preceding these commands suppress their display as they are executed. Instead a message is output tell what member is being updated in what library. You can, of course, do away with the suffix rules listed here, and rely on the standard suffix rules to determine how to update object code files and libraries.

The dependency lines follow beginning with the **bookrecs** dependency line. In this line, both object code files and libraries form the list of dependent files. Its Unix command uses the `cc` compiler to create an executable program called **bookrecs**. The $@ holds the name of the target, in this case, **bookrecs**. The `CC` variable is a builtin variable that holds the name of the compiler command, cc.

The next two dependency lines lack any Unix commands. They will rely on suffix rules to update their targets. If **types.h** is out of date, then its target, **main.o**, needs to be updated and will make use of the suffix rule for updating .o files. The next dependency line makes the library **iolib.a** dependent on its members. Should the source code for any of its members be changed, then **iolib.a** will need to be updated. Since there is no Unix command, the suffix rule for updating libraries will be used.

The next dependency line is used to print source code files that have been recently modified. It target is the zero-length file called print. The C source code files forms the list of dependent files. The $? special variable in the lp command holds only the names of those files that were modified since the last printing. $? literally holds the filenames in the list of dependent files on a dependency line whose timestamp is more recent than that of the targets. Following the lp command, the touch command updates the print file. The @ operator preceding the touch command suppresses its display when it is executed.

Finally the .DEFAULT: special target displays an error message should the user specify a target that does not exist.

makefile

```
CFILES = main.c input.c print.c
OBJECTS = main.o
LIBS = iolib.a
IOLIBMEMS = iolib.a(input.o) iolib.a(print.o)
SYSLIBS = -lm
CFLAGS = -g -O

.PRECIOUS: print

.c.o:
        $(CC) $(CFLAGS) -c $<

.c.a:
        @$(CC) $(CFLAGS) -c $<
        @ar r $@ $%
        @echo Member $% updated in library $@

bookrecs : $(OBJECTS) $(LIBS)
        $(CC) $(CFLAGS) $(OBJECTS) $(LIBS) $(SYSLIBS) -o $@

main.o: types.h

iolib.a: $(IOLIBMEMS)
        @ranlib iolib.a

print : $(CFILES)
        lp $?
        @touch print

.DEFAULT:
        @echo Unknown target $@
```

Run of make command.

```
$ touch main.c print.c
$ make
cc -O -c main.c
Member print.o updated in library iolib.a
cc -g -O main.o iolib.a -lm -o bookrecs
$
```

Table 24-5: The make Utility, managing programs

Make

The make utility manages programs, keeping track of what source code files have been changed and compiling only those files when creating a new executable file. Below is an example of make.

```
$ make
cc -c io.c
cc main.o io.o -o bookrecs
$
```

make updates programs by reading dependency lines from a file. These dependency lines instruct make on dependencies between files. You enter these files in a file called makefile. You can specify your own file with the `-f` option and the filename. Below is the syntax for a dependency line.

      target file : dependent files ; command

      target file : dependent files
      tab   Unix command
      empty line

A dependency line without a dependency list will always execute its command.
      target file :
      tab   command
      empty line

You can define variables in the makefile in the same way that you define shell variables. However the evaluation is different. To evaluate a variable you need to encase it in parentheses first and then precede it with a `$` sign.

      variable-name = string
      `$(variable-name)`

```
        CFILES = main.c io.c
        $(CFILES)
```

You can select a certain dependency line for execution by using its target as an argument on the command line. The next example will select the dependency line whose target is "print".
```
$ make print
```

You define suffix rules using as a target two suffixes. The first is used to make the second. A suffix rule is applied if there is no dependency line with which to make a target. The `$<` special variable is used in suffix rule to hold the name of the out-of-date file. `$*` holds the name of the target without its suffix.
```
    .c.o:
        cc -c $<
```

Options

      `-f` filename   This option allows you to specify your own makefile that has the name filename. The default name is makefile.
```
$ make -f disp.mak
```

-n   This option only displays the commands that make would currently execute. It does not actually execute the commands.

-t   This option by itself updates the time stamp of all the target files. No commands are executed.

Formatted IO

Conversion Specifiers and Modifiers

Formatted Output

Formatted Input

Conversion Specifiers

Conversion Modifiers

25. Formatted I/O

Formatted I/O allows input or output characters to be converted into different types of values. There are two functions for formatted I/O: printf and scanf. printf converts different types of values into output characters for printing to the screen. scanf converts input characters into different types of values and assigns them to variables and arrays.

Formatted Output: printf

printf consists of a format string followed by a list of values. The list of values is optional. The format string is enclosed in double quotes and consists of constants and conversion specifiers. A conversion specifier is a special code that indicates the type of conversion that needs to take place on a listed value. In the format list, a conversion specifier is always preceded by a percent sign. For example, the conversion specifier for an integer value is a %d. See Table 25-1 for a list of C conversion specifiers. The syntax for a printf function call is shown here, along with an example of such a function call.

```
printf(" format string in quotes " , list of values );
printf("There are %d pages in this book", 75);
```

Long and long double values require the conversion modifiers l and L, as well as their respective conversion specifiers. A conversion modifier is placed between the percent sign and the conversion specifier. The correct conversion specifier for a long is %ld. For a long double it is %Lf. printf does not require an l modifier for a double. In printf, the %f conversion modifier works equally well with both floats and doubles. Since expressions always promote floats to doubles, the argument expressions in a printf will always pass a double which %f is designed operate on. scanf, however, distinguishes between floats and doubles. scanf requires that the lowercase l conversion specifier be included when converting a double. In scanf, %f converts floats only, whereas %lf converts doubles. In LISTING 25-1, integer and floating point, as well as long and double values are printed out. Notice the conversion specifiers.

LISTING 25-1:

```
#include <stdio.h>

int main(void)
        {
        int num = 35;
        float price = 7.50;
        long total = 750001;
        double cost = 100000.00;

        printf ("The number is %d\n", num);
        printf ("The price is %f\n", price);
        printf ("The total is %ld\n", total);
        printf ("The cost is %.2f\n", cost);
        printf("The num = %d, price is %.2f\n", num,price);

        return 0;
        }
```

Output for LISTING 25-1:

```
The number is 35
The price is 7.500000
The total is 75000
The cost is 100000.00
The num = 35, price is 7.50
```

There is a sequential correspondence between a conversion specifier and a value in the value list. The first conversion specifier will convert the first value. The second conversion specifier in the format string will convert the second value. In the next example and in LISTING 25-1, the value of num and price are printed out in the same printf operation.

```
printf("The num = %d, price is %.2f.\n", num,price);
```

The first conversion specifier, %d, matches up with the first value, the value held by the num variable, 35. It informs printf that the first value is an integer and needs to be converted from an integer to its character equivalent. The integer value 35 will be converted to the characters '3' and '5' for output. The second conversion specifier, %.2f, matches up with the second value, the value held by the price variable, 7.50. It notifies printf that the second value is a float. The floating point value 7.50 will be converted to the characters '7', '.', '5', and '0'.

Table 25-1: Output Conversion Specifiers

%c	character
%d	integer (decimal)
%i	integer (decimal, octal, or hexadecimal)
%f	float
%e	float, exponential notation
%E	float, E notation
%g	float, use shorter of f or e notation
%G	float, use shorter of F or E notation
%u	unsigned integer
%p	pointer
%o	octal integer
%x	hexadecimal integer, 0-f
%X	hexadecimal with 0-F
%s	string (character array)
%%	percent sign (percent sign character)

Formatted Input: scanf

scanf formats character input into values that can be assigned to corresponding variables. Whereas printf has a list of values to be formatted into characters, scanf has a list of variables into which converted character input will be assigned. A scanf format string usually consists of a series of conversion specifiers. There usually are no other characters in the format string. The same conversion specifiers used for printf are used for scanf.

scanf conversion specifiers indicate the type of value the input characters are to be converted to. The %d specifier converts characters into an integer value. Numeric characters will be converted into an integer value and assigned to a corresponding variable. For example, the characters '4', '5', and '8' will be converted to the integer value 458, and then assigned to a variable.

scanf operates on a list of variables, not on values as printf does. Variable names are listed after the format string. However, you need more than just a variable's name. You need to place an ampersand, &. before each variable's name. For the num variable you need to enter &num. If you fail to do so, your program will crash when you try to run it. scanf actually requires the memory addresses of variables, and this is provided by the & placed before the variable name. This process is examined in detail in Chapters 5 and 6. The following shows the syntax for scanf and an example of its use.

```
scanf("conversion specifier", &variable);
scanf("%d", &num);
```

Using scanf in your program allows you to let the user enter in values to variables. Often, scanf is preceded by a prinf that outputs a prompt, telling the user what value needs to be entered. Notice that prinf has no values listed or conversion specifiers. It is only being used here to output the string of characters making up the format string.

```
printf("Please enter a number: ");
scanf("%d", &num);
```

It is very important to match the right conversion specifier with the type of the corresponding variable. If they do not match, an invalid value will be assigned to the variable. Though scanf and printf share many of the same conversion specifiers, there is one crucial difference. Unlike printf, scanf requires the lowercase l conversion modifier when converting a double. The conversion specifier for a double is %lf. Without the l modifier, attempts to input data to a double will fail.

In the following example input operations are performed on floating point values, using scanf to read in values from the keyboard. Notice the use of the l and L modifiers to read in double and long double values. The value for salary is read in as a fixed field of five numbers.

```
int main(void)
    {
    double cost;
    long double total;

    scanf("%lf", &cost);
    scanf("%5Lf", &total);
    }
```

In LISTING 25-2, the user is prompted to enter in the values for the different variables. Notice the conversion specifers in the scanf function calls. The conversion specifier for cost is %lf using the l conversion modifier required for a double. However, when cost is printed out by printf, the conversion speccifier has no l modifier, %f.

LISTING 25-2:

```
#include <stdio.h>

int main(void)
        {
        int num;
        float price ;
        long total;
        double cost;

        printf ("Please enter a number: ");
        scanf ("%d", &num);

        printf ("Please enter a price: ");
        scanf ("%f", &price);

        printf ("Please enter a total: ");
        scanf ("%ld", &total);

        printf ("Please enter a cost: ");
        scanf ("%lf", &cost);

        printf ("\n");
        printf ("The number is %d\n", num);
        printf ("The price is %f\n", price);
        printf ("The total is %ld\n", total);
        printf ("The cost is %.2f\n", cost);

        return 0;
        }
```

Output for LISTING 25-2:

```
        Please enter a number: 23
        Please enter a price: 14.50
        Please enter a total: 93000
        Please enter a cost: 450000.00

        The number is 23.
        The price is 14.50.
        The total is 93000.
        The cost is 450000.00.
```

A scanf conversion specifier works by reading valid input until it reaches invalid input. The reading always stops at invalid input. A space, tab, or newline is considered invalid input for almost all kinds of conversion specifiers. Technically, the space, tab, and newline are referred to as white spaces. A conversion specifier will pass over white spaces at the start of its input. After the white space, it will read in and convert all valid characters until the next invalid character. The next invalid character may be a white space.

The [] Field Specifier

When dealing with strings, formatted input suffer from a frustrating limitation. Since the space delimits the end of a field, spaces cannot be allowed in a string. There is a way around this using a different string conversion specifier represented by braces, `[]`. Braces literally specify a set of characters considered valid for a string field. Whereas `%s` reads in all characters except delimiters, you can use the braces to read in a specific range of characters for a string. `%[a-m]` specifies as valid input characters between a and m. `%[A-Za-z ]` specifies all letters and the space as valid input. This would override the space as a delimiter, but then you could not use the space itself as a delimiter for this field. In this case, you could use a tab as the delimiter instead of a space.

If tabs are used as delimiters, the format string could be more easily written using another feature of braces, the circumflex symbol, `^`. The circumflex symbol specifies invalid input. Characters are accepted until the invalid character is reached. The conversion specifier `%[^\t]` reads any character into a string until a tab is reached. In the next example, the string conversion specifier for the name field has been replaced by the braces conversion specifier with the circumflex and tab characters. The format string for the `scanf` statement is `"%[^\t]%d%f"`. For this to work, a tab character needs to be entered after each name field that the user inputs. The tab character itself will not show up. Instead you will see what appears to be several spaces between fields, that are in fact one tab character.

```
scanf("%[^\t]%d%f\n",name,&id,&salary)
```

The format string has a newline constant at the end, \n. There is a problem with the `%[^\t]` conversion modifier. It will also read in any preceding spaces and newlines. In this case, it will include not only the name, but also the newline character from the preceding input. You can use several strategies to overcome this problem. The simplest, in this case, is to place a newline constant in the format string. Constants on the format string will match and skip corresponding characters in the file. At the end of the line, the newline constant matches and skips the newline in the file. The `%[^\t]` conversion modifier is then poised to read the name data in the next input line. You can also implement a more flexible method using the field skipper modifier described later in this section.

Input Conversion Problems

It is possible to read in more than one value on the same line. In such a situation, you can think of input as organized into fields. The fields are separated by a delimiter consisting of a space or tab. The carriage return is the delimiter for the last field. In the next example, the values for num, id, and price are read in all at once. The format string of the `scanf` contains a conversion specifier for each variable.

```
scanf ("%d%d%f", &num, &id, &price);
```

Input Line:
```
    76  5  7.89
```

In the previous example, the first conversion specifier, `%d`, starts reading valid input. Valid characters for an integer are the numeric characters from 0 to 9. Anything else, white space or any other character, is invalid. It reads 7 and 6 and then stops at the invalid character, the space. The specifier then converts the characters '7' and '6' into the integer value 76 and assigns that value to the variable num. The second specifier then skips over the intervening white space and starts to read valid input. It reads the character 5 and then reaches an invalid character, a space (white space). It stops reading and then converts the character '5' into an integer value 5. It then assigns 5 to the variable id. The third specifier skips over the intervening white space and reads the valid input characters 7, ., 8, and 9, and then reaches an invalid character, the newline. The specifier then converts the characters '7', '.', '8', and '9' into the floating point value 7.89. It then assigns 7.89 to the variable price.

The reading of input progresses only over valid characters or white spaces. Invalid characters are not read out. The next conversion specifier will attempt to read the same input that was invalid for the previous specifier. Even if there are no more specifiers in the current `scanf` statement, the invalid input will remain for the next conversion specifier in the next `scanf` statement. If input is not correctly organized, there can be strange and absurd results. With the input below, `scanf` will fail on the second conversion. The character 'B' in Bill is invalid input for both integer and floating point conversions. Subsequent calls to `scanf` will also attempt to read and convert 'Bill'.

```
Input Line:
     76   Bill   7.89
```

`scanf` is a function and, as a function, has a return value. `scanf` returns as its value the number of successful conversions. In the next example, the return value of `scanf` is assigned to the variable valid. If all conversions were successful, `scanf` would return the value 3.

```
valid = scanf("%s%d%f",name,&id,&salary);
```

You can use this return value of `scanf` to detect invalid input. The return value of `scanf` is the number of successful conversions. If one of the conversions fail, the return value will be less than the number of conversion specifiers in the format string. In the next example, valid holds the return value of `scanf`. If its value is less than the number of conversion specifiers in the format string, then a conversion has failed.

```
valid = scanf("%s%d%f",name,&id,&salary));
if (valid < 3)
       printf ("Invalid Input\n");
else
       printf("%s %d %f\n", name, id, salary);
```

This solution is not yet complete. For the program to continue successfully it must skip over the bad data record. This can be done by using another feature of the format string, the asterisk, `*`. A conversion specifier, when used with an asterisk, skips over the data field for that conversion specifier. The asterisk can be thought of as a field skipper. Conversion modifiers:input:field skipper;

```
valid = scanf("%s%d%f",name, &id, &salary);
if (valid < 3)
           {
           scanf("%*[^\n]");
           printf("Invalid Input \n");
           }
else
           printf("%s %d %.2f\n", name, id, salary);
```

The field-skipping feature can then be combined with the braces conversion specifier to skip over the rest of the bad data record. This technique takes advantage of the fact that the programmer has set up the carriage return as the end of the record. A newline placed within braces with a circumflex symbol, [^\n], will process everything until the carriage return is reached. Add an asterisk, "%*[^\n]", and scanf simply skips over all the rest of the data in the line, until the newline.

In LISTING 25-3, input is read and printed out. scanf is set up to read three fields. Each time scanf executes, it effectively reads a line of input. Notice the test for the while statement. scanf is actually a macro that is a function call to fscanf with the stdin file pointer. Like fscanf, scanf will return an EOF value if and end of file character is detected. On most systems, you can enter the end of file character on your input line by pressing Ctrl-d. Entering the Ctrl-d will stop the loop. On MS WINDOWS systems you enter a Ctrl-z.

The return value for scanf is saved in a variable valid that is then tested to check and see if all conversions were successful. If not, then the user entered invalid input. A second call to scanf then skips over this invalid input using the field skipper modifier and brackets conversion specifier.

LISTING 25: 3:

```
#include <stdio.h>
int main(void)
{
char name[10];
int num, id;
float salary;
int valid;

while( (valid = scanf("%s%d%f",name, &id, &salary)) != EOF)
        {
        if (valid < 3)
                {
                scanf("%*[^\n]");
                printf("Invalid Input \n\n");
                }
        else
                printf("%s %d %.2f\n\n", name, id, salary);

        }
return 0;
}
```

Run of LISTING 25-3

```
Dylan 43 9.50
Dylan 43 9.50

George 2 seven
Invalid Input

Chris 36 2000.00
Chris 36 2000.00

Robert 4 Mark
Invalid Input

Robert 4 27.82
Robert 4 27.82

^D
```

Output Conversion Modifiers

Both `scanf` and `printf` may use conversion modifiers. Some modifiers are essential for correct conversion. The `l` and `L` modifiers are required for correct conversion of long integers, doubles, and long doubles. Other modifiers are used only to format output or to constrain input. Some modifiers are specific to either `printf` or `scanf`. For example, the + modifier is used with `printf` to print a plus sign before an numeric value.

Table 25-3 lists and describes several of the most commonly used conversion modifiers. They are divided into three categories: long and short conversion modifiers, output modifiers used with `printf`, and input modifiers used with `scanf`. As described in the previous sections, the long and short conversion modifiers are required for the correct conversion of long, double, and short values. They are used in much the same way by both `printf` and `scanf`. Some modifiers are used by both `printf` and `scanf`, but in slightly different ways. For example the field width modifier specifies the number of character read in or output. However in `scanf` this modifier strictly limits the number of characters read, whereas in `printf` it just padds output. Other modifiers are used exclusively for either output or input. The justification, sign, and form modifiers are used only with `printf` to format output. The field skipper modifier only applies to input. Certain modifiers apply only to a certain type of data. The precision modifier applies only to floating point values, whether for input or ouput.

Table 25-2: Input Conversion Specifiers

`%c`	character
`%d`	integer (decimal)
`%i`	integer (decimal, octal, or hexadecimal)
`%f`	float
`%e`	float, exponential notation
`%g`	float, use shorter of `f` or `e` notation
`%u`	unsigned integer
`%p`	pointer
`%o`	octal integer
`%x`	hexadecimal integer, `0-f`
`%s`	string (character array)
`%[a-b]`	string. Specifies valid input for a string.
`%[^a-b]`	string. Specifies invalid input for a string.
`%`	percent sign (literal)

Field Width Modifier

The field width is used to determine the number of characters read in or printed out. The field width is specified with a number placed after the percent sign and before the conversion specifier. In the conversion specifier `%5d` the number 5 is the field width modifier. In `printf` the field width modifier causes the output to be padded with blanks, if the number of characters in the output is less than the field width number. The conversion specifier, `%5d`, will print out three preceding blanks for the value 25, giving you ' 25'. By default the character used for padding is a space. However you can make the padding character a zero by preceding the field with modifier with a 0. The conversion specifier %05d, will print out three preceding zeros for the value 25, giving you 00025.

The `printf` field width modifier will not restrict output. If a value takes more characters than that specified by the field width modifier, then those extra characters will be output. For example, given a conversion specifier of %051d , the entire value of 643000 will be output, even though there are 6 digits in this value instead of 5.

The program in LISTING 25-4 uses the field width and justification modifiers in `printf` output operations. Notice how the zero padding modifier is applied in the second `printf`. The value output in the third `printf` overflows its field width modifier.

LISTING 25-4: Field Width and Justification Modifiers

```
#include <stdio.h>

int main(void)
        {
        printf("Decimal is padded with 3 blanks %5d\n", 25);
        printf("Decimal is padded with 3 zeros %05d\n", 25);
        printf("Decimal overflows with %5ld \n", 6437500);
        printf("String w padded 7 blanks ,%10s\n","RIC");
        return 0;
        }
```

Output for LISTING 25-4:

```
        Decimal is padded with 3 blanks     25
        Decimal is padded with 3 zeros  00025
        Decimal overflows with 6437500
        String padded w 7 blanks ,        RIC.
```

Precision Modifiers

The precision modifier is used for converting floating point values. The precision modifier is simply a period followed by a number specifying the number of places to be printed out after the decimal. The precision modifier will round off the last place printed. The conversion specifier %.2f will only print out two places after the decimal in a floating point value. The value 3.568 will be printed out as 3.57. You saw an application of the precision modifier in the LISTING 25-4 when the floating point value of cost was output. Below is the `printf` function called used in that program.

```
        printf("The cost is %.2f \n", cost);
```

Often the precision and field width modifier are combined. The conversion specifier %6.2f will pad the value 3.56 with two spaces. The field width modifier refers to the number of characters used to print out the value. In a floating point value the period is counted as one of those characters. The conversion specifier %6.2 will allow three characters before the decimal. The decimal and two characters after it, make up the remaining three characters. In the next example, cost would be output with preceding zeros if its value took less than 6 characters to represent. Given that price has a value of 7.50, then the output would be 7.50 preceded by two spaces, ' 7.50'

```
printf("The price is %6.2f \n", price);
```

The program in LISTING 25-5 uses the field width and precision modifiers in `printf` output operations. Notice how the precision modifier is applied to a floating point value. The left justification modifier, - , is added in the last two `printf` examples.

LISTING 25-5: Field Width, Precision, and Justification Modifiers

```
#include <stdio.h>

int main(void)
    {
    printf("Float has 2 pl 3 blanks,%7.2f.\n",3.58);
    printf("Float is left justified,%-7.2f.\n",3.58);

    return 0;
    }
```

Output for LISTING 25-5:

```
Float has 2 pl 3 blanks,   3.58.
Float is left justified,3.58   .
```

Justification, Sign, and Form Modifiers

Certain output modifiers are used exclusively with `printf` to format output. They are organized into three categories: justification, the sign modifiers, and the full form modifiers. The justification modifiers are used to align output. The sign modifiers prints out the sign of a value. The form modifier prints out the full form of the value, including octal and hexadecimal symbols.

Output can be justified to the right or left. By default the output is always justified to the right. Any needed blanks will be placed before the output value. A minus sign, -, placed before the field width modifier will justify the output to the left. Needed blanks will be placed after the output value. The conversion specifier `%-5d` will print out three blanks after the value 25.

LISTING 25-6: Field Width and Justification Modifiers

```
#include <stdio.h>

int main(void)
    {
    printf("Decimal is left justified %-5d.\n",25);
    printf("String padded w 7 blanks ,%10s.\n","RIC");
    printf("String is left justified ,%-10s.\n","RIC");

    printf("Float has 2 pl 3 blanks,%7.2f.\n",3.58);
    printf("Float is left justified,%-7.2f.\n",3.58);

    return 0;
    }
```

Output for LISTING 25-6:

```
Decimal is left justified 25   .
String padded w 7 blanks ,        RIC.
String is left justified ,RIC        .
Float has 2 pl 3 blanks,    3.58.
Float is left justified,3.58    .
```

The program in LISTING 25-6 uses the field width and justification modifiers in `printf` output operations. Notice how the zero padding modifier is applied in the second `printf`. The value output in the third `printf` overflows its field width modifier. The left justification modifier, - , is added in the last `printf` examples.

The sign modifiers will display the sign of a value, indicating whether it is plus or minus. Though a minus sign will normally be displayed for negative values, the plus sign is not displayed for positive values, unless you use the + sign modifier. The + modifier placed in the conversion specifier will display a + symbol before any positive value. The conversion specifier `%+d` will output +25 for the value 25. A minus sign will be output for any minus value. In the next example, the `printf` operation outputs a +39.

```
printf("The number is %+d", 39);
```

```
Output:
        The number is +39
```

An alternative sign modifier consists of a space entered in a conversion specifier instead of a plus sign. This space sign modifier will output a space in place of a plus sign for positive values. The conversion specifier `%d` will output a preceding space before the value 25 , ' 25'. Negative values still have a minus sign output for them. The space sign modifier is helpful when you want to line up negative and positive numbers underneath each other in your output, as shown in the next example.

```
printf("Oct. Count =  % d\n", -42);
printf("Nov. Count =  % d\n", 63);
```

```
Output:
        Oct. Count = -42
        Nov. Count =  63
```

The standard conversion modifiers will often take shortcuts when outputting values. For example, trailing zeros in a floating point value are often dropped. Octal values do not include a preceding 0, and hexadecimal values do not contain a preceding 0x. To force `printf` to output the full form of a value, you need to use the form modifier. The form modifier is a sharp sign, #. You place it in the conversion modifier after the % sign. The conversion modifier `%#x` will output the full form of a hexadecimal value, including the preceding 0x characters.

```
printf("The Hex value is %#x \n", 42);
printf("The Octal value is %#o \n", 63);
```

```
Output:
        The Hex value is 0x
        The Octal value is 0
```

In the next example, a floating point value is output first without the form modifier and then with the form modifier. With the form modifier, the floating point value includes its trailing zeros in the decimal places.

```
printf("The price is %.2f \n", 35.00);
printf("The price is %#.2f \n", 35.00);

Output:
        The price is 35.
        The price is 35.00
```

Input Conversion Modifiers

In `scanf` the field width modifier specifies a specific number of characters to be read from input. The conversion specifier, `%5d`, will read exactly five characters from the input, including white spaces. Unlike the `printf` field width specifier, the `scanf` field width specifier is very restrictive. It will only read the specified number of characters, no matter what they may be. In the next example, `scanf` read only the first five characters that the user has input and converts them to a floating point value for salary.

```
scanf("%5f", &salary);
```

You still need to include any requires conversion modifiers. In the next example, cost is a double and as such requires the `l` conversion modifier. This modifier is combined with the fields width modifier to read in the next 8 characters and convert them to a double.

```
scanf("%8lf", &cost);
```

In the following example input operations are performed, using `scanf` to read in values from the keyboard. The value for salary is read in as a fixed field of five numbers.

```
int main(void)
        {
        double cost;
        float salary;

        scanf("%lf", &cost);
        scanf("%5f", &salary);
        }
```

Table 25-3: Conversion Modifiers

Long and Short Conversion Modifiers: l, L, h

%ld	Convert long integer.

```
printf("long decimal %ld \n",25000000);
```

%Lf	Convert long double.

```
printf("long double %Lf",989000000.34);
```

%hd	Convert a short integer. (%hu for short unsigned)

```
printf("Decimal is a short %hd", 26);
```

Output Conversion Modifiers: printf

Long and Short Conversion Modifiers: l, L, h

%ld   Convert long integer.
```
printf("long decimal %ld \n",25000000);
```
%Lf   Convert long double.
```
printf("long double %Lf",989000000.34);
```
%lf   Convert a double. Required for scanf when reading a double.
```
scanf("%lf", &price);
```
%hd   Convert a short integer. (%hu for short unsigned)
```
printf("Decimal is a short %hd", 26);
```

Field Width Modifiers:

Number for decimal and string specifiers: %d, %i, %s

%5d	Number less than three places padded.	___25
%05d	Specifies padding with leading zeros.	00025
%10s	String less than 10 pad with spaces.	_____RIC

Precision Modifiers: floating point

Precision for floating point specifiers: %f, %e, %g, %G, %E

%7.2f	Seven total spaces - two past decimal point.	___3.58

Justification:

Right justification with blanks is the default.
– indicates left justification with blanks.

%-5d	Number less than five places padded to right.	25___
%-7.2f	Seven total spaces - two past decimal point.	3.58___
%-10s	A string less than 10 pad with spaces.	RIC_____

Sign Symbols

+	Specifies that sign of value will be displayed, plus or minus

```
printf("%+d", 25);    +25
```

(space)	Print leading space instead of + sign for positive values.

```
printf("% d,% d",-30,+25);  -30, 25
```

Full Form

#	Specifies that full form is printed out.
%#o	Octal. Prints leading 0 for octal number.
%#x	Hexadecimal. Prints leading 0x for hex number.

`%#7.2f` Floating Point: `%f`, `%e`, `%g`, %G, `%E`. Prints out decimal point even if
there are only zeros after the decimal.

`%#7.2g` Floating Point: `%g`, `%G`. Prevents trailing zeros from being removed.

Input Conversion Modifiers: `scanf`

Long and Short Conversion Modifiers: `l`, `L`, h

    `%ld`   Convert long integer.

    `%Lf`   Convert long double.

    `%lf`   Convert a double. Required for scanf when reading a double.

                `scanf("%lf", &price);`

    `%hd`   Convert a short integer. (`%hu` for short unsigned)

Field Width Modifiers:

Restricted Number of characters read: `%d`, `%i`, `%s`

    `%5d`   Read 5 characters for decimal conversion

    `%05d`   The 5 characters read may be padded with leading zeros

    `%5f`   Read 5 characters for float, including period used for decimal.

Precision Modifiers: floating point

Read specified number of characters after the decimal: `%f`, `%e`, `%g`, `%G`, `%E`

    `%7.2f`   Read 7 characters for float, having two decimal places

Input Field Modifiers

    `%*`   Field skipping modifier. Skips an input field.

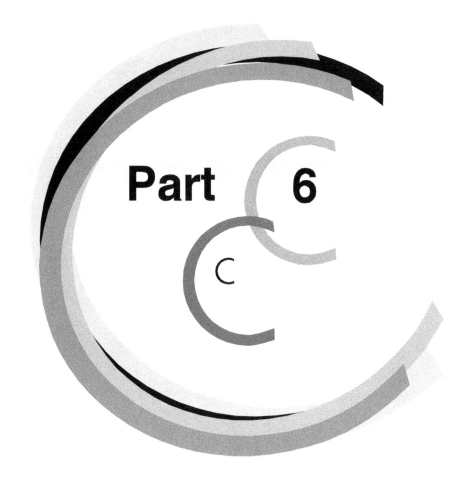

Part 6

Appendixes

The ASCII Code

Decimal, Octal, and Hexadecimal

Part 6: Appendices

A: The ASCII Code

Dec	Octal	Hex	Binary	Key	ASCII Symbol
0	00	00	0 000 000	Ctrl 1	NULL
1	01	01	0 000 001	Ctrl A	SOH
Dec	Octal	Hex	Binary	Key	ASCII Symbol
2	02	02	0 000 010	Ctrl B	STX
3	03	03	0 000 011	Ctrl C	ETX
4	04	04	0 000 100	Ctrl D	EOT
5	05	05	0 000 101	Ctrl E	ENQ
6	06	06	0 000 110	Ctrl F	ACK
7	07	07	0 000 111	Ctrl G	BELL
8	10	08	0 001 000	Ctrl H	BS (Backspace)
9	11	09	0 001 001	Ctrl I	HT (Tab)
10	12	0A	0 001 010	Ctrl J	LF (Line Feed)
11	13	0B	0 001 011	Ctrl K	VT (Vertical TAb
12	14	0C	0 001 100	Ctrl L	FF (Form Feed)
13	15	0D	0 001 101	Ctrl M	CR (Carriage Return)
14	16	0E	0 001 110	Ctrl N	SO
15	17	0F	0 001 111	Ctrl O	SI
16	20	10	0 010 000	Ctrl P	DLE
17	21	11	0 010 001	Ctrl Q	DC1
18	22	12	0 010 010	Ctrl R	DC2
19	23	13	0 010 011	Ctrl S	DC3
20	24	14	0 010 100	Ctrl T	DC4
21	25	15	0 010 101	Ctrl U	NAK
22	26	16	0 010 110	Ctrl V	SYN
23	27	17	0 010 111	Ctrl W	ETB
Dec	Octal	Hex	Binary	Key	ASCII Symbol
24	30	18	0 011 000	Ctrl X	CAN
25	31	19	0 011 001	Ctrl Y	EM
26	32	1A	0 011 010	Ctrl Z	SUB
27	33	1B	0 011 011	ESC, Escape	ESC, Escape
28	34	1C	0 011 100	Ctrl \	^ \
29	35	1D	0 011 101	Ctrl }	^ }
30	36	1E	0 011 110	Ctrl =	^ =
31	37	1F	0 011 111	Ctrl -	^ -

Dec	Octal	Hex	Binary	Key	ASCII Symbol
32	40	20	0 100 000	Spacebar	Spacebar
33	41	21	0 100 001	!	!
34	42	22	0 100 010	"	"
35	43	23	0 100 011	#	#
36	44	24	0 100 100	$	$
37	45	25	0 100 101	%	%
38	46	26	0 100 110	&	&
39	47	27	0 100 111	,	,
40	50	28	0 101 000	(	(
41	51	29	0 101 001	)	)
42	52	2A	0 101 010	*	*
43	53	2B	0 101 011	+	+
44	54	2C	0 101 100	'	'
45	55	2D	0 101 101	−	−
46	56	2E	0 101 110	.	.
47	57	2F	0 101 111	/	/
48	60	30	0 110 000	0	0
49	61	31	0 110 001	1	1
50	62	32	0 110 010	2	2
51	63	33	0 110 011	3	3
52	64	34	0 110 100	4	4
53	65	35	0 110 101	5	5
54	66	36	0 110 110	6	6
55	67	37	0 110 111	7	7
56	70	38	0 111 000	8	8
57	71	39	0 111 001	9	9
58	72	3A	0 111 010	:	:
59	73	3B	0 111 011	;	;
60	74	3C	0 111 100	<	<
61	75	3D	0 111 101	=	=
62	76	3E	0 111 011	>	>
63	77	3F	0 111 111	?	?
64	100	40	1 000 000	@	@
65	101	41	1 000 001	A	A
66	102	42	1 000 010	B	B
67	103	43	1 000 011	C	C
68	104	44	1 000 100	D	D
69	105	45	1 000 101	E	E
70	106	46	1 000 110	F	F
71	107	47	1 000 111	G	G
72	110	48	1 001 000	H	H
73	111	49	1 001 001	I	I
74	112	4A	1 001 010	J	J
75	113	4B	1 001 011	K	K
76	114	4C	1 001 100	L	L
77	115	4D	1 001 101	M	M
78	116	4E	1 001 110	N	N
79	117	4F	1 001 111	O	O
80	120	50	1 010 000	P	P
81	121	51	1 010 001	Q	Q

Dec	Octal	Hex	Binary	Key	ASCII Symbol
82	122	52	1 010 010	R	R
83	123	53	1 010 011	S	S
84	124	54	1 010 100	T	T
85	125	55	1 010 101	U	U
86	126	56	1 010 110	V	V
87	127	57	1 010 111	W	W
88	130	58	1 011 000	X	X
89	131	59	1 011 001	Y	Y
90	132	5A	1 011 010	Z	Z
91	133	5B	1 011 011	[	[
92	134	5C	1 011 100	\	\
93	135	5D	1 011 101	]	]
94	136	5E	1 011 110	^	^
95	137	5F	1 011 111	_	_
96	140	60	1 100 000	`	`
97	141	61	1 100 001	a	a
Dec	**Octal**	**Hex**	**Binary**	**Key**	**ASCII Symbol**
98	142	62	1 100 010	b	b
99	143	63	1 100 011	c	c
100	144	64	1 100 100	d	d
101	145	65	1 100 101	e	e
102	146	66	1 100 110	f	f
103	147	67	1 100 111	g	g
104	150	68	1 101 000	h	h
105	151	69	1 101 001	i	i
106	152	6A	1 101 010	j	j
107	153	6B	1 101 011	k	k
108	154	6C	1 101 100	l	l
109	155	6D	1 101 101	m	m
110	156	6E	1 101 110	n	n
111	157	6F	1 101 111	o	o
112	160	70	1 110 000	p	p
113	161	71	1 110 001	q	q
114	162	72	1 110 010	r	r
115	163	73	1 110 011	s	s
116	164	74	1 110 100	t	t
117	165	75	1 110 101	u	u
118	166	76	1 110 110	v	v
119	167	77	1 110 111	w	w
120	170	78	1 111 000	x	x
121	171	79	1 111 001	y	y
122	172	7A	1 111 010	z	z
123	173	7B	1 111 011	{	{
124	174	7C	1 111 100				
125	175	7D	1 111 101	}	}
126	176	7E	1 111 011	~	~
127	177	7F	1 111 111	Del, delete key	Del, delete key

The Standard Library

I/O, String, Math, and Utility Functions

B. The Standard Library

Input and Output Functions: stdio.h

File Operations

FILE *fopen(const char*fn, const char*mode)	Open a file with the name fn and mode mode and return a pointer to FILE
FILE*freopen(const char *f, const char *mode, FILE *fp)	Open a file and associate it with a stream already opened. Used to reassign stdin or stdout with a specific file.
int fclose(FILE *fp)	Close the file
int fflush(FILE *fp)	Write buffered but not yet written data to a file
int remove(const char *fn)	Erase a file
int rename(const char*fn,const char*newfn)	Rename a file
FILE *tmpfile(void)	Generate a temporary file
int setvbuf(FILE *fp, char *b, int cfg, size_t sz)	Configure the buffer used for a file stream. There are three possible buffer configurations: full buffer, line buffer, and unbuffered. IOFBF, IOLBF, IONBF.
FILE *tmpfile(void)	Create a temporary file that is automatically removed with program ceases
char *tmpnam(char s[L_tmpnam])	Create a string that is not the name of a file and return a pointer to an internal static array.

Character Text File Functions

int getc(FILE *fp)	Retrieves the next character in a file or EOF if the end of the file is reached.
int putc(int ch , FILE *fp)	Write a character to a file.
int getchar(void)	Retrieve a character from the standard input, getc(stdin).
int putchar(int ch)	Output a character to the standard output, putc(ch, stdout)
int fgetc(FILE *fp)	Equivalent to getc
int fputc(int ch, FILE *fp)	Equivalent to putc
int ungetc(int ch, FILE *fp)	Place a character back into the file, to be the next character read.
char *fgets(char*s,int n,FILE*fp)	Reads a line of characters into an array placing a null at the end. NULL is returned for end-of-file.
int fputs(const char *s, FILE *fp)	Write a string to a file
char *gets(char *s)	Reads the nexct input line into the array s, replacing the terminating newline with '\0'.

| cint puts(const char *s) | Writes the strng s and a newline to stdout. Ret urns EOF is error occurs and non-negative otherwise. |

Formatted Text File Functions

int fprintf(FILE*fp,const char*s,...)	Convert values to character data and write to a file.
int fscanf(FILE*fp, const char*s,...)	Read character data from a file, convert to specified values, and assign to listed objects.
int printf(const char* s, ...)	Perform conversion of values to character data and print to the standard output, stdout
int scanf(const char *s, ...)	Read characters from standard input, stdin, and convert to specified values, and assign to listed objects.
int sprintf(char*s,const char*s,...)	Perform conversion of values to character data and write as a string to an array of characters.
int sscanf(char*s,const char*s, ...)	Read characters from a string, convert to values, and assign to listed objects
int vprintf(const char *s, va_list arg)	Convert values in a variable argument list and print to standard output
int vfprintf(FILE *fp, const char *s, va_list arg)	Convert values in a variable argument list and write to a file
int vsprintf(char *s, const char *s, va_list arg)	Convert values in a variable argument list and copy as string to array of characters.

Record and File Position File Functions

size_t fread(void* s, size_t n, size_t r, FILE *fp)	Read data without conversion from a file into a block of bytes, s. n is the number of bytes read, r is the repeat factor.
size_t fwrite(void* s, size_t, size_t, FILE *fp)	Write data from a block of bytes to a file. n is the number of bytes read, r is the repeat factor.
int fseek(FILE *fp,long n,int ori)	Set the file position indicator to a specific byte offset in a file. The three points of origin are SEEK_SET, SEEK_END, SEEK_CUR.
long ftell(FILE *fp)	Returns the byte offset of the current file position or a -1L on an error.
void rewind(FILE *fp)	Reset file position indicator to the beginning of the file
int fgetpos(FILE *fp, fpos_t *p)	Records a file offset position in the fpos_t argument
int fsetpos(FILE *fp, const fpos_t *p)	Sets the file position to that recorded in the fpos_t argument.

File Error File Functions

void clearerr(FILE* fp)	Clears end-of-file and error indicators.
int feof(FILE *fp)	Returns non-zero if end-of-file was reached and 0 if an error occured
int ferror(FILE *fp)	Returns non-zero if error occured for a file.
void perror(const char *s)	Prints to stderr the string s and the system defined string for the error that has occured.

String Functions: string.h

char* strcpy(char *t, char *s)	Copy source string, s, to target string, t.
char* strncpy(char *t,char *s, int n)	Copy a maximum of n characters from string s to string t
char *strcat(char *t, char *s)	Append string s to string.t
char* strncat(char*t, char *s, int n)	Append a maximum of n characters from string s to t.
int strcmp(char *t, char *s)	Compare string t to s: return 0 if equal, return < 0 if t<s , return >0 if t>s.
int strncmp(char*t,char *s,int n)	Compare a maximum of n characters in strings s and t. Return the same values as for strcmp
char* strchr(char *t, int c)	return address of first occurrence of character c in string t. Otherwise return NULL
char* strrchr(char *t, int c)	Return address of first occurence of string s in string t.
size_t strspn(char *t,char *s)	Return length of the largest segment of string t whose charcters are not composed of the characters in string s
size_t strcspn(char*t,char* s)	Return length of largest segment of string t whose characters are composed of the characters in string s
char* strpbrk(char *t,char *s)	Return first address of any characters in string t contained string s
char* strstr(char *t, char *s)	Return address of first occurrence of string s in string t.
size_t strlen(char *s)	Return length of string
char *strerror(int n)	Return address of system-defined string associated with error number n
char *strtok(char *t, char *s)	Search for a token in t delimited by characters in s.
void *memcpy(char *t, char *s, int n)	Copy n bytes from array s to array t.
void *memmove(char *t, char *s, int n)	Copy n bytes from array s to array t even if arrays overlap.
int memcmp(char *t,char *s,int n)	Compare first n bytes in array t to array s. Return same values as strcmp.
void *memchr(char *t,int c,int n)	Return address of first occurrence of c in first n bytes of array t.
void *memset(char *t,int c,int n)	Copy the character value c to the first n bytes of array t.

Utility Functions: stdlib.h

double atof(const char *s)	Convert a string to a double
int atoi(const char *s)	Convert a string to an integer
long atol(const char *s)	Convert a string to a long
double strtod(const char*s,char **p)	Convert a prefix of s to a double and place remaining unconverted characters in *p.
long strtol(const char*s,char**p,int b)	Convert prefix of s to a long and place remaining unconverted characters in *p. b indicates a base for the conversion.
unsigned long stroul(const char*s, char**p, int b)	Convert prefix as strtol does but for an unsigned long
int abs(int n)	Returns absolute value of an integer n
long labs(long n)	Returns absolute value of an long, n.
div_t div(int n, ind d)	Returns a structure of type div_t that contains both the quotient and remainder resulting from the division of n by d. The member names for div_t are quot and rem.
ldiv_t ldiv(long n, long d)	Performs the same operation as div but for long values.
int rand(void)	Returns a random integer value
void srand(unsigned int seed)	Set the seed for a new sequence of random numbers
void*calloc(int nobj,size_t n)	Allocates memory for nobj number of objects of size n bytes. Returns the address of that memory or a NULL if it fails. All bytes will be initialized to 0.
void *malloc(size_t n)	Allocates memory of size n bytes and returns the address. Bytes are not initialized.
void*realloc(void *p,size_t n)	Change the size of the memory pointed to by p.
void free(void *p)	Frees allocated memory pointed by p.
void abort(void)	Terminates program abnormally
void exit (int status)	Normal program termination. 0 for status indicates successful termination. Non-zero for status indicates unsuccessful termination.
int atexit(void(*f)(void))	Specifies a function, f, to be executed when program ends.
int system(char* s)	Send string s as an operating system command to the system
char *getenv(char* e)	Returns environment string for e.
void *bsearch(const void *key, const void*ar, size_t n, size_t sz, int(*cmp)(const void*keyval,const void*d))	Search array ar for entry that matches key. Use the function cmp to perform the comparisons. The number of elements in the array is n and the size of each element is sz
void qsort(void*base,size_t n, size_t sz, int(*cmp)(const void*,const void*))	Sort an array using function cmp. n is the number of elements and sz is the the size of each element.

Character Test Operations: ctype.h

isalnum(char c)	Letter or digit
isalpha(char c)	Letter
iscntrl(char c)	A control character
isdigit(char c)	Digit
isgraph(char c)	Printable character, except space
islower(char c)	Lower case character
isprint(char c)	Printable character including space
ispunct(char c)	Printable character, except space, letter, or number
isspace(char c)	Whitespace character, \f, \n, t, \v, \r, space
isupper(char c)	Upper case character
isxdigit(char c)	Hexadecimal digit
int tolower(int)	Change upper case character to lower case and return the lower case value
int toupper(int)	Change lower case character to upper case and return the upper case value

Variable Argument Macros: stdarg.h

va_list ap;	Variable of type va_list is used to point to each argument in a variable argument list in turn
va_start(va_list ap, par)	Initialize va_list variable, ap, to first argument in a variable argument list. par is last declared parameter.
va_arg(va_list ap, data type)	Sequentially references each argument in a variable argument list. The type of each argument must be provided
void va_end(va_list ap)	Called before function ends to close down variable argument processing.

Mathematical Operations: math.h

sin(double x)	Sine of x
cos(double x)	Cosine of x
tan(double x)	Tangent of x
asin(double x)	Arc sine of x
acos(double x)	Arc cosine of x
atan(double x)	Arc tangent of x with range of $-1/2$ to $+1/2$
atan2(double x, double y)	Arc tangent of x with range of -1 to $+1$
sinh(double x)	Hyperbolic sine of x
cosh(double x)	Hyperbolic cosine of x
tanh(double x)	Hperbolic tangent of x
exp(double x)	Exponential function
log(double x)	Natural log
log10(double x)	Log base 10

pow(double x, double y)	Power function, x to power of y
sqrt(double x)	Square root
ceil(double x)	Smallest integer not less than x
floor(double x)	Largest integer not greater than x
fags(double x)	Absolute value of x
ldexp(double x, int e)	x * 2e
frexp(double x, int *fr)	Divides x into a normalized fraction and an exponent that is a power of 2. The power of 2 is placed in *fr and the fraction is returned. x = fr * 2exp
modf(double x, double *fr)	Seperate x into integral and fractional parts. Fraction is place in *fr and integral part is returned
fmod(double x, double y)	Floating point remaineder of x divided by y

Jumps : setjmp.h

int setjump(jmp_buf env)	Save environment information in env
void longjump(jump_buf env, int v)	Jump to location across function boundaries, referencing environment set up by setjump

Diagnostics: assert.h

void assert(int expressio0)	Used to add diagnositcs to program. If expression returns 0, assert will output message to standard error.specifying the expression, the filename, and the line number. Then calls abort to end execution of the program.

Signals: signal.h

void (*signal(int sig, void(*sigfunc)(int)))(int)	Set configuration for interrupt signals received. There is a set of possible signals each with an associated fucntion. User can specify own function to be executed on a given signal. signal is a function that returns a pointer to a function.
int raise(int sig)	Send signal sig to program.
SIG_IGN	Function to ignore signals
SIG_DFL	Function to respond to signal with default functions
void (*signal(int sig, void(*sigfunc)(int)))(int)	Set configuration for interrupt signals received. There is a set of possible signals each with an associated fucntion. User can specify own function to be executed on a given signal. signal is a function that returns a pointer to a function.
int raise(int sig)	Send signal sig to program.
SIG_IGN	Function to ignore signals
SIG_DFL	Function to respond to signal with default functions

Time Operations: time.h

clock_t cloack(void)	Returns processor time for session.
clock_t time(time_t *tp)	Returns the current calendar time
double difftime(time_t t2, time_t1)	Difference in seconds between two times
time_t mktime (struct tme *tp)	Converts time in tp to calendar time
char *asctime(const struct tme *tp)	Converted time in tp to a string.
char *ctime(const time_t *tp)	Converts calendar time in tp to local time
struct tm *gmtime(const time_t *tp)	Converts time in tp to Coordinated Universal Time
struct tme *localtime(const time_t *tp)	Convert calendar time in tp to local time
size_t strftime(char*s, int smax, const char*fmt, const struct tm *tp)	Format output of time in tp to string s. Conversion specifiers: %a weekday name, %b month name, %d day of month, %H hour.

System-defined Integral Limits: limits.h

CHAR_BIT	8	Number of bits in a char data type
CHAR_MAX	UCHAR_MAX/SCHAR_MAX	Max value of char
CHAR_MIN	0 OR SCHAR_MIN	Min value of char
INT_MAX	+32767	Max value of int
INT_MIN	-32767	Min value of int
LONG_MIN	+2147483647L	Max value of long
LONG_MAX	-2147483647L	Min value of long
SCHAR_MAX	+127	Max value of signed char
SCHAR_MIN	-127	Min value of signed char
SHRT_MAX	+32767	Max value of short
SHRT_MIN	-32767	Min value of short
UCHAR_MAX	255U	Max value of unsigned char
UNINT_MAX	65535U	Max value of unsigned int
ULONG_MAX	4294967295UL	Max value of unsigned long
USHRT_MAX	65535U	Max value of unsigned short

System-defined Floating-point Limits: floats.h

FLT_RADIX	2	Radix of exponent representation
FLT_ROUNDS		Floating point round off mode
FLT_DIG	6	Decimal digits in fraction for a float
FLT_EPSILON	1E-5	Smallest number that changes a float
FLT_MANT_DIG		Number of digits in mantissa
FLT_MAX	1E+37	Largest floating point value
FLT_MAX_EXP		Maximum exponent for FLT_RADIX
FLT_MIN	1E-37	Minimum floating point value
FLT_MIN_EXP		Minimum exponent for FLT_RADIX

DBL_DIG	10	Decimal digits in fraction for double.
DBL_EPSILON	1E-9	Smallest number that changes a double
DBL_MANT_DIG		Number of digits in double mantissa
DBL_MAX	1E+37	Maximum floating point double value
DBL_MAX_EXP		Maximum exponent for FLT_RADIX
DBL_MIN	1E-37	Minimum floating point double value
DBL_MIN_EXP		Minimum exponent for FLT_RADIX

K & R   C

Functions and Pointers

C. K&R C

There is an earlier version of the C programming language known as K&R C. K&R C is the original programming language as it was developed by Dennis Ritchie at Bell Laboratories. ANSI C is the newer standard version, incorporating many new features and syntax changes. To a great extent the two versions are the same. However, ANSI C introduces new keywords and syntactic structures unknown to K&R C. For this reason, a K&R C compiler cannot compile ANSI C code. Depending upon the compiler, an ANSI C compiler may or may not be able to compile K&R C code.

      C++ further complicates the situation. A C++ compiler will be able to compile ANSI C programs. C++ compilers cannot compile K&R C programs. C++ adheres to a strict ANSI C syntax.

      ANSI C is the current standard. For this reason, all examples in this text are presented in ANSI C. However, since some older code may be written in K&R C, K&R C examples are provided here. C was originally developed in a research environment and was not intended for widespread use. Its original design (K&R) allowed for concise and sometimes obscure coding. In addition, many new features were later developed for the language. An ANSI C version of the language was established to provide a standard for the language. New features were incorporated and, in some cases, the syntax was altered.

K&R C differs primarily in the way a parameter list is specified. In K&R C, the parameter list is separated into the list of parameters followed by a list of parameter declarations. In ANSI C, the parameter declarations are included in the parameter list. If a function returns no value or has no parameters, the void type is used for the return type or parameter list. In K&R C, there is no void type. The return type and parameter list, in this case, would be left empty.

Function Definitions in K&R C

In K&R C, the parameter list consists only of the names of the parameter variables. The parameter declarations follow the parameter list and are arranged like regular variable declarations. Each declaration is terminated with a semicolon. The declarations of the parameter variables do not have to have the same order as that of the parameter names in the parameter list.

```
float calc (num, cost)
      int num;
      float cost;
      {
      }
```

In K&R C, there is a default return type of int. This allows functions to be defined with no return type in the header. Such functions will automatically have a return type of **int**.

```
addfunc (num1, num2)
int addfunc (num1, num2)
```

There is no keyword void in K&R C. If a function has no return type, it is simply written without specifying a return type. The function will still have the default return type of int, but this can be ignored. In the same way, the lack of parameters is indicated with an empty parameter list and no parameter declarations. In the next example, the function printname is defined in a K&R style. The empty parameter list means that this function takes no arguments, and the lack of a return type means that it does not return a value.

```
printname()
      {
      printf("The author's name is Dickens");;
      }
```

LISTING C.1 is an example of K&R C function definitions. Notice how the parameter list and parameter declarations are separated in K&R C. The parameter declarations are placed before the opening brace of the function block. Both num and calc_rate are declared before the opening block of the calc function. Local variable declarations, such as cost, are placed after the opening brace of the function block. The function declaration for calc does not include the parameter types.

LISTING C-1: K&R C Parametersprecalc.c

```
#include <stdio.h>

      float calc();   /* K&R C Function declaration*/

      main()
            {
            float rate;

            rate = 2.0;
            calc ( 5, rate);        /* Function call*/
            }

float calc (num, calc_rate) /* Parameter Names */
            int num;
            float calc_rate;        /* Parameter Declarations */
            {
            float cost;

            cost = calc_rate * num;
            }
```

In the K&R **calcerr.c** program in LISTING C.2, there is no return type in the function definition of calc, while, at the same time, there is a return type in the function declaration of calc. This will result in a compiler error that says calc is re-defined. In C, there can be only one unique name per function. There cannot be two functions with the same name. The compiler thinks that is happening here.

LISTING C-2: K&R

calcerr.c

```
#include <stdio.h>

      float calc();

      main()
            {
            float result;
            result = calc();
            }

   calc ()                /* return type missing */
            {
            float cost;
            cost = (3.00 * 3.56);
            return (cost);
            }
```

The problem occurs because there is no return type explicitly defined for calc. If there is no return type given in the function definition, the return type defaults to integer. calc is seen by the compiler as `int calc()`. A type also uniquely identifies a function name. `float calc()` and `int calc()` are two different functions. One returns a float, and the other returns an int. But they use the same name, which is invalid. So the compiler now has float calc() and `int calc()`. The compiler thinks that the calc declared in main is a different calc from the one defined below. This is easily corrected making the defined return type and the declared return type the same. As shown in the **calctype.c** program in LISTING C.3 both the function declaration and function definition of calc have the same return value, float.

In K&R C, the function declaration cannot include parameter types. A K&R C function declaration consists of only the function name and the return type. This means that function declarations do not have type information about the function's parameters. Only the return type is specified. This requires the programmer to take great care to match the types of the argument values and the types of the parameter variables. If they do not match, the parameter's values will be undefined.

There is a limited built-in promotion of parameter variables to avoid this problem. In K&R C expressions, float and character operands are always promoted to doubles and ints. This means that a floating point expression will always have a result that is a double. The floats are first promoted to doubles and then operated on. As expressions, argument expressions will never pass a float or char value. The float or char will always be promoted to a double or int. Taking this fact into consideration, in K&R C, any parameter variable declared as a char is defined as an int, and float is defined as a double, even if you should explicitly define them as char or float. You cannot have float or char parameter variables. They are automatically changed to doubles or ints by the compiler. This avoids conflicts between chars and ints, and between floats and double, but not between any other types. . A float value passed to an integer parameter variable will give the integer parameter an absurd value.

LISTING C-3: K&R

calctype.c
```
#include <stdio.h>
        float calc();

                main()
                        {
                        float result;
                        result = calc();
                        }

        float calc ()
                        {
                        float cost;
                        cost = (3.00 * 3.56);
                        return (cost);
                        }
```

In ANSI Standard C, the function declaration was expanded to deal with this problem. Whereas function declarations in K&R C only specify the return type, function declarations in ANSI C provide information about parameter types.

K&R Arithmetic conversion rules

Convert all chars and shorts to int. Convert all floats to double.

If one operand is a double, convert the other to a double
        else
            if one operand is a long, convert the other to a long
                    else
                            if one operand is unsigned, convert the other to unsigned

LISTING C-4: K&R, PARAMETERS AND RETURN VALUES

pricearg.c
```c
#include <stdio.h>
#define MARGIN 0.05
double input_cost();
double input_wholesale();
double calc_price();
double calc_profit();

  main()
        {
        double price, cost, profit, wholesale_price;
        int response = 'y';

        while (response != 'n'){
                cost = input_cost();
                wholesale_price = input_wholesale();
                price = calc_price( wholesale_price );
                profit = calc_profit( cost, price);
                printf("Profit = %.2f\n", profit);
                printf("Do you wish to continue:");
                while (getchar() != '\n');
                response = getchar();
                }
        return 0;
        }

double input_cost()
        {
        double user_cost;
        printf("\nPlease enter cost: ");
        scanf ("%lf", &user_cost);
        return (user_cost);
        }

double input_wholesale()
        {
        double user_wholesale;
        printf("\nPlease enter wholesale price: ");
        scanf ("%lf", &user_wholesale);
        return (user_wholesale);
        }

double calc_price ( w_price )
        double  w_price;
        {
        double calc_price;
        calc_price = w_price + (w_price * MARGIN);
        return (calc_price);
        }

double calc_profit (cost, price )
        double cost, price;
        {
        return (price - cost);
        }
```

LISTING C-5: K&R, PARAMETERS AND POINTERS

priceptr.c

```c
#include <stdio.h>
#define MARGIN 0.05

/* K&R FUNCTION DECLARATIONS */
int user_input();
int calc_price();
int calc_profit();


  main()
        {
        double price, cost, profit, wholesale_price;
        int response = 'y';

        while (response != 'n'){
                user_input( &cost, &wholesale_price);
                calc_price( wholesale_price, &price );
                calc_profit( cost, price, &profit );
                printf("Profit = %.2f\n", profit);
                printf("Do you wish to continue:");
                response = getchar();
                }
        }


 user_input(costptr, wholesaleptr)
        double *costptr;
        double *wholesaleptr;
        {
        printf("\nPlease enter cost: ");
        scanf ("%lf", costptr);
        printf("\nPlease enter wholesale price: ");
        scanf ("%lf", wholesaleptr);
        while (getchar() != '\n');
        }


 calc_price( w_price, priceptr )
        double w_price, *priceptr;
        {
        *priceptr = w_price + (w_price * MARGIN);
        }


 calc_profit( cost, price, profitptr)
        double cost, price;
        double *profitptr;
        {
        *profitptr = (price - cost);
        }
```

Function Type Errors in K&R C

In K&R C, if the types do not match, the results will be undefined. The types of arguments are not checked for inconsistencies against the types of corresponding parameters. If they are different, no corrections are made. The parameters will end up with absurd values. To understand how this happens, you must take a closer look at the relationship between the calling function, arguments, and parameters.

The definition of a variable requires name and type information as well as the allocation of memory for its use and the address of that memory. When local variables are defined, they allocate memory for their use. However, parameter variable do not allocate any memory. They are, instead, given the address of memory previously allocated by the calling function for argument values. The calling function allocates memory for the results of its argument expressions. The type and size of each piece of memory allocated is determined by the type of each argument value. The memory allocated for an argument is initialized with the argument's value. Parameters, when they are defined, are assigned parts of that previously allocated memory. The definition of a parameter variable does not include an actual new allocation of memory. It simply references part of the memory already allocated by the calling function for argument values. In other words, argument values and parameter variables will share the same memory.

There must be a match between the memory allocated by the calling function for the argument values and the parameter definitions. Memory is marked off for parameters sequentially according the size of their types. The first parameter will be given the address of the first byte in the argument allocated memory. If the first parameter is an integer, the second parameter will start at the third byte. If the second parameter is a double, then the third parameter will start at the 10th byte in memory. The first two bytes are used for the integer and the next eight bytes for the double.

If the types of the parameters do not match the types of the arguments then a mismatch occurs. The memory they share will be out of sync. A double argument will take up eight bytes of memory. If its corresponding parameter is an integer, the integer will use only the first two bytes of the double's memory. The size of an integer is only two bytes. It expects its argument value also to be an integer, using only two bytes, not eight.

In Figure C.1, both `mytot` and `mycount` parameters are declared as integers. However, they are passed two arguments, `subtot` and count, one of which is a floating point value. The calling function allocates memory beginning with the first argument. The eight-byte floating point value obtained from `subtot` is followed by the two-byte integer value obtained from count. The parameter `mytot` expects to find a two-byte integer value as the first value. Instead, it accesses the first two bytes of the floating point value. `mycount` expects to find its integer value placed right after mytot's. Instead, it accesses the third and fourth bytes of the floating point value.

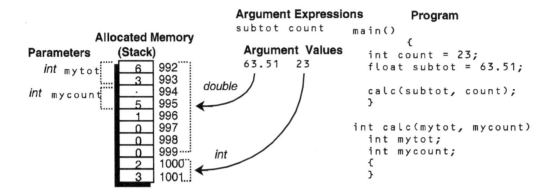

Figure C-1: Program stack and invalid arguments.

The **pcallref.c** program in LISTING C.6 is the same program, but in a K&R format. Notice the function declaration does not specify any parameter types.

LISTING C-6: K&R

pcallref.c

```
#include <stdio.h>

    int calc();           /* Function declaration */

    main()
         {
         int num;

         num = 7;
         calc (&num);    /* Address as argument */
         }
 int calc(cptr)                /*Paramater names*/
         int *cptr;                /* Parameter declarations*/
         {
         *cptr = 8;
         }
```

If a function declaration is missing, a K&R C compiler will make assumptions about the nature of the function. This will not cause a compiler error but may cause the linker to link incorrectly. The incorrect linking may or may not be detected. Instead, runtime errors will occur.

The K&R C program in LISTING C.7 contains a very subtle link error. Everything looks as if it should work. The `calc` function returns a float. The receiving variable `res` in `main` is also a float. Everything looks in sync. It is not. At runtime, the variable `res` will have a nonsense value in it.

How does this happen? **main.c** and **calc.c** are compiled separately. There is no function declaration for calc. When **main.c** is compiled, the compiler has no idea what the actual characteristics of calc are. It does not know that calc returns a float. Since it has no idea of what kind of value the calc function returns, it assumes that calc returns the default value, an integer. In K&R C, the default return value of a function is an integer.

When **calc.c** is compiled, the calc function returns a float. The linker then links the two. The linker does not check the return types for the function call of calc and the definition of calc function. Now main expects to receive an integer from calc, but calc is really returning a float. When the program runs and calc executes, calc sets up a return value that is a float. A float may consist of eight bytes. When the calc function returns to main, main then fetches calc's return value. main thinks that the return value is an integer, while, in fact, it is really a float. An integer is two bytes. main takes the first two bytes of the return value and treats whatever is in them as an integer. It may evaluate to an absurd value. This absurd integer value will then be converted to a float and assigned to res.

LISTING C-7:

main.c
```
main()
        {
        float res;

        res = calc(4,5);
        }
```

calc.c
```
float calc(x,y)
        int x,y;
        {
        float calcres;
        calcres = (x * y) * 0.05;
        return (calcres);
        }
```

Arrays and Pointers in K&R C

In K&R C, array initialization is allowed for static and external arrays, but not for automatic arrays. To make the **arinit.c** program in LISTING 10-1 from Chapter 10 to work in K&R C, the arrays myletters and totals need to be declared as either external or static. The **parinit.c** program in LISTING C.8 is a K&R version of LISTING 10-1. Here myletters is declared as static using the static type, and totals is declared as external by placing its declaration outside of any function.

LISTING C-8: K&R

parinit.c

```
#include <stdio.h>

 int totals[]={23, 8, 11, 31};

 main()
        {
        static char myletters[]={'C','D','E'};

        putchar (myletters[1]);
        }
```

Keep in mind that in K&R C, automatic arrays cannot be initialized. This means that any strings you want to declare initialize within a function must be static. You would need to precede the array declaration by the keyword static. Of course even in K&R C, external arrays can be initialized.

In K&R C, there is no special conversion specifier for addresses. An address is treated as an unsigned integer. The conversion specifier for unsigned integers is the letter u, %u. This can lead to problems because the size of an address may not be the same as that of an unsigned integer. Sometimes an address is the same as a long integer, requiring an 'l' modifier for output, %lu. Even then, there may be systems in which an address is larger than an unsigned integer and smaller than an unsigned long. In this case, the only safe solution is to use a cast to convert the smaller address to an unsigned long.

```
printf("Value in numptr is address %u.",numptr);
printf("Value in numptr is address %lu.",
                                           (unsigned long) numptr);
```

```
        Value in numptr is address 534.
        Value in numptr is address 534.
```

In K&R C, there is no void type for pointers. Instead, the pointer type pointer-to-char, char*, is used as a kind of generic pointer type. However, a pointer-to-char is still a pointer to a character type of object. In K&R C, `malloc` returns an address whose type is that of a pointer-to-char. In order to assign this address of type pointer-to-char to a different type of pointer variable, you need to use a cast operation on the address to change its pointer type. In the next example, a cast operation is applied the address returned by `malloc` to generate a pointer to an integer. In the cast operation, the type of a pointer is not only the asterisk, which indicates it is a pointer, but also the kind of object the pointer points to, in this case an int, `(int*)`.

```
        (int *) malloc(sizeof(int));

        int *numptr;

        numptr = (int *) malloc(sizeof(int));
```

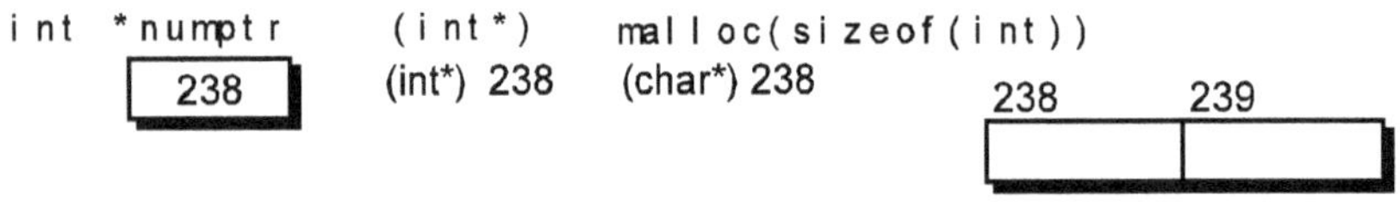

Figure C-2: malloc and pointer variable.

In K&R C there is a slight variation on how you need to specify the address of the block used in `fread` and `fwrite` function calls. In K&R C, the first argument for `fread` and fwrite is the address of a character. The address passed must be an address of a char, char *. However, in the address operation `&employee`, the address is an address of an EMP structure, not a char. The address can be easily changed to an address of a char with a cast. The address of employee, `&employee`, can be cast as `(char *)` `&employee`.

```
        fread((char*) &employee,sizeof(EMP),1,fileptr);
```

D. Answers to Exercises

The complete set of source code files for both examples and exercise answers for this book are available at **www.surfingturtlepress.com**.

Chapter 6: Structures

ANSWER 6-1:

```c
/* RETURN VALUES */
#include <stdio.h>
#define MARGIN  0.05

double calc(double);
double user_input(void);
int user_response(void);

int main(void)
     {
     double price, cost;
     int response = 'y';

     while (response != 'n'){
          cost = user_input();
          price = calc(cost);
          while (getchar() != '\n');
          printf("\nPrice is %.2f\n", price);
          response = user_response();
          }
     return 0;
     }


 double user_input(void)
     {
     double  user_cost;

     printf("\nPlease enter cost: ");
     scanf ("%lf", &user_cost);
     return (user_cost);
     }

double calc(double cost)
     {
     double calc_price;

     calc_price = cost + (cost * MARGIN);
     return (calc_price);
     }

int user_response(void)
     {
     int res;

     printf ("\nDo you wish to continue ? ");
     res = getchar();
     return (res);
     }
```

ANSWER 6-2: PARAMATERS AND POINTERS, ANSI

```c
#include <stdio.h>
#define MARKUP1 0.05
#define MARKUP2 0.10
#define CUTOFF 10

void user_input(double*, int*);
double calc(double, double);
double markup(int);

int main(void)
        {
        double price, cost, total = 0;
        double markup_percent;
        int product_number;
        int response = 'y';

        while (response != 'n'){
                user_input( &cost, &product_number);
                markup_percent = markup(product_number);
                price = calc(cost, markup_percent );
                total = total + price;
                printf("Price = %.2lf\n", price);
                printf("Do you wish to continue : ");
                response = getchar();
                }
        printf("\nTotal is %.2lf\n", total);
        return 0;
        }

void user_input(double *costptr, int *prodptr)
        {
        printf("\nPlease enter cost: ");
        scanf ("%lf", costptr);
        printf("\nPlease enter product number: ");
        scanf ("%lf", prodptr);
        while (getchar() !='\n');
        }

double calc (double cost, double markup_percent)
        {
        return (cost + (cost * markup_percent));
        }

double markup(int prodnum)
        {
        double res;

        if (prodnum < CUTOFF)
                res = MARKUP1;
         else
                res = MARKUP2;

        return res;
        }
```

Chapter 7: Structures

ANSWER 7-1:

```c
#include <stdio.h>
#define FACTOR 10000.00

/* EMP structure */
typedef  struct emp {
                int  id;
                float salary;
                } EMP;

EMP input_rec(void);
void output_rec(EMP);
float calc_sal(void);

int main(void)
        {
        EMP employee;

        employee = input_rec();
        output_rec(employee);
        return 0;
        }


EMP input_rec(void)
        {
        EMP in_emp;

        printf("\nplease enter employee id: ");
        scanf("%d", &in_emp.id);
        in_emp.salary = calc_sal();

        return(in_emp);
        }

void output_rec(EMP out_emp)
        {
        printf("\n\n Employee Record \n");
        printf("\n\t ID    : %d \n", out_emp.id);
        printf("\n\t SALARY: %.2f \n\n", out_emp.salary);
        }

float calc_sal(void)
        {
        int years;
        float result;

        printf("\nplease enter years experience:");
        scanf("%d", &years);
        result = years * FACTOR;
        return(result);
        }
```

ANSWER 7-2:

```c
#include <stdio.h>
#define FACTOR 10000.00

        typedef struct emp {
                int id;
                float salary;
                }EMP;

void input_rec(EMP*);
void output_rec(EMP*);
float calc_sal(void);
void menu(void);
int user_response(void);

int main(void)
        {
        EMP employee;
        int more = 0;
        int response;

        while (more == 0){
                menu();
                response = user_response();

                switch(response){
                        case  'i':
                                input_rec(&employee);
                                break;
                        case  'p':
                                output_rec(&employee);
                                break;
                        case  'q':
                                more = 1;
                                break;
                        default:
                                printf("invalid input\n");
                        }
                while (getchar() != '\n');
                }
        return 0;
        }

void input_rec(EMP *in_emptr)
        {
        printf("\nplease enter employee id: ");
        scanf("%d", &in_emptr->id);
        in_emptr->salary = calc_sal();
        }

void output_rec(EMP *out_emptr)
        {
        printf("\n\n Employee Record \n");
        printf("\n\t ID   :  %d \n", out_emptr->id);
        printf("\n\tSALARY:%.2f\n\n",out_emptr->salary);
        }
```

```
void menu(void){
        printf("\ni = Input a record\n");
        printf("p = Print the record\n");
        printf("q = Quit program\n\n");
        }

float calc_sal(void)
        {
        int years;
        float result;

        printf("\nplease enter years experience: ");
        scanf("%d", &years);
        result = years * FACTOR;
        return(result);
        }

 int user_response(void)
        {
        int res;
        printf ("\nPlease enter menu option? ");
        res = getchar();
        return (res);
        }
```

Chapter 9: Program Organization

ANSWER 9-1:

protos.h

```
#define    MARKUP1 0.05
#define    MARKUP2 0.10

void user_input(double*, int*);
double calc(double, double);
double markup(int);
int newcutoff(int);
```

main.c
```
/* PARAMATERS AND POINTERS - ANSI */

#include <stdio.h>
#include "protos.h"

int main(void)
        {
        double price, cost, total = 0;
        double markup_percent;
        int product_number;
        int response = 'y';

        while (response != 'n')
                {
                user_input(&cost, &product_number);
```

```
                markup_percent = markup(product_number);
                price = calc(cost, markup_percent);
                total = total + price;
                printf("Price = %.2lf\n", price);
                printf("Do you wish to continue");
                response = getchar();
                }
        printf("\nTotal is %.2lf\n", total);
        return 0;
        }
```

input.c

```
#include <stdio.h>
#include "protos.h"

void user_input(double *costptr, int *prodptr)
        {
        int res;
        int newcut;

        printf("\nPlease enter cost: ");
        scanf ("%lf", costptr);
        printf("\nPlease enter product number: ");
        scanf ("%lf", prodptr);
        while (getchar() !='\n');

        printf ("Do you have a new cutoff?");
        res = getchar();
        if (res == 'y')
                {
                printf ("please enter new cutoff\n");
                scanf ("%d", &newcut);
                newcutoff(newcut);
                }
        while (getchar() !='\n');
        }
```

calc.c

```
#include <stdio.h>
#include "protos.h"
static int cutoff = 10;

int newcutoff(int cut)
                {
                cutoff = cut;
                }

double calc (double cost, double markup_percent)
        {
        return (cost + (cost * markup_percent));
        }

double markup(int prodnum)
        {
        double res;
        if (prodnum < cutoff)
                res = MARKUP1;
         else
                res = MARKUP2;
        return res;
        }
```

ANSWER 9-2:

types.h
```
#define FACTOR 10000.00
typedef  struct emp {  /* EMP structure */
                int  id;
                float salary;
                } EMP;

EMP input_rec(void);
void output_rec(EMP);
float calc_sal(void);
void menu(void);
int user_response(void);

main.c
#include <stdio.h>
#include "types.h"

int main(void)
        {
        EMP employee;
        int more = 0, response;

        while (more == 0){
                menu();
                response = user_response();
                switch(response){
                        case  'i':
                                employee = input_rec();
                                break;
                        case  'p':
                                output_rec(employee);
                                break;
                        case  'q':
                                more = 1;
                                break;
                        default:
                                printf("invalid input\n");
                        }
                while (getchar() != '\n');
                }
        return 0;
        }

void menu(void){
        printf("\ni = Input a record\n");
        printf("p = Print the record\n");
        printf("q = Quit program\n\n");
        }
```

input.c
```c
#include <stdio.h>
#include "types.h"

EMP input_rec(void)
        {
        EMP in_emp;

        printf("\nplease enter employee id: ");
        scanf("%d", &in_emp.id);
        in_emp.salary = calc_sal();
        return(in_emp);
        }

 int user_response(void){
        int res;
        printf ("\nPlease enter menu option? ");
        res = getchar();
        return (res);
        }

output.c

#include <stdio.h>
#include "types.h"

void output_rec(EMP out_emp)
        {
        printf("\n\n Employee Record \n");
        printf("\n\t ID:    %d \n", out_emp.id);
        printf("\n\t SALARY:%.2f \n\n", out_emp.salary);
        }

calc.c

#include <stdio.h>
#include "types.h"

float calc_sal(void)
        {
        float years;
        float result;

        printf("\nplease enter years experience:");
        scanf("%f", &years);
        result = years * FACTOR;
        return(result);
        }
```

Chapter 10: Arrays and Pointers

ANSWER 10-1:

```c
#include <stdio.h>
int main(void)
        {
        int mynums[10];
        int * numptr;

        numptr = mynums;
        while(numptr < (mynums + 10) )
                {
                printf("Enter number :");
                scanf("%d", numptr);
                numptr++;
                }
        for(numptr=mynums;numptr<(mynums+10);numptr++)
                {
                printf("%d \n",  *numptr);
                }
        }
```

ANSWER 10-3:

```c
#include <stdio.h>

int main(void)
        {
        int mynums[5];
        int * numptr;
        int indexnum, searchnum;

        numptr = mynums;
        while (numptr < (mynums + 5) )
                {
                printf("Enter number :");
                scanf("%d", numptr);
                numptr++;
                }

        for(numptr=mynums;numptr<(mynums+5);numptr++)
                {
                printf("%d \n",  *numptr);
                }

        printf("\nEnter number to be searched :");
        scanf("%d", &searchnum);

        for(numptr=mynums; (*numptr!=searchnum)&&
                                (numptr<(mynums+10));numptr++);
        if (*numptr == searchnum)
                {
                indexnum = numptr - mynums ;
                printf("\nIndex = %d \n",  indexnum);
                }
         else
                printf("\nNumber not found\n");
        return 0;
        }
```

Chapter 11: Arrays of Characters: Strings

ANSWER 11-2: MYGETS ANSWER with POINTERS

```c
#include <stdio.h>

void mygets(char *);

int main(void)
        {
        int i;
        char name[30];
        printf("please enter name?:");
        mygets(name);
        printf("%s", name);
        return 0;
        }
void mygets(char *nameptr)
        {
        char *cptr;

        for(cptr=nameptr;(*cptr=getchar())!='\n';cptr++);
        *cptr = '\0';
        }
```

ANSWER 11-3: STRINGLEN and STRINGCAT

```c
#include <stdio.h>
#include <string.h>

int stringlen(char*);
void stringcat(char*, char*);

int main(void)
        {
        int i,len;
        char firstname[30];
        char lastname[30];
        char wholename[30];

        printf("please enter first name?:");
        gets(firstname);
        printf("please enter last name?:");
        gets(lastname);

        strcpy(wholename, firstname);
        stringcat(wholename, " ");
        stringcat(wholename, lastname);
        len = stringlen(wholename);
        printf("\nLength = %d", len);
        printf("\nName = %s\n", wholename);
        return 0;
        }
```

```
int stringlen(char *nameptr)
        {
        char *cptr;
        int i = 0;

        for (cptr = nameptr;  *cptr != '\0'; cptr++ )
                        i++;
        return(i);
        }

void stringcat(char *strptr, char *cpstrptr)
        {
        char *cptr;
        char *sptr;
        int len;

        cptr = cpstrptr;
        len = stringlen(strptr);
        sptr = &strptr[len];

        while(*cptr != '\0')
                {
                *sptr = *cptr;
                sptr++;
                cptr++;
                }
        *sptr = '\0';
        }
```

ANSWER 11-5:

main.c

```
#include <stdio.h>
#include <string.h>
#define MAXLINE  80
#define USERMAX 20

int index_str (char *, char *);

int main(void)
        {
        int pos, len, count;
        char buffer[MAXLINE];
        char pattern[USERMAX];
        char *bufptr;

        printf("\nplease enter pattern: ");
        gets(pattern);
        len = strlen(pattern);
        printf("Enter line: ");
        gets(buffer);

        count = 0;
        while (buffer[0] != '\0')
                {
                bufptr = buffer;
```

```
                    while((pos=index_str(bufptr,pattern)) >= 0)
                        {
                        printf ("\n%s",buffer);
                        bufptr = bufptr + (pos + len);
                        count++;
                        }
                    printf("\nEnter line: ");
                    gets(buffer);
                    }

            printf("Count found = %d",count);
            return 0;
            }
```

lib.c

```
int index_str (char *strp, char *patp)
        {
        char *ip, *jp, *kp;

        for(ip = strp; *ip!= '\0'; ip++)
                {
                for(jp=ip,kp=patp; (*kp!='\0')&&(*jp==*kp);jp++,kp++);
                if (*kp == '\0')
                        return (ip - strp);
                }
        return(-1);
        }
```

Chapter 12: Arrays of Structures

ANSWER 12-3:

types.h

```
#define MAX_FIELD_LEN 20
#define MAXRECS 20
#define STORE_COUNT 5

        typedef  struct rec_type {
                char name[MAX_FIELD_LEN];
                int store_id;
                double sales;
                } REC;

REC *add_recs (REC *);
void fill_rec (REC *);
void store_report (REC *, REC*);
void outputrecs(REC*, REC*);
int get_user_ok(void);
```

main.c
```
#include "types.h"

        REC recs[MAXRECS];

int main(void)
        {
        REC *lastrecptr;

        lastrecptr = add_recs (recs);
        outputrecs(recs, lastrecptr);
        store_report (recs, lastrecptr);
        return 0;
        }
```

```
add.c
#include <stdio.h>
#include  "types.h"

REC *add_recs (REC recs[])
        {
        int more = 1;
        REC *recptr;

        recptr = recs;
        while((more==1) && (recptr<(recs+MAXRECS)))
                {
                fill_rec(recptr);
                recptr++;
                more = get_user_ok();
                }
        recptr--;
        return (recptr);
        }

void fill_rec (REC *recptr)
        {
        printf("Please enter Last name : ");
        scanf("%s",recptr->name);

        printf("Please enter store id : ");
        scanf("%d",&recptr->store_id);

        printf("Please enter sales : ");
        scanf("%lf",&recptr->sales);
        }

int get_user_ok(void)
        {
        char response[2];

        printf("Do you wish to enter another record?");
        scanf("%s", response);
        if(response[0] =='y')
                return 1;
        else
                return 0;
        }
```

report.c
```c
#include <stdio.h>
#include "types.h"

void store_report (REC *recs, REC *lastrecptr)
        {
        int i;
        double store_rep [STORE_COUNT];
        REC *recptr;

        for  (i = 0; i < STORE_COUNT ; i++)
                store_rep[i] = 0.00 ;

        for(recptr=recs;recptr<=lastrecptr;recptr++)
         {
         store_rep[recptr->store_id] += recptr->sales;
         }

        printf ("\n\tREPORT OF STORETOTALS \n\n");
        for(i = 0; i < STORE_COUNT ; i++)
                        printf("\t%.2f\n",store_rep[i]);


        }

void outputrecs(REC *recs, REC *lastrecptr)
        {
        REC *recptr;

        recptr = recs;
        while(recptr <= lastrecptr)
                {
                printf("\n\n Transaction Record\n");
                printf("\n\t NAME : %s \n", recptr->name);
                printf("\n\t STORE ID: %d \n",recptr->store_id);
                printf("\n\t SALES:%.2f\n\n",recptr->sales);
                recptr++;
                }
    }
```

Chapter 13: Arrays of Arrays

ANSWER 13-1 POINTERS TO ARRAYS

```c
int strfind(char (*strptr)[40], char *fstr)
{
char (*sptr)[40];
char *cptr;
int res;
sptr=strptr;
while((strcmp(*sptr,fstr)!=0)&&(sptr<(strptr+10)))
        {
        sptr++;
        }
if(sptr < (strptr + 10))
        res = (sptr - strptr);
 else
        res = -1;
}
```

Chapter 14: Arrays of Pointers

ANSWER 14-2: ARGC, Number of Arguments

```c
#include <stdio.h>
#include <stdlib.h>

int main(int argc, char *argv[])
        {

        if (argc > 4)
                {
                printf("Too many arguments \n");
                exit(1);
                }
          else
                if (argc < 4)
                {
                printf("Too few arguments \n");
                exit(1);
                }

        printf("\n My first name is %s\n", argv[1]);
        printf(" My last name is %s\n", argv[2]);
        printf(" My age is %s\n", argv[3]);
        return 0;
        }
```

Chapter 16: Text Files

ANSWER 16-1: TEXT FILE

```c
#include <stdio.h>
#define MAX 80

int main(int argc, char *argv[])
                {
                FILE *fptr;
                char buffer[100];

                fptr = fopen(argv[1], "r");

                while(fgets(buffer, MAX, fptr) != NULL)
                        {
                        puts(buffer);
                        }

                fclose(fptr);
                return 0;
                }
```

ANSWER 16-2: TEXT FILE

```
#include <stdio.h>

int main(void)
                {
                FILE *fptr;
                char buffer[100];

                printf("Enter line: ");
                gets(buffer);
                fptr = fopen("newfile", "w");

                while (buffer[0] != '\0')
                        {
                        fputs(buffer, fptr);
                        printf("Enter line: ");
                        gets(buffer);
                        }
                fclose(fptr);
                return 0;
                }
```

ANSWER 16-3: TEXT FILE

```
void print_text (FILE *fptr )
                {
                char buffer[MAX];

                while(fgets(buffer, MAX, fptr) != NULL)
                        {
                        puts(buffer);
                        }
                }


void write_text(FILE *fptr)
                {

                char buffer[MAX];

                printf("Enter line");
                gets(buffer);

                while (buffer[0] != '\0')
                        {
                        fputs(buffer, fptr);
                        printf("Enter line");
                        gets(buffer);
                        }
                }
```

ANSWER 16-4: TEXT FILE

```c
#include <stdio.h>
#define MAXLINE  80
extern int index_str(char*, char*);

int main(int argc, char *argv[])
        {
        extern int index_str();
        int pos;
        char buffer[MAXLINE];
        FILE *fileptr;

        fileptr = fopen(argv[1], "r");
        while(fgets (buffer, MAXLINE, fileptr) != NULL)
                {
                if((pos = index_str (buffer,argv[2])) >= 0)
                        {
                        printf ("%s",buffer);
                        }
                }
        fclose (fileptr);
        return 0;
        }
```

ANSWER 16-5: FORMATED FILE

```c
#include <stdio.h>
#include "months.h"
#define RATE 0.10
float calc(float);

int main(void)
        {
        int  month, day;
        char store[20];
        float  price, cost, total = 0.00;
        FILE *fileptr;

        fileptr = fopen("costd", "r");
        while ((fscanf(fileptr, "%d %d %f %s\n",
                            &month,&day,&price,store))!=EOF)
                {
                if(((month==SEPTEMBER) || (month==AUGUST))
                            && (day==MONDAY))
                        {
                        cost = calc(price) ;
                        printf( "%.2f %s\n",price ,store );
                        total = total + cost;
                        }
                }
        printf("Total in Sept and Aug = %.2f\n",total);
        fclose(fileptr);
        return 0;
        }
```

```
float calc(float price)
     {
     float cost;
     cost = price - (price * RATE);
     return (cost);
     }
```

Chapter 17: Record File

ANSWER 17-1: RECORD FILE COPY

```
#include <stdio.h>

typedef  struct emp_type {
     char name [20];
     int id;
     double salary;
     } EMP;

int main(argc, argv)
     int argc;
     char ** argv;
     {
     EMP rec;
     FILE *orig_fptr;
     FILE *copy_fptr;

     orig_fptr = fopen (argv[1], "r");
     copy_fptr = fopen (argv[2], "w");

while((fread(&rec,sizeof(EMP),1,orig_fptr))!=NULL)
             {
             fwrite(&rec,sizeof(EMP),1,copy_fptr);
             }
     fclose (orig_fptr);
     fclose (copy_fptr);
     return 0;
     }
```

ANSWER 17-2: Find and Update Functions

```
Include in emp.c file
static long findrec(EMP *emptr)
                {
                long id;
                EMP emprec;

                printf("Please enter record id: ");
                scanf("%ld", &id);
                readrec((char*)emptr, id);
                return(id);
                }
void updaterec(void)
        {
        long recno;
        EMP employee;

        recno = findrec(&employee);
        output_rec(employee);
        selectfield(&employee);
        writerec((char*)&employee,recno);
        }

static void selectfield(EMP *emptr)
                {
                int more = 0, response;

                while (more == 0){
                        menurec( *emptr );
                        response = user_response();
                        switch(response){
                                case '1':
                                        printf("enter new name: ");
                                        gets(emptr->name);
                                        break;
                                case '2':
                                        printf("\n enter employee id:");
                                        scanf("%d", &emptr->id);
                                        break;
                                case '3':
                                        emptr->salary = calc_sal();
                                        break;
                                case 'q':
                                        more = 1;
                                        break;
                                default:
                                        printf("invalid input\n");
                                }
                        }
                }
static void menurec(EMP out_emp)
        {
        printf("\n\n Employee Record \n");
        printf("\n\t 1.NAME  : %s \n", out_emp.name);
        printf("\n\t 2.ID    : %d \n", out_emp.id);
        printf("\n\t 3.SALARY: %f \n", out_emp.salary);
        printf("\n Choose field to be changed");
        }
```

Table Listing

Figure Listing

Program Listing

Index

Index

www.ingramcontent.com/pod-product-compliance
Lightning Source LLC
LaVergne TN
LVHW062257060326

832902LV00013B/1928